PENGUIN BOOKS

The Corfu Trilogy

Gerald Durrell (1925–95) moved from England to Corfu with his family when he was eight. He immediately became fascinated by the island's natural history and spent much of his time studying the local wildlife and keeping numerous, and often unusual, pets. He grew up to be a famous naturalist, animal-collector, and conservationist.

Durrell dedicated his life to the conservation of wildlife and it is through his efforts that creatures such as the Mauritius pink pigeon and the Mallorcan midwife toad have avoided extinction. Over his lifetime he wrote thirty-seven books, went on dozens of animal-collecting trips and presented numerous TV shows. He founded the Durrell Wildlife Conservation Trust in 1959 as a centre for the conservation of endangered species – of which his wife Lee is still Honorary Director. He was awarded the OBE in 1982.

The Corfu Trilogy

My Family and Other Animals
Birds, Beasts, and Relatives
The Garden of the Gods

GERALD DURRELL

PENGUIN BOOKS

PENGUIN BOOKS

UK | USA | Canada | Ireland | Australia
India | New Zealand | South Africa

Penguin Books is part of the Penguin Random House group of companies
whose addresses can be found at global.penguinrandomhouse.com.

My Family and Other Animals
First published in Great Britain by Rupert Hart-Davis Limited 1956
First published in the United States of America by The Viking Press, Inc. 1957
First published in Penguin Books 1977
Copyright © Gerald M. Durrell, 1984
Copyright renewed Gerald M. Durrell, 1984
Portions of this book appeared in *Mademoiselle*

Birds, Beasts, and Relatives
First published in the United States of America by The Viking Press, Inc. 1969
Published in Penguin Books 2004
Copyright © Gerald M. Durrell, 1969

The Garden of the Gods
First published by Collins 1978
Copyright © The Estate of Gerald Durrell, 1978, 2003

All three books first published together as *The Corfu Trilogy* by Penguin Books 2006
024
All rights reserved

The moral right of the author has been asserted

Set in 11/13 pt Monotype Dante
Typeset by Rowland Phototypesetting Ltd, Bury St Edmunds, Suffolk
Printed in England by Clays Ltd, St Ives plc

ISBN-13: 978–0–141–02841–5
ISBN-10: 0–141–02841–6

www.greenpenguin.co.uk

My Family and Other Animals

To My Mother

Contents

It is a melancholy of mine own, compounded of many simples, extracted from many objects, and indeed the sundry contemplation of my travels, which, by often rumination, wraps me in a most humorous sadness.

— SHAKESPEARE, *As You Like It*

The Speech for the Defence

'Why, sometimes I've believed as many as six impossible
things before breakfast.'

The White Queen – *Through the Looking Glass*

This is the story of a five-year sojourn that I and my family made
on the Greek island of Corfu. It was originally intended to be a
mildly nostalgic account of the natural history of the island, but
I made a grave mistake by introducing my family into the book
in the first few pages. Having got themselves on paper, they then
proceeded to establish themselves and invite various friends to
share the chapters. It was only with the greatest difficulty, and
by exercising considerable cunning, that I managed to retain a
few pages here and there which I could devote exclusively to
animals.

I have attempted to draw an accurate and unexaggerated
picture of my family in the following pages; they appear as I saw
them. To explain some of their more curious ways, however, I
feel that I should state that at the time we were in Corfu the
family were all quite young: Larry, the eldest, was twenty-three;
Leslie was nineteen; Margo eighteen; while I was the youngest,
being of the tender and impressionable age of ten. We have never
been very certain of my mother's age, for the simple reason that
she can never remember her date of birth; all I can say is that she
was old enough to have four children. My mother also insists
that I explain that she is a widow for, as she so penetratingly
observed, you never know what people might think.

5

In order to compress five years of incident, observation, and pleasant living into something a little less lengthy than the *Encyclopædia Britannica*, I have been forced to telescope, prune, and graft, so that there is little left of the original continuity of events. Also I have been forced to leave out many happenings and characters that I would have liked to describe.

It is doubtful if this would have been written without the help and enthusiasm of the following people. I mention this so that blame can be laid in the right quarter. My grateful thanks, then, to:

Dr Theodore Stephanides. With typical generosity, he allowed me to make use of material from his unpublished work on Corfu, and supplied me with a number of dreadful puns, some of which I have used.

My family. They, after all, unconsciously provided a lot of the material and helped me considerably during the writing of the book by arguing ferociously and rarely agreeing about any incident on which I consulted them.

My wife, who pleased me by laughing uproariously when reading the manuscript, only to inform me that it was my spelling that amused her.

Sophie, my secretary, who was responsible for the introduction of commas and the ruthless eradication of the split infinitive.

I should like to pay a special tribute to my mother, to whom this book is dedicated. Like a gentle, enthusiastic, and understanding Noah, she has steered her vessel full of strange progeny through the stormy seas of life with great skill, always faced with the possibility of mutiny, always surrounded by the dangerous shoals of overdraft and extravagance, never being sure that her navigation would be approved by the crew, but certain that she would be blamed for anything that went wrong. That she survived the voyage is a miracle, but survive it she did, and, moreover, with her reason more or less intact. As my brother Larry rightly points out, we can be proud of the way we have brought her up; she is a credit to us. That she has reached that happy Nirvana where nothing shocks or startles is exemplified by the fact that one weekend recently, when all alone in the house, she was treated to the sudden arrival of a series of crates containing two pelicans, a scarlet ibis, a vulture, and eight monkeys. A lesser mortal might have quailed at such a contingency, but not Mother. On Monday morning I found her in the garage being pursued round and round by an irate pelican which she was trying to feed with sardines from a tin.

'I'm glad you've come, dear,' she panted; 'this pelican is a *little* difficult to handle.'

When I asked her how she *knew* the animals belonged to me, she replied, 'Well, of course I knew they were yours, dear; who else would send pelicans to me?'

Which goes to show how well she knows at least one of her family.

Lastly, I would like to make a point of stressing that all the anecdotes about the island and the islanders are absolutely true. Living in Corfu was rather like living in one of the more flamboyant and slapstick comic operas. The whole atmosphere and charm of the place was, I think, summed up neatly on an Admiralty map we had, which showed the island and the adjacent coastline in great detail. At the bottom was a little inset which read:

CAUTION: *As the buoys marking the shoals are often out of position, mariners are cautioned to be on their guard when navigating these shores.*

Part One

There is a pleasure sure
In being mad, which none but madmen know.

— DRYDEN, *The Spanish Friar, II, i*

The Migration

July had been blown out like a candle by a biting wind that ushered in a leaden August sky. A sharp, stinging drizzle fell, billowing into opaque grey sheets when the wind caught it. Along the Bournemouth sea-front the beach huts turned blank wooden faces towards a greeny-grey, froth-chained sea that leaped eagerly at the cement bulwark of the shore. The gulls had been tumbled inland over the town, and they now drifted above the house-tops on taut wings, whining peevishly. It was the sort of weather calculated to try anyone's endurance.

Considered as a group my family was not a very prepossessing sight that afternoon, for the weather had brought with it the usual selection of ills to which we were prone. For me, lying on the floor, labelling my collection of shells, it had brought catarrh, pouring it into my skull like cement, so that I was forced to breathe stertorously through open mouth. For my brother Leslie, hunched dark and glowering by the fire, it had inflamed the convolutions of his ears so that they bled delicately but persistently. To my sister Margo it had delivered a fresh dappling of acne spots to a face that was already blotched like a red veil. For my mother there was a rich, bubbling cold, and a twinge of rheumatism to season it. Only my eldest brother, Larry, was untouched, but it was sufficient that he was irritated by our failings.

It was Larry, of course, who started it. The rest of us felt too apathetic to think of anything except our own ills, but Larry was designed by Providence to go through life like a small, blond firework, exploding ideas in other people's minds, and then curling up with catlike unctuousness and refusing to take any blame for the consequences. He had become increasingly irritable as the afternoon wore on. At length, glancing moodily round the room, he decided to attack Mother, as being the obvious cause of the trouble.

'Why do we stand this bloody climate?' he asked suddenly, making a gesture towards the rain-distorted window. 'Look at it! And, if it comes to that, look at us . . . Margo swollen up like a plate of scarlet porridge . . . Leslie wandering around with four-teen fathoms of cotton wool in each ear . . . Gerry sounds as though he's had a cleft palate from birth . . . And look at you: you're looking more decrepit and hagridden every day.'

Mother peered over the top of a large volume entitled *Easy Recipes from Rajputana*.

'Indeed I'm not,' she said indignantly.

'You *are*,' Larry insisted; 'you're beginning to look like an Irish washerwoman . . . and your family looks like a series of illustrations from a medical encyclopædia.'

Mother could think of no really crushing reply to this, so she contented herself with a glare before retreating once more behind her book.

'What we need is sunshine,' Larry continued; 'don't you agree, Les? . . . Les . . . *Les!*'

Leslie unravelled a large quantity of cotton wool from one ear.

'What d'you say?' he asked.

'There you are!' said Larry, turning triumphantly to Mother, 'it's become a major operation to hold a conversation with him. I ask you, what a position to be in! One brother can't hear what you say, and the other one can't be understood. Really, it's time something was done. I can't be expected to produce deathless prose in an atmosphere of gloom and eucalyptus.'

'Yes, dear,' said Mother vaguely.

'What we all need,' said Larry, getting into his stride again, 'is sunshine . . . a country where we can *grow*.'

'Yes, dear, that would be nice,' agreed Mother, not really listening.

'I had a letter from George this morning – he says Corfu's wonderful. Why don't we pack up and go to Greece?'

'Very well, dear, if you like,' said Mother unguardedly. Where Larry was concerned she was generally very careful not to commit herself.

'When?' asked Larry, rather surprised at this cooperation.

Mother, perceiving that she had made a tactical error, cautiously lowered *Easy Recipes from Rajputana*.

'Well, I think it would be a sensible idea if you were to go on ahead, dear, and arrange things. Then you can write and tell me if it's nice, and we all can follow,' she said cleverly.

Larry gave her a withering look.

'You said *that* when I suggested going to Spain,' he reminded her, 'and I sat for two interminable months in Seville, waiting for you to come out, while you did nothing except write me massive letters about drains and drinking water, as though I was the town clerk or something. No, if we're going to Greece, let's all go together.'

'You do *exaggerate*, Larry,' said Mother plaintively; 'anyway, I can't go just like that. I have to arrange something about this house.'

'Arrange? Arrange what, for heaven's sake? Sell it.'

'I can't do that, dear,' said Mother, shocked.

'Why not?'

'But I've only just bought it.'

'Sell it while it's still untarnished, then.'

'Don't be ridiculous, dear,' said Mother firmly; 'that's quite out of the question. It would be madness.'

So we sold the house and fled from the gloom of the English summer, like a flock of migrating swallows.

We all travelled light, taking with us only what we considered to be the bare essentials of life. When we opened our luggage for customs inspection, the contents of our bags were a fair indication of character and interests. Thus Margo's luggage contained a multitude of diaphanous garments, three books on slimming, and a regiment of small bottles, each containing some elixir guaranteed to cure acne. Leslie's case held a couple of roll-top pullovers and a pair of trousers which were wrapped round two revolvers, an air-pistol, a book called *Be Your Own Gunsmith*, and a large bottle of oil that leaked. Larry was accompanied by two trunks of books and a briefcase containing his clothes. Mother's luggage was sensibly divided between clothes and various volumes on cooking and gardening. I travelled with only those items that I thought necessary to relieve the tedium of a long journey: four books on natural history, a butterfly net, a dog, and a jam jar full of caterpillars all in imminent danger of turning into chrysalids. Thus, by our standards fully equipped, we left the clammy shores of England.

France rain-washed and sorrowful, Switzerland like a Christmas cake, Italy exuberant, noisy, and smelly, were passed, leaving only confused memories. The tiny ship throbbed away from the heel of Italy out into the twilit sea, and as we slept in our stuffy cabins, somewhere in that tract of moon-polished water we passed the invisible dividing line and entered the bright, looking-glass world of Greece. Slowly this sense of change seeped down to us, and so, at dawn, we awoke restless and went on deck.

The sea lifted smooth blue muscles of wave as it stirred in the dawn light, and the foam of our wake spread gently behind us like a white peacock's tail, glinting with bubbles. The sky was pale and stained with yellow on the eastern horizon. Ahead lay a chocolate-brown smudge of land, huddled in mist, with a frill of foam at its base. This was Corfu, and we strained our eyes to make out the exact shapes of the mountains, to discover valleys, peaks, ravines, and beaches, but it remained a silhouette. Then suddenly the sun lifted over the horizon, and the sky turned the smooth enamelled blue of a jay's eye. The endless, meticulous curves of the sea flamed for an instant and then changed to a deep royal purple flecked with green. The mist lifted in quick, lithe ribbons, and before us lay the island, the mountains as though sleeping beneath a crumpled blanket of brown, the folds stained with the green of olive groves. Along the shore curved beaches as white as tusks among tottering cities of brilliant gold, red, and white rocks. We rounded the northern cape, a smooth shoulder of rust-red cliff carved into a series of giant caves. The dark waves lifted our wake and carried it gently towards them, and then, at their very mouths, it crumpled and hissed thirstily among the rocks. Rounding the cape, we left the mountains, and the island sloped gently down, blurred with the silver and green iridescence of olives, with here and there an admonishing finger of black cypress against the sky. The shallow sea in the bays was butterfly blue, and even above the sound of the ship's engines we could hear, faintly ringing from the shore like a chorus of tiny voices, the shrill, triumphant cries of the cicadas.

The Unsuspected Isle

We threaded our way out of the noise and confusion of the customs shed into the brilliant sunshine on the quay. Around us the town rose steeply, tiers of multi-coloured houses piled haphazardly, green shutters folded back from their windows like the wings of a thousand moths. Behind us lay the bay, smooth as a plate, smouldering with that unbelievable blue.

Larry walked swiftly, with head thrown back and an expression of such regal disdain on his face that one did not notice his diminutive size, keeping a wary eye on the porters who struggled with his trunks. Behind him strolled Leslie, short, stocky, with an air of quiet belligerence, and then Margo, trailing yards of muslin and scent. Mother, looking like a tiny, harassed missionary in an uprising, was dragged unwillingly to the nearest lamp post by an exuberant Roger and forced to stand there, staring into space, while he relieved the pent-up feelings that had accumulated in his kennel. Larry chose two magnificently dilapidated horse-drawn cabs, had the luggage installed in one and seated himself in the second. Then he looked round irritably.

'Well?' he asked. 'What are we waiting for?'

'We're waiting for Mother,' explained Leslie. 'Roger's found a lamp post.'

'Dear God!' said Larry, and then hoisted himself upright in the cab and bellowed, 'Come *on*, Mother, come on. Can't the dog wait?'

'Coming, dear,' called Mother passively and untruthfully, for Roger showed no signs of quitting the post.

'That dog's been a damned nuisance all the way,' said Larry.

'Don't be so impatient,' said Margo indignantly; 'the dog can't help it . . . and anyway, we had to wait an hour in Naples for *you*.'

'My stomach was out of order,' explained Larry coldly.

'Well, probably *his* stomach's out of order,' said Margo triumphantly. 'It's six of one and a dozen of the other.'

'You mean half a dozen of the other.'

'Whatever I mean, it's the same thing.'

At this moment Mother arrived, slightly dishevelled, and we had to turn our attentions to the task of getting Roger into the cab. He had never been in such a vehicle, and treated it with suspicion. Eventually we had to lift him bodily and hurl him inside, yelping frantically, and then pile in breathlessly after him and hold him down. The horse, frightened by this activity, broke into a shambling trot, and we ended in a tangled heap on the floor of the cab with Roger moaning loudly underneath us.

'What an entry,' said Larry bitterly. 'I had hoped to give an impression of gracious majesty, and this is what happens . . . we arrive in town like a troupe of mediæval tumblers.'

'Don't keep *on*, dear,' Mother said soothingly, straightening her hat; 'we'll soon be at the hotel.'

So our cab clopped and jingled its way into the town, while we sat on the horsehair seats and tried to muster the appearance of gracious majesty Larry required. Roger, wrapped in Leslie's powerful grasp, lolled his head over the side of the vehicle and rolled his eyes as though at his last gasp. Then we rattled past an alley-way in which four scruffy mongrels were lying in the sun. Roger stiffened, glared at them, and let forth a torrent of deep barks. The mongrels were immediately galvanized into activity, and they sped after the cab, yapping vociferously. Our pose was irretrievably shattered, for it took two people to restrain the raving Roger, while the rest of us leaned out of the cab and made wild gestures with magazines and books at the pursuing horde. This only had the effect of exciting them still further, and at each alley-way we passed their numbers increased, until by the time we were rolling down the main thoroughfare of the town there were some twenty-four dogs swirling about our wheels, almost hysterical with anger.

'Why doesn't somebody *do* something?' asked Larry, raising his voice above the uproar. 'This is like a scene from *Uncle Tom's Cabin*.'

'Why don't *you* do something; instead of criticizing?' snapped Leslie, who was locked in combat with Roger.

Larry promptly rose to his feet, snatched the whip from our astonished driver's hand, made a wild swipe at the herd of dogs, missed them, and caught Leslie across the back of the neck.

'What the hell d'you think you're playing at?' Leslie snarled, twisting a scarlet and angry face towards Larry.

'Accident,' explained Larry airily. 'I'm out of practice . . . it's so long since I used a horse whip.'

'Well, watch what you're bloody well doing,' said Leslie loudly and belligerently.

'Now, now, dear, it was an accident,' said Mother.

Larry took another swipe at the dogs and knocked off Mother's hat.

'You're more trouble than the dogs,' said Margo.

'Do be careful, dear,' said Mother, clutching her hat; 'you might hurt someone. I should put the whip down.'

At that moment the cab shambled to a halt outside a doorway over which hung a board with 'Pension Suisse' inscribed on it. The dogs, feeling that they were at last going to get to grips with this effeminate black canine who rode in cabs, surrounded us in a solid, panting wedge. The door of the hotel opened and an ancient bewhiskered porter appeared and stood staring glassily at the turmoil in the street. The difficulties of getting Roger out of the cab and into the hotel were considerable, for he was a heavy dog and it took the combined efforts of the family to lift, carry, and restrain him. Larry had by now forgotten his majestic pose and was rather enjoying himself. He leaped down and danced about the pavement with the whip, cleaving a path through the dogs, along which Leslie, Margo, Mother, and I hurried, bearing the struggling, snarling Roger. We staggered into the hall, and the porter slammed the front door and leaned against it, his moustache quivering. The manager came forward, eyeing us with a mixture of apprehension and curiosity. Mother faced him, hat on one side of her head, clutching in one hand my jam jar of caterpillars.

'Ah!' she said, smiling sweetly, as though our arrival had been the most normal thing in the world. 'Our name's Durrell. I believe you've got some rooms booked for us?'

'Yes, madame,' said the manager, edging round the still grumbling Roger; 'they are on the first floor . . . four rooms and a balcony.'

'How nice,' beamed Mother; 'then I think we'll go straight up and have a little rest before lunch.'

And with considerable majestic graciousness she led her family upstairs.

Later we descended to lunch in a large and gloomy room full of dusty potted palms and contorted statuary. We were served by the bewhiskered porter, who had become the head waiter simply by donning tails and a celluloid dicky that creaked like a convention of crickets. The meal, however, was ample and well cooked, and we ate hungrily. As coffee was served, Larry sat back in his chair with a sigh.

'That was a passable meal,' he said generously. 'What do you think of this place, Mother?'

'Well, the *food's* all right, dear,' said Mother, refusing to commit herself.

'They seem a helpful crowd,' Larry went on. 'The manager himself shifted my bed nearer the window.'

'He wasn't very helpful when I asked for paper,' said Leslie.

'Paper?' asked Mother. 'What did you want paper for?'

'For the lavatory . . . there wasn't any in there,' explained Leslie.

'Shhh! Not at the table,' whispered Mother.

'You obviously don't look,' said Margo in a clear and penetrating voice; 'they've got a little box full by the pan.'

'Margo, dear!' exclaimed Mother, horrified.

'What's the matter? Didn't you see the little box?'

Larry gave a snort of laughter.

'Owing to the somewhat eccentric plumbing system of the town,' he explained to Margo kindly, 'that little box is provided for the . . . er . . . debris, as it were, when you have finished communing with nature.'

Margo's face turned scarlet with a mixture of embarrassment and disgust.

'You mean . . . you mean . . . that was . . . My God! I might have caught some foul disease,' she wailed, and, bursting into tears, fled from the dining-room.

'Most insanitary,' said Mother severely; 'it really is a *disgusting* way to do things. Quite apart from the mistakes one can make, I should think there's a danger of getting typhoid.'

'Mistakes wouldn't happen if they'd organize things properly,' Leslie pointed out, returning to his original complaint.

'Yes, dear; but I don't think we ought to discuss it now. The best thing we can do is to find a house as soon as possible, before we all go down with something.'

Upstairs Margo was in a state of semi-nudity, splashing disinfectant over herself in quantities, and Mother spent an exhausting afternoon being forced to examine her at intervals for the symptoms of the diseases which Margo felt sure she was hatching. It was unfortunate for Mother's peace of mind that the Pension Suisse happened to be situated in the road leading to the local cemetery. As we sat on our small balcony overhanging the street an apparently endless succession of funerals passed beneath us. The inhabitants of Corfu obviously believed that the best part of a bereavement was the funeral, for each seemed more ornate than the last. Cabs decorated with yards of purple and black crêpe were drawn by horses so enveloped in plumes and canopies that it was a wonder they could move. Six or seven of these cabs, containing the mourners in full and uninhibited grief, preceded the corpse itself. This came on another cartlike vehicle, and was ensconced in a coffin so large and lush that it looked more like an enormous birthday cake. Some were white, with purple, black-and-scarlet, and deep blue decorations; others were gleaming black with complicated filigrees of gold and silver twining abundantly over them, and glittering brass handles. I had never seen anything so colourful and attractive. This, I decided, was really the way to die, with shrouded horses, acres of flowers, and a horde of most satisfactorily grief-stricken relatives. I hung over the balcony rail watching the coffins pass beneath, absorbed and fascinated.

As each funeral passed, and the sounds of mourning and the clopping of hooves died away in the distance, Mother became more and more agitated.

'I'm sure it's an epidemic,' she exclaimed at last, peering down nervously into the street.

'Nonsense, Mother; don't fuss,' said Larry airily.

'But, dear, so *many* of them . . . it's unnatural.'

'There's nothing unnatural about dying. People do it all the time.'

'Yes, but they don't die like flies unless there's something wrong.'

'Perhaps they save 'em up and bury 'em in a bunch,' suggested Leslie callously.

'Don't be silly,' said Mother. 'I'm sure it's something to do with the drains. It can't be healthy for people to have *those* sort of arrangements.'

'My God!' said Margo sepulchrally, 'then I suppose I'll get it.'

'No, no, dear; it doesn't follow,' said Mother vaguely; 'it might be something that's not catching.'

'I don't see how you can have an epidemic unless it's something catching,' Leslie remarked logically.

'Anyway,' said Mother, refusing to be drawn into any medical arguments, 'I think we ought to find out. Can't you ring up the health authorities, Larry?'

'There probably aren't any health authorities here,' Larry pointed out, 'and even if there were, I doubt if they'd tell me.'

'Well,' Mother said with determination, 'there's nothing for it. We'll have to move. We must get out of the town. We must find a house in the country *at once.*'

The next morning we started on our house-hunt, accompanied by Mr Beeler, the hotel guide. He was a fat little man with cringing eyes and sweat-polished jowls. He was quite sprightly when we set off, but then he did not know what was in store for him. No one who has not been house-hunting with my mother can possibly imagine it. We drove around the island in a cloud of dust while Mr Beeler showed us villa after villa in a bewildering selection of sizes, colours, and situations, and Mother shook her head firmly at them all. At last we had contemplated the tenth and final villa on Mr Beeler's list, and Mother had shaken her head once again. Brokenly Mr Beeler seated himself on the stairs and mopped his face with his handkerchief.

'Madame Durrell,' he said at last, 'I have shown you every villa I know, yet you do not want any. Madame, what is it you require? What is the matter with these villas?'

Mother regarded him with astonishment.

'Didn't you *notice?*' she asked. 'None of them had a bathroom.'

Mr Beeler stared at Mother with bulging eyes.

'But Madame,' he wailed in genuine anguish, 'what for you want a bathroom? Have you not got the sea?'

We returned in silence to the hotel.

By the following morning Mother had decided that we would hire a car and go out house-hunting on our own. She was convinced that somewhere on the island there lurked a villa with a bathroom. We did not share Mother's belief, and so it was a slightly irritable and argumentative group that she herded down to the taxi rank in the main square. The taxi drivers, perceiving our innocent appearance, scrambled from inside their cars and flocked round us like vultures, each trying to out-shout his compatriots. Their voices grew louder and louder, their eyes flashed, they clutched each other's arms and ground their teeth at one another, and then they laid hold of us as though they would tear us apart. Actually, we were being treated to the mildest of mild altercations, but we were not used to the Greek temperament, and to us it looked as though we were in danger of our lives.

'Can't you *do* something, Larry?' Mother squeaked, disentangling herself with difficulty from the grasp of a large driver.

'Tell them you'll report them to the British consul,' suggested Larry, raising his voice above the noise.

'Don't be silly, dear,' said Mother breathlessly. 'Just explain that we don't understand.'

Margo, simpering, stepped into the breach.

'We English,' she yelled at the gesticulating drivers; 'we no understand Greek.'

'If that man pushes me again I'll poke him in the eye,' said Leslie, his face flushed red.

'Now, now, dear,' panted Mother, still struggling with the driver who was propelling her vigorously towards his car; 'I don't think they mean any harm.'

At that moment everyone was startled into silence by a voice that rumbled out above the uproar, a deep, rich, vibrant voice, the sort of voice you would expect a volcano to have.

'Hoy!' roared the voice. 'Whys donts yous have someones who can talks your own language?'

Turning, we saw an ancient Dodge parked by the curb, and behind the wheel sat a short, barrel-bodied individual, with hamlike hands and a great, leathery, scowling face surmounted by a jauntily tilted peaked cap. He opened the door of the car, surged out onto the pavement, and waddled across to us. Then he stopped, scowling even more ferociously, and surveyed the group of silent cab drivers.

'Thems been worrying yous?' he asked Mother.

'No, no,' said Mother untruthfully; 'it was just that we had difficulty in understanding them.'

'Yous wants someones who can talks your own language,' repeated the new arrival; 'thems bastards . . . if yous will excuses the words . . . would swindles their own mothers. Excuses me a minute and I'll fix thems.'

He turned on the drivers a blast of Greek that almost swept them off their feet. Aggrieved, gesticulating, angry, they were herded back to their cars by this extraordinary man. Having given them a final and, it appeared, derogatory blast of Greek, he turned to us again.

'Wheres yous wants to gos?' he asked, almost truculently.

'Can you take us to look for a villa?' asked Larry.

'Sure. I'll takes yous anywheres. Just yous says.'

'We are looking,' said Mother firmly, 'for a villa with a bath-room. Do you know of one?'

The man brooded like a great, suntanned gargoyle, his black eyebrows twisted into a knot of thoughtfulness.

'Bathrooms?' he said. 'Yous wants a bathrooms?'

'None of the ones we have seen so far had them,' said Mother.

'Oh, I knows a villa with a bathrooms,' said the man. 'I was wondering if its was goings to be bigs enough for yous.'

'Will you take us to look at it, please?' asked Mother.

'Sure, I'll takes yous. Gets into the cars.'

We climbed into the spacious car, and our driver hoisted his bulk behind the steering wheel and engaged his gears with a terrifying sound. We shot through the twisted streets on the outskirts of the town, swerving in and out among the loaded donkeys, the carts, the groups of peasant women, and innumer-able dogs, our horn honking a deafening warning. During this our driver seized the opportunity to engage us in conversation.

Each time he addressed us he would crane his massive head round to see our reactions, and the car would swoop back and forth across the road like a drunken swallow.

'Yous English? Thought so . . . English always wants bathrooms . . . I gets a bathroom in my house . . . Spiro's my name, Spiro Hakiaopulos . . . they alls calls me Spiro Americano on accounts of I lives in America . . . Yes, spent eight years in Chicago . . . That's where I learnt my goods English . . . Wents there to makes moneys . . . Then after eight years I says, "Spiros," I says, "yous mades enough . . ." sos I comes backs to Greece . . . brings this car . . . best ons the islands . . . no one else gets a car like this . . . All the English tourists knows me, theys all asks for me when theys comes here . . . Theys knows theys wonts be swindled . . . I likes the English . . . best kinds of peoples . . . Honest to Gods, ifs I wasn't Greek I'd likes to be English.'

We sped down a white road covered in a thick layer of silky dust that rose in a boiling cloud behind us, a road lined with prickly pears like a fence of green plates each cleverly balanced on another's edge, and splashed with knobs of scarlet fruit. We passed vineyards where the tiny, stunted vines were laced in green leaves, olive groves where the pitted trunks made a hundred astonished faces at us out of the gloom of their own shadow, and great clumps of zebra-striped cane that fluttered their leaves like a multitude of green flags. At last we roared to the top of a hill, and Spiro crammed on his brakes and brought the car to a dust-misted halt.

'Theres you ares,' he said, pointing with a great stubby forefinger; 'thats the villa with the bathrooms, likes yous wanted.'

Mother, who had kept her eyes firmly shut throughout the drive, now opened them cautiously and looked. Spiro was pointing at a gentle curve of hillside that rose from the glittering sea. The hill and the valleys around it were an eiderdown of olive groves that shone with a fishlike gleam where the breeze touched the leaves. Halfway up the slope, guarded by a group of tall, slim cypress trees, nestled a small strawberry-pink villa, like some exotic fruit lying in the greenery. The cypress trees undulated gently in the breeze, as if they were busily painting the sky a still brighter blue for our arrival.

2

The Strawberry-Pink Villa

The villa was small and square, standing in its tiny garden with an air of pink-faced determination. It shutters had been faded by the sun to a delicate creamy green, cracked and bubbled in places. The garden, surrounded by tall fuchsia hedges, had flower beds worked in complicated geometrical patterns, marked with smooth white stones. The white cobbled paths, scarcely as wide as a rake's head, wound laboriously round beds hardly larger than a big straw hat, beds in the shape of stars, half-moons, triangles, and circles, all overgrown with a shaggy tangle of flowers run wild. Roses dropped petals that seemed as big and smooth as saucers, flame red, moon white, glossy, and un-wrinkled; marigolds like broods of shaggy suns stood watching their parents' progress through the sky. In the low growth the pansies pushed their velvety, innocent faces through the leaves, and the violets drooped sorrowfully under their heart-shaped leaves. The bougainvillæa that sprawled luxuriously over the tiny front balcony was hung, as though for a carnival, with its lantern-shaped magenta flowers. In the darkness of the fuchsia hedge a thousand ballerina-like blooms quivered expectantly. The warm air was thick with the scent of a hundred dying flowers, and full of the gentle, soothing whisper and murmur of insects. As soon as we saw it, we wanted to live there; it was as though the villa had been standing there waiting for our arrival. We felt we had come home.

Having lumbered so unexpectedly into our lives, Spiro now took over complete control of our affairs. It was better, he explained, for him to do things, as everyone knew him, and he would make sure we were not swindled.

'Donts you worrys yourselfs about anythings, Mrs Durrells,' he had scowled; 'leaves everythings to me.'

So he would take us shopping, and after an hour's sweating and roaring he would get the price of an article reduced by perhaps two drachmas. This was approximately a penny; it was not the cash, but the principle of the thing, he explained. The fact that he was Greek and adored bargaining was, of course, another reason. It was Spiro who, on discovering that our money had not yet arrived from England, subsidized us, and took it upon himself to go and speak severely to the bank manager about his lack of organization. That it was not the poor manager's fault did not deter him in the least. It was Spiro who paid our hotel bill, who organized a car to carry our luggage to the villa, and who drove us out there himself, his car piled high with groceries that he had purchased for us.

That he knew everyone on the island, and that they all knew him, we soon discovered was no idle boast. Wherever his car stopped, half a dozen voices would shout out his name, and hands would beckon him to sit at the little tables under the trees and drink coffee. Policemen, peasants, and priests waved and smiled as he passed; fishermen, grocers, and café owners greeted him like a brother. 'Ah, Spiro!' they would say, and smile at him affectionately as though he were a naughty but lovable child. They respected his honesty and his belligerence, and above all they adored his typically Greek scorn and fearlessness when dealing with any form of governmental red tape. On arrival, two of our cases containing linen and other things had been confiscated by the customs on the curious grounds that they were merchandise. So, when we moved out to the strawberry-pink villa and the problem of bed linen arose, Mother told Spiro about our cases languishing in the customs, and asked his advice.

'Gollys, Mrs Durrells,' he bellowed, his huge face flushing red with wrath; 'whys you never tells me befores? Thems bastards in the customs. I'll take you down theres tomorrows and fix thems: I knows thems alls, and they knows *me*. Leaves everythings to me – I'll fix thems.'

The following morning he drove Mother down to the customs shed. We all accompanied them, for we did not want to miss the fun. Spiro rolled into the customs house like an angry bear.

'Wheres these peoples things?' he inquired of the plump little customs man.

'You mean their boxes of merchandise?' asked the customs official in his best English.

'Whats you thinks I means?'

'They are here,' admitted the official cautiously.

'We've comes to takes thems,' scowled Spiro; 'gets thems ready.'

He turned and stalked out of the shed to find someone to help carry the luggage, and when he returned he saw that the customs man had taken the keys from Mother and was just lifting the lid of one of the cases. Spiro, with a grunt of wrath, surged forward and slammed the lid down on the unfortunate man's fingers.

'Whats fors you open it, you sonofabitch?' he asked, glaring.

The customs official, waving his pinched hand about, protested wildly that it was his duty to examine the contents.

'Dutys?' said Spiro with fine scorn. 'Whats you means, dutys? Is it your dutys to attacks innocent foreigners, eh? Treats thems like smugglers, eh? Thats whats yous calls dutys?'

Spiro paused for a moment, breathing deeply; then he picked up a large suitcase in each great hand and walked towards the door. He paused and turned to fire his parting shot.

'I knows you, Christaki, sos donts you go talkings about dutys to me. I remembers when you was fined twelve thousand drachmas for dynamitings fish. I won't have any criminal talkings to *me* abouts dutys.'

We rode back from the customs in triumph, all our luggage intact and unexamined.

'Thems bastards thinks they owns the islands,' was Spiro's

comment. He seemed quite unaware of the fact that he was acting as though he did.

Once Spiro had taken charge he stuck to us like a burr. Within a few hours he had changed from a taxi driver to our champion, and within a week he was our guide, philosopher, and friend. He became so much a member of the family that very soon there was scarcely a thing we did, or planned to do, in which he was not involved in some way. He was always there, bull-voiced and scowling, arranging things we wanted done, telling us how much to pay for things, keeping a watchful eye on us all and reporting to Mother anything he thought she should know. Like a great, brown, ugly angel he watched over us as tenderly as though we were slightly weak-minded children. Mother he frankly adored, and he would sing her praises in a loud voice wherever we happened to be, to her acute embarrassment.

'You oughts to be carefuls whats you do,' he would tell us, screwing up his face earnestly; 'we donts wants to worrys your mothers.'

'Whatever for, Spiro?' Larry would protest in well-simulated astonishment. 'She's never done anything for us . . . why should we consider her?'

'Gollys, Master Lorrys, donts *jokes* like that,' Spiro would say in anguish.

'He's quite right, Spiro,' Leslie would say very seriously; 'she's really not much good as a mother, you know.'

'Donts says that, *donts says that*,' Spiro would roar. 'Honest to Gods, if I hads a mother likes yours I'd gos down every mornings and kisses her feets.'

So we were installed in the villa, and we each settled down and adapted ourselves to our surroundings in our respective ways. Margo, merely by donning a microscopic swim suit and sun-bathing in the olive groves, had collected an ardent band of handsome peasant youths who appeared like magic from an apparently deserted landscape whenever a bee flew too near her or her deck chair needed moving. Mother felt forced to point out that she thought this sun-bathing was rather *unwise*.

'After all, dear, that costume doesn't cover an awful lot, does it?' she pointed out.

'Oh, Mother, don't be so old-fashioned,' Margo said impatiently. 'After all, you only die once.'

This remark was as baffling as it was true, and successfully silenced Mother.

It had taken three husky peasant boys half an hour's sweating and panting to get Larry's trunks into the villa, while Larry bustled round them, directing operations. One of the trunks was so big it had to be hoisted in through the window. Once they were installed, Larry spent a happy day unpacking them, and the room was so full of books that it was almost impossible to get in or out. Having constructed battlements of books round the outer perimeter, Larry would spend the whole day in there with his typewriter, only emerging dreamily for meals. On the second morning he appeared in a highly irritable frame of mind, for a peasant had tethered his donkey just over the hedge. At regular intervals the beast would throw out its head and let forth a prolonged and lugubrious bray.

'I ask you! Isn't it laughable that future generations should be deprived of my work simply because some horny-handed idiot has tied that stinking beast of burden near my window?' Larry asked.

'Yes, dear,' said Mother, 'why don't you move it if it disturbs you?'

'My dear Mother, I can't be expected to spend my time chasing donkeys about the olive groves. I threw a pamphlet on Theosophy at it; what more do you expect me to do?'

'The poor thing's tied up. You can't expect it to untie itself,' said Margo.

'There should be a law against parking those loathsome beasts anywhere near a house. Can't one of you go and move it?'

'Why should we? It's not disturbing us,' said Leslie.

'That's the trouble with this family,' said Larry bitterly; 'no give and take, no consideration for others.'

'You don't have much consideration for others,' said Margo.

'It's all your fault, Mother,' said Larry austerely; 'you shouldn't have brought us up to be so selfish.'

'I like that!' exclaimed Mother. 'I never did anything of the sort!'

'Well, we didn't get as selfish as this without *some* guidance,' said Larry.

In the end, Mother and I unhitched the donkey and moved it farther down the hill.

Leslie meanwhile had unpacked his revolvers and startled us all with an apparently endless series of explosions while he fired at an old tin can from his bedroom window. After a particularly deafening morning, Larry erupted from his room and said he could not be expected to work if the villa was going to be rocked to its foundations every five minutes. Leslie, aggrieved, said that he had to practise. Larry said it didn't sound like practice, but more like the Indian Mutiny. Mother, whose nerves had also been somewhat frayed by the reports, suggested that Leslie practise with an empty revolver. Leslie spent half an hour explaining why this was impossible. At length he reluctantly took his tin farther away from the house where the noise was slightly muffled but just as unexpected.

In between keeping a watchful eye on us all, Mother was settling down in her own way. The house was redolent with the scent of herbs and the sharp tang of garlic and onions, and the kitchen was full of a bubbling selection of pots, among which she moved, spectacles askew, muttering to herself. On the table was a tottering pile of books which she consulted from time to time. When she could drag herself away from the kitchen, she would drift happily about the garden, reluctantly pruning and cutting, enthusiastically weeding and planting.

For myself, the garden held sufficient interest; together Roger and I learned some surprising things. Roger, for example, found that it was unwise to smell hornets, that the peasant dogs ran screaming if he glanced at them through the gate, and that the chickens that leaped suddenly from the fuchsia hedge, squawking wildly as they fled, were unlawful prey, however desirable.

This doll's-house garden was a magic land, a forest of flowers through which roamed creatures I had never seen before. Among the thick, silky petals of each rose bloom lived tiny, crablike spiders that scuttled sideways when disturbed. Their small, translucent bodies were coloured to match the flowers they inhabited: pink, ivory, wine red, or buttery yellow. On the rose stems, encrusted with green flies, lady-birds moved like newly painted toys; lady-birds pale red with large black spots; lady-birds apple red with brown spots; lady-birds orange with grey-and-black freckles. Rotund and amiable, they prowled and fed among the anæmic flocks of greenfly. Carpenter bees, like furry, electric-blue bears, zigzagged among the flowers, growling fatly and busily. Humming bird hawk-moths, sleek and neat, whipped up and down the paths with a fussy efficiency, pausing occasionally on speed-misty wings to lower a long, slender proboscis into a bloom. Among the white cobbles large black ants staggered and gesticulated in groups round strange trophies: a dead caterpillar, a piece of rose petal or a dried grass-head fat with seeds. As an accompaniment to all this activity there came from the olive groves outside the fuchsia hedge the incessant shimmering cries of the cicadas. If the curious, blurring heat haze produced a sound, it would be exactly the strange, chiming cries of these insects.

At first I was so bewildered by this profusion of life on our very doorstep that I could only move about the garden in a daze, watching now this creature, now that, constantly having my attention distracted by the flights of brilliant butterflies that drifted over the hedge. Gradually, as I became more used to the bustle of insect life among the flowers, I found I could concentrate more. I would spend hours squatting on my heels or lying on my stomach watching the private lives of the creatures around me, while Roger sat nearby, a look of resignation on his face. In this way I learned a lot of fascinating things.

I found that the little crab spiders could change colour just as successfully as any chameleon. Take a spider from a wine-red rose, where he had been sitting like a bead of coral, and place him in the depths of a cool white rose. If he stayed there – and most of them did – you would see his colour gradually ebb away, as though the change had given him anæmia, until, some two days later, he would be crouching among the white petals like a pearl.

I discovered that in the dry leaves under the fuchsia hedge lived another type of spider, a fierce little huntsman with the cunning and ferocity of a tiger. He would stalk about his continent of leaves, eyes glistening in the sun, pausing now and then to raise himself up on his hairy legs to peer about. If he saw a fly settle to enjoy a sun-bath he would freeze; then, as slowly as a leaf growing, he would move forward, imperceptibly, edging nearer and nearer, pausing occasionally to fasten his life-line of silk to the surface of the leaves. Then, when close enough, the huntsman would pause, his legs shift minutely as he got a good purchase, and then he would leap, legs spread out in a hairy embrace, straight onto the dreaming fly. Never did I see one of these little spiders miss its kill, once it had manœuvred into the right position.

All these discoveries filled me with a tremendous delight, so that they had to be shared, and I would burst suddenly into the house and startle the family with the news that the strange, spiky black caterpillars on the roses were not caterpillars at all, but the young of lady-birds, or with the equally astonishing news that lacewing flies laid eggs on stilts. This last miracle I was lucky enough to witness. I found a lacewing fly on the roses and watched her as she climbed about the leaves, admiring her beautiful, fragile wings like green glass, and her enormous liquid golden eyes. Presently she stopped on the surface of a rose leaf and lowered the tip of her abdomen. She remained like that for a moment and then raised her tail, and from it, to my astonishment, rose a slender thread, like a pale hair. Then, on the very tip of this stalk, appeared the egg. The female had a rest, and then repeated the performance until the surface of the rose leaf looked as though it were covered with a forest of tiny club moss. The laying over, the female rippled her antennæ briefly and flew off in a mist of green gauze wings.

Perhaps the most exciting discovery I made in this multi-coloured Lilliput to which I had access was an earwig's nest. I had long wanted to find one and had searched everywhere without success, so the joy of stumbling upon one unexpectedly was overwhelming, like suddenly being given a wonderful present. I moved a piece of bark and there beneath it was the nursery, a small hollow in the earth that the insect must have burrowed out for herself. She squatted in the middle of it, shielding underneath her a few white eggs. She crouched over them like a hen, and did not move when the flood of sunlight struck her as I lifted the bark. I could not count the eggs, but there did not seem to be many, so I presumed that she had not yet laid her full complement. Tenderly I replaced her lid of bark.

From that moment I guarded the nest jealously. I erected a protecting wall of rocks round it, and as an additional precaution I wrote out a notice in red ink and stuck it on a pole nearby as a warning to the family. The notice read: 'BEWAR – EARWIG NEST – QUIAT PLESE.' It was only remarkable in that the two correctly spelled words were biological ones. Every hour or so I would subject the mother earwig to ten minutes' close scrutiny. I did not dare examine her more often for fear she might desert her nest. Eventually the pile of eggs beneath her grew, and she seemed to have become accustomed to my lifting off her bark roof. I even decided that she had begun to recognize me, from the friendly way she waggled her antennæ.

To my acute disappointment, after all my efforts and constant sentry duty, the babies hatched out during the night. I felt that, after all I had done, the female might have held up the hatching until I was there to witness it. However, there they were, a fine brood of young earwigs, minute, frail, looking as though they had been carved out of ivory. They moved gently under their mother's body, walking between her legs, the more venturesome even climbing onto her pincers. It was a heart-warming sight. The next day the nursery was empty: my wonderful family had scattered over the garden. I saw one of the babies some time later; he was bigger, of course, browner and stronger, but I recognized him immediately. He was curled up in a maze of rose petals, having a sleep, and when I disturbed him he merely raised his pincers irritably over his back. I would have liked to think that it was a salute, a cheerful greeting, but honesty compelled me to admit that it was nothing more than an earwig's warning to a potential enemy. Still, I excused him. After all, he had been very young when I last saw him.

I came to know the plump peasant girls who passed the garden every morning and evening. Riding side-saddle on their slouching, drooping-eared donkeys, they were shrill and colourful as parrots, and their chatter and laughter echoed among the olive trees. In the mornings they would smile and shout greetings as their donkeys pattered past, and in the evenings they would lean over the fuchsia hedge, balancing precariously on their steeds' backs, and, smiling, hold out gifts for me – a bunch of amber grapes still sun-warmed, some figs black as tar striped with pink where they had burst their seams with ripeness, or a giant watermelon with an inside like pink ice. As the days passed, I came gradually to understand them. What had at first been a confused babble became a series of recognizable separate sounds. Then, suddenly, these took on meaning, and slowly and haltingly

I started to use them myself; then I took my newly acquired words and strung them into ungrammatical and stumbling sentences. Our neighbours were delighted, as though I had conferred some delicate compliment by trying to learn their language. They would lean over the hedge, their faces screwed up with concentration, as I groped my way through a greeting or a simple remark, and when I had successfully concluded they would beam at me, nodding and smiling, and clap their hands. By degrees I learned their names, who was related to whom, which were married and which hoped to be, and other details. I learned where their little cottages were among the olive groves, and should Roger and I chance to pass that way the entire family, vociferous and pleased, would tumble out to greet us, to bring a chair, so that I might sit under their vine and eat some fruit with them.

Gradually the magic of the island settled over us as gently and clingingly as pollen. Each day had a tranquillity, a timelessness, about it, so that you wished it would never end. But then the dark skin of night would peel off and there would be a fresh day waiting for us, glossy and colourful as a child's transfer and with the same tinge of unreality.

3

The Rose-Beetle Man

In the morning, when I woke, the bedroom shutters were luminous and barred with gold from the rising sun. The morning air was full of the scent of charcoal from the kitchen fire, full of eager cock-crows, the distant yap of dogs, and the unsteady, melancholy tune of the goat bells as the flocks were driven out to pasture.

We ate breakfast out in the garden, under the small tangerine trees. The sky was fresh and shining, not yet the fierce blue of noon, but a clear milky opal. The flowers were half asleep, roses dew-crumpled, marigolds still tightly shut. Breakfast was, on the whole, a leisurely and silent meal, for no member of the family was very talkative at that hour. By the end of the meal the influence of the coffee, toast, and eggs made itself felt, and we started to revive, to tell each other what we intended to do, why we intended to do it, and then argue earnestly as to whether each had made a wise decision. I never joined in these discussions, for I knew perfectly well what I intended to do, and would concentrate on finishing my food as rapidly as possible.

'*Must* you gulp and slush your food like that?' Larry would inquire in a pained voice, delicately picking his teeth with a matchstick.

'Eat it slowly, dear,' Mother would murmur; 'there's no hurry.'

No hurry? With Roger waiting at the garden gate, an alert black shape, watching for me with eager brown eyes? No hurry, with the first sleepy cicadas starting to fiddle experimentally among the olives? No hurry, with the island waiting, morning cool, bright as a star, to be explored? I could hardly expect the family to understand this point of view, however, so I would slow down until I felt that their attention had been attracted elsewhere, and then stuff my mouth again.

Finishing at last, I would slip from the table and saunter towards the gate, where Roger sat gazing at me with a questioning air. Together we would peer through the wrought-iron gates into the olive groves beyond. I would suggest to Roger that perhaps it wasn't worth going out today. He would wag his stump in hasty denial, and his nose would butt at my hand. No, I would say, I really didn't think we ought to go out. It looked as though it was going to rain, and I would peer up into the clear, burnished sky with a worried expression. Roger, ears cocked, would peer into the sky too, and then look at me imploringly. Anyway, I would go on, if it didn't look like rain now it was almost certain to rain later, and so it would be much safer just to sit in the garden with a book. Roger, in desperation, would place a large black paw on the gate, and then look at me, lifting one side of his upper lip, displaying his white teeth in a lopsided, ingratiating grin, his stump working itself into a blur of excitement. This was his trump card, for he knew I could never resist his ridiculous grin. So I would stop teasing him, fetch my match-boxes and my butterfly net, the garden gate would creak open and clang shut, and Roger would be off through the olive groves swiftly as a cloud-shadow, his deep bark welcoming the new day.

In those early days of exploration Roger was my constant companion. Together we ventured farther and farther afield, discovering quiet, remote olive groves which had to be investigated and remembered, working our way through a maze of blackbird-haunted myrtles, venturing into narrow valleys where the cypress trees cast a cloak of mysterious, inky shadow. He was the perfect companion for an adventure, affectionate without exuberance, brave without being belligerent, intelligent and full of good-humoured tolerance for my eccentricities. If I slipped when climbing a dew-shiny bank, Roger appeared suddenly, gave a snort that sounded like suppressed laughter, a quick look over, a rapid lick of commiseration, shook himself, sneezed, and gave me his lopsided grin. If I found something that interested me – an ant's nest, a caterpillar on a leaf, a spider wrapping up a fly in swaddling clothes of silk – Roger sat down and waited until I had finished examining it. If he thought I was taking too long, he shifted nearer, gave a gentle, whiny yawn, and then sighed deeply and started to wag his tail. If the matter was of no great importance, we would move on, but if it was something absorbing that had to be pored over, I had only to frown at Roger and he would realize it was going to be a long job. His ears would droop, his tail slow down and stop, and he would slouch off to the nearest bush and fling himself down in the shade, giving me a martyred look as he did so.

During these trips Roger and I came to know and be known by a great number of people in various parts of the surrounding countryside. There was, for example, a strange, mentally defective youth with a round face as expressionless as a puffball. He was always dressed in tattered shirt, shiny blue serge trousers that were rolled up to the knee, and on his head the elderly remains of a bowler hat without a brim. Whenever he saw us he came hurrying through the olives, raised his absurd hat politely, and wished us good day in a voice as childish and sweet as a flute. He would stand, watching us without expression, nodding at any remark I happened to make, for ten minutes or so. Then, raising his hat politely, he would go off through the trees. And there was the immensely fat and cheerful Agathi, who lived in a tiny tumbledown cottage high up the hill. She was always sitting outside her house with a spindle of sheep's wool, twining and pulling it into coarse thread. She must have been well over seventy, but her hair was still black and lustrous, plaited carefully and wound round a pair of polished cow's horns, an ornament that some of the older peasant women adopted. As she sat in the sun, like a great black toad with a scarlet head-dress draped over the cow's horns, the bobbin of wool would rise and fall, twisting like a top, her fingers busy unravelling and plucking, and her drooping mouth with its hedge of broken and discoloured teeth wide open as she sang, loudly and harshly, but with great vigour.

It was from Agathi that I learned some of the most beautiful and haunting of the peasant songs. Sitting on an old tin in the sun, eating grapes or pomegranates from her garden, I would sing with her, and she would break off now and then to correct my pronunciation. We sang, verse by verse, the gay, rousing song of the river, *Vangelió*, and of how it dropped from the mountains, making the gardens rich, the fields fertile, and the trees heavy with fruit. We sang, rolling our eyes at each other in exaggerated coquetry, the funny little love song called 'False-hood'. 'Lies, lies,' we warbled, shaking our heads, 'all lies, but it is my fault for teaching you to go round the countryside telling people I love you.' Then we would strike a mournful note and sing, perhaps, the slow, lilting song called 'Why Are You Leaving Me?' We were almost overcome by this one, and would wail out the long, soulful lyrics, our voices quavering. When we came to the last bit, the most heart-rending of all, Agathi would clasp her hands to her great breasts, her black eyes would become misty and sad, and her chins would tremble with emotion. As the last discordant notes of our duet faded away, she would turn to me, wiping her nose on the corner of her head-dress.

'What fools we are, eh? What fools, sitting here in the sun, singing. And of love, too! I am too old for it and you are too young, and yet we waste our time singing about it. Ah, well, let's have a glass of wine, eh?'

Apart from Agathi, the person I liked best was the old shepherd Yani, a tall, slouching man with a great hooked nose like an eagle's, and incredible moustaches. I first met him one hot afternoon when Roger and I had spent an exhausting hour trying to dig a large green lizard out of its hole in a stone wall. At length, unsuccessful, sweaty and tired, we had flung ourselves down beneath five little cypress trees that cast a neat square of shadow on the sun-bleached grass. Lying there, I heard the gentle, drowsy tinkling of a goat bell, and presently the herds wandered past us, pausing to stare with vacant yellow eyes, bleat sneeringly, and then move on. The soft sound of their bells, and of their mouths ripping and tearing at the undergrowth, had a soothing effect on me, and by the time they had drifted slowly past and the shepherd appeared I was nearly asleep. He stopped and looked at me, leaning heavily on his brown olive-wood stick, his little black eyes fierce under his shaggy brows, his big boots planted firmly in the heather.

'Good afternoon,' he greeted me gruffly; 'you are the foreigner . . . the little English lord?'

By then I was used to the curious peasant idea that all English people were lords, and I admitted that that's who I was. He turned and roared at a goat which had reared onto its hind legs and was tearing at a young olive, and then turned back.

'I will tell you something, little lord,' he said; 'it is dangerous for you to lie here, beneath these trees.'

I glanced up at the cypresses, but they seemed safe enough to me, and so I asked why he thought they were dangerous.

'Ah, you may *sit* under them, yes. They cast a good shadow, cold as well-water; but that's the trouble, they tempt you to sleep. And you must never, for any reason, sleep beneath a cypress.'

He paused, stroked his moustache, waited for me to ask why, and then went on:

'Why? Why? Because if you did you would be changed when you woke. Yes, the black cypresses, they are dangerous. While you sleep, their roots grow into your brains and steal them, and when you wake up you are mad, head as empty as a whistle.'

I asked whether it was only the cypress that could do this, or did it apply to other trees.

'No, only the cypress,' said the old man, peering up fiercely at the trees above me as though to see whether they were listening; 'only the cypress is the thief of intelligence. So be warned, little lord, and don't sleep here.'

He nodded briefly, gave another fierce glance at the dark blades of the cypress, as if daring them to make some comment, and then picked his way carefully through the myrtle bushes to where his goats grazed scattered about the hill, their great udders swinging like bagpipes beneath their bellies.

I got to know Yani very well, for I was always meeting him during my explorations, and occasionally I visited him in his little house, when he would ply me with fruit, and give me advice and warnings to keep me safe on my walks.

Perhaps one of the most weird and fascinating characters I met during my travels was the Rose-Beetle Man. He had a fairy-tale air about him that was impossible to resist, and I used to look forward eagerly to my infrequent meetings with him. I first saw him on a high, lonely road leading to one of the remote mountain villages. I could hear him long before I could see him, for he was playing a rippling tune on a shepherd's pipe, breaking off now and then to sing a few words in a curious nasal voice. As he rounded the corner both Roger and I stopped and stared at him in amazement.

He had a sharp, foxlike face with large, slanting eyes of such a dark brown that they appeared black. They had a weird, vacant look about them, and a sort of bloom such as one finds on a plum, a pearly covering almost like a cataract. He was short and slight, with a thinness about his wrists and neck that argued a lack of food. His dress was fantastic, and on his head was a shapeless hat with a very wide, floppy brim. It had once been bottle green, but was now speckled and smeared with dust, wine stains, and cigarette burns. In the band were stuck a fluttering forest of feathers: cock feathers, hoopoe feathers, owl feathers, the wing of a kingfisher, the claw of a hawk, and a large dirty white feather that may have come from a swan. His shirt was worn and frayed, grey with sweat, and round the neck dangled an enormous cravat of the most startling blue satin. His coat was dark and shapeless, with patches of different hues here and there; on the sleeve a bit of white cloth with a design of rosebuds; on the shoulder a triangular patch of wine-red and white spots. The pockets of this garment bulged, the contents almost spilling out: combs, balloons, little highly coloured pictures of the saints, olive-wood carvings of snakes, camels, dogs, and horses, cheap mirrors, a riot of handkerchiefs, and long twisted rolls of bread decorated with seeds. His trousers, patched like his coat, drooped over a pair of scarlet *charouhias*, leather shoes with upturned toes decorated with a large black-and-white pompon. This extraordinary character carried on his back bamboo cages full of pigeons and young chickens, several mysterious sacks, and a large bunch of fresh green leeks. With one hand he held his pipe to his mouth, and in the other a number of lengths of cotton, to each of which was tied an almond-size rose-beetle, glittering golden green in the sun, all of them flying round his hat with desperate, deep buzzings, trying to escape from the threads tied firmly round their waists. Occasionally, tired of circling round and round without success, one of the beetles would settle for a moment on his hat, before launching itself off once more on its endless merry-go-round.

When he saw us the Rose-Beetle Man stopped, gave a very exaggerated start, doffed his ridiculous hat, and swept us a low bow. Roger was so overcome by this unlooked-for attention that he let out a volley of surprised barks. The man smiled at us, put on his hat again, raised his hands, and waggled his long, bony fingers at me. Amused and rather startled by this apparition, I politely bade him good day. He gave another courtly bow. I asked him if he had been to some fiesta. He nodded his head vigorously, raised his pipe to his lips and played a lilting little tune on it, pranced a few steps in the dust of the road, and then stopped and jerked his thumb over his shoulder, pointing back the way he had come. He smiled, patted his pockets, and rubbed his forefinger and thumb together in the Greek way of expressing money. I suddenly realized that he must be dumb. So, standing in the middle of the road, I carried on a conversation with him and he replied with a varied and very clever pantomime. I asked what the rose-beetles were for, and why he had them tied with pieces of cotton. He held his hand out to denote small boys, took one of the lengths of cotton from which a beetle hung, and whirled it rapidly round his head. Immediately the insect came to life and started on its planet-like circling of his hat, and he beamed at me. Pointing up at the sky, he stretched his arms out and gave a deep nasal buzzing, while he banked and swooped across the road. Aeroplane, any fool could see that. Then he pointed to the beetles, held out his hand to denote children and whirled his stock of beetles round his head so that they all started to buzz peevishly.

Exhausted by his explanation, he sat down by the edge of the road, played a short tune on his flute, breaking off to sing in his curious nasal voice. They were not articulate words he used, but a series of strange gruntings and tenor squeaks, that appeared to be formed at the back of his throat and expelled through his nose. He produced them, however, with such verve and such wonderful facial expressions that you were convinced the curious sounds really meant something. Presently he stuffed his flute into his bulging pocket, gazed at me reflectively for a moment, and then swung a small sack off his shoulder, undid it, and, to my delight and astonishment, tumbled half a dozen tortoises into the dusty road. Their shells had been polished with oil until they shone, and by some means or other he had managed to decorate their front legs with little red bows. Slowly and ponderously they unpacked their heads and legs from their gleaming shells and set off down the road, doggedly and without enthusiasm. I watched them, fascinated; the one that particularly took my fancy was quite a small one with a shell about the size of a tea-cup. It seemed more sprightly than the others, and its shell was a paler colour – chestnut, caramel, and amber. Its eyes were bright and its walk was as alert as any tortoise's could be. I sat contemplating it for a long time. I convinced myself that the family would greet its arrival at the villa with tremendous enthusiasm, even, perhaps, congratulating me on finding such an elegant specimen. The fact that I had no money on me did not worry me in the slightest, for I would simply tell the man to call at the villa for payment the next day. It never occurred to me that he might not trust me. The fact that I was English was sufficient, for the islanders had a love and respect for the Englishman out of all proportion to his worth. They would trust an Englishman where they would not trust each other. I asked the Rose-Beetle Man the price of the little tortoise. He held up both hands, fingers spread out. However, I hadn't watched the peasants transacting business for nothing. I shook my head firmly and held up two fingers, unconsciously imitating the man. He closed his eyes in horror at the thought, and held up nine fingers; I held up three; he shook his head, and after some thought held up six fingers; I, in return, shook my head and held up five. The Rose-Beetle Man shook his head, and sighed deeply and sorrowfully, so we sat in silence and stared at the tortoises crawling heavily and uncertainly about the road, with the curious graceless determination of babies. Presently the Rose-Beetle Man indicated the little tortoise and held up six fingers again. I shook my head and held up five. Roger yawned loudly; he was thoroughly bored by this silent bargaining. The Rose-Beetle Man picked up the reptile and showed me in panto-mime how smooth and lovely its shell was, how erect its head, how pointed its nails. I remained implacable. He shrugged, handed me the tortoise, and held up five fingers.

Then I told him I had no money, and that he would have to come the next day to the villa, and he nodded as if it were the most natural thing in the world. Excited by owning this new pet, I wanted to get back home as quickly as possible in order to show it to everyone, so I said good-bye, thanked him, and hurried off along the road. When I reached the place where I had to cut down through the olive groves, I stopped and examined my acquisition carefully. He was undoubtedly the finest tortoise I had ever seen, and worth, in my opinion, at least twice what I had paid for him. I patted his scaly head with my finger and placed him carefully in my pocket. Before diving down the hillside I glanced back. The Rose-Beetle Man was still in the same place on the road, but he was doing a little jig, prancing and swaying, his flute warbling, while in the road at his feet the tortoises ambled to and fro, dimly and heavily.

The new arrival was duly christened Achilles, and turned out to be a most intelligent and lovable beast, possessed of a peculiar sense of humour. At first he was tethered by a leg in the garden, but as he grew tamer we let him go where he pleased. He learned his name in a very short time, and we had only to call out once or twice and then wait patiently for a while and he would appear, lumbering along the narrow cobbled paths on tip-toe, his head and neck stretched out eagerly. He loved being fed, and would squat regally in the sun while we held out bits of lettuce, dandelions, or grapes for him. He loved grapes as much as Roger did, so there was always great rivalry. Achilles would sit mumbling the grapes in his mouth, the juice running down his chin, and Roger would lie nearby, watching him with agonized eyes, his mouth drooling saliva. Roger always had his fair share of the fruit, but even so he seemed to think it a waste to give such delicacies to a tortoise. When the feeding was over, if I didn't keep an eye on him, Roger would creep up to Achilles and lick his front vigorously in an attempt to get the grape juice that the reptile had dribbled down himself. Achilles, affronted at such a liberty, would snap at Roger's nose, and then, when the licks became too overpowering and moist, he would retreat into his shell with an indignant wheeze, and refuse to come out until we had removed Roger from the scene.

But the fruit that Achilles liked best were wild strawberries. He would become positively hysterical at the mere sight of them, lumbering to and fro, craning his head to see if you were going to give him any, gazing at you pleadingly with his tiny shoe-button eyes. The very small strawberries he could devour at a gulp, for they were only the size of a fat pea. But if you gave him a big one, say the size of a hazel nut, he behaved in a way that I had never seen another tortoise emulate. He would grab the fruit and, holding it firmly in his mouth, would stumble off at top speed until he reached a safe and secluded spot among the flower beds, where he would drop the fruit and then eat it at leisure, returning for another one when he had finished.

As well as developing a passion for strawberries, Achilles also developed a passion for human company. Let anyone come into the garden to sit and sun-bathe, to read, or for any other reason, and before long there would be a rustling among the sweet-williams, and Achilles's wrinkled and earnest face would be poked through. If you were sitting in a chair, he contented himself with getting as close to your feet as possible, and there he would sink into a deep and peaceful sleep, his head drooping out of his shell, his nose resting on the ground. If, however, you were lying on a rug, sun-bathing, Achilles would be convinced that you were lying on the ground simply in order to provide him with amusement. He would surge down the path and onto the rug with an expression of bemused good humour on his face. He would pause, survey you thoughtfully, and then choose a portion of your anatomy on which to practise mountaineering. Suddenly to have the sharp claws of a determined tortoise embedded in your thigh as he tries to lever himself up onto your stomach is not conducive to relaxation. If you shook him off and moved the rug it would only give you temporary respite, for Achilles would circle the garden grimly until he found you again. This habit became so tiresome that, after many complaints and threats from the family, I had to lock him up whenever we lay in the garden.

Then one day the garden gate was left open and Achilles was nowhere to be found. Search parties were immediately organized, and the family, who up till then had spent most of their time openly making threats against the reptile's life, wandered about the olive groves, shouting, 'Achilles . . . strawberries, Achilles . . . Achilles . . . strawberries . . .' At length we found him. Ambling along in his usual detached manner, he had fallen into a disused well, the wall of which had long since disintegrated, and the mouth of which was almost covered by ferns. He was, to our regret, quite dead. Even Leslie's attempts at artificial respiration and Margo's suggestion of forcing strawberries down his throat (to give him, as she explained, something to live for) failed to get any response. So, mournfully and solemnly, his corpse was buried in the garden under a small strawberry plant (Mother's sugges-tion). A short funeral address, written and read in a trembling voice by Larry, made the occasion a memorable one. It was only marred by Roger, who, in spite of all my protests, insisted on wagging his tail throughout the burial service.

Not long after Achilles had been taken from us I obtained another pet from the Rose-Beetle Man. This time it was a pigeon. He was still very young and had to be force-fed on bread-and-milk and soaked corn. He was the most revolting bird to look at, with his feathers pushing through the wrinkled scarlet skin, mixed with the horrible yellow down that covers baby pigeons and makes them look as though they have been peroxiding their hair. Owing to his repulsive and obese appearance, Larry suggested we called him Quasimodo, and, liking the name without realizing the implications, I agreed. For a long time after he could feed himself, and when all his feathers had grown, Quasimodo re-tained a sprig of yellow down on his head which gave him the appearance of a rather pompous judge wearing a wig several sizes too small.

Owing to his unorthodox upbringing, and the fact that he had no parents to teach him the facts of life, Quasimodo became convinced that he was not a bird at all, and refused to fly. Instead he walked everywhere. If he wanted to get onto a table or a chair, he stood below it, ducking his head and cooing in a rich contralto until someone lifted him up. He was always eager to join us in anything we did, and would even try to come for walks with us. This, however, we had to stop, for either you carried him on your shoulder, which was risking an accident to your clothes, or else you let him walk behind. If you let him walk, then you had to slow down your own pace to suit his, for should you get too far ahead you would hear the most frantic and imploring coos and turn round to find Quasimodo running desperately after you, his tail wagging seductively, his iridescent chest pouted out with indignation at your cruelty.

Quasimodo insisted on sleeping in the house; no amount of coaxing or scolding would get him to inhabit the pigeon loft I had constructed for him. He preferred to sleep on the end of Margo's bed. Eventually, however, he was banished to the drawing-room sofa, for if Margo turned over in bed at night Quasimodo would wake, hobble up the bed, and perch on her face, cooing loudly and lovingly.

It was Larry who discovered that Quasimodo was a musical pigeon. Not only did he like music, but he actually seemed to recognize two different varieties, the waltz and the military march. For ordinary music he would waddle as close to the gramophone as possible and sit there with pouting chest, eyes half closed, purring softly to himself. But if the tune was a waltz he would move round and round the machine, bowing, twisting, and cooing tremulously. For a march, on the other hand – Sousa for preference – he drew himself up to his full height, inflated his chest, and stamped up and down the room, while his coo became so rich and throaty that he seemed in danger of strangling himself. He never attempted to perform these actions for any other kind of music than marches and waltzes. Occasionally, however, if he had not heard any music for some time, he would (in his enthusiasm at hearing the gramophone) do a march for a waltz, or vice versa, but he invariably stopped and corrected himself half-way through.

One sad day we found, on waking Quasimodo, that he had duped us all, for there among the cushions lay a glossy white egg. He never quite recovered from this. He became embittered, sullen, and started to peck irritably if you attempted to pick him up. Then he laid another egg, and his nature changed completely. He, or rather she, became wilder and wilder, treating us as though we were her worst enemies, slinking up to the kitchen door for food as if she feared for her life. Not even the gramophone would tempt her back into the house. The last time I saw her she was sitting in an olive tree, cooing in the most pretentious and coy manner, while further along the branch a large and very masculine-looking pigeon twisted and cooed in a perfect ecstasy of admiration.

For some time the Rose-Beetle Man would turn up at the villa fairly regularly with some new addition to my menagerie: a frog, perhaps, or a sparrow with a broken wing. One afternoon Mother and I, in a fit of extravagant sentimentalism, bought up his entire stock of rose-beetles and, when he had left, let them all go in the garden. For days the villa was full of rose-beetles, crawling on the beds, lurking in the bathroom, banging against the light at night, and falling like emeralds into our laps.

The last time I saw the Rose-Beetle Man was one evening when I was sitting on a hill-top overlooking the road. He had obviously been to some fiesta and had been plied with much wine, for he swayed to and fro across the road, piping a melancholy tune on his flute. I shouted a greeting, and he waved extravagantly without looking back. As he rounded the corner he was silhouetted for a moment against the pale lavender evening sky. I could see his battered hat with the fluttering feathers, the bulging pockets of his coat, the bamboo cages full of sleepy pigeons on his back, and above his head, circling drowsily round and round,

I could see the dim specks that were the rose-beetles. Then he rounded the curve of the road and there was only the pale sky with a new moon floating in it like a silver feather, and the soft twittering of his flute dying away in the dusk.

4

A Bushel of Learning

Scarcely had we settled into the strawberry-pink villa before Mother decided that I was running wild, and that it was necessary for me to have some sort of education. But where to find this on a remote Greek island? As usual when a problem arose the entire family flung itself with enthusiasm into the task of solving it. Each member had his or her own idea of what was best for me, and each argued with such fervour that any discussion about my future generally resulted in an uproar.

'Plenty of time for him to learn,' said Leslie; 'after all, he can read, can't he? I can teach him to shoot, and if we bought a boat I could teach him to sail.'

'But, dear, that wouldn't *really* be much use to him later on,' Mother pointed out, adding vaguely, 'unless he was going into the Merchant Navy or something.'

'I think it's essential that he learns to dance,' said Margo, 'or else he'll grow up into one of these awful tongue-tied hobbledehoys.'

'Yes, dear; but that sort of thing can come *later*. He should be getting some sort of grounding in things like mathematics and French . . . and his spelling's appalling.'

'Literature,' said Larry, with conviction, 'that's what he wants, a good solid grounding in literature. The rest will follow naturally. I've been encouraging him to read some good stuff.'

'But don't you think Rabelais is a little *old* for him?' asked Mother doubtfully.

'Good, clean fun,' said Larry airily; 'it's important that he gets sex in its right perspective now.'

'You've got a mania about sex,' said Margo primly; 'it doesn't matter what we're discussing, you always have to drag it in.'

'What he wants is a healthy, outdoor life; if he learned to shoot and sail –' began Leslie.

'Oh, stop talking like a bishop. You'll be advocating cold baths next.'

'The trouble with you is you get in one of these damned supercilious moods where you think you know best, and you won't even listen to anyone else's point of view.'

'With a point of view as limited as yours, you can hardly expect me to listen to it.'

'Now, now, there's no sense in fighting,' said Mother.

'Well, Larry's so bloody unreasonable.'

'I like that!' said Larry indignantly; 'I'm far and away the most reasonable member of the family.'

'Yes, dear, but fighting doesn't solve the problem. What we want is someone who can teach Gerry and who'll encourage him in his interests.'

'He appears to have only one interest,' said Larry bitterly, 'and that's this awful urge to fill things with animal life. I don't think he ought to be encouraged in *that*. Life is fraught with danger as it is. I went to light a cigarette only this morning and a damn' great bumble-bee flew out of the box.'

'It was a grasshopper with me,' said Leslie gloomily.

'Yes, I think that sort of thing ought to be stopped,' said Margo. 'I found the *most revolting* jar of wriggling things on the dressing-table, of all places.'

'He doesn't mean any harm, poor little chap,' said Mother pacifically; 'he's so interested in all these things.'

'I wouldn't mind being attacked by bumble-bees, if it *led* anywhere,' Larry pointed out. 'But it's just a phase . . . he'll grow out of it by the time he's fourteen.'

'He's been in this phase from the age of two,' said Mother, 'and he's showing no signs of growing out of it.'

'Well, if you insist on stuffing him full of useless information, I suppose George would have a shot at teaching him,' said Larry.

'*That's* a brain-wave,' said Mother delightedly. 'Will you go over and see him? I think the sooner he starts the better.'

Sitting under the open window in the twilight, with my arm round Roger's shaggy neck, I had listened with interest, not unmixed with indignation, to the family discussion on my fate. Now that it was settled, I wondered vaguely who George was, and why it was so necessary for me to have lessons. But the dusk was thick with flower scents, and the olive groves were dark, mysterious, and fascinating. I forgot about the imminent danger of being educated, and went off with Roger to hunt for glow-worms in the sprawling brambles.

I discovered that George was an old friend of Larry's, who had come to Corfu to write. There was nothing very unusual about this, for all Larry's acquaintances in those days were either authors, poets, or painters. It was George, moreover, who was really responsible for our presence in Corfu, for he had written such eulogistic letters about the place that Larry had become convinced we could live nowhere else. Now George was to pay the penalty for his rashness. He came over to the villa to discuss my education with Mother, and we were introduced. We regarded each other with suspicion. George was a very tall and extremely thin man who moved with the odd disjointed grace of a puppet. His lean, skull-like face was partially concealed by a finely pointed brown beard and a pair of large tortoise-shell spectacles. He had a deep, melancholy voice, a dry and sarcastic sense of humour. Having made a joke, he would smile in his beard with a sort of vulpine pleasure which was quite unaffected by anyone else's reactions.

Gravely George set about the task of teaching me. He was undeterred by the fact that there were no school-books available on the island; he simply ransacked his own library and appeared on the appointed day armed with a most unorthodox selection of tomes. Sombrely and patiently he taught me the rudiments of geography from the maps in the back of an ancient copy of

Pears Cyclopædia, English from books that ranged from Wilde to Gibbon, French from a fat and exciting book called *Le Petit Larousse*, and mathematics from memory. From my point of view, however, the most important thing was that we devoted some of our time to natural history, and George meticulously and carefully taught me how to observe and how to note down observations in a diary. At once my enthusiastic but haphazard interest in nature became focused, for I found that by writing things down I could learn and remember much more. The only mornings that I was ever on time for my lessons were those which were given up to natural history.

Every morning at nine George would come stalking through the olive trees, clad in shorts, sandals, and an enormous straw hat with a frayed brim, clutching a wedge of books under one arm, swinging a walking-stick vigorously.

'Good morning. The disciple awaits the master agog with anticipation, I trust?' he would greet me, with a saturnine smile.

In the little dining-room of the villa the shutters would be closed against the sun, and in the green twilight George would loom over the table, methodically arranging the books. Flies, heat-drugged, would crawl slowly on the walls or fly drunkenly about the room, buzzing sleepily. Outside the cicadas were greeting the new day with shrill enthusiasm.

'Let me see, let me see,' George would murmur, running a long forefinger down our carefully prepared time-table; 'yes, yes, mathematics. If I remember rightly, we were involved in the Herculean task of discovering how long it would take six men to build a wall if three of them took a week. I seem to recall that we have spent almost as much time on this problem as the men spent on the wall. Ah, well, let us gird our loins and do battle once again. Perhaps it's the *shape* of the problem that worries you, eh? Let us see if we can make it more exciting.'

He would droop over the exercise book pensively, pulling at

his beard. Then in his large, clear writing he would set the problem out in a fresh way.

'If it took two caterpillars a week to eat eight leaves, how long would four caterpillars take to eat the same number? Now, apply yourself to that.'

While I struggled with the apparently insoluble problem of the caterpillars' appetites, George would be otherwise occupied. He was an expert fencer, and was at that time engaged in learning some of the local peasant dances, for which he had a passion. So, while waiting for me to finish the sum, he would drift about in the gloom of the room, practising fencing stances or complicated dancing steps, a habit that I found disconcerting, to say the least, and to which I shall always attribute my inability to do mathematics. Place any simple sum before me, even now, and it immediately conjures up a vision of George's lanky body swaying and jerking round the dimly lit dining-room. He would accompany the dancing sequences with a deep and tuneless humming, like a hive of distraught bees.

'Tum-ti-tum-ti-tum . . . tiddle tiddle tumty *dee* . . . left leg over . . . three steps right . . . tum-ti-tum-ti-tum-ti – *dum* . . . back, round, down, and up . . . tiddle iddle umpty *dee* . . .,' he would drone, as he paced and pirouetted like a dismal crane. Then, suddenly, the humming would stop, a steely look would creep into his eyes, and he would throw himself into an attitude of defence, pointing an imaginary foil at an imaginary enemy. His eyes narrowed, his spectacles a-glitter, he would drive his adversary back across the room, skilfully avoiding the furniture. When his enemy was backed into the corner, George would dodge and twist round him with the agility of a wasp, stabbing, thrusting, guarding. I could almost see the gleam of steel. Then came the final moment, the upward and outward flick that would catch his opponent's weapon and twist it harmlessly to one side, the swift withdrawal, followed by the long, straight lunge that drove the point of his foil right through the adversary's heart.

Through all this I would be watching him, fascinated, the exercise book lying forgotten in front of me. Mathematics was not one of our more successful subjects.

In geography we made better progress, for George was able to give a more zoological tinge to the lesson. We would draw giant maps, wrinkled with mountains, and then fill in the various places of interest, together with drawings of the more exciting fauna to be found there. Thus for me the chief products of Ceylon were tapirs and tea, of India tigers and rice, of Australia kangaroos and sheep, while the blue curves of currents we drew across the oceans carried whales, albatross, penguins, and walrus, as well as hurricanes, trade winds, fair weather and foul. Our maps were works of art. The principal volcanoes belched such flames and sparks one feared they would set the paper continents alight; the mountain ranges of the world were so blue and white with ice and snow that it made one chilly to look at them. Our brown, sun-drenched deserts were lumpy with camel humps and pyramids, and our tropical forests so tangled and luxuriant that it was only with difficulty that the slouching jaguars, lithe snakes, and morose gorillas managed to get through them, while on their outskirts emaciated natives hacked wearily at the painted trees, forming little clearings apparently for the purpose of writing 'coffee' or perhaps 'cereals' across them in unsteady capitals. Our rivers were wide, and blue as forget-me-nots, freckled with canoes and crocodiles. Our oceans were anything but empty, for where they had not frothed themselves into a fury of storms or drawn themselves up into an awe-inspiring tidal wave that hung over some remote, palm-shaggy island, they were full of life. Good-natured whales allowed unseaworthy galleons, armed with a forest of harpoons, to pursue them relentlessly; bland and inno-cent-looking octopi tenderly engulfed small boats in their arms; Chinese junks, with jaundiced crews, were followed by shoals of well-dentured sharks, while fur-clad Eskimos pursued obese herds of walrus through ice fields thickly populated by polar bears and penguins. They were maps that lived, maps that one could study, frown over, and add to; maps, in short, that really *meant* something.

Our attempts at history were not, at first, conspicuously successful, until George discovered that by seasoning a series of unpalatable facts with a sprig of zoology and a sprinkle of completely irrelevant detail, he could get me interested. Thus I became conversant with some historical data which, to the best of my knowledge, have never been recorded before. Breathlessly, history lesson by history lesson, I followed Hannibal's progress over the Alps. His reason for attempting such a feat and what he intended to do on the other side were details that scarcely worried me. No, my interest in what I considered to be a very badly planned expedition lay in the fact that *I knew the name of each and every elephant*. I also knew that Hannibal had appointed a special man not only to feed and look after the elephants, *but to give them hot-water bottles when the weather got cold*. This interesting fact seems to have escaped most serious historians. Another thing that most history books never seem to mention is that Columbus's first words on setting foot ashore in America were, 'Great heavens, look . . . a jaguar!' With such an introduction, how could one fail to take an interest in the continent's subsequent history? So George, hampered by inadequate books and a reluctant pupil, would strive to make his teaching interesting, so that the lessons did not drag.

Roger, of course, thought that I was simply wasting my mornings. However, he did not desert me, but lay under the table asleep while I wrestled with my work. Occasionally, if I had to fetch a book, he would wake, get up, shake himself, yawn loudly, and wag his tail. Then, when he saw me returning to the table, his ears would droop and he would walk heavily back to his private corner and flop down with a sigh of resignation. George did not mind Roger's being in the room, for he behaved himself well, and did not distract my attention. Occasionally, if he was sleeping very heavily and heard a peasant dog barking, Roger would wake up with a start and utter a raucous roar of rage before realizing where he was. Then he would give an embarrassed look at our disapproving faces, his tail would twitch, and he would glance round the room sheepishly.

For a short time Quasimodo also joined us for lessons, and behaved very well as long as he was allowed to sit in my lap. He would drowse there, cooing to himself, the entire morning. It was I who banished him, in fact, for one day he upset a bottle of green ink in the exact centre of a large and very beautiful map that we had just completed. I realized, of course, that this vandalism was not intentional, but even so I was annoyed. Quasimodo tried for a week to get back into favour by sitting outside the door and cooing seductively through the crack, but each time I weakened I would catch a glimpse of his tail-feathers, a bright and horrible green, and harden my heart again.

Achilles also attended one lesson, but he did not approve of being inside the house. He spent the morning wandering about the room and scratching at the skirting-boards and door. Then he kept getting wedged under bits of furniture and scrabbling frantically until we lifted the object and rescued him. The room being small, it meant that in order to move one bit of furniture we had to move practically everything else. After a third upheaval George said that as he was unused to such exertions, he thought Achilles would be happier in the garden.

So there was only Roger left to keep me company. It was comforting, it's true, to be able to rest my feet on his woolly bulk while I grappled with a problem, but even then it was hard to concentrate, for the sun would pour through the shutters, tiger-striping the table and floor, reminding me of all the things I might be doing.

There around me were the vast, empty olive groves echoing with cicadas; the moss-grown stone walls that made the vineyards into steps where the painted lizards ran; the thickets of myrtle alive with insects, and the rough headland where the flocks of garish goldfinches fluttered with excited pipings from thistle-head to thistle-head.

Realizing this, George wisely instituted the novel system of outdoor lessons. Some mornings he arrived, carrying a large furry towel, and together we would make our way down through the olive groves and along the road that was like a carpet of white velvet under its layer of dust. Then we branched off onto a goat track that ran along the top of miniature cliffs, until it led us to a bay, secluded and small, with a crescent-shaped fringe of white sand running round it. A grove of stunted olives grew there, providing a pleasant shade. From the top of the little cliff the water in the bay looked so still and transparent that it was hard to believe there was any at all. Fishes seemed to drift over the wave-wrinkled sand as though suspended in mid-air, while through six feet of clear water you could see rocks on which anemones lifted frail, coloured arms, and hermit crabs moved, dragging their top-shaped homes.

We would strip beneath the olives and walk out into the warm, bright water, to drift, face down, over the rocks and clumps of seaweed, occasionally diving to bring up something that caught our eye: a shell more brightly coloured than the rest; or a hermit crab of massive proportions, wearing an anemone on his shell, like a bonnet with a pink flower on it. Here and there on the sandy bottom grew rib-shaped beds of black ribbon-weed, and it was among these beds that the sea-slugs lived. Treading water and peering down, we could see below the shining, narrow fronds of green and black weeds growing close and tangled, over which we hung like hawks suspended in air above a strange woodland. In the clearing among the weed-bed lay the sea-slugs, perhaps the ugliest of the sea fauna. Some six inches long, they looked exactly like overgrown sausages made out of thick, brown, carunculated leather – dim, primitive beasts that just lie in one spot, rolling gently with the sea's swing, sucking in sea-water at one end of their bodies and passing it out at the other. The minute vegetable and animal life in the water is filtered off somewhere inside the sausage, and passed to the simple mechanism of the sea-slug's stomach. No one could say that the sea-slugs led interesting lives. Dully they rolled on the sand, sucking in the sea with monotonous regularity. It was hard to believe that these obese creatures could defend themselves in any way, or that they would ever need to, but in fact they had an unusual method of showing their displeasure. Pick them up out of the water, and they would squirt a jet of sea-water out of either end of their bodies, apparently without any muscular effort. It was this water-pistol habit of theirs that led us to invent a game. Each armed with a sea-slug, we would make our weapons squirt, noting how and where the water struck the sea. Then we moved over to that spot, and the one who discovered the greatest amount of sea fauna in his area won a point. Occasionally, as in any game, feeling would run high, indignant accusations of cheating would be made and denied. It was then we found our sea-slugs useful for turning on our opponent. Whenever we had made use of the sea-slugs' services we always swam out and returned them to their forest of weed. Next time we came down they would still be there, probably in exactly the same position as we had left them, rolling quietly to and fro.

Having exhausted the possibilities of the slugs, we would hunt for new shells for my collection, or hold long discussions on the other fauna we had found; George would suddenly realize that all this, though most enjoyable, could hardly be described as education in the strictest sense of the word, so we would drift back to the shallows and lie there. The lesson then proceeded, while the shoals of little fish would gather about us and nibble gently at our legs.

'So the French and British Fleets were slowly drawing together for what was to be the decisive sea battle of the war. When the enemy was sighted, Nelson was on the bridge bird-watching through his telescope . . . He had already been warned of the Frenchmen's approach by a friendly gull . . . eh? . . . oh, a greater black-backed gull I think it was. Well, the ships manœuvred round each other . . . of course they couldn't move so fast in those days, for they did everything by sail . . . no engines . . . no, not even outboard engines . . . The British sailors were a bit worried because the French seemed so strong, but when they saw that Nelson was so little affected by the whole thing that he was sitting on the bridge labelling his birds'-egg collection, they decided that there was really nothing to be scared about . . .'

The sea was like a warm, silky coverlet that moved my body gently to and fro. There were no waves, only this gentle underwater movement, the pulse of the sea, rocking me softly. Around my legs the coloured fish flicked and trembled, and stood on their heads while they mumbled at me with toothless gums. In the drooping clusters of olives a cicada whispered gently to itself.

'. . . and so they carried Nelson down below as quickly as possible, so that none of the crew would know he had been hit . . . He was mortally wounded, and lying below decks with the battle still raging above, he murmured his last words, 'Kiss me, Hardy,' and then he died . . . What? Oh, yes. Well, he had already told Hardy that if anything happened to him he could have his birds' eggs . . . so, though England had lost her finest seaman, the battle had been won, and it had far-reaching effects in Europe . . .'

Across the mouth of the bay a sun-bleached boat would pass, rowed by a brown fisherman in tattered trousers, standing in the stern and twisting an oar in the water like a fish's tail. He would raise one hand in lazy salute, and across the still, blue water you could hear the plaintive squeak of the oar as it twisted, and the soft clop as it dug into the sea.

5

A Treasure of Spiders

One hot, dreamy afternoon, when everything except the shouting cicadas seemed to be asleep, Roger and I set out to see how far we could climb over the hills before dark. We made our way up through the olive groves, striped and dappled with white sunlight, where the air was hot and still, and eventually we clambered above the trees and out onto a bare, rocky peak, where we sat down for a rest. The island dozed below us, shimmering like a water picture in the heat-haze: grey-green olives; black cypresses; multicoloured rocks of the sea-coast; and the sea smooth and opalescent, kingfisher blue, jade green, with here and there a pleat or two in its sleek surface where it curved round a rocky, olive-tangled promontory. Directly below us was a small bay with a crescent-shaped rim of white sand, a bay so shallow, and with a floor of such dazzling sand, that the water was a pale blue, almost white. I was sweaty after the ascent, and Roger sat with flopping tongue and froth-flecked whiskers. We decided that we would not climb the hills after all; we would go for a bathe instead. So we hurried down the hillside until we reached the little bay, empty, silent, asleep under the brilliant shower of sun-light. We sat in the warm, shallow waters, drowsily, and I delved in the sand around me. Occasionally I found a smooth pebble, or a piece of bottle which had been rubbed and licked by the sea until it was like an astonishing jewel, green and translucent. These finds I handed to Roger, who sat watching me. He, not certain what I expected him to do but not wishing to offend me, took them deli-cately in his mouth. Then, when he thought I was not looking, he would drop them back into the water and sigh deeply.

Later I lay on a rock to dry, while Roger sneezed and clopped his way along the shallows in an attempt to catch one of the blue-finned blennies, with their pouting, vacant faces, which flipped from rock to rock with the speed of swallows. Breathing heavily and staring down into the clear water, Roger followed them, a look of intense concentration on his face. When I was dry, I put on my shorts and shirt and called to Roger. He came reluctantly, with many a backward glance at the blennies which still flicked across the sandy, sun-ringed floor of the bay. Coming as close to me as possible, he shook himself vigorously, showering me with water from his curly coat.

After the swim, my body felt heavy and relaxed, and my skin as though it were covered with a silky crust of salt. Slowly and dreamily we made our way onto the road. Discovering that I was hungry, I wondered which was the nearest cottage where I could get something to eat. I stood kicking up puffs of fine white dust from the road as I considered this problem. If I went to see Leonora, who undoubtedly lived the nearest, she would give me figs and bread, but she would also insist on giving me the latest bulletin on her daughter's state of health. Her daughter was a husky-voiced virago with a cast in one eye, whom I cordially disliked, so I had no interest in her health. I decided not to go to Leonora; it was a pity, for she had the best fig trees for miles around, but there was a limit to what I could endure for the sake of black figs. If I went to see Taki, the fisherman, he would be having his siesta, and would merely shout, 'Go away, little corn-top,' from the depths of his tightly shuttered house. Christaki and his family would probably be about, but in return for food they would expect me to answer a lot of tedious questions: was England bigger than Corfu? How many people lived there? Were they all lords? What was a train like? Did trees grow in England? and so on, interminably. If it had been morning I could have cut through the fields and vineyards, and before reaching home I would have fed well on contributions from various of my friends on the way: olives, bread, grapes, figs, ending perhaps with a short detour that would take me through Philomena's fields, where I could be sure of ending my snack with a crisp, pink slice of watermelon, cold as ice. But now it was siesta time, and most of the peasants were asleep in their houses behind tightly closed doors and shutters. It was a difficult problem, and while I thought about it the pangs of hunger grew, and I kicked more energetically at the dusty road, until Roger sneezed protestingly and gave me an injured look.

Suddenly I had an idea. Just over the hill lived Yani, the old shepherd, and his wife, in a minute, sparkling white cottage. Yani, I knew, had his siesta in front of his house, in the shade of his grapevine, and if I made enough noise approaching the house he would wake up. Once awake, it was certain that he would offer me hospitality. There was not a single peasant house you could visit and come empty away. Cheered by this thought, I set off up the stony, meandering pathway created by the pattering hooves of Yani's goats, over the brow of the hill and into the valley, where the red roof of the shepherd's house gleamed among the giant olive trunks. When I judged I was close enough, I stopped and threw a stone for Roger to retrieve. This was one of Roger's favourite pastimes, but once having started it you had to continue, or else he would stand in front of you and bark hideously until you repeated the performance in sheer desperation. He retrieved the stone, dropped it at my feet, and backed away expectantly, ears cocked, eyes gleaming, muscles taut and ready for action. I ignored both him and the stone. He looked faintly surprised; he examined the stone carefully, and then looked at me again. I whistled a short tune and looked up into the sky. Roger gave an experimental yap; then, seeing I still took no notice, he followed it up with a volley of deep, rich barks that echoed among the olives. I let him bark for about five minutes. By this time I felt sure Yani must be aware of our arrival. Then I threw the stone for Roger, and, as he fled after it joyfully, I made my way round to the front of the house.

The old shepherd, as I expected, was in the tattered shade of the vine that sprawled on its iron trellis-work above my head, but to my intense annoyance he had not woken up. He was sprawling in a plain deal chair, which was tilted back against the wall at a dangerous angle. His arms dangled limply, his legs were spread out, and his magnificent moustache, orange and white with nicotine and age, lifted and trembled with his snores, like some strange seaweed that is raised and lowered by a gentle swell. The thick fingers of his stumpy hands twitched as he slept, and I could see the thick-ribbed yellow nails, like flakes cut from a tallow candle. His brown face, wrinkled and furrowed as the bark of a pine, was expressionless, the eyes tightly shut. I stared at him, trying to will him to wake up, but with no result. It was not etiquette for me to wake him, and I was debating whether it would be worth while waiting until he awoke naturally, or whether it would be better to go and be bored by Leonora, when Roger came in search of me, bustling round the side of the house, ears pricked, tongue drooping. He saw me, wagged his tail in brief greeting, and glanced round with the air of a visitor who knows he is welcome. Suddenly he froze, his moustache bristled, and he started to walk forward slowly, stiff-legged and quivering. He had seen something that I had failed to observe: curled up under Yani's tilted chair sat a large, lanky grey cat, who was watching us with insolent green eyes. Before I could reach out and grab him, Roger had pounced. The cat, in a lithe movement that argued long practice, fled like a skimming stone to where the gnarled grapevine twisted drunkenly round the trellis, and shot up it with a scutter of sharp claws. Crouched among the bunches of white grapes, she stared down at Roger and spat delicately. Roger, frustrated and angry, threw back his head and barked threats and insults. Yani's eyes flew open, his chair rocked, and his arms flailed violently in an effort to keep his balance. The chair teetered uncertainly and then settled onto all four legs with a thud.

'Saint Spiridion save me!' he implored loudly. 'God have mercy!'

He glared round, his moustache quivering, to find the cause of the uproar, and saw me sitting demurely on the wall. I greeted him sweetly and politely, as though nothing had happened, and asked if he had slept well. He rose to his feet, grinning, and scratched his stomach vigorously.

'Ah, it's you making enough noise to split my head. Your health, your health. Sit down, little lord,' he said, dusting off his chair and placing it for me; 'it is good to see you. You will eat with me, and have a drink, perhaps? It is a very hot afternoon, very hot – hot enough to melt a bottle.'

He stretched and, yawning loudly, displayed gums as innocent of teeth as a baby's. Then, turning towards the house, he roared:

'Aphrodite . . . *A*phrodite . . . wake, woman . . . foreigners have come . . . the little lord is sitting with me . . . Bring food . . . d'you hear?'

'I heard, I heard,' came a muffled voice from behind the shutters.

Yani grunted, wiped his moustache, and made his way to the nearest olive tree and retired discreetly behind it. He reappeared, doing up his trousers and yawning, and came over to sit on the wall near me.

'Today I should have taken my goats to Gastouri. But it was too hot, much too hot. In the hills the rocks will be so hot you could light a cigarette from them. So I went instead and tasted Taki's new white wine. Spiridion! What a wine . . . like the blood of a dragon and as smooth as a fish . . . What a wine! When I came back the air was full of sleep, so here I am.'

He sighed deeply but impenitently, and fumbled in his pocket for his battered tin of tobacco and thin grey cigarette papers. His brown, calloused hand cupped to catch the little pile of golden leaf, and the fingers of his other hand tugged and pulled at it gently. He rolled the cigarette swiftly, nipped off the tobacco that dangled from the ends and replaced it in the tin, and then lit his smoke with the aid of a huge tin lighter from which a wick curled like an angry snake. He puffed reflectively for a moment, pulled a shred of tobacco off his moustache, and reached into his pocket again.

'Here, you are interested in the little ones of God; look at this that I caught this morning, crouching under a rock like the devil,' he said, pulling from his pocket a tiny bottle, firmly corked and filled with golden olive oil. 'A fine one this, a fighter. The only fighter I know who can do damage with his backside.'

The bottle, filled to the brim with oil, looked as though it were made of pale amber, and enshrined in the centre, held suspended by the thickness of the oil, was a small chocolate-brown scorpion, his tail curved like a scimitar over his back. He was quite dead, suffocated by the glutinous grave. Around his corpse was a faint wisp of discoloration, like a mist in the golden oil.

'See that?' said Yani. 'That's the poison. He was full, that one.'

I asked, curiously, why it was necessary to put the scorpion in oil.

Yani chuckled richly, and wiped his moustache.

'You do not know, little lord, though you spend all your time on your stomach catching these things, eh?' he said, greatly amused. 'Well, I will tell you. You never know, it may be of use to you. First catch the scorpion, catch him alive and catch him as gently as a falling feather. Then you put him, alive – mark you, alive – in a bottle of oil. Let him simmer, let him die in it, let the sweet oil soak up the poison. Then, should you ever be stung by one of his brothers (and Saint Spiridion protect you from that), you must rub the place with that oil. That will cure the sting for you so that it is of no more discomfort than the prick of a thorn.'

While I digested this curious information, Aphrodite appeared from the house, her wrinkled face as red as a pomegranate seed, bearing a tin tray on which was a bottle of wine, a jug of water, and a plate with bread, olives, and figs on it. Yani and I drank the wine, watered to a delicate pale pink, and ate the food in silence. In spite of his toothless gums, Yani tore large pieces of the bread off and champed them hungrily, swallowing great lumps that made his wrinkled throat swell. When we had finished, he sat back, wiped his moustache carefully, and took up the conversation again, as if there had been no pause.

'I knew a man once, a shepherd like myself, who had been to a fiesta in a distant village. On the way back, as his stomach was warm with wine, he decided to have a sleep, so he found a spot beneath some myrtles. But while he slept a scorpion crept out from under the leaves and crawled into his ear, and when he awoke it stung him.'

Yani paused at this psychological moment to spit over the wall and roll himself another cigarette.

'Yes,' he sighed at last, 'it was very sad . . . one so young. The tiny scorpion stung him in the ear . . . phut! . . . like that. The poor fellow flung himself about in his agony. He ran screaming through the olives, tearing at his head . . . Ah! it was dreadful. There was no one to hear his cries and help him . . . no one at all. In terrible pain he started to run for the village, but he never reached it. He fell down dead, down there in the valley, not far from the road. We found him the next morning when we were going to the fields. What a sight! What a sight! With that one little bite his head had swollen up as though his brains were pregnant, and he was dead, quite dead.'

Yani sighed deeply and lugubriously, twirling the little bottle of oil in his fingers.

'That is why,' he went on, 'I never go up into the hills and sleep. And, in case I should perhaps share some wine with a friend and forget the danger, I always carry a scorpion bottle with me.'

The talk drifted to other and equally absorbing topics, and after an hour or so I rose, dusted the crumbs off my lap, thanked

the old man and his wife for their hospitality, accepted a bunch
of grapes as a parting present, and set off towards home. Roger
walked close to me, his eyes fixed on my pocket, for he had
noticed the grapes. At length, finding an olive grove, dark and
cool with the long shadows of evening, we sat down by a mossy
bank and shared the fruit. Roger ate his whole, pips and all. I
spat out my pips into a circle around me, and imagined with
satisfaction the flourishing vineyard that would grow up on the
spot. When the grapes were finished I rolled over onto my
stomach and, with my chin in my hands, examined the bank
behind me.

A tiny green grasshopper with a long, melancholy face sat
twitching his hind legs nervously. A fragile snail sat on a moss
sprig, meditating and waiting for the evening dew. A plump
scarlet mite, the size of a match-head, struggled like a tubby
huntsman through the forest of moss. It was a microscopic world,
full of fascinating life. As I watched the mite making his slow
progress I noticed a curious thing. Here and there on the green
plush surface of the moss were scattered faint circular marks,
each the size of a shilling. So faint were they that it was only
from certain angles they were noticeable at all. They reminded
me of a full moon seen behind thick clouds, a faint circle that
seemed to shift and change. I wondered idly what could have
made them. They were too irregular, too scattered to be the
prints of some beast, and what was it that would walk up an
almost vertical bank in such a haphazard manner? Besides, they
were not like imprints. I prodded the edge of one of these circles
with a piece of grass. It remained unmoved. I began to think the
mark was caused by some curious way in which the moss grew.
I probed again, more vigorously, and suddenly my stomach
gave a clutch of tremendous excitement. It was as though my
grass-stalk had found a hidden spring, for the whole circle lifted
up like a trapdoor. As I stared, I saw to my amazement that it
was in fact a trapdoor, lined with silk, and with a neatly bevelled

edge that fitted snugly into the mouth of the silk-lined shaft it concealed. The edge of the door was fastened to the lip of the tunnel by a small flap of silk that acted as a hinge. I gazed at this magnificent piece of workmanship and wondered what on earth could have made it. Peering down the silken tunnel, I could see nothing; I poked my grass-stalk down, but there was no response. For a long time I sat staring at this fantastic home, trying to decide what sort of beast had made it. I thought that it might be a wasp of some sort, but had never heard of a wasp that fitted its nest with secret doors. I felt that I must get to the bottom of this problem immediately. I would go down and ask George if he knew what this mysterious beast was. Calling Roger, who was busily trying to uproot an olive tree, I set off at a brisk trot.

I arrived at George's villa out of breath, bursting with suppressed excitement, gave a perfunctory knock at the door, and dashed in. Only then did I realize he had company. Seated in a chair near him was a figure which, at first glance, I decided must be George's brother, for he also wore a beard. He was, however, in contrast to George, immaculately dressed in a grey flannel suit with waistcoat, a spotless white shirt, a tasteful but sombre tie, and large, solid, highly polished boots. I paused on the threshold, embarrassed, while George surveyed me sardonically.

'Good evening,' he greeted me. 'From the joyful speed of your entry I take it that you have not come for a little extra tuition.'

I apologized for the intrusion, and then told George about the curious nests I had found.

'Thank heavens you're here, Theodore,' he said to his bearded companion. 'I shall now be able to hand the problem over to expert hands.'

'Hardly an expert . . .' mumbled the man called Theodore, deprecatingly.

'Gerry, this is Doctor Theodore Stephanides,' said George. 'He is an expert on practically everything you care to mention. And what you don't mention, he does. He, like you, is an eccentric nature-lover. Theodore, this is Gerry Durrell.'

I said how do you do, politely, but to my surprise the bearded man rose to his feet, stepped briskly across the room and held out a large white hand.

'Very pleased to meet you,' he said, apparently addressing his beard, and gave me a quick, shy glance from twinkling blue eyes.

I shook his hand and said I was very pleased to meet him, too. Then we stood in awkward silence, while George watched us, grinning.

'Well, Theodore,' he said at last, 'and what d'you think produced these strange secret passages?'

Theodore clasped his hands behind his back, lifted himself on his toes several times, his boots squeaking protestingly, and gravely considered the floor.

'Well . . . er . . .' he said, his words coming slowly and meticulously, 'it sounds to me as though they might be the burrows of the trapdoor spider . . . er . . . it is a species which is quite common here in Corfu . . . that is to say, when I say common, I suppose I have found some thirty or . . . er . . . forty specimens during the time I have been here.'

'Ah,' said George, 'trapdoor spiders, eh?'

'Yes,' said Theodore. 'I feel that it's more than probable that that is what they are. However, I may be mistaken.'

He rose and fell on his toes, squeaking gently, and then he shot me a keen glance.

'Perhaps, if they are not too far away, we could go and verify it,' he suggested tentatively. 'I mean to say, if you have nothing better to do, and it's not too far . . .' His voice trailed away on a faintly interrogative note.

I said that they were only just up the hill, not really far.

'Um,' said Theodore.

'Don't let him drag you about all over the place, Theodore,' said George. 'You don't want to be galloped about the countryside.'

'No, no, not at all,' said Theodore. 'I was just about to leave, and I can easily walk that way back. It is quite a simple matter for me to . . . er . . . cut down through the olive groves and reach Canoni.'

He picked up a neat grey Homburg and placed it squarely on his head. At the door he held out his hand and shook George's briefly.

'Thank you for a delightful tea,' he said, and stumped gravely off along the path by my side.

As we walked along I studied him covertly. He had a straight, well-shaped nose; a humorous mouth lurking in the ash-blond beard; straight, rather bushy eyebrows under which his eyes, keen but with a twinkle in them and laughter-wrinkles at the corners, surveyed the world. He strode along energetically, humming to himself. When we came to a ditch full of stagnant water he stopped for a moment and stared down into it, his beard bristling.

'Um,' he said conversationally, '*daphnia magna.*'

He rasped at his beard with his thumb, and then set off down the path again.

'Unfortunately,' he said to me, 'I was coming out to see some people . . . er . . . *friends* of mine, and so I did not bring my collecting bag with me. It is a pity, for that ditch might have contained something.'

When we branched off the fairly smooth path we had been travelling along and started up the stony goat-track, I expected some sort of protest, but Theodore strode behind me with unabated vigour, still humming. At length we came to the gloomy olive grove, and I led Theodore to the bank and pointed out the mysterious trapdoor.

He peered down at it, his eyes narrowed.

'Ah-ha,' he said, 'yes . . . um . . . yes.'

He produced from his waistcoat pocket a tiny penknife, opened it, inserted the point of the blade delicately under the little door, and flipped it back.

'Um, yes,' he repeated; *'cteniza.'*

He peered down the tunnel, blew down it and then let the trapdoor fall into place again.

'Yes, they are the burrows of the trapdoor spiders,' he said, 'but this one does not appear to be inhabited. Generally, the creature will hold on to the . . . er . . . *trapdoor* . . . with her legs, or rather, her *claws*, and she holds on with such tenacity that you have to be careful or you will damage the door, trying to force it open. Um . . . yes . . . these are the burrows of the females, of course. The male makes a similar burrow, but it is only about half the size.'

I remarked that it was the most curious structure I had seen.

'Ah-ha! yes,' said Theodore, 'they are certainly very curious. A thing that always puzzles me is how the female knows when the male is approaching.'

I must have looked blank, for he teetered on his toes, shot me a quick look and went on:

'The spider, of course, waits inside its burrow until some insect – a fly or a grasshopper, or something similar – chances to walk past. They can judge, it seems, whether the insect is close enough to be caught. If it is, the spider . . . er . . . pops out of its hole and catches the creature. Now when the male comes in search of the female he must walk over the moss to the trapdoor, and I have often wondered why it is that he is not . . . er . . . devoured by the female in mistake. It is possible, of course, that his footsteps sound different. Or he may make some sort of . . . you know . . . some sort of *sound* which the female recognizes.'

We walked down the hill in silence. When we reached the place where the paths forked I said that I must leave him.

'Ah, well, I'll say good-bye,' he said, staring at his boots. 'I have enjoyed meeting you.'

We stood in silence for a moment. Theodore was afflicted with the acute embarrassment that always seemed to overwhelm him when greeting or saying good-bye to someone. He stared hard at his boots for a moment longer, and then he held out his hand and shook mine gravely.

'Good-bye,' he said. 'I . . . er . . . I expect we shall meet again.'

He turned and stumped off down the hill, swinging his stick, staring about him with observant eyes. I watched him out of sight and then walked slowly in the direction of the villa. I was at once confused and amazed by Theodore. First, since he was obviously a scientist of considerable repute (and I could have told this by his beard), he was to me a person of great importance. In fact he was the only person I had met until now who seemed to share my enthusiasm for zoology. Secondly, I was extremely flattered to find that he treated me and talked to me exactly as though I were his own age. I liked him for this, as I was not talked down to by my family, and I took rather a poor view of any outsider who tried to do so. But Theodore not only talked to me as though I were grown up, but also as though I were as knowledgeable as he.

The facts he told me about the trapdoor spider haunted me: the idea of the creature crouching in its silken tunnel, holding the door closed with its hooked claws, listening to the movement of the insects on the moss above. What, I wondered, did things sound like to a trapdoor spider? I could imagine that a snail would trail over the door with a noise like sticking-plaster being slowly torn off. A centipede would sound like a troop of cavalry. A fly would patter in brisk spurts, followed by a pause while it washed its hands – a dull rasping sound like a knife-grinder at work. The larger beetles, I decided, would sound like steam-rollers, while the smaller ones, the lady-birds and others, would probably purr over the moss like clockwork motor cars. Fascinated by this thought, I made my way back home through the darkening fields, to tell the family of my new discovery and of my meeting with

Theodore. I hoped to see him again, for there were many things I wanted to ask him, but I felt it would be unlikely that he would have very much time to spare for me. I was mistaken, however, for two days later Leslie came back from an excursion into the town and handed me a small parcel.

'Met that bearded johnny,' he said laconically; 'you know, that scientist bloke. Said this was for you.'

Incredulously I stared at the parcel. Surely it couldn't be for me? There must be some mistake, for a great scientist would hardly bother to send me parcels. I turned it over, and there, written on it in neat, spidery writing, was my name. I tore off the paper as quickly as I could. Inside was a small box and a letter.

My dear Gerry Durrell,

I wondered, after our conversation the other day, if it might not assist your investigations of the local natural history to have some form of magnifying instrument. I am therefore sending you this pocket microscope, in the hope that it will be of some use to you. It is, of course, not of very high magnification, but you will find it sufficient for field work.

With best wishes,

Yours sincerely,

Theo. Stephanides

P.S. *If you have nothing better to do on Thursday, perhaps you would care to come to tea, and I could then show you some of my microscope slides.*

6

The Sweet Spring

During the last days of the dying summer, and throughout the warm, wet winter that followed, tea with Theodore became a weekly affair. Every Thursday I would set out, my pockets bulging with match-boxes and test-tubes full of specimens, to be driven into the town by Spiro. It was an appointment that I would not have missed for anything.

Theodore would welcome me in his study, a room that met with my full approval. It was, in my opinion, just what a room should be. The walls were lined with tall bookshelves filled with volumes on freshwater biology, botany, astronomy, medicine, folklore and similar fascinating and sensible subjects. Interspersed with these were selections of ghost and crime stories. Thus Sherlock Holmes rubbed shoulders with Darwin, and Le Fanu with Fabre, in what I considered to be a thoroughly well-balanced library. At one window of the room stood Theodore's telescope, its nose to the sky like a howling dog, while the sills of every window bore a parade of jars and bottles containing minute freshwater fauna, whirling and twitching among the delicate fronds of green weed. On one side of the room was a massive desk, piled high with scrapbooks, micro-photographs, X-ray plates, diaries, and notebooks. On the opposite side of the room was the microscope table, with its powerful lamp on the jointed stem leaning like a lily over the flat boxes that housed Theodore's collection of slides. The microscopes themselves, gleaming like magpies, were housed under a series of beehive-like domes of glass.

'How are you?' Theodore would inquire, as if I were a complete stranger, and give me his characteristic handshake – a sharp downward tug, like a man testing a knot in a rope. The formalities being over, we could then turn our minds to more important topics.

'I was . . . er . . . you know . . . looking through my slides just before your arrival, and I came across one which may interest you. It is a slide of the mouth-parts of the rat flea . . . *ceratophyllus fasciatus*, you know. Now, I'll just adjust the microscope . . . There! . . . You see? Very curious. I mean to say, you could almost imagine it was a human face, couldn't you? Now I had another . . . er . . . slide here . . . That's funny. Ah! got it. Now this one is of the spinnerets of the garden or cross spider . . . er . . . *epeira fasciata* . . .'

So, absorbed and happy, we would pore over the microscope. Filled with enthusiasm, we would tack from subject to subject, and if Theodore could not answer my ceaseless flow of questions himself, he had books that could. Gaps would appear in the bookcase as volume after volume was extracted to be consulted, and by our side would be an ever-growing pile of volumes.

'Now this one is a cyclops . . . *cyclops viridis* . . . which I caught out near Govino the other day. It is a female with egg-sacs . . . Now, I'll just adjust . . . you'll be able to see the eggs quite clearly . . . I'll just put her in the live box . . . er . . . hum . . . there are several species of cyclops found here in Corfu . . .'

Into the brilliant circle of white light a weird creature would appear, a pear-shaped body, long antennæ that twitched indignantly, a tail like sprigs of heather, and on each side of it (slung like sacks of onions on a donkey) the two large sacs bulging with pink beads.

'. . . called cyclops because, as you can see, it has a single eye situated in the centre of its forehead. That's to say, in the centre of what *would* be its forehead if a cyclops had one. In Ancient Greek mythology, as you know, a cyclops was one of a group of giants . . . er . . . each of whom had one eye. Their task was to forge iron for Hephæstus.'

Outside, the warm wind would shoulder the shutters, making them creak, and the rain-drops would chase each other down the window-pane like transparent tadpoles.

'Ah-ha! It is curious that you should mention that. The peasants in Salonika have a very similar . . . er . . . superstition . . . No, no, merely a superstition. I have a book here that gives a most *interesting* account of vampires in . . . um . . . Bosnia. It seems that the local people there . . .'

Tea would arrive, the cakes squatting on cushions of cream, toast in a melting shawl of butter, cups agleam and a faint wisp of steam rising from the teapot spout.

'. . . but, on the other hand, it is impossible to say that there is *no* life on Mars. It is, in my opinion, quite possible that some form of life will be found . . . er . . . *discovered* there, should we ever succeed in *getting* there. But there is no reason to suppose that any form of life found there would be identical . . .'

Sitting there, neat and correct in his tweed suit, Theodore would chew his toast slowly and methodically, his beard bristling, his eyes kindling with enthusiasm at each new subject that swam into our conversation. To me his knowledge seemed inexhaustible. He was a rich vein of information, and I mined him assiduously. No matter what the subject, Theodore could contribute something interesting to it. At last I would hear Spiro honking his horn in the street below, and I would rise reluctantly to go.

'Good-bye,' Theodore would say, tugging my hand. 'It's been a pleasure having you . . . er . . . no, no, not at all. See you next Thursday. When the weather gets better . . . er . . . less damp . . . in the *spring*, you know . . . perhaps we might go for some walks together . . . see what we can obtain. There are some most interesting ditches in the Val de Ropa . . . um, yes . . . Well, good-bye . . . Not at all.'

Driving back along the dark, rain-washed road, Spiro humming richly as he squatted behind the wheel, I would dream of the spring to come, and of all the wonderful creatures that Theodore and I would capture.

Eventually the warm wind and the rain of winter seemed to polish the sky, so that when January arrived it shone a clear, tender blue . . . the same blue as that of the tiny flames that devoured the olive logs in the charcoal pits. The nights were still and cool, with a moon so fragile it barely freckled the sea with silver points. The dawns were pale and translucent until the sun rose, mist-wrapped, like a gigantic silkworm cocoon, and washed the island with a delicate bloom of gold dust.

With March came the spring, and the island was flower-filled, scented, and aflutter with new leaves. The cypress trees that had tossed and hissed during the winds of winter now stood straight and sleek against the sky, covered with a misty coat of greenish-white cones. Waxy yellow crocuses appeared in great clusters, bubbling out among the tree roots and tumbling down the banks. Under the myrtles, the grape-hyacinths lifted buds like magenta sugar-drops, and the gloom of the oak thickets was filled with the dim smoke of a thousand blue day-irises. Anemones, delicate and easily wind-bruised, lifted ivory flowers the petals of which seemed to have been dipped in wine. Vetch, marigold, asphodel, and a hundred others flooded the fields and woods. Even the ancient olives, bent and hollowed by a thousand springs, decked themselves in clusters of minute creamy flowers, modest and yet decorative, as became their great age. It was no half-hearted spring, this: the whole island vibrated with it as though a great, ringing chord had been struck. Everyone and everything heard it and responded. It was apparent in the gleam of flower petals, the flash of bird wings and the sparkle in the dark, liquid eyes of the peasant girls. In the water-filled ditches the frogs that looked newly en-amelled snored a rapturous chorus in the lush weeds. In the vill-age coffee shops the wine seemed redder and, somehow, more potent. Blunt, work-calloused fingers plucked at guitar strings with strange gentleness, and rich voices rose in lilting, haunting song.

Spring affected the family in a variety of ways. Larry bought himself a guitar and a large barrel of strong red wine. He interspersed his bouts of work by playing haphazardly on the instrument and singing Elizabethan love songs in a meek tenor voice, with frequent pauses for refreshment. This would soon induce a mood of melancholy, and the love songs would become more doleful, while between each Larry would pause to inform whichever member of the family happened to be present that spring, for him, did not mean the beginning of a new year, but the death of the old one. The grave, he would proclaim, making the guitar rumble ominously, yawned a little wider with each season.

One evening the rest of us had gone out and left Mother and Larry alone together. Larry had spent the evening singing more and more dismally, until he had succeeded in working them both into a fit of acute depression. They attempted to alleviate this state with the aid of wine, but unfortunately this had the reverse effect, for they were not used to the heavy wines of Greece. When we returned we were somewhat startled to be greeted by Mother, standing at the door of the villa with a hurricane lantern. She informed us with lady-like precision and dignity that she wished to be buried under the rose bushes. The novelty of this lay in the fact that she had chosen such an accessible place for the disposal of her remains. Mother spent a lot of her spare time choosing places to be buried in, but they were generally situated in the most remote areas, and one had visions of the funeral cortège dropping exhausted by the wayside long before it had reached the grave.

When left undisturbed by Larry, however, spring for Mother meant an endless array of fresh vegetables with which to experiment, and a riot of new flowers to delight her in the garden. There streamed from the kitchen a tremendous number of new dishes, soups, stews, savouries, and curries, each richer, more fragrant, and more exotic than the last. Larry began to suffer from dyspepsia. Scorning the simple remedy of eating less, he procured an immense tin of bicarbonate of soda, and would solemnly take a dose after every meal.

'Why do *you eat* so much if it upsets you, dear?' Mother asked.

'It would be an insult to your cooking to eat less,' Larry replied unctuously.

'You're getting terribly fat,' said Margo; 'it's very bad for you.'

'Nonsense!' said Larry in alarm. 'I'm not getting fat, Mother, am I?'

'You look as though you've put on a little weight,' Mother admitted, surveying him critically.

'It's your fault,' Larry said unreasonably. 'You will keep tempting me with these aromatic delicacies. You're driving me to ulcers. I shall have to go on a diet. What's a good diet, Margo?'

'Well,' said Margo, launching herself with enthusiasm into her favourite topic, 'you could try the orange-juice-and-salad one; that's awfully good. There's the milk-and-raw-vegetable one . . . that's good too, but it takes a little time. Or there's the boiled-fish-and-brown-bread one. I don't know what that's like, I haven't tried it yet.'

'Dear God!' exclaimed Larry, genuinely shocked. 'Are those diets?'

'Yes, and they're all very good ones,' said Margo earnestly. 'I've been trying the orange-juice one and it's done wonders for my acne.'

'No,' said Larry firmly. 'I'm not going to do it if it means that I have to champ my way like a damned ungulate through bushels of raw fruit and vegetables. You will all have to resign yourselves to the fact that I shall be taken from you at an early age, suffering from fatty degeneration of the heart.'

At the next meal he took the precaution of having a large dose of bicarbonate beforehand, and then protested bitterly that the food tasted queer.

Margo was always badly affected by the spring. Her personal appearance, always of absorbing interest to her, now became

84

almost an obsession. Piles of freshly laundered clothes filled her bedroom, while the washing-line sagged under the weight of clothes newly washed. Singing shrilly and untunefully she would drift about the villa, carrying piles of flimsy underwear or bottles of scent. She would seize every opportunity to dive into the bathroom, in a swirl of white towels, and once in there she was as hard to dislodge as a limpet from a rock. The family in turn would bellow and batter on the door, getting no more satisfaction than an assurance that she was nearly finished, an assurance which we had learned by bitter experience not to have any faith in. Eventually she would emerge, glowing and immaculate, and drift from the house, humming, to sun-bathe in the olive groves or go down to the sea and swim. It was during one of these excursions to the sea that she met an over-good-looking young Turk. With unusual modesty she did not inform anyone of her frequent bathing assignations with this paragon, feeling, as she told us later, that we would not be interested. It was, of course, Spiro who discovered it. He watched over Margo's welfare with the earnest concern of a St Bernard, and there was precious little she could do without Spiro's knowing about it. He cornered Mother in the kitchen one morning, glanced surreptitiously round to make sure they were not overheard, sighed deeply, and broke the news to her.

'I'm very sorrys to haves to tells you this, Mrs Durrells,' he rumbled, 'buts I thinks you oughts to knows.'

Mother had by now become quite used to Spiro's conspiratorial air when he came to deliver some item of information about the family, and it no longer worried her.

'What's the matter now, Spiro?' she asked.

'It's Missy Margo,' said Spiro sorrowfully.

'What about her?'

Spiro glanced round uneasily.

'Dos you knows shes meetings a *mans?*' he inquired in a vibrant whisper.

'A man? Oh . . . er . . . yes, I did know,' said Mother, lying valiantly.

Spiro hitched up his trousers over his belly and leaned forward.

'But dids you knows he's a *Turk?*' he questioned in tones of bloodcurdling ferocity.

'A Turk?' said Mother vaguely. 'No, I didn't know he was a Turk. What's wrong with that?'

Spiro looked horrified.

'Gollys, Mrs Durrells, whats wrongs with it? He's a *Turk*. I wouldn'ts trust a sonofabitch Turk with any girls. He'll cuts her throats, thats what he'll do. Honest to Gods, Mrs Durrells, its not safe, Missy Margo swimmings with hims.'

'All right, Spiro,' said Mother soothingly, 'I'll speak to Margo about it.'

'I just thoughts you oughts to knows, thats all. Buts donts you worrys . . . if he dids anythings to Missy Margo I'd fix the bastard,' Spiro assured her earnestly.

Acting on the information received, Mother mentioned the matter to Margo, in a slightly less bloodcurdling manner than Spiro's, and suggested that the young Turk be brought up to tea. Delighted, Margo went off to fetch him, while Mother hastily made a cake and some scones, and warned the rest of us to be on our best behaviour. The Turk, when he arrived, turned out to be a tall young man, with meticulously waved hair and a flashy smile that managed to convey the minimum of humour with the maximum of condescension. He had all the sleek, smug self-possession of a cat in season. He pressed Mother's hand to his lips as though he were conferring an honour on her, and scattered the largesse of his smile for the rest of us. Mother, feeling the hackles of the family rising, threw herself desperately into the breach.

'Lovely having you . . . wanted so often . . . never seems time, you know . . . days simply *fly* past . . . Margo's told us so much about you . . . do have a scone . . .' she said breathlessly, smiling with dazzling charm and handing him a piece of cake.

'So kind,' murmured the Turk, leaving us in some doubt as to whether he was referring to us or himself. There was a pause.

'He's on holiday here,' announced Margo suddenly, as though it were something quite unique.

'Really?' said Larry waspishly. 'On holiday? Amazing!'

'I had a holiday once,' said Leslie indistinctly through a mouthful of cake; 'remember it clearly.'

Mother rattled the tea things nervously, and glared at them.

'Sugar?' she inquired fruitily. 'Sugar in your tea?'

'Thank you, yes.'

There was another short silence, during which we all sat and watched Mother pouring out the tea and searching her mind desperately for a topic of conversation. At length the Turk turned to Larry.

'You write, I believe?' he said with complete lack of interest.

Larry's eyes glittered. Mother, seeing the danger signs, rushed in quickly before he could reply.

'Yes, yes,' she smiled, 'he writes away, day after day. Always tapping at the typewriter.'

'I always feel that I could write superbly if I tried,' remarked the Turk.

'Really?' said Mother. 'Yes, well, it's a gift, I suppose, like so many things.'

'He swims well,' remarked Margo, 'and he goes out terribly far.'

'I have no fear,' said the Turk modestly. 'I am a superb swimmer, so I have no fear. When I ride the horse, I have no fear, for I ride superbly. I can sail the boat magnificently in the typhoon without fear.'

He sipped his tea delicately, regarding our awestruck faces with approval.

'You see,' he went on, in case we had missed the point, 'you see, I am not a fearful man.'

The result of the tea party was that the next day Margo

received a note from the Turk asking her if she would accompany him to the cinema that evening.

'Do you think I ought to go?' she asked Mother.

'If you want to, dear,' Mother answered, adding firmly, 'but tell him I'm coming too.'

'That should be a jolly evening for you,' remarked Larry.

'Oh, Mother, you can't,' protested Margo; 'he'll think it so queer.'

'Nonsense, dear,' said Mother vaguely. 'Turks are quite used to chaperones and things . . . look at their harems.'

So that evening Mother and Margo, dressed becomingly, made their way down the hill to meet the Turk. The only cinema was an open-air one in the town, and we calculated that the show should be over by ten at the latest. Larry, Leslie, and I waited eagerly for their return. At half-past one in the morning Margo and Mother, in the last stages of exhaustion, crept into the villa and sank into chairs.

'Oh, so you've come back?' said Larry. 'We thought you'd flown with him. We imagined you galloping about Constantinople on camels, your yashmaks rippling seductively in the breeze.'

'We've had the most awful evening,' said Mother, easing her shoes off, 'really awful.'

'What happened?' asked Leslie.

'Well, to begin with he stank of the most frightful perfume,' said Margo, 'and that put me off straight away.'

'We went in the cheapest seats, so close to the screen that I got a headache,' said Mother, 'and simply crammed together like sardines. It was so oppressive I couldn't breathe. And then, to crown it all, I got a flea. It was nothing to laugh at, Larry; really I didn't know what to do. The blessed thing got inside my corsets and I could feel it running about. I couldn't very well scratch, it would have looked so peculiar. I had to keep pressing myself against the seat. I think he noticed, though . . . he kept giving me funny looks from the corner of his eye. Then in the interval he went out and came back with some of that horrible, sickly Turkish Delight, and before long we were all covered with white sugar, and I had a dreadful thirst. In the second interval he went out and came back with flowers. I ask you, dear, flowers in the middle of the cinema. That's Margo's bouquet, on the table.'

Mother pointed to a massive bunch of spring flowers, tied up in a tangle of coloured ribbons. She delved into her bag and produced a minute bunch of violets that looked as though they had been trodden on by an exceptionally hefty horse.

'This,' she said, 'was for me.'

'But the worst part was coming home,' said Margo.

'A dreadful journey!' Mother agreed. 'When we came out of the cinema I thought we were going to get a car, but no, he hustled us into a cab, and a very smelly one at that. Really, I think he must be mental to try and come all that way in a cab. Anyway, it took us hours and *hours*, because the poor horse was tired, and I was sitting there trying to be polite, dying to scratch myself, and longing for a drink. All the fool could do was to sit there grinning at Margo and singing Turkish love songs. I could have cheerfully hit him. I thought we were *never* going to get back. We couldn't even get rid of him at the bottom of the hill. He insisted on coming up with us, armed with a huge stick, because he said the forests were full of serpents at this time of the year. I was *so* glad to see the back of him. I'm afraid you'll just *have* to choose your boy friends more carefully in future, Margo. I can't go through that sort of thing again. I was terrified he'd come right up to the door and we'd have to ask him in. I thought we'd *never* get away.'

'You obviously didn't make yourself fearful enough,' said Larry.

For Leslie the coming of spring meant the soft pipe of wings as the turtle-doves and wood-pigeons arrived, and the sudden flash and scuttle of a hare among the myrtles. So, after visiting numerous gun shops and after much technical argument, he returned to the villa one day proudly carrying a double-barrelled shotgun. His first action was to take it to his room, strip it down, and clean it, while I stood and watched, fascinated by the gleaming barrels and stock, sniffing rapturously at the rich heavy scent of the gun oil.

'Isn't she a beauty?' he crooned, more to himself than to me, his vivid blue eyes shining. 'Isn't she a honey?'

Tenderly he ran his hands over the silken shape of the weapon. Then he whipped it suddenly to his shoulder and followed an imaginary flock of birds across the ceiling of the room.

'Pow! . . . pow!' he intoned, jerking the gun against his shoulder. 'A left and a right, and down they come.'

He gave the gun a final rub with the oily rag and set it carefully in the corner of the room by his bed.

'We'll have a try for some turtle-doves tomorrow, shall we?' he continued, splitting open a packet and spilling the scarlet shells onto the bed. 'They start coming over about six. That little hill across the valley is a good place.'

So at dawn he and I hurried through the hunched and misty olive groves, up the valley where the myrtles were wet and squeaky with dew, and on to the top of the little hill. We stood waist-deep among the vines, waiting for the light to strengthen and for the birds to start flighting. Suddenly the pale morning sky was flecked with dark specks, moving as swiftly as arrows, and we could hear the quick wheep of wings. Leslie waited, standing stockily with legs apart, gun-stock resting on his hip, his eyes, intense and gleaming, following the birds. Nearer and nearer they flew, until it seemed that they must fly past us and be lost in the silvery, trembling olive tops behind. At the very last moment the gun leaped smoothly to his shoulder, the beetle-shiny barrels lifted their mouths to the sky, the gun jerked as the report echoed briefly, like the crack of a great branch in a still forest. The turtle-dove, one minute so swift and intent in its flight, now fell languidly to earth, followed by a swirl of soft, cinnamon-coloured feathers. When five doves hung from his belt, limp, bloodstained, with demurely closed eyes, he lit a cigarette, pulled his hat-brim down over his eyes and cuddled the gun under his arm.

'Come on,' he said; 'we've got enough. Let's give the poor devils a rest.'

We returned through the sun-striped olive groves where the chaffinches were pinking like a hundred tiny coins among the leaves. Yani, the shepherd, was driving his herd of goats out to graze. His brown face, with its great sweep of nicotine-stained moustache, wrinkled into a smile; a gnarled hand appeared from the heavy folds of his sheepskin cloak and was raised in salute.

'*Chairete*,' he called in his deep voice, the beautiful Greek greeting, '*chairete, kyrioi* . . . be happy.'

The goats poured among the olives, uttering stammering cries to each other, the leader's bell clonking rhythmically. The chaffinches tinkled excitedly. A robin puffed out his chest like a tangerine among the myrtles and gave a trickle of song. The island was drenched with dew, radiant with early morning sun, full of stirring life. Be happy. How could one be anything else in such a season?

Conversation

As soon as we had settled down and started to enjoy the island, Larry, with characteristic generosity, wrote to all his friends and asked them to come out and stay. The fact that the villa was only just big enough to house the family apparently had not occurred to him.

'I've asked a few people out for a week or so,' he said casually to Mother one morning.

'That will be nice, dear,' said Mother unthinkingly.

'I thought it would do us good to have some intelligent and stimulating company around. We don't want to stagnate.'

'I hope they're not too *highbrow*, dear,' said Mother.

'Good Lord, Mother, of course they're *not*; just extremely charming, ordinary people. I don't know why you've got this phobia about people being highbrow.'

'I don't like the highbrow ones,' said Mother plaintively. 'I'm not highbrow, and I can't talk about poetry and things. But they always seem to imagine, just because I'm your mother, that I should be able to discuss literature at great length with them. And they always come and ask me silly questions just when I'm in the middle of cooking.'

'I don't ask you to discuss art with them,' said Larry testily, 'but I think you might try and conceal your revolting taste in literature. Here I fill the house with good books and I find your bedside table simply groaning under the weight of cookery books, gardening books, and the most lurid-looking mystery stories. I can't think where you get hold of these things.'

'They're very good detective stories,' said Mother defensively. 'I borrowed them from Theodore.'

Larry gave a short, exasperated sigh and picked up his book again.

'You'd better let the Pension Suisse know when they're coming,' Mother remarked.

'What for?' asked Larry, surprised.

'So they can reserve the rooms,' said Mother, equally surprised.

'But I've invited them to stay here,' Larry pointed out.

'Larry! You haven't! Really, you are most *thoughtless*. How can they possibly stay here?'

'I really don't see what you're making a fuss about,' said Larry coldly.

'But where are they going to *sleep?*' said Mother, distraught. 'There's hardly enough room for us, as it is.'

'Nonsense, Mother, there's plenty of room if the place is organized properly. If Margo and Les sleep out on the veranda, that gives you two rooms; you and Gerry could move into the drawing-room, and that would leave those rooms free.'

'Don't be silly, dear. We can't all camp out all over the place like gipsies. Besides, it's still chilly at night, and I don't think Margo and Les ought to sleep outside. There simply isn't room to entertain in this villa. You'll just have to write to these people and put them off.'

'I can't put them off,' said Larry. 'They're on their way.'

'Really, Larry, you are the most annoying creature. Why on earth didn't you tell me before? You wait until they're nearly here, and then you tell me.'

'I didn't know you were going to treat the arrival of a few friends as if it was a major catastrophe,' Larry explained.

'But, dear, it's so silly to invite people when you know there's no room in the villa.'

'I do wish you'd stop fussing,' said Larry irritably; 'there's quite a simple solution to the whole business.'

'What?' asked Mother suspiciously.

'Well, since the villa isn't big enough, let's move to one that is.'

'Don't be ridiculous. Whoever heard of moving into a larger house because you've invited some friends to stay?'

'What's the matter with the idea? It seems a perfectly sensible solution to me; after all, if you say there's no room here, the obvious thing to do is to move.'

'The obvious thing to do is not to invite people,' said Mother severely.

'I don't think it's good for us to live like hermits,' said Larry. 'I only really invited them for you. They're a charming crowd. I thought you'd like to have them. Liven things up a bit for you.'

'I'm quite lively enough, thank you,' said Mother with dignity.

'Well, I don't know what we're going to do.'

'I really don't see why they can't stay in the Pension Suisse, dear.'

'You can't ask people out to stay with you and then make them live in a third-rate hotel.'

'How many have you invited?' asked Mother.

'Oh, just a few . . . two or three . . . They won't all be coming at once. I expect they'll turn up in batches.'

'I think at least you might be able to tell me how many you've invited,' said Mother.

'Well, I can't remember now. Some of them didn't reply, but that doesn't mean anything . . . they're probably on their way and thought it was hardly worth letting us know. Anyway, if you budget for seven or eight people I should think that would cover it.'

'You mean, including ourselves?'

'No, no, I mean seven or eight people as well as the family.'

'But it's absurd, Larry; we can't possibly fit thirteen people into this villa, with all the good will in the world.'

'Well, let's *move*, then. I've offered you a perfectly sensible solution. I don't know what you're arguing about.'

'But don't be ridiculous, dear. Even if we did move into a villa large enough to house thirteen people, what are we going to do with the extra space when they've gone?'

'Invite some more people,' said Larry, astonished that Mother should not have thought of this simple answer for herself.

Mother glared at him, her spectacles askew.

'Really, Larry, you do make me cross,' she said at last.

'I think it's rather unfair that you should blame me because your organization breaks down with the arrival of a few guests,' said Larry austerely.

'A few guests!' squeaked Mother. 'I'm glad you think eight people are a few guests.'

'I think you're adopting a most unreasonable attitude.'

'I suppose there's nothing unreasonable in inviting people and not letting me know?'

Larry gave her an injured look, and picked up his book.

'Well, I've done all I can,' he said; 'I can't do any more.'

There was a long silence, during which Larry placidly read his book and Mother piled bunches of roses into vases and placed them haphazardly round the room, muttering to herself.

'I wish you wouldn't just *lie* there,' she said at last. 'After all, they're your friends. It's up to you to do something.'

Larry, with a long-suffering air, put down his book.

'I really don't know what you expect me to do,' he said. 'Every suggestion I've made you've disagreed with.'

'If you made sensible suggestions I wouldn't disagree.'

'I don't see anything ludicrous in anything I suggested.'

'But, Larry dear, do be reasonable. We can't just rush to a new villa because some people are coming. I doubt whether we'd find one in time, anyway. And there's Gerry's lessons.'

'All that could easily be sorted out if you put your mind to it.'

'We are *not* moving to another villa,' said Mother firmly; 'I've made up my mind about that.'

She straightened her spectacles, gave Larry a defiant glare, and strutted off towards the kitchen, registering determination in every inch.

Part Two

Be not forgetful to entertain strangers:
for thereby some have entertained angels unawares.

– HEBREWS xiii, 2

7

The Daffodil-Yellow Villa

The new villa was enormous, a tall, square Venetian mansion, with faded daffodil-yellow walls, green shutters, and a fox-red roof. It stood on a hill overlooking the sea, surrounded by unkempt olive groves and silent orchards of lemon and orange trees. The whole place had an atmosphere of ancient melancholy about it: the house with its cracked and peeling walls, its tremendous echoing rooms, its verandas piled high with drifts of last year's leaves and so overgrown with creepers and vines that the lower rooms were in a perpetual green twilight; the little walled and sunken garden that ran along one side of the house, its wrought-iron gates scabby with rust, had roses, anemones, and geraniums sprawling across the weed-grown paths, and the shaggy, untended tangerine trees were so thick with flowers that the scent was almost overpowering; beyond the garden the orchards were still and silent, except for the hum of bees and an occasional splutter of birds among the leaves. The house and land were gently, sadly decaying, lying forgotten on the hillside overlooking the shining sea and the dark, eroded hills of Albania. It was as though villa and landscape were half asleep, lying there drugged in the spring sunshine, giving themselves up to the moss, the ferns, and the crowds of tiny toadstools.

It was Spiro, of course, who had found the place, and who organized our move with the minimum of fuss and the maximum of efficiency. Within three days of seeing the villa for the first time the long wooden carts were trailing in a dusty procession along the roads, piled high with our possessions, and on the fourth day we were installed.

At the edge of the estate was a small cottage inhabited by the gardener and his wife, an elderly, rather decrepit pair who seemed to have decayed with the estate. His job was to fill the water tanks, pick the fruit, crush the olives, and get severely stung once a year extracting honey from the seventeen bee-hives that simmered beneath the lemon trees. In a moment of misguided enthusiasm Mother engaged the gardener's wife to work for us in the villa. Her name was Lugaretzia, and she was a thin, lugubrious individual, whose hair was forever coming adrift from the ramparts of pins and combs with which she kept it attached to her skull. She was extremely sensitive, as Mother soon discovered, and the slightest criticism of her work, however tactfully phrased, would make her brown eyes swim with tears in an embarrassing display of grief. It was such a heart-rending sight to watch that Mother very soon gave up criticizing her altogether.

There was only one thing in life that could bring a smile to Lugaretzia's gloomy countenance, a glint to her spaniel eyes, and that was a discussion of her ailments. Where most people are hypochondriacs as a hobby, Lugaretzia had turned it into a full-time occupation. When we took up residence it was her stomach that was worrying her. Bulletins on the state of her stomach would start at seven in the morning when she brought up the tea. She would move from room to room with the trays, giving each one of us a blow-by-blow account of her nightly bout with her inside. She was a master of the art of graphic description; groaning, gasping, doubling up in agony, stamping about the rooms, she would give us such a realistic picture of her suffering that we would find our own stomachs aching in sympathy.

'Can't you *do* something about that woman?' Larry asked Mother one morning, after Lugaretzia's stomach had been through a particularly bad night.

'What do you expect me to do?' she asked. 'I gave her some of your bicarbonate of soda.'

'That probably accounts for her bad night.'

'I'm sure she doesn't *eat* properly,' said Margo. 'What she probably wants is a good diet.'

'Nothing short of a bayonet would do her stomach any good,' said Larry caustically, 'and I know . . . during the last week I have become distressingly familiar with every tiny convolution of her larger intestine.'

'I know she's a bit trying,' said Mother, 'but, after all, the poor woman is obviously suffering.'

'Nonsense,' said Leslie; 'she enjoys every minute of it. Like Larry does when he's ill.'

'Well, anyway,' said Mother hurriedly, 'we'll just have to put up with her; there's no one else we can get locally. I'll get Theodore to look her over next time he comes out.'

'If all she told me this morning was true,' said Larry, 'you'll have to provide him with a pick and a miner's lamp.'

'Larry, don't be disgusting,' said Mother severely.

Shortly afterwards, to our relief, Lugaretzia's stomach got better, but almost immediately her feet gave out, and she would hobble pitifully round the house, groaning loudly and frequently. Larry said that Mother hadn't hired a maid, but a ghoul, and suggested buying her a ball and chain. He pointed out that this would at least let us know when she was coming, and allow us time to escape, for Lugaretzia had developed the habit of creeping up behind one and groaning loudly and unexpectedly in one's ear. Larry started having breakfast in his bedroom after the morning when Lugaretzia took off her shoes in the dining-room in order to show us exactly which toes were hurting.

But, apart from Lugaretzia's ailments, there were other snags in the house. The furniture (which we had rented with the villa) was a fantastic collection of Victorian relics that had been locked in the rooms for the past twenty years. They crouched every-where, ugly, ungainly, unpractical, creaking hideously to each other and shedding bits of themselves with loud cracks like musket-shots, accompanied by clouds of dust if you walked past them too heavily. The first evening the leg came off the dining-room table, cascading the food onto the floor. Some days later Larry sat down on an immense and solid-looking chair, only to have the back disappear in a cloud of acrid dust. When Mother went to open a wardrobe the size of a cottage and the entire door came away in her hand, she decided that something must be done.

'We simply can't have people to stay in a house where everything comes to bits if you look at it,' she said. 'There's nothing for it, we'll have to buy some new furniture. Really, these guests are going to be the most expensive we've ever had.'

The next morning Spiro drove Mother, Margo, and myself into the town to buy furniture. We noticed that the town was more crowded, more boisterous, than usual, but it never occurred to us that anything special was happening until we had finished bargaining with the dealer and made our way out of his shop into the narrow, twisted streets. We were jostled and pushed as we struggled to get back to the place where we had left the car. The crowd grew thicker and thicker, and the people were so tightly wedged together that we were carried forward against our will.

'I think there must be something going on,' said Margo observantly. 'Maybe it's a fiesta or something interesting.'

'I can't care *what* it is, as long as we get back to the car,' said Mother.

But we were swept along, in the opposite direction to the car, and eventually pushed out to join a vast crowd assembled in the main square of the town. I asked an elderly peasant woman near me what was happening, and she turned to me, her face lit up with pride.

'It is Saint Spiridion, *kyria*,' she explained. 'Today we may enter the church and kiss his feet.'

Saint Spiridion was the patron saint of the island. His mummified body was enshrined in a silver coffin in the church, and once a year he was carried in procession round the town. He was very powerful, and could grant requests, cure illness, and do a number of other wonderful things for you if he happened to be in the right mood when asked. The islanders worshipped him, and every second male on the island was called Spiro in his honour. Today was a special day; apparently they would open the coffin and allow the faithful to kiss the slippered feet of the mummy, and make any request they cared to. The composition of the crowd showed how well loved the saint was by the Corfiots: there were elderly peasant women in their best black clothes, and their husbands, hunched as olive trees, with sweeping white moustaches; there were fishermen, bronzed and muscular, with the dark stains of octopus ink on their shirts; there were the sick too, the mentally defective, the consumptive, the crippled, old people who could hardly walk, and babies wrapped and bound like cocoons, their pale, waxy little faces crumpled up as they coughed and coughed. There were even a few tall, wild-looking Albanian shepherds, moustached and with shaven heads, wearing great sheepskin cloaks. This great multicoloured wedge of humanity moved slowly towards the dark door of the church, and we were swept along with it, wedged like pebbles in a lava-flow. By now Margo had been pushed well ahead of me, while Mother was equally far behind. I was caught firmly between five fat peasant women, who pressed on me like cushions and exuded sweat and garlic, while Mother was hopelessly entangled between two of the enormous Albanian shepherds. Steadily, firmly, we were pushed up the steps and into the church.

Inside, it was dark as a well, lit only by a bed of candles that bloomed like yellow crocuses along one wall. A bearded, tall-hatted priest clad in black robes flapped like a crow in the gloom, making the crowd form into a single line that filed down the church, past the great silver coffin and out through another door into the street. The coffin was standing upright, looking like a silver chrysalis, and at its lower end a portion had been removed so that the saint's feet, clad in the richly embroidered slippers, peeped out. As each person reached the coffin he bent, kissed the feet, and murmured a prayer, while at the top of the sarcophagus the saint's black and withered face peered out of a glass panel with an expression of acute distaste. It became evident that, whether we wanted to or not, we were going to kiss Saint Spiridion's feet. I looked back and saw Mother making frantic efforts to get to my side, but the Albanian bodyguard would not give an inch, and she struggled ineffectually. Presently she caught my eye and started to grimace and point at the coffin, shaking her head vigorously. I was greatly puzzled by this, and so were the two Albanians, who were watching her with undisguised suspicion. I think they came to the conclusion that Mother was about to have a fit, and with some justification, for she was scarlet in the face, and her grimaces were getting wilder and wilder. At last, in desperation, she threw caution to the winds and hissed at me over the heads of the crowd, 'Tell Margo . . . *not* to kiss . . . kiss the air . . . kiss the *air*.'

I turned to deliver Mother's message to Margo, but it was too late; there she was, crouched over the slippered feet, kissing them with an enthusiasm that enchanted and greatly surprised the crowd. When it came to my turn I obeyed Mother's instructions, kissing loudly and with a considerable show of reverence a point some six inches above the mummy's left foot. Then I was pushed along and disgorged through the church door and out into the street, where the crowd was breaking up into little groups, laughing and chattering. Margo was waiting on the steps, looking extremely self-satisfied. The next moment Mother appeared, shot from the door by the brawny shoulders of her shepherds. She staggered wildly down the steps and joined us.

'Those *shepherds*,' she exclaimed faintly. 'So ill-mannered . . . the smell nearly killed me . . . a mixture of incense and garlic . . . How do they manage to smell like that?'

'Oh, well,' said Margo cheerfully. 'It'll have been worth it if Saint Spiridion answers my request.'

'A most *insanitary* procedure,' said Mother, 'more likely to spread disease than cure it. I dread to think what we would have caught if we'd *really* kissed his feet.'

'But I kissed his feet,' said Margo, surprised.

'Margo! You didn't!'

'Well, everyone else was doing it.'

'And after I expressly told you *not* to.'

'You never told me not to . . .'

I interrupted and explained that I had been too late with Mother's warning.

'After all those people have been slobbering over those slippers you have to go and kiss them.'

'I was only doing what the others did.'

'I can't think what on earth possessed you to *do* such a thing.'

'Well, I thought he might cure my acne.'

'Acne!' said Mother scornfully. 'You'll be lucky if you don't catch something to go with the acne.'

The next day Margo went down with a severe attack of influenza, and Saint Spiridion's prestige with Mother reached rock bottom. Spiro was sent racing into the town for a doctor, and he returned bringing a little dumpy man with patent-leather hair, a faint wisp of moustache, and shoe-button eyes behind great horn-rimmed spectacles.

This was Doctor Androuchelli. He was a charming man, with a bedside manner that was quite unique.

'Po-po-po,' he said, strutting into the bedroom and regarding Margo with scorn, 'po-po-*po!* Remarkably unintelligent you have been, no? Kissing the saint's feet! Po-po-po-po-po! Nearly you might have caught some bugs unpleasant. You are lucky; she is influenza. Now you will do as I tell you, or I will rinse my hands of you. And please do not increase my work with such stupidity. If you kiss another saint's feet in the future I will not come to cure you . . . Po-po-po . . . such a thing to do.'

So while Margo languished in bed for three weeks, with

Androuchelli po-po-ing over her every two or three days, the rest of us settled into the villa. Larry took possession of one enormous attic and engaged two carpenters to make bookshelves; Leslie converted the large covered veranda behind the house into a shooting gallery, and hung an enormous red flag up outside whenever he was practising; Mother pottered absent-mindedly round the vast, subterranean, stone-flagged kitchen, preparing gallons of beef tea and trying to listen to Lugaretzia's monologues and worry about Margo at the same time. For Roger and myself, of course, there were fifteen acres of garden to explore, a vast new paradise sloping down to the shallow, tepid sea. Being temporarily without a tutor (for George had left the island) I could spend the whole day out, only returning to the villa for hurried meals.

In this varied terrain so close at hand I found many creatures which I now regarded as old friends: the rose-beetles, the blue carpenter-bees, the lady-birds, and the trapdoor spiders. But I also discovered many new beasts to occupy me. In the crumbling walls of the sunken garden lived dozens of little black scorpions, shining and polished as if they had been made out of Bakelite; in the fig and lemon trees just below the garden were quantities of emerald-green tree-frogs, like delicious satiny sweets among the leaves; up on the hillside lived snakes of various sorts, brilliant lizards, and tortoises. In the fruit orchards there were many kinds of birds: goldfinches, greenfinches, redstarts, wagtails, orioles, and an occasional hoopoe, salmon-pink, black, and white, probing the soft ground with long curved beaks, erecting their crests in astonishment when they saw me, and flying off.

Under the eaves of the villa itself the swallows had taken up residence. They had arrived a short time before we had, and their knobbly mud houses were only just completed, still dark brown and damp like rich plum-cake. As these were drying to a lighter biscuit brown, the parent birds were busy lining them, foraging round the garden for rootlets, lambs' wool, or feathers. Two of the swallows' nests were lower than the others, and it was on these that I concentrated my attention. Over a period of days I leaned a long ladder against the wall, midway between the two nests, and then slowly, day by day, I climbed higher and higher, until I could sit on the top rung and look into the nests, now some four feet away from me. The parent birds seemed in no way disturbed by my presence, and continued their stern work of preparing for a family, while I crouched on top of the ladder, and Roger lay at the bottom.

I grew to know these swallow families very well, and watched their daily work with considerable interest. What I took to be the two females were very similar in behaviour, earnest, rather preoccupied, over-anxious, and fussy. The two males, on the other hand, displayed totally different characters. One of them, during the work of lining the nest, brought excellent material, but he refused to treat it as a job of work. He would come swooping home, carrying a wisp of sheep's wool in his mouth, and would waste several minutes skating low over the flowers in the garden, drawing figures of eight, or else weaving in and out of the columns that held up the grape-vine. His wife would cling to the nest and chitter at him exasperatedly, but he refused to take life seriously. The other female also had trouble with her mate, but it was trouble of a different sort. He was, if anything, over-enthusiastic. He seemed determined to leave no stone unturned in his efforts to provide his young with the finest nest-lining in the colony. But, unfortunately, he was no mathematician, and, try as he would, he could not remember the size of his nest. He would come flying back, twittering in an excited if somewhat muffled manner, carrying a chicken or turkey feather as big as himself, and with such a thick quill it was impossible to bend it. It would generally take his wife several minutes to convince him that, no matter how they struggled and juggled, the feather would not fit into the nest. Acutely disappointed, he would eventually drop the feather so that it whirlpooled down to join the ever-increasing pile on the ground beneath, and then fly off in search of something more suitable. In a little while he would be back, struggling under a load of sheep's wool so matted and hard with earth and dung that he would have difficulty in getting up to the eaves, let alone into the nest.

When at last the nests were lined, the freckled eggs laid and hatched, the two husbands' characters seemed to change. The one who had brought so much futile nest-lining now swooped and hawked about the hillsides in a carefree manner, and would come drifting back carelessly carrying a mouthful of insect life of just the right size and softness to appeal to his fuzzy, trembling brood. The other male now became terribly harassed and apparently a prey to the dreadful thought that his babies might starve. So he would wear himself to a shadow in the pursuit of food, and return carrying the most unsuitable items, such as large spiky beetles, all legs and wing-case, and immense, dry, and completely indigestible dragon-flies. He would cling to the edge of the nest and make valiant but vain attempts to get these gigantic offerings rammed down the ever-open gullets of his young. I dread to think what would have happened if he had succeeded in wedging one of these spiky captures down their throats. Luckily, however, he never succeeded, and eventually, looking more harassed than ever, he would drop the insect to the ground and fly off hurriedly in search of something else. I was very grateful to this swallow, for he provided me with three species of butterfly, six dragon-flies and two ant-lions which were new to my collection.

The females, once the young were hatched, behaved in much the same way as they had always done: they flew a little faster, there was an air of brisk efficiency about them, but that was all. It intrigued me to see for the first time the hygienic arrangements of a bird's nest. I had often wondered, when hand-rearing a young bird, why it hoisted its bottom skywards with much waggling when it wanted to excrete. Now I discovered the reason. The excreta of the baby swallows was produced in globules which were coated with mucus that formed what was almost a gelatine packet round the dropping. The young would stand on their heads waggle their bottoms in a brief but enthusiastic rumba, and deposit their little offering on the rim of the nest. When the females arrived they would cram the food they had collected down the gaping throats, and then delicately pick up the dropping in their beaks and fly off to deposit it somewhere over the olive groves. It was an admirable arrangement, and I would watch the whole performance fascinated, from the bottom-waggle – which always made me giggle – to the final swoop of the parent over the tree-top, and the dropping of the little black-and-white bomb earthwards.

Owing to the male swallow's habit of collecting strange and unsuitable insects for his young, I always used to examine the area below the nest twice a day, in the hope of finding new specimens to add to my collection. It was here that, one morning, I found the most extraordinary-looking beetle crawling about. I did not think that even that mentally defective swallow could have brought back such a large creature, or even that he could have caught it, but it was certainly there, underneath the colony. It was a large, clumsy, blue-black beetle, with a large round head, long jointed antennæ, and a bulbous body. The weird thing about it was its wing-cases; it looked as though it had sent them to the laundry and they had shrunk, for they were very small and appeared to have been constructed for a beetle half the size. I toyed with the idea that it may have found itself without a pair of clean wing-cases to put on that morning and had to borrow its younger brother's pair, but I eventually decided that this idea, however enchanting, could not be described as scientific. I noticed, after I had picked it up, that my fingers smelled faintly acrid and oily, though it had not appeared to have exuded any liquid that I could see. I gave it to Roger to smell, to see if he agreed with me, and he sneezed violently and backed away, so I concluded that it must be the beetle and not my hand. I preserved it carefully, so that Theodore could identify it when he came.

Now that the warm days of spring had arrived, Theodore would come out to the villa every Thursday for tea, arriving in a horse-drawn cab from the town, his immaculate suit, stiff collar, and Homburg hat making a strange contrast to the nets, bags, and boxes full of test-tubes with which he was surrounded. Before tea we would examine any new specimens I had acquired and identify them. After tea we would wander about the grounds in search of creatures, or else make what Theodore would call an excursion to some neighbouring pond or ditch in search of new microscopic life for Theodore's collection. He identified my strange beetle, with its ill-fitting electra, without much trouble, and proceeded to tell me some extraordinary things about it.

'Ah-ha! Yes,' he said, closely scrutinizing the beast, 'it's an oil-beetle . . . *meloe proscaraboeus* . . . Yes . . . they are certainly very curious-looking beetles. What d'you say? Ah, yes, the wing-cases . . . Well, you see they are flightless. There are several species of coleoptera that have lost the power of flight, for one reason or another. It is the life history of this beetle that is very curious. This, of course, is a female. The male is considerably smaller – I should say approximately half the size. It appears that the female lays a number of small yellow eggs in the soil. When these hatch out into larvæ they climb up any flowers nearby and wait inside the blooms. There is a certain type of solitary bee which they must wait for, and when it enters the flower, the larvæ . . . hitch-hike . . . er . . . get a good grip with their claws on the bee's fur. If they are lucky, the bee is a female who is collecting honey to put in the cells with her egg. Then as soon as the bee has completed the filling of the cell and lays her egg, the larva jumps off onto the egg, and the bee closes the cell. Then the larva eats the egg and develops inside the cell. The thing that always strikes me as curious is that there is only *one* species of bee that the larvæ prey on. I should have thought that a great many of the larvæ catch hold of the wrong species of bee, and so eventually *die*. Then, of course, even if it's the *right* kind of bee, there is no . . . um . . . guarantee that it's a female about to lay eggs.'

He paused for a moment, raised himself on his toes several times, and thoughtfully contemplated the floor. Then he looked up, his eyes twinkling.

'I mean to say,' he continued, 'it's rather like backing a horse in a race . . . um . . . with the odds heavily against you.'

He waggled the glass-topped box gently so that the beetle slid from one end to the other, waving its antennæ in surprise. Then he put it carefully back on the shelf among my other specimens.

'Talking of horses,' said Theodore happily, placing his hands on his hips and rocking gently, 'did I ever tell you about the time when I led the triumphant entry into Smyrna on a white charger? Well, it was in the First World War, you know, and the commander of my battalion was determined that we should march into Smyrna in a . . . er . . . triumphal column, led, if possible, by a man on a white horse. Unfortunately, they gave me the doubtful privilege of leading the troops. Of course, I had learned to ride, you know, but I would not consider myself . . . um . . . an expert horseman. Well, everything went very well, and the horse behaved with great decorum, until we got into the outskirts of the town. It is custom in parts of Greece, as you know, to throw scent, perfume, rose-water, or something of the sort over the . . . er . . . conquering heroes. As I was riding along at the head of the column, an old woman darted out of a side street and started to hurl eau-de-Cologne about. The horse did not mind *that*, but most unfortunately a small quantity of the scent must have splashed into his *eye*. Well, he was quite used to parades and so forth, and cheering crowds and things, but he was not used to having his eye squirted full of eau-de-Cologne. He became . . . er . . . most upset about it and was acting more like a circus horse than a charger. I only managed to stay on because my feet had become wedged in the stirrups. The column had to break ranks to try to calm him down, but he was so upset that eventually the commander decided it would be unwise to let him take part in the rest of the triumphal entry. So while the column marched through the main streets with bands playing and people cheering and so forth, I was forced to slink through the back streets on my white horse, both of us, to add insult to injury, by now smelling very strongly of eau-de-Cologne. Um . . . I have never really *enjoyed* horse-riding since then.'

8

The Tortoise Hills

Behind the villa there were a series of small hills that raised shaggy crests above the surrounding olive groves. They were hills covered with great beds of green myrtle, tall heather, and a patchy feathering of cypress trees. This was probably the most fascinating area of the whole garden, for it was overflowing with life. In the sandy paths the ant-lion larvæ dug their little cone-shaped pits, and lay in wait to spatter any unwary ant that stepped over the edge with a bombardment of sand that would send it tumbling down to the bottom of the trap, to be seized in the ant-lion larva's terrible, pincer-like jaws. In the red sand-banks the hunting wasps were digging their tunnels, and hawking low in pursuit of spiders; they would stab with their sting, paralysing them, and carry them off to serve as food for their larvæ. Among the heather blooms the great, fat, furry caterpillars of emperor moths fed slowly, looking like animated fur collars. Among the myrtles in the warm, scented twilight of their leaves, the mantids prowled, heads turning this way and that as they watched for prey. Among the cypress branches the chaffinches had their neat nests, full of gawping, goggle-eyed babies; and on the lower branches the goldcrests weaved their tiny, fragile cups of moss and hair, or foraged for insects, hanging upside down on the ends of the branches, giving almost inaudible squeaks of joy at the discovery of a tiny spider or a gnat, their golden crests gleaming like little forge caps as they flipped daintily through the gloom of the tree.

It was not long after we arrived at the villa that I discovered these hills really belonged to the tortoises. One hot afternoon Roger and I were concealed behind a bush, waiting patiently for a large swallow-tail butterfly to return to its favourite sunning patch, so that we might capture it. It was the first really hot day we had had that year, and everything seemed to be lying drugged and asleep, soaking up the sun. The swallow-tail was in no hurry; he was down by the olive groves doing a ballet dance by himself, twisting, diving, pirouetting in the sun. As we watched him, I saw, from the corner of my eye, a faint movement at one side of the bush we were sheltering behind. I glanced quickly to see what it was, but the brown earth was sun-drenched and empty of life. I was just about to turn my attention to the butterfly again when I saw something that I could hardly believe: the patch of earth I had been looking at suddenly heaved upwards, as though pushed by a hand from beneath; the soil cracked and a tiny seedling waved about wildly before its pale roots gave way and it fell on its side.

What, I wondered, could be the cause of this sudden eruption? An earthquake? Surely not so small and confined. A mole? Not in such dry and waterless terrain. As I was speculating, the earth gave another heave, clods of it cracked off and rolled away, and I was looking at a brown and yellow shell. More earth was swept out of the way as the shell bucked upwards, and then, slowly and cautiously, a wrinkled, scaly head appeared out of the hole and a long, skinny neck followed it. The bleary eyes blinked once or twice as the tortoise surveyed me; then, deciding I must be harmless, he hoisted himself with infinite care and effort out of his earthy cell, walked two or three steps, and sank down in the sunshine, drowsing gently. After the long winter under the damp and chilly soil, that first sun-bath must have been like a drink of wine to the reptile. His legs were spread out from his shell, his neck extended as far as it could, his head resting on the ground; with eyes closed, the creature seemed to be absorbing sunshine through every bit of his body and shell. He remained lying there for about ten minutes, and then he rose, slowly and deliberately, and rolled off down the path to where a patch of dandelion and clover spread in the shade of a cypress. Here his legs seemed to give way and he collapsed onto the bottom of his shell with a thump. Then his head appeared from his shell, bent slowly down towards the rich green pile of the clover patch, his mouth opened wide, there was a moment's suspense, and then his mouth closed round the succulent leaves, his head jerked back to tear them off, and he sat there munching happily, his mouth stained with the first food of the year.

This must have been the first tortoise of spring, and as if his appearance from the subterranean dormitory were a signal, the hills suddenly became covered with tortoises. I have never seen so many congregated in so small an area: big ones the size of a soup plate and little ones the size of a cup, chocolate-coloured great-grandfathers and pale, horn-coloured youngsters, all lumbering heavily along the sandy paths, in and out of the heather and myrtles, occasionally descending to the olive groves where the vegetation was more succulent. Sitting in one spot for an hour or so you could count as many as ten tortoises pass you, and on one afternoon, as an experiment, I collected thirty-five specimens in two hours, just walking about the hillside and picking them up as they wandered about with an air of preoccupied determination, their club feet thumping on the ground.

No sooner had the shelled owners of the hills appeared from their winter quarters and had their first meal, than the males became romantically inclined. Stalking along on tip-toe with stumbling rapidity, their necks stretched out to the fullest extent, they would set out in search of a mate, pausing now and then to give a strange, yawping cry, the passionate love song of a male tortoise. The females, ambling heavily through the heather and pausing now and then for a snack, would answer in an off-hand manner. Two or three males, travelling at what – for a tortoise – was a gallop, would generally converge on the same female. They would arrive, out of breath and inflamed with passion, and glare at each other, their throats gulping convulsively. Then they would prepare to do battle.

These battles were exciting and interesting to watch, resembling all-in wrestling more than boxing, for the combatants did not possess either speed or the physical grace to indulge in fancy footwork. The general idea was for one to charge his rival as rapidly as possible, and just before impact to duck his head into his shell. The best blow was considered to be the broadside, for this gave the opportunity – by wedging yourself against your rival's shell and pushing hard – of overturning him and leaving him flapping helplessly on his back. If they couldn't manage to get in a broadside, any other part of the rival's anatomy did just as well. Charging each other, straining and pushing, their shells clattering together, occasionally taking a slow-motion bite at each other's neck or retreating into their shells with a hiss, the males would do battle. Meanwhile the object of their frenzy would amble slowly onwards, pausing now and then for a bite to eat, apparently unconcerned by the scraping and cracking of shells behind her. On more than one occasion these battles became so furious that a male in a fit of misplaced enthusiasm would deliver a broadside to his lady-love by mistake. She would merely fold herself into her shell with an outraged sniff, and wait patiently until the battle had passed her by. These fights seemed to me the most ill-organized and unnecessary affairs, for it was not always the strongest tortoise that won; with good terrain in his favour a small specimen could easily overturn one twice his size. Nor, indeed, was it invariably one of the warriors that got the lady, for on several occasions I saw a female wander away from a pair of fighting males to be accosted by a complete stranger (who had not even chipped his shell on her behalf) and go off with him quite happily.

Roger and I would squat by the hour in the heather, watching the tortoise knights in their ill-fitting armour jousting for the ladies, and the contests never failed to entertain us. Sometimes we would lay bets with each other as to which one was going to win, and by the end of the summer Roger had backed so many losers that he owed me a considerable amount of money. Sometimes, when the battle was very fierce, Roger would get carried away by the spirit of the thing and want to join in, and I would have to restrain him.

When the lady had eventually made her choice, we would follow the happy couple on their honeymoon among the myrtles, and even watch (discreetly hidden behind the bushes) the final acts in the romantic drama. The wedding night – or rather day – of a tortoise is not exactly inspiring. To begin with, the female performs in a disgracefully coy manner, and becomes heavily skittish in evading her bridegroom's attentions. She irritates him in this way until he is forced to adopt cave-man tactics, and subdues her maidenly antics with a few short, sharp broadsides. The actual sexual act was the most awkward and fumbling thing I had ever seen. The incredibly heavy-handed and inexpert way the male would attempt to hoist himself onto the female's shell, slipping and slithering, clawing desperately for a foothold on the shiny shields, overbalancing and almost overturning, was extremely painful to watch; the urge to go and assist the poor creature was almost overwhelming, and I had the greatest difficulty in restraining myself from interference. Once a male was infinitely more bungling than usual, and fell down three times during the mounting, and generally behaved in such an imbecile manner I was beginning to wonder if he was going to take all summer about it . . . At last, more by luck than skill, he hoisted himself up, and I was just heaving a sigh of relief when the female, obviously bored by the male's inadequacy, moved a few steps towards a dandelion leaf. Her husband clawed wildly at her moving shell, but could get no foothold; he slipped off, teetered for a minute, and then rolled ignominiously over onto his back. This final blow seemed to be too much for him, because, instead of trying to right himself, he simply folded himself up in his shell and lay there mournfully. The female, meanwhile, ate the dandelion leaf. At last, since his passion seemed to have died, I rolled the male over, and after a minute or so he wandered off, peering about him in a dazed fashion, and ignoring his erstwhile bride, who regarded him unemotionally, her mouth full of food. As a punishment for her callous behaviour I carried her up to the most barren and desiccated part of the hillside and left her there, so that she would have an extremely long walk to the nearest clover patch.

I came to know many of the tortoises by sight, so closely and enthusiastically did I watch their daily lives. Some I could recognize by their shapes and colours, others by some physical defect – a chip from the edge of a shell, the loss of a toe-nail, and so on. There was one large honey-and-tar-coloured female who was unmistakable, for she had only one eye. I got on such intimate terms with her that I christened her Madame Cyclops. She came to know me quite well, and, realizing that I meant her no harm, she would not disappear into her shell at my approach, but stretch up her neck to see if I had brought her a tit-bit in the shape of a lettuce leaf or some tiny snails, of which she was inordinately fond. She would roll about her business quite happily, while Roger and I followed her, and occasionally, as a special treat, we would carry her down to the olive groves for a picnic lunch on the clover. To my infinite regret I was not present at her wedding, but I was lucky enough to witness the outcome of the honeymoon.

I found her one day busily engaged in digging a hole in the soft soil at the base of a bank. She had dug to a fair depth when I arrived, and seemed quite glad to have a rest and a little refreshment in the shape of some clover flowers. Then she set to work once more, scraping the earth out with her fore-feet and barging it to one side with her shell. Not being quite certain what she was trying to achieve, I did not attempt to help her, but merely lay on my stomach in the heather and watched. After some time, when she had excavated quite a pile of earth, she carefully scrutinized the hole from all angles and was apparently satisfied. She turned round, lowered her hind end over the hole, and sat there with a rapt look on her face while she absent-mindedly laid nine white eggs. I was most surprised and delighted, and congratulated her heartily on this achievement, while she gulped at me in a meditative sort of way. She then proceeded to scrape the soil back over the eggs and pat it down firmly by the simple method of standing over it and flopping down on her tummy several times. This task accomplished, she had a rest and accepted the remains of the clover blooms.

I found myself in an awkward position, for I dearly wanted one of the eggs to add to my collection; I did not like to take it while she was there, for fear that she might feel insulted and perhaps dig up the remaining eggs and eat them, or do something equally horrible. So I had to sit and wait patiently while she finished her snack, had a short doze, and then ambled off among the bushes. I followed her for some distance to make sure she did not turn back, and then hurried to the nest and carefully unearthed one of the eggs. It was about the size of a pigeon's, oval in shape and with a rough, chalky shell. I patted the earth back over the nest so that she would never know it had been disturbed, and carried my trophy triumphantly back to the villa. I blew the sticky yolk out of it with great care, and enshrined the shell among my natural-history collection in a small glass-topped box of its own. The label, which was a nice blend of scientific and sentimental, read: *Egg of Greek Tortoise* (*Testudo græca*). *Laid by Madame Cyclops.*

Throughout the spring and early summer, while I was studying the courtship of the tortoises, the villa was filled with an apparently endless stream of Larry's friends. No sooner had we seen one lot off, and sighed with relief, than another steamer would arrive, and the line of taxis and horse-carriages would hoot and clatter their way up the drive, and the house would be filled once more. Sometimes the fresh load of guests would turn up before we had got rid of the previous group, and the chaos was indescribable; the house and garden would be dotted with poets, authors, artists, and playwrights arguing, painting, drinking, typing, and composing. Far from being the ordinary, charming people that Larry had promised, they all turned out to be the most extraordinary eccentrics, who were so highbrow that they had difficulty in understanding one another.

One of the first to arrive was Zatopec, an Armenian poet, a short, stocky individual with a swooping eagle nose, a shoulder-length mane of silvery hair, and hands bulbous and twisted by arthritis. He arrived wearing an immense, swirling black cloak and a broad-brimmed black hat, riding in a carriage piled high with wine. His voice shook the house like a sirocco as he swept into it, his cloak rippling, his arms full of bottles. He scarcely stopped talking the whole time he stayed. He talked from morning till night, drinking prodigious quantities of wine, snatching forty winks wherever he happened to be, and rarely going to bed at all. In spite of his advanced years he had lost none of his enthusiasm for the opposite sex, and, while he treated Mother and Margo with a sort of creaking, antique courtesy, no peasant girl for miles was free from his attentions. He would hobble through the olive groves after them, roaring with laughter, shouting endearments, his cloak flapping behind him, his pocket bulging with a bottle of wine. Even Lugaretzia was not safe, and had her bottom pinched while she was sweeping under the sofa. This proved something of a blessing, as it made her forget her ailments for a few days, and blush and giggle kittenishly whenever Zatopec appeared. Eventually Zatopec departed as he had arrived, lying back regally in a cab, his cloak wrapped round him, shouting endearments to us as it clopped off down the drive, promising to return soon from Bosnia and bring some more wine for us.

The next invasion consisted of three artists, Jonquil, Durant, and Michael. Jonquil looked, and sounded, like a cockney owl with a fringe; Durant was lank and mournful and so nervous that he would almost jump out of his skin if you spoke to him suddenly; by contrast, Michael was a short, fat, somnambulistic little man who looked like a well-boiled prawn with a mop of dark, curly hair. These three had only one thing in common, and that was a desire to get some work done. Jonquil, on striding into the house for the first time, made this quite clear to a startled Mother.

'I didn't come for no bleeding 'oliday,' she said severely; 'I came to get some work done, so I'm not interested in picnics and such, see?'

'Oh . . . er . . . no, no, of course not,' said Mother guiltily, as though she had been planning vast banquets among the myrtle bushes for Jonquil's benefit.

'Jus' so long as you know,' said Jonquil. 'I didn't want to upset nothing, see? I jus' want to get some work done.'

So she promptly retired to the garden, clad in a bathing costume, and slept peacefully in the sun throughout her stay.

Durant, he informed us, wanted to work too, but first he had to get his nerve back. He was shattered, he told us, quite shattered by his recent experience. Apparently, while in Italy he had suddenly been seized with the desire to paint a masterpiece. After much thought he decided that an almond orchard in full bloom should give a certain scope to his brush. He spent considerable time and money driving about the countryside in search of the right orchard. At long last he found the perfect one; the setting was magnificent and the blooms were full and thick. Feverishly he set to work, and by the end of the first day he had got the basis down on canvas. Tired, but satisfied, he packed up his things and returned to the village. After a good night's sleep he awoke refreshed and invigorated, and rushed back to the orchard to complete his picture. On arrival there he was struck dumb with horror and amazement, for every tree was gaunt and bare, while the ground was thickly carpeted with pink and white petals. Apparently during the night a spring storm had playfully stripped all the orchards in the vicinity of their blossom, including Durant's special one.

'I vas stricken,' he told us, his voice quivering, his eyes filled with tears. 'I swore I vould never paint again . . . never! But slowly I am recovering my nerves . . . I am feeling less shattered . . . Sometime I vill start to paint again.'

On inquiry, it turned out that this unfortunate experience had taken place two years previously, and he had still not recovered.

Michael got off to a bad start. He was captivated by the colouring of the island, and told us enthusiastically that he would begin work on an immense canvas that would capture the very essence of Corfu. He could hardly wait to start. It was most unfortunate that he happened to be a prey to asthma. It was equally unfortunate that Lugaretzia had placed on a chair in his room a blanket which I used for horse-riding, there being no saddles available. In the middle of the night we were awakened by a noise that sounded like a troop of bloodhounds being slowly strangled. Assembling sleepily in Michael's room we found him wheezing and gasping, the sweat running down his face. While Margo rushed to make some tea and Larry to get some brandy, Leslie opened the windows and Mother put Michael back to bed, and, since he was now clammy with sweat, tenderly covered him with the horse-blanket. To our surprise, in spite of all remedies, he got worse. While he could still speak, we questioned him interestedly about his complaint and its cause.

'Psychological, purely psychological,' said Larry. 'What does the wheezing sound remind you of?'

Michael shook his head mutely.

'I think he ought to sniff something up . . . something like ammonia or something,' said Margo. 'It's wonderful if you're going to faint.'

'Well, he's not going to faint,' said Leslie tersely, 'but he probably would if he sniffed ammonia.'

'Yes, dear, it is a bit strong,' said Mother. 'I wonder what could have brought it on . . . Are you allergic to something, Michael?'

Between gasps Michael informed us that he was only allergic to three things: the pollen of the lilac flowers, cats, and horses. We all peered out of the window, but there was not a lilac tree for miles. We searched the room, but there was no cat hidden anywhere. I indignantly denied Larry's accusation that I had smuggled a horse into the house. It was only when Michael seemed on the verge of death that we noticed the horse-rug, which Mother had tucked carefully under his chin. This incident had such a bad effect on the poor man that he was quite unable to put a brush to canvas during his stay; he and and Durant lay side by side in deck-chairs, recovering their nerve together.

While we were still coping with these three, another guest arrived in the shape of Melanie, Countess de Torro. She was tall, thin, with a face like an ancient horse, crow-black eyebrows and an enormous cushion of scarlet hair on her head. She had hardly been in the house five minutes before she complained of the heat, and to Mother's consternation and my delight, she caught hold of her scarlet hair and removed it, revealing a head as bald as a mushroom top. Seeing Mother's startled gaze, the Countess explained in her harsh, croaking voice. 'I've just recovered from erysipelas,' she said; 'lost all my hair . . . couldn't find eyebrows and wig to match in Milan . . . might get something in Athens.'

It was unfortunate that, owing to a slight impediment due to ill-fitting false teeth, the Countess was inclined to mumble, so Mother was under the impression that the disease she had just recovered from was of a much more unlady-like character. At the first available opportunity she got Larry into a corner.

'Disgusting!' she said in a vibrant whisper. 'Did you *hear* what she's had? And you call her a friend.'

'Friend?' said Larry in surprise. 'Why, I hardly know her . . . can't stand the woman; but she's an interesting character and I wanted to study her at close hand.'

'I like that,' said Mother indignantly. 'So you invite that *creature* here and we all catch some revolting disease while you take notes. No, I'm sorry, Larry, but she'll have to go.'

'Don't be silly, Mother,' said Larry irritably; 'you can't catch it . . . not unless you intend to share a bed with her.'

'Don't be *revolting*,' said Mother, glaring. 'I won't stand that obscene person in this house.'

They argued in whispers for the rest of the day, but Mother was adamant. Eventually Larry suggested asking Theodore out and getting his opinion on the matter, and to this Mother agreed. So a note was dispatched, asking Theodore to come out and spend the day. His reply accepting the invitation was brought by a carriage in which reclined the cloak-swathed form of Zatopec, who, it turned out, had drunk a farewell of prodigious size to Corfu, got on the wrong boat, and ended up in Athens. As by then he had missed his appointment in Bosnia, he had philosophically boarded the next vessel back to Corfu, bringing with him several crates of wine. Theodore turned up the next day, wearing, as a concession to summer, a panama instead of his usual Homburg. Before Mother had a chance to warn him about our hairless guest, Larry had introduced them.

'A doctor?' said Melanie, Countess de Torro, her eyes gleaming. 'How interesting. Perhaps you can advise me . . . I've just had erysipelas.'

'Ah-ha! Really?' said Theodore, eyeing her keenly. 'Which . . . er . . . treatment did you have?'

They embarked on a long and technical discussion with enthusiasm, and it was only the most determined efforts on Mother's part that got them away from what she still considered to be an indelicate subject.

'Really, Theodore's as bad as that woman,' she said to Larry.

'I do *try* and be broad-minded, but there is a limit, and I don't think things like that should be discussed at tea.'

Later Mother got Theodore alone, and the subject of the Countess's disease was explained. Mother was then stricken with a guilty conscience at having misjudged the woman, and was immensely affable to her for the rest of the day, even telling her to take her wig off if she felt the heat.

The dinner that night was colourful and extraordinary, and I was so fascinated by the assembly of characters and the various conversations that I did not know which one to listen to with undivided attention. The lamps smoked gently and cast a warm, honey-coloured light over the table, making the china and glass glitter, and setting fire to the red wine as it splashed into the glasses.

'But, dear boy, you have missed the meaning of it . . . yes, yes, you have!' Zatopec's voice booming out, his nose curving over his wine glass. 'You cannot discuss poetry as if it were house painting . . .'

'. . . so I says to 'im, "I'm not doing a bleeding drawing for less than a tenner a time, and that's dirt cheap," I says . . .'

'. . . and the next morning I vas paralysed . . . shocked beyond everything . . . thousands of blossoms, bruised and torn . . . I say I vill never paint again . . . my nerves had been shattered . . . the whole orchard gone . . . phuit! like that . . . and there vas I . . .'

'. . . and then, of course, I had the sulphur baths.'

'Ah, yes . . . um . . . though, mind you, I think the bath treatment is . . . er . . . a little . . . er . . . you know . . . a little *over-rated*. I believe that ninety-two per cent of sufferers . . .'

The plates of food, piled like volcanoes, steaming gently; the early fruit in a polished pile in the centre dish; Lugaretzia hobbling round the table, groaning gently to herself; Theodore's beard twinkling in the lamplight; Leslie carefully manufacturing bread pellets to shoot at a moth that hovered round the lamps; Mother, ladling out the food, smiling vaguely at everyone and keeping a watchful eye on Lugaretzia; under the table Roger's cold nose pressed hard against my knee in mute appeal.

Margo and the still-wheezing Michael discussing art: '. . . but then I think that Lawrence does that sort of thing so much *better*. He has a certain rich bloom, as it were . . . don't you agree? I mean, take Lady Chatterley, eh?'

'Oh, yes, quite. And then, of course, he did wonderful things in the desert, didn't he? . . . and writing that wonderful book . . . the . . . er . . . *The Seven Pillows of Wisdom*, or whatever it was called . . .'

Larry and the Countess discussing art: '. . . but you must have the straightforward simplicity, the clarity of a child's eyes . . . Take the finest *fundamental* verse . . . take "Humpty Dumpty". . . . Now, there's poetry for you . . . the simplicity and freedom from clichés and outdated shibboleths . . .'

'. . . but then it's useless prating about the simple approach to poetry if you're going to produce jingles which are about as straightforward and uncomplicated as a camel's stomach . . .'

Mother and Durant: '. . . and you can imagine the effect it had on me . . . I vas shattered.'

'Yes, you must have been. Such a shame, after all that trouble. Will you have a little more rice?'

Jonquil and Theodore: '. . . and the Latvian peasants . . . well, I've never seen anything like it . . .'

'Yes, here in Corfu and . . . er . . . I believe . . . in some parts of Albania, the peasants have a very . . . er . . . similar custom . . .'

Outside, the moon's face was peering through a filigree of vine-leaves, and the owls were giving their strange, chiming cries. Coffee and wine were served on the balcony, between the vine-shaggy pillars. Larry strummed on the guitar and sang an Elizabethan marching song. This reminded Theodore of one of his fantastic but true Corfu anecdotes, which he related to us with impish glee.

'As you know, here in Corfu nothing is ever done the correct way. Everyone starts out with the . . . er . . . *best intentions*, but something always seems to go wrong. When the Greek king visited the island some years ago the . . . er . . . climax of his tour was to be a . . . er . . . sort of stage show . . . a play. The climax of the drama was the Battle of Thermopylæ, and, as the curtain fell, the Greek army was supposed to drive . . . um . . . the Persian army triumphantly into the . . . what d'you call them? Ah, yes, the *wings*. Well, it appears that the people playing the part of the Persians were a bit disgruntled at the thought of having to retreat in front of the king, and the fact that they had to play the part of Persians also . . . you know . . . rankled. It only required a little incident to set things off. Unfortunately, during the battle scene the leader of the Greek army . . . um . . . misjudged the distance and caught the leader of the Persian army quite a heavy blow with his wooden sword. This, of course, was an accident. I mean to say, the poor fellow didn't *mean* to do it. But nevertheless it was sufficient to . . . er . . . inflame the Persian army to such an extent that instead of . . . er . . . retreating, they *advanced*. The centre of the stage became a milling mob of helmeted soldiers locked in mortal combat. Two of them were thrown into the orchestra pit before someone had the sense to lower the curtain. The king remarked later that he had been greatly impressed by the . . . um . . . *realism* shown in the battle scene.'

The burst of laughter sent the pale geckos scuttling up the wall in alarm.

'Theodore!' Larry laughed mockingly. 'I'm sure you made that up.'

'No, no!' Theodore protested; 'it's quite true . . . I saw it myself.'

'It sounds the most unlikely story.'

'Here in Corfu,' said Theodore, his eyes twinkling with pride, '*anything* can happen.'

The sea striped with moonlight gleamed through the olives. Down by the well the tree-frogs croaked excitedly to each other.

Two owls were having a contest in the tree below the veranda. In the grape-vine above our heads the geckos crept along the gnarled branches, eagerly watching the drifts of insects that were drawn, like a tide, by the lamplight.

9

The World in a Wall

The crumbling wall that surrounded the sunken garden alongside the house was a rich hunting ground for me. It was an ancient brick wall that had been plastered over, but now this outer skin was green with moss, bulging and sagging with the damp of many winters. The whole surface was an intricate map of cracks, some several inches wide, others as fine as hairs. Here and there large pieces had dropped off and revealed the rows of rose-pink bricks lying beneath like ribs. There was a whole landscape on this wall if you peered closely enough to see it; the roofs of a hundred tiny toadstools, red, yellow, and brown, showed in patches like villages on the damper portions; mountains of bottle-green moss grew in tuffets so symmetrical that they might have been planted and trimmed; forests of small ferns sprouted from cracks in the shady places, drooping languidly like little green fountains. The top of the wall was a desert land, too dry for anything except a few rust-red mosses to live in it, too hot for anything except sun-bathing by the dragon-flies. At the base of the wall grew a mass of plants – cyclamen, crocus, asphodel – thrusting their leaves among the piles of broken and chipped roof-tiles that lay there. This whole strip was guarded by a labyrinth of blackberry hung, in season, with fruit that was plump and juicy and black as ebony.

The inhabitants of the wall were a mixed lot, and they were divided into day and night workers, the hunters and the hunted. At night the hunters were the toads that lived among the brambles, and the geckos, pale, translucent, with bulging eyes, that lived in the cracks higher up the wall. Their prey was the population of stupid, absent-minded crane-flies that zoomed and barged their way among the leaves; moths of all sizes and shapes, moths striped, tessellated, checked, spotted, and blotched, that fluttered in soft clouds along the withered plaster; the beetles, rotund and neatly clad as business men, hurrying with portly efficiency about their night's work. When the last glow-worm had dragged his frosty emerald lantern to bed over the hills of moss, and the sun rose, the wall was taken over by the next set of inhabitants. Here it was more difficult to differentiate between the prey and the predators, for everything seemed to feed indiscriminately off everything else. Thus the hunting wasps searched out caterpillars and spiders; the spiders hunted for flies; the dragon-flies, big, brittle and hunting-pink, fed off the spiders and the flies; and the swift, lithe, and multicoloured wall lizards fed off everything.

But the shyest and most self-effacing of the wall community were the most dangerous; you hardly ever saw one unless you looked for it, and yet there must have been several hundred living in the cracks of the wall. Slide a knife-blade carefully under a piece of the loose plaster and lever it gently away from the brick, and there, crouching beneath it, would be a little black scorpion an inch long, looking as though he were made out of polished chocolate. They were weird-looking little things, with their flattened, oval bodies, their neat, crooked legs, and enormous crablike claws, bulbous and neatly jointed as armour, and the tail like a string of brown beads ending in a sting like a rose-thorn. The scorpion would lie there quite quietly as you examined him, only raising his tail in an almost apologetic gesture of warning if you breathed too hard on him. If you kept him in the sun too long he would simply turn his back on you and walk away, and then slide slowly but firmly under another section of plaster.

I grew very fond of these scorpions. I found them to be pleasant, unassuming creatures with, on the whole, the most charming habits. Provided you did nothing silly or clumsy (like putting your hand on one) the scorpions treated you with respect, their one desire being to get away and hide as quickly as possible. They must have found me rather a trial, for I was always ripping sections of the plaster away so that I could watch them, or capturing them and making them walk about in jam jars so that I could see the way their feet moved. By means of my sudden and unexpected assaults on the wall I discovered quite a bit about the scorpions. I found that they would eat bluebottles (though how they caught them was a mystery I never solved), grass-hoppers, moths, and lacewing flies. Several times I found one of them eating another, a habit I found most distressing in a creature otherwise so impeccable.

By crouching under the wall at night with a torch, I managed to catch some brief glimpses of the scorpions' wonderful courtship dances. I saw them standing, claws clasped, their bodies raised to the skies, their tails lovingly entwined; I saw them waltzing slowly in circles among the moss cushions, claw in claw. But my view of these performances was all too short, for almost as soon as I switched on the torch the partners would stop, pause for a moment, and then, seeing that I was not going to extinguish the light, would turn round and walk firmly away, claw in claw, side by side. They were definitely beasts that believed in keep-ing themselves to themselves. If I could have kept a colony in captivity I would probably have been able to see the whole of the courtship, but the family had forbidden scorpions in the house, despite my arguments in favour of them.

Then one day I found a fat female scorpion in the wall, wearing what at first glance appeared to be a pale fawn fur coat. Closer inspection proved that this strange garment was made up of a mass of tiny babies clinging to the mother's back. I was enraptured by this family, and I made up my mind to smuggle them into the house and up to my bedroom so that I might keep them and watch them grow up. With infinite care I manœuvred the mother and family into a match-box, and then hurried to the villa. It was rather unfortunate that just as I entered the door lunch should be served; however, I placed the match-box carefully on the mantelpiece in the drawing-room, so that the scorpions should get plenty of air, and made my way to the dining-room and joined the family for the meal. Dawdling over my food, feeding Roger surreptitiously under the table, and listening to the family arguing, I completely forgot about my exciting new captures. At last Larry, having finished, fetched the cigarettes from the drawing-room, and lying back in his chair he put one in his mouth and picked up the match-box he had brought. Oblivious of my impending doom I watched him interestedly as, still talking glibly, he opened the match-box.

Now I maintain to this day that the female scorpion meant no harm. She was agitated and a trifle annoyed at being shut up in a match-box for so long, and so she seized the first opportunity to escape. She hoisted herself out of the box with great rapidity, her babies clinging on desperately, and scuttled onto the back of Larry's hand. There, not quite certain what to do next, she paused, her sting curved up at the ready. Larry, feeling the movement of her claws, glanced down to see what it was, and from that moment things got increasingly confused.

He uttered a roar of fright that made Lugaretzia drop a plate and brought Roger out from beneath the table, barking wildly. With a flick of his hand he sent the unfortunate scorpion flying down the table, and she landed midway between Margo and Leslie, scattering babies like confetti as she thumped onto the cloth. Thoroughly enraged at this treatment, the creature sped towards Leslie, her sting quivering with emotion. Leslie leaped to his feet, overturning his chair, and flicked out desperately with his napkin, sending the scorpion rolling across the cloth towards Margo, who promptly let out a scream that any railway engine would have been proud to produce. Mother, completely bewildered by this sudden and rapid change from peace to chaos, put on her glasses and peered down the table to see what was causing the pandemonium, and at that moment Margo, in a vain attempt to stop the scorpion's advance, hurled a glass of water at it. The shower missed the animal completely, but successfully drenched Mother, who, not being able to stand cold water, promptly lost her breath and sat gasping at the end of the table, unable even to protest. The scorpion had now gone to ground under Leslie's plate, while her babies swarmed wildly all over the table. Roger, mystified by the panic, but determined to do his share, ran round and round the room, barking hysterically.

'It's that bloody boy again . . .' bellowed Larry.

'Look out! Look out! They're coming!' screamed Margo.

'All we need is a book,' roared Leslie; 'don't panic, hit 'em with a book.'

'What on earth's the *matter* with you all?' Mother kept imploring, mopping her glasses.

'It's that bloody boy . . . he'll kill the lot of us . . . Look at the table . . . knee-deep in scorpions . . .'

'Quick . . . quick . . . do something . . . Look out, look out!'

'Stop screeching and get a book, for God's sake . . . You're worse than the dog . . . Shut *up*, Roger . . .'

'By the grace of God I wasn't bitten . . .'

'Look out . . . there's another one . . . Quick . . . quick . . .'

'Oh, shut up and get me a book or something . . .'

'But *how* did the scorpions get on the table, dear?'

'That bloody boy . . . Every match-box in the house is a death-trap . . .'

'Look out, it's coming towards me . . . Quick, quick, do something . . .'

'Hit it with your knife . . . *your knife* . . . Go on, hit it . . .'

Since no one had bothered to explain things to him, Roger was under the mistaken impression that the family were being attacked, and that it was his duty to defend them. As Lugaretzia was the only stranger in the room, he came to the logical conclusion that she must be the responsible party, so he bit her in the ankle. This did not help matters very much.

By the time a certain amount of order had been restored, all the baby scorpions had hidden themselves under various plates and bits of cutlery. Eventually, after impassioned pleas on my part, backed up by Mother, Leslie's suggestion that the whole lot be slaughtered was quashed. While the family, still simmering with rage and fright, retired to the drawing-room, I spent half an hour rounding up the babies, picking them up in a teaspoon, and returning them to their mother's back. Then I carried them outside on a saucer and, with the utmost reluctance, released them on the garden wall. Roger and I went and spent the afternoon on the hillside, for I felt it would be prudent to allow the family to have a siesta before seeing them again.

The results of this incident were numerous. Larry developed a phobia about match-boxes and opened them with the utmost caution, a handkerchief wrapped round his hand. Lugaretzia limped round the house, her ankle enveloped in yards of bandage, for weeks after the bite had healed, and came round every morning, with the tea, to show us how the scabs were getting on. But, from my point of view, the worst repercussion of the whole affair was that Mother decided I was running wild again, and that it was high time I received a little more education. While the problem of finding a full-time tutor was being solved, she was determined that my French, at least, should be kept in trim. So arrangements were made, and every morning Spiro would drive me into the town for my French lesson with the Belgian consul.

The consul's house was situated in the maze of narrow, smelly alley-ways that made up the Jewish quarter of the town. It was a fascinating area, the cobbled streets crammed with stalls that were piled high with gaily coloured bales of cloth, mountains of shining sweetmeats, ornaments of beaten silver, fruit, and vegetables. The streets were so narrow that you had to stand back against the wall to allow the donkeys to stagger past with their loads of merchandise. It was a rich and colourful part of the town, full of noise and bustle, the screech of bargaining women, the cluck of hens, the barking of dogs, and the wailing cry of the men carrying great trays of fresh hot loaves on their heads. Right in the very centre, in the top flat of a tall, rickety building that leaned tiredly over a tiny square, lived the Belgian consul.

He was a sweet little man, whose most striking attribute was a magnificent three-pointed beard and carefully waxed moustache. He took his job rather seriously, and was always dressed as though he were on the verge of rushing off to some important official function, in a black cut-away coat, striped trousers, fawn spats over brightly polished shoes, an immense cravat like a silk waterfall, held in place by a plain gold pin, and a tall and gleaming top hat that completed the ensemble. One could see him at any hour of the day, clad like this, picking his way down the dirty, narrow alleys, stepping daintily among the puddles, drawing himself back against the wall with a magnificently courteous gesture to allow a donkey to pass, and tapping it coyly on the rump with his malacca cane. The people of the town did not find his garb at all unusual. They thought that he was an Englishman, and as all Englishmen were lords it was not only right but necessary that they should wear the correct uniform.

The first morning I arrived, he welcomed me into a living-room whose walls were decorated with a mass of heavily framed photographs of himself in various Napoleonic attitudes. The Victorian chairs, covered with red brocade, were patched with antimacassars by the score; the table on which we worked was draped in a wine-red cloth of velvet, with a fringe of bright green tassels round the edge. It was an intriguingly ugly room. In order to test the extent of my knowledge of French, the consul sat me down at the table, produced a fat and battered edition of *Le Petit Larousse*, and placed it in front of me, open at page one.

'You will please to read zis,' he said, his gold teeth glittering amicably in his beard.

He twisted the points of his moustache, pursed his lips, clasped his hands behind his back, and paced slowly across to the window, while I started down the list of words beginning with A. I had hardly stumbled through the first three when the consul stiffened and uttered a suppressed exclamation. I thought at first he was shocked by my accent, but it apparently had nothing to do with me. He rushed across the room, muttering to himself, tore open a cupboard, and pulled out a powerful-looking air rifle, while I watched him with increasing mystification and interest, not unmixed with a certain alarm for my own safety. He loaded the weapon, dropping pellets all over the carpet in his frantic haste. Then he crouched and crept back to the window, where, half concealed by the curtain, he peered out eagerly. Then he raised the gun, took careful aim at something, and fired. When he turned round, slowly and sadly shaking his head, and laid the gun aside, I was surprised to see tears in his eyes. He drew a yard or so of silk handkerchief out of his breast pocket and blew his nose violently.

'Ah, ah, ah,' he intoned, shaking his head dolefully, 'ze poor lizzle fellow. Buz we musz work . . . please to continuez wiz your reading, *mon ami.*'

For the rest of the morning I toyed with the exciting idea that the consul had committed a murder before my very eyes, or, at least, that he was carrying out a blood feud with some neighbouring householder. But when, after the fourth morning, the consul was still firing periodically out of his window, I decided that my explanation could not be the right one, unless it was an exceptionally large family he was feuding with, and a family, moreover, who were apparently incapable of firing back. It was a week before I found out the reason for the consul's incessant fusillade, and the reason was cats. In the Jewish quarter, as in other parts of the town, the cats were allowed to breed unchecked. There were literally hundreds of them. They belonged to no one and were uncared for, so that most of them were in a frightful state, covered with sores, their fur coming out in great bald patches, their legs bent with rickets, and all of them so thin that it was a wonder they were alive at all. The consul was a great cat-lover, and he possessed three large and well-fed Persians to prove it. But the sight of all these starving, sore-ridden felines stalking about on the roof-tops opposite his window was too much for his sensitive nature.

'I cannot feed zem all,' he explained to me, 'so I like to make zem happiness by zooting zem. Zey are bezzer so, buz iz makes me feel so zad.'

He was, in fact, performing a very necessary and humane service, as anyone who had seen the cats would agree. So my lessons in French were being continuously interrupted while the consul leaped to the window to send yet another cat to a happier hunting ground. After the report of the gun there would be a moment's silence, in respect for the dead; then the consul would blow his nose violently and sigh tragically, and we would plunge once more into the tangled labyrinth of French verbs.

For some inexplicable reason the consul was under the impression that Mother could speak French, and he would never lose an opportunity of engaging her in conversation. If she had the good fortune, while shopping in the town, to notice his top hat bobbing through the crowd towards her, she would hastily retreat into the nearest shop and buy a number of things she had no use for, until the danger was past. Occasionally, however, the consul would appear suddenly out of an alley-way and take her by surprise. He would advance, smiling broadly and twirling his cane, sweep off his top hat, and bow almost double before her, while clasping her reluctantly offered hand and pressing it passionately into his beard. Then they would stand in the middle of the street, occasionally being forced apart by a passing donkey, while the consul swamped Mother under a flood of French, gesturing elegantly with his hat and stick, apparently unaware of the blank expression on Mother's face. Now and then he would punctuate his speech with a questioning '*N'est-ce pas, madame?*'

and this was Mother's cue. Summoning up all her courage, she would display her complete mastery over the French tongue.

'*Oui, oui!*' she would exclaim, smiling nervously, and then add, in case it had sounded rather unenthusiastic, 'OUI, OUI.'

This procedure satisfied the consul, and I'm sure he never realized that this was the only French word that Mother knew. But these conversations were a nerve-racking ordeal for her, and we had only to hiss 'Look out, Mother, the consul's coming,' to set her tearing off down the street at a lady-like walk that was dangerously near to a gallop.

In some ways these French lessons were good for me; I did not learn any French, it's true, but by the end of the morning I was so bored that my afternoon sorties into the surrounding country were made with double the normal enthusiasm. And then, of course, there was always Thursday to look forward to. Theodore would come out to the villa as soon after lunch as was decent, and stay until the moon was high over the Albanian mountains. Thursday was happily chosen, from his point of view, because it was on this day that the seaplane from Athens arrived and landed in the bay not far from the house. Theodore had a passion for watching seaplanes land. Unfortunately the only part of the house from which you could get a good view of the bay was the attic, and then it meant leaning perilously out of the window and craning your neck. The plane would invariably arrive in the middle of tea; a dim, drowsy hum could be heard, so faint one could not be sure it was not a bee. Theodore, in the middle of an anecdote or an explanation, would suddenly stop talking, his eyes would take on a fanatical gleam, his beard would bristle, and he would cock his head on one side.

'Is that . . . er . . . you know . . . is that the sound of a *plane?*' he would inquire.

Everyone would stop talking and listen; slowly the sound would grow louder and louder. Theodore would carefully place his half-eaten scone on his plate.

'Ah-ha!' he would say, wiping his fingers carefully. 'Yes, that certainly *sounds* like a plane . . . er . . . um . . . yes.'

The sound would grow louder and louder, while Theodore shifted uneasily in his seat. At length Mother would put him out of his misery.

'Would you like to go up and watch it land?' she would ask.

'Well . . . er . . . if you're sure . . .' Theodore would mumble, vacating his seat with alacrity. 'I . . . er . . . find the sight very attractive . . . if you're sure you don't mind.'

The sound of the plane's engines would now be directly overhead; there was not a moment to lose.

'I have always been . . . er . . . you know . . . attracted . . .'

'Hurry up, Theo, or you'll miss it,' we would chorus.

The entire family then vacated the table, and, gathering Theodore *en route*, we sped up the four flights of stairs, Roger racing ahead, barking joyfully. We burst into the attic, out of breath, laughing, our feet thumping like gun-fire on the uncarpeted floor, threw open the windows, and leaned out, peering over the olive tops to where the bay lay like a round blue eye among the trees, its surface as smooth as honey. The plane, like a cumbersome overweight goose, flew over the olive groves, sinking lower and lower. Suddenly it would be over the water, racing its reflection over the blue surface. Slowly the plane dropped lower and lower. Theodore, eyes narrowed, beard bristling, watched it with bated breath. Lower and lower, and then suddenly it touched the surface briefly, left a widening petal of foam, flew on, and then settled on the surface and surged across the bay, leaving a spreading fan of white foam behind it. As it came slowly to rest, Theodore would rasp the side of his beard with his thumb, and ease himself back into the attic.

'Um . . . yes,' he would say, dusting his hands, 'it is certainly a . . . very . . . er . . . *enjoyable* sight.'

The show was over. He would have to wait another week for the next plane. We would shut the attic windows and troop noisily downstairs to resume our interrupted tea. The next week exactly the same thing would happen all over again.

It was on Thursdays that Theodore and I went out together, sometimes confining ourselves to the garden, sometimes venturing further afield. Loaded down with collecting boxes and nets, we wended our way through the olives, Roger galloping ahead of us, nose to the ground. Everything that we came across was grist to our mill: flowers, insects, rocks, or birds. Theodore had an apparently inexhaustible fund of knowledge about everything, but he imparted this knowledge with a sort of meticulous diffidence that made you feel he was not so much teaching you something new as reminding you of something which you were already aware of, but which had, for some reason or other, slipped your mind. His conversation was sprinkled with hilarious anecdotes, incredibly bad puns, and even worse jokes, which he would tell with great relish, his eyes twinkling, his nose wrinkled as he laughed silently in his beard, as much at himself as at his own humour.

Every water-filled ditch or pool was, to us, a teeming and unexplored jungle, with the minute cyclops and water-fleas, green and coral pink, suspended like birds among the underwater branches, while on the muddy bottom the tigers of the pool would prowl: the leeches and the dragon-fly larvæ. Every hollow tree had to be closely scrutinized in case it should contain a tiny pool of water in which mosquito-larvæ were living, every mossy-wigged rock had to be overturned to find out what lay beneath it, and every rotten log had to be dissected. Standing straight and immaculate at the edge of a pool, Theodore would carefully sweep his little net through the water, lift it out, and peer keenly into the tiny glass bottle that dangled at the end, into which all the minute water life had been sifted.

'Ah-ha!' he might say, his voice ringing with excitement, his beard bristling, 'I believe it's *ceriodaphnia laticaudata*.'

He would whip a magnifying glass from his waistcoat pocket
and peer more closely.

'Ah, um . . . yes . . . very curious . . . it is *laticaudata*. Could
you just . . . er . . . hand me a clean test-tube . . . um . . . thank
you . . .'

He would suck the minute creature out of the bottle with a
fountain-pen filler, enshrine it carefully in the tube, and then
examine the rest of the catch.

'There doesn't seem to be anything else that's particularly
exciting . . . Ah, yes, I didn't notice . . . there is rather a curious
caddis larva . . . there, d'you see it? . . . um . . . it appears to have
made its case of the shells of certain molluscs . . . It's certainly
very pretty.'

At the bottom of the little bottle was an elongated case, half
an inch long, constructed out of what appeared to be silk, and
thick with tiny flat snail-shells like buttons. From one end of this
delightful home the owner peered, an unattractive maggot-like
beast with a head like an ant's. Slowly it crawled across the glass,
dragging its beautiful house with it.

'I tried an interesting experiment once,' Theodore said. 'I
caught a number of these . . . er . . . larvæ, and removed their
shells. Naturally it doesn't *hurt* them. Then I put them in some
jars which contained perfectly clear water and nothing in the
way of . . . er . . . materials with which to build new cases. Then
I gave each set of larvæ different-coloured materials to build with:
some I gave very tiny blue and green beads, and some I gave
chips of brick, white sand, even some . . . er . . . fragments of
coloured glass. They all built new cases out of these different
things, and I must say the result was very curious and . . . er . . .
colourful. They are certainly very clever *architects*.'

He emptied the contents of the bottle back into the pool, put
his net over his shoulder, and we walked on our way.

'Talking of *building*,' Theodore continued, his eyes sparkling, 'did I tell you what happened to . . . a . . . er . . . a friend of mine? Um, yes. Well, he had a small house in the country, and, as his family . . . um . . . increased, he decided that it was not big enough. He decided to add another floor to the house. He was, I think, a little *over-confident* of his own architectural . . . um . . . prowess, and he insisted on designing the new floor himself. Um, ha, yes. Well, everything went well and in next to no time the new floor was ready, complete with bedrooms, bathrooms, and so forth. My friend had a party to celebrate the completion of the work, we all drank toasts to the . . . um . . . new piece of building, and with great ceremony the scaffolding was taken down . . . um . . . removed. No one noticed anything . . . um . . . anything *amiss*, until a late arrival at the celebration wanted to look round the new rooms. It was then discovered that there was no staircase. It appears that my friend had forgotten to put a staircase in his plans, you know, and during the actual . . . er . . . the actual *building* operations he and the workmen had got so used to climbing to the top floor by means of the scaffolding that no one apparently noticed the . . . er . . . the *defect*.'

So we would walk on through the hot afternoon, pausing by the pools and ditches and stream, wading through the heavily scented myrtle bushes, over the hillsides crisp with heather, along white, dusty roads where we were occasionally passed by a drooping, plodding donkey carrying a sleepy peasant on its back.

Towards evening, our jars, bottles, and tubes full of strange and exciting forms of life, we would turn for home. The sky would be fading to a pale gold as we marched through the olive groves, already dim with shadow, and the air would be cooler and more richly scented. Roger would trot ahead of us, his tongue flapping out, occasionally glancing over his shoulder to make sure we were following him. Theodore and I, hot and dusty and tired, our bulging collecting bags making our shoulders ache pleasantly, would stride along singing a song that Theodore had taught me. It had a rousing tune that gave a new life to tired feet,

and Theodore's baritone voice and my shrill treble would ring
out gaily through the gloomy trees:

> 'There was an old man who lived in Jerusalem,
> Glory Halleluiah, Hi-ero-jerum.
> He wore a top hat and he looked very sprucelum,
> Glory Halleluiah, Hi-ero-jerum.
> Skinermer rinki doodle dum, skinermer rinki doodle dum,
> Glory Halleluiah, Hi-ero-jerum . . .'

10

The Pageant of Fireflies

Spring merged slowly into the long, hot, sun-sharp days of summer sung in by cicadas, shrill and excited, making the island vibrate with their cries. In the fields the maize was starting to fill out, the silken tassels turning from brown to butter-blond; when you tore off the wrapping of leaves and bit into the rows of pearly seeds the juice would spurt into your mouth like milk. On the vines the grapes hung in tiny clusters, freckled and warm. The olives seemed weighed down under the weight of their fruit, smooth drops of green jade among which the choirs of cicadas zithered. In the orange groves, among the dark and shiny leaves, the fruit was starting to glow redly, like a blush spreading up the green, pitted skins.

Up on the hills, among the dark cypress and the heather, shoals of butterflies danced and twisted like wind-blown confetti, pausing now and then on a leaf to lay a salvo of eggs. The grasshoppers and locusts whirred like clockwork under my feet, and flew drunkenly across the heather, their wings shining in the sun. Among the myrtles the mantids moved, lightly, carefully, swaying slightly, the quintessence of evil. They were lank and green, with chinless faces and monstrous globular eyes, frosty gold, with an expression of intense, predatory madness in them. The crooked arms, with their fringes of sharp teeth, would be raised in mock supplication to the insect world, so humble, so fervent, trembling slightly when a butterfly flew too close.

Towards evening, when it grew cooler, the cicadas stopped singing, their place being taken by the green tree-frogs, glued damply to the lemon-tree leaves down by the well. With bulging eyes staring as though hypnotized, their backs as shiny as the leaves they sat amongst, they swelled out their vocal sacs and croaked harshly and with such violence that they seemed in danger of splitting their damp bodies with the effort. When the sun sank there was a brief, apple-green twilight which faded and became mauve, and the air cooled and took on the scents of evening. The toads appeared, putty-coloured with strange, map-like blotches of bottle-green on their skins. They hopped furtively among the long grass clumps in the olive groves, where the crane-flies' unsteady flight seemed to cover the ground with a drifting curtain of gauze. They sat there blinking, and then would suddenly snap at a passing crane-fly; sitting back, looking a trifle embarrassed, they stuffed the trailing ends of wing and leg into their great mouths with the aid of their thumbs. Above them, on the crumbling walls of the sunken garden, the little black scorpions walked solemnly, hand in hand, among the plump mounds of green moss and the groves of tiny toadstools.

The sea was smooth, warm and as dark as black velvet, not a ripple disturbing the surface. The distant coastline of Albania was dimly outlined by a faint reddish glow in the sky. Gradually, minute by minute, this glow deepened and grew brighter, spreading across the sky. Then suddenly the moon, enormous, wine-red, edged herself over the fretted battlement of mountains, and threw a straight, blood-red path across the dark sea. The owls appeared now, drifting from tree to tree as silently as flakes of soot, hooting in astonishment as the moon rose higher and higher, turning to pink, then gold, and finally riding in a nest of stars, like a silver bubble.

With the summer came Peter to tutor me, a tall, handsome young man, fresh from Oxford, with decided ideas on education which I found rather trying to begin with. But gradually the atmosphere of the island worked its way insidiously under his skin, and he relaxed and became quite human. At first the lessons were painful to an extreme: interminable wrestling with fractions and percentages, geological strata and warm currents, nouns, verbs, and adverbs. But, as the sunshine worked its magic on Peter, the fractions and percentages no longer seemed to him an overwhelmingly important part of life and they were gradually pushed more and more into the background; he discovered that the intricacies of geological strata and the effects of warm currents could be explained much more easily while swimming along the coast, while the simplest way of teaching me English was to allow me to write something each day which he would correct. He had suggested a diary, but I was against this, pointing out that I already kept one on nature, in which was recorded everything of interest that happened each day. If I were to keep another diary, what was I to put in it? Peter could find no answer to this argument. I suggested that I might try something a little more ambitious and interesting than a diary. Diffidently, I suggested I write a book, and Peter, somewhat startled, but not being able to think of any reason why I should *not* write a book, agreed. So every morning I spent a happy hour or so adding another chapter to my epic, a stirring tale which involved a voyage round the world with the family, during which we captured every conceivable kind of fauna in the most unlikely traps. I modelled my style on the *Boy's Own Paper*, and so each chapter ended on a thrilling note, with Mother being attacked by a jaguar, or Larry struggling in the coils of an enormous python. Sometimes these climaxes were so complicated and fraught with danger that I had great difficulty in extricating the family intact on the following day. While I was at work on my masterpiece, breathing heavily, tongue protruding, breaking off for discussions with Roger on the finer points of the plot, Peter and Margo would take a stroll in the sunken garden to look at the flowers. To my surprise, they had both suddenly become very botanically minded. In this way the mornings passed very pleasantly for all concerned. Occasionally, in the early days, Peter suffered from sudden spasms of conscience, my epic would be relegated to a drawer, and we would pore over mathematical problems. But as the summer days grew longer, and Margo's interest in gardening became more sustained, these irritating periods became less frequent.

After the unfortunate affair of the scorpion, the family had given me a large room on the first floor in which to house my beasts, in the vague hope that this would confine them to one particular portion of the house. This room – which I called my study, and which the rest of the family called the Bug House – smelled pleasantly of ether and methylated spirits. It was here that I kept my natural-history books, my diary, microscope, dissecting instruments, nets, collecting bags, and other important items. Large cardboard boxes housed my birds'-egg, beetle, butterfly, and dragon-fly collections, while on the shelves above were a fine range of bottles full of methylated spirits in which were preserved such interesting items as a four-legged chicken (a present from Lugaretzia's husband), various lizards and snakes, frog-spawn in different stages of growth, a baby octopus, three half-grown brown rats (a contribution from Roger), and a minute tortoise, newly hatched, that had been unable to survive the winter. The walls were sparsely, but tastefully, decorated with a slab slate containing the fossilized remains of a fish, a photograph of myself shaking hands with a chimpanzee, and a stuffed bat. I had prepared the bat myself, without assistance, and I was extremely proud of the result. Considering how limited my knowledge of taxidermy was, it looked, I thought, extremely *like* a bat, especially if you stood at the other side of the room. With wings outstretched it glowered down from the wall from its slab of cork. When summer came, however, the bat appeared to feel the heat; it sagged a little, its coat no longer glossy, and a new and mysterious smell started to make itself felt above the ether and methylated spirits. Poor Roger was wrongly accused at first, and it was only later, when the smell had penetrated even to Larry's bedroom, that a thorough investigation traced the odour to my bat. I was surprised and not a little annoyed. Under pressure I was forced to get rid of it. Peter explained that I had not cured it properly, and said that if I could obtain another specimen he would show me the correct procedure. I thanked him profusely, but tactfully suggested that we keep the whole thing a secret; I explained that I felt the family now looked with a suspicious eye on the art of taxidermy, and it would require a lot of tedious persuasion to get them into an agreeable frame of mind.

My efforts to secure another bat were unsuccessful. Armed with a long bamboo I waited for hours in the moon-splashed corridors between the olive trees, but the bats flickered past like quicksilver and vanished before I could use my weapon. But, while waiting in vain for a chance to hit a bat, I saw a number of other night creatures which I would not otherwise have seen. I watched a young fox hopefully digging for beetles in the hillside, scrabbling with slim paws at the earth, and scrunching the insects up hungrily as he unearthed them. Once, five jackals appeared out of the myrtle bushes, paused in surprise at seeing me, and then melted away among the trees, like shadows. The nightjars on silent, silky wings would slide as smoothly as great black swallows along the rows of olives, sweeping across the grass in pursuit of the drunken, whirling crane-flies. One night a pair of squirrel dormice appeared in the tree above me, and chased each other in wild exuberance up and down the grove, leaping from branch to branch like acrobats, skittering up and down the tree-trunks, their bushy tails like puffs of grey smoke in the moonlight. I was so fascinated by these creatures that I was determined to try to catch one. The best time to search for them was, of course, during the day, when they would be asleep. So, I hunted laboriously through the olive groves for their hideout, but it was a hopeless quest, for every gnarled and twisted trunk was hollow, and each contained half a dozen holes. However, my patience did not go entirely unrewarded, for one day I thrust my arm into a hole and my fingers closed round something small and soft, something that wiggled as I pulled it out. At first glance my capture appeared to be an outsize bundle of dandelion seeds, furnished with a pair of enormous golden eyes; closer inspection proved it to be a young Scops owl, still clad in his baby down. We regarded each other for a moment, and then the bird, apparently indignant at my ill-mannered laughter at his appearance, dug his tiny claws deeply into my thumb, and I lost my grip on the branch, so that we fell out of the tree together.

I carried the indignant owlet back home in my pocket, and introduced him to the family with a certain trepidation. To my surprise, he was greeted with unqualified approval, and no objection was raised to my keeping him. He took up residence in a basket kept in my study and, after much argument, he was christened Ulysses. From the first he showed that he was a bird of great strength of character, and not to be trifled with. Although he would have fitted comfortably into a tea-cup, he showed no fear and would unhesitatingly attack anything and everyone, regardless of size. As we all had to share the room, I felt it would be a good idea if he and Roger got on intimate terms, so, as soon as the owl had settled down, I performed the introductions by placing Ulysses on the floor, and telling Roger to approach and make friends. Roger had become very philosophical about having to make friends with the various creatures that I adopted, and he took the appearance of an owl in his stride. Wagging his tail briskly, in an ingratiating manner, he approached Ulysses, who squatted on the floor with anything but a friendly expression on his face. He watched Roger's approach in an unwinking stare of ferocity. Roger's advance became less confident. Ulysses continued to glare as though trying to hypnotize the dog. Roger stopped, his ears drooped, his tail wagging only feebly, and he glanced at me for inspiration. I ordered him sternly to continue his overtures of friendship. Roger looked nervously at the owl, and then with great nonchalance walked round him, in an effort, to approach him from the back. Ulysses, however, let his head revolve too, and kept his eyes still fixed on the dog. Roger, never having met a creature that could look behind itself without turning round, seemed a trifle nonplussed. After a moment's thought he decided to try the skittish, let's-all-have-a-jolly-game approach. He lay down on his stomach, put his head between his paws and crept slowly towards the bird, whining gently and wagging his tail with abandon. Ulysses continued to look as though he were stuffed. Roger, still progressing on his stomach, managed to get quite close, but then he made a fatal mistake. He pushed his woolly face forward and sniffed loudly and interestedly at the bird. Now, Ulysses would stand a lot, but he was not going to be sniffed at by a mountainous dog covered with black curls. He decided that he would have to show this ungainly and wingless beast exactly where he got off. He lowered his eyelids, clicked his beak, hopped up into the air and landed squarely on the dog's muzzle, burying his razor-sharp claws in the black nose. Roger, with a stricken yelp, shook the bird off and retired beneath the table; no amount of coaxing would get him to come out until Ulysses was safely back in his basket.

When Ulysses grew older he lost his baby down and developed the fine ash-grey, rust-red, and black plumage of his kind, with the pale breast handsomely marked with Maltese crosses in black. He also developed long ear-tufts, which he would raise in indignation when you attempted to take liberties with him. As he was now far too old to be kept in a basket, and strongly opposed to the idea of a cage, I was forced to give him the run of the study. He performed his flying lessons between the table and the door-handle, and, as soon as he had mastered the art, chose the pelmet above the window as his home, and would spend the day sleeping up there, eyes closed, looking exactly like an olive stump. If you spoke to him he would open his eyes a fraction, raise his ear-tufts and elongate his whole body, so that he looked like some weird, emaciated Chinese idol. If he was feeling particularly affectionate he would click his beak at you, or, as a great concession, fly down and give you a hurried peck on the ear.

As the sun sank and the geckos started to scuttle about the shadowy walls of the house, Ulysses would wake up. He would yawn delicately, stretch his wings, clean his tail, and then shiver violently so that all his feathers stood out like the petals of a wind-blown chrysanthemum. With great nonchalance he would regurgitate a pellet of undigested food onto the newspaper spread below for this and other purposes. Having prepared himself for the night's work, he would utter an experimental 'Tywhoo?' to make sure his voice was in trim, and then launch himself on soft wings, to drift round the room as silently as a flake of ash and land on my shoulder. For a short time he would sit there, nibbling my ear, and then he would give himself another shake, put sentiment to one side, and become business-like. He would fly onto the window-sill and give another questioning 'Tywhoo?' staring at me with his honey-coloured eyes. This was the signal that he wanted the shutters opened. As soon as I threw them back he would float out through the window, to be silhouetted for a moment against the moon before diving into the dark olives. A moment later a loud challenging 'Tywhoo! Tywhoo!' would ring out, the warning that Ulysses was about to start his hunting.

The length of time Ulysses spent on his hunts varied; sometimes he would swoop back into the room after only an hour, and on other occasions he would be out all night. But, wherever he went, he never failed to come back to the house between nine and ten for his supper. If there was no light in my study, he would fly down and peer through the drawing-room window to see if I was there. If I was not there, he would fly up the side of the house again to land on my bedroom window-sill and tap briskly on the shutters, until I opened them and served him with his saucer of mince, or chopped chicken's heart, or whatever delicacy was on the menu that day. When the last gory morsel had been swallowed he would give a soft, hiccoughing chirrup, sit meditating for a moment, and then fly off over the moon-bright tree tops.

Since he had proved himself an able fighter, Ulysses became fairly friendly towards Roger, and if we were going down for a late evening swim I could sometimes prevail upon him to honour us with his company. He would ride on Roger's back, clinging tight to the black wool; if, as occasionally happened, Roger forgot his passenger and went too fast, or skittishly jumped over a stone, Ulysses' eye would blaze, his wings would flap in a frantic effort to keep his balance, and he would click his beak loudly and indignantly until I reprimanded Roger for his carelessness. On the shore Ulysses would perch on my shorts and shirt, while Roger and I gambolled in the warm, shallow water. Ulysses would watch our antics with round and faintly disapproving eyes, sitting up as straight as a guardsman. Now and then he would leave his post to skim out over us, click his beak, and return to shore, but whether he did this in alarm for our safety or in order to join in our game I could never decide. Sometimes, if we took too long over the swim, he would get bored and fly up the hill to the garden, crying 'Tywhoo!' in farewell.

In the summer, when the moon was full, the family took to bathing at night, for during the day the sun was so fierce that the sea became too hot to be refreshing. As soon as the moon had risen we would make our way down through the trees to the creaking wooden jetty, and clamber into the *Sea Cow*. With Larry and Peter on one oar, Margo and Leslie on the other, and Roger and myself in the bows to act as look-outs, we would drift down the coast for half a mile or so to where there was a small bay with a lip of white sand and a few carefully arranged boulders, smooth and still sun-warm, ideal for sitting on. We would anchor the *Sea Cow* in deep water and then dive over the side to gambol and plunge, and set the moonlight shaking across the waters of the bay. When tired, we swam languidly to the shore and lay on the warm rocks, gazing up into the star-freckled sky. Generally after half an hour or so I would get bored with the conversation and slip back into the water and swim slowly out across the bay, to lie on my back, cushioned by the warm sea, gazing up at the moon.

One night, while I was thus occupied, I discovered that our bay was used by other creatures as well. Lying spread-eagled in the silky water, gazing into the sky, only moving my hands and feet slightly to keep afloat, I was looking at the Milky Way stretched like a chiffon scarf across the sky and wondering how many stars it contained. I could hear the voices of the others laughing and talking on the beach, echoing over the water, and by lifting my head I could see their position on the shore by the pulsing lights of their cigarettes. Drifting there, relaxed and dreamy, I was suddenly startled to hear, quite close to me, a clop and gurgle of water, followed by a long, deep sigh, and a series of gentle ripples rocked me up and down. Hastily I righted myself and trod water, looking to see how far from the beach I had drifted. To my alarm I found that I was some considerable distance not only from the shore but from the *Sea Cow* as well, and I was not at all sure what sort of creature was swimming around in the dark waters beneath me. I could hear the others laughing on the shore at some joke or other, and I saw someone flip a cigarette-end high into the sky like a red star that curved over and extinguished itself at the rim of the sea. I was feeling more and more uncomfortable, and I was just about to call for assistance when, some twenty feet away from me, the sea seemed to part with a gentle swish and gurgle and a gleaming back appeared, gave a deep, satisfied sigh, and sank below the surface again. I had hardly time to recognize it as a porpoise before I found I was right in the midst of them. They rose all around me, sighing luxuriously, their black backs shining as they humped in the moonlight. There must have been about eight of them, and one rose so close that I could have swum forward three strokes and touched his ebony head. Heaving and sighing heavily, they played across the bay, and I swam with them, watching fascinated as they rose to the surface, crumpling the water, breathed deeply, and then dived beneath the surface again, leaving only an expanding hoop of foam to mark the spot. Presently, as if obeying a signal, they turned and headed out of the bay towards the distant coast of Albania, and I trod water and watched them go, swimming up the white chain of moonlight, backs agleam as they rose and plunged with heavy ecstasy in the water as warm as fresh milk. Behind them they left a trail of great bubbles that rocked and shone briefly like miniature moons before vanishing under the ripples.

After this we often met the porpoises when we went moonlight bathing, and one evening they put on an illuminated show for our benefit, aided by one of the most attractive insects that inhabited the island. We had discovered that in the hot months of the year the sea became full of phosphorescence. When there was moonlight this was not so noticeable – a faint greenish flicker round the bows of the boat, a brief flash as someone dived into the water. We found that the best time for the phosphorescence was when there was no moon at all. Another illuminated inhabitant of the summer months was the firefly. These slender brown beetles would fly as soon as it got dark, floating through the olive groves by the score, their tails flashing on and off, giving a light that was greenish-white, not golden-green as the sea was. Again, however, the fireflies were at their best when there was no bright moonlight to detract from their lights. Strangely enough, we would never have seen the porpoises, the fireflies, and the phosphorescence acting together if it had not been for Mother's bathing-costume.

For some time Mother had greatly envied us our swimming, both in the daytime and at night, but, as she pointed out when we suggested she join us, she was far too old for that sort of thing. Eventually, however, under constant pressure from us, Mother paid a visit into town and returned to the villa coyly bearing a mysterious parcel. Opening this she astonished us all by holding up an extraordinary shapeless garment of black cloth, covered from top to bottom with hundreds of frills and pleats and tucks.

'Well, what d'you think of it?' Mother asked.

We stared at the odd garment and wondered what it was for.

'What is it?' asked Larry at length.

'It's a bathing-costume, of course,' said Mother. 'What on earth did you think it was?'

'It looks to me like a badly skinned whale,' said Larry, peering at it closely.

'You can't *possibly* wear that, Mother,' said Margo, horrified, 'why, it looks as though it was made in nineteen-twenty.'

'What are all those frills and things for?' asked Larry with interest.

'Decoration, of course,' said Mother indignantly.

'What a jolly idea! Don't forget to shake the fish out of them when you come out of the water.'

'Well, *I* like it, anyway,' Mother said firmly, wrapping the monstrosity up again, 'and I'm going to wear it.'

'You'll have to be careful you don't get waterlogged, with all that cloth around you,' said Leslie seriously.

'Mother, it's *awful*; you can't wear it,' said Margo. 'Why on earth didn't you get something more up to date?'

'When you get to my age, dear, you can't go around in a two-piece bathing-suit . . . you don't have the figure for it.'

'I'd love to know what sort of figure that was designed for,' remarked Larry.

'You really are *hopeless*, Mother,' said Margo despairingly.

'But I *like* it . . . and I'm not asking you to wear it,' Mother pointed out belligerently.

'That's right, you do what you want to do,' agreed Larry; 'don't be put off. It'll probably suit you very well if you can grow another three or four legs to go with it.'

Mother snorted indignantly and swept upstairs to try on her costume. Presently she called to us to come and see the effect, and we all trooped up to the bedroom. Roger was the first to enter, and, on being greeted by this strange apparition clad in its voluminous black costume rippling with frills, he retreated hurriedly through the door, backwards, barking ferociously. It was some time before we could persuade him that it really was Mother, and even then he kept giving her vaguely uncertain looks from the corner of his eye. However, in spite of all opposition, Mother stuck to her tentlike bathing-suit, and in the end we gave up.

In order to celebrate her first entry into the sea we decided to have a moonlight picnic down at the bay, and sent an invitation to Theodore, who was the only stranger that Mother would tolerate on such a great occasion. The day for the great immersion arrived, food and wine were prepared, the boat was cleaned out and filled with cushions, and everything was ready when Theodore turned up. On hearing that we had planned a moonlight picnic and swim he reminded us that on that particular night there was no moon. Everyone blamed everyone else for not having checked on the moon's progress, and the argument went on until dusk. Eventually we decided that we would go on the picnic in spite of everything, since all the arrangements were made, so we staggered down to the boat, loaded down with food, wine, towels, and cigarettes, and set off down the coast. Theodore and I sat in the bows as look-outs, and the rest took it in turn to row while Mother steered. To begin with, her eyes not having become accustomed to the dark, Mother skilfully steered us in a tight circle, so that after ten minutes' strenuous rowing the jetty suddenly loomed up and we ran into it with a splintering crash. Unnerved by this, Mother went to the opposite extreme and steered out to sea, and we would eventually have made a landfall somewhere on the Albanian coastline if Leslie had not noticed in time. After this Margo took over the steering, and she did it quite well, except that she would, in a crisis, get flurried and forget that to turn right one had to put the tiller over to the left. The result was that we had to spend ten minutes straining and tugging at the boat which Margo had, in her excitement, steered onto, instead of away from, a rock. Taken all round it was an auspicious start to Mother's first bathe.

Eventually we reached the bay, spread out the rugs on the sand, arranged the food, placed the battalion of wine-bottles in a row in the shallows to keep cool, and the great moment had arrived. Amid much cheering Mother removed her housecoat and stood revealed in all her glory, clad in the bathing-costume which made her look, as Larry pointed out, like a sort of marine Albert Memorial. Roger behaved very well until he saw Mother wade into shallow water in a slow and dignified manner. He then got terribly excited. He seemed to be under the impression that the bathing-costume was some sort of sea monster that had enveloped Mother and was now about to carry her out to sea. Barking wildly, he flung himself to the rescue, grabbed one of the frills dangling so plentifully round the edge of the costume and tugged with all his strength in order to pull Mother back to safety. Mother, who had just remarked that she thought the water a little cold, suddenly found herself being pulled backwards. With a squeak of dismay she lost her footing and sat down heavily in two feet of water, while Roger tugged so hard that a large section of the frill gave way. Elated by the fact that the enemy appeared to be disintegrating, Roger, growling encouragement to Mother, set to work to remove the rest of the offending monster from her person. We writhed on the sand, helpless with laughter, while Mother sat gasping in the shallows, making desperate attempts to regain her feet, beat Roger off, and retain at least a portion of her costume. Unfortunately, owing to the extreme thickness of the material from which the costume was constructed, the air was trapped inside; the effect of the water made it inflate like a balloon, and trying to keep this airship of frills and tucks under control added to Mother's difficulties. In the end it was Theodore who shooed Roger away and helped

Mother to her feet. Eventually, after we had partaken of a glass of wine to celebrate and recover from what Larry referred to as Perseus's rescue of Andromeda, we went in to swim, and Mother sat discreetly in the shallows, while Roger crouched nearby, growling ominously at the costume as it bulged and fluttered round Mother's waist.

The phosphorescence was particularly good that night. By plunging your hand into the water and dragging it along you could draw a wide golden-green ribbon of cold fire across the sea, and when you dived as you hit the surface it seemed as though you had plunged into a frosty furnace of glinting light. When we were tired we waded out of the sea, the water running off our bodies so that we seemed to be on fire, and lay on the sand to eat. Then, as the wine was opened at the end of the meal, as if by arrangement, a few fireflies appeared in the olives behind us – a sort of overture to the show.

First of all there were just two or three green specks, sliding smoothly through the trees, winking regularly. But gradually more and more appeared, until parts of the olive grove were lit with a weird green glow. Never had we seen so many fireflies congregated in one spot; they flicked through the trees in swarms, they crawled on the grass, the bushes and the olive trunks, they drifted in swarms over our heads and landed on the rugs like green embers. Glittering streams of them flew out over the bay, swirling over the water, and then, right on cue, the porpoises appeared, swimming in line into the bay, rocking rhythmically through the water, their backs as if painted with phosphorus. In the centre of the bay they swam round, diving and rolling, occasionally leaping high in the air and falling back into a conflagration of light. With the fireflies above and the illuminated porpoises below it was a fantastic sight. We could even see the luminous trails beneath the surface where the porpoises swam in fiery patterns across the sandy bottom, and when they leaped high in the air the drops of emerald glowing water flicked from them, and you could not tell if it was phosphorescence or fireflies you were looking at. For an hour or so we watched this pageant, and then slowly the fireflies drifted back inland and farther down the coast. Then the porpoises lined up and sped out to sea, leaving a flaming path behind them that flickered and glowed, and then died slowly, like a glowing branch laid across the bay.

II

The Enchanted Archipelago

As the summer grew hotter and hotter we decided that it required too much effort to row the *Sea Cow* down the coast to our bathing bay, so we invested in an outboard engine. The acquisition of this machine opened up a vast area of coastland for us, for we could now venture much farther afield, making trips along the jagged coastline to remote and deserted beaches golden as wheat, or lying like fallen moons among the contorted rocks. It was thus that I became aware of the fact that stretching along the coast for miles was a scattered archipelago of small islands, some fairly extensive, some that were really outsize rocks with a wig of greenery perched precariously on top. For some reason, which I could not discover, the sea faunæ were greatly attracted by this archipelago, and round the edges of the islands, in rock-pools and sandy bays the size of a large table, there was a bewildering assortment of life. I managed to inveigle the family into several trips to these islets, but as these had few good bathing spots the family soon got bored with having to sit on sun-baked rocks while I fished interminably in the pools and unearthed at intervals strange and, to them, revolting sea-creatures. Also, the islands were strung out close to the coast, some of them being separated from the mainland only by a channel twenty feet wide, and there were plenty of reefs and rocks. So guiding the *Sea Cow* through these hazards and making sure the propeller did not strike and break made any excursion to the islands a difficult navigational problem. Our trips there became less and less frequent, in spite of all arguments on my part, and I was tortured by the thought of all the wonderful animal life waiting in the limpid pools to be caught; but I was unable to do anything about it, simply because

I had no boat. I suggested that I might be allowed to take the *Sea Cow* out myself, say once a week, but the family were, for a variety of reasons, against this. But then, just when I had almost given up hope, I was struck with a brilliant idea: my birthday was due fairly soon, and if I dealt with the family skilfully I felt sure I could get not only a boat but a lot of other equipment as well. I therefore suggested to the family that, instead of letting them choose my birthday presents, I might tell them the things which I wanted most. In this way they could be sure of not disappointing me. The family, rather taken aback, agreed, and then, somewhat suspiciously, asked me what I wanted. Innocently, I said that I hadn't thought about it much, but that I would work out a list for each person, and they could then choose one or more items on it.

My list took a lot of time and thought to work out, and a considerable amount of applied psychology. Mother, for instance, I knew would buy me everything on her list; so I put down some of the most necessary and expensive equipment: five wooden cases, glass-topped, cork-lined, to house my insect collection; two dozen test-tubes; five pints of methylated spirits, five pints of formalin, and a microscope. Margo's list was a little more difficult, for the items had to be chosen so that they would encourage her to go to her favourite shops. So from her I asked for ten yards of butter muslin, ten yards of white calico, six large packets of pins, two bundles of cotton wool, two pints of ether, a pair of forceps, and two fountain-pen fillers. It was, I realized resignedly, quite useless to ask Larry for anything like formalin or pins, but if my list showed some sort of literary leaning I stood a good chance. Accordingly I made out a formidable sheet covered with the titles, authors' names, publishers, and prices of all the natural history books I felt in need of, and put an asterisk against those that would be most gratefully received. Since I had only one request left, I decided to tackle Leslie verbally instead of handing him a list, but I knew I should have to choose my moment with care. I had to wait some days for what I considered to be a propitious moment.

I had just helped him to the successful conclusion of some ballistic experiments he was making, which involved tying an ancient muzzle-loader to a tree and firing it by means of a long string attached to the trigger. At the fourth attempt we achieved what apparently Leslie considered to be success: the barrel burst and bits of metal whined in all directions. Leslie was delighted and made copious notes on the back of an envelope. Together we set about picking up the remains of the gun. While we were thus engaged I casually asked him what he would like to give me for my birthday.

'Hadn't thought about it,' he replied absently, examining with evident satisfaction a contorted piece of metal. 'I don't mind . . . anything you like . . . you choose.'

I said I wanted a boat. Leslie, realizing how he had been trapped, said indignantly that a boat was far too large a present for a birthday, and anyway he couldn't afford it. I said, equally indignantly, that he had *told* me to choose what I liked. Leslie said yes, he had, but he hadn't meant a boat, as they were terribly expensive. I said that when one said *anything* one meant anything, which included boats, and anyway I didn't expect him to buy me one. I had thought, since he knew so much about boats, he would be able to build me one. However, if he thought that would be too difficult . . .

'Of course it's not difficult,' said Leslie, unguardedly, and then added hastily, 'Well . . . not terribly difficult. But it's the *time*. It would take ages and ages to do. Look, wouldn't it be better if I took you out in the *Sea Cow* twice a week?'

But I was adamant; I wanted a boat and I was quite prepared to wait for it.

'Oh, all right, all right,' said Leslie exasperatedly, 'I'll build you a boat. But I'm not having you hanging around while I do it, understand? You're to keep well away. You're not to see it until it's finished.'

Delightedly I agreed to these conditions, and so for the next two weeks Spiro kept turning up with car-loads of planks, and the sounds of sawing, hammering, and blasphemy floated round from the back veranda. The house was littered with wood shavings, and everywhere he walked Leslie left a trail of sawdust. I found it fairly easy to restrain my impatience and curiosity, for I had, at that time, something else to occupy me. Some repairs had just been completed to the back of the house, and three large bags of beautiful pink cement had been left over. These I had appropriated, and I set to work to build a series of small ponds in which I could keep not only my freshwater fauna, but also all the wonderful sea creatures I hoped to catch in my new boat. Digging ponds in midsummer was harder work than I had anticipated, but eventually I had some reasonably square holes dug, and a couple of days splashing around in a sticky porridge of lovely coral-pink cement soon revived me. Leslie's trails of sawdust and shavings through the house were now interwoven with a striking pattern of pink footprints.

The day before my birthday the entire family made an expedition into the town. The reasons were threefold. Firstly, they wanted to purchase my presents. Secondly, the larder had to be stocked up. We had agreed that we would not invite a lot of people to the party; we said we didn't like crowds, and so ten guests, carefully selected, were the most we were prepared to put up with. It would be a small but distinguished gathering of people we liked best. Having unanimously decided on this, each member of the family then proceeded to invite ten people. Unfortunately they didn't all invite the same ten, with the exception of Theodore, who received five separate invitations. The result was that Mother, on the eve of the party, suddenly discovered we were going to have not ten guests but forty-six. The third reason for going to town was to make sure that Lugaretzia attended the dentist. Recently her teeth had been her chief woe, and Doctor Androuchelli, having peered into her mouth, had uttered a series of popping noises indicative of horror, and said that she must have all her teeth out, since it was obvious that they were the cause of all her ailments. After a week's arguing, accompanied by floods of tears, we managed to get Lugaretzia to consent, but she had refused to go without moral support. So, bearing her, white and weeping, in our midst, we swept into town.

We returned in the evening, exhausted and irritable, the car piled high with food, and Lugaretzia lying across our laps like a corpse, moaning frightfully. It was perfectly obvious that she would be in no condition to assist with the cooking and other work on the morrow.

Spiro, when asked to suggest a solution, gave his usual answer. 'Nevers you minds,' he scowled; 'leaves everything to me.'

The following morning was full of incident. Lugaretzia had recovered sufficiently to undertake light duties, and she followed us all round the house, displaying with pride the gory cavities in her gums, and describing in detail the agonies she had suffered with each individual tooth. My presents having been duly inspected and the family thanked, I then went round to the back veranda with Leslie, and there lay a mysterious shape covered with a tarpaulin. Leslie drew this aside with the air of a conjuror, and there lay my boat. I gazed at it rapturously; it was surely the most perfect boat that anyone had ever had. Gleaming in her coat of new paint she lay there, my steed to the enchanted archipelago.

The boat was some seven feet long, and almost circular in shape. Leslie explained hurriedly – in case I thought the shape was due to defective craftsmanship – that the reason for this was that the planks had been too short for the frame, an explanation I found perfectly satisfactory. After all, it was the sort of irritating thing that could have happened to anyone. I said stoutly that I thought it was a lovely shape for a boat, and indeed I thought it was. She was not sleek, slim, and rather predatory looking, like most boats, but rotund, placid, and somehow comforting in her circular solidarity. She reminded me of an earnest dungbeetle, an insect for which I had great affection. Leslie, pleased at my evident delight, said deprecatingly that he had been forced to make her flat-bottomed, since, for a variety of technical reasons, this was the safest. I said that I liked flat-bottomed boats the best, because it was possible to put jars of specimens on the floor without so much risk of them upsetting. Leslie asked me if I liked the colour scheme, as he had not been too sure about it. Now, in my opinion, the colour scheme was the best thing about it, the final touch that completed the unique craft. Inside she was painted green and white, while her bulging sides were tastefully covered in white, black, and brilliant orange stripes, a combination of colours that struck me as being both artistic and friendly. Leslie then showed me the long, smooth cypress pole he had cut for a mast, but explained that it could not be fitted into position until the boat was launched. Enthusiastically I suggested launching her at once. Leslie, who was a stickler for procedure, said you couldn't launch a ship without naming her, and had I thought of a name yet? This was a difficult problem, and the whole family were called out to help me solve it. They stood clustered round the boat, which looked like a gigantic flower in their midst, and racked their brains.

'Why not call it the *Jolly Roger?*' suggested Margo.

I rejected this scornfully; I explained that I wanted a sort of *fat* name that would go with the boat's appearance and personality.

'*Arbuckle,*' suggested Mother vaguely.

That was no use, either; the boat simply didn't look like an Arbuckle.

'Call it the *Ark,*' said Leslie, but I shook my head.

There was another silence while we all stared at the boat.

Suddenly I had it, the perfect name: *Bootle*, that's what I'd call her.

'Very nice, dear,' approved Mother.

'I was just about to suggest the *Bumtrinket*,' said Larry.

'Larry, dear!' Mother reproved. 'Don't teach the boy things like that.'

I turned Larry's suggestion over in my mind; it was certainly an unusual name, but then so was *Bootle*. They both seemed to conjure up the shape and personality of the boat. After much thought I decided what to do. A pot of black paint was produced and laboriously, in rather trickly capitals, I traced her name along the side: THE BOOTLE-BUMTRINKET. There it was; not only an *unusual* name, but an aristocratically hyphenated one as well. In order to ease Mother's mind I had to promise that I would refer to the boat only as the *Bootle* in conversation with strangers. The matter of the name being settled, we set about the task of launching her. It took the combined efforts of Margo, Peter, Leslie, and Larry to carry the boat down the hill to the jetty, while Mother and I followed behind with the mast and a small bottle of wine with which to do the launching properly. At the end of the jetty the boat-bearers stopped, swaying with exhaustion, and Mother and I struggled with the cork of the wine-bottle.

'What are you *doing?*' asked Larry irritably. 'For Heaven's sake hurry up; I'm not used to being a slipway.'

At last we got the cork from the bottle, and I announced in a clear voice that I christened this ship the *Bootle-Bumtrinket*. Then I slapped her rotund backside with the bottle, with the unhappy result that half a pint of white wine splashed over Larry's head.

'Look out, look out,' he remonstrated. 'Which one of us are you supposed to be launching?'

At last they cast the *Bootle-Bumtrinket* off the jetty with a mighty heave, and she landed on her flat bottom with a report like a cannon, showering sea-water in all directions, and then bobbed steadily and confidently on the ripples. She had the faintest suggestion of a list to starboard, but I generously attributed this to the wine and not to Leslie's workmanship.

'Now!' said Leslie, organizing things. 'Let's get the mast in . . . Margo, you hold her nose . . . that's it . . . Now, Peter, if you'll get into the stern, Larry and I will hand you the mast . . . all you have to do is stick it in that socket.'

So, while Margo lay on her tummy holding the nose of the boat, Peter leaped nimbly into the stern and settled himself, with legs apart, to receive the mast which Larry and Leslie were holding.

'This mast looks a bit long to me, Les,' said Larry, eyeing it critically.

'Nonsense! It'll be fine when it's in,' retorted Leslie. 'Now . . . are you ready, Peter?'

Peter nodded, braced himself, clasped the mast firmly in both hands, and plunged it into the socket. Then he stood back, dusted his hands, and the *Bootle-Bumtrinket*, with a speed remarkable for a craft of her circumference, turned turtle. Peter, clad in his one decent suit which he had put on in honour of my birthday, disappeared with scarcely a splash. All that remained on the surface of the water was his hat, the mast, and the *Bootle-Bumtrinket*'s bright orange bottom.

'He'll drown! He'll drown!' screamed Margo, who always tended to look on the dark side in a crisis.

'Nonsense! It's not deep enough,' said Leslie.

'I told you that mast was too long,' said Larry unctuously.

'It *isn't* too long,' Leslie snapped irritably; 'that fool didn't set it right.'

'Don't you dare call him a fool,' said Margo.

'You can't fit a twenty-foot mast onto a thing like a washtub and expect it to keep upright,' said Larry.

'If you're so damn clever why didn't *you* make the boat?'

'I wasn't asked to . . . Besides, you're supposed to be the expert, though I doubt if they'd employ you on Clydeside.'

'Very funny. It's easy enough to criticize . . . just because that fool —'

'Don't you call him a fool . . . How dare you?'

'Now, now, don't argue about it, dears,' said Mother peaceably.

'Well, Larry's so damn patronizing . . .'

'Thank God! He's come up,' said Margo in fervent tones as the bedraggled and spluttering Peter rose to the surface.

We hauled him out and Margo hurried him up to the house to try to get his suit dry before the party. The rest of us followed, still arguing. Leslie, incensed at Larry's criticism, changed into trunks and, armed with a massive manual on yacht construction and a tape measure, went down to salvage the boat. For the rest of the morning he kept sawing bits off the mast until she eventually floated upright, but by then the mast was only about three feet high. Leslie was very puzzled, but he promised to fit a new mast as soon as he'd worked out the correct specification. So the *Bootle-Bumtrinket*, tied to the end of the jetty, floated there in all her glory, looking like a very vivid, overweight Manx cat.

Spiro arrived soon after lunch, bringing with him a tall, elderly man who had the air of an ambassador. This, Spiro explained, was the King of Greece's ex-butler, who had been prevailed upon to come out of retirement and help with the party. Spiro then turned everyone out of the kitchen and he and the butler closeted themselves in there together. When I went round and peered through the window, I saw the butler in his waistcoat, polishing glasses, while Spiro, scowling thoughtfully and humming to himself, was attacking a vast pile of vegetables. Occasionally he would waddle over and blow vigorously at the seven charcoal fires along the wall, making them glow like rubies.

The first guest to arrive was Theodore, sitting spick and span in a carriage, his best suit on, his boots polished, and, as a concession to the occasion, without any collecting gear. He clasped in one hand a walking-stick, and in the other a neatly tied parcel. 'Ah-ha! Many . . . er . . . happy returns of the day,' he said,

shaking my hand. 'I have brought you a . . . er . . . small . . . er
. . . memento . . . a small gift, that is to say, *present* to er . . .
commemorate the occasion . . . um.'

On opening the parcel I was delighted to find that it contained
a fat volume entitled *Life in Ponds and Streams*.

'I think you will find it a useful . . . um . . . addition to your
library,' said Theodore, rocking on his toes. 'It contains some
very interesting information on . . . er . . . *general* freshwater life.'

Gradually the guests arrived, and the front of the villa was a
surging mass of carriages and taxis. The great drawing-room
and dining-room were full of people, talking and arguing and
laughing, and the butler, who to Mother's dismay had donned a
tail-coat, moved swiftly through the throng like an elderly penguin, serving drinks and food with such a regal air that a lot of
the guests were not at all sure if he was a real butler, or merely
some eccentric relative we had staying with us. Down in the
kitchen Spiro drank prodigious quantities of wine as he moved
among the pots and pans, his scowling face glowing redly in the
light from the fires, his deep voice roaring out in song. The air
was full of the scent of garlic and herbs, and Lugaretzia was kept
hobbling to and fro from kitchen to drawing-room at considerable
speed. Occasionally she would succeed in backing some unfortunate guest into a corner and, holding a plate of food under his
nose, would proceed to give him the details of her ordeal at the
dentist, giving the most lifelike and repulsive imitation of what a
molar sounded like when it was torn from its socket, and opening
her mouth wide to show her victims the ghastly havoc that had
been wrought inside.

More and more guests arrived, and with them came presents.
Most of these were, from my point of view, useless, as they could
not be adapted for natural-history work. The best of the presents
were, in my opinion, two puppies brought by a peasant family I
knew who lived not far away. One puppy was liver and white
with large ginger eyebrows, and the other was coal black with

large ginger eyebrows. As they were presents, the family had, of course, to accept them. Roger viewed them with suspicion and interest, so in order that they should all get acquainted I locked them in the dining-room with a large plate of party delicacies between them. The results were not quite what I had anticipated, for when the flood of guests grew so large that we had to slide back the doors and let some of them into the dining-room, we found Roger seated gloomily on the floor, the two puppies gambolling round him, while the room was decorated in a fashion that left us in no doubt that the new additions had both eaten and drunk to their hearts' content. Larry's suggestion that they be called Widdle and Puke was greeted with disgust by Mother, but the names stuck and Widdle and Puke they remained.

Still the guests came, overflowing the drawing-room into the dining-room, and out of the French windows onto the veranda. Some of them had come thinking that they would be bored, and after an hour or so they enjoyed themselves so much that they called their carriages, went home, and reappeared with the rest of their families. The wine flowed, the air was blue with cigarette smoke, and the geckos were too frightened to come out of the cracks in the ceiling because of the noise and laughter. In one corner of the room Theodore, having daringly removed his coat, was dancing the *Kalamatiano* with Leslie and several other of the more exhilarated guests, their feet crashing and shuddering on the floor as they leaped and stamped. The butler, having perhaps taken a little more wine than was good for him, was so carried away by the sight of the national dance that he put his tray down and joined in, leaping and stamping as vigorously as anyone in spite of his age, his coat-tails flapping behind him. Mother, smiling in a rather forced and distraught manner, was wedged between the English padre, who was looking with increasing disapproval at the revelry, and the Belgian consul, who was chattering away in her ear and twirling his moustache. Spiro appeared from the kitchen to find out where the butler had got to, and promptly joined in the *Kalamatiano*. Balloons drifted across the room, bouncing against the dancers' legs, exploding suddenly with loud bangs; Larry, out on the veranda, was endeavouring to teach a group of Greeks some of the finer English limericks. Puke and Widdle had gone to sleep in someone's hat. Doctor Androuchelli arrived and apologized to Mother for being late.

'It was my wife, madame; she has just been delivered of a baby,' he said with pride.

'Oh, congratulations, doctor,' said Mother; 'we must drink to them.'

Spiro, exhausted by the dance, was sitting on the sofa nearby, fanning himself. 'Whats?' he roared at Androuchelli, scowling ferociously. 'You gets anothers babys?'

'Yes, Spiro, a boy,' said Androuchelli, beaming.

'How manys you gets now?' asked Spiro.

'Six, only six,' said the doctor in surprise. 'Why?'

'You oughts to be ashames of yourself,' said Spiro in disgust. 'Six . . . Gollys! Carrying on like cats and dogses.'

'But I like children,' protested Androuchelli.

'When I gots married I asks my wifes how many she wants,' said Spiro in a loud voice, 'and she says twos, so I gives her twos and then I gets her sewed ups. Six childrens . . . Honest to Gods, you makes me wants to throws . . . cats and dogses.'

At this point the English padre decided that he would, most reluctantly, have to leave, as he had a long day ahead of him tomorrow. Mother and I saw him out, and when we returned Androuchelli and Spiro had joined the dancers.

The sea was dawn-calm, and the eastern horizon flushed with pink, when we stood yawning at the front door and the last carriage clopped its way down the drive. As I lay in bed with Roger across my feet, a puppy on each side of me, and Ulysses sitting fluffed out on the pelmet, I gazed through the window at the sky, watching the pink spread across the olive tops, extinguishing the stars one by one, and thought that, taken all round, it had been an extremely good birthday party.

Very early next morning I packed my collecting gear and some food, and with Roger, Widdle, and Puke as company set off on a voyage in the *Bootle-Bumtrinket*. The sea was calm, the sun was shining out of a gentian-blue sky, and there was just the faintest breeze; it was a perfect day. The *Bootle-Bumtrinket* wallowed up the coast in a slow and dignified manner, while Roger sat in the bows as look-out, and Widdle and Puke ran from one side of the boat to the other, fighting, trying to lean over the side and drink the sea, and generally behaving in a pathetically landlubberish fashion.

The joy of having a boat of your own! The feeling of pleasant power as you pulled on the oars and felt the boat surge forward with a quick rustle of water, like someone cutting silk; the sun gently warming your back and making the sea surface flicker with a hundred different colours; the thrill of wending your way through the complex maze of weed-shaggy reefs that glowed just beneath the surface of the sea. It was even with pleasure that I contemplated the blisters that were rising on my palms, making my hands feel stiff and awkward.

Though I spent many days voyaging in the *Bootle-Bumtrinket*, and had many adventures, there was nothing to compare with that very first voyage. The sea seemed bluer, more limpid and transparent, the islands seemed more remote, sun-drenched, and enchanting than ever before, and it seemed as though the life of the sea had congregated in the little bays and channels to greet me and my new boat. A hundred feet or so from an islet I shipped the oars and scrambled up to the bows, where I lay side by side with Roger, peering down through a fathom of crystal water at the sea bottom, while the *Bootle-Bumtrinket* floated towards the shore with the placid buoyancy of a celluloid duck. As the boat's turtle-shaped shadow edged across the sea-bed, the multi-coloured, ever-moving tapestry of sea life was unfolded.

In the patches of silver sand the clams were stuck upright in small clusters, their mouths gaping. Sometimes, perched between the shell's horny lips, here would be a tiny, pale ivory pea-crab, the frail, soft-shelled, degenerate creature that lived a parasitic life in the safety of the great shell's corrugated walls. It was interesting to set off the clam colony's burglar alarm. I drifted over a group of them until they lay below, gaping up at me, and then gently edged the handle of the butterfly net down and tapped on the shell. Immediately the shell snapped shut, the movement causing a small puff of white sand to swirl up like a tornado. As the currents of this shell's alarm slid through the water the rest of the colony felt them. In a moment clams were slamming their front doors shut left and right, and the water was full of little whirls of sand, drifting and swirling about the shells, falling back to the sea-bed like silver dust.

Interspersed with the clams were the serpulas, beautiful feathery petals, forever moving round and round, perched on the end of a long, thick, greyish tube. The moving petals, orange-gold and blue, looked curiously out of place on the end of these stubby stalks, like an orchid on a mushroom stem. Again the serpulas had a burglar-alarm system, but it was much more sensitive than the clams; the net handle would get within six inches of the whirlpool of shimmering petals, and they would suddenly all point skywards, bunch together and dive head-first down the stalk, so that all that was left was a series of what looked like bits of miniature hosepipe stuck in the sand.

On the reefs that were only a few inches below the water, and that were uncovered at low tide, you found the thickest congregation of life. In the holes were the pouting blennies, which stared at you with their thick lips, giving their faces an expression of insolence as they fluttered their fins at you. In the shady clefts among the weeds the sea urchins would be gathered in clusters, like shiny brown horse-chestnut seed-cases, their spines moving gently like compass needles towards possible danger. Around them the anemones clung to the rocks, plump and lustrous, their arms waving in an abandoned and somehow Eastern-looking dance in an effort to catch the shrimps that flipped past, transparent as glass. Routing in the dark underwater caverns, I unearthed a baby octopus, who settled on the rocks like a Medusa head, blushed to a muddy brown, and regarded me with rather sad eyes from beneath the bald dome of its head. A further movement on my part and it spat out a small storm-cloud of black ink that hung and rolled in the clear water, while the octopus skimmed off behind it, shooting through the water with its arms trailing, looking like a streamer-decorated balloon. There were crabs too, fat, green, shiny ones on the tops of the reef, waving their claws in what appeared to be a friendly manner, and down below, on the weedy bed of the sea, the spider-crabs with their strange spiky-edged shells, their long, thin legs, each wearing a coat of weeds, sponges, or occasionally an anemone which they had carefully planted on their backs. Everywhere on the reefs, the weed patches, the sandy bottom, moved hundreds of top shells, neatly striped and speckled in blue, silver, grey, and red, with the scarlet and rather indignant face of a hermit crab peering out from underneath. They were like small ungainly caravans moving about, bumping into each other, barging through the weeds, or rumbling swiftly across the sand among the towering clam-shells and sea-fans.

The sun sank lower, and the water in the bays and below the tottering castles of rock was washed with the slate grey of evening shadow. Slowly, the oars creaking softly to themselves, I rowed the *Bootle-Bumtrinket* homewards. Widdle and Puke lay asleep, exhausted by the sun and sea air, their paws twitching, their ginger eyebrows moving as they chased dream crabs across endless reefs. Roger sat surrounded by glass jars and tubes in which tiny fish hung suspended, anemones waved their arms, and spider-crabs touched the sides of their glass prisons with delicate claws. He sat staring down into the jars, ears pricked, occasionally looking up at me and wagging his tail briefly, before becoming absorbed once again in his studies. Roger was a keen student of marine life. The sun gleamed like a coin behind the olive trees, and the sea was striped with gold and silver when the *Bootle-Bumtrinket* brought her round behind bumping gently against the jetty. Hungry, thirsty, tired, with my head buzzing full of the colours and shapes I had seen, I carried my precious specimens slowly up the hill to the villa, while the three dogs, yawning and stretching, followed behind.

12

The Woodcock Winter

As the summer drew to a close I found myself, to my delight, once more without a tutor. Mother had discovered that, as she so delicately put it, Margo and Peter were becoming '*too* fond of one another.' As the family was unanimous in its disapproval of Peter as a prospective relation by marriage, something obviously had to be done. Leslie's only contribution to the problem was to suggest shooting Peter, a plan that was, for some reason, greeted derisively. I thought it was a splendid idea, but I was in the minority. Larry's suggestion that the happy couple should be sent to live in Athens for a month, in order, as he explained, to get it out of their systems, was quashed by Mother on the grounds of immorality. Eventually Mother dispensed with Peter's services, he left hurriedly and furtively, and we had to cope with a tragic, tearful, and wildly indignant Margo, who, dressed in her most flowing and gloomy clothing for the event, played her part magnificently. Mother soothed and uttered gentle platitudes, Larry gave Margo lectures on free love, and Leslie, for reasons best known to himself, decided to play the part of the outraged brother and kept appearing at intervals, brandishing a revolver and threatening to shoot Peter down like a dog if he set foot in the house again. In the midst of all this Margo, tears trickling effectively down her face, made tragic gestures and told us her life was blighted. Spiro, who loved a good dramatic situation as well as anyone, spent his time weeping in sympathy with Margo and posting various friends of his along the docks to make sure that Peter did not attempt to get back onto the island. We all enjoyed ourselves very much. Just as the thing seemed to be dying a natural death, and Margo was able to eat a whole meal without bursting into tears, she got a note from Peter saying he would return for her. Margo, rather panic-stricken by the idea, showed the note to Mother, and once more the family leaped with enthusiasm into the farce. Spiro doubled his guard on the docks, Leslie oiled his guns and practised on a large cardboard figure pinned to the front of the house, Larry went about alternately urging Margo to disguise herself as a peasant and fly to Peter's arms or to stop behaving like Camille. Margo, insulted, locked herself in the attic and refused to see anyone except me, as I was the only member of the family who had not taken sides. She lay there, weeping copiously, and reading a volume of Tennyson; occasionally she would break off to consume a large meal – which I carried up on a tray – with undiminished appetite.

Margo stayed closeted in the attic for a week. She was eventually brought down from there by a situation which made a fitting climax to the whole affair. Leslie had discovered that several small items had been vanishing from the *Sea Cow*, and he suspected the fishermen who rowed past the jetty at night. He decided that he would give the thieves something to think about, so he attached to his bedroom window three long-barrelled shotguns aiming down the hill at the jetty. By an ingenious arrangement of strings he could fire one barrel after the other without even getting out of bed. The range was, of course, too far to do any damage, but the whistling of shot through the olive leaves and the splashing as it pattered into the sea would, he felt, act as a fairly good deterrent. So carried away was he by his own brilliance that he omitted to mention to anyone that he had constructed his burglar trap.

We had all retired to our rooms and were variously occupied. The house was silent. Outside came the gentle whispering of crickets in the hot night air. Suddenly there came a rapid series of colossal explosions that rocked the house and set all the dogs barking downstairs. I rushed out onto the landing, where pandemonium reigned; the dogs had rushed upstairs in a body to join in the fun, and were leaping about, yelping excitedly. Mother, looking wild and distraught, had rushed out of her bedroom in her voluminous nightie, under the impression that Margo had committed suicide. Larry burst angrily from his room to find out what the row was about, and Margo, under the impression that Peter had returned to claim her and was being slaughtered by Leslie, was fumbling madly at the lock on the attic door and screaming at the top of her voice.

'She's done something silly . . . she's done something silly . . .' wailed Mother, making frantic endeavours to get herself free from Widdle and Puke, who, thinking this was all a jolly nocturnal romp, had seized the end of her nightie and were tugging at it, growling ferociously.

'It's the limit . . . You can't even sleep in peace . . . This family's driving me mad,' bellowed Larry.

'Don't hurt him . . . leave him alone . . . you cowards,' came Margo's voice, shrill and tearful, as she scrabbled wildly in an attempt to get the attic door opened.

'Burglars . . . Keep calm . . . it's only burglars,' yelled Leslie, opening his bedroom door.

'She's still alive . . . she's still alive . . . Get these dogs away . . .'

'You brutes . . . how dare you shoot him? . . . Let me out, *let me out* . . .'

'Stop fussing; it's only burglars . . .'

'Animals and explosions all day, and then bloody great twelve-gun salutes in the middle of the night . . . It's carrying eccentricity too far . . .'

Eventually Mother struggled up to the attic, trailing Widdle and Puke from the hem of her night attire, and, white and shaking, threw open the door to find an equally white and shaking Margo. After a lot of confusion we discovered what had happened, and what each of us had thought. Mother, trembling with shock, reprimanded Leslie severely.

'You mustn't do things like that, dear,' she pointed out. 'It's really stupid. If you fire your guns off do at least let us *know.*'

'Yes,' said Larry bitterly, 'just give us a bit of warning, will you? Shout "Timber," or something of the sort.'

'I don't see how I can be expected to take burglars by surprise if I've got to shout out warnings to you all,' said Leslie aggrievedly.

'I'm damned if I see why we should be taken by surprise too,' said Larry.

'Well, ring a bell or something, dear. Only please don't do that again . . . it's made me feel quite queer.'

But the episode got Margo out of the attic, which, as Mother said, was one mercy.

In spite of being on nodding acquaintance with the family once again, Margo still preferred to nurse her broken heart in private, so she took to disappearing for long periods with only the dogs for company. She waited until the sudden, fierce siroccos of autumn had started before deciding that the ideal place for her to be alone was a small island situated in the bay opposite the house, about half a mile out. One day, when her desire for solitude became overwhelming, she borrowed the *Bootle-Bumtrinket* (without my permission), piled the dogs into it, and set off to the island to lie in the sun and meditate on Love.

It was not until tea-time, and with the aid of field-glasses, that I discovered where my boat and Margo had got to. Irately, and somewhat unwisely, I told Mother of Margo's whereabouts, and pointed out that she had no business to borrow my boat without permission. Who, I asked acidly, was going to build me a new boat if the *Bootle-Bumtrinket* was wrecked? By now the sirocco was howling round the house like a pack of wolves, and Mother, actuated by what I at first considered to be acute worry regarding the fate of the *Bootle-Bumtrinket*, panted upstairs and hung out of the bedroom window, scanning the bay with the field-glasses. Lugaretzia, sobbing and wringing her hands, hobbled up as well, and the two of them, trembling and anxious, kept chasing from window to window peering out at the foam-flecked bay. Mother was all for sending someone out to rescue Margo, but there was no one available. So all she could do was squat at the window with the glasses glued to her eyes while Lugaretzia offered up prayers to Saint Spiridion and kept telling Mother a long and involved story about her uncle who had been drowned in just such a sirocco. Fortunately, Mother could only understand about one word in seven of Lugaretzia's tale.

Eventually it apparently dawned on Margo that she had better start for home before the sirocco got any worse, and we saw her come down through the trees to where the *Bootle-Bumtrinket* bobbed and jerked at her moorings. But Margo's progress was slow and, to say the least, curious; first she fell down twice, then she ended up on the shore about fifty yards away from the boat, and wandered about in circles for some time, apparently looking for it. Eventually, attracted by barks from Roger, she stumbled along the shore and found the boat. Then she had great difficulty in persuading Widdle and Puke to get into it. They did not mind boating when the weather was calm, but they had never been in a rough sea and they had no intention of starting now. As soon as Widdle was safely installed in the boat she would turn to catch Puke, and by the time she had caught him Widdle had leaped ashore again. This went on for some time. At last she managed to get them both in together, leaped in after them, and rowed strenuously for some time before realizing that she had not untied the boat.

Mother watched her progress across the bay with bated breath. The *Bootle-Bumtrinket*, being low in the water, was not always visible, and whenever it disappeared behind a particularly large wave Mother would stiffen anxiously, convinced that the boat had foundered with all hands. Then the brave orange-and-white blob would appear once more on the crest of a wave and Mother would breathe again. The course Margo steered was peculiar, for the *Bootle-Bumtrinket* tacked to and fro across the bay in a haphazard fashion, occasionally even reappearing above the waves with her nose pointing towards Albania. Once or twice Margo rose unsteadily to her feet and peered around the horizon, shading her eyes with her hand; then she would sit down and start rowing once more. Eventually, when the boat had, more by accident than design, drifted within hailing distance, we all went down to the jetty and yelled instructions above the hiss and splash of the waves and the roar of the wind. Guided by our shouts Margo pulled valiantly for the shore, hitting the jetty with such violence that she almost knocked Mother off into the sea. The dogs scrambled out and fled up the hill, obviously scared that we might make them undertake another trip with the same captain. When we had helped Margo ashore we discovered the reason for her unorthodox navigation. Having reached the island, she had draped herself out in the sun and fallen into a deep sleep, to be woken by the noise of the wind. Having slept for the better part of three hours in the fierce sun, she found her eyes so puffy and swollen that she could hardly see out of them. The wind and spray had made them worse, and by the time she reached the jetty she could hardly see at all. She was red and raw with sunburn and her eyelids so puffed out that she looked like a particularly malevolent Mongolian pirate.

'Really, Margo, I sometimes wonder if you're quite *right*,' said Mother, as she bathed Margo's eyes with cold tea; 'you do the most stupid things.'

'Oh, rubbish, Mother. You do *fuss*,' said Margo. 'It could have happened to anyone.'

But this incident seemed to cure her broken heart, for she no longer took solitary walks, nor did she venture out in the boat again; she behaved once more as normally as it was possible for her to do.

Winter came to the island gently as a rule. The sky was still clear, the sea blue and calm, and the sun warm. But there would be an uncertainty in the air. The gold and scarlet leaves that littered the countryside in great drifts whispered and chuckled among themselves, or took experimental runs from place to place, rolling like coloured hoops among the trees. It was as if they were practising something, preparing for something, and they would discuss it excitedly in rustly voices as they crowded round the tree-trunks. The birds, too, congregated in little groups, puffing out their feathers, twittering thoughtfully. The whole air was one of expectancy, like a vast audience waiting for the curtain to go up. Then one morning you threw back the shutters and looked down over the olive trees, across the blue bay to the russet mountains of the mainland, and became aware that winter had arrived, for each mountain peak would be wearing a tattered skull-cap of snow. Now the air of expectancy grew almost hourly.

In a few days small white clouds started their winter parade, trooping across the sky, soft and chubby, long, languorous, and unkempt, or small and crisp as feathers, and driving them before it, like an ill-assorted flock of sheep, would come the wind. This was warm at first, and came in gentle gusts, rubbing through the olive groves so that the leaves trembled and turned silver with excitement, rocking the cypresses so that they undulated gently, and stirring the dead leaves into gay, swirling little dances that died as suddenly as they began. Playfully it ruffled the feathers on the sparrows' backs, so that they shuddered and fluffed themselves; and it leaped without warning at the gulls, so that they were stopped in mid-air and had to curve their white wings against it. Shutters started to bang and doors chattered suddenly in their frames. But still the sun shone, the sea remained placid, and the mountains sat complacently, summer-bronzed, wearing their splintered snow hats.

For a week or so the wind played with the island, patting it, stroking it, humming to itself among the bare branches. Then there was a lull, a few days' strange calm; suddenly, when you least expected it, the wind would be back. But it was a changed wind, a mad, hooting, bellowing wind that leaped down on the island and tried to blow it into the sea. The blue sky vanished as a cloak of fine grey cloud was thrown over the island. The sea turned a deep blue, almost black, and became crusted with foam. The cypress trees were whipped like dark pendulums against the sky, and the olives (so fossilized all summer, so still and witchlike) were infected with the madness of the wind and swayed creaking on their misshapen, sinewy trunks, their leaves hissing as they turned, like mother of pearl, from green to silver. This is what the dead leaves had whispered about, this is what they had practised for; exultantly they rose in the air and danced, whirli-gigging about, dipping, swooping, falling exhausted when the wind tired of them and passed on. Rain followed the wind, but it was a warm rain that you could walk in and enjoy, great fat drops that rattled on the shutters, tapped on the vine leaves like drums, and gurgled musically in the gutters. The rivers up in the Albanian mountains became swollen and showed white teeth in a snarl as they rushed down to the sea, tearing at their banks, grabbing the summer debris of sticks, logs, grass tussocks, and other things and disgorging them into the bay, so that the dark-blue waters became patterned with great coiling veins of mud and other flotsam. Gradually all these veins burst, and the sea changed from blue to yellow-brown; then the wind tore at the surface, piling the water into ponderous waves, like great tawny lions with white manes that stalked and leaped upon the shore.

This was the shooting season; on the mainland the great lake of Butrinto had a fringe of tinkling ice round its rim, and its surface was patterned with flocks of wild duck. On the brown hills, damp and crumbling with rain, the hares, roe deer, and wild boar gathered in the thickets to stamp and gnaw at the frozen ground, unearthing the bulbs and roots beneath. On the island the swamps and pools had their wisps of snipe, probing the mushy earth with their long rubbery beaks, humming like arrows as they flipped up from under your feet. In the olive groves, among the myrtles, the woodcock lurked, fat and ungainly, leaping away when disturbed with a tremendous purring of wings, looking like bundles of wind-blown autumn leaves.

Leslie, of course, was in his element at this time. With a band of fellow enthusiasts he made trips over to the mainland once a fortnight, returning with the great bristly carcass of wild boar, cloaks of bloodstained hares, and huge baskets brimming over with the iridescent carcasses of ducks. Dirty, unshaven, smelling strongly of gun-oil and blood, Leslie would give us the details of the hunt, his eyes gleaming as he strode about the room demonstrating where and how he had stood, where and how the boar had broken cover, the crash of the gun rolling and bouncing among the bare mountains, the thud of the bullet, and the skidding somersault that the boar took into the heather. He described it so vividly that we felt we had been present at the hunt. Now he was the boar, testing the wind, shifting uneasily in the cane thicket, glaring under its bristling eyebrows, listening to the sound of the beaters and dogs; now he was one of the beaters, moving cautiously through waist-high undergrowth, looking from side to side, making the curious bubbling cry to drive the game from cover; now, as the boar broke cover and started down the hill, snorting, he flung the imaginary gun to his shoulder and fired, the gun kicked realistically, and in the corner of the room the boar somersaulted and rolled to his death.

Mother thought little about Leslie's hunting trips until he brought the first wild boar back. Having surveyed the ponderous, muscular body and the sharp tusks that lifted the upper lip in a snarl, she gasped faintly.

'Goodness! I never realized they were so big,' she said. 'I do hope you'll be careful, dear.'

'Nothing to worry about,' said Leslie, 'unless they break cover right at your feet; then it's a bit of a job, because if you miss they're on you.'

'Most *dangerous*,' said Mother. 'I never realized they were so big . . . you might easily be injured or killed by one of those brutes, dear.'

'No, no, Mother; it's perfectly safe unless they break right under your feet.'

'I don't see why it should be dangerous even then,' said Larry.

'Why not?' asked Leslie.

'Well, if they charge you, and you miss, why not just jump over them?'

'Don't be ridiculous,' said Leslie, grinning. 'The damn' things stand about three feet at the shoulder, and they're hellish fast. You haven't got time to jump over them.'

'I really don't see why not,' said Larry; 'after all, it would be no more difficult than jumping over a chair. Anyway, if you couldn't jump over them, why not vault over them?'

'You do talk nonsense, Larry; you've never seen these things move. It would be impossible to vault *or* jump.'

'The trouble with you hunting blokes is lack of imagination,' said Larry critically. 'I supply magnificent ideas – all you have to do is to try them out. But no, you condemn them out of hand.'

'Well, you come on the next trip and demonstrate how to do it,' suggested Leslie.

'I don't profess to being a hairy-chested man of action,' said Larry austerely. 'My place is in the realm of ideas – the brainwork, as it were. I put my brain at your disposal for the formation of schemes and stratagems, and then you, the muscular ones, carry them out.'

'Yes; well, I'm not carrying *that* one out,' said Leslie with conviction.

'It sounds most foolhardy,' said Mother. 'Don't you do anything silly, dear. And, Larry, stop putting dangerous ideas into his head.'

Larry was always full of ideas about things of which he had no experience. He advised me on the best way to study nature, Margo on clothes, Mother on how to manage the family and pay up her overdraft, and Leslie on shooting. He was perfectly safe, for he knew that none of us could retaliate by telling him the best way to write. Invariably, if any member of the family had a problem, Larry knew the best way to solve it; if anyone boasted of an achievement, Larry could never see what the fuss was about – the thing was perfectly easy to do, providing one used one's brain. It was due to this attitude of pomposity that he set the villa on fire.

Leslie had returned from a trip to the mainland, loaded with game, and puffed up with pride. He had, he explained to us, pulled off his first left-and-a-right. He had to explain in detail, however, before we grasped the full glory of his action. Apparently a left-and-a-right in hunting parlance meant to shoot and kill two birds or animals in quick succession, first with your left barrel and then with your right. Standing in the great stone-flagged kitchen, lit by the red glow of the charcoal fires, he explained how the flock of ducks had come over in the wintry dawn, spread out across the sky. With a shrill whistle of wings they had swept overhead and Leslie had picked out the leader, fired, turned his gun onto the second bird, and fired again with terrific speed, so that when he lowered his smoking barrels the two ducks splashed into the lake almost as one. Gathered in the kitchen, the family listened spellbound to his graphic description. The broad wooden table was piled high with game, Mother and Margo were plucking a brace of ducks for dinner, I was examining the various species and making notes on them in my diary (which was rapidly becoming more bloodstained and feather-covered), and Larry was sitting on a chair, a neat, dead mallard in his lap, stroking its crisp wings and watching as Leslie, up to the waist in an imaginary swamp, for the third time showed us how he achieved his left-and-a-right.

'Very good, dear,' said Mother, when Leslie had described the scene for the fourth time. 'It must have been very difficult.'

'I don't see why,' said Larry.

Leslie, who was just about to describe the whole thing over again, broke off and glared at him. 'Oh, you don't?' he asked belligerently. 'And what d'you know about it? You couldn't hit an olive tree at three paces, let alone a flying bird.'

'My dear fellow, I'm not belittling you,' said Larry in his most irritating and unctuous voice. 'I just don't see why it is considered so difficult to perform what seems to me a simple task.'

'*Simple?* If you'd had any experience of shooting you wouldn't call it simple.'

'I don't see that it's necessary to have had shooting experience. It seems to me to be merely a matter of keeping a cool head and aiming reasonably straight.'

'Don't be silly,' said Leslie disgustedly. 'You always think the things other people do are simple.'

'It's the penalty of being versatile,' sighed Larry. 'Generally they turn out to be ridiculously simple when I try them. That's why I can't see what you're making a fuss for, over a perfectly ordinary piece of marksmanship.'

'Ridiculously simple when *you* try them?' repeated Leslie incredulously. 'I've never seen you carry out one of your suggestions yet.'

'A gross slander,' said Larry, nettled. 'I'm always ready to prove my ideas are right.'

'All right, let's see you pull off a left-and-a-right, then.'

'Certainly. You supply the gun and the victims and I'll show you that it requires no ability whatsoever; it's a question of a mercurial mind that can weigh up the mathematics of the problem.'

'Right. We'll go after snipe down in the marsh tomorrow. You can get your mercurial mind to work on those.'

'It gives me no pleasure to slaughter birds that have every appearance of having been stunted from birth,' said Larry, 'but, since my honour is at stake, I suppose they must be sacrificed.'

'If you get *one* you'll be lucky,' said Leslie with satisfaction.

'Really, you children do argue about the stupidest things,' said Mother philosophically, wiping the feathers off her glasses.

'I agree with Les,' said Margo unexpectedly; 'Larry's too fond of telling people how to do things, and doing nothing himself. It'll do him good to be taught a lesson. I think it was jolly clever of Les to kill two birds with one stone, or whatever it's called.'

Leslie, under the impression that Margo had misunderstood his feat, started on a new and more detailed recital of the episode.

It had rained all night, so early next morning, when we set off to see Larry perform his feat, the ground was moist and squelchy underfoot, and smelled as rich and fragrant as plum-cake. To honour the occasion Larry had placed a large turkey feather in his tweed hat, and he looked like a small, portly, and immensely dignified Robin Hood. He complained vigorously all the way down to the swamp in the valley where the snipe congregated. It was cold, it was extremely slippery, he didn't see why Leslie couldn't take his word for it without this ridiculous farce, his gun was heavy, there probably wouldn't be any game at all, for he couldn't see anything except a mentally defective penguin being out on a day like this. Coldly and relentlessly we urged him down to the swamp, turning a deaf ear to all his arguments and protests.

The swamp was really the level floor of a small valley, some ten acres of flat land which were cultivated during the spring and summer months. In the winter it was allowed to run wild, and it became a forest of bamboos and grass, intersected by the brimming irrigation ditches. These ditches that criss-crossed about the swamp made hunting difficult, for most of them were too wide to jump, and you could not wade them, since they consisted of about six feet of liquid mud and four feet of dirty water. They were spanned, here and there, by narrow plank bridges, most of which were rickety and decayed, but which were the only means of getting about the swamp. Your time during a hunt was divided between looking for game and looking for the next bridge.

We had hardly crossed the first little bridge when three snipe purred up from under our feet and zoomed away, swinging from side to side as they flew. Larry flung the gun to his shoulder and pulled the triggers excitedly. The hammers fell, but there was no sound.

'It would be an idea to load it,' said Leslie with a certain quiet triumph.

'I thought *you'd* done that,' Larry said bitterly; 'you're acting as the blasted gunbearer, after all. I'd have got that pair if it hadn't been for your inefficiency.'

He loaded the gun and we moved slowly on through the bamboos. Ahead we could hear a pair of magpies cackling fiendishly whenever we moved. Larry muttered threats and curses on them for warning the game. They kept flying ahead of us, cackling loudly, until Larry was thoroughly exasperated. He stopped at the head of a tiny bridge that sagged over a wide expanse of placid water.

'Can't we do something about those birds?' he inquired heatedly. 'They'll scare everything for miles.'

'Not the snipe,' said Leslie; 'the snipe stick close until you almost walk on them.'

'It seems quite futile to continue,' said Larry. 'We might as well send a brass band ahead of us.'

He tucked the gun under his arm and stamped irritably on to the bridge. It was then that the accident occurred. He was in the middle of the groaning, shuddering plank when two snipe which had been lying concealed in the long grass at the other end of the bridge rocketed out of the grass and shot skywards. Larry, forgetting in his excitement his rather peculiar situation, shipped the gun to his shoulder and, balancing precariously on the swaying bridge, fired both barrels. The gun roared and kicked, the snipe flew away undamaged, and Larry with a yell of fright fell backwards into the irrigation ditch.

'Hold the gun above your head! Hold it above your head!' roared Leslie.

'Don't stand up or you'll sink,' screeched Margo. 'Sit still.'

But Larry, spreadeagled on his back, had only one idea, and that was to get out as quickly as possible. He sat up and then tried to get to his feet, using, to Leslie's anguish, the gun barrels as a support. He raised himself up, the liquid mud shuddered and boiled, the gun sank out of sight, and Larry disappeared up to his waist.

'Look what you've done to the gun,' yelled Leslie furiously; 'you've choked the bloody barrels.'

'What the hell do you expect me to do?' snarled Larry. 'Lie here and be sucked under? Give me a hand, for heaven's sake.'

'Get the gun out,' said Leslie angrily.

'I refuse to save the gun if you don't save me,' Larry yelled. 'Damn it, I'm not a seal . . . *get me out!*'

'If you give me the end of the gun I can pull you out, you idiot,' shouted Leslie. 'I can't reach you otherwise.'

Larry groped wildly under the surface for the gun and sank several inches before he retrieved it, clotted with black and evil-smelling mud.

'Dear God! Just *look* at it,' moaned Leslie, wiping the mud off it with his handkerchief, 'just look at it.'

'Will you stop carrying on over that beastly weapon and get me out of here?' asked Larry vitriolically. 'Or do you want me to sink beneath the mud like a sort of sportsmen's Shelley?'

Leslie handed him the ends of the barrels, and we all heaved mightily. It seemed to make no impression whatsoever, except that when we stopped, exhausted, Larry sank a little deeper.

'The idea is to *rescue* me,' he pointed out, panting, 'not deliver the *coup de grâce*.'

'Oh, stop yapping and try to heave yourself out,' said Leslie.

'What d'you think I've been doing, for heaven's sake? I've ruptured myself in three places as it is.'

At last, after much effort, there came a prolonged belch from the mud and Larry shot to the surface and we hauled him up the bank. He stood there, covered with the black and stinking slush, looking like a chocolate statue that has come in contact with a blast furnace; he appeared to be melting as we watched.

'Are you all right?' asked Margo.

Larry glared at her. 'I'm fine,' he said sarcastically, 'simply fine Never enjoyed myself more. Apart from a slight touch of pneumonia, a ricked back, and the fact that one of my shoes lies full fathom five, I'm having a wonderful time.'

As he limped homewards he poured scorn and wrath on our heads, and by the time we reached home he was convinced that the whole thing had been a plot. As he entered the house, leaving a trail like a ploughed field, Mother uttered a gasp of horror.

'What *have* you been doing, dear?' she asked.

'Doing? What do you think I've been doing? I've been shooting.'

'But how did you get like that, dear? You're *sopping*. Did you fall in?'

'Really, Mother, you and Margo have such remarkable perspicacity I sometimes wonder how you survive.'

'I only *asked*, dear,' said Mother.

'Well, of course I fell in; what did you think I'd been doing?'

'You must change, dear, or you'll catch cold.'

'I can manage,' said Larry with dignity; 'I've had quite enough attempts on my life for one day.'

He refused all offers of assistance, collected a bottle of brandy from the larder, and retired to his room, where, on his instructions, Lugaretzia built a huge fire. He sat muffled up in bed, sneezing and consuming brandy. By lunch-time he sent down for another bottle, and at tea-time we could hear him singing lustily, interspersed with gigantic sneezes. At supper-time Lugaretzia had paddled upstairs with the third bottle, and Mother began to get worried. She sent Margo up to see if Larry was all right. There was a long silence, followed by Larry's voice raised in wrath, and Margo's pleading plaintively. Mother, frowning, stumped upstairs to see what was happening, and Leslie and I followed her.

In Larry's room a fire roared in the grate, and Larry lay concealed under a towering pile of bedclothes. Margo, clasping a glass, stood despairingly by the bed.

'What's the matter with him?' asked Mother, advancing determinedly.

'He's drunk,' said Margo despairingly, 'and I can't get any sense out of him. I'm trying to get him to take this Epsom salts, otherwise he'll feel awful tomorrow, but he won't touch it. He keeps hiding under the bedclothes and saying I'm trying to poison him.'

Mother seized the glass from Margo's hand and strode to the bedside.

'Now come on, Larry, and stop being a fool,' she snapped briskly; 'drink this down *at once.*'

The bedclothes heaved and Larry's tousled head appeared from the depths. He peered blearily at Mother, and blinked thoughtfully to himself. 'You're a horrible old woman . . . I'm sure I've seen you somewhere before,' he remarked, and before Mother had recovered from the shock of this observation he had sunk into a deep sleep.

'Well,' said Mother, aghast, 'he must have had a lot. Anyway, he's asleep now, so let's just build up the fire and leave him. He'll feel better in the morning.'

It was Margo who discovered, early the following morning, that a pile of glowing wood from the fire had slipped down between the boards of the room and set fire to the beam underneath. She came flying downstairs in her nightie, pale with emotion, and burst into Mother's room.

'The house is on fire . . . Get out! Get out!' she yelled dramatically.

Mother leaped out of bed with alacrity. 'Wake Gerry . . . wake Gerry,' she shouted, struggling, for some reason best known to herself, to get her corsets on over her nightie.

'Wake up . . . wake up . . . Fire . . . fire!' screamed Margo at the top of her voice.

Leslie and I tumbled out onto the landing

'What's going on?' demanded Leslie.

'Fire!' screamed Margo in his ear. 'Larry's on fire!'

Mother appeared, looking decidedly eccentric with her corsets done up crookedly over her nightie.

'Larry's on fire? Quick, save him,' she screamed, and rushed up stairs to the attic, closely followed by the rest of us. Larry's room was full of acrid smoke, which poured up from between the floorboards. Larry himself lay sleeping peacefully. Mother dashed over to the bed and shook him vigorously.

'Wake *up*, Larry; for heaven's sake wake up.'

'What's the matter?' he asked, sitting up sleepily.

'The room's on fire.'

'I'm not surprised,' he said, lying down again. 'Ask Les to put it out.'

'Pour something on it,' shouted Les, 'get something to pour on it.'

Margo, acting on these instructions, seized a half-empty brandy bottle and scattered the contents over a wide area of floor. The flames leaped up and crackled merrily.

'You fool, not *brandy!*' yelled Leslie; 'water . . . get some water.'

But Margo, overcome at her contribution to the holocaust, burst into tears. Les, muttering wrathfully, hauled the bedclothes off the recumbent Larry and used them to smother the flames. Larry sat up indignantly.

'What the hell's going on?' he demanded.

'The room's on fire, dear.'

'Well, I don't see why I should freeze to death. Why tear all the bedclothes off? Really, the fuss you all make. It's quite simple to put out a fire.'

'Oh, shut up,' snapped Leslie, jumping up and down on the bedclothes.

'I've never known people for panicking like you all do,' said Larry; 'it's simply a matter of keeping your head. Les has the worst of it under control; now if Gerry fetches the hatchet, and you, Mother, and Margo fetch some water, we'll soon have it out.'

Eventually, while Larry lay in bed and directed operations, the rest of us managed to rip up the planks and put out the smouldering beam. It must have been smouldering throughout the night, for the beam, a twelve-inch-thick slab of olive wood, was charred half-way through. When, eventually, Lugaretzia appeared and started to clean up the mass of smouldering bedclothes, wood splinters, water, and brandy, Larry lay back on the bed with a sigh.

'There you are,' he pointed out; 'all done without fuss and panic. It's just a matter of keeping your head. I would like someone to bring me a cup of tea, please; I've got the most splitting headache.'

'I'm not surprised; you were as tiddled as an owl last night,' said Leslie.

'If you can't tell the difference between a high fever due to exposure and a drunken orgy it's hardly fair to besmirch my character,' Larry pointed out.

'Well, the fever's left you with a good hangover, anyway,' said Margo.

'It's not a hangover,' said Larry with dignity, 'it's just the strain of being woken up at the crack of dawn by an hysterical pack of people and having to take control of a crisis.'

'Fat lot of controlling you did, lying in bed,' snorted Leslie.

'It's not the action that counts, it's the brainwork behind it, the quickness of wit, the ability to keep your head when all about you are losing theirs. If it hadn't been for me you would probably all have been burnt in your beds.'

Conversation

Spring had arrived and the island was sparkling with flowers. Lambs with flapping tails gambolled under the olives, crushing the yellow crocuses under their tiny hooves. Baby donkeys with bulbous and uncertain legs munched among the asphodels. The ponds and streams and ditches were tangled in chains of spotted toads' spawn, the tortoises were heaving aside their winter bed-clothes of leaves and earth, and the first butterflies, winter-faded and frayed, were flitting wanly among the flowers.

In this crisp, heady weather the family spent most of its time on the veranda, eating, sleeping, reading, or just simply arguing. It was here, once a week, that we used to congregate to read our mail which Spiro had brought out to us. The bulk of it consisted of gun catalogues for Leslie, fashion magazines for Margo, and animal journals for myself. Larry's post generally contained books and interminable letters from authors, artists, and musicians, about authors, artists, and musicians. Mother's contained a wedge of mail from various relatives, sprinkled with a few seed cata-logues. As we browsed we would frequently pass remarks to one another, or read bits aloud. This was not done with any motive of sociability (for no other member of the family would listen, anyway), but merely because we seemed unable to extract the full flavour of our letters and magazines unless they were shared. Occasionally, however, an item of news would be sufficiently startling to rivet the family's attention on it, and this happened one day in spring when the sky was like blue glass, and we sat in the dappled shade of the vine, devouring our mail.

'Oh, this is nice . . . Look . . . organdie with puffed sleeves . . . I think I would prefer it in *velvet*, though . . . or maybe a brocade top with a *flared* skirt. Now, that's nice . . . it would look good with long white gloves and one of those sort of summery hats, wouldn't it?'

A pause, the faint sound of Lugaretzia moaning in the dining-room, mingled with the rustle of paper. Roger yawned loudly, followed in succession by Puke and Widdle.

'God! What a beauty! . . . Just *look* at her . . . telescopic sight, bolt action . . . What a beaut! Um . . . a hundred and fifty . . . not really expensive, I suppose . . . Now *this* is good value . . . Let's see . . . double-barrelled . . . choke . . . yes . . . I suppose one really needs something a bit heavier for ducks.'

Roger scratched his ears in turn, twisting his head on one side, a look of bliss on his face, groaning gently with pleasure. Widdle lay down and closed his eyes. Puke vainly tried to catch a fly, his jaws clopping as he snapped at it.

'Ah! Antoine's had a poem accepted at last! Real talent there, if he can only dig down to it. Varlaine's starting a printing press in a stable . . . Pah! Limited editions of his own works. Oh, God, George Bullock's trying his hand at portraits . . . portraits, I ask you! He couldn't paint a candlestick. Good book here you should read, Mother: *The Elizabethan Dramatists* . . . a wonderful piece of work . . . some fine stuff in it . . .'

Roger worked his way over his hind-quarters in search of a flea, using his front teeth like a pair of hair-clippers, snuffling noisily to himself. Widdle twitched his legs and tail minutely, his ginger eyebrows going up and down in astonishment at his own dream. Puke lay down and pretended to be asleep, keeping an eye cocked for the fly to settle.

'Aunt Mabel's moved to Sussex . . . She says Henry's passed all his exams and is going into a bank . . . at least, I *think* it's a bank . . . her writing really is awful, in spite of that expensive education she's always boasting about . . . Uncle Stephen's broken his leg, poor old dear . . . and done something to his *bladder*? . . . Oh, no, I see . . . really this writing . . . he broke his leg falling off a ladder . . . You'd think he'd have more sense than to go up a ladder at his age . . . ridiculous . . . Tom's married . . . one of the Garnet girls . . .'

Mother always left until the last a fat letter, addressed in large, firm, well-rounded handwriting, which was the monthly instalment from Great-Aunt Hermione. Her letters invariably created an indignant uproar among the family, so we all put aside our mail and concentrated when Mother, with a sigh of resignation, unfurled the twenty-odd pages, settled herself comfortably, and began to read.

'She says that the doctors don't hold out much hope for her,' observed Mother.

'They haven't held out any hope for her for the last forty years and she's still as strong as an ox,' said Larry.

'She says she always thought it a little peculiar of us, rushing off to Greece like that, but they've just had a bad winter and she thinks that perhaps it was wise of us to choose such a salubrious climate.'

'Salubrious! What a word to use!'

'Oh, heavens! . . . Oh, no . . . oh, Lord! . . .'

'What's the matter?'

'She says she wants to come and stay . . . the doctors have advised a warm climate!'

'No, I refuse! I couldn't bear it,' shouted Larry, leaping to his feet; 'it's bad enough being shown Lugaretzia's gums every morning, without having Great-Aunt Hermione dying by inches all over the place. You'll have to put her off, Mother . . . tell her there's no room.'

'But I can't, dear; I told her in the last letter what a big villa we had.'

'She's probably forgotten,' said Leslie hopefully.

'She hasn't. She mentions it here . . . where is it? . . . oh, yes, here you are: "As you now seem able to afford such an extensive establishment, I am sure, Louie dear, that you would not begrudge a small corner to an old woman who has not much longer to live." There you are! What on earth can we *do*?'

'Write and tell her we've got an epidemic of smallpox raging out here, and send her a photograph of Margo's acne,' suggested Larry.

'Don't be silly, dear. Besides, I told her how healthy it is here.'

'Really, Mother, you are impossible!' exclaimed Larry angrily. 'I was looking forward to a nice quiet summer's work, with just a few select friends, and now we're going to be invaded by that evil old camel, smelling of mothballs and singing hymns in the lavatory.'

'Really, dear, you do *exaggerate*. And I don't know why you have to bring lavatories into it – I've never heard her sing hymns anywhere.'

'She does nothing else *but* sing hymns . . . "Lead, Kindly Light," while everyone queues on the landing.'

'Well, anyway, we've got to think of a good excuse. I can't write and tell her we don't want her because she sings hymns.'

'Why not?'

'Don't be unreasonable, dear; after all, she *is* a relation.'

'What on earth's that got to do with it? Why should we have to fawn all over the old hag because she's a relation, when the really sensible thing to do would be to burn her at the stake.'

'She's not as bad as that,' protested Mother half-heartedly.

'My dear mother, of all the foul relatives with which we are cluttered, she is definitely the worst. Why you keep in touch which her I cannot, for the life of me, imagine.'

'Well, I've got to answer her *letters*, haven't I?'

'Why? Just write "Gone away" across them and send them back.'

'I couldn't do that, dear; they'd recognize my handwriting,' said Mother vaguely; 'besides, I've opened this now.'

'Can't one of us write and say you're ill?' suggested Margo.

'Yes, we'll say the doctors have given up hope,' said Leslie.

'*I'll* write the letter,' said Larry with relish. 'I'll get one of those lovely black-edged envelopes . . . that will add an air of verisimilitude to the whole thing.'

'You'll do nothing of the sort,' said Mother firmly. 'If you did that she'd come straight out to nurse me. You know what she is.'

'Why keep in touch with them? That's what I want to know,' asked Larry despairingly. 'What satisfaction does it give you? They're all either fossilized or mental.'

'Indeed, they're *not* mental,' said Mother indignantly.

'Nonsense, Mother . . . Look at Aunt Bertha, keeping flocks of imaginary cats . . . and there's Great-Uncle Patrick, who wanders about nude and tells complete strangers how he killed whales with a penknife . . . They're *all* bats.'

'Well, they're *queer*; but they're all very old, and so they're bound to be. But they're not *mental*,' explained Mother, adding candidly, 'Anyway, not enough to be put away.'

'Well, if we're going to be invaded by relations, there's only one thing to do,' said Larry resignedly.

'What's that?' inquired Mother, peering over her spectacles expectantly.

'We must move, of course.'

'Move? Move where?' asked Mother, bewildered.

'Move to a smaller villa. Then you can write to all these zombies and tell them we haven't any room.'

'But don't be stupid, Larry. We can't *keep* moving. We moved here in order to cope with your friends.'

'Well, now we'll have to move to cope with the relations.'

'But we can't *keep* rushing to and fro about the island. People will think we've gone mad.'

'They'll think we're even madder if that old harpy turns up. Honestly, Mother, I couldn't stand it if she came. I should probably borrow one of Leslie's guns and blow a hole in her corsets.'

'Larry! I do wish you *wouldn't* say things like that in front of Gerry.'

'I'm just warning you.'

There was a pause, while Mother polished her spectacles feverishly.

'But it seems so . . . so . . . *eccentric* to keep changing villas like that, dear,' she said at last.

'There's nothing eccentric about it,' said Larry, surprised; 'it's a perfectly logical thing to do.'

'Of course it is,' agreed Leslie; 'it's a sort of self-defence, anyway.'

'Do be sensible, Mother,' said Margo; 'after all, a change is as good as a feast.'

So, bearing that novel proverb in mind, we moved.

Part Three

As long liveth the merry man (they say)
As doth the sorry man, and longer by a day.

– UDALL, *Ralph Roister Doister*

13

The Snow-White Villa

Perched on a hill-top among olive trees, the new villa, white as snow, had a broad veranda running along one side, which was hung with a thick pelmet of grape-vine. In front of the house was a pocket-handkerchief-sized garden, neatly walled, which was a solid tangle of wild flowers. The whole garden was overshadowed by a large magnolia tree, the glossy dark green leaves of which cast a deep shadow. The rutted driveway wound away from the house, down the hillside through olive groves, vineyards, and orchards, before reaching the road. We had liked the villa the moment Spiro had shown it to us. It stood, decrepit but immensely elegant, among the drunken olives, and looked rather like an eighteenth-century exquisite reclining among a congregation of charladies. Its charms had been greatly enhanced, from my point of view, by the discovery of a bat in one of the rooms, clinging upside down to a shutter and chittering with dark malevolence. I had hoped that he would continue to spend the day in the house, but as soon as we moved in he decided that the place was getting overcrowded and departed to some peaceful olive trunk. I regretted his decision, but, having many other things to occupy me, I soon forgot about him.

It was at the white villa that I got on really intimate terms with the mantids; up till then I had seen them, occasionally, prowling through the myrtles, but I had never taken very much notice of them. Now they forced me to take notice of them, for the hill-top on which the villa stood contained hundreds, and most of them were much larger than any I had seen before. They squatted disdainfully on the olives, among the myrtles, on the smooth green magnolia leaves, and at night they would converge on the house whirring into the lamplight with their green wings churning like the wheels of ancient paddle-steamers, to alight on the tables or chairs and stalk mincingly about, turning their heads from side to side in search of prey, regarding us fixedly from bulbous eyes in chinless faces. I had never realized before that mantids could grow so large, for some of the specimens that visited us were fully four and a half inches long; these monsters feared nothing, and would, without hesitation, attack something as big as or bigger than themselves. These insects seemed to consider that the house was their property, and the walls and ceilings their legitimate hunting grounds. But the geckos that lived in the cracks in the garden wall also considered the house their hunting ground, and so the mantids and the geckos waged a constant war against each other. Most of the battles were mere skirmishes between individual members of the two forms of animals, but as they were generally well matched the fights rarely came to much. Occasionally, however, there would be a battle really worth watching. I was lucky enough to have a grandstand view of such a fight, for it took place above, on, and in my bed.

During the day most of the geckos lived under the loose plaster on the garden wall. As the sun sank and the cool shadow of the magnolia tree enveloped the house and garden they would appear, thrusting their small heads out of the cracks and staring interestedly around with their golden eyes. Gradually they slid out into the wall, their flat bodies and stubby, almost conical tails looking ash-grey in the twilight. They would move cautiously across the moss-patched wall until they reached the safety of the vine over the veranda, and there wait patiently until the sky grew dark and the lamps were lit. Then they would choose their hunting areas and make their way to them across the wall of the house, some to the bedrooms, some to the kitchen, while others remained on the veranda among the vine leaves.

There was a particular gecko that had taken over my bedroom as his hunting ground, and I grew to know him quite well and christened him Geronimo, since his assaults on the insect life seemed to me as cunning and well planned as anything that famous Red Indian had achieved. Geronimo seemed to be a cut above the other geckos. To begin with, he lived alone, under a large stone in the zinnia bed beneath my window, and he would not tolerate another gecko anywhere near his home; nor, for that matter, would he allow any strange gecko to enter my bedroom. He rose earlier than the others of his kind, coming out from beneath his stone while the wall and house were still suffused with pale sunset light. He would scuttle up the flaky white plaster precipice until he reached my bedroom window, and poke his head over the sill, peering about curiously and nodding his head rapidly, two or three times, whether in greeting to me or in satisfaction at finding the room as he had left it, I could never make up my mind. He would sit on the windowsill, gulping to himself, until it got dark and a light was brought in; in the lamp's golden gleam he seemed to change colour, from ash-grey to a pale, translucent pinky-pearl that made his neat pattern of goose-pimples stand out, and made his skin look so fine and thin that you felt it should be transparent so that you could see the viscera, coiled neatly as a butterfly's proboscis, in his fat tummy. His eyes glowing with enthusiasm, he would waddle up the wall to his favourite spot, the left-hand outside corner of the ceiling, and hang there upside down, waiting for his evening meal to appear.

The food was not long in arriving. The first shoal of gnats, mosquitoes, and lady-birds, which Geronimo ignored, was very soon followed by the daddy-longlegs, the lacewing flies, the smaller moths, and some of the more robust beetles. Watching Geronimo's stalking tactics was quite an education. A lacewing or a moth, having spun round the lamp until it was dizzy, would flutter up and settle on the ceiling in the white circle of lamplight printed there. Geronimo, hanging upside down in his corner, would stiffen. He would nod his head two or three times very rapidly, and then start to edge across the ceiling cautiously, millimetre by millimetre, his bright eyes on the insect in a fixed stare. Slowly he would slide over the plaster until he was six inches or so away from his prey, whereupon he stopped for a second and you could see his padded toes moving as he made his grip on the plaster more secure. His eyes would become more protuberant with excitement, what he imagined to be a look of blood-curdling ferocity would spread over his face, the tip of his tail would twitch minutely, and then he would skim across the ceiling as smoothly as a drop of water, there would be a faint snap, and he would turn round, an expression of smug happiness on his face, the lacewing inside his mouth with its legs and wings trailing over his lips like a strange, quivering walrus moustache. He would wag his tail vigorously, like an excited puppy, and then trot back to his resting place to consume his meal in comfort. He had incredibly sharp eyesight, for I frequently saw him spot a minute moth from the other side of the room and circle the ceiling in order to get near enough for the capture.

His attitude towards rivals who tried to usurp his territory was very straightforward. No sooner had they hauled themselves over the edge of the sill and settled down for a short rest after the long climb up the side of the villa, than there would be a scuffling noise, and Geronimo would flash across the ceiling and down the wall, to land on the window-sill with a faint thump. Before the newcomer could make a move, Geronimo would rush forward and leap on him. The curious thing was that, unlike the other geckos, he did not attack the head or body of his enemy. He made straight for his opponent's tail, and seizing it in his mouth, about half an inch from the tip, he would hang on like a bulldog and shake it from side to side. The newcomer, unnerved by this dastardly and unusual mode of attack, immediately took refuge in the time-honoured protective device of the lizards: he would drop his tail and scuttle over the edge of the sill and down the wall to the zinnia bed as fast as he could. Geronimo, panting a little from the exertion, would be left standing triumphantly on the sill, his opponent's tail hanging out of his mouth and thrashing to and fro like a snake. Having made sure his rival had departed, Geronimo would then settle down and proceed to eat the tail, a disgusting habit of which I strongly disapproved. However, it was apparently his way of celebrating a victory, and he was not really happy until the tail was safely inside his bulging stomach.

Most of the mantids that flew into my room were fairly small. Geronimo was always eager to tackle them, but they were too quick for him. Unlike the other insects the mantids seemed unaffected by the lamplight; instead of whirling round and round drunkenly, they would calmly settle in a convenient spot and proceed to devour the dancers whenever they settled to regain their strength. Their bulbous eyes seemed just as keen as the gecko's, and they would always spot him and move hurriedly, long before he had crept within fighting range. The night of the great fight, however, he met a mantis that not only refused to fly away, but actually went to meet him, and it was almost more than he could cope with.

I had for some time been intrigued by the breeding habits of the mantids. I had watched the unfortunate male crouching on the back of a female who, with complete equanimity, was browsing on him over her shoulder. Even after his head and thorax had disappeared into the female's neat mouth his hinder end continued to do its duty. Having watched their rather savage love life, I was now very anxious to see the laying and hatching of the eggs. My chance came one day when I was in the hills and I came face to face, as it were, with an exceptionally large female mantis who was stalking regally through the grass. Her belly was distended, and I felt sure that she was expecting a happy event. Having paused, swaying from side to side on her slender legs, and surveyed me coldly, she continued on her way, mincing through the grass-stalks. I decided that the best thing to do would be to capture her so that she could lay her eggs in a box where I could watch over them in comfort. As soon as she realized that I was attempting to capture her, she whirled round and stood up on end, her pale, jade-green wings outspread, her toothed arms curved upwards in a warning gesture of defiance. Amused at her belligerence towards a creature so much bigger than herself, I casually caught her round the thorax between finger and thumb. Instantly her long, sharp arms reached over her back and closed on my thumb, and it felt as though half a dozen needles had been driven through the skin. In my surprise I dropped her and sat back to suck my wound; I found that three of the little punctures had gone really deep, and that, by squeezing, tiny drops of blood appeared. My respect for her increased; she was obviously an insect to be reckoned with. At the next attempt I was more cautious and used two hands, grabbing her round the thorax with one and holding on to her dangerous front arms with the other. She wiggled ineffectually, and tried to bite me with her jaws, lowering her evil little pointed face and nibbling at my skin, but her jaws were too weak to have any effect. I carried her home and imprisoned her in a large gauze-covered cage in my bedroom, tastefully decorated with ferns, heather, and rocks, among which she moved with light-footed grace. I christened her Cicely, for no obvious reason, and spent a lot of time catching butterflies for her, which she ate in large quantities and with apparently undiminishing appetite, while her stomach got bigger and bigger. Just when I was certain that at any moment she would lay her eggs, she somehow or other found a hole in her cage and escaped.

I was sitting in bed reading one night when, with a great whirring of wings, Cicely flew across the room and landed heavily on the wall, some ten feet away from where Geronimo was busily cleaning up the last bits of an exceptionally furry moth. He paused with bits of fluff adhering to his lips, and gazed in astonishment at Cicely. He had, I am sure, never seen such a large mantis before, for Cicely was a good half inch longer than he was. Amazed by her size and taken aback by her effrontery at settling in his room, Geronimo could do nothing but stare at her for a few seconds. Meanwhile Cicely turned her head from side to side and looked about with an air of grim interest, like an angular spinster in an art gallery. Recovering from his surprise, Geronimo decided that this impertinent insect would have to be taught a lesson. He wiped his mouth on the ceiling, and then nodded his head rapidly and lashed his tail from side to side, obviously working himself up into a death-defying fury. Cicely took no notice at all, but continued to stare about her, swaying slightly on her long, slender legs. Geronimo slid slowly from the wall, gulping with fury, until about three feet away from the mantis he paused and shifted his feet in turn to make sure that his grip was good. Cicely, with well-simulated astonishment, appeared to notice him for the first time. Without changing her position she turned her head round and peered over her shoulder. Geronimo glared at her and gulped harder. Cicely, having surveyed him coolly with her bulging eyes, continued her inspection of the ceiling as if the gecko did not exist. Geronimo edged forward a few inches, scuffled his toes once more and the tip of his tail twitched. Then he launched himself forward, and a strange thing happened. Cicely, who up till then was apparently absorbed in the inspection of a crack in the plaster, leaped suddenly into the air, turned round, and landed in the same spot, but with her wings spread out like a cloak, reared up on her hind legs, and curved both serviceable forefeet at the ready. Geronimo had not been prepared for this spiky reception, and he skidded to a halt about three inches away and stared at her. She returned his stare with one of scornful belligerence. Geronimo seemed a little puzzled by the whole thing; according to his experience the mantis should have taken flight and zoomed away across the room at his approach, and yet here she was standing on end, arms ready to stab, her green cloak of wings rustling gently as she swayed from side to side. However, he could not back out now, having got so far, so he braced himself and leaped in for the kill.

His speed and weight told, for he crashed into the mantis and made her reel, and grabbed the underside of her thorax in his jaws. Cicely retaliated by snapping both her front legs shut on Geronimo's hind legs. They rustled and staggered across the ceiling and down the wall, each seeking to gain some advantage. Then there was a pause while the contestants had a rest and prepared for the second round, without losing their grips. I wondered whether I ought to interfere; I did not want either of them to get killed, but at the same time the fight was so intriguing that I was loath to separate them. Before I could decide, they started once again.

For some reason or other Cicely was bent on trying to drag Geronimo down the wall to the floor, while he was equally determined that he should drag her up to the ceiling. They lurched to and fro for some time, first one and then the other gaining the upper hand, but nothing decisive really happening. Then Cicely made her fatal mistake; seizing the opportunity during one of their periodic pauses, she hurled herself into the air in what seemed to be an attempt to fly across the room with Geronimo dangling from her claws, like an eagle with a lamb. But she had not taken his weight into consideration. Her sudden leap took the gecko by surprise and tore the suction-pads on his toes free from their grip on the ceiling, but no sooner were they in mid-air than he became a dead weight, and a weight that not even Cicely could cope with. In an intricate tangle of tail and wings they fell onto the bed.

The fall surprised them both so much that they let go of each other, and sat on the blanket regarding each other with blazing eyes. Thinking this was a suitable opportunity to come between them and call it a draw, I was just about to grab the contestants when they launched themselves at each other once again. This time Geronimo was wiser and grasped one of Cicely's sharp forearms in his mouth. She retaliated by grabbing him round the neck with the other arm. Both were at an equal disadvantage on the blanket, for their toes and claws got caught in it and tripped them up. They struggled to and fro across the bed, and then started to work their way up towards the pillow. By now they were both looking very much the worse for wear; Cicely had a wing crushed and torn and one leg bent and useless, while Geronimo had a great number of bloody scratches across his back and neck caused by Cicely's front claws. I was now far too interested to see who was going to win to dream of stopping them, so I vacated the bed as they neared the pillow, for I had no desire to have one of Cicely's claws dug into my chest.

It looked as though the mantis was tiring, but as her feet made contact with the smooth surface of the sheet it seemed as if she was given a new lease of life. It was a pity that she applied her new-found strength towards the wrong objective. She released her grip on Geronimo's neck and seized his tail instead; whether she thought that by doing so she could hoist him into the air and thus immobilize him, I don't know, but it had the opposite effect. As soon as the claws dug into his tail Geronimo dropped it, but the furious wiggle he gave to accomplish this made his head wag rapidly from side to side, and the result was that he tore Cicely's forearm off in his mouth. So there was Cicely with Geronimo's lashing tail clasped in one claw, while Geronimo, tailless and bloody, had Cicely's left forearm twitching in his mouth. Cicely might still have saved the fight if she had grabbed Geronimo quickly, before he spat out his mouthful of arm; but she was too wrapped up in the thrashing tail, which I think she thought was a vital part of her adversary, and with her one claw she maintained a firm grip on it. Geronimo spat out the forearm and leaped forward, his mouth snapped, and Cicely's head and thorax disappeared into his mouth.

This was really the end of the fight; now it was merely a matter of Geronimo's hanging on until Cicely was dead. Her legs twitched, her wings unfurled like green fans and rustled crisply as they flapped, her great abdomen pulsed, and the movements of her dying body toppled them both into a cleft in the rumpled bedclothes. For a long time I could not see them; all I could hear was the faint crackle of the mantis's wings, but presently even this ceased. There was a pause, and then a small, scratched, and blood-stained head poked above the edge of the sheet, and a pair of golden eyes contemplated me triumphantly as Geronimo crawled tiredly into view. A large piece of skin had been torn from his shoulder, leaving a raw, red patch; his back was freckled with beads of blood where the claws had dug into him, and his gory tail-stump left a red smear on the sheet when he moved. He was battered, limp, and exhausted, but victorious. He sat there for some time, gulping to himself, and allowed me to mop his back with a ball of cotton wool on the end of a match-stick. Then, as a prize, I caught five fat flies and gave them to him, and he ate them with enjoyment. Having recovered his strength somewhat, he made his way slowly round the wall, over the window-sill, and down the outside wall of the house to his home under the stone in the zinnia bed. Obviously he had decided that a good night's rest was needed after such a hectic brawl. The following night he was back in his usual corner, perky as ever, wagging his stump of a tail with pleasure as he eyed the feast of insects drifting about the lamp.

It was a couple of weeks after his great battle that Geronimo appeared one night over the window-sill, and, to my astonishment, he had with him another gecko. The newcomer was quite tiny, only about half Geronimo's size, and a very delicate pearly-pink with large and lustrous eyes. Geronimo took up his usual stand in one corner while the newcomer chose a spot in the centre of the ceiling. They set about the task of insect hunting with immense concentration, completely ignoring each other. I thought at first that the newcomer, being so dainty, was Geronimo's bride, but investigation in the zinnia bed proved that he still maintained a bachelor establishment under his stone. The new gecko apparently slept elsewhere, appearing only at night to join Geronimo as he shinned up the wall to the bedroom. In view of Geronimo's pugnacious attitude towards other geckos I found it difficult to understand his toleration of this newcomer. I toyed with the idea that it might be his son or daughter, but I knew that geckos had no family life whatsoever, simply laying their eggs and leaving the young (when hatched) to fend for themselves, so this did not seem probable. I was still undecided as to what name I should bestow on this new inhabitant of my bedroom when it met with a dreadful fate.

To the left of the villa was a large valley like a bowl of greensward, thickly studded with the twisted columns of the olive trunks. This valley was surrounded by clay and gravel cliffs about twenty feet high, along the base of which grew a thick bed of myrtles that covered a tumbled mass of rocks. This was a fertile hunting ground from my point of view, for a great quantity of various animals lived in and round this area. I was hunting among these boulders one day when I found a large, half-rotten olive trunk lying under the bushes. Thinking there might be something of interest beneath it, I heaved valiantly until it rolled over and settled on its back soggily. In the trough left by its weight crouched two creatures that made me gasp with astonishment.

They were, as far as I could see, common toads, but they were the largest I had ever seen. Each one had a girth greater than the average saucer. They were greyish-green, heavily carunculated, and with curious white patches here and there on their bodies where the skin was shiny and lacking in pigment. They squatted there like two obese, leprous Buddhas, peering at me and gulping in the guilty way that toads have. Holding one in each hand was like handling two flaccid, leathery balloons, and the toads blinked their fine golden filigreed eyes at me, and settled themselves more comfortably on my fingers, gazing at me trustfully, their wide, thick-lipped mouths seeming to spread in embarrassed and uncertain grins. I was delighted with them, and so excited at their discovery that I felt I must immediately share them with someone or I would burst with suppressed joy. I tore back to the villa, clutching a toad in each hand, to show my new acquisitions to the family.

Mother and Spiro were in the larder checking the groceries when I burst in. I held the toads aloft and implored them to look at the wonderful amphibians. I was standing fairly close to Spiro so that when he turned round he found himself staring into a toad's face. Spiro's scowl faded, his eyes bulged and his skin took on a greenish hue; the resemblance between him and the toad was quite remarkable. Whipping out his handkerchief and holding it to his mouth, Spiro waddled uncertainly out onto the veranda and was violently sick.

'You shouldn't show Spiro things like that, dear,' Mother remonstrated. 'You know he's got a weak stomach.'

I pointed out that although I was aware of Spiro's weak stomach I had not thought that the sight of such lovely creatures as the toads would affect him so violently. What was wrong with them? I asked, greatly puzzled.

'There's nothing wrong with them, dear; they're lovely,' said Mother, eyeing the toads suspiciously. 'It's just that *everyone* doesn't like them.'

Spiro waddled in again, looking pale, mopping his forehead with his handkerchief. I hastily hid the toads behind my back.

'Gollys, Master Gerrys,' he said dolefully, 'whys you shows me things like that? I'm sorrys I had to rush outs, Mrs Durrells, but honest to Gods when I sees one of them bastards I haves to throws, and I thought it was betters if I throws out theres than in heres. Donts you ever shows me them things again, Master Gerrys, please.'

To my disappointment the rest of the family reacted in much the same way as Spiro had done to the toad twins, and so, finding that I could not stir up any enthusiasm among the others, I sadly took the creatures up to my room and placed them carefully under my bed.

That evening, when the lamps were lit, I let the toads out for a walk about the room, and amused myself by knocking down insects that swirled round the lamp for them to eat. They flopped ponderously to and fro, gulping up these offerings, their wide mouths snapping shut with a faint clopping sound as their sticky tongues flipped the insect inside. Presently an exceptionally large and hysterical moth came barging into the room, and, thinking what a fine titbit it would make, I pursued it relentlessly. Presently it settled on the ceiling, out of my reach, within a few inches of Geronimo's friend. Since the moth was at least twice its size, the gecko wisely ignored it. In an effort to knock it down for the toads I hurled a magazine at it, which was a stupid thing to do. The magazine missed the moth but caught the gecko amidships, just as it was staring at an approaching lacewing fly. The book flew into the corner of the room, and the gecko fell with a plop onto the carpet right in front of the larger of the two toads. Before the reptile had recovered its breath, and before I could do anything to save it, the toad leaned forward with a benign expression on its face, the wide mouth fell open like a drawbridge, the tongue flicked out and in again, carrying the gecko with it, and the toad's mouth closed once more and assumed its expression of shy good humour. Geronimo, hanging upside down in his corner, seemed quite indifferent to the fate of his companion, but I was horrified by the whole incident and mortified to feel that it was my fault. I hastily gathered up the toads and locked them in their box, for fear that Geronimo himself might be the next victim of their ferocity.

I was very intrigued by these giant toads for a number of reasons. First, they appeared to be the common species, yet they were blotched with the curious white patches on body and legs. Also all the other common toads I had seen had been only a quarter of the size of these monsters. Another curious thing was that I had found them together under the log; to find one such monster would have been unusual, but to find a pair sitting side by side like that was, I felt sure, a unique discovery. I even wondered if they might turn out to be something quite new to science. Hopefully I kept them imprisoned under my bed until the following Thursday, when Theodore arrived. Then I rushed breathlessly up to the bedroom and brought them down for him to see.

'Ah-ha!' Theodore observed, peering at them closely and prodding one with his forefinger; 'yes, they are certainly very large specimens.'

He lifted one out of the box and placed it on the floor, where it sat staring at him mournfully, bulging and sagging like a blob of mildewed dough.

'Um . . . yes,' said Theodore; 'they seem to be . . . er . . . the common toad, though, as I say, they are exceptionally *fine* specimens. These curious marks are due to lack of pigmentation. I should think it's due to age, though of course I . . . er . . . I may be wrong. They must be a considerable age to have reached . . . er . . . to have attained such proportions.'

I was surprised, for I had never looked upon toads as being particularly long-lived creatures. I asked Theodore what the usual age was that they attained.

'Well, it's difficult to say . . . um . . . there are no statistics to go on,' he pointed out, his eyes twinkling, 'but I should imagine that ones as large as these might well be twelve or even twenty years old. They seem to have a great tenacity for life. I have read somewhere of toads being walled up in houses and so forth, and it appears that they must have been confined like that for a number of years. In one case I believe it was something like twenty-five years.'

He lifted the other toad out of the box and set it down beside its companion. They sat side by side, gulping and blinking, their flabby sides wobbling as they breathed. Theodore contemplated them fully for a moment, and then took a pair of forceps out of his waistcoat pocket. He strode into the garden and overturned several rocks until he found a large, moist, and liver-coloured earthworm. He picked it up neatly with his forceps and strode back to the veranda. He stood over the toads and dropped the writhing earthworm onto the stone flags. It coiled itself into a knot, and then slowly started to unravel itself. The nearest toad lifted its head, blinked its eyes rapidly, and turned slightly so that it was facing the worm. The worm continued to writhe like a piece of wool on a hot coal. The toad bent forward, staring down at it with an expression of extreme interest on its broad face.

'Ah-ha!' said Theodore, and smiled in his beard.

The worm performed a particularly convulsive figure eight, and the toad leaned farther forward with excitement. Its great mouth opened, the pink tongue flicked out, and the forepart of the worm was carried into the gaping maw. The toad shut its mouth with a snap, and most of the worm, which hung outside, coiled about wildly. The toad sat back and with great care proceeded to stuff the tail end of the worm into its mouth, using its thumbs. As each section of thrashing worm was pushed in, the toad would gulp hard, closing its eyes with an expression as if of acute pain. Slowly but surely, bit by bit, the worm disappeared between the thick lips, until at last there was only a fraction of an inch dangling outside, twitching to and fro.

'Um,' said Theodore in an amused tone of voice. 'I always like watching them do that. It reminds me of those conjurers, you know, that pull yards and yards of tapes or coloured ribbons out of their mouths . . . er . . . only, of course, the other way *round.*'

The toad blinked, gulped desperately, its eyes screwed up, and the last bit of worm disappeared inside its mouth.

'I wonder,' said Theodore meditatively, his eyes twinkling – 'I wonder if one could teach toads to swallow *swords?* It would be interesting to try.'

He picked up the toads carefully and replaced them in their box.

'Not sharp swords, of course,' he said, straightening up and rocking on his toes, his eyes gleaming. 'If the swords were sharp you might get your toad *in a hole*.'

He chuckled quietly to himself, rasping the side of his beard with his thumb.

14
The Talking Flowers

It was not long before I received the unwelcome news that yet
another tutor had been found for me. This time it was a certain
individual named Kralefsky, a person descended from an intricate
tangle of nationalities but predominantly English. The family
informed me that he was a very nice man and was, moreover,
interested in birds, so we should get on together. I was not,
however, the least impressed by this last bit of information; I had
met a number of people who professed to be interested in
birds, and who had turned out (after careful questioning) to be
charlatans who did not know what a hoopoe looked like, or
could not tell the difference between a black redstart and an
ordinary one. I felt certain that the family had invented this
bird-loving tutor simply in an effort to make me feel happier
about having to start work once again. I was sure that his
reputation as an ornithologist would turn out to have grown
from the fact that he once kept a canary when he was fourteen.
Therefore I set off for town to my first lesson in the gloomiest
possible frame of mind.

Kralefsky lived in the top two storeys of a square, mildewed
old mansion that stood on the outskirts of the town. I climbed
the wide staircase and, with disdainful bravado, rapped a sharp
tattoo on the knocker that decorated the front door. I waited,
glowering to myself and digging the heel of my shoe into the
wine-red carpet with considerable violence; presently, just as I
was about to knock again, there came the soft pad of footsteps,
and the front door was flung wide to reveal my new tutor.

I decided immediately that Kralefsky was not a human being
at all, but a gnome who had disguised himself as one by donning

an antiquated but very dapper suit. He had a large, egg-shaped head with flattened sides that were tilted back against a smoothly rounded hump-back. This gave him the curious appearance of being permanently in the middle of shrugging his shoulders and peering up into the sky. A long, fine-bridged nose with widely flared nostrils curved out of his face, and his extremely large eyes were liquid and of a pale sherry colour. They had a fixed, faraway look in them, as though their owner were just waking up out of a trance. His wide, thin mouth managed to combine primness with humour, and now it was stretched across his face in a smile of welcome, showing even but discoloured teeth.

'Gerry Durrell?' he asked, bobbing like a courting sparrow, and flapping his large, bony hands at me. 'Gerry Durrell, is it not? Come in, my dear boy, do come in.'

He beckoned me with a long forefinger, and I walked past him into the dark hall, the floorboards creaking protestingly under their mangy skin of carpet.

'Through here; this is the room we shall work in,' fluted Kralefsky, throwing open a door and ushering me into a small, sparsely furnished room. I put my books on the table and sat down in the chair he indicated. He leaned over the table, balancing on the tips of his beautifully manicured fingers, and smiled at me in a vague way. I smiled back, not knowing quite what he expected.

'Friends!' he exclaimed rapturously. 'It is most *important* that we are friends. I am quite, quite certain we will become friends, aren't you?'

I nodded seriously, biting the inside of my cheeks to prevent myself from smiling.

'Friendship,' he murmured, shutting his eyes in ecstasy at the thought, 'friendship! That's the ticket!'

His lips moved silently, and I wondered if he was praying, and if so whether it was for me, himself, or both of us. A fly circled his head and then settled confidently on his nose. Kralefsky started, brushed it away, opened his eyes, and blinked at me.

'Yes, yes, that's it,' he said firmly; 'I'm sure we shall be friends. Your mother tells me that you have a great love of natural history. This, you see, gives us something in common straight away . . . a bond, as it were, eh?'

He inserted a forefinger and thumb into his waistcoat pocket, drew out a large gold watch, and regarded it reproachfully. He sighed, replaced the watch, and then smoothed the bald patch on his head that gleamed like a brown pebble through his licheny hair.

'I am by way of being an aviculturist, albeit an amateur,' he volunteered modestly. 'I thought perhaps you might care to see my collection. Half an hour or so with the feathered creatures will, I venture to think, do us no harm before we start work. Besides, I was a *little* late this morning, and one or two of them need fresh water.'

He led the way up a creaking staircase to the top of the house, and paused in front of a green baize door. He produced an immense bunch of keys that jangled musically as he searched for the right one; he inserted it, twisted it round, and drew open the heavy door. A dazzle of sunlight poured out of the room, blinding me, and with it came a deafening chorus of bird-song; it was as though Kralefsky had opened the gates of Paradise in the grubby corridor at the top of his house. The attic was vast, stretching away across almost the whole top of the house. It was uncarpeted, and the only piece of furniture was a large deal table in the centre of the room. But the walls were lined, from floor to ceiling, with row upon row of big, airy cages containing dozens of fluttering, chirruping birds. The floor of the room was covered with a fine layer of bird-seed, so that as you walked your feet scrunched pleasantly, as though you were on a shingle beach. Fascinated by this mass of birds I edged slowly round the room, pausing to gaze into each cage, while Kralefsky (who appeared to have forgotten my existence) seized a large watering-can from the table and danced nimbly from cage to cage, filling water pots.

My first impression, that the birds were all canaries, was quite wrong; to my delight I found there were goldfinches painted like clowns in vivid scarlet, yellow, and black; greenfinches as green and yellow as lemon leaves in midsummer; linnets in their neat chocolate-and-white tweed suiting; bullfinches with bulging, rose-pink breasts; and a host of other birds. In one corner of the room I found small French windows that led me out onto a balcony. At each end a large aviary had been built, and in one lived a cock blackbird, black and velvety with a flaunting, banana-yellow beak; while in the other aviary opposite was a thrushlike bird which was clad in the most gorgeous blue feathering, a celestial combination of shades from navy to opal.

'Rock-thrush,' announced Kralefsky, poking his head round the door suddenly and pointing at this beautiful bird; 'I had it sent over as a nestling last year . . . from Albania, you know. Unfortunately I have not, as yet, been able to obtain a lady for him.'

He waved the watering-can amiably at the thrush, and disappeared inside again. The thrush regarded me with a roguish eye, fluffed his breast out, and gave a series of little clucks that sounded like an amused chuckle. Having gazed long and greedily at him, I went back into the attic, where I found Kralefsky still filling water-pots.

'I wonder if you would care to assist?' he asked, staring at me with vacant eyes, the can drooping in his hand so that a fine stream of water dribbled onto the highly polished toe of one shoe. 'A task like this is so much easier if two pairs of hands work at it, I always think. Now, if you hold the watering-can . . . so . . . I will hold out the pots to be filled . . . excellent! That's the ticket! We shall accomplish this in no time at all.'

So, while I filled the little earthenware pots with water, Kralefsky took them carefully between finger and thumb and inserted them deftly through the cage doors, as though he were popping sweets into a child's mouth. As he worked he talked to both me and the birds with complete impartiality, but as he did not vary his tone at all I was sometimes at a loss to know whether the remark was addressed to me or to one of the occupants of the cages.

'Yes, they're in fine fettle today; it's the sunshine, you know . . . As soon as it gets to this side of the house they start to sing, don't you? You must lay more next time . . . only two, my dear, only two. You couldn't call *that* a clutch, with all the good will in the world. Do you like this new seed? Do you keep any yourself, eh? There are a number of most interesting seed-eaters found here . . . Don't do that in your clean water . . . Breeding some of them is, of course, a task, but a most rewarding one, I find, especially the crosses. I have generally had great success with crosses . . . except when you only lay two, of course . . . rascal, *rascal!*'

Eventually the watering was done, and Kralefsky stood surveying his birds for a moment or so, smiling to himself and wiping his hands carefully on a small towel. Then he led me round the room, pausing before each cage to give me an account of the bird's history, its ancestors, and what he hoped to do with it. We were examining – in a satisfied silence – a fat, flushed bullfinch, when suddenly a loud, tremulous ringing sound rose above the clamour of bird-song. To my astonishment the noise appeared to emanate from somewhere inside Kralefsky's stomach.

'By Jove!' he exclaimed in horror, turning agonized eyes on me, 'by Jove!'

He inserted finger and thumb into his waistcoat and drew out his watch. He depressed a tiny lever and the ringing sound ceased. I was a little disappointed that the noise should have such a commonplace source; to have a tutor whose inside chimed at intervals would, I felt, have added greatly to the charm of the lessons. Kralefsky peered eagerly at the watch and then screwed up his face in disgust.

'By Jove!' he repeated faintly, 'twelve o'clock already . . .

winged time indeed . . . Dear me, and you leave at half-past, don't you?'

He slipped the watch back into its pocket and smoothed his bald patch.

'Well,' he said at last, 'we cannot, I feel, achieve any scholastic advancement in half an hour. Therefore, if it would pass the time pleasantly for you, I suggest we go into the garden below and pick some groundsel for the birds. It's so good for them, you know, especially when they're laying.'

So we went into the garden and picked groundsel until Spiro's car honked its way down the street like a wounded duck.

'Your car, I believe,' observed Kralefsky politely. 'We have certainly managed to gather a good supply of green stuff in the time. Your assistance was invaluable. Now, tomorrow you will be here at nine o'clock sharp, won't you? That's the ticket! We may consider this morning was not wasted; it was a form of introduction, a measuring up of each other. And I hope a chord of friendship has been struck. By Jove, yes, that's very important! Well, *au revoir* until tomorrow, then.'

As I closed the creaking, wrought-iron gates he waved at me courteously and then wandered back towards the house, leaving a trail of golden-flowered groundsel behind him, his hump-back bobbing among the rose bushes.

When I got home the family asked me how I liked my new tutor. Without going into details, I said that I found him very nice, and that I was sure we should become firm friends. To the query as to what we had studied during our first morning I replied, with a certain amount of honesty, that the morning had been devoted to ornithology and botany. The family seemed satisfied. But I very soon found that Mr Kralefsky was a stickler for work, and he had made up his mind to educate me in spite of any ideas I might have on the subject. The lessons were boring to a degree, for he employed a method of teaching that must have been in fashion round about the middle of the eighteenth century. History was served in great, indigestible chunks, and the dates were learned by heart. We would sit and repeat them in a monotonous, sing-song chorus, until they became like some incantation that we chanted automatically, our minds busy with other things. For geography I was confined, to my annoyance, to the British Isles, and innumerable maps had to be traced and filled in with the bevies of counties and the county towns. Then the counties and the towns had to be learned by heart, together with the names of the important rivers, the main produce of places, the populations, and much other dreary and completely useless information.

'Somerset?' he would trill, pointing at me accusingly.

I would frown in a desperate attempt to remember something about that county. Kralefsky's eyes would grow large with anxiety as he watched my mental struggle.

'Well,' he would say at length, when it became obvious that my knowledge of Somerset was non-existent – 'well, let us leave Somerset and try Warwickshire. Now then, Warwickshire. County town? Warwick! That's the ticket! Now, what do they produce in Warwick, eh?'

As far as I was concerned they did not produce anything in Warwick, but I would hazard a wild guess at coal. I had discovered that if one went on naming a product relentlessly (regardless of the county or town under discussion), sooner or later you would find the answer to be correct. Kralefsky's anguish at my mistakes was very real; the day I informed him that Essex produced stainless steel there were tears in his eyes. But these long periods of depression were more than made up for by his extreme pleasure and delight when, by some strange chance, I answered a question correctly.

Once a week we tortured ourselves by devoting a morning to French. Kralefsky spoke French beautifully, and to hear me massacring the language was almost more than he could bear. He very soon found that it was quite useless to try to teach me from the normal text-books, so these were set aside in favour of a three-volume set of bird books; but even with these it was uphill going. Occasionally, when we were reading the description of the robin's plumage for the twentieth time, a look of grim determination would settle on Kralefsky's face. He would slam the book shut and rush out into the hall, to reappear a minute later wearing a jaunty panama.

'I think it would freshen us up a little . . . blow the cobwebs away . . . if we went for a short *walk*,' he would announce, giving a distasteful glance at *Les Petits Oiseaux de l'Europe*. 'I think we will make our way through the town and come back along the esplanade, eh? Excellent! Now, we must not waste time, must we? It will be a good opportunity for us to practise our *conversational* French, won't it? So no English, please – everything to be said in French. It is in this way that we become familiar with a language.'

So, in almost complete silence, we would wend our way through the town. The beauty of these walks was that, no matter which direction we set out in, we invariably found ouselves, somehow or other, in the bird market. We were rather like Alice in the looking-glass garden: no matter how determinedly we strode off in the opposite direction, in no time at all we found ourselves in the little square where the stalls were piled high with wicker cages and the air rang with the song of birds. Here French would be forgotten; it would fade away into the limbo to join algebra, geometry, history dates, county towns, and similar subjects. Our eyes sparkling, our faces flushed, we would move from stall to stall, examining the birds carefully and bargaining fiercely with the vendors, and gradually our arms would become laden with cages.

Then we would be brought suddenly back to earth by the watch in Kralefsky's waistcoat pocket, chiming daintily, and he would almost drop his tottering burden of cages in his efforts to extract the watch and stop it.

'By Jove! Twelve o'clock! Who would have thought it, eh?

Just hold this linnet for me, will you, while I stop the watch . . . Thank you . . . We will have to be quick, eh? I doubt whether we can make it on foot, laden as we are. Dear me! I think we had better have a cab. An extravagance, of course, but needs must where the devil drives, eh?'

So we would hurry across the square, pile our twittering, fluttering purchases into a cab and be driven back to Kralefsky's house, the jingle of the harness and the thud of hooves mingling pleasantly with the cries of our bird cargo.

I had worked for some weeks with Kralefsky before I discovered that he did not live alone. At intervals during the morning he would pause suddenly, in the middle of a sum or a recitation of county towns, and cock his head on one side, as if listening.

'Excuse me a moment,' he would say. 'I must go and see Mother.'

At first this rather puzzled me, for I was convinced that Kralefsky was far too old to have a mother still living. After considerable thought, I came to the conclusion that this was merely his polite way of saying that he wished to retire to the lavatory, for I realized that not everyone shared my family's lack of embarrassment when discussing this topic. It never occurred to me that, if this was so, Kralefsky closeted himself more often than any other human being I had met. One morning I had consumed for breakfast a large quantity of loquats, and they had distressing effects on me when we were in the middle of a history lesson. Since Kralefsky was so finicky about the subject of lavatories I decided that I would have to phrase my request politely, so I thought it best to adopt his own curious term. I looked him firmly in the eye and said that I would like to pay a visit to his mother.

'My mother?' he repeated in astonishment. 'Visit my mother? Now?'

I could not see what the fuss was about, so I merely nodded.

'Well,' he said doubtfully, 'I'm sure she'll be delighted to see you, of course, but I'd better just go and see if it's convenient.'

He left the room, still looking a trifle puzzled, and returned after a few minutes.

'Mother would be delighted to see you,' he announced, 'but she says will you please excuse her being a little untidy?'

I thought it was carrying politeness to an extreme to talk about the lavatory as if it were a human being, but, since Kralefsky was obviously a bit eccentric on the subject, I felt I had better humour him. I said I did not mind a bit if his mother was in a mess, as ours frequently was as well.

'Ah . . . er . . . yes, yes, I expect so,' he murmured, giving me rather a startled glance. He led me down the corridor, opened a door, and, to my complete surprise, ushered me into a large shadowy bedroom. The room was a forest of flowers; vases, bowls, and pots were perched everywhere, and each contained a mass of beautiful blooms that shone in the gloom like walls of jewels in a green-shadowed cave. At one end of the room was an enormous bed, and in it, propped up on a heap of pillows, lay a tiny figure not much bigger than a child. She must have been very old, I decided as we drew nearer, for her fine, delicate features were covered with a network of wrinkles that grooved a skin as soft and velvety-looking as a baby mushroom's. But the astonishing thing about her was her hair. It fell over her shoulders in a thick cascade, and then spread half-way down the bed. It was the richest and most beautiful auburn colour imaginable, glinting and shining as though on fire, making me think of autumn leaves and the brilliant winter coat of a fox.

'Mother dear,' Kralefsky called softly, bobbing across the room and seating himself on a chair by the bed, 'Mother dear, here's Gerry come to see you.'

The minute figure on the bed lifted thin, pale lids and looked at me with great tawny eyes that were as bright and intelligent as a bird's. She lifted a slender, beautifully shaped hand, weighed down with rings, from the depths of the auburn tresses and held it out to me, smiling mischievously.

'I am so very flattered that you asked to see me,' she said in a soft, husky voice. 'So many people nowadays consider a person of my age a bore.'

Embarrassed, I muttered something, and the bright eyes looked at me, twinkling, and she gave a fluting blackbird laugh, and patted the bed with her hand.

'Do sit down,' she invited; 'do sit down and talk for a minute.'

Gingerly I picked up the mass of auburn hair and moved it to one side so that I could sit on the bed. The hair was soft, silky, and heavy, like a flame-coloured wave swishing through my fingers. Mrs Kralefsky smiled at me, and lifted a strand of it in her fingers, twisting it gently so that it sparkled.

'My one remaining vanity,' she said; 'all that is left of my beauty.'

She gazed down at the flood of hair as though it were a pet, or some other creature that had nothing to do with her, and patted it affectionately.

'It's strange,' she said, 'very strange. I have a theory, you know, that some beautiful things fall in love with themselves, as Narcissus did. When they do that, they need no help in order to live; they become so absorbed in their own beauty that they live for that alone, feeding on themselves, as it were. Thus, the more beautiful they become, the stronger they become; they live in a circle. That's what my hair has done. It is self-sufficient, it grows only for itself, and the fact that my old body has fallen to ruin does not affect it a bit. When I die they will be able to pack my coffin deep with it, and it will probably go on growing after my body is dust.'

'Now, now, Mother, you shouldn't talk like that,' Kralefsky chided her gently. 'I don't like these morbid thoughts of yours.'

She turned her head and regarded him affectionately, chuckling softly.

'But it's not morbid, John; it's only a theory I have,' she explained. 'Besides, think what a beautiful shroud it will make.'

She gazed down at her hair, smiling happily. In the silence Kralefsky's watch chimed eagerly, and he started, pulled it out of his pocket and stared at it.

'By Jove!' he said, jumping to his feet, 'those eggs should have hatched. Excuse me a minute, will you, Mother? I really must go and see.'

'Run along, run along,' she said. 'Gerry and I will chat until you come back . . . don't worry about *us*.'

'That's the ticket!' exclaimed Kralefsky, and bobbed rapidly across the room between the banks of flowers, like a mole burrowing through a rainbow. The door sighed shut behind him, and Mrs Kralefsky turned her head and smiled at me.

'They say,' she announced – 'they *say* that when you get old, as I am, your body slows down. I don't believe it. No, I think that is quite wrong. I have a theory that you do *not* slow down at all, but that *life slows down for you*. You understand me? Everything becomes languid, as it were, and you can notice so much more when things are in slow motion. The things you see! The extraordinary things that happen all around you, that you never even suspected before! It is really a delightful adventure, quite delightful!'

She sighed with satisfaction, and glanced round the room.

'Take flowers,' she said, pointing at the blooms that filled the room. 'Have you heard flowers *talking*?'

Greatly intrigued, I shook my head; the idea of flowers talking was quite new to me.

'Well, I can assure you that they *do* talk,' she said. 'They hold long conversations with each other . . . at least I presume them to be conversations, for I don't understand what they're saying, naturally. When you're as old as I am you'll probably be able to hear them as well; that is, if you retain an open mind about such matters. *Most* people say that as one gets older one believes nothing and is surprised at nothing, so that one becomes more receptive to ideas. Nonsense! All the old people I know have had their minds locked up like grey, scaly oysters since they were in their teens.'

She glanced at me sharply.

'D'you think I'm queer? Touched, eh? Talking about flowers holding conversations?'

Hastily and truthfully I denied this. I said that I thought it was more than likely that flowers conversed with each other. I pointed out that bats produced minute squeaks which I was able to hear, but which would be inaudible to an elderly person, since the sound was too high-pitched.

'That's it, that's it!' she exclaimed delightedly. 'It's a question of wave-length. I put it all down to this slowing-up process. Another thing that you don't notice when you're young is that flowers have personality. They are different from each other, just as people are. Look, I'll show you. D'you see that rose over there, in the bowl by itself?'

On a small table in the corner, enshrined in a small silver bowl, was a magnificent velvety rose, so deep a garnet red that it was almost black. It was a gorgeous flower, the petals curled to perfection, the bloom on them as soft and unblemished as the down on a newly hatched butterfly's wing.

'Isn't he a beauty?' inquired Mrs Kralefsky. 'Isn't he wonderful? Now, I've had him two weeks. You'd hardly believe it, would you? And he was not a bud when he came. No, no, he was fully open. But, do you know, he was so sick that I did not think he would live? The person who plucked him was careless enough to put him in with a bunch of Michaelmas daisies. Fatal, absolutely fatal! You have no idea how cruel the daisy family is, on the whole. They are very rough-and-ready sort of flowers, very down to earth, and, of course, to put such an aristocrat as a rose amongst them is just *asking* for trouble. By the time he got here he had drooped and faded to such an extent that I did not even notice him among the daisies. But, luckily, I heard them at it. I was dozing here when they started, particularly, it seemed to me, the yellow ones, who always seem so belligerent. Well, of course, I didn't know what they were saying, but it sounded *horrible*. I couldn't think *who* they were talking to at first; I thought they were quarrelling among themselves. Then I got out of bed to have a look and I found that poor rose, crushed in the middle of them, being harried to death. I got him out and put him by himself and gave him half an aspirin. Aspirin is so good for roses. Drachma pieces for the chrysanthemums, aspirin for roses, brandy for sweet peas, and a squeeze of lemon-juice for the fleshy flowers, like begonias. Well, removed from the company of the daisies and given that pick-me-up, he revived in no time, and he seems so grateful; he's obviously making an effort to remain beautiful for as long as possible in order to thank me.'

She gazed at the rose affectionately, as it glowed in its silver bowl.

'Yes, there's a lot I have learned about flowers. They're just like people. Put too many together and they get on each other's nerves and start to wilt. Mix some kinds and you get what appears to be a dreadful form of class distinction. And, of course, the water is so important. Do you know that some people think it's kind to change the water every day? Dreadful! You can *hear* the flowers dying if you do that. I change the water once a week, put a handful of earth in it, and they thrive.'

The door opened and Kralefsky came bobbing in, smiling triumphantly.

'They've all hatched!' he announced, 'all four of them. I'm so glad. I was quite worried, as it's her first clutch.'

'Good, dear; I'm so glad,' said Mrs Kralefsky delightedly. 'That is nice for you. Well, Gerry and I have been having a most interesting conversation. At least, I found it interesting, anyway.'

Getting to my feet, I said that I had found it most interesting as well.

'You must come and see me again, if it would not bore you,' she said. 'You will find my ideas a little eccentric, I think, but they are worth listening to.'

She smiled up at me, lying on the bed under her great cloak of hair, and lifted a hand in a courteous gesture of dismissal. I followed Kralefsky across the room, and at the door I looked back and smiled. She was lying quite still, submissive under the weight of her hair. She lifted her hand again and waved. It seemed to me, in the gloom, that the flowers had moved closer to her, had crowded eagerly about her bed, as though waiting for her to tell them something. A ravaged old queen, lying in state, surrounded by her whispering court of flowers.

15

The Cyclamen Woods

Half a mile or so from the villa rose a fairly large conical hill, covered with grass and heather, and crowned with three tiny olive groves, separated from each other by wide beds of myrtle. I called these three little groves the Cyclamen Woods, for in the right season the ground beneath the olive trees was flushed magenta and wine-red with the flowers of cyclamen that seemed to grow more thickly and more luxuriantly·here than anywhere else in the countryside. The flashy, circular bulbs, with their flaky peeling skin, grew in beds like oysters, each with its cluster of deep green, white-veined leaves, a fountain of beautiful flowers that looked as though they had been made from magenta-stained snowflakes.

The Cyclamen Woods were an excellent place to spend an afternoon. Lying beneath the shade of the olive trunks, you could look out over the valley, a mosaic of fields, vineyards, and orchards, to where the sea shone between the olive trunks, a thousand fiery sparkles running over it as it rubbed itself gently and languorously along the shore. The hill-top seemed to have its own breeze, albeit a baby one, for no matter how hot it was below in the valley, up in the three olive groves the tiny wind played constantly, the leaves whispered, and the drooping cyclamen flowers bowed to each other in endless greeting. It was an ideal spot in which to rest after a hectic lizard hunt, when your head was pounding with the heat, your clothes limp and discoloured with perspiration, and the three dogs hung out their pink tongues and panted like ancient miniature railway engines. It was while the dogs and I were resting after just such a hunt that I acquired two new pets, and, indirectly, started off a chain of coincidences that affected both Larry and Mr Kralefsky.

The dogs, tongues rippling, had flung themselves down among the cyclamens, and lay on their stomachs, hindlegs spread out, in order to get as much of the cool earth against their bodies as possible. Their eyes were half closed and their jowls dark with saliva. I was leaning against an olive trunk that had spent the past hundred years growing itself into the right shape for a perfect back-rest, and gazing out over the fields and trying to identify my peasant friends among the tiny coloured blobs that moved there. Far below, over a blond square of ripening maize, a small black-and-white shape appeared, like a piebald Maltese cross, skimming rapidly across the flat areas of cultivation, heading determinedly for the hill-top on which I sat. As it flew up towards me the magpie uttered three brief, harsh chucks that sounded rather muffled, as though its beak were full of food. It dived as neatly as an arrow into the depths of an olive tree some distance away; there was a pause, and then there arose a chorus of shrill wheezing shrieks from among the leaves, which swept to a crescendo and died slowly away. Again I heard the magpie chuck, softly and warningly, and it leaped out of the leaves and glided off down the hillside once more. I waited until the bird was a mere speck, like a dust-mote floating over the frilly triangle of vineyard on the horizon, and then got to my feet and cautiously circled the tree from which the curious sounds had come. High up among the branches, half hidden by the green and silver leaves, I could make out a large, oval bundle of twigs, like a huge, furry football wedged among the branches. Excitedly I started to scramble up the tree, while the dogs gathered at the bottom of the trunk and watched me with interest; when I was near to the nest I looked down and my stomach writhed, for the dogs' faces, peering up at me eagerly, were the size of pimpernel flowers. Carefully, my palms sweating, I edged my way out along the branches until I crouched side by side with the nest among the breeze-ruffled leaves. It was a massive structure, a great basket of carefully interwoven sticks, a deep cup of mud and rootlets in its heart. The entrance hole through the wall was small, and the twigs that surrounded it bristled with sharp thorns, as did the sides of the nest and the neatly domed wickerwork roof. It was the sort of nest designed to discourage the most ardent ornithologist.

Trying to avoid looking down, I lay on my stomach along the branch and pushed my hand carefully inside the thorny bundle, groping in the mud cup. Under my fingers I could feel soft, quivering skin and fluff, while a shrill chorus of wheezes rose from inside the nest. Carefully I curved my fingers round one fat, warm baby and drew it out. Enthusiastic though I was, even I had to admit it was no beauty. Its squat beak, with a yellow fold at each corner, the bald head, and the half-open bleary eyes gave it a drunken and rather imbecile look. The skin hung in folds and wrinkles all over its body, apparently pinned loosely and haphazardly to its flesh by black feather-stubs. Between the lanky legs drooped a huge flaccid stomach, the skin of it so fine that you could dimly see the internal organs beneath. The baby squatted in my palm, its belly spreading out like a water-filled balloon, and wheezed hopefully. Groping about inside the nest I found that there were three other youngsters, each as revolting as the one I had in my hand. After some thought, and having examined each of them with care, I decided to take two and leave the other pair for the mother. This struck me as being quite fair, and I did not see how the mother could possibly object. I chose the largest (because he would grow up quickly) and the smallest (because he looked so pathetic), put them carefully inside my shirt, and climbed cautiously back to the waiting dogs. On being shown the new additions to the menagerie Widdle and Puke immediately decided that they must be edible, and tried to find out if their conclusion was correct. After I had reprimanded them, I showed the birds to Roger. He sniffed at them in his usual benign way, and then retreated hastily when the babies shot their heads up on long, scrawny necks, red mouths gaping wide, and wheezed lustily.

As I carried my new pets back homewards I tried to decide what to call them; I was still debating this problem when I reached the villa and found the family, who had just been on a shopping expedition into town, disgorging from the car. Holding out the babies in my cupped hands, I inquired if anyone could think of a suitable pair of names for them. The family took one look and all reacted in their individual ways.

'Aren't they *sweet?*' said Margo.

'What are you going to feed them on?' asked Mother.

'What revolting things!' said Leslie.

'Not *more* animals?' asked Larry with distaste.

'Gollys, Master Gerrys,' said Spiro, looking disgusted, 'whats thems?'

I replied, rather coldly, that they were baby magpies, that I hadn't asked anyone's opinion on them, but merely wanted some help in christening them. What should I call them?

But the family were not in a helpful mood.

'Fancy taking them away from their mother, poor little things,' said Margo.

'I hope they're old enough to eat, dear,' said Mother.

'Honest to gods! The things Master Gerrys *finds*,' said Spiro.

'You'll have to watch out they don't steal,' said Leslie.

'Steal?' said Larry in alarm. 'I thought that was jackdaws.'

'Magpies too,' said Leslie; 'awful thieves, magpies.'

Larry took a hundred-drachma note from his pocket and waved it over the babies, and they immediately shot their heads skywards, necks wavering, mouths gaping, wheezing and bubbling frantically. Larry jumped back hastily.

'You're right, by God!' he exclaimed excitedly. 'Did you see that? They tried to attack me and get the money!'

'Don't be ridiculous, dear; they're only hungry,' said Mother.

'Nonsense, Mother . . . you saw them leap at me, didn't you?

It's the money that did it . . . even at that age they have criminal instincts. He can't possibly keep them; it will be like living with Arsène Lupin. Go and put them back where you found them, Gerry.'

Innocently and untruthfully I explained that I couldn't do that, as the mother would desert them, and they would then starve to death. This, as I had anticipated, immediately got Mother and Margo on my side.

'We can't let the poor little things starve,' protested Margo.

'I don't see that it would do any harm to keep them,' said Mother.

'You'll regret it,' said Larry; 'it's asking for trouble. Every room in the house will be rifled. We'll have to bury all our valuables and post an armed guard over them. It's lunacy.'

'Don't be silly, dear,' said Mother soothingly. 'We can keep them in a cage and only let them out for exercise.'

'Exercise!' exclaimed Larry. 'I suppose you'll call it exercise when they're flapping round the house with hundred-drachma notes in their filthy beaks.'

I promised faithfully that the magpies should not, in any circumstance, be allowed to steal. Larry gave me a withering look. I pointed out that the birds had still to be named, but nobody could think of anything suitable. We stood and stared at the quivering babies, but nothing suggested itself.

'Whats you goings to do with them bastards?' asked Spiro.

Somewhat acidly I said that I intended to keep them as pets, and that, furthermore, they were not bastards, but magpies.

'*Whats* you calls them?' asked Spiro, scowling.

'Magpies, Spiro, magpies,' said Mother, enunciating slowly and clearly.

Spiro turned this new addition to his English vocabulary over in his mind, repeating it to himself, getting it firmly embedded.

'Magenpies,' he said at last, 'magenpies, eh?'

'Magpies, Spiro,' corrected Margo.

'Thats what I says,' said Spiro indignantly, 'magenpies.'

So from that moment we gave up trying to find a name for them and they became known simply as the Magenpies.

By the time the Magenpies had gorged themselves to a size where they were fully fledged, Larry had become so used to seeing them around that he had forgotten their allegedly criminal habits. Fat, glossy, and garrulous, squatting on top of their basket and flapping their wings vigorously, the Magenpies looked the very picture of innocence. All went well until they learned to fly. The early stages consisted in leaping off the table on the veranda, flapping their wings frantically, and gliding down to crash onto the stone flags some fifteen feet away. Their courage grew with the strength of their wings, and before very long they accomplished their first real flight, a merry-go-round affair around the villa. They looked so lovely, their long tails glittering in the sun, their wings hissing as they swooped down to fly under the vine, that I called the family out to have a look at them. Aware of their audience, the Magenpies flew faster and faster, chasing each other, diving within inches of the wall before banking to one side, and doing acrobatics on the branches of the magnolia tree. Eventually one of them, made over-confident by our applause, misjudged his distance, crashed into the grape-vine, and fell onto the veranda, no longer a bold, swerving ace of the air, but a woebegone bundle of feathers that opened its mouth and wheezed plaintively at me when I picked it up and soothed it. But, once having mastered their wings, the Magenpies quickly mapped out the villa and then they were all set for their banditry.

The kitchen, they knew, was an excellent place to visit, providing they stayed on the doorstep and did not venture inside; the drawing-room and dining-room they never entered if someone was there; of the bedrooms they knew that the only one in which they were assured of a warm welcome was mine. They would certainly fly into Mother's or Margo's, but they were constantly being told not to do things, and they found this boring. Leslie would allow them on his window-sill but no farther, but they gave up visiting him after the day he let off a gun by accident. It unnerved them, and I think they had a vague idea that Leslie had made an attempt on their lives. But the bedroom that really intrigued and fascinated them was, of course, Larry's, and I think this was because they never managed to get a good look inside. Before they had even touched down on the window-sill they would be greeted with such roars of rage, followed by a rapidly discharged shower of missiles, that they would be forced to flap rapidly away to the safety of the magnolia tree. They could not understand Larry's attitude at all; they decided that – since he made such a fuss – it must be that he had something to hide, and that it was their duty to find out what it was. They chose their time carefully, waiting patiently until one afternoon Larry went off for a swim and left his window open.

I did not discover what the Magenpies had been up to until Larry came back; I had missed the birds, but thought they had flown down the hill to steal some grapes. They were obviously well aware that they were doing wrong, for though normally loquacious they carried out their raid in silence, and (according to Larry) took it in turns to do sentry duty on the window-sill. As he came up the hill he saw, to his horror, one of them sitting on the sill, and shouted wrathfully at it. The bird gave a chuck of alarm and the other one flew out of the room and joined it; they flapped off into the magnolia tree, chuckling hoarsely, like schoolboys caught raiding an orchard. Larry burst into the house, and swept up to his room, grabbing me *en route*. When he opened the door Larry uttered a moan like a soul in torment.

The Magenpies had been through the room as thoroughly as any Secret Service agent searching for missing plans. Piles of manuscript and typing paper lay scattered about the floor like drifts of autumn leaves, most of them with an attractive pattern of holes punched in them. The Magenpies never could resist paper. The typewriter stood stolidly on the table, looking like a disembowelled horse in a bull ring, its ribbon coiling out of its interior, its keys bespattered with droppings. The carpet, bed, and table were aglitter with a layer of paper clips like frost. The Magenpies, obviously suspecting Larry of being a dope smuggler, had fought valiantly with the tin of bicarbonate of soda, and had scattered its contents along a line of books, so that they looked like a snow-covered mountain range. The table, the floor, the manuscript, the bed, and especially the pillow, were decorated with an artistic and unusual chain of footprints in green and red ink. It seemed almost as though each bird had overturned his favourite colour and walked in it. The bottle of blue ink, which would not have been so noticeable, was untouched.

'This is the last straw,' said Larry in a shaking voice, 'positively the last straw. Either you do something about those birds or I will personally wring their necks.'

I protested that he could hardly blame the Magenpies. They were interested in things, I explained; they couldn't help it, they were just made like that. All members of the crow tribe, I went on, warming to my defence work, were naturally curious. They didn't know they were doing wrong.

'I did not ask for a lecture on the crow tribe,' said Larry ominously, 'and I am not interested in the moral sense of magpies, either inherited or acquired. I am just telling you that you will have to either get rid of them or lock them up; otherwise I shall tear them wing from wing.'

The rest of the family, finding they could not siesta with the argument going on, assembled to find out the trouble.

'Good heavens! Dear, what *have* you been doing?' asked Mother, peering round the wrecked room.

'Mother, I am in no mood to answer imbecile questions.'

'Must be the Magenpies,' said Leslie, with the relish of a prophet proved right. 'Anything missing?'

'No, nothing missing,' said Larry bitterly; 'they spared me that.'

'They've made an awful mess of your papers,' observed Margo.

Larry stared at her for a moment, breathing deeply. 'What a masterly understatement,' he said at last; 'you are always ready with the apt platitude to sum up a catastrophe. How I envy you your ability to be inarticulate in the face of Fate.'

'There's no need to be rude,' said Margo.

'Larry didn't mean it, dear,' explained Mother untruthfully; 'he's naturally upset.'

'Upset? *Upset?* Those scab-ridden vultures come flapping in here like a pair of critics and tear and bespatter my manuscript before it's even finished, and you say I'm *upset?*'

'It's *very* annoying, dear,' said Mother, in an attempt to be vehement about the incident, 'but I'm sure they didn't mean it. After all, they don't understand . . . they're only birds.'

'Now don't you start,' said Larry fiercely. 'I've already been treated to a discourse on the sense of right and wrong in the crow tribe. Its disgusting the way this family carries on over animals; all this anthropomorphic slush that's drooled out as an excuse. Why don't you all become magpie worshippers, and erect a prison to pray in? The way *you* all carry on one would think that *I* was to blame, and that it's *my* fault that my room looks as though it's been plundered by Attila the Hun. Well, I'm telling you: if something isn't done about those birds right away, I shall deal with them myself.'

Larry looked so murderous that I decided it would probably be safer if the Magenpies were removed from danger, so I lured them into my bedroom with the aid of a raw egg and locked them up in their basket while I considered the best thing to do. It was obvious that they would have to go into a cage of sorts, but I wanted a really large one for them, and I did not feel that I could cope with the building of a really big aviary by myself. It was useless asking the family to help me, so I decided that I would have to inveigle Mr Kralefsky into the constructional work. He could come out and spend the day, and once the cage was finished he would have the opportunity of teaching me how to wrestle. I had waited a long time for a favourable opportunity of getting these wrestling lessons, and this seemed to me to be ideal. Mr Kralefsky's ability to wrestle was only one of his many hidden accomplishments, as I had found out.

Apart from his mother and his birds I had discovered that Kralefsky had one great interest in life, and that was an entirely imaginary world he had evoked in his mind, a world in which rich and strange adventures were always happening, adventures in which there were only two major characters: himself (as hero) and a member of the opposite sex who was generally known as a Lady. Finding that I appeared to believe the anecdotes he related to me, he got bolder and bolder, and day by day allowed me to enter a little farther into his private paradise. It all started one morning when we were having a break for coffee and biscuits. The conversation somehow got onto dogs, and I confessed to an overwhelming desire to possess a bulldog – creatures that I found quite irresistibly ugly.

'By Jove, yes! Bulldogs!' said Krafelsky. 'Fine beasts, trust-worthy and brave. One cannot say the same of *bull-terriers*, unfortunately.'

He sipped his coffee and glanced at me shyly; I sensed that I was expected to draw him out, so I asked why he thought bull-terriers particularly untrustworthy.

'Treacherous!' he explained, wiping his mouth. '*Most* treacherous.'

He leaned back in his chair, closed his eyes, and placed the tips of his fingers together, as if praying.

'I recall that once – many years ago when I was in England – I was instrumental in saving a Lady's life when she was attacked by one of those brutes.'

He opened his eyes and peeped at me; seeing that I was all attention, he closed them again and continued. 'It was a fine morning in spring, and I was taking a constitutional in Hyde

Park. Being so early, there was no one else about, and the park was silent except for the bird-songs. I had walked quite some distance when I suddenly became aware of a deep, powerful baying.'

His voice sank to a thrilling whisper and, with his eyes still closed, he cocked his head on one side as if listening. So realistic was it that I, too, felt I could hear the savage, regular barks echoing among the daffodils.

'I thought nothing of it at first. I supposed it to be some dog out enjoying itself chasing squirrels. Then, suddenly, I heard cries for help mingling with the ferocious baying.' He stiffened in his chair, frowned, and his nostrils quivered. 'I hurried through the trees, and suddenly came upon a terrible sight.'

He paused, and passed a hand over his brow, as though even now he could hardly bear to recall the scene.

'There, with her back to a tree, stood a Lady. Her skirt was torn and ripped, her legs bitten and bloody, and with a deckchair she was fending off a ravening bull-terrier. The brute, froth flecking its yawning mouth, leaped and snarled, waiting for an opening. It was obvious that the Lady's strength was ebbing. There was not a moment to be lost.'

Eyes still firmly closed, the better to see the vision, Kralefsky drew himself up in his chair, straightened his shoulders and fixed his features into an expression of sneering defiance, a devil-may-care expression – the expression of a man about to save a Lady from a bull-terrier.

'I raised my heavy walking-stick and leaped forward, giving a loud cry to encourage the Lady. The hound, attracted by my voice, immediately sprang at me, growling horribly, and I struck it such a blow on the head that my stick broke in half. The animal, though of course dazed, was still full of strength; I stood there, defenceless, as it gathered itself and launched itself at my throat with gaping jaws.'

Kralefsky's forehead had become quite moist during this

recital, and he paused to take out his handkerchief and pat his brow with it. I asked eagerly what had happened then. Kralefsky reunited his finger-tips and went on.

'I did the only thing possible. It was a thousand-to-one chance, but I had to take it. As the beast leaped at my face I plunged my hand into his mouth, seized his tongue, and twisted it as hard as I could. The teeth closed on my wrist, blood spurted out, but I hung on grimly, knowing my life was at stake. The dog lashed to and fro for what seemed like an age. I was exhausted. I felt I could not hold on any longer. Then, suddenly, the brute gave a convulsive heave and went limp. I had succeeded. The creature had been suffocated by its own tongue.'

I sighed rapturously. It was a wonderful story, and might well be true. Even it if wasn't true, it was the sort of thing that *should* happen, I felt; and I sympathized with Kralefsky if, finding that life had so far denied him a bull-terrier to strangle, he had supplied it himself. I said that I thought he had been very brave to tackle the dog in that way. Kralefsky opened his eyes, flushed with pleasure at my obvious enthusiasm, and smiled deprecatingly.

'No, no, not really brave,' he corrected. 'The Lady was in distress, you see, and a gentleman could do nothing else. By Jove, no!'

Having found in me a willing and delighted listener, Kralefsky's confidence grew. He told me more and more of his adventures, and each became more thrilling than the last. I discovered that, by skilfully planting an idea in his mind one morning, I could be sure of an adventure dealing with it the following day, when his imagination had had a chance to weave a story. Enthralled, I heard how he and a Lady had been the sole survivors of a shipwreck on a voyage to Murmansk ('I had some business to attend to there'). For two weeks he and the Lady drifted on an iceberg, their clothes frozen, feeding on an occasional raw fish or sea-gull, until they were rescued. The ship that spotted them might easily have overlooked them if it had not been for Kralefsky's quick wit: he used the Lady's fur coat to light a signal fire.

I was enchanted with the story of the time he had been held up by bandits in the Syrian desert ('while taking a Lady to see some tombs') and, when the ruffians threatened to carry his fair companion off and hold her to ransom, he offered to go in her place. But the bandits obviously thought the Lady would make a more attractive hostage, and refused. Kralefsky hated bloodshed, but, in the circumstances, what could a gentleman do? He killed all six of them with a knife he had concealed in his mosquito boot. During the First World War he had, naturally, been in the Secret Service. Disguised in a beard, he had been dropped behind the enemy lines to contact another English spy and obtain some plans. Not altogether to my surprise, the other spy turned out to be a Lady. Their escape (with the plans) from the firing squad was a masterpiece of ingenuity. Who but Kralefsky would have thought of breaking into the armoury, loading all the rifles with blanks, and then feigning death as the guns roared out?

I became so used to Kralefsky's extraordinary stories that on the rare occasions when he told me one that was faintly possible I generally believed it. This was his downfall. One day he told me a story of how, when he was a young man in Paris, he was walking along one evening and came across a great brute of a man ill-treating a Lady. Kralefsky, his gentlemanly instincts outraged, promptly hit the man on the head with his walking-stick. The man turned out to be the champion wrestler of France, and he immediately demanded that his honour be satisfied; Kralefsky agreed. The man suggested that they meet in the ring and wrestle it out; Kralefsky agreed. A date was fixed and Kralefsky started to go into training for the fight ('a vegetable diet and many exercises'), and when the great day came he had never felt fitter. Kralefsky's opponent – who, to judge from his description, bore a close resemblance, both in size and mentality, to Neanderthal Man – was surprised to find Kralefsky was a match for him. They struggled round the ring for an hour, neither succeeding in throwing the other. Then, suddenly, Kralefsky remembered a throw he had been taught by a Japanese friend of his. With a twist and a jerk he heaved his massive adversary up, twirled him round, and hurled him right out of the ring. The unfortunate man was in hospital for three months, so badly was he hurt. As Kralefsky rightly pointed out, this was a just and fitting punishment for a cad who was so low as to raise his hand to a Lady.

Intrigued by this tale, I asked Kralefsky if he would teach me the rudiments of wrestling, as I felt it would be most useful to me should I ever come across a Lady in distress. Kralefsky seemed rather reluctant; perhaps at some later date, when we had plenty of room, he might show me a few throws, he said. He had forgotten the incident, but I had not, and so the day he came out to help me build the Magenpies their new home I determined to remind him of his promise. During tea I waited until there was a suitable pause in the conversation and then reminded Kralefsky of his famous fight with the French Champion Wrestler.

Kralefsky was not at all pleased to be reminded of this exploit, it appeared. He turned pale, and shushed me hurriedly. 'One does not boast in public about such things,' he whispered hoarsely.

I was quite willing to respect his modesty, providing he gave me a wrestling lesson. I pointed out that all I wanted was to be shown a few of the more simple tricks.

'Well,' said Kralefsky, licking his lips, 'I suppose I can show you a few of the more *elementary* holds. But it takes a long time to become a proficient wrestler, you know.'

Delighted, I asked him if we should wrestle out on the veranda, where the family could watch us, or in the seclusion of the drawing-room? Kralefsky decided on the drawing-room. It was important not to be distracted, he said. So we went into the house and moved the furniture out of the way, and Kralefsky reluctantly took off his coat. He explained that the basic and most important principle of wrestling was to try to throw your opponent off balance. You could do this by seizing him round the waist and giving a quick sideways twitch. He demonstrated what he meant, catching me and throwing me gently onto the sofa.

'Now!' he said, holding up a finger, 'have you got the idea?'

I said yes, I thought I'd got the idea all right.

'That's the ticket!' said Kralefsky. 'Now you throw *me.*'

Determined to be a credit to my instructor, I threw him with great enthusiasm. I hurled myself across the room, seized him round the chest, squeezed as hard as I could to prevent his escape, and then flung him with a dextrous twist of my wrist towards the nearest chair. Unfortunately, I did not throw him hard enough, and he missed the chair altogether and crashed to the floor, uttering a yell that brought the family rushing in from the veranda. We lifted the white-faced, groaning wrestling champion onto the couch, and Margo went to bring some brandy.

'What on earth did you *do* to him?' Mother asked.

I said that all I had done was to follow instructions. I'd been invited to throw him and I had thrown him. It was perfectly simple, and I didn't see that any blame could possibly be attached to me.

'You don't know your own *strength*, dear,' said Mother; 'you should be more careful.'

'Damn' silly thing to do,' said Leslie. 'Might have killed him.'

'I knew a man once who was crippled for life by a wrestling throw,' remarked Larry conversationally.

Kralefsky groaned more loudly.

'Really, Gerry, you do some very silly things,' said Mother, distraught, obviously with visions of Kralefsky being confined to a wheel-chair for the rest of his days.

Irritated by what I considered to be quite unfair criticisms, I pointed out again that it was not my fault. I had been shown how to throw a person, and then invited to demonstrate. So I had thrown him.

'I'm sure he didn't mean you to lay him out like *that*,' said Larry; 'you might have damaged his spine. Like this fellow I knew, his spine was split like a banana. Very curious. He told me that bits of the bone were sticking out . . .'

Kralefsky opened his eyes and gave Larry an anguished look. 'I wonder if I might have some water?' he said faintly.

At this moment Margo returned with the brandy, and we made Kralefsky take some. A little colour came into his cheeks again, and he lay back and closed his eyes once more.

'Well, you can sit up, and that's one good sign,' said Larry cheerfully; 'though I believe it's not really a trustworthy indication. I knew an artist who fell off a ladder and broke his back, and he was walking round for a week before they discovered it.'

'Good God, really?' asked Leslie, deeply interested. 'What happened to him?'

'He died,' said Larry.

Kralefsky raised himself into a sitting position and gave a wan smile. 'I think perhaps, if you would be kind enough to let Spiro drive me, it would be wiser if I went into town and consulted a doctor.'

'Yes, of course Spiro will take you,' said Mother. 'I should go along to Theodore's laboratory and get him to take an x-ray, just to put your mind at rest.'

So we wrapped Kralefsky, pale but composed, in quantities of rugs and placed him tenderly in the back of the car.

'Tell Theodore to send us a note with Spiro to let us know how you are,' said Mother. 'I do hope you'll soon be better. I'm really so sorry this had to happen; it was so very careless of Gerry.'

It was Kralefsky's big moment. He smiled a smile of pain-racked nonchalance and waved a hand feebly. 'Please, please don't distress yourself. Think nothing more about it,' he said.

'Don't blame the boy; it was not his fault. You see, I'm a *little* out of practice.'

Much later that evening Spiro returned from his errand of mercy, bearing a note from Theodore.

Dear Mrs Durrell,

It appears from the x-ray photographs I have taken of Mr Kralefsky's chest that he has cracked two ribs: one of them, I'm sorry to say, quite severely. He was reticent as to the cause of the damage, but quite considerable force must have been employed. However, if he keeps them bound up for a week or so he should suffer no permanent injury.

With kindest regards to you all,
Yours,
Theodore

P.S. *I didn't by any chance leave a small black box at your house when I came out last Thursday, did I? It contains some very interesting Anopheles mosquitoes I had obtained, and it seems I must have mislaid it. Perhaps you would let me know?*

16

The Lake of Lilies

The Magenpies were most indignant at their imprisonment, in spite of the large size of their quarters. Suffering from insatiable curiosity as they did, they found it most frustrating not to be able to investigate and comment on everything that happened. Their field of view was limited to the front of the house, and so if anything happened round the back they would go almost frantic, cackling and chucking indignantly as they flew round and round their cage, poking their heads through the wire in an effort to see what was going on. Confined as they were, they were able to devote a lot of time to their studies, which consisted of getting a solid grounding in the Greek and English language, and producing skilful imitations of natural sounds. Within a very short time they were able to call all members of the family by name, and they would, with extreme cunning, wait until Spiro had got into the car and coasted some distance down the hill, before rushing to the corner of their cage and screaming 'Spiro . . . *Spiro* . . . *Spiro*,' making him cram on his brakes and return to the house to find out who was calling him. They would also derive a lot of innocent amusement by shouting 'Go away' and 'Come here' in rapid succession, in both Greek and English, to the complete confusion of the dogs. Another trick, out of which they got endless pleasure, was deluding the poor unfortunate flock of chickens, which spent the day scratching hopefully round the olive groves. Periodically the maid would come to the kitchen door and utter a series of piping noises, interspersed with strange hiccuping cries, which the hens knew was a signal for food, and they would assemble at the back door like magic. As soon as the Magenpies had mastered the chicken-food call they worried the poor hens into a decline. They would wait until the most awkward time before using it – until the hens, with infinite effort and much squawking, had gone to roost in the smaller trees, or, in the heat of the day, when they had all settled down for a pleasant siesta in the shade of the myrtles. No sooner were they drowsing pleasantly than the Magenpies would start the food call, one doing the hiccups while the other did the piping. The hens would all glance nervously round, each waiting for one of the others to show signs of life. The Magenpies would call again, more seductively and urgently. Suddenly, one hen with less self-control than the rest would leap squawking to her feet and bounce towards the Magenpies' cage, and the rest, clucking and flapping, would follow her with all speed. They would rush up to the wire of the cage, barging and squawking, treading on one another's feet, pecking at each other, and then stand in a disorderly, panting crowd looking up into the cage where the Magenpies, sleek and elegant in their black-and-white suits, would stare down at them and chuckle, like a pair of city slickers that have successfully duped a crowd of bumbling and earnest villagers.

The Magenpies liked the dogs, although they seized every opportunity to tease them. They were particularly fond of Roger, and he would frequently go and call on them, lying down close to the wire netting, ears pricked, while the Magenpies sat on the ground inside the cage, three inches away from his nose, and talked to him in soft, wheezy chucks, with an occasional raucous guffaw, as though they were telling him dirty jokes. They never teased Roger as much as they teased the other two, and they never attempted to lure him close to the wire with soft blandishments so that they could flap down and pull his tail, as they frequently did with both Widdle and Puke. On the whole the Magenpies approved of dogs, but they liked them to look *and* behave like dogs; so, when Dodo made her appearance in our midst the Magenpies absolutely refused to believe that she was a dog, and treated her from the beginning with a sort of rowdy, jeering disdain.

Dodo was a breed known as a Dandy Dinmont. They look like long, fat, hair-covered balloons, with minute bow legs, enormous and protuberant eyes, and long flopping ears. Strangely enough it was due to Mother that this curious misshapen breed of dog made its appearance among us. A friend of ours had a pair of these beasts which had suddenly (after years of barrenness) produced a litter of six puppies. The poor man was at his wits' end trying to find good homes for all these offspring, and so Mother, good-naturedly and unthinkingly, said she would have one. She set off one afternoon to choose her puppy and, rather unwisely, selected a female. At the time it did not strike her as impudent to introduce a bitch into a household exclusively populated by very masculine dogs. So, clasping the puppy, like a dimly conscious sausage, under one arm, Mother climbed into the car and drove home in triumph to show the new addition to the family. The puppy, determined to make the occasion a memorable one, was violently and persistently sick from the moment she got in the car to the moment she got out. The family, assembled on the veranda, viewed Mother's prize as it waddled up the path towards them, eyes bulging, minute legs working frantically to keep the long, drooping body in motion, ears flapping wildly, pausing now and then to vomit into a flower bed.

'Oh, isn't he *sweet*?' cried Margo.

'Good God! It looks like a sea-slug,' said Leslie.

'Mother! Really!' said Larry, contemplating Dodo with loathing. 'Where did you dig up that canine Frankenstein?'

'Oh, but he's *sweet*,' repeated Margo. 'What's wrong with him?'

'It's not a him, it's a her,' said Mother, regarding her acquisition proudly; 'she's called Dodo.'

'Well, that's two things wrong with it for a start,' said Larry. 'It's a ghastly name for an animal, and to introduce a bitch into the house with those other three lechers about is asking for trouble. Apart from that, just look at it! Look at the shape! How did it get like that? Did it have an accident, or was it born like that?'

'Don't be silly, dear; it's the breed. They're *meant* to be like that.'

'Nonsense, Mother; it's a monster. Who would want to deliberately produce a thing that shape?'

I pointed out that dachshunds were much the same shape, and they had been bred specially to enable them to get down holes after badgers. Probably the Dandy Dinmont had been bred for a similar reason.

'She looks as though she was bred to go down holes after sewage,' said Larry.

'Don't be disgusting, dear. They're very nice little dogs, and very faithful, apparently.'

'I should imagine they have to be faithful to anyone who shows interest in them; they can't possibly have many admirers in the world.'

'I think you're being very nasty about her, and, anyway, you're in no position to talk about beauty; it's only skin deep after all, and before you go throwing stones you should look for the beam in *your* eye,' said Margo triumphantly.

Larry looked puzzled. 'Is that a proverb, or a quotation from the *Builders' Gazette*?' he inquired.

'I think she means that it's an ill wind that gathers no moss,' said Leslie.

'You make me sick,' said Margo, with dignified scorn.

'Well, join little Dodo in the flower bed.'

'Now, now,' said Mother, 'don't argue about it. It's my dog and I like her, so that's all that matters.'

So Dodo settled in, and almost immediately showed faults in

her make-up which caused us more trouble than all the other dogs put together. To begin with she had a weak hind-leg, and at any time during the day or night her hip joint was liable to come out of its socket, for no apparent reason. Dodo, who was no stoic, would greet this catastrophe with a series of piercing shrieks that worked up to a crescendo of such quivering intensity that it was unbearable. Strangely enough, her leg never seemed to worry her when she went out for walks, or gambolled with elephantine enthusiasm after a ball on the veranda. But invariably in the evening when the family were all sitting quietly, absorbed in writing or reading or knitting, Dodo's leg would suddenly leap out of its socket and she would roll on her back and utter a scream that would make everybody jump and lose control of whatever they were doing. By the time we had massaged her leg back into place Dodo would have screamed herself to exhaustion, and immediately fall into a deep and peaceful sleep, while we would be so unnerved that we would be unable to concentrate on anything for the rest of the evening.

We soon discovered that Dodo had an extremely limited intelligence. There was only room for one idea at a time in her skull, and once it was there Dodo would retain it grimly in spite of all opposition. She decided quite early in her career that Mother belonged to her, but she was not over-possessive at first until one afternoon Mother went off to town to do some shopping and left Dodo behind. Convinced that she would never see Mother again, Dodo went into mourning and waddled, howling sorrowfully, round the house, occasionally being so overcome with grief that her leg would come out of joint. She greeted Mother's return with incredulous joy, but made up her mind that from that moment she would not let Mother out of her sight, for fear she might escape again. So she attached herself to Mother with the tenacity of a limpet, never moving more than a couple of feet away at the most. If Mother sat down, Dodo would lie at her feet; if Mother had to get up and cross the room for a book or a cigarette, Dodo would accompany her, and then they would return together and sit down again, Dodo giving a deep sigh of satisfaction at the thought that once more she had foiled Mother's attempts at escape. She even insisted on being present when Mother had a bath, sitting dolefully by the tub and staring at Mother with embarrassing intensity. Any attempts to leave her outside the bathroom door resulted in Dodo's howling madly and hurling herself at the door-panels, which almost invariably resulted in her hip's slipping out of its socket. She seemed to be under the impression that it was not safe to let Mother go alone into the bathroom, even if she stood guard over the door. There was always the possibility, she seemed to think, that Mother might give her the slip by crawling down the plug-hole.

At first Dodo was regarded with tolerant scorn by Roger, Widdle, and Puke; they did not think much of her, for she was too fat and too low slung to walk far, and if they made any attempts to play with her it seemed to bring on an attack of persecution mania, and Dodo would gallop back to the house, howling for protection. Taken all round they were inclined to consider her a boring and useless addition to the household, until they discovered that she had one superlative and overwhelmingly delightful characteristic: she came into season with monotonous regularity. Dodo herself displayed an innocence about the facts of life that was rather touching. She seemed not only puzzled but positively scared at her sudden bursts of popularity, when her admirers arrived in such numbers that Mother had to go about armed with a massive stick. It was owing to this Victorian innocence that Dodo fell an easy victim to the lure of Puke's magnificent ginger eyebrows, and so met a fate worse than death when Mother inadvertently locked them in the drawing-room together while she supervised the making of tea. The sudden and unexpected arrival of the English padre and his wife, ushering them into the room in which the happy couple were disporting themselves, and the subsequent efforts to maintain a normal conversation, left Mother feeling limp and with a raging headache.

To everyone's surprise (including Dodo's) a puppy was born of this union, a strange, mewling blob of a creature with its mother's figure and its father's unusual liver-and-white markings. To suddenly become a mother like that, Dodo found, was very demoralizing, and she almost had a nervous breakdown, for she was torn between the desire to stay in one spot with her puppy and the urge to keep as close to Mother as possible. We were, however, unaware of this psychological turmoil. Eventually Dodo decided to compromise, so she followed Mother around and carried the puppy in her mouth. She had spent a whole morning doing this before we discovered what she was up to; the unfortunate baby hung from her mouth by its head, its body swinging to and fro as Dodo waddled along at Mother's heels. Scolding and pleading having no effect, Mother was forced to confine herself to the bedroom with Dodo and her puppy, and we carried their meals up on a tray. Even this was not altogether successful, for if Mother moved out of the chair, Dodo, ever alert, would seize her puppy and sit there regarding Mother with starting eyes, ready to give chase if necessary.

'If this goes on much longer that puppy'll grow into a giraffe,' observed Leslie.

'I know, poor little thing,' said Mother; 'but what can I *do*? She picks it up if she sees me lighting a cigarette.'

'Simplest thing would be to drown it,' said Larry. 'It's going to grow into the most horrifying animal, anyway. Look at its parents.'

'No, indeed you won't drown it!' exclaimed Mother indignantly.

'Don't be *horrible*,' said Margo; 'the poor little thing.'

'Well, I think it's a perfectly ridiculous situation, allowing yourself to be chained to a chair by a dog.'

'It's my dog, and if I want to sit here I *shall*,' said Mother firmly.

'But for how long? This might go on for months.'

'I shall think of something,' said Mother with dignity.

The solution to the problem that Mother eventually thought of was simple. She hired the maid's youngest daughter to carry the puppy for Dodo. This arrangement seemed to satisfy Dodo very well, and once more Mother was able to move about the house. She pottered from room to room like some Eastern potentate, Dodo pattering at her heels, and young Sophia bringing up the end of the line, tongue protruding and eyes squinting with the effort, bearing in her arms a large cushion on which reposed Dodo's strange offspring. When Mother was going to be in one spot for any length of time Sophia would place the cushion reverently on the ground, and Dodo would surge onto it and sigh deeply. As soon as Mother was ready to go to another part of the house, Dodo would get off her cushion, shake herself, and take up her position in the cavalcade, while Sophia lifted the cushion aloft as though it carried a crown. Mother would peer over her spectacles to make sure the column was ready, give a little nod, and they would wind their way off to the next job.

Every evening Mother would go for a walk with the dogs, and the family would derive much amusement from watching her progress down the hill. Roger, as senior dog, would lead the procession, followed by Widdle and Puke. Then came Mother, wearing an enormous straw hat, which made her look like an animated mushroom, clutching in one hand a large trowel with which to dig any interesting wild plants she found. Dodo would waddle behind, eyes protruding and tongue flapping, and Sophia would bring up the rear, pacing along solemnly, carrying the imperial puppy on its cushion. Mother's circus, Larry called it, and would irritate her by bellowing out of the window, 'Oi! Lady, wot time does the big top go up, hay?'

He purchased a bottle of hair restorer for her so that, as he explained, she could conduct experiments on Sophia and try to turn her into a bearded lady. 'That's wot your show *needs*, lady,' he assured her in a hoarse voice – 'a bit of clarse, see? Nothing like a bearded lady for bringin' a bit o' clarse to a show.'

But in spite of all this Mother continued to lead her strange caravan off into the olive groves at five o'clock every evening.

Up in the north of the island lay a large lake with the pleasant, jingling name of Antiniotissa, and this place was one of our favourite haunts. It was about a mile long, an elongated sheet of shallow water surrounded by a thick mane of cane and reed, and separated from the sea at one end by a wide, gently curving dune of fine white sand. Theodore always accompanied us when we paid our visits to the lake, for he and I would find a rich field of exploration in the ponds, ditches, and marshy pot-holes that lay around the shore of the lake. Leslie invariably took a battery of guns with him, since the cane forest rustled with game, while Larry insisted on taking an enormous harpoon, and would stand for hours in the stream that marked the lake's entry into the sea, endeavouring to spear the large fish that swam there. Mother would be laden with baskets full of food, empty baskets for plants, and various gardening implements for digging up her finds. Margo was perhaps the most simply equipped, with a bathing-costume, a large towel, and a bottle of sun-tan lotion. With all this equipment our trips to Antiniotissa were something in the nature of major expeditions.

There was, however, a certain time of the year when the lake was at its best, and that was the season of lilies. The smooth curve of the dune that ran between the bay and the lake was the only place on the island where these sand lilies grew, strange, misshapen bulbs buried in the sand, that once a year sent up thick green leaves and white flowers above the surface, so that the dune became a glacier of flowers. We always visited the lake at this time, for the experience was a memorable one. Not long after Dodo had become a mother, Theodore informed us that the time of the lilies was at hand, and we started to make preparations for our trip to Antiniotissa. We soon found that having a nursing mother in our midst was going to complicate matters considerably.

'We'll have to go by boat this time,' Mother said, frowning at a complicated, jigsaw-like jersey she was knitting.

'Why, by boat it takes twice as long,' said Larry.

'We can't go by car, dear, because Dodo will be sick, and anyway there wouldn't be room for all of us.'

'You're *not* going to take that animal, are you?' asked Larry in horror.

'But I have to, dear . . . purl two, cast off one . . . I can't leave her behind . . . purl three . . . you know what she's like.'

'Well, hire a special car for her then. I'm damned if I'm going to drive about the countryside looking as though I've just burgled Battersea Dogs' Home.'

'She can't travel by car. That's what I'm explaining to you. You know she gets car-sick . . . Now be quiet a minute, dear, I'm counting.'

'It's ridiculous . . .' began Larry exasperatedly.

'Seventeen, eighteen, *nineteen, twenty,*' said Mother loudly and fiercely.

'It's ridiculous that we should have to go the longest way round just because Dodo vomits every time she sees a car.'

'There!' said Mother irritably, 'you've made me lose count. I do wish you wouldn't argue with me when I'm knitting.'

'How d'you know she won't be sea-sick?' inquired Leslie interestedly.

'People who are car-sick are never sea-sick,' explained Mother.

'I don't believe it,' said Larry. 'That's an old wives' tale, isn't it, Theodore?'

'Well, I wouldn't like to say,' said Theodore judicially. 'I have heard it before, but whether there's any . . . um . . . you know . . . any *truth* in it, I can't say. All I know is that I have, so far, not felt sick in a car.'

Larry looked at him blankly. 'What does that prove?' he asked, bewildered.

'Well, I am always sick in a boat,' explained Theodore simply.

'That's wonderful!' said Larry. 'If we travel by car Dodo will be sick, and if we travel by boat Theodore will. Take your choice.'

'I didn't know you got sea-sick, Theodore,' said Mother.

'Oh, yes, unfortunately I do. I find it a great drawback.'

'Well, in weather like this the sea will be very calm, so I should think you'll be all right,' said Margo.

'Unfortunately,' said Theodore, rocking on his toes, 'that does not make any difference at all. I suffer from the . . . er . . . *slightest* motion. In fact on several occasions when I have been in the cinema and they have shown films of ships in rough seas I have been forced to . . . um . . . forced to leave my seat.'

'Simplest thing would be to divide up,' said Leslie; 'half go by boat and the other half go by car.'

'That's a brain-wave!' said Mother. 'The problem is solved.'

But it did not settle the problem at all, for we discovered that the road to Antiniotissa was blocked by a minor landslide, and so to get there by car was impossible. We would have to go by sea or not at all.

We set off in a warm pearly dawn that foretold a breathlessly warm day and a calm sea. In order to cope with the family, the dogs, Spiro, and Sophia, we had to take the *Bootle-Bumtrinket* as well as the *Sea Cow*. Having to trail the *Bootle-Bumtrinket*'s rotund shape behind her cut down on the *Sea Cow*'s speed, but it was the only way to do it. At Larry's suggestion the dogs, Sophia, Mother, and Theodore travelled in the *Bootle-Bumtrinket* while the rest of us piled into the *Sea Cow*. Unfortunately Larry had not taken into consideration one important factor: the wash caused by the *Sea Cow*'s passage. The wave curved like a wall of blue glass from her stern and reached its maximum height just as it struck the broad breast of the *Bootle-Bumtrinket*, lifting her up into the air and dropping her down again with a thump. We did not notice the effect the wash was having for some considerable time, for the noise of the engine drowned the frantic cries for help from Mother. When we eventually stopped and let the *Bootle-Bumtrinket* bounce up to us, we found that not only were both Theodore and Dodo ill, but everyone else was as well, including such a hardened and experienced sailor as Roger. We had to get them all into the *Sea Cow* and lay them out in a row, and Spiro, Larry, Margo, and myself took up our positions in the *Bootle-Bumtrinket*. By the time we were nearing Antiniotissa everyone was feeling better, with the exception of Theodore, who still kept as close to the side of the boat as possible, staring hard at his boots and answering questions monosyllabically. We rounded the last headland of red and gold rocks, lying in wavy layers like piles of gigantic fossilized newspapers, or the rusty and mould-covered wreckage of a colossus's library, and the *Sea Cow* and the *Bootle-Bumtrinket* turned into the wide blue bay that lay at the mouth of the lake. The curve of pearl-white sand was backed by the great lily-covered dune behind, a thousand white flowers in the sunshine like a multitude of ivory horns lifting their lips to the sky and producing, instead of music, a rich, heavy scent that was the distilled essence of summer, a warm sweetness that made you breathe deeply time and again in an effort to retain it within you. The engine died away in a final splutter that echoed briefly among the rocks, and then the two boats whispered their way shorewards, and the scent of the lilies came out over the water to greet us.

Having got the equipment ashore and installed it on the white sand, we each wandered off about our own business. Larry and Margo lay in the shallow water half asleep, being rocked by the faint, gentle ripples. Mother led her cavalcade off on a short walk, armed with a trowel and a basket. Spiro, clad only in his underpants and looking like some dark, hairy prehistoric man, waddled into the stream that flowed from the lake to the sea and stood knee deep, scowling down into the transparent waters, a trident held at the ready as the shoals of fish flicked around his feet. Theodore and I drew lots with Leslie as to which side of the lake we should have, and then set off in opposite directions. The boundary marking the half-way mark on the lake shore was a large and particularly misshapen olive. Once we reached there we would turn back and retrace our footsteps, and Leslie would do the same on his side. This cut out the possibility of his shooting us, by mistake, in some dense and confusing cane brake. So, while Theodore and I dipped and pottered among the pools and streamlets, like a pair of eager herons, Leslie strode stockily through the undergrowth on the other side of the lake, and an occasional explosion would echo across to us to mark his progress.

Lunch-time came and we assembled hungrily on the beach, Leslie with a bulging bag of game, hares damp with blood, partridge and quail, snipe and wood pigeons; Theodore and I with our test-tubes and bottles a-shimmer with small life. A fire blazed, the food was piled on the rugs, and the wine was fetched from the sea's edge where it had been put to cool. Larry pulled his corner of the rug up the dune so that he could stretch full-length surrounded by the white trumpets of the lilies. Theodore sat upright and neat, his beard wagging as he chewed his food slowly and methodically. Margo sprawled elegantly in the sun, picking daintily at a pile of fruit and vegetables. Mother and Dodo were installed in the shade of a large umbrella. Leslie squatted on his haunches in the sand, his gun across his thighs, eating a huge hunk of cold meat with one hand and stroking the barrels of the weapon meditatively with the other. Nearby Spiro crouched by the fire, sweat running down his furrowed face and dropping in gleaming drops into the thick pelt of black hair on his chest, as he turned an improvised olive-wood spit, with seven fat snipe on it, over the flames.

'What a heavenly place!' mumbled Larry through a mouthful of food, lying back luxuriously among the shining flowers. 'I feel this place was designed for me. I should like to lie here for ever, having food and wine pressed into my mouth by groups of naked and voluptuous dryads. Eventually, of course, over the centuries, by breathing deeply and evenly I should embalm myself with this scent, and then one day my faithful dryads would find me gone, and only the scent would remain. Will someone throw me one of those *delicious*-looking figs?'

'I read a most interesting book on embalming once,' said Theodore enthusiastically. 'They certainly seemed to go to a great deal of trouble to prepare the bodies in Egypt. I must say I thought the method of . . . er . . . extracting the brain through the nose was *most* ingenious.'

'Dragged them down through the nostrils with a sort of hook arrangement, didn't they?' inquired Larry.

'Larry, dear, not while we're *eating*.'

Lunch being over we drifted into the shade of the nearby olives and drowsed sleepily through the heat of the afternoon, while the sharp, soothing song of the cicadas poured over us. Occasionally one or another of us would rise, wander down to the sea, and flop into the shallows for a minute before coming back, cooled, to resume his siesta. At four o'clock Spiro, who had been stretched out massive and limp, bubbling with snores, regained consciousness with a snort and waddled down the beach to relight the fire for tea. The rest of us awoke slowly, dreamily, stretching and sighing, and drifted down over the sand towards the steaming, chattering kettle. As we crouched with the cups in our hands, blinking and musing, still half asleep, a robin appeared among the lilies and hopped down towards us, his breast glowing, his eyes bright. He paused some ten feet away and surveyed us critically. Deciding that we needed some entertainment, he hopped to where a pair of lilies formed a beautiful arch, posed beneath them theatrically, puffed out his chest, and piped a liquid, warbling song. When he had finished he suddenly ducked his head in what appeared to be a ludicrously conceited bow, and then flipped off through the lilies, frightened by our burst of laughter.

'They *are* dear little things, robins,' said Mother. 'There was one in England that used to spend hours by me when I was gardening. I love the way they puff up their little chests.'

'The way that one bobbed looked exactly as if he was bowing,' said Theodore. 'I must say when he . . . er . . . puffed up his chest he looked very like a rather . . . you know . . . a rather *outsize* opera singer.'

'Yes, singing something rather frothy and light . . . Strauss, I should think,' agreed Larry.

'Talking of operas,' said Theodore, his eyes gleaming, 'did I ever tell you about the last opera we had in Corfu?'

We said no, he hadn't told us, and settled ourselves comfortably, getting almost as much amusement from the sight of Theodore telling the story as from the story itself.

'It was . . . um . . . one of those travelling opera companies, you know. I think it came from Athens, but it may have been Italy. Anyway, their first performance was to be *Tosca*. The singer who took the part of the heroine was exceptionally . . . er . . . *well developed*, as they always seem to be. Well, as you know, in the final act of the opera the heroine casts herself to her doom from the battlements of a fortress – or, rather, a *castle*. On the first night the heroine climbed up onto the castle walls, sang her final song, and then cast herself to her . . . you know . . . her *doom* on the rocks below. Unfortunately it seems that the stage hands had forgotten to put anything beneath the walls for her to *land* on. The result was that the crash of her landing and her subsequent . . . er . . . yells of pain detracted somewhat from the impression that she was a shattered corpse on the rocks far below. The singer who was just bewailing the fact that she was dead had to sing quite . . . er . . . quite *powerfully* in order to drown her cries. The heroine was, rather naturally, somewhat upset by the incident, and so the following night the stage hands threw themselves with enthusiasm into the job of giving her a pleasant landing. The heroine, somewhat battered, managed to hobble her way through the opera until she reached the . . . er . . . final scene. Then she again climbed onto the battlements, sang her last song, and cast herself to her death. Unfortunately the stage hands, having made the landing *too* hard on the first occasion, had gone to the opposite extreme. The huge pile of mattresses and . . . er . . . you know, those springy bed things, was so *resilient* that the heroine hit them and then bounced up again. So while the cast was down at the . . . er . . . what d'you call them? . . . ah, yes, the *footlights*, telling each other she was dead, the upper portions of the heroine reappeared two or three times above the battlements, to the mystification of the audience.'

The robin, who had hopped nearer during the telling of the story, took fright and flew off again as we exploded in a burst of laughter.

'Really, Theodore, I'm sure you spend your spare time making up these stories,' protested Larry.

'No, no,' said Theodore, smiling happily in his beard; 'if it were anywhere else in the world I would have to, but here in Corfu they . . . er . . . anticipate art, as it were.'

Tea over, Theodore and I returned to the lake's edge once more and continued our investigation until it grew too shadowy to see properly; then we walked slowly back to the beach, where the fire Spiro had built pulsed and glowed like an enormous chrysanthemum among the ghostly white lilies. Spiro, having speared three large fish, was roasting them on a grid, absorbed and scowling, putting now a flake of garlic, now a squeeze of lemon-juice or a sprinkle of pepper on the delicate white flesh that showed through where the charred skin was starting to peel off. The moon rose above the mountains, turned the lilies to silver except where the flickering flames illuminated them with a flush of pink. The tiny ripples sped over the moonlit sea and breathed with relief as they reached the shore at last. Owls started to chime in the trees, and in the gloomy shadows fireflies gleamed as they flew, their jade-green, misty lights pulsing on and off.

Eventually, yawning and stretching, we carried our things down to the boats. We rowed out to the mouth of the bay, and then, in the pause while Leslie fiddled with the engine, we looked back at Antiniotissa. The lilies were like a snow-field under the moon, and the dark backcloth of olives was pricked with the lights of fireflies. The fire we had built, stamped and ground underfoot before we left, glowed like a patch of garnets at the edge of the flowers.

'It is certainly a very . . . er . . . *beautiful* place,' said Theodore with immense satisfaction.

'It's a glorious place,' agreed Mother, and then gave it her highest accolade, 'I should like to be buried there.'

The engine stuttered uncertainly, then broke into a deep roar; the *Sea Cow* gathered speed and headed along the coast-line, trailing the *Bootle-Bumtrinket* behind, and beyond that our wash fanned out, white and delicate as a spider's web on the dark water, flaming here and there with a momentary spark of phosphorescence.

17

The Chessboard Fields

Below the villa, between the line of hills on which it stood and the sea, were the Chessboard Fields. The sea curved into the coast in a great, almost landlocked bay, shallow and bright, and on the flat land along its edges lay the intricate pattern of narrow waterways that had once been salt pans in the Venetian days. Each neat little patch of earth, framed with canals, was richly cultivated and green with crops of maize, potatoes, figs, and grapes. These fields, small coloured squares edged with shining waters, lay like a sprawling, multicoloured chessboard on which the peasants' coloured figures moved from place to place.

This was one of my favourite areas for hunting in, for the tiny waterways and the lush undergrowth harboured a multitude of creatures. It was easy to get lost there, for if you were enthusiastically chasing a butterfly and crossed the wrong little wooden bridge from one island to the next you could find yourself wandering to and fro, trying to get your bearings in a bewildering maze of fig-trees, reeds, and curtains of tall maize. Most of the fields belonged to friends of mine, peasant families who lived up in the hills, and so when I was walking there I was always sure of being able to rest and gossip over a bunch of grapes with some acquaintance, or to receive interesting items of news, such as the fact that there was a lark's nest under the melon plants on Georgio's land. If you walked straight across the chessboard without being distracted by friends, side-tracked by terrapins sliding down the mud banks and plopping into the water, or the sudden crackling buzz of a dragon-fly swooping past, you eventually came to the spot where all the channels widened and vanished into a great flat acreage of sand, moulded into endless neat pleats by the previous night's tides. Here long winding chains of flotsam marked the sea's slow retreat, fascinating chains full of coloured seaweed, dead pipe-fish, fishing-net corks that looked good enough to eat – like lumps of rich fruit cake – bits of bottle-glass emeried and carved into translucent jewels by the tide and the sand, shells as spiky as hedgehogs, others smooth, oval, and delicate pink, like the finger-nails of some drowned goddess. This was the sea-birds' country: snipe, oyster-catcher, dunlin, and terns strewn in small pattering groups at the edge of the sea, where the long ripples ran towards the land and broke in long curving ruffs round the little humps of sand. Here, if you felt hungry, you could wade out into the shallows and catch fat, transparent shrimps that tasted as sweet as grapes when eaten raw, or you could dig down with your toes until you found the ribbed, nutlike cockles. Two of these, placed end to end, hinge to hinge, and then twisted sharply in opposite directions, opened each other neatly; the contents, though slightly rubbery, were milky and delicious to eat.

One afternoon, having nothing better to do, I decided to take the dogs and visit the fields. I would make yet another attempt to catch Old Plop, cut across to the sea for a feed of cockles and a swim, and make my way home via Petro's land so that I could sit and exchange gossip with him over a watermelon or a few plump pomegranates. Old Plop was a large and ancient terrapin that lived in one of the canals. I had been trying to capture him for a month or more, but in spite of his age he was very wily and quick, and no matter how cautiously I stalked him when he lay asleep on the muddy bank, he would always wake up at the crucial moment, his legs would flail frantically, and he would slide down the mud slope and plop into the water like a corpulent lifeboat being launched. I had caught a great many terrapins, of course, both the black ones with the thick freckling of golden pin-head spots on them, and the slim grey ones with fawny-cream lines; but Old Plop was something I had set my heart on. He was bigger than any terrapin I had seen, and so old that his battered shell and wrinkled skin had become completely black, losing any markings they may have had in his distant youth. I was determined to possess him, and as I had left him alone for a whole week I thought it was high time to launch another attack.

With my bag of bottles and boxes, my net, and a basket to put Old Plop in should I catch him, I set off down the hill with the dogs. The Magenpies called 'Gerry! . . . Gerry! . . . Gerry!' after me in tones of agonized entreaty, and then, finding I did not turn, they fell to jeering and cackling and making rude noises. Their harsh voices faded as we entered the olive groves, and were then obliterated by the choir of cicadas whose song made the air tremble. We made our way along the road, hot, white, and as soft as a powder-puff underfoot. I paused at Yani's well for a drink, and then leaned over the rough sty made from olive branches in which the two pigs lived, wallowing with sonorous content in a sea of glutinous mud. Having sniffed deeply and appreciatively at them, and slapped the largest on his grubby, quivering behind, I continued down the road. At the next bend I had a brisk argument with two fat peasant ladies, balancing baskets of fruit on their heads, who were wildly indignant at Widdle. He had crept up on them when they were engrossed in conversation and after sniffing at them had lived up to his name over their skirts and legs. The argument as to whose fault it was kept all of us happily occupied for ten minutes, and was then continued as I walked on down the road, until we were separated by such a distance that we could no longer hear and appreciate each other's insults.

Cutting across the first three fields, I paused for a moment in Taki's patch to sample his grapes. He wasn't there, but I knew he wouldn't mind. The grapes were the small fat variety, with a sweet, musky flavour. When you squeezed them the entire contents, soft and seedless, shot into your mouth, leaving the flaccid skin between your finger and thumb. The dogs and I ate four bunches and I put another two bunches in my collecting bag for future reference, after which we followed the edge of the canal towards the place where Old Plop had his favourite mud slide. As we were drawing near to this spot, I was just about to caution the dogs on the need for absolute silence when a large green lizard flashed out of a wheat-patch and scuttled away. The dogs, barking wildly, galloped in eager pursuit. By the time I reached Old Plop's mud slide there was only a series of gently expanding ripples on the water to tell me that he had been present. I sat down and waited for the dogs to rejoin me, running through in my mind the rich and colourful insults with which I would bombard them. But to my surprise they did not come back. Their yelping in the distance died away, there was a pause, and then they started to bark in a chorus – monotonous, evenly spaced barks that meant they had found something. Wondering what it could be I hurried after them.

They were clustered in a half-circle round a clump of grass at the water's edge, and came gambolling to meet me, tails thrashing, whining with excitement, Roger lifting his upper lip in a pleased grin because I had come to examine their find. At first I could not see what it was they were so excited over; then what I had taken to be a rootlet moved, and I was looking at a pair of fat brown water-snakes, coiled passionately together in the grass, regarding me with impersonal silvery eyes from their spade-shaped heads. This was a thrilling find, and one that almost compensated for the loss of Old Plop. I had long wanted to catch one of these snakes, but they were such fast and skilful swimmers that I had never succeeded in getting close enough to accomplish a capture. Now the dogs had found this fine pair, lying in the sun – there for the taking, as it were.

The dogs, having done their duty by finding these creatures and leading me to them, now retreated to a safe distance (for they did not trust reptiles) and sat watching me interestedly. Slowly I manoeuvred my butterfly net round until I could unscrew the handle; having done this, I had a stick with which to do the catching, but the problem was *how* to catch two snakes with one stick? While I was working this out, one of them decided the thing for me, uncoiling himself unhurriedly and sliding into the water as cleanly as a knife-blade. Thinking that I had lost him, I watched irritably as his undulating length merged with the water reflection. Then, to my delight, I saw a column of mud rise slowly through the water and expand like a rose on the surface; the reptile had buried himself at the bottom, and I knew he would stay there until he thought I had gone. I turned my attention to his mate, pressing her down in the lush grass with the stick; she twisted herself into a complicated knot, and, opening her pink mouth, hissed at me. I grabbed her firmly round the neck between finger and thumb, and she hung limp in my hand while I stroked her handsome white belly, and the brown back where the scales were raised slightly like the surface of a fir-cone. I put her tenderly into the basket, and then prepared to capture the other one. I walked a little way down the bank and stuck the handle of the net into the canal to test the depth, and discovered that about two feet of water lay on a three-foot bed of soft, quivering mud. Since the water was opaque, and the snake was buried in the bottom slush, I thought the simplest method would be to feel for him with my toes (as I did when searching for cockles) and, having located him, to make a quick pounce.

I took off my sandals and lowered myself into the warm water, feeling the liquid mud squeeze up between my toes and stroke up my legs, as soft as ashes. Two great black clouds bloomed about my thighs and drifted across the channel. I made my way towards the spot where my quarry lay hidden, moving my feet slowly and carefully in the shifting curtain of mud. Suddenly, under my foot, I felt the slithering body, and I plunged my arms elbow-deep into the water and grabbed. My fingers closed only on mud which oozed between them and drifted away in turbulent, slow-motion clouds. I was just cursing my ill-luck when the snake shot to the surface a yard away from me, and started to swim sinuously along the surface. With a yell of triumph I flung myself full length on top of him.

There was a confused moment as I sank beneath the dark waters and the silt boiled up into my eyes, ears, and mouth, but I could feel the reptile's body thrashing wildly to and fro, firmly clasped in my left hand, and I glowed with triumph. Gasping and spluttering under my layer of mud, I sat up in the canal and grabbed the snake round the neck before he could recover his wits and bite me; then I spat for a long time, to rid my teeth and lips of the fine, gritty layer which coated them. When I at last rose to my feet and turned to wade ashore I found to my surprise that my audience of dogs had been enlarged by the silent arrival of a man, who was squatting comfortably on his haunches and watching me with a mixture of interest and amusement.

He was a short, stocky individual whose brown face was topped by a thatch of close-cropped fair hair, the colour of tobacco. He had large, very blue eyes that had a pleasant humorous twinkle in them, and crows' feet in the fine skin at the corners. A short, hawk's-beak nose curved over a wide and humorous mouth. He was wearing a blue cotton shirt that was bleached and faded to the colour of a forget-me-not dried by the sun, and old grey flannel trousers. I did not recognize him, and supposed him to be a fisherman from some village farther down the coast. He regarded me gravely as I scrambled up the bank, and then smiled.

'Your health,' he said in a rich, deep voice.

I returned his greeting politely, and then busied myself with the job of trying to get the second snake into the basket without letting the first one escape. I expected him to deliver a lecture to me on the deadliness of the harmless water-snakes and the dangers I ran by handling them, but to my surprise he remained silent, watching with interest while I pushed the writhing reptile into the basket. This done, I washed my hands and produced the grapes I had filched from Taki's fields. The man accepted half the fruit and we sat without talking, sucking the pulp from the grapes with noisy enjoyment. When the last skin had plopped into the canal, the man produced tobacco and rolled a cigarette between his blunt, brown fingers.

'You are a stranger?' he asked, inhaling deeply and with immense satisfaction.

I said that I was English, and that I and my family lived in a villa up in the hills. Then I waited for the inevitable questions as to the sex, number, and age of my family, their work and aspirations, followed by a skilful cross-examination as to why we lived in Corfu. This was the usual peasant way; it was not done unpleasantly, nor with any motive other than friendly interest. They would vouchsafe their own private business to you with great simplicity and frankness, and would be hurt if you did not do the same. But, to my surprise, the man seemed satisfied with my answer, and asked nothing further, but sat there blowing fine streamers of smoke into the sky and staring about him with dreamy blue eyes. With my finger-nail I scraped an attractive pattern in the hardening carapace of grey mud on my thigh, and decided that I would have to go down to the sea and wash both myself and my clothes before returning home. I got to my feet and shouldered my bag and nets; the dogs got to their feet, shook themselves, and yawned. More out of politeness than anything, I asked the man where he was going. It was, after all, peasant etiquette to ask questions. It showed your interest in the person. So far I hadn't asked him anything at all.

'I'm going down to the sea,' he said, gesturing with his cigarette – 'down to my boat . . . Where are you going?'

I said I was making for the sea too, first to wash and secondly to find some cockles to eat.

'I will walk with you,' he said, rising and stretching. 'I have a basketful of cockles in my boat; you may have some of those if you like.'

We walked through the fields in silence, and when we came out onto the sands he pointed at the distant shape of a rowing-boat, lying comfortably on her side, with a frilly skirt of ripples round her stern. As we walked towards her I asked if he was a fisherman, and if so, where he came from.

'I come from here . . . from the hills,' he replied. 'At least, my home is here, but I am now at Vido.'

The reply puzzled me, for Vido was a tiny islet lying off the town of Corfu, and as far as I knew it had no one on it at all except convicts and warders, for it was the local prison island. I pointed this out to him.

'That's right,' he agreed, stooping to pat Roger as he ambled past, 'that's right. I'm a convict.'

I thought he was joking, and glanced at him sharply, but his expression was quite serious. I said I presumed he had just been let out.

'No, no, worse luck,' he smiled. 'I have another two years to do. But I'm a good prisoner, you see. Trustworthy and make no trouble. Any like me, those they feel they can trust, are allowed to make boats and sail home for the week-end, if it's not too far. I've got to be back there first thing Monday morning.'

Once the thing was explained, of course, it was simple. It never even occurred to me that the procedure was unusual. I knew one wasn't allowed home for week-ends from an English prison, but this was Corfu, and in Corfu anything could happen. I was bursting with curiosity to know what his crime had been, and I was just phrasing a tactful inquiry in my mind when we reached the boat, and inside it was something that drove all other thoughts from my head. In the stern, tethered to the seat by one yellow leg, sat an immense black-backed gull, who contemplated me with sneering yellow eyes. I stepped forward eagerly and stretched out my hand to the broad, dark back.

'Be careful . . . watch out; he is a bully, that one!' said the man urgently.

His warning came too late, for I had already placed my hand on the bird's back and was gently running my fingers over the silken feathering. The gull crouched, opened his beak slightly, and the dark iris of his eye contracted with surprise, but he was so taken aback by my audacity that he did nothing.

'Spiridion!' said the man in amazement, 'he must like you; he's never let anyone else touch him without biting.'

I buried my fingers in the crisp white feathers on the bird's neck, and as I scratched gently the gull's head drooped forwards and his yellow eyes became dreamy. I asked the man where he had managed to catch such a magnificent bird.

'I sailed over to Albania in the spring to try to get some hares, and I found him in a nest. He was small then, and fluffy as a lamb. Now he's like a great duck,' the man said, staring pensively at the gull. 'Fat duck, ugly duck, biting duck, aren't you, eh?'

The gull at being thus addressed opened one eye and gave a short, harsh yarp, which may have been repudiation or agreement. The man leaned down and pulled a big basket from under the seat; it was full to the brim with great fat cockles that chinked musically. We sat in the boat and ate the shellfish, and all the time I watched the bird, fascinated by the snow-white breast and head, his long hooked beak and fierce eyes, as yellow as spring crocuses, the broad back and powerful wings, sooty black. From the soles of his great webbed feet to the tip of his beak he was, in my opinion, quite admirable. I swallowed a final cockle, wiped my hands on the side of the boat, and asked the man if he could get a baby gull for me the following spring.

'You want one?' he said in surprise; 'you like them?'

I felt this was understanding my feelings. I would have sold my soul for such a gull.

'Well, have him if you want him,' said the man casually, jerking a thumb at the bird.

I could hardly believe my ears. For someone to possess such a wonderful creature and to offer him as a gift so carelessly was incredible. Didn't he *want* the bird, I asked?

'Yes, I like him,' said the man, looking at the bird meditatively, 'but he eats more than I can catch for him, and he is such a wicked one that he bites everybody; none of the other prisoners or the warders like him. I've tried letting him go, but he *won't* go – he keeps coming back. I was going to take him over to Albania one week-end and leave him there. So if you're sure you want him you can have him.'

Sure I wanted him? It was like being offered an angel. A slightly sardonic-looking angel, it's true, but one with the most magnificent wings. In my excitement I never even stopped to wonder how the family would greet the arrival of a bird the size of a goose with a beak like a razor. In case the man changed his mind I hastily took off my clothes, beat as much of the dried mud off them as possible, and had a quick swim in the shallows. I put on my clothes again, whistled the dogs, and prepared to carry my prize home. The man untied the string, lifted the gull up, and handed him to me; I clasped it under one arm, surprised that such a huge bird should be so feather-light. I thanked the man profusely for his wonderful present.

'He knows his name,' he remarked, clasping the gull's beak between his fingers and waggling it gently. 'I call him Alecko. He'll come when you call.'

Alecko, on hearing his name, paddled his feet wildly and looked up into my face with questioning yellow eyes.

'You'll be wanting some fish for him,' remarked the man. 'I'm going out in the boat tomorrow, about eight. If you like to come we can catch a good lot for him.'

I said that would be fine, and Alecko gave a yarp of agreement. The man leaned against the bows of the boat to push it out, and I suddenly remembered something. As casually as I could I asked him what his name was, and why he was in prison. He smiled charmingly over his shoulder.

'My name's Kosti,' he said, 'Kosti Panopoulos. I killed my wife.'

He leaned against the bows of the boat and heaved; she slid whispering across the sand and into the water, and the little ripples leaped and licked at her stern like excited puppies. Kosti scrambled into the boat and took up the oars.

'Your health,' he called. 'Until tomorrow.'

The oars creaked musically, and the boat skimmed rapidly over the limpid waters. I turned, clasping my precious bird under my arm, and started to trudge back over the sand, towards the chessboard fields.

The walk home took me some time. I decided that I had misjudged Alecko's weight, for he appeared to get heavier and heavier as we progressed. He was a dead weight that sagged lower and lower, until I was forced to jerk him up under my arm again, whereupon he would protest with a vigorous yarp. We were half-way through the fields when I saw a convenient fig tree which would, I thought, provide both shade and sustenance, so I decided to take a rest. While I lay in the long grass and munched figs, Alecko sat nearby as still as though he were carved out of wood, watching the dogs with unblinking eyes. The only sign of life were his irises, which would expand and contract excitedly each time one of the dogs moved.

Presently, rested and refreshed, I suggested to my band that we tackle the last stage of the journey; the dogs rose obediently, but Alecko fluffed out his feathers so that they rustled like dry leaves, and shuddered all over at the thought. Apparently he disapproved of my hawking him around under my arm like an old sack, ruffling his feathers. Now that he had persuaded me to put him down in such a pleasant spot he had no intention of continuing what appeared to him to be a tedious and unnecessary journey. As I stooped to pick him up he snapped his beak, uttered a loud, harsh scream, and lifted his wings above his back in the posture usually adopted by tombstone angels. He glared at me. Why, his look seemed to imply, leave this spot? There was shade, soft grass to sit on, and water nearby; what point was there in leaving it to be humped about the countryside in a manner both uncomfortable and undignified? I pleaded with him for some time, and, as he appeared to have calmed down, I made another attempt to pick him up. This time he left me in no doubt as to his desire to stay where he was. His beak shot out so fast I could not avoid it, and it hit my approaching hand accurately. It was as though I had been slashed by an ice-pick. My knuckles were bruised and aching, and a two-inch gash welled blood in great profusion. Alecko looked so smug and satisfied with this attack that I lost my temper. Grabbing my butterfly net I brought it down skilfully and, to his surprise, enveloped him in its folds. I jumped on him before he could recover from the shock and grabbed his beak in one hand. Then I wrapped my handkerchief round and round his beak and tied it securely in place with a bit of string, after which I took off my shirt and wrapped it round him, so that his flailing wings were pinioned tightly to his body. He lay there, trussed up as though for market, glaring at me and uttering muffled screams of rage. Grimly I picked up my equipment, put him under my arm, and stalked off towards home. Having got the gull, I wasn't going to stand any nonsense about getting him back to the villa. For the rest of the journey Alecko proceeded to produce, uninterruptedly, a series of wild, strangled cries of piercing quality, so by the time we reached the house I was thoroughly angry with him.

I stamped into the drawing-room, put Alecko on the floor, and started to unwrap him, while he accompanied the operation raucously. The noise brought Mother and Margo hurrying in from the kitchen. Alecko, now freed from my shirt, stood in the middle of the room with the handkerchief still tied round his beak and trumpeted furiously.

'What on earth's that?' gasped Mother.

'What an *enormous* bird!' exclaimed Margo. 'What is it, an eagle?'

My family's lack of ornithological knowledge had always been a source of annoyance to me. I explained testily that it was not an eagle but a black-backed gull, and told them how I had got him.

'But, dear, how on earth are we going to *feed* him?' asked Mother. 'Does he eat fish?'

Alecko, I said hopefully, would eat anything. I tried to catch him to remove the handkerchief from his beak, but he was obviously under the impression that I was trying to attack him, so he screamed and trumpeted loudly and ferociously through the handkerchief. This fresh outburst brought Larry and Leslie down from their rooms.

'Who the hell's playing *bagpipes?*' demanded Larry as he swept in.

Alecko paused for a moment, surveyed this newcomer coldly, and, having summed him up, yarped loudly and scornfully.

'My God!' said Larry, backing hastily and bumping into Leslie. 'What the devil's *that?*'

'It's a new bird Gerry's got,' said Margo; 'doesn't it look *fierce?*'

'It's a gull,' said Leslie, peering over Larry's shoulder; 'what a whacking great thing!'

'Nonsense,' said Larry; 'it's an albatross.'

'No, it's a gull.'

'Don't be silly. Whoever saw a gull that size? I tell you it's a bloody great albatross.'

Alecko padded a few paces towards Larry and yarped at him again.

'Call him off,' Larry commanded. 'Gerry, get the damn thing under *control;* it's attacking me.'

'Just stand still. He won't hurt you,' advised Leslie.

'It's all very well for you; you're behind me. Gerry, catch that bird at once, before it does me irreparable damage.'

'Don't shout so, dear; you'll frighten it.'

'I like that! A thing like a roc flapping about on the floor attacking everyone, and you tell me not to frighten it.'

I managed to creep up behind Alecko and grab him; then, amid his deafening protests, I removed the handkerchief from his beak. When I let him go again he shuddered indignantly, and snapped his beak two or three times with a sound like a whip-crack.

'Listen to it!' exclaimed Larry. 'Gnashing its teeth!'

'They haven't got teeth,' observed Leslie.

'Well, it's gnashing *something*. I hope you're not going to let him keep it, Mother? It's obviously a dangerous brute; look at his eyes. Besides, it's unlucky.'

'Why unlucky?' asked Mother, who had a deep interest in superstition.

'It's a well-known thing. Even if you have just the *feathers* in the house everyone goes down with plague, or goes mad or something.'

'That's peacocks you're thinking of, dear.'

'No, I tell you it's albatrosses. It's well known.'

'No, dear, it's peacocks that are unlucky.'

'Well, anyway, we can't have that thing in the house. It would be sheer lunacy. Look what happened to the Ancient Mariner. We'll all have to sleep with crossbows under our pillows.'

'Really, Larry, you do *complicate* things,' said Mother. 'It seems quite tame to me.'

'You wait until you wake up one morning and find you've had your eyes gouged out.'

'What nonsense you talk, dear. It looks quite harmless.'

At this moment Dodo, who always took a little while to catch up with rapidly moving events, noticed Alecko for the first time. Breathing heavily, her eyes protruding with interest, she waddled forward and sniffed at him. Alecko's beak flashed out, and if Dodo had not turned her head at that moment – in response to my cry of alarm – her nose would have been neatly sliced off; as it was she received a glancing blow on the side of the head that surprised her so much that her leg leaped out of joint. She threw back her head and let forth a piercing yell. Alecko, evidently under the impression that it was a sort of vocal contest, did his best to out-scream Dodo, and flapped his wings so vigorously that he blew out the nearest lamp.

'There you are,' said Larry in triumph. 'What did I say? Hasn't been in the house five minutes and it kills the dog.'

Mother and Margo massaged Dodo back to silence, and Alecko sat and watched the operation with interest. He clicked his beak sharply, as if astonished at the frailty of the dog tribe, decorated the floor lavishly, and wagged his tail with the swagger of one who had done something clever.

'How nice!' said Larry. 'Now we're expected to wade about the house waist deep in guano.'

'Hadn't you better take him outside, dear?' suggested Mother. 'Where are you going to keep him?'

I said that I had thought of dividing the Magenpies' cage and keeping Alecko there. Mother said this was a very good idea. Until his cage was ready I tethered him on the veranda, warning each member of the family in turn as to his whereabouts.

'Well,' observed Larry as we sat over dinner, 'don't blame *me* if the house is hit by a cyclone. I've warned you; I can do no more.'

'Why a cyclone, dear?'

'Albatrosses always bring bad weather with them.'

'It's the first time I've heard a cyclone described as bad weather,' observed Leslie.

'But it's *peacocks* that are unlucky, dear, I keep telling you,' Mother said plaintively. 'I know, because an aunt of mine had some of the tail-feathers in the house and the cook died.'

'My dear Mother, the albatross is world famous as a bird of ill-omen. Hardened old salts are known to go white and faint when they see one. I tell you, we'll find the chimney covered with Saint Elmo's fire one night, and before we know where we are we'll be drowned in our beds by a tidal wave.'

'You said it would be a cyclone,' Margo pointed out.

'A cyclone *and* a tidal wave,' said Larry, 'with probably a touch of earthquake and one or two volcanic eruptions thrown in. It's tempting Providence to keep that beast.'

'Where did you get him, anyway?' Leslie asked me.

I explained about my meeting with Kosti (omitting any mention of the water-snakes, for all snakes were taboo with Leslie) and how he had given me the bird.

'Nobody in their right senses would give somebody a present like that,' observed Larry. 'Who is this man, anyway?'

Without thinking, I said he was a convict.

'A *convict?*' quavered Mother. 'What d'you mean, a convict?'

I explained about Kosti's being allowed home for the weekends, because he was a trusted member of the Vido community. I added that he and I were going fishing the next morning.

'I don't know whether it's very wise, dear,' Mother said doubtfully. 'I don't like the idea of your going about with a convict. You never know what he's done.'

Indignantly, I said I knew perfectly well what he'd done. He killed his wife.

'A *murderer?*' said Mother, aghast. 'But what's he doing wandering round the countryside? Why didn't they hang him?'

'They don't have the death penalty here for anything except bandits,' explained Leslie; 'you get three years for murder and five years if you're caught dynamiting fish.'

'Ridiculous!' said Mother indignantly. 'I've never heard of anything so scandalous.'

'I think it shows a nice sense of the importance of things,' said Larry. 'Whitebait before women.'

'Anyway, I won't have you wandering around with a murderer,' said Mother to me. 'He might cut your throat or something.'

After an hour's arguing and pleading I finally got Mother to agree that I should go fishing with Kosti, providing that Leslie came down and had a look at him first. So the next morning I went fishing with Kosti, and when we returned with enough food to keep Alecko occupied for a couple of days, I asked my friend to come up to the villa, so that Mother could inspect him for herself.

Mother had, after considerable mental effort, managed to commit to memory two or three Greek words. This lack of vocabulary had a restrictive effect on her conversation at the best of times, but when she was faced with the ordeal of exchanging small talk with a murderer she promptly forgot all the Greek she knew. So she had to sit on the veranda, smiling nervously, while Kosti in his faded shirt and tattered pants drank a glass of beer, and while I translated his conversation.

'He seems such a *nice* man,' Mother said, when Kosti had taken his leave; 'he doesn't look a bit like a murderer.'

'What did you think a murderer looked like?' asked Larry – 'someone with a hare lip and a club foot, clutching a bottle marked "Poison" in one hand?'

'Don't be silly, dear; of course not. But I thought he'd look . . . well, you know, a little more *murderous*.'

'You simply can't judge by physical appearance,' Larry pointed out; 'you can only tell by a person's actions. I could have told you he was a murderer at once.'

'How, dear?' asked Mother, very intrigued.

'Elementary,' said Larry with a deprecating sigh. 'No one but a murderer would have thought of giving Gerry that albatross.'

An Entertainment with Animals

The house was humming with activity. Groups of peasants, loaded with baskets of produce and bunches of squawking hens, clustered round the back door. Spiro arrived twice, and sometimes three times, a day, the car piled high with crates of wine, chairs, trestle tables, and boxes of foodstuffs. The Magenpies, infected with the excitement, flapped from one end of their cage to the other, poking their heads through the wire and uttering loud raucous comments on the bustle and activity. In the dining-room Margo lay on the floor, surrounded by huge sheets of brown paper on which she was drawing large and highly coloured murals in chalk; in the drawing-room Leslie was surrounded by huge piles of furniture, and was mathematically working out the number of chairs and tables the house could contain without becoming uninhabitable; in the kitchen Mother (assisted by two shrill peasant girls) moved in an atmosphere like the interior of a volcano, surrounded by clouds of steam, sparkling fires, and the soft bubbling and wheezing of pots; the dogs and I wandered from room to room helping where we could, giving advice and generally making ourselves useful; upstairs in his bedroom Larry slept peacefully. The family was preparing for a party.

As always, we had decided to give the party at a moment's notice, and for no other reason than that we suddenly felt like it. Overflowing with the milk of human kindness, the family had invited everyone they could think of, including people they cordially disliked. Everyone threw themselves into the preparations with enthusiasm. Since it was early September we decided to call it a Christmas party, and, in order that the whole thing should not be too straightforward, we invited our guests to lunch, as well as to tea and dinner. This meant the preparation of a vast quantity of food, and Mother (armed with a pile of dog-eared recipe books) disappeared into the kitchen and stayed there for hours at a time. Even when she did emerge, her spectacles misted with steam, it was almost impossible to conduct a conversation with her that was not confined exclusively to food.

As usual, on the rare occasions when the family were unanimous in their desire to entertain, they started organizing so far in advance, and with such zest, that by the time the day of the festivities dawned they were generally exhausted and irritable. Our parties, needless to say, never went as we envisaged. No matter how we tried there was always some last-minute hitch that switched the points and sent our carefully arranged plans careering off on a completely different track from the one we had anticipated. We had, over the years, become used to this, which is just as well, for otherwise our Christmas party would have been doomed from the outset, for it was almost completely taken over by the animals. It all started, innocently enough, with goldfish.

I had recently captured, with the aid of Kosti, the ancient terrapin I called Old Plop. To have obtained such a regal and interesting addition to my collection of pets made me feel that I should do something to commemorate the event. The best thing would be, I decided, to reorganize my terrapin pond, which was merely an old tin wash-tub. I felt it was far too lowly a hovel for such a creature as Old Plop to inhabit, so I obtained a large, square stone tank (which had once been used as an olive-oil store) and proceeded to furnish it artistically with rocks, water-plants, sand, and shingle. When completed it looked most natural, and the terrapins and water-snakes seemed to approve. However, I was not quite satisfied. The whole thing, though undeniably a remarkable effort, seemed to lack something. After considerable thought I came to the conclusion that what it needed to add the final touch was goldfish. The problem was, where to get them? The nearest place to purchase such a thing would be Athens, but this would be a complicated business, and, moreover, take time. I wanted my pond to be complete for the day of the party. The family were, I knew, too occupied to be able to devote any time to the task of obtaining goldfish, so I took my problem to Spiro. He, after I had described in graphic detail what goldfish were, said that he thought my request was impossible; he had never come across any such fish in Corfu. Anyway, he said he would see what he could do. There was a long period of waiting, during which I thought he had forgotten, and then, the day before the party, he beckoned me into a quiet corner, and looked around to make sure we were not overheard.

'Master Gerrys, I thinks I can gets you them golden fishes,' he rumbled hoarsely. 'Donts says anythings to anyones. You comes into towns with me this evenings, whens I takes your Mothers in to haves her hairs done, and brings somethings to puts them in.'

Thrilled with this news, for Spiro's conspiratorial air lent a pleasant flavour of danger and intrigue to the acquisition of goldfish, I spent the afternoon preparing a can to bring them home in. That evening Spiro was late, and Mother and I had been waiting on the veranda some considerable time before his car came honking and roaring up the drive, and squealed to a halt in front of the villa.

'Gollys, Mrs Durrells, I'm sorrys I'm lates,' he apologized as he helped Mother into the car.

'That's all right, Spiro. We were only afraid that you might have had an accident.'

'Accidents?' said Spiro scornfully. 'I never has accidents. No, it was them piles again.'

'Piles?' said Mother, mystified.

'Yes, I always gets them piles at this times,' said Spiro moodily.

'Shouldn't you see a doctor if they're worrying you?' suggested Mother.

'Doctors?' repeated Spiro, puzzled. 'Whats fors?'

'Well, piles can be dangerous, you know,' Mother pointed out.

'*Dangerous?*'

'Yes, they can be if they're neglected.'

Spiro scowled thoughtfully for a minute. 'I mean them aeroplane piles,' he said at last.

'*Aeroplane* piles?'

'Yes. French I thinks theys are.'

'You mean aeroplane *pilots*.'

'Thats whats I says, piles,' Spiro pointed out indignantly.

It was dusk when we dropped Mother at the hairdressers, and Spiro drove me over to the other side of the town, parking outside some enormous wrought-iron gates. He surged out of the car, glanced around surreptitiously, then lumbered up to the gates and whistled. Presently an ancient and bewhiskered individual appeared out of the bushes, and the two of them held a whispered consultation. Spiro came back to the car.

'Gives me the cans, Master Gerrys, and yous stay heres,' he rumbled. 'I wonts be longs.'

The bewhiskered individual opened the gates, Spiro waddled in, and they both tip-toed off into the bushes. Half an hour later Spiro reappeared, clutching the tin to his massive chest, his shoes squelching, his trouser legs dripping water.

'Theres you ares, Master Gerrys,' he said, thrusting the tin at me. Inside swam five fat and gleaming goldfish.

Immensely pleased, I thanked Spiro profusely.

'Thats all rights,' he said, starting the engine; 'only donts says a things to anyones, eh?'

I asked where it was he had got them; whom did the garden belong to?

'Nevers you minds,' he scowled; 'jus' you keeps thems things hidden, and donts tells a soul about them.'

It was not until some weeks later that, in company with Theodore, I happened to pass the same wrought-iron gates, and

I asked what the place was. He explained that it was the palace in which the Greek King (or any other visiting royalty) stayed when he descended on the island. My admiration for Spiro knew no bounds; to actually burgle a palace and steal goldfish from the King's pond struck me as being a remarkable achievement. It also considerably enhanced the prestige of the fish as far as I was concerned, and gave an added lustre to their fat forms as they drifted casually among the terrapins.

It was on the morning of the party that things really started to happen. To begin with, Mother discovered that Dodo had chosen this day, of all days, to come into season. One of the peasant girls had to be detailed to stand outside the back door with a broom to repel suitors so that Mother could cook uninterruptedly, but even with this precaution there were occasional moments of panic when one of the bolder Romeos found a way into the kitchen via the front of the house.

After breakfast I hurried out to see my goldfish and discovered, to my horror, that two of them had been killed and partially eaten. In my delight at getting the fish, I had forgotten that both terrapins and the water-snakes were partial to a plump fish occasionally. So I was forced to move all the reptiles into kerosene tins until I could think of a solution to the problem. By the time I had cleaned and fed the Magenpies and Alecko I had still thought of no way of being able to keep the fish and reptiles together, and it was nearing lunch-time. The arrival of the first guests was imminent. Moodily I wandered round to my carefully arranged pond, to discover, to my horror, that someone had moved the water-snakes' tin into the full glare of the sun. They lay on the surface of the water so limp and hot that for a moment I thought they were dead; it was obvious that only immediate first aid could save them, and picking up the tin I rushed into the house. Mother was in the kitchen, harassed and absent-minded, trying to divide her attention between the cooking and Dodo's followers.

I explained the plight of the snakes and said that the only thing that would save them was a long, cool immersion in the bath. Could I put them in the bath for an hour or so?

'Well, yes, dear; I suppose that would be all right. Make sure everyone's finished, though, and don't forget to disinfect it, will you?' she said.

I filled the bath with nice cool water and placed the snakes tenderly inside; in a few minutes they showed distinct signs of reviving. Feeling well satisfied, I left them for a good soak, while I went upstairs to change. On coming down again I sauntered out onto the veranda to have a look at the lunch table, which had been put out in the shade of the vine. In the centre of what had been a very attractive floral centrepiece perched the Magenpies, reeling gently from side to side. Cold with dismay I surveyed the table. The cutlery was flung about in a haphazard manner, a layer of butter had been spread over the side plates, and buttery footprints wandered to and fro across the cloth. Pepper and salt had been used to considerable effect to decorate the smeared remains of a bowl of chutney. The water jug had been emptied over everything to give it that final, inimitable Magenpie touch.

There was something decidedly queer about the culprits, I decided; instead of flying away as quickly as possible they remained squatting among the tattered flowers, swaying rhythmically, their eyes bright, uttering tiny chucks of satisfaction to each other. Having gazed at me with rapt attention for a moment, one of them walked very unsteadily across the table, a flower in his beak, lost his balance on the edge of the cloth, and fell heavily to the ground. The other one gave a hoarse cluck of amusement, put his head under his wing, and went to sleep. I was mystified by this unusual behaviour. Then I noticed a smashed bottle of beer on the flagstones. It became obvious that the Magenpies had indulged in a party of their own, and were very drunk. I caught them both quite easily, though the one on the table tried to hide under a butter-bespattered napkin and pretend he was not there. I was just standing with them in my hands, wondering if I could slip them back in their cage and deny all knowledge of the outrage, when Mother appeared carrying a jug of sauce. Caught, as it were, red-handed I had no chance of being believed if I attributed the mess to a sudden gale, or to rats, or any one of the excuses that had occurred to me. The Magenpies and I had to take our medicine.

'Really, dear, you *must* be careful about their cage door. You know what they're like,' Mother said plaintively. 'Never mind, it was an accident. And I suppose they're not really responsible if they're *drunk*.'

On taking the bleary and incapable Magenpies back to their cage I discovered, as I had feared, that Alecko had seized the opportunity to escape as well. I put the Magenpies back in their compartment and gave them a good telling off; they had by now reached the belligerent stage, and attacked my shoe fiercely. Squabbling over who should have the honour of eating the lace, they then attacked each other. I left them flapping round in wild, disorderly circles, making ineffectual stabs with their beaks, and went in search of Alecko. I hunted through the garden and all over the house, but he was nowhere to be seen. I thought he must have flown down to the sea for a quick swim, and felt relieved that he was out of the way.

By this time the first of the guests had arrived, and were drinking on the veranda. I joined them, and was soon deep in a discussion with Theodore; while we were talking, I was surprised to see Leslie appear out of the olive groves, his gun under his arm, carrying a string bag full of snipe, and a large hare. I had forgotten that he had gone out shooting in the hope of getting some early woodcock.

'Ah-ha!' said Theodore with relish, as Leslie vaulted over the veranda rail and showed us his game bag. 'Is that your own hare or is it . . . um . . . a *wig*?'

'Theodore! You pinched that from Lamb!' said Larry accusingly.

'Yes . . . er . . . um . . . I'm afraid I did. But it seemed such a good *opportunity*,' explained Theodore contritely.

Leslie disappeared into the house to change, and Theodore and I resumed our conversation. Mother appeared and seated herself on the wall, Dodo at her feet. Her gracious-hostess act was somewhat marred by the fact that she kept breaking off her conversation to grimace fiercely and brandish a large stick at the panting group of dogs gathered in the front garden. Occasionally an irritable, snarling fight would flare up among Dodo's boy-friends, and whenever this occurred the entire family would turn round and bellow 'Shut up' in menacing tones. This had the effect of making the more nervous of our guests spill their drinks. After every such interruption Mother would smile round brightly and endeavour to steer the conversation back to normal. She had just succeeded in doing this for the third time when all talk was abruptly frozen again by a bellow from inside the house. It sounded like the sort of cry the minotaur would have produced if suffering from toothache.

'Whatever's the matter with Leslie?' asked Mother.

She was not left long in doubt, for he appeared on the veranda clad in nothing but a small towel.

'Gerry,' he roared, his face a deep red with rage. 'Where's that boy?'

'Now, *now*, dear,' said Mother soothingly, 'whatever's the matter?'

'Snakes,' snarled Leslie, making a wild gesture with his hands to indicate extreme length, and then hastily clutching at his slipping towel, 'snakes, that's what's the matter.'

The effect on the guests was interesting. The ones that knew us were following the whole scene with avid interest; the uninitiated wondered if perhaps Leslie was a little touched, and were not sure whether to ignore the whole incident and go on talking, or to leap on him before he attacked someone.

'What *are* you talking about, dear?'

'That bloody *boy's* filled the sodding *bath* full of bleeding *snakes*,' said Leslie, making things quite clear.

'Language, dear, language!' said Mother automatically, adding absently, 'I do wish you'd put some clothes on; you'll catch a chill like that.'

'Damn great things like *hosepipes* . . . It's a wonder I wasn't bitten.'

'Never mind, dear, it's really my fault. I told him to put them there,' Mother apologized, and then added, feeling that the guests needed some explanation, 'they were suffering from sunstroke, poor things.'

'Really, Mother!' exclaimed Larry, 'I think that's carrying things too far.'

'Now don't *you* start, dear,' said Mother firmly; 'it was Leslie who was bathing with the snakes.'

'I don't know why Larry always has to interfere,' Margo remarked bitterly.

'Interfere? I'm not interfering. When Mother conspires with Gerry in filling the bath with snakes I think it's my duty to complain.'

'Oh, shut up,' said Leslie. 'What I want to know is, when's he going to remove the bloody things?'

'I think you're making a lot of fuss about nothing,' said Margo.

'If it has become necessary for us to perform our ablutions in a nest of hamadryads I shall be forced to move,' Larry warned.

'Am I going to get a bath or not?' asked Leslie throatily.

'Why can't you take them out yourself?'

'Only Saint Francis of Assisi would feel really at *home* here . . .'

'Oh, for heaven's sake be quiet!'

'I've got just as much right to air my views—'

'I want a *bath*, that's all. Surely it is not too much to ask—'

'Now, now, dears, don't quarrel,' said Mother. 'Gerry, you'd better go and take the snakes out of the bath. Put them in the basin or somewhere for the moment.'

'No! They've got to go right outside!'

'All right, dear; don't shout.'

Eventually I borrowed a saucepan from the kitchen and put my water-snakes in that. They had, to my delight, recovered completely, and hissed vigorously when I removed them from the bath. On returning to the veranda I was in time to hear Larry holding forth at length to the assembled guests.

'I assure you the house is a death-trap. Every conceivable nook and cranny is stuffed with malignant faunæ waiting to pounce. How I have escaped being maimed for life is beyond me. A simple, innocuous action like lighting a cigarette is fraught with danger. Even the sanctity of my bedroom is not respected. First, I was attacked by a scorpion, a hideous beast that dripped venom and babies all over the place. Then my room was torn asunder by magpies. Now we have snakes in the bath and huge flocks of albatrosses flapping round the house, making noises like defective plumbing.'

'Larry, dear, you do *exaggerate*,' said Mother, smiling vaguely at the guests.

'My dear Mother, if anything I am understating the case. What about the night Quasimodo decided to sleep in my room?'

'That wasn't very dreadful, dear.'

'Well,' said Larry with dignity, 'it may give *you* pleasure to be woken at half-past three in the morning by a pigeon who seems intent on pushing his rectum into your eye . . .'

'Yes, well, we've talked quite enough about animals,' said Mother hurriedly. 'I think lunch is ready, so shall we all sit down?'

'Well, anyway,' said Larry as we moved down the veranda to the table, 'that boy's a menace . . . he's got beasts in his belfry.'

The guests were shown their places, there was a loud scraping as chairs were drawn out, and then everyone sat down and smiled at each other. The next moment two of the guests uttered yells of agony and soared out of their seats, like rockets.

'Oh, dear, *now* what's happened?' asked Mother in agitation.

'It's probably scorpions again,' said Larry, vacating his seat hurriedly.

'Something bit me . . . bit me in the leg!'

'There you are!' exclaimed Larry, looking round triumphantly. '*Exactly* what I said! You'll probably find a brace of bears there.'

The only one not frozen with horror at the thought of some hidden menace lurking round his feet was Theodore, and he gravely bent down, lifted the cloth, and poked his head under the table.

'Ah-ha!' he said interestedly, his voice muffled.

'What is it?' asked Mother.

Theodore reappeared from under the cloth. 'It seems to be some sort of a . . . er . . . some sort of a *bird*. A large black-and-white one.'

'It's that albatross!' said Larry excitedly.

'No, no,' corrected Theodore; 'it's some species of *gull*, I think.'

'Don't move . . . keep quite still, unless you want your legs taken off at the knee!' Larry informed the company.

As a statement calculated to quell alarm it left a lot to be desired. Everybody rose in a body and vacated the table.

From beneath the cloth Alecko gave a long, menacing yarp – whether in dismay at losing his victims or protest at the noise, it was difficult to say.

'Gerry, catch that bird up immediately!' commanded Larry from a safe distance.

'Yes, dear,' Mother agreed. 'You'd better put him back in his cage. He can't stay under there.'

I gently lifted the edge of the cloth, and Alecko, squatting regally under the table, surveyed me with angry yellow eyes. I stretched out a hand towards him, and he lifted his wings and clicked his beak savagely. He was obviously in no mood to be trifled with. I got a napkin and started to try to manœuvre it towards his beak.

'Do you require any assistance, my dear boy?' inquired

Kralefsky, obviously feeling that his reputation as an ornithologist required him to make some sort of offer.

To his obvious relief I refused his help. I explained that Alecko was in a bad mood and would take a little while to catch.

'Well, for heaven's sake hurry up; the soup's getting cold,' snapped Larry irritably. 'Can't you tempt the brute with something? What do they eat?'

'All the nice gulls love a sailor,' observed Theodore with immense satisfaction.

'Oh, Theodore, please!' protested Larry, pained; 'not in moments of crisis.'

'By Jove! It does look savage!' said Kralefsky as I struggled with Alecko.

'It's probably hungry,' said Theodore happily, 'and the sight of us sitting down to eat was gull and wormwood to it.'

'*Theodore!*'

I succeeded at last in getting a grip on Alecko's beak, and I hauled him screaming and flapping out from under the table. I was hot and dishevelled by the time I had pinioned his wings and carried him back to his cage. I left him there, screaming insults and threats at me, and went back to resume my interrupted lunch.

'I remember a very dear friend of mine being molested by a large gull, once,' remarked Kralefsky reminiscently, sipping his soup.

'Really?' said Larry. 'I didn't know they were such depraved birds.'

'He was walking along the cliffs with a lady,' Kralefsky went on without listening to Larry, 'when the bird swooped out of the sky and attacked them. My friend told me he had the greatest difficulty in beating it off with his umbrella. Not an enviable experience, by Jove, eh?'

'Extraordinary!' said Larry.

'What he *should* have done,' Theodore pointed out gravely,

'was to point his umbrella at it and shout, "Stand back or I'll fire."'

'Whatever for?' inquired Kralefsky, very puzzled.

'The gull would have believed him and flown away in terror,' explained Theodore blandly.

'But I don't quite understand . . .' began Kralefsky, frowning.

'You see, they're terribly *gullible* creatures,' said Theodore in triumph.

'Honestly, Theodore, you're like an ancient copy of *Punch*,' groaned Larry.

The glasses clinked, knives and forks clattered, and the wine-bottles glugged as we progressed through the meal. Delicacy after delicacy made its appearance, and after the guests had shown their unanimous approval of each dish Mother would smile deprecatingly. Naturally, the conversation revolved around animals.

'I remember when I was a child being sent to visit one of our numerous elderly and eccentric aunts. She had a bee fetish; she kept vast quantities of them; the garden was overflowing with hundreds of hives humming like telegraph poles. One afternoon she put on an enormous veil and a pair of gloves, locked us all in the cottage for safety, and went out to try to get some honey out of one of the hives. Apparently she didn't stupefy them properly, or whatever it is you do, and when she took the lid off, a sort of waterspout of bees poured out and settled on her. We were watching all this through the window. We didn't know much about bees, so we thought this was the correct procedure, until we saw her flying round the garden making desperate attempts to evade the bees, getting her veil tangled up in the rose bushes. Eventually she reached the cottage and flung herself at the door. We couldn't open it because she had the key. We kept trying to impress this on her, but her screams of agony and the humming of the bees drowned our voices. It was, I believe, Leslie who had the brilliant idea of throwing a bucket of water over her from the bedroom window. Unfortunately in his enthusiasm he threw the bucket as well. To be drenched with cold water and then hit on the head with a large galvanized-iron bucket is irritating enough, but to have to fight off a mass of bees at the same time makes the whole thing extremely trying. When we eventually got her inside she was so swollen as to be almost unrecognizable.' Larry paused in his story and sighed sorrowfully.

'Dreadful, by Jove,' exclaimed Kralefsky, his eyes wide. 'She might have been killed.'

'Yes, she might,' agreed Larry. 'As it was, it completely ruined my holiday.'

'Did she recover?' asked Kralefsky. It was obvious that he was planning a thrilling Infuriated Bee Adventure that he could have with his lady.

'Oh, yes, after a few weeks in hospital,' Larry replied carelessly. 'It didn't seem to put her off bees though. Shortly afterwards a whole flock of them swarmed in the chimney, and in trying to smoke them out she set fire to the cottage. By the time the fire brigade arrived the place was a mere charred shell, surrounded by bees.'

'Dreadful, *dreadful*,' murmured Kralefsky.

Theodore, meticulously buttering a piece of bread, gave a tiny grunt of amusement. He popped the bread into his mouth, chewed it stolidly for a minute or so, swallowed, and wiped his beard carefully on his napkin.

'Talking of fires,' he began, his eyes alight with impish humour, 'did I tell you about the time the Corfu Fire Brigade was modernized? It seems that the chief of the fire service had been to Athens and had been greatly . . . er . . . *impressed* by the new fire-fighting equipment there. He felt it was high time that Corfu got rid of its horse-drawn fire engine and should obtain a new one . . . um . . . preferably a nice, shiny *red* one. There were several other improvements he had thought of as well. He came back here alight with . . . um . . . with *enthusiasm*. The first thing

298

he did was to cut a round hole in the ceiling of the fire station, so that the firemen could slide down a pole in the correct manner. It appears that in his haste to become modernized he forgot the pole, and so the first time they had a *practice* two of the firemen broke their legs.'

'No, Theodore, I refuse to believe that. It couldn't be true.'

'No, no, I assure you it's perfectly true. They brought the men to my laboratory to be x-rayed. Apparently what had happened was that the chief had not explained to the men about the pole, and they thought they had to *jump* down the hole. That was only the beginning. At quite considerable cost an extremely . . . er . . . large fire engine was purchased. The chief insisted on the *biggest* and *best*. Unfortunately it was so big that there was only one way they could drive it through the town – you know how narrow most of the streets are. Quite often you would see it rushing along, its bell clanging like mad, in the *opposite* direction to the fire. Once outside the town, where the roads are somewhat . . . er . . . broader, they could cut round to the fire. The most curious thing, I thought, was the business about the very modern fire alarm the chief had sent for: you know, it was one of those ones where you break the glass and there is a little sort of . . . um . . . telephone inside. Well, there was great argument as to where they should put this. The chief told me that it was a very difficult thing to decide, as they were not sure *where* the fires were going to break out. So, in order to avoid any confusion, they fixed the fire alarm on the *door* of the fire station.'

Theodore paused, rasped his beard with his thumb, and took a sip of wine.

'They had hardly got things organized before they had their first fire. Fortunately I happened to be in the vicinity and could watch the whole thing. The place was a garage, and the flames had got a pretty good hold before the owner had managed to run to the fire station and break the glass on the fire alarm. Then there were angry words exchanged, it seems, because the chief was annoyed at having his fire alarm broken so *soon*. He told the man that he should have knocked on the door; the fire alarm was brand new, and it would take weeks to replace the glass. Eventually the fire engine was wheeled out into the street and the firemen assembled. The chief made a short speech, urging each man to do his . . . um . . . duty. Then they took their places. There was a bit of a fuss about who should have the honour of ringing the bell, but eventually the chief did the job himself. I must say that when the engine *did* arrive it looked very impressive. They all leaped off and bustled about, and looked very efficient. They uncoiled a very large hose, and then a fresh hitch became apparent. No one could find the key which was needed to unlock the back of the engine so that the hose could be attached. The chief said he had given it to Yani, but it was Yani's night off, it seems. After a lot of argument someone was sent running to Yani's house, which was . . . er . . . *fortunately*, not too far away. While they were waiting, the firemen admired the blaze, which by now was quite considerable. The man came back and said that Yani was not at his house, but his wife said he had gone to the fire. A search through the crowd was made and to the chief's indignation they found Yani among the onlookers, the key in his pocket. The chief was very angry, and pointed out that it was *this* sort of thing that created a bad impression. They got the back of the engine open, attached the hose, and turned on the water. By that time, of course, there was hardly any garage left to . . . er . . . *put out.*'

Lunch over, the guests were too bloated with food to do anything except siesta on the veranda, and Kralefsky's attempts to organize a cricket match were greeted with complete lack of enthusiasm. A few of the more energetic of us got Spiro to drive us down for a swim, and we lolled in the sea until it was time to return for tea, another of Mother's gastronomic triumphs. Tottering mounds of hot scones; crisp, paper-thin biscuits; cakes like snowdrifts, oozing jam; cakes dark, rich, and moist, crammed with fruit; brandy snaps brittle as coral and overflowing with honey. Conversation was almost at a standstill; all that could be heard was the gentle tinkle of cups, and the heartfelt sigh of some guest, already stuffed to capacity, accepting another slice of cake. Afterwards we lay about on the veranda in little groups, talking in a desultory, dreamy fashion as the tide of green twilight washed through the olive groves and deepened the shade beneath the vine so that faces became obscured in the shadow.

Presently Spiro, who had been off in the car on some mysterious expedition of his own, came driving through the trees, his horn blaring to warn everything and everyone of his arrival.

'Why *does* Spiro have to shatter the evening calm with that ghastly noise?' inquired Larry in a pained voice.

'I agree, I agree,' murmured Kralefsky sleepily; 'one should have nightingales at this time of day, not motor car horns.'

'I remember being very puzzled,' remarked Theodore's voice out of the shadows, with an undertone of amusement, 'on the first occasion when I drove with Spiro. I can't recall exactly what the conversation was about, but he suddenly remarked to me, "Yes, Doctors, peoples are scarce when I drive through a village." I had a . . . um . . . curious mental picture of villages quite empty of people, and huge piles of corpses by the side of the road. Then Spiro went on, "Yes, when I goes through a village I blows my horns like hells and scares them all to death."'

The car swept round to the front of the house, and the headlight raked along the veranda briefly, showing up the frilly ceiling of misty green vine leaves, the scattered groups of guests talking and laughing, the two peasant girls with their scarlet headscarves, padding softly to and fro, their bare feet scuffing on the flags, laying the table. The car stopped, the sound of the engine died away, and Spiro came waddling up the path, clutching an enormous and apparently heavy brown-paper parcel to his chest.

'Good God! Look!' exclaimed Larry dramatically, pointing a

trembling finger. 'The publishers have returned my manuscript again.'

Spiro, on his way into the house, stopped and scowled over his shoulder.

'Golly, nos, Master Lorrys,' he explained seriously, 'this is thems three turkeys my wifes cooked for your mothers.'

'Ah, then there is still hope,' sighed Larry in exaggerated relief; 'the shock has made me feel quite faint. Let's all go inside and have a drink.'

Inside, the rooms glowed with lamplight, and Margo's brilliantly coloured murals moved gently on the walls as the evening breeze straightened them carefully. Glasses started to titter and chime, corks popped with a sound like stones dropping into a well, the siphons sighed like tired trains. The guests livened up; their eyes gleamed, the talk mounted into a crescendo.

Bored with the party, and being unable to attract Mother's attention, Dodo decided to pay a short visit to the garden by herself. She waddled out into the moonlight and chose a suitable patch beneath the magnolia tree to commune with nature. Suddenly, to her dismay, she was confronted by a pack of bristling, belligerent, and rough-looking dogs who obviously had the worst possible designs on her. With a yell of fright she turned tail and fled back into the house as quickly as her short, fat little legs would permit. But the ardent suitors were not going to give up without a struggle. They had spent a hot and irritating afternoon trying to make Dodo's acquaintance, and they were not going to waste this apparently Heaven-sent opportunity to try to get their relationship with her on a more intimate footing. Dodo galloped into the crowded drawing-room, screaming for help, and hot on her heels came the panting, snarling, barging wave of dogs. Roger, Puke, and Widdle, who had slipped off to the kitchen for a snack, returned with all speed and were horrified by the scene. If anyone was going to seduce Dodo, they felt, it was going to be one of them, not some scrawny village pariah. They hurled themselves with gusto upon Dodo's pursuers, and in a moment the room was a confused mass of fighting, snarling dogs and leaping hysterical guests trying to avoid being bitten.

'It's wolves! . . . It means we're in for a hard winter,' yelled Larry, leaping nimbly onto a chair.

'Keep calm, keep calm!' bellowed Leslie, as he seized a cushion and hurled it at the nearest knot of struggling dogs. The cushion landed and was immediately seized by five angry mouths and torn asunder. A great whirling cloud of feathers gushed up into the air and drifted over the scene.

'Where's Dodo?' quivered Mother. 'Find Dodo; they'll hurt her.'

'Stop them! Stop them! They're killing each other,' shrilled Margo, and seizing a soda siphon she proceeded to spray both guests and dogs with complete impartiality.

'I believe *pepper* is a good thing for dog-fights,' observed Theodore, the feathers settling on his beard like snow, 'though of course I have never tried it *myself*.'

'By Jove!' yelped Kralefsky, 'watch out . . . save the ladies!'

He followed this advice by helping the nearest female onto the sofa and climbing up beside her.

'Water also is considered to be good,' Theodore went on musingly, and as if to test this he poured his glass of wine with meticulous accuracy over a passing dog.

Acting on Theodore's advice, Spiro surged out to the kitchen and returned with a kerosene tin of water clasped in his hamlike hands. He paused in the doorway and raised it above his head. 'Watch outs,' he roared; 'I'll fixes the bastards.'

The guests fled in all directions, but they were not quick enough. The polished, glittering mass of water curved through the air and hit the floor, to burst up again and then curve and break like a tidal wave over the room. It had the most disastrous results as far as the nearest guests were concerned, but it had the most startling and instantaneous effect on the dogs. Frightened by the boom and swish of water, they let go of each other and fled out into the night, leaving behind them a scene of carnage that was breath-taking. The room looked like a hen-roost that had been hit by a cyclone; our friends milled about, damp and feather-encrusted; feathers had settled on the lamps and the acrid smell of burning filled the air.

Mother, clasping Dodo in her arms, surveyed the room. 'Leslie, dear, go and get some towels so that we can dry ourselves. The room *is* in a mess. Never mind, let's all go out onto the veranda, shall we?' she said, and added sweetly, 'I'm so sorry this happened. It's Dodo, you see; she's very *interesting* to the dogs at the moment.'

Eventually the party was dried, the feathers plucked off them, their glasses were filled, and they were installed on the veranda where the moon was stamping the flags with ink-black shadows of the vine leaves. Larry, his mouth full of food, strummed softly on his guitar and hummed indistinctly; through the French windows we could see Leslie and Spiro both scowling with concentration, skilfully dismembering the great brown turkeys; Mother drifted to and fro through the shadows, anxiously asking everyone if they were getting enough to eat; Kralefsky was perched on the veranda wall – his body crablike in silhouette, the moon peering over his hump – telling Margo a long and involved story; Theodore was giving a lecture on the stars to Dr Androuchelli, pointing out the constellations with a half-eaten turkey leg.

Outside, the island was striped and patched in black and silver by moonlight. Far down in the dark cypress trees the owls called to each other comfortingly. The sky looked as black and soft as a mole-skin covered with a delicate dew of stars. The magnolia tree loomed vast over the house, its branches full of white blooms, like a hundred miniature reflections of the moon, and their thick, sweet scent hung over the veranda languorously, the scent that was an enchantment luring you out into the mysterious, moonlit countryside.

The Return

With a gentlemanly honesty which I found hard to forgive, Mr Kralefsky had informed Mother that he had taught me as much as he was able; the time had come, he thought, for me to go to somewhere like England or Switzerland to finish my education. In desperation I argued against any such idea; I said I *liked* being half-educated; you were so much more *surprised* at everything when you were ignorant. But Mother was adamant. We were to return to England and spend a month or so there consolidating our position (which meant arguing with the bank) and then we would decide where I was to continue my studies. In order to quell the angry mutterings of rebellion in the family she told us that we should look upon it merely as a holiday, a pleasant trip. We should soon be back again in Corfu.

So our boxes, bags, and trunks were packed, cages were made for birds and tortoises, and the dogs looked uncomfortable and slightly guilty in their new collars. The last walks were taken among the olives, the last tearful good-byes exchanged with our numerous peasant friends, and then the cars, piled high with our possessions, moved slowly down the drive in procession, looking, as Larry pointed out, rather like the funeral of a successful rag-and-bone merchant.

Our mountain of possessions was arranged in the customs shed, and Mother stood by it jangling an enormous bunch of keys. Outside in the brilliant white sunlight the rest of the family talked with Theodore and Kralefsky, who had come to see us off. The customs officer made his appearance and wilted slightly at the sight of our mound of baggage, crowned with a cage from which the Magenpies peered malevolently. Mother smiled

305

nervously and shook her keys, looking as guilty as a diamond smuggler.

The customs man surveyed Mother and the luggage, tightened his belt, and frowned. 'Theese your?' he inquired, making quite sure.

'Yes, yes, all mine,' twittered Mother, playing a rapid solo on her keys. 'Did you want me to open anything?'

The customs man considered, pursing his lips thoughtfully. 'Hoff yew any noo clooes?' he asked.

'I'm sorry?' said Mother.

'Hoff yew any noo clooes?'

Mother cast a desperate glance round for Spiro. 'I'm so sorry. I didn't quite catch . . .'

'Hoff yew any noo clooes . . . *any noo clooes?*'

Mother smiled with desperate charm. 'I'm sorry I can't quite . . .'

The customs man fixed her with an angry eye.

'Madame,' he said ominously, leaning over the counter, 'do yew spik English?'

'Oh, yes,' exclaimed Mother, delighted at having understood him, 'yes, a *little.*'

She was saved from the wrath of the man by the timely arrival of Spiro. He lumbered in, sweating profusely, soothed Mother, calmed the customs man, explained that we had not had any new clothes for years, and had the luggage shifted outside onto the quay almost before anyone could draw breath. Then he borrowed the customs man's piece of chalk and marked all the baggage himself, so there would be no further confusion.

'Well, I won't say good-bye but only *au revoir*,' mumbled Theodore, shaking hands precisely with each of us. 'I hope we shall have you back with us . . . um . . . *very soon.*'

'Good-bye, good-bye,' fluted Kralefsky, bobbing from one person to the other. 'We shall so look forward to your return. By Jove, yes! And have a good time, make the most of your stay in old England. Make it a *real* holiday, eh? That's the ticket!'

Spiro shook each of us silently by the hand, and then stood staring at us, his face screwed up into the familiar scowl, twisting his cap in his huge hands.

'Wells, I'll says good-byes,' he began and his voice wavered and broke, great fat tears squeezing themselves from his eyes and running down his furrowed cheeks. 'Honest to Gods, I didn't means to cry,' he sobbed, his vast stomach heaving, 'but it's just likes saying goods-bye to my own peoples. I feels you belongs to me.'

The tender had to wait patiently while we comforted him. Then, as its engine throbbed and it drew away across the dark blue water, our three friends stood out against the multicoloured background, the tottering houses sprawled up the hillside, Theodore neat and erect, his stick raised in grave salute, his beard twinkling in the sun; Kralefsky bobbing and ducking and waving extravagantly; Spiro, barrel-bodied and scowling, alternately wiping his eyes with his handkerchief and waving it to us.

As the ship drew across the sea and Corfu sank shimmering into a pearly heat haze on the horizon a black depression settled on us, which lasted all the way back to England. The grimy train scuttled its way up from Brindisi towards Switzerland, and we sat in silence, not wishing to talk. Above our heads, on the rack, the finches sang in their cages, the Magenpies chucked and hammered with their beaks, and Alecko gave a mournful yarp at intervals. Around our feet the dogs lay snoring. At the Swiss frontier our passports were examined by a disgracefully efficient official. He handed them back to Mother, together with a small slip of paper, bowed unsmilingly, and left us to our gloom. Some moments later Mother glanced at the form the official had filled in, and as she read it, she stiffened.

'Just look what he's put,' she exclaimed indignantly, '*impertinent* man.'

Larry stared at the little form and snorted. 'Well, that's the penalty you pay for leaving Corfu,' he pointed out.

On the little card, in the column headed *Description of Passengers* had been written, in neat capitals: ONE TRAVELLING CIRCUS AND STAFF.

'What a thing to write,' said Mother, still simmering. 'Really, some people are *peculiar*.'

The train rattled towards England.

Birds, Beasts, and Relatives

Contents

Conversation

It had been a hard winter, and even when spring was supposed to have taken over, the crocuses – which seemed to have a touching and unshaken faith in the seasons – were having to push their way grimly through a thin crust of snow. The sky was low and grey, liable to discharge another fall of snow at any minute, and a biting wind howled round the house. Taken altogether, weather conditions were not ideal for a family reunion, particularly when it was my family.

It was a pity, I felt, that when they had all forgathered in England for the first time since World War II, they should be treated to something approaching a blizzard. It did not bring out the best in them; it made them more touchy than usual, quicker to take offence, and less likely to lend a sympathetic ear to anyone's point of view but their own.

They were grouped, like a pride of moody lions, round a fire so large and flamboyant that there was immediate danger of its setting fire to the chimney. My sister Margo had just added to it by the simple method of dragging in the carcass of a small tree from the garden and pushing one end into the fireplace, while the remainder of the trunk lay across the hearth-rug. My mother was knitting, but you could tell by the slightly vacant look on her face and the way her lips moved occasionally, as if she were in silent prayer, that she was really occupied with the menu for tomorrow's lunch. My brother Leslie was buried behind a large manual on ballistics, while my elder brother Lawrence, clad in a roll-top pullover of the type usually worn by fishermen (several sizes too large for him), was standing by the window sneezing wetly and regularly into a large scarlet handkerchief.

'Really, this is a *frightful* country,' he said, turning on us belligerently, as though we were all directly responsible for the climatic conditions prevailing. 'You set foot on shore at Dover and you're met by a positive barrage of cold germs . . . D'you realize that this is the first cold I've had in twelve years? Simply because I had the sense to keep away from Pudding Island. Everyone I've met so far has a cold. The entire population of the British Isles seems to do absolutely nothing from one year's end to another except shuffle round in small circles sneezing voluptuously into each other's faces . . . a sort of merry-go-round of reinfection. What chance of survival has one got?'

'Just because *you've* got a cold you carry on as though the world was coming to an end,' said Margo. 'I can't understand why men always make such a fuss.'

Larry gave her a withering look from watering eyes. 'The trouble with you all is that you like being martyrs. No one free from masochistic tendencies would stay in this – this virus's paradise. You've all stagnated; you *like* wallowing here in a sea of infection. One excuses people who have never known anything else, but you all had a taste of the sun in Greece; you should know better.'

'Yes, dear,' said Mother soothingly, 'but you've just come at a bad time. It can be very nice, you know. In the spring, for example.'

Larry glared at her. 'I hate to jolt you out of your Rip Van Winkle-like trance,' he said, 'but this is supposed to *be* the spring . . . and look at it! You need a team of huskies to go down to post a letter.'

'Half an inch of snow,' snorted Margo. 'You do exaggerate.'

'I agree with Larry,' Leslie said, appearing from behind his book suddenly. 'It's bloody cold out. Makes you feel you don't want to do anything. You can't even get any decent shooting.'

'Exactly,' said Larry triumphantly, 'while in a sensible country like Greece one would be having breakfast outside and then going down to the sea for a morning bathe. Here my teeth chatter so much it's only with difficulty that I can eat any breakfast.'

'I do wish you'd stop harping on Greece,' said Leslie. 'It reminds me of that bloody book of Gerry's. It took me ages to live that down.'

'Took *you* ages?' said Larry caustically. 'What about me? You've no idea what damage that Dickens-like caricature did to my literary image.'

'But the way he wrote about me, you would think I never thought about anything but guns and boats,' said Leslie.

'Well, you never do think about anything but guns and boats.'

'I was the one that suffered most,' said Margo. 'He did nothing but talk about my acne.'

'I thought it was quite an accurate picture of you all,' said Mother, 'but he made me out to be a *positive imbecile.*'

'I wouldn't mind being lampooned in decent prose,' Larry pointed out, blowing his nose vigorously, 'but to be lampooned in bad English is unbearable.'

'The title alone is insulting,' said Margo. '*My Family and Other Animals*! I get sick of people saying, "And which other animal are you?"'

'I thought the title was rather funny, dear,' said Mother. 'The only thing I thought was that he hadn't used all the best stories.'

'Yes, I agree,' said Leslie.

'What best stories?' Larry demanded suspiciously.

'Well, what about the time you sailed Max's yacht round the island? That was damned funny.'

'If that story had appeared in print I would have sued him.'

'I don't see why, it was very funny,' said Margo.

'And what about the time you took up spiritualism – supposing he'd written about that? I suppose you'd enjoy *that*?' inquired Larry caustically.

'No, I would not – he couldn't write that,' said Margo in horror.

'Well, there you are,' said Larry in triumph. 'And what about Leslie's court case?'

'I don't see why you have to bring me into it,' said Leslie.

'You were the one who was going on about him not using the best incidents,' Larry pointed out.

'Yes, I'd forgotten about those stories,' said Mother, chuckling. 'I think they were funnier than the ones you used, Gerry.'

'I'm glad you think that,' I said thoughtfully.

'Why?' asked Larry, glaring at me.

'Because I've decided to write another book on Corfu and use all those stories,' I explained innocently.

The uproar was immediate.

'I forbid it,' roared Larry, sneezing violently. 'I absolutely forbid it.'

'You're not to write about my spiritualism,' Margo cried out. 'Mother, tell him he's not to write about that.'

'Nor my court case,' snarled Leslie. 'I won't have it.'

'And if you so much as mention yachts . . .' Larry began.

'Larry dear, do keep your voice down,' said Mother.

'Well, forbid him to write a sequel then,' shouted Larry.

'Don't be silly, dear, I can't stop him,' said Mother.

'Do you want it all to happen again?' demanded Larry hoarsely. 'The bank writing to ask if you will kindly remove your overdraft, the tradesmen looking at you askance, anonymous parcels full of strait-jackets being left on the doorstep, being cut dead by all the relatives. You are supposed to be head of the family – stop him writing it.'

'You do exaggerate, Larry dear,' said Mother. 'Anyway, I can't stop him if he wants to write it. I don't think it will do any harm and those stories are the best ones, I think. I don't see why he shouldn't write a sequel.'

The family rose in a body and told her loudly and vociferously why I should not write a sequel. I waited for the noise to die down.

'And apart from those stories, there are quite a number of others,' I said.

'Which ones, dear?' inquired Mother.

The family, red-faced, bristling, glowered at me in an expectant silence.

'Well,' I said thoughtfully, 'I want to give a description of your love affair with Captain Creech, Mother.'

'What?' squeaked Mother. 'You'll do no such thing . . . love affair with that disgusting old creature, indeed. I won't have you writing about *that*.'

'Well, I think that's the best story of the lot,' said Larry unctuously, 'the vibrant passion of the romance, the sweet, archaic charm of the leading man . . . the way you led the poor old chap on . . .'

'Oh, do be quiet, Larry,' said Mother crossly. 'You do make me angry when you talk like that. I don't think it's a good idea for you to write this book, Gerry.'

'I second that,' said Larry. 'If you publish we'll sue you in a body.'

Faced with such a firm and united family, bristling in their resolve to prevent me at all costs, there was only one thing I could do. I sat down and wrote this book.

Writing something of this sort presents many pitfalls for the author. His new readers do not want to be constantly irritated by references to a previous book that they have not read, and the ones who have read the previous book do not want to be irritated by constant repetition of events with which they are familiar. I hope that I have managed to steer a fairly steady course between the two.

PART ONE

Perama

*Here great trees cool-shaded grow, pear, pomegranate, rich apple,
honey-sweet fig and blossoming olive, forever bearing fruit, winter and
summer never stripped, but everblowing the western wind brings fruit
to birth and ripens others. Pear follows pear, apple after apple grows,
fig after fig, and grape yields grape again.*

– Homer

PART THREE

Epilogue

I

The Christening

The island lies off the Albanian and Greek coast-lines like a long, rust-eroded scimitar. The hilt of the scimitar is the mountain region of the island, for the most part barren and stony, with towering rock cliffs haunted by blue rock-thrushes and peregrine falcons. In the valleys in this mountain region, however, where water gushes plentifully from the red-and-gold rocks, you get forests of almond and walnut trees, casting shade as cool as a well, thick battalions of spear-like cypress and silver-trunked fig trees with leaves as large as a salver. The blade of the scimitar is made up of rolling greeny-silver eiderdowns of giant olive trees, some reputedly over five hundred years old and each one unique in its hunched, arthritic shape, its trunk pitted with a hundred holes like pumice-stone. Towards the tip of the blade you have Lefkimi, with its twinkling, eye-aching sand dunes and great salt marshes, decorated with acres of bamboos that creak and rustle and whisper to each other surreptitiously. The island is called Corfu.

That August, when we arrived, the island lay breathless and sun-drugged in a smouldering, peacock-blue sea under a sky that had been faded to a pale powder-blue by the fierce rays of the sun. Our reasons for packing up and leaving the gloomy shores of England were somewhat nebulous, but based loosely on the fact that we were tired of the drab suburbanness of life in England and its accompanying bleak and unpleasant climate. So we had fled to Corfu, hoping that the sunshine of Greece would cure us of the mental and physical inertia which so long a sojourn in England had brought about. Very soon after we had landed, we had acquired our first villa and our first friend on the island.

The friend was Spiro, a waddling, barrel-shaped man with huge powerful hands and a brown, leathery, scowling face. He had perfected an odd but adequate command over English and he possessed an ancient Dodge which he used as a taxi. We soon found that Spiro, like most of the Corfu characters, was unique. There seemed to be no one that he did not know and nothing that he could not obtain or get done for you. Even the most bizarre requests from the family would be met by him with the remark, 'Don'ts yous worries about thats. I'll fixes thats.' And fix it he would. His first major piece of fixing was the acquisition of our villa, for Mother had been insistent that we must have a bathroom, and this very necessary adjunct of wholesome living was in short supply in Corfu. But, needless to say, Spiro knew of a villa with a bath, and very soon, after much shouting and roaring, gesticulation, sweating, and waddling to and fro carrying armfuls of our goods and chattels, Spiro had us safely installed. From that moment he ceased to be merely a taxi driver that we hired and became our guide, philosopher, and friend.

The villa that Spiro had found was shaped not unlike a brick and was a bright crushed-strawberry pink with green shutters. It crouched in a cathedral-like grove of olives that sloped down the hillside to the sea, and it was surrounded by a pocket-handkerchief-size garden, the flower-beds laid out with a geometrical accuracy so dear to the Victorians, and the whole thing guarded by a tall, thick hedge of fuchsias that rustled mysteriously with birds. Coming, as we had done, from a number of years' torture in the cold grey of England, the sunshine and the brilliant colours and scents it evoked acted on us all like a heady draught of wine.

It affected each member of the family in a different way. Larry wandered about in a sort of daze, periodically quoting long stanzas of poetry to Mother, who either did not listen or else said, 'Very nice, dear,' absently. She, entranced by the variety of fruit and vegetables available, spent most of her time closeted in the kitchen preparing complicated and delicious menus for every meal. Margo, convinced that the sunshine would do for her acne what all the pills and potions of the medical profession had so far failed to do, sun-bathed with strenuous earnestness in the olive groves and in consequence got herself badly burned. Leslie discovered, to his delight, that one could purchase lethal weapons without a permit in Greece and so he kept disappearing into town and reappearing carrying a variety of fowling pieces ranging from ancient Turkish muzzle-loaders to revolvers and shot guns. As he insisted on practising with each new acquisition, our nerves became somewhat frayed, and as Larry remarked somewhat bitterly, it was rather like living in a villa surrounded by revolutionary forces.

The garden, for long untended, was an overgrown riot of uninhibited flowers and weeds in which whirled, squeaked, rustled, and jumped a multi-coloured merry-go-round of insect life, and so it was the garden that held my immediate attention.

However luxurious our various gardens had been in England, they had never provided me with such an assortment of living creatures. I found myself prey to the most curious sensation of unreality. It was rather like being born for the first time. In that brilliant, brittle light I could appreciate the true huntsman's-red of a lady-bird's wing case, the magnificent chocolate and amber of an earwig, and the deep shining agate of the ants. Then I could feast my eyes on a bewildering number of creatures unfamiliar to me: the great, furry carpenter-bees, which prowled like electric-blue teddy bears, humming to themselves, from flower to flower; the sulphur-yellow, black-striped swallow-tailed butterflies, with their elegant cut-away coats, that pirouetted up and down the fuchsia hedge doing complicated minuets with each other; and the humming-bird hawk-moths that hung, stationary, suspended by a blur of wings, in front of the flowers, while they probed each bloom with their long, delicate proboscises.

I was exceedingly ignorant as to even the simplest facts about these creatures and I had no books to guide me. All I could do was to watch them as they went about their business in the garden or capture them so that I could study them more carefully at first hand. Very soon my bedroom was filled with a battalion of jam jars and biscuit tins containing the prizes that I had found in our tiny garden. These had to be smuggled surreptitiously into the house, for the family, with the possible exception of Mother, viewed the introduction of this fauna into the villa with considerable alarm.

Each brilliant day brought some new puzzles of behaviour to underline my ignorance. One of the creatures that intrigued and irritated me most was the dung-beetle. I would lie on my stomach with Roger, my dog, squatting like a mountain of black curls, panting, by my side, watching two shiny black dung-beetles, each with a delicately curved rhino horn on its head, rolling between them (with immense dedication) a beautifully shaped ball of cow dung. To begin with I wanted to know how they managed to make the ball so completely and beautifully round. I knew from my own experiments with clay and Plasticine that it was extremely difficult to get a completely round ball, however hard you rubbed and manipulated the material, yet the dung-beetles, with only their spiky legs as instruments, devoid of calipers or any other aid, managed to produce these lovely balls of dung, as round as the moon. Then there was the second problem. Why had they made it and where were they taking it?

I solved this problem, or part of it, by devoting one entire morning to a pair of dung-beetles, refusing to be deviated from my task by the other insects in the garden or by the faint moans and yawns of boredom that came from Roger. Slowly, on all fours, I followed them foot by laborious foot across the garden, which was so small to me and yet such a vast world to the beetles. Eventually they came to a small hummock of soft earth under the fuchsia hedge. Rolling the ball of dung uphill was a mammoth task, and several times the beetles' foot-work was at fault and the ball would break away and roll back to the bottom of the little incline, the beetles hurrying after it and, I liked to imagine, shouting abuse at each other. Eventually, however, they got it to the top of the rise and started down the opposite slope. At the bottom of the slope, I noticed for the first time, was a round hole like a well, which had been sunk into the earth, and it was for this that the beetles were heading. When they were within a couple of inches of the hole, one of the beetles hurried ahead and backed into the hole where he sat, gesticulating wildly with his front legs, while the other beetle, with a considerable effort (I could almost convince myself that I heard him panting), rolled the ball of dung up to the mouth of the burrow. After a considerable length of time spent in pushing and pulling, the ball slowly disappeared into the depths of the earth and the beetles with it. This annoyed me. After all, they were obviously going to do something with the ball of dung, but if they did it under ground, how could I be expected to see what they did? Hoping for some enlightenment on this problem, I put it to the family at lunch-time. What, I inquired, did dung-beetles do with dung? There was a moment's startled silence.

'Well, I expect they find it useful, dear,' said Mother vaguely.

'I trust you're not hoping to smuggle some into the house?' Larry inquired. 'I refuse to live in a villa whose decor consists of balls of dung all over the floor.'

'No, no, dear, I'm sure he won't,' said Mother peaceably and untruthfully.

'Well, I'm just warning you, that's all,' said Larry. 'As it is, he appears to have all the more dangerous insects out of the garden closeted in his bedroom.'

'They probably want it for warmth,' said Leslie, who had been giving the matter of dung-beetles some thought. 'Very warm stuff, dung. Ferments.'

'Should we, at any time, require central heating,' said Larry, 'I'll bear that in mind.'

'They probably eat it,' said Margo.

'Margo, dear,' said Mother. 'Not while we're having lunch.'

As usual, my family's lack of biological knowledge had let me down.

'What you want to read,' said Larry, absentmindedly helping himself to another plateful of stew, which he had just described to Mother as being lacking in flavour, 'what you want to read is some Fabre.'

I inquired what or who Fabre was, more out of politeness than anything else, because, as the suggestion had come from Larry, I was convinced that Fabre would turn out to be some obscure medieval poet.

'Naturalist,' said Larry, his mouth full, waving his fork at me. 'Wrote about insects and things. I'll try and get you a copy.'

Overwhelmed with such unlooked-for magnanimity on the part of my elder brother, I made a point of being very careful within the next two or three days not to do anything to incur his wrath; but the days passed and no book appeared and eventually I forgot about it and devoted my time to the other insects in the garden.

But the word 'why' pursued and frustrated me on every hand. Why did the carpenter-bees cut out little circular pieces from the rose leaves and fly away with them? Why did the ants conduct what appeared to be passionate love affairs with the massed battalions of green fly that infested many of the plants in the garden? What were the strange, amber, transparent insect corpses or shells that I found sticking to grass stalks and to olive trees? They were the empty skins, as fragile as ash, of some creature with a bulbous body, bulbous eyes, and a pair of thick, well-barbed forelegs. Why did each of these shells have a split down its back? Had they been attacked and had all their life juices sucked out of them? If so, what had attacked them and what were they? I was a bubbling cauldron of questions which the family were unable to answer.

I was in the kitchen when Spiro arrived one morning some days later, as I was showing Mother my latest acquisition, a long, thin, caramel-coloured centipede which I was insisting, in spite of her disbelief, glowed with a white light at night. Spiro waddled into the kitchen, sweating profusely, looking, as he always did, truculent and worried.

'I've broughts yours mails, Mrs Durrells,' he said to Mother, and then, glancing at me, 'Mornings, Masters Gerrys.'

Thinking, in my innocence, that Spiro would share my enthusiasm for my latest pet, I pushed the jam jar under his nose and urged him to feast his eyes upon it. He took one swift look at the centipede, now going round and round in the bottom of the jar like a clock-work train, dropped the mail on the floor, and retreated hurriedly behind the kitchen table.

'Gollys, Masters Gerrys,' he said, 'what's you doing with *thats?*'

I explained it was only a centipede, puzzled at his reaction.

'Thems bastards are poisonous, Mrs Durrells,' said Spiro earnestly, to Mother. 'Honest to Gods Masters Gerrys shouldn't *have* things like thats.'

'Well, perhaps not,' said Mother vaguely. 'But he's so interested in all these things. Take it outside, dear, where Spiro can't see it.'

'Makes me scarce,' I heard Spiro say as I left the kitchen with my precious jar. 'Honest to Gods, Mrs Durrells, makes me scarce what that boy *finds.*'

I managed to get the centipede into my bedroom without meeting any other members of the family and I bedded him down in a small dish, tastefully decorated with moss and bits of bark. I was determined that the family should appreciate the fact that I had found a centipede that glowed in the dark. I had planned that night to put on a special pyrotechnic display after dinner. However, all thoughts of the centipede and his phosphorescence were completely driven from my mind, for in with the mail was a fat, brown parcel which Larry, having glanced at, tossed across to me while we were eating lunch.

'Fabre,' he said succinctly.

Forgetting my food, I tore the parcel open, and there inside was a squat, green book entitled *The Sacred Beetle and Others* by Jean Henri Fabre. Opening it, I was transported by delight, for the frontispiece was a picture of two dung-beetles, and they looked so familiar they might well have been close cousins of my own dung-beetles. They were rolling a beautiful ball of dung between them. Enraptured, savouring every moment, I turned the pages slowly. The text was charming. No erudite or confusing tome, this. It was written in such a simple and straightforward way that even I could understand it.

'Leave the book till later, dear. Eat your lunch before it gets cold,' said Mother.

Reluctantly I put the book on my lap and then attacked my food with such speed and ferocity that I had acute indigestion for the rest of the afternoon. This in no way detracted from the charm of delving into Fabre for the first time. While the family siestaed, I lay in the garden in the shade of the tangerine trees and devoured the book, page by page, until by tea-time – to my disappointment – I had reached the end. But nothing could describe my elation. I was now armed with knowledge. I knew, I felt, everything there was to know about dung-beetles. Now they were not merely mysterious insects crawling ponderously throughout the olive groves – they were my intimate friends.

About this time another thing that extended and encouraged my interest in natural history – though I cannot say that I appreciated it at the time – was the acquisition of my first tutor, George. George was a friend of Larry's, tall, lanky, brown-bearded and bespectacled, possessed of a quiet and sardonic sense of humour. It is probable that no tutor has ever had to battle with such a reluctant pupil. I could see absolutely no reason for having to learn anything that was not connected with natural history, and so our early lessons were fraught with difficulty. Then George discovered that, by correlating such subjects as history, geography, and mathematics with zoology, he could get some results, and so we made fair progress. However, the best thing as far as I was concerned was that one morning a week was devoted exclusively to natural history, when George and I would peer earnestly at my newly acquired specimens and endeavour to identify them and work out their life histories. A meticulous diary was kept which contained a large number of flamboyant and somewhat shaky pictures, purporting to be of the specimens in question, done by me in a variety of coloured inks and water-colours.

Looking back, I have a sneaking feeling that George enjoyed the mornings devoted to natural history as much as I did. It was, for example, the only morning during the week that I would go to meet him. I would amble through the olive groves half-way to the tiny villa that he occupied, and then Roger and I would conceal ourselves in a clump of myrtle and await his approach. Presently he would appear, clad in nothing but a pair of sandals, faded shorts, and a gigantic, tattered straw hat, carrying under one arm a pile of books and swinging a long, slender walking-stick in the other hand. The reason for going to meet George, I regret to say, was of an entirely mercenary nature. Roger and I would squat in the sweet-scented myrtles and lay bets with each other as to whether or not, on this particular morning, George was going to fight an olive tree.

George was an expert fencer and had a quantity of cups and medals to prove it, so the desire to fight something frequently overcame him. He would be striding along the path, his spectacles glittering, swinging his walking-stick, when suddenly one olive tree would become an evil and malignant thing that had to be taught a lesson. Dropping his books and hat by the side of the path, he would advance cautiously towards the tree in question, his walking-stick, now transformed into a sword, held in his right hand at the ready, his left arm held out elegantly behind him. Slowly, stiff-legged, like a terrier approaching a bull mastiff, he would circle the tree, watching with narrowed eyes for its first unfriendly move. Suddenly he would lunge forward and the point of his stick would disappear in one of the holes in the olive tree's trunk and he would utter a pleased 'Ha,' and immediately dodge back out of range, before the tree could retaliate. I noticed that if he succeeded in driving his sword into one of the smaller of the olive tree's holes, this did not constitute a death wound, merely a slight scratch, which apparently had the effect of rousing his antagonist to a fury, for in a second he would be fighting grimly for his life, dancing nimble-footed round the olive tree, lunging and parrying, leaping away with a downward slash of his sword, turning aside the vicious lunge that the olive tree had aimed at him, but so rapidly that I had missed the move. Some olive trees he would finish off quickly with a deadly thrust through one of the larger holes, into which his sword disappeared almost up to the hilt, but on several occasions he met with an olive tree that was almost more than a match for him, and for perhaps a quarter of an hour or so, it would be a fight to the death, with George, grim-faced, using every cunning trick he knew to break through the defences of the giant tree and kill it. Once he had successfully killed his antagonist, George would wipe the blood off his sword fastidiously, put on his hat, pick up his books, and continue, humming to himself, down the path. I always let him get a considerable distance away before joining him, for fear he should realize I had watched his imaginary battle and become embarrassed by it.

It was about this time that George introduced me to someone who was going to become immediately the most important person in my life, Dr Theodore Stephanides. To me, Theodore was one of the most remarkable people I had ever met (and thirty-three years later I am still of the same opinion). With his ash-blond hair and beard and his handsome aquiline features,

Theodore looked like a Greek god, and certainly he seemed as omniscient as one. Apart from being medically qualified, he was also a biologist (his particular study being freshwater biology), poet, author, translator, astronomer, and historian, and he found time between these multifarious activities to help run an X-ray laboratory, the only one of its kind, in the town of Corfu. I had first met him over a little problem of trap-door spiders, a creature that I had only recently discovered, and he had imparted to me such fascinating information about them, so diffidently and shyly, that I was captivated, not only by the information, but by Theodore himself, for he treated me exactly as though I were an adult.

After our first meeting, I was convinced that I should probably never see him again, as anyone as omniscient and famous as he was could not possibly have the time to spare for a ten-year-old. But the following day I received a present of a small pocket microscope from him and a note asking me to go to tea with him in his flat in town. Here I plied him with eager questions and breathlessly ran riot through the enormous library in his study and peered for hours through the gleaming barrels of microscopes at the strange and beautiful forms of pond life that Theodore, like a magician, seemed able to conjure out of any drab, dirty stretch of water. After my first visit to Theodore, I asked Mother tentatively whether I might ask him to come to tea with us.

'I suppose so, dear,' said Mother. 'I hope he speaks English, though.'

Mother's battle with the Greek language was a losing one. Only the day previously she had spent an exhausting morning preparing a particularly delicious soup for lunch, and having concluded this to her satisfaction, she put it into a soup tureen and handed it to the maid. The maid looked at her inquiringly, whereupon Mother used one of the few Greek words that she had managed to commit to memory. '*Exo*,' she had said firmly, waving her arms. '*Exo*.' She then went on with her cooking and turned round just in time to see the maid pouring the last of the soup down the sink. This had, not unnaturally, given her a phobia about her linguistic abilities.

I said indignantly that Theodore could speak excellent English – in fact, if anything, better English than we could. Soothed by this, Mother suggested that I write Theodore a note and invite him out for the following Thursday. I spent an agonizing two hours hanging about in the garden waiting for him to arrive, peering every few minutes through the fuchsia hedge, a prey to the most terrible emotions. Perhaps the note had never reached him. Or perhaps he had put it in his pocket and forgotten about it and was, at this moment, gallivanting eruditely at the southernmost tip of the island. Or perhaps he had heard about the family and just didn't want to come. If that was the case, I vowed, I would not lightly forgive them. But presently I saw him, neatly tweed-suited, his Homburg squarely on his head, striding up through the olive trees, swinging his stick and humming to himself. Hung over his shoulder was his collecting bag, which was as much a part of him as his arms and legs, for he was rarely seen anywhere without it.

To my delight, Theodore was an immediate, uproarious success with the family. He could, with a shy urbanity, discuss mythology, Greek poetry, and Venetian history with Larry, ballistics and the best hunting areas on the island with Leslie, good slimming diets and acne cures with Margo, and peasant recipes and detective stories with Mother. The family behaved much in the same way that I had behaved when I went to tea with him. He seemed such an endless mine of information that they bombarded him ceaselessly with questions, and Theodore, as effortlessly as a walking encyclopaedia, answered them all, adding for good measure a sprinkling of incredibly bad puns and hilarious anecdotes about the island and the islanders.

At one point, to my indignation, Larry said that Theodore ought to desist from encouraging me in my interest in natural history, for, as he pointed out, the villa was a small one and already stuffed to capacity with practically every revolting bug and beetle that I could lay my hands on.

'It isn't that,' said Mother, 'that worries me. It's the mess that he gets himself into. Really, Theodore, after he's been out for a walk with Roger he has to change into completely clean clothes. I don't know what he does with them.'

Theodore gave a tiny grunt of amusement.

'I remember once,' he said, popping a piece of cake into his mouth and chewing it methodically, his beard bristling and his eyes kindling happily, 'I was coming to tea with some . . . um . . . you know, *friends* of mine here in Perama. At that time I was in the army and I was rather proud of the fact that I had just been made a captain. So . . . er . . . you know . . . er . . . to show off I wore my uniform, which included beautifully polished boots and spurs. I was rowed across by the ferry to Perama, and as I was walking through the little marshy bit I saw a plant that was new to me. So I stepped over to collect it. Treading on what . . . you know . . . seemed to be firm ground, I suddenly found that I had sunk up to my armpits in very foul smelling mud. Fortunately there was a small tree near by and I . . . er . . . managed to grab hold of it and pull myself *out*. But now I was covered from the waist downwards with stinking black mud. The sea was . . . er, you know . . . quite close, so I . . . er . . . thought it would be better to be wet with clean sea-water than covered with mud, so I waded out into it and walked up and down. Just at that moment, a bus happened to pass on the road above and as soon as they saw me with my cap on and my uniform coat, walking about in the sea, the bus driver immediately stopped so that all his passengers could . . . er . . . get a better view of the spectacle. They all seemed considerably puzzled, but they were even more astonished when I walked out of the sea and they saw that I was wearing boots and spurs as well.'

Solemnly, Theodore waited for the laughter to subside.

'I think, you know,' he said meditatively and quite seriously, 'that I definitely undermined their faith in the sanity of the army.'

Theodore was a huge success with the family and ever after that he came out to spend at least one day a week with us, preferably more if we could inveigle him away from his numerous activities.

By this time we had made innumerable friends among the peasant families that lived around us, and so vociferously hospitable were they that even the shortest walk was almost indefinitely prolonged, for at every little house we came to we would have to sit down and drink a glass of wine or eat some fruit with its owners and pass the time of day. Indirectly, this was very good for us, for each of these meetings strengthened our rather shaky command over the Greek language, so that soon we found that we were fairly proficient in conducting quite complicated conversations with our peasant friends.

Then came the accolade, the gesture that proved to us we had been accepted by the community in general. We were asked to a wedding. It was the wedding of Katerina, the sister of our maid, Maria. Katerina was a voluptuous girl, with a wide, glittering smile and brown eyes as large and as soft as pansies. Gay, provocative, and as melodious as a nightingale, she had been breaking hearts in the district for most of her twenty years. Now she had settled on Stephanos, a sturdy, handsome boy whom the mere sight of Katerina rendered tongue-tied, inarticulate, and blushing with love.

When you were invited to a wedding, we soon discovered, the thing was not done in half-measures. The first festivity was the engagement party, when you all went to the bride's house carrying your presents and she thanked you prettily for them and plied you with wine. Having suitably mellowed the guests, the future bride and groom would start walking to what was to be their future home, preceded by the village band (two violins, a flute, and a guitar) playing sprightly airs, and followed by the guests, all carrying their presents. Katerina's presents were a fairly mixed bag. The most important was a gigantic double brass bed and this led the procession, carried by four of Stephanos' friends. Thereafter followed a string of guests carrying sheets, pillow cases, cushions, a wooden chair, frying pans, large bottles of oil, and similar gifts. Having installed the presents in the new cottage, we then drank to the health of the couple and thus warmed their future home for them. We then all retired to our homes, slightly light-headedly, and waited for the next act in the drama, which was the wedding itself.

We had asked, somewhat diffidently, if Theodore might attend the wedding with us and the bride and her parents were enchanted with the idea, since, as they explained with becoming ingenuousness, very few weddings in the district could boast of having a whole English family *and* a genuine doctor as guests.

The great day came, and donning our best clothes and collecting Theodore from town, we made our way down to Katerina's parents' house, which stood among olive trees overlooking the sparkling sea. This was where the ceremony was to take place. When we got there we found it a hive of activity. Relatives had come on their donkeys from villages as far as ten miles away. All round the house, groups of ancient men and decrepit old women sat engulfing wine in vast quantities, gossiping as ceaselessly and as animatedly as magpies. For them this was a great day, not only because of the wedding, but because, living as much as ten miles distant, they were probably having their first opportunity in twenty years to exchange news and scandal. The village band was in full spate – the violins whining, the guitar rumbling, and the flute making periodic squeaks like a neglected puppy – and to this all the younger guests were dancing under the trees, while near by the carcasses of four lambs were sizzling and bubbling on spits over a great chrysanthemum blaze of charcoal.

'Aha!' said Theodore, his eyes alight with interest. 'Now that dance they are doing is the Corfu dance. It and the . . . er . . . tune *originated* here in Corfu. There are some authorities, of course, who believe that the dance . . . that is to say, the *steps* . . . originated in Crete, but for myself, I believe it is . . . um . . . an entirely Corfu product.'

The girls in their goldfinch-bright costumes revolved prettily in a half-moon while ahead of them pranced a swarthy young male with a crimson handkerchief, bucking, leaping, twisting, and bowing like an exuberant cockerel to his admiring entourage of hens. Katerina and her family came forward to greet us and ushered us to the place of honour, a rickety wooden table that had been spread with a white cloth and at which was already sitting a magnificent old priest who was going to perform the ceremony. He had a girth like that of a whale, snow-white eyebrows, and moustache and beard so thick and luxuriant that almost all that could be seen of his face were two twinkling, olive-black eyes and a great, jutting, wine-red nose. On hearing that Theodore was a doctor, the priest, out of the kindness of his heart, described in graphic detail the innumerable symptoms of his several diseases (which God had seen fit to inflict him with) and at the end of the recital laughed uproariously at Theodore's childish diagnosis that a little less wine and a little more exercise might alleviate his ailments.

Larry eyed Katerina, who, clad in her white bridal gown, had joined the circle of the dancers. In her tight, white satin, Katerina's stomach was more prominent and noticeable than it would have been otherwise.

'This wedding,' said Larry, 'is taking place not a moment too soon.'

'Do be quiet, dear,' whispered Mother. 'Some of them might speak English.'

'It's a curious fact,' said Theodore, oblivious to Mother's stricture, 'that at a lot of the weddings you will find the bride in . . . er . . . um . . . a *similar* condition. The peasants here are very Victorian in their outlook. If a young man is . . . er . . . seriously *courting* a girl, neither family dreams for a moment that he will not marry her. In fact, if he did try to . . . um . . . you know . . . run off, both his family and the bride's family would be after him. This leads to a situation where, when the young man is courting, he is . . . er . . . chaffed, that is to say, has his *leg* pulled by all the young men of the district, who say that they doubt his . . . um . . . prowess as a . . . um . . . you know . . . potential father. They get the poor fellow into such a state that he is almost forced to . . . er . . . you know . . . um . . . *prove* himself.'

'Very unwise, I would have thought,' said Mother.

'No, no,' said Theodore, endeavouring to correct Mother's unscientific approach to the problem. 'In fact, it is considered quite a *good* thing for the bride to be pregnant. It proves her . . . um . . . fecundity.'

Presently the priest heaved his vast bulk onto his gouty feet and made his way into the main room of the house, which had been prepared for the ceremony. When he was ready, Stephanos, perspiring profusely, his suit half a size too small for him and looking slightly dazed at his good fortune, was propelled towards the house by a laughing, joking band of young men, while a group of shrilly chattering young women fulfilled the same function for Katerina.

The main room of the house was extremely tiny, so that by the time the bulk of the well-larded priest had been inserted into it, plus all the accoutrements of his trade, there was only just about enough room for the happy couple to stand in front of him. The rest of us had to be content with peering through the door or through the windows. The service was incredibly long and, to us, incomprehensible, though I could hear Theodore translating bits of it to Larry. It seemed to me to involve quite an unnecessary amount of intoning, accompanied by innumerable signs of the cross and the splashing of tidal waves of holy water. Then two little garlands of flowers like twin haloes were held over the heads of Katerina and Stephanos, and while the priest droned on, these were exchanged at intervals. As it had been some considerable time since the people who held these garlands had been to a wedding, they occasionally misinterpreted the priest's instructions and there was, so to speak, a clash of garlands over the heads of the bridal pair; but at long last rings were exchanged and placed upon the brown, work-calloused fingers, and Katerina and Stephanos were truly and, we hoped, irretrievably wed.

The silence during the ceremony had been almost complete, broken only by the odd, drowsy chuckle of a hen or the shrill, and instantly repressed, squall of a baby; but now the stern part of the ceremony was over and the party blossomed once again. The band dug down into its repertoire and produced gayer and more sprightly tunes. Laughter and raucous badinage arose on every side. The wine flowed guggling from the bottles and the guests danced round and round and round, flushed and happy, as inexorably as the hands on a clock face.

The party did not end till well after twelve. All the older guests had already made their way homewards on drooping donkeys. The great fires, with the remains of the sheep carcasses over them, had died in a shroud of grey ash with only a sprinkling of garnet embers winking in it. We took a last glass of wine with Katerina and Stephanos and then made our way sleepily through the olive groves, silvered by a moon as large and as white as a magnolia blossom. The scops owls chimed mournfully to each other, and the odd firefly winked emerald-green as we passed. The warm air smelled of the day's sunshine, of dew, and of a hundred aromatic leaf scents. Mellow and drugged with wine, walking between the great hunched olives, their trunks striped with cool moonlight, I think we all felt we had arrived, that we had been accepted by the island. We were now, under the quiet, bland eye of the moon, christened Corfiotes. The night was beautiful, and tomorrow, we knew, another tiger-golden day lay ahead of us. It was as though England had never really existed.

2

The Bay of Olives

As you left the villa and walked down through the olive groves, you eventually reached the road with its thick coating of white dust, as soft as silk. If you walked along this for half a mile or so, you came to a goat track which led down a steep slope through the olives and then you reached a small half-moon bay, rimmed with white sands and great piles of dried ribbon-weed that had been thrown up by the winter storms and lay along the beach like large, badly made birds' nests. The two arms of the bay were composed of small cliffs, at the base of which were innumerable rock pools, filled with the glint and glitter of sea life.

As soon as George realized that to incarcerate me every morning of the week in the villa impaired my concentration, he instituted the novel educational gambit of 'outdoor lessons'. The sandy beach and the shaggy piles of weed soon became scorching deserts or impenetrable jungles, and with the aid of a reluctant crab or sand-hopper to play the part of Cortez or Marco Polo, we would explore them diligently. Geography lessons done under these circumstances I found had immense charm. We once decided, with the aid of rocks, to do a map of the world along the edge of the sea, so that we had real sea. It was an immensely absorbing task, for, to begin with, it was not all that easy to find rocks shaped like Africa or India or South America, and sometimes two or three rocks had to be joined together to give the required shape to the continent. Then, of course, when you were obtaining a rock, you turned it over very carefully and found a host of sea life underneath it which would keep us both happily absorbed for a quarter of an hour or so, till George realized with a start that this was not getting on with our map of the world.

This little bay became one of my favourite haunts, and nearly every afternoon while the family were having their siesta, Roger and I would make our way down through the breathless olive groves, vibrating with the cries of the cicadas, and pad our way along the dusty road, Roger sneezing voluptuously as his great paws stirred up the dust, which went up his nose like snuff. Once we reached the bay, whose waters in the afternoon sun were so still and transparent they did not seem to be there at all, we would swim for a while in the shallows and then each of us would go about his own particular hobbies.

For Roger, this consisted of desperate and unsuccessful attempts to catch some of the small fish that flicked and trembled in the shallow water. He would stalk along slowly, muttering to himself, his ears cocked, gazing down into the water. Then, suddenly, he would plunge his head beneath the surface, and you heard his jaws clop together and he would pull his head out, sneeze violently, and shake the water off his fur, while the goby or blenny that he had attempted to catch would flip a couple of yards farther on and squat on a rock pouting at him and trembling its tail seductively.

For me the tiny bay was so full of life that I scarcely knew where to begin my collecting. Under and on top of the rocks were the chalky white tunnels of the tube-worms, like some swirling and complicated pattern of icing on a cake, and in the slightly deeper water there were stuck in the sand what appeared to be lengths of miniature hose pipe. If you stood and watched carefully, a delicate, feathery, flowerlike cluster of tentacles would appear at the ends of the hose pipes – tentacles of iridescent blue and red and brown that would revolve slowly round and round. These were the bristle-worms; a rather ugly name, I felt, for such a beautiful creature. Sometimes there would be little clusters of them and they looked like a flower-bed whose flowers could move. You had to approach them with infinite caution, for should you move your feet too rapidly through the water you would set up currents that telegraphed your approach and the tentacles would bunch together and dive with incredible speed back into the tube.

Here and there on the sandy floor of the bay were half-moons of black, shiny ribbon-weed, looking like dark feather boas, anchored to the sand, and in these you would find pipefish, whose heads looked extraordinarily like elongated seahorses, perched on the end of a long, slender body. The pipefishes would float upright among the ribbon-weeds, which they resembled so closely it required a lot of concentrated searching to find them.

Along the shore, under the rocks, you could find tiny crabs or beadlet anemones like little scarlet-and-blue jewelled pin-cushions, or the snakelocks anemones, their slender, coffee-coloured stalks and long, writhing tentacles giving them a hair style that Medusa might well have envied. Every rock was encrusted with pink or white or green coral, fine forests of minute seaweeds, including a delicate growth of *acetabularia mediterranea* with slender threadlike stalks, and perched on the top of each stalk something that looked like a small green parasol turned inside out by some submarine wind. Occasionally a rock would be encrusted with a great black lump of sponge covered with gaping, protuberant mouths like miniature volcanoes. You could pull these sponges off the rocks and split them open with a razor blade, for sometimes, inside, you would find curious forms of life; but the sponge, in retaliation, would coat your hands with a mucus that smelt horribly of stale garlic and took hours to wear off.

Scattered along the shore and in the rock pools, I would find new shells to add to my collection; half the delight of collecting these was not only the beautiful shapes of the shells themselves, but the extraordinary evocative names that had been given to them. A pointed shell like a large winkle, the lip of whose mouth had been elongated into a series of semi-webbed fingers, was, I discovered to my delight, called the pelican's foot. An almost circular, white, conical, limpet-like shell went under the name of Chinaman's hat. Then there were the ark-shells, and the two sides of these strange, boxlike shells, when separated, did look (if one used a modicum of imagination) like the hulks of two little arks. Then there were the tower-shells, twisted and pointed as a narwhal's horn, and the top-shells, gaily striped with a zigzag pattern of scarlet, black, or blue. Under some of the bigger rocks, you would find keyhole limpets, each one of which had, as the name implied, a strange keyhole-like aperture in the top of the shell, through which the creature breathed. And then, best of all, if you were lucky, you would find the flattened ormers, scaly grey with a row of holes along one side; but if you turned it over and extracted its rightful occupant, you would find the whole interior of the shell glowing in opalescent, sunset colours, magical in their beauty. I had at that time no aquariums, so I was forced to construct for myself, in one corner of the bay, a rock pool some eight feet long by four feet wide. Into this I would put my various captures so that I could be almost certain of knowing where they were on the following day.

It was in this bay that I caught my first spider-crab, and I would have walked right past him, thinking him to be a weed-covered rock, if he had not made an incautious movement. His body was about the size and shape of a small flattened pear, and at the pointed end it was decorated with a series of spikes, ending in two hornlike protuberances over his eyes. His legs and his pincers were long, slender, and spindly. But the thing that intrigued me most about him was the fact that he was wearing, on his back and on his legs, a complete suit of tiny seaweeds, which appeared to be growing out of his shell. Enchanted by this weird creature, I carried him triumphantly along the beach to my rock pool and placed him in it. The firm grip with which I had had to hold him (for once having discovered that he was recognized as a crab, he made desperate efforts to escape) had rubbed off quite a lot of his seaweed suit by the time I got him to the pool. I placed him in the shallow, clear water, and lying on my stomach, watched him to see what he would do. Standing high on his toes, like a spider in a hurry, he scuttled a foot or so away from where I had put him and then froze. He sat like this for a long time, so long in fact that I was just deciding that he was going to remain immobile for the rest of the morning, recovering from the shock of capture, when he suddenly extended a long, delicate claw and very daintily, almost shyly, proceeded to pluck a tiny piece of seaweed that was growing on a near-by rock. He put the seaweed to his mouth and I could see him mumbling at it. At first I thought he was eating it, but I soon realized I was mistaken, for, with an angular grace, he placed his claw over his back, felt around in a rather fumbling sort of way, and then proceeded to plant the tiny piece of weed on his carapace. I presumed that he had been making the base of the weed sticky with saliva or some similar substance to make it adhere to his back. As I watched him, he trundled slowly round the pool, collecting a variety of seaweed with the assiduous dedication of a professional botanist in a hitherto unexplored jungle. Within an hour or so his back was covered with such a thick layer of growth that, if he sat still and I took my eyes off him for a moment, I had difficulty in knowing exactly where he was.

Being intrigued by this cunning form of camouflage, I searched the bay carefully until I found another spider-crab. For him I built a special small pool with a sandy floor, completely devoid of weed. I put him in and he settled down quite happily. The following day I returned, carrying with me a nail brush (which subsequently, rather unfortunately, turned out to be Larry's) and taking up the unfortunate spider-crab, I scrubbed him vigorously until not an atom of weed remained upon his back or legs. Then I dropped into his pool a variety of things: a number of tiny top-shells and some broken fragments of coral, some small sea anemones and some minute bits of bottle-glass that had been sandpapered by the sea so that they looked like misty jewels. Then I sat down to watch.

The crab, when returned to his pool, sat quite still for several minutes, obviously recovering from the indignity of the scrubbing I had given him. Then, as if he could not quite believe the terrible fate that had overtaken him, he put his two pincers over his head and proceeded to feel his back with the utmost delicacy, presumably hoping against hope that at least one frond of sea-weed remained. But I had done my task well and his back was shining and bare. He walked a few paces tentatively and then squatted down and sulked for half an hour. Then he roused himself out of his gloom and walked over to the edge of the pond, where he endeavoured to wedge himself under a dark ridge of rock. There he sat brooding miserably over his lack of camouflage until it was time for me to go home.

I returned very early the following morning, and to my delight, I saw that the crab had been busy while I had been away. Making the best of a bad job, he had decorated the top of his shell with a number of the ingredients that I had left for him. He looked extremely gaudy and had an air of carnival about him. Striped top-shells had been pasted on, interspersed with bits of coral, and up near his head he was wearing two beadlet anemones, like an extremely saucy bonnet with ribbons. I thought, as I watched him crawling about the sand, that he looked exceedingly conspicuous, but, curiously enough, when he went over and squatted by his favourite overhang of rock, he turned into what appeared to be a little pile of shell and coral debris, with a couple of anemones perched on top of it.

To the left of the little bay, a quarter of a mile or so from the shore, lay an island called Pondikonissi, or Mouse Island. It was shaped not unlike an isosceles triangle and was thick with elderly cypress trees and oleander bushes, which guarded a small snow-white church and tiny living quarters adjoining it. This island was inhabited by an elderly and extremely verminous monk, with long black robes and a stove-pipe hat, whose major function in life appeared to be ringing the bell in the match-box-size church at intervals and rowing slowly over to a neighbouring headland in the evening, where there was a small nunnery, inhabited by three ancient nuns. Here he would partake of ouzo and a cup of coffee and discuss, presumably, the state of sin in the world today, and then, as the sun set and turned the calm waters round his island to a multi-coloured sheet of shot-silk, he would row back again, like a hunched black crow, in his creaking, leaking boat.

Margo, having discovered that constant sun-bathing, if anything, inflamed her acne, now decided on another of Mother Nature's cures – sea-bathing. Every morning she would get up at about half past five, rout me out of bed, and together we would make our way down to the shore and plunge into the clear water, still chilly from the moon's gaze, and then swim slowly and languidly across to Pondikonissi. Here Margo would drape herself on a rock and I would potter happily in the rock pools on the shore. Unfortunately, our visitations to the island seemed to have a detrimental effect upon the monk, for no sooner had Margo landed and arranged herself attractively on a rock than he would come stamping down the long flight of stone steps that led up to the church, shaking his fist at her, and mouthing incomprehensible Greek from the depths of his long, unkempt beard. Margo would always greet him with a bright smile and a cheerful wave of her hand, and this generally made him almost apoplectic with rage. He would stamp to and fro, his black robes swishing, pointing one dirty and trembling finger at the heavens above and another at Margo. After this had happened on numerous occasions, I managed to commit to memory several of the monk's favourite phrases, for his vocabulary was not an extensive one. I then asked my friend Philemon what they meant.

Philemon was convulsed with laughter. He laughed so much that he was almost incapable of explaining to me, but I at length understood that the monk had several derogatory terms that he used for Margo, the mildest of these being 'white witch'.

When I related this to Mother, she was, to my astonishment, considerably shocked.

'Really,' she said, 'we ought to report him to somebody. They'd never be able to carry on like that in the Church of England.'

Eventually, however, the whole thing became a sort of game. When Margo and I swam across, we would take some cigarettes over for the monk and he would come flying down the stone steps, shaking his fist and threatening us with the wrath of God, and then, having done his duty, as it were, he would hitch up his robes, squat on the wall, and with great good humour smoke the cigarettes we had brought him. Occasionally he would even trot back to the church to bring us a handful of figs from his tree or a few almonds, milky and fresh, which we would crack between the smooth stones on the beach.

Between Pondikonissi and my favourite bay there stretched a whole string of reefs. Most of these were flat-topped, some of them only the size of a table and others the size of a small garden. The majority of them lay perhaps two inches below the surface of the water, so that if you hauled yourself out and stood on them, from a distance it looked exactly as though you were walking on the surface of the sea. I had long wanted to investigate these reefs, for they contained a lot of sea life that you did not find in the shallow waters of the bay. But this presented insurmountable difficulties, for I could not get my equipment out there. I had tried to swim out to one reef with two large jam jars slung round my neck on a string and carrying my net in one hand, but half-way there the jam jars suddenly and maliciously filled with water, and their combined weight dragged me under. It was a few seconds before I managed to disentangle myself from them and rise gasping and spluttering to the surface, by which time my jars were lying glinting and rolling in a fathom of water, as irretrievable as though they had been on the moon.

Then, one hot afternoon, I was down in the bay turning over rocks in an effort to find some of the long, multi-coloured ribbon-worms that inhabited that sort of terrain. So absorbed was I in my task that the prow of a rowing-boat had scrunched and whispered its way into the sandy shore beside me before I was aware of it. Standing in the stern, leaning on his single oar – which he used, as did all the fishermen, twisting it in the water like a fish's tail – was a young man, burnt almost black by the sun. He had a mop of dark, curly hair, eyes as bright and as black as mulberries, and his teeth gleamed astonishingly white in his brown face.

'*Yasu,*' he said. 'Your health.'

I returned his greeting and watched him as he jumped nimbly out of the boat, carrying a small rusty anchor which he wedged firmly behind a great double bed of drying seaweed on the beach. He was wearing nothing but a very tattered singlet and a pair of trousers that had once been blue, but were now bleached almost white by the sun. He came over and squatted companionably beside me and produced from his pocket a tin containing tobacco and cigarette papers.

'It is hot today,' he said, making a grimace, while his blunt, calloused fingers rolled a cigarette with extraordinary deftness. He stuck it in his mouth and lit it with the aid of a large, tin lighter, inhaled deeply, and then sighed. He cocked an eyebrow at me, his eyes as bright as a robin's.

'You're one of the strangers that live up on the hill?' he inquired.

By this time my Greek had become reasonably fluent, so I admitted that, yes, I was one of the strangers.

'And the others?' he asked. 'The others in the villa, who are they?'

I had quickly learned that every Corfiote, particularly the peasants, loved to know all about you and would, in return for this information, vouchsafe to you the most intimate details of their private lives. I explained that the others at the villa were my mother, my two brothers, and my sister. He nodded gravely, as though this information were of the utmost importance.

'And your father?' he continued. 'Where is your father?'

I explained that my father was dead.

'Poor thing,' he said, quickly commiserating. 'And your poor mother with four children to bring up.'

He sighed lugubriously at this terrible thought and then brightened.

'Still,' he said philosophically, 'thus is life. What are you looking for here under these stones?'

I explained as best I could, though I always found it difficult to get the peasants to understand why I was so interested in such a variety of creatures that were either obnoxious or not worth worrying about and all of which were inedible.

'What's your name?' he asked.

I said that it was Gerasimos, which was the closest approach to Gerald that one could come to in Greek. But, I explained, my friends called me Gerry.

'I'm Taki,' he said. 'Taki Thanatos. I live at Benitses.'

I asked him what he was doing up here so comparatively far from his village. He shrugged.

'I have come from Benitses,' he said, 'and I fish on the way. Then I eat and I sleep and when it's night I light my lights and go back to Benitses, fishing again.'

This news excited me, for not long before, we had been returning late from town, and standing on the road by the little path that led up to the villa, we had seen a boat passing below us, being rowed very slowly, with a large carbon lamp fixed to the bows. As the fisherman manœuvred the boat slowly through the dark, shallow waters, the pool of light cast by his lamp had illuminated great patches of sea-bed with the utmost vividness, reefs smouldering citron green, pink, yellow, and brown as the boat moved slowly along. I had thought at the time that this must be a fascinating occupation, but I had known no fishermen. Now I began to view Taki with some enthusiasm.

I asked him eagerly what time he intended to start his fishing and whether he meant to go round the reefs that lay scattered between the bay and Pondikonissi.

'I start about ten,' he said. 'I work round the island, then I head towards Benitses.'

I asked him whether it would be possible for me to join him, because, as I explained, there were lots of strange creatures living on the reef which I could not obtain without the aid of a boat.

'Why not?' he said. 'I shall be down below Menelaos'. You come at ten. I'll take you round the reefs and then drop you back at Menelaos' before I go to Benitses.'

I assured him fervently that I would be there at ten o'clock. Then, gathering up my net and bottles and whistling for Roger, I beat a hasty retreat before Taki could change his mind. Once I was safely out of earshot, I slowed down and gave a considerable amount of thought to how I was going to persuade the family in general, and Mother in particular, to let me go out to sea at ten o'clock at night.

Mother, I knew, had always been worried about my refusal to have a siesta during the heat of the day. I had explained to her that this was generally the best time for insects and things like that, but she was not convinced that this was a valid argument. However, the result was that at night, just when something interesting was happening (such as Larry locked in a verbal battle with Leslie), Mother would say, 'It's time you went to bed, dear. After all, remember, you don't have a siesta.'

This I felt might be the answer to the night-fishing. It was scarcely three o'clock and I knew that the family would be lying supine behind closed shutters, only to awake and start to buzz at each other, drowsily, like sun-drugged flies, at about half past five.

I made my way back to the villa with the utmost speed. When I was a hundred yards away, I took off my shirt and wrapped it carefully round my jam jars full of specimens so that not a chink or a rattle would betray my presence; then, cautioning Roger upon pain of death not to utter a sound, we made our way cautiously into the villa and slipped like shadows into my bedroom. Roger squatted panting in the middle of the floor and viewed me with considerable surprise as I took off all my clothes and climbed into bed. He was not at all sure that he approved of this untoward behaviour. As far as he was concerned, the whole afternoon stretched ahead of us, littered with exciting adventures, and here was I preparing to go to sleep. He whined experimentally and I shushed him with such fierceness that his ears drooped, and putting his stumpy tail between his legs, he crept under the bed and curled up with a rueful sigh. I took a book and tried to concentrate on it. The half-closed shutters made the room look like a cool, green aquarium, but in fact the air was still and hot and the sweat rolled in rivulets down my ribs. What on earth, I thought, shifting uncomfortably on the already sodden sheet, could the family possibly see in a siesta? What good did it do them? In fact, how they managed to sleep at all was a mystery to me. At this moment I sank swiftly into oblivion.

I woke at half past five and staggered out, half-asleep, to the veranda, where the family were having tea.

'Good heavens,' said Mother. 'Have you been sleeping?'

I said, as casually as I could, that I thought a siesta a good thing that afternoon.

'Are you feeling well, dear?' she asked anxiously.

I said, yes, I felt fine. I had decided to have a siesta in order to prepare myself for that evening.

'Why, what's happening, dear?' asked Mother.

I said, with all the nonchalance I could muster, that I was

going out at ten o'clock with a fisherman who was going to take me night-fishing, for, as I explained, there were certain creatures that came out only at night and this was the best method of obtaining them.

'I hope this does not mean,' said Larry ominously, 'that we're going to have octopus and conger eels flopping around the floor. Better stop him, Mother. Before you know where you are the whole villa will look and smell like Grimsby.'

I replied, somewhat heatedly, that I did not intend to bring the specimens back to the villa, but to put them straight into my special rock pool.

'Ten o'clock's rather *late*, dear,' said Mother. 'What time will you be back?'

Lying valiantly, I said I thought I would be back at about eleven.

'Well, mind you wrap up warmly,' said Mother, who was always convinced that, in spite of the nights' being warm and balmy, I would inevitably end up with double pneumonia if I did not wear a jersey. Promising faithfully to wrap up warmly, I finished my tea and then spent an exciting and satisfying hour or so in marshalling my collecting gear. There was my long-handled net, a long bamboo with three wire hooks on the end for pulling interesting clumps of seaweed nearer to one, eight wide-mouthed jam jars, and several tins and boxes for putting such things as crabs or shells in. Making sure that Mother was not around, I put on my bathing trunks under my shorts and hid a towel in the bottom of my collecting bag, for I felt sure that I might have to dive for some of the specimens. I knew that Mother's fears of double pneumonia would increase a hundredfold if she thought I was going to do this.

Then at a quarter to ten I slung my bag on my back and, taking a torch, made my way down through the olive groves. The moon was a pale, smudged sickle in a star-lit sky, shedding only the feeblest light. In the black recesses among the olive roots, glow-worms gleamed like emeralds, and I could hear the scops owls calling 'toink, toink' to each other from the shadows.

When I reached the beach I found Taki squatting in his boat, smoking. He had already lighted the carbon lamp and it hissed angrily to itself and smelt strongly of garlic as it cast a brilliant circle of white light into the shallow water by the bows. Already I could see that a host of life had been attracted to it. Gobies and blennies had come out of their holes and were sitting on the seaweed-covered rocks, pouting and gulping expectantly like an audience in the theatre waiting for the curtain to go up. Shore-crabs scuttled to and fro, pausing now and then to pluck some seaweed delicately and stuff it carefully into their mouths; and everywhere there trundled top-shells, dragged by small, choleric-looking hermit-crabs, who now occupied the shells in place of their rightful owners.

I arranged my collecting gear in the bottom of the boat and sat down with a contented sigh. Taki pushed off and then, using the oar, punted us along through the shallow water and the beds of ribbon-weed that rustled and whispered along the side of the boat. As soon as we were in deeper water, he fixed both his oars and then rowed standing up. We progressed very slowly, Taki keeping a careful eye on the nimbus of light that illuminated the sea bottom for some twelve feet in every direction. The oars squeaked musically and Taki hummed to himself. Along one side of the boat lay an eight-foot pole ending in a five-pronged, savagely barbed trident. In the bow I could see the little bottle of olive oil, such a necessary accoutrement to the fisherman, for should a slight wind blow up and ruffle the waters, a sprinkling of oil would have a magically calming effect on the pleated surface of the sea. Slowly and steadily we crept out towards the black triangular silhouette of Pondikonissi to where the reefs lay. When we neared them Taki rested on his oars for a moment and looked at me.

'We'll go round and round for five minutes,' he said, 'so that

I may catch what there is. Then after that I will take you round to catch the things that you want.'

I readily agreed to this, for I was anxious to see how Taki fished with his massive trident. Very slowly we edged our way round the biggest of the reefs, the light illuminating the strange submarine cliffs covered with pink and purple seaweeds that looked like fluffy oak trees. Peering down into the water, one felt as though one were a kestrel, floating smoothly on outstretched wings over a multi-coloured autumn forest.

Suddenly Taki stopped rowing and dug his oars gently into the water to act as a brake. The boat came to an almost complete standstill as he picked up the trident.

'Look,' he said, pointing to the sandy bottom under a great bulwark of submarine cliff. 'Scorpios.'

At first glance I could see nothing then suddenly I saw what he meant. Lying on the sand was a fish some two feet long with a great filigree of sharp spines like a dragon's crest along its back, and enormous pectoral fins spread out on the sand. It had a tremendously wide head with golden eyes and a sulky, pouting mouth. But it was the colours that astonished me, for it was decked out in a series of reds ranging from scarlet to wine, pricked out and accentuated here and there with white. It looked immensely sure of itself as it lay there, flamboyant, on the sand, and immensely dangerous, too.

'This is good eating,' whispered Taki to my surprise, for the fish, if anything, looked highly poisonous.

Slowly and delicately he lowered the trident into the water, easing the barbed fork inch by inch towards the fish. There was no sound except the peevish hissing of the lamp. Slowly, inexorably, the trident got closer and closer. I held my breath. Surely that great fish with its gold-flecked eyes must notice its approaching doom? A sudden flip of the tail, I thought, and a swirl of sand and it would be gone. But no. It just lay there gulping methodically and pompously to itself. When the trident was within a foot of it, Taki paused. I saw him gently shift his grip on the haft. He stood immobilc for a second, although it seemed an interminable time to me, and then suddenly, so speedily that I did not actually see the movement, he drove the five prongs swiftly and neatly through the back of the great fish's head. There was a swirl of sand and blood and the fish twisted and writhed on the prongs, curling its body so that the spines along its back jabbed at the trident. But Taki had driven the trident home too skilfully and it could not escape. Quickly, hand over hand, he pulled in the pole, and the fish came over the side and into the boat, flapping and writhing. I came forward to help him get it off the prongs, but he pushed me back roughly.

'Take care,' he said, 'the scorpios is a bad fish.'

I watched while, with the aid of the oar blade, he got the fish off the trident, and although to all intents and purposes it must have been dead, it still wriggled and flapped and tried to drive the spines on its back into the side of the boat.

'Look, look,' said Taki. 'You see now why we call it scorpios. If he can stab you with those spines, Saint Spiridion, what pain you would have! You would have to go to the hospital quickly.'

With the aid of the oar and the trident, and a dexterous bit of juggling, he managed to lift the scorpion fish up and drop it into an empty kerosene tin where it could do no harm. I wanted to know why, if it was poisonous, it was supposed to be good eating.

'Ah,' said Taki, 'it's only the spines. You cut those off. The flesh is sweet, as sweet as honey. I will give it to you to take home with you.'

He bent over his oars once more and we proceeded to squeak our way along the edge of the reef again. Presently he paused once more. Here the sea-bed was sandy with just a few scattered tufts of young green ribbon-weed. Again, he slowed the boat to a standstill and picked up his trident.

'Look,' he said. 'Octopus.'

My stomach gave a clutch of excitement, for the only octopuses

I had seen had been the dead ones on sale in the town, and these, I felt sure, bore no resemblance to the living creature. But peer as hard as I could, the sandy bottom appeared to be completely devoid of life.

'There, *there*,' said Taki, lowering the trident gently into the water and pointing. 'Can't you see it? Did you leave your eyes behind? There, *there*. Look, I am almost touching it.'

Still I could not see it. He lowered the trident another foot.

'Now can you see it, foolish one?' he chuckled. 'Just at the end of the prongs.'

And suddenly I could see it. I had been looking at it all the time, but it was so grey and sandlike that I had mistaken it for part of the sea-bed. It squatted on the sand in a nest of tentacles, and there under its bald, domed head its eyes, uncannily human, peered up at us forlornly.

'It's a big one,' said Taki.

He shifted the trident slightly in his grasp, but the movement was incautious. Suddenly the octopus turned from a drab sandy colour to a bright and startling iridescent green. It squirted a jet of water out of its syphon, and projected by this, in a swirl of sand, it shot off the sea-bed. Its tentacles trailed out behind it, and as it sped through the water, it looked like a runaway balloon.

'Ah, *gammoto!*' said Taki.

He threw the trident down and seizing the oars he rowed swiftly in the wake of the octopus. The octopus obviously possessed a touching faith in its camouflage, for it had come to rest on the sea-bed some thirty-five feet away.

Once again, Taki eased the boat up to it and once again he lowered the trident carefully into the water. This time he took no risks and made no incautious movements. When the pronged fork was within a foot of the octopus's domed head, Taki strengthened his grip on the pole and plunged it home. Immediately the silver sand boiled up in a cloud as the octopus's tentacles threshed and writhed and wound themselves round the trident. Ink spurted from its body and hung like a trembling curtain of black lace or coiled like smoke across the sand. Taki was chuckling now with pleasure. He hauled the trident up swiftly, and as the octopus came into the boat, two of its tentacles seized and adhered to the side. Taki gave a sharp tug and the tentacles were pulled free with a ripping, rasping noise that was like the sound of sticking plaster being removed, a thousand times magnified. Swiftly, Taki grabbed the round, slimy body of the octopus and deftly removed it from the prongs and then, to my astonishment, he lifted this writhing Medusa head and put it to his face so that the tentacles wound round his forehead, his cheeks, and his neck, the suckers leaving white impressions against his dark skin. Then, choosing his spot carefully, he suddenly buried his teeth in the very core of the creature with a snap and a sideways jerk, reminiscent of a terrier breaking the back of a rat. He had obviously bitten through some vital nerve-centre, for immediately the tentacles released their grip on his head and fell limply, only their very extremities twitching and curling slightly. Taki threw the octopus into the tin with the scorpion fish and spat over the side of the boat and then, reaching over, cupped a handful of sea-water and swilled his mouth out with it.

'You have brought me luck,' he said, grinning and wiping his mouth. 'It is not many nights that I get an octopus *and* a scorpios.'

But apparently Taki's luck stopped short at the octopus, for although we circled the reef several times, we caught nothing more. We did see the head of a moray eel sticking out of its hole in the reef, an extremely vicious-looking head the size of a small dog's. But when Taki lowered the trident, the moray eel, very smoothly and with much dignity, retreated with fluid grace into the depths of the reef and we did not see him again. For myself, I was quite glad, for I imagined he must have been about six feet long, and to wrestle about in a dimly lit boat with a six-foot moray eel was an experience that even I, ardent naturalist though I was, felt I could do without.

'Ah, well,' said Taki philosophically. 'Now let's go and do your fishing.'

He rowed me out to the largest of the reefs and landed me with my gear on its flat top. Armed with my net, I prowled along the edge of the reef while Taki rowed the boat some six feet behind me, illuminating the smouldering beauty of the rocks. There was so much life that I despaired of being able to capture it all.

There were fragile blennies, decked out in gold and scarlet; tiny fish half the size of a match-stick with great black eyes and pillar-box red bodies; and others, the same size, whose colouring was a combination of deep Prussian- and pale powder-blue. There were blood-red starfish and purple, brittle starfish, their long, slender, spiky arms forever coiling and uncoiling. These had to be lifted in the net with the utmost delicacy, for the slightest shock and they would, with gay abandon, shed all their arms lavishly. There were slipper limpets that, when you turned them over, you found had half the underside covered by a neat flange of shell, so that the whole thing *did* look rather like a baggy, shapeless carpet-slipper designed for a gouty foot. Then there were cowries, some as white as snow and delicately ribbed, others a pale cream, heavily blotched and smudged with purple-black markings. Then there were the coat-of-mail shells, or chitons, some two and a half inches long, that clung to crannies in the rocks, looking like gigantic wood-lice. I saw a baby cuttlefish the size of match-box and almost fell off the edge of the reef in my efforts to capture him, but to my immense chagrin, he escaped. After only half an hour's collecting I found that my jars, tins, and boxes were crammed to overflowing with life, and I knew that, albeit reluctantly, I would have to stop.

Taki, very goodhumouredly, rowed me over to my favourite bay and stood watching with amusement while I carefully emptied my jars of specimens into my rock pool. Then he rowed me back to the jetty below Menelaos'. Here he strung a cord through the gills of the now dead scorpion fish and handed it to me.

'Tell your mother,' he said, 'to cook it with hot paprika and oil and potatoes and little marrows. It is very sweet.'

I thanked him for this and for the fact that he had been so patient with me.

'Come fishing again,' he said. 'I shall be up here next week. Probably Wednesday or Thursday. I'll send a message to you when I arrive.'

I thanked him and said I would look forward to it. He pushed the boat off and poled his way through the shallow waters heading in the direction of Benitses.

I shouted 'Be happy' after him.

'*Pasto calo*,' he answered. 'Go to the good.'

I turned and trudged my way wearily up the hill. I discovered to my horror that it was half past two and I knew Mother would by now have convinced herself that I had been drowned or eaten by a shark or overtaken by some similar fate. However, I hoped that the scorpion fish would placate her.

3

The Myrtle Forests

About half a mile north of the villa the olive grove thinned out and there was a great flat basin, fifty or sixty acres in extent, on which no olives grew. Here was only a great green forest of myrtle bushes, interspersed with dry, stony grassland, decorated with the strange candelabras of the thistles, glowing a vivid electric blue, and the huge flaky bulb of squills. This was one of my favourite hunting grounds, for it contained a remarkable selection of insect life. Roger and I would squat in the heavily scented shade of the myrtle bushes and watch the array of creatures that passed us; at certain times of the day the branches were as busy as the main street of a town.

The myrtle forests were full of mantises some three inches long, with vivid green wings. They would sway through the myrtle branches on their slender legs, their wickedly barbed front arms held up in an attitude of hypocritical prayer, their little pointed faces with their bulbous straw-coloured eyes turning this way and that, missing nothing, like angular, embittered spinsters at a cocktail party. Should a cabbage white or a fritillary land on the glossy myrtle leaves, the mantises would approach them with the utmost caution, moving almost imperceptibly, pausing now and then to sway gently to and fro on their legs, beseeching the butterfly to believe they were really wind-ruffled leaves.

I once saw a mantis stalk and finally launch himself at a large swallow-tail which was sitting in the sun gently moving its wings and meditating. At the last minute, however, the mantis missed its footing and instead of catching the swallow-tail by the body, as it had intended to do, caught it by one wing. The swallow-tail came out of its trance with a start and flapped its wings so vigorously that it succeeded in lifting the forequarters of the mantis off the leaves. A few more vigorous flappings and, to the mantis' annoyance, the swallow-tail flew lopsidedly away with a large section missing from one wing. The mantis philosophically sat down and ate the piece of wing that it had retained in its claws.

Under the rocks that littered the ground among the thistles there lived a surprising variety of creatures, in spite of the fact that the earth was baked rock-hard by the sun and was almost hot enough to poach an egg. Here lived a beast that always gave me the creeps. It was a flattened centipede some two inches long, with a thick fringe of long spiky legs along each side of its body. It was so flat that it could get into the most minute crevice and it moved with tremendous speed, seeming more to glide over the ground than run, as smoothly as a flat pebble skims across ice. These creatures were called Scutigeridae, and I could think of no other name which would be so apt in conjuring up their particularly obnoxious form of locomotion.

Scattered among the rocks, you would find holes that had been driven into the hard ground, each the size of a half-crown or larger. They were silk-lined and with a web spread to a three-inch circle around the mouth of the burrow. These were the lairs of the tarantulas, great, fat, chocolate-coloured spiders with fawn-and-cinnamon markings. With their legs spread out, they covered an area perhaps the size of a coffee saucer and their bodies were about the size of half a small walnut. They were immensely powerful spiders, quick and cruel in their hunting, and displaying a remarkable sort of inimical intelligence. For the most part, they hunted at night, but occasionally you would see them during the day, striding swiftly through the thistles on their long legs, in search of their prey. Generally, as soon as they saw you, they would scuttle off and soon be lost among the myrtles, but one day I saw one who was so completely absorbed that he let me approach quite close.

He was some six or seven feet away from his burrow, and he was standing half-way up a blue thistle, waving his front legs and peering about him, reminding me irresistibly of a hunter who had climbed up a tree in order to see if there was any game about. He continued to do this for about five minutes while I squatted on my haunches and watched him. Presently he climbed carefully down the thistle and set off in a very determined manner. It was almost as though he had seen something from his lofty perch, but searching the ground around, I could see no sign of life, and in any case I was not at all sure that a tarantula's eyesight was as good as all that. But he marched along in a determined fashion until he came to a large clump of Job's tears, a fine trembling grass whose seed heads look like little white plaited rolls of bread. Going closer to this, I suddenly realized what the tarantula appeared to be after, for under the delicate fountain of white grass there was a lark's nest. It had four eggs in it and one of them had just hatched, and the tiny, pink, downy offspring was still struggling feebly in the remains of the shell.

Before I could do anything sensible to save it, the tarantula had marched up over the edge of the nest. He loomed there for a moment, monstrous and terrifying, and then swiftly he drew the quivering baby to him and sank his long, curved mandibles into its back. The baby gave two minute, almost inaudible squeaks and opened its mouth wide as it writhed briefly in the hairy embrace of the spider. The poison took effect and it went rigid for a brief moment and then hung limply. The spider waited, immobile, till he was certain the poison had done its work, and then he turned and marched off, the baby hanging limply from his jaws. He looked like some strange, leggy retriever, bringing in his first grouse of the season. Without a pause, he hurried back to his burrow and disappeared inside it, carrying the limp, pathetic little body of the fledgling.

I was amazed by this encounter, for two reasons: firstly, because I did not realize that tarantulas would tackle anything the size of a baby bird, and secondly, because I could not see how he knew the nest was there – and he obviously *did* know, for he walked, unhesitatingly, straight to it. The distance from the thistle he had climbed to the nest was about thirty-five feet, as I found out by pacing it, and I was positive that no spider had the eyesight to be able to spot such a well-camouflaged nest and the fledgling from that distance. This left only smell, and here again, although I knew animals could smell subtle scents which our blunted nostrils could not pick up, I felt that on a breathlessly still day at thirty-five feet it would take a remarkable olfactory sense to be able to pinpoint the baby lark. The only solution I could come to was that the spider had, during his perambulations, discovered the nest and kept checking on it periodically to see whether the young had hatched. But this did not satisfy me as an explanation, for it attributed a thought process to an insect which I was pretty certain it did not possess. Even my oracle, Theodore, could not explain this puzzle satisfactorily. All I knew was that that particular pair of larks did not succeed in rearing a single young one that year.

Other creatures that fascinated me greatly in the myrtle forests were the ant-lion larvae. Adult ant-lions come in a variety of sizes and, for the most part, rather drab colouring. They look like extremely untidy and demented dragon-flies. They have wings that seem to be out of all proportion to their bodies and these they flap with a desperate air, as though it required the maximum amount of energy to prevent them from crashing to the earth. They were a good-natured, bumbling sort of beast, and did no harm to anybody. But the same could not be said of their larvae. What the rapacious dragon-fly larvae were to the pond, the ant-lion larvae were to the dry, sandy areas that lay between the myrtle bushes. The only sign that there were ant-lion larvae about was a series of curious, cone-shaped depressions in areas where the soil was fine and soft enough to be dug. The first time I discovered these cones, I was greatly puzzled as to what had made them. I wondered if perhaps some mice had been excavating for roots or something similar; I was unaware that at the base of each cone was the architect, waiting taut and ready in the sand, as dangerous as a hidden man-trap. Then I saw one of these cones in action and realized for the first time that it was not only the larva's home, but also a gigantic trap.

An ant would come trotting along (I always felt they hummed to themselves as they went about their work); it might be one of the little, busy, black variety or one of the large, red, solitary ants that staggered about the countryside with their red abdomens pointing to the sky, for some obscure reason, like anti-aircraft guns. Whichever species it was, if it happened to walk over the edge of one of the little pits, it immediately found that the sloping sides shifted so that it very soon started to slide down towards the base of the cone. It would then turn and try to climb out of the pit, but the earth or sand would shift in little avalanches under its feet. As soon as one of these avalanches had trickled down to the base of the cone, it would be the signal for the larva to come into action. Suddenly the ant would find itself bombarded with a rapid machine-gun fire of sand or earth, projected up from the bottom of the pit with incredible speed by the head of the larva. With the shifting ground underfoot and being bombarded with earth or sand, the ant would miss its foothold and roll ignominiously down to the bottom of the pit. Out of the sand, with utmost speed, would appear the head of the ant-lion larva, a flattened, ant-like head, with a pair of enormous curved jaws, like sickles. These would be plunged into the unfortunate ant's body and the larva would sink back beneath the sand, dragging the kicking and struggling ant with it to its grave. As I felt the ant-lion larvae took an unfair advantage over the dim-witted and rather earnest ants, I had no compunction in digging them up when I found them, taking them home, and making them hatch out eventually in little muslin cages, so that if they were a species new to me, I could add them to my collection.

One day we had one of those freak storms when the sky turned blue-black and the lightning fretted a silver filigree across it. And then had come the rain – great, fat, heavy drops, as warm as blood. When the storm had passed, the sky had been washed to the clear blue of a hedge-sparrow's egg and the damp earth sent out wonderfully rich, almost gastronomic smells as of fruit-cake or plum pudding; and the olive trunks steamed as the rain was dried off them by the sun, each trunk looking as though it were on fire. Roger and I liked these summer storms. It was fun to be able to splash through the puddles and feel one's clothes getting wetter and wetter in the warm rain. In addition to this, Roger derived considerable amusement by barking at the lightning. When the rain ceased we were passing the myrtle forests, and I went in on the off-chance that the storm might have brought out some creatures that would normally be sheltering from the heat of the day. Sure enough, on a myrtle branch there were two fat, honey- and amber-coloured snails gliding smoothly towards each other, their horns waving provocatively. Normally, I knew, in the height of the summer, these snails would aestivate. They would attach themselves to a convenient branch, construct a thin, paperlike front door over the mouth of the shell, and then retreat deep into its convolutions in order to husband the moisture in their bodies from the fierce heat of the sun. This freak storm had obviously awakened them and made them feel gay and romantic. As I watched them they glided up to each other until their horns touched. Then they paused and gazed long and earnestly into each other's eyes. One of them then shifted his position slightly so that he could glide alongside the other one. When he was alongside, something happened that made me doubt the evidence of my own eyes. From his side, and almost simultaneously from the side of the other snail, there shot what appeared to be two minute, fragile white darts, each attached to a slender white cord. The dart from snail one pierced the side of snail two and disappeared, and the dart from snail two performed a similar function on snail one. So, there they were, side by side attached to each other by the two little white cords. And there they sat like two curious sailing ships roped together. This was amazing enough, but stranger things were to follow. The cords gradually appeared to get shorter and shorter and drew the two snails together. Peering at them so closely that my nose was almost touching them, I came to the incredulous conclusion that each snail, by some incredible mechanism in its body, was winching its rope in, thus hauling the other until presently their bodies were pressed tightly together. I knew they must be mating, but their bodies had become so amalgamated that I could not see the precise nature of the act. They stayed rapturously side by side for some fifteen minutes and then, without so much as a nod or a thank you, they glided away in opposite directions, neither one displaying any signs of darts or ropes, or indeed any sign of enthusiasm at having culminated their love affair successfully.

I was so intrigued by this piece of behaviour that I could hardly wait until the following Thursday, when Theodore came to tea, to tell him about it. Theodore listened, rocking gently on his toes and nodding gravely while I graphically described what I had witnessed.

'Aha, yes,' he said when I had finished. 'You were . . . um . . . you know . . . um . . . extremely lucky to see that. I have watched any number of snails and I have never seen it.'

I asked whether I had imagined the little darts and the ropes.

'No, no,' said Theodore. 'That's quite correct. The darts are formed of a sort of . . . um . . . calcium-like substance and once they have penetrated the snail, they, you know, disappear . . . dissolve. It seems there is some evidence to think that the darts cause a *tingling* sensation which the snails . . . um . . . apparently find pleasant.'

I asked whether I was right in assuming that each snail had winched its rope in.

'Yes, yes, that's quite correct,' said Theodore. 'They apparently have some . . . um . . . sort of mechanism inside which can pull the rope back again.'

I said I thought it was one of the most remarkable things I had ever seen.

'Yes, indeed. Extremely curious,' said Theodore, and then added a bomb-shell that took my breath away. 'Once they are alongside, the . . . um . . . male half of one snail mates with the, um . . . female half of the other snail and . . . um, *vice versa*, as it were.'

It took me a moment or so to absorb this astonishing information. Was I correct in assuming, I inquired cautiously, that each snail was both male *and* female?

'Um. Yes,' said Theodore, 'hermaphrodite.'

His eyes twinkled at me and he rasped the side of his beard with his thumb. Larry, who had been wearing the pained expression he normally wore when Theodore and I discussed natural history, was equally astonished by this amazing revelation of the snails' sex life.

'Surely you're joking, Theodore?' he protested. 'You mean to say that each snail is both a male and a female?'

'Yes, indeed,' said Theodore, adding with masterly understatement, 'it's very curious.'

'Good God,' cried Larry. 'I think it's unfair. All those damned slimy things wandering about seducing each other like mad all over the bushes, and having the pleasures of both sensations. Why couldn't such a gift be given to the human race? That's what I want to know.'

'Aha, yes. But then you would have to lay eggs,' Theodore pointed out.

'True,' said Larry, 'but what a marvellous way of getting out of cocktail parties – "I'm terribly sorry I can't come," you would say. "I've got to sit on my eggs." '

Theodore gave a little snort of laughter.

'But snails don't sit on their eggs,' he explained. 'They bury them in damp earth and leave them.'

'The ideal way of bringing up a family,' said Mother, unexpectedly but with immense conviction. 'I wish I'd been able to bury you all in some damp earth and leave you.'

'That's an extremely harsh and ungrateful thing to say,' said Larry. 'You've probably given Gerry a complex for the rest of his life.'

But if the conversation had given me a complex, it was one about snails, for I was already planning vast snail-hunting expeditions with Roger, so that I could bring dozens of them back to the villa and keep them in tins, where I could observe them shooting their love darts at each other to my heart's content. But, in spite of the fact that I caught hundreds of snails during the next few weeks, kept them incarcerated in tins and lavished every care and attention on them (even gave them simulated thunder-storms with the aid of a watering can), I could not get them to mate.

The only other time I saw snails indulging in this curious love-play was when I succeeded in obtaining a pair of the giant Roman, or apple, snails that lived on the stony outcrops of the Mountain of the Ten Saints, and the only reason I was able to get up there and capture these snails was because, on my birthday, Mother had purchased for me my heart's desire, a sturdy baby donkey.

Although, ever since we arrived in Corfu, I had been aware that there were vast quantities of donkeys there – indeed the entire agricultural economy of the island depended on them – I had not really concentrated on them until we had gone to Katerina's wedding. Here a great number of the donkeys had brought with them their babies, many of them only a few days old. I was enchanted by their bulbous knees, their great ears, and their wobbling, uncertain walk and I had determined then, come what might, that I would possess a donkey of my own.

As I explained to Mother, while trying to argue her into agreeing to this, if I had a donkey to carry me and my equipment, I could go so much farther afield. Why couldn't I have it for Christmas, I asked? Because, Mother replied, firstly, they were too expensive, and secondly, there were not any babies available at that precise time. But if they were too expensive, I argued, why couldn't I have one as a Christmas *and* birthday present? I would willingly forgo all other presents in lieu of a donkey. Mother said she would see, which I knew from bitter experience generally meant that she would forget about the matter as rapidly and as comprehensively as possible. As it got near to my birthday, I once again reiterated all the arguments in favour of having a donkey. Mother just repeated that we would see.

Then one day, Costas, the brother of our maid, made his appearance in the olive grove just outside our little garden carrying on his shoulders a great bundle of tall bamboos. Whistling happily to himself he proceeded to dig holes in the ground and to set the bamboos upright so that they formed a small square. Peering at him through the fuchsia hedge, I wondered what on earth he was doing, so, whistling Roger, I went round to see.

'I am building,' said Costas, 'a house for your mother.'

I was astonished. What on earth could Mother want a bamboo house for? Had she, perhaps, decided to sleep out of doors? I felt this was unlikely. What, I inquired of Costas, did Mother want with a bamboo house?

He gazed at me wall-eyed.

'Who knows?' he said shrugging. 'Perhaps she wants to keep plants in it or store sweet potatoes for the winter.'

I thought this was extremely unlikely as well, but having watched Costas for half an hour I grew bored and went off for a walk with Roger.

By the next day the framework of the bamboo hut had been finished and Costas was now busy twining bundles of reeds between the bamboos to form solid walls and the roof. By the next day it was completed and looked exactly like one of Robinson Crusoe's earlier attempts at house-building. When I inquired of Mother what she intended to use the house for, she said that she was not quite sure, but she felt it would come in useful. With that vague information I had to be content.

The day before my birthday, everybody started acting in a slightly more eccentric manner than usual. Larry, for some reason best known to himself, went about the house shouting 'Tantivy!' and 'Tally-ho' and similar hunting slogans. As he was fairly frequently afflicted in this way, I did not take much notice.

Margo kept dodging about the house carrying mysterious bundles under her arms, and at one point I came face to face with her in the hall and noted, with astonishment, that her arms were full of multi-coloured decorations left over from Christmas. On seeing me she uttered a squeak of dismay and rushed into her bedroom in such a guilty and furtive manner that I was left staring after her with open mouth.

Even Leslie and Spiro were afflicted, it seemed, and they kept going into mysterious huddles in the garden. From the snippets of their conversation that I heard, I could not make head or tail of what they were planning.

'In the backs seats,' Spiro said, scowling. 'Honest to Gods, Masters Leslies, I have dones it befores.'

'Well, if you're sure, Spiro,' Leslie replied doubtfully, 'but we don't want any broken legs or anything.'

Then Leslie saw me undisguisedly eavesdropping and asked me truculently what the hell I thought I was doing, eavesdropping on people's private conversations? Why didn't I go down to the nearest cliff and jump off? Feeling that the family were in no mood to be amicable, I took Roger off into the olive groves and for the rest of the day we ineffectually chased green lizards.

That night I had just turned down the lamp and snuggled down in bed when I heard sounds of raucous singing, accompanied by gales of laughter, coming through the olive groves. As the uproar got closer, I could recognize Leslie's and Larry's voices, combined with Spiro's, each of them appearing to be singing a different song. It seemed as though they had been somewhere and celebrated too well. From the indignant whispering and shuffling going on in the corridor, I could tell that Margo and Mother had reached the same conclusion.

They burst into the villa, laughing hysterically at some witticism that Larry had produced, and were shushed fiercely by Margo and Mother.

'Do be quiet,' said Mother. 'You'll wake Gerry. What have you been drinking?'

'Wine,' said Larry in a dignified voice. He hiccuped.

'Wine,' said Leslie. 'And then we danced, and Spiro danced, and I danced, and Larry danced. And Spiro danced and then Larry danced and then I danced.'

'I think you had better go to bed,' said Mother.

'And then Spiro danced again,' said Leslie, 'and then Larry danced.'

'All right, dear, all right,' said Mother. 'Go to *bed*, for heaven's sake. Really, Spiro, I do feel that you shouldn't have let them drink so much.'

'Spiro danced,' said Leslie, driving the point home.

'I'll take him to bed,' said Larry. 'I'm the only sober member of the party.'

There was the sound of lurching feet on the tiles as Leslie and Larry, clasped in each other's arms, staggered down the corridor.

'I'm now dancing with *you*,' came Leslie's voice as Larry dragged him into his bedroom and put him to bed.

'I'm sorrys, Mrs Durrells,' said Spiro, his deep voice thickened with wine, 'but I couldn't stops thems.'

'Did you get it?' said Margo.

'Yes, Missy Margos. Don'ts you worrys,' said Spiro. 'It's down with Costas.'

Eventually Spiro left and I heard Mother and Margo going to bed. It made a fittingly mysterious end to what had been a highly confusing day as far as I was concerned. But I soon forgot about the family's behaviour, as, lying in the dark wondering what my presents were going to be the following day, I drifted off to sleep.

The following morning I woke and lay for a moment wondering what was so special about that day, and then I remembered. It was my birthday. I lay there savouring the feeling of having a whole day to myself when people would give me presents and the family would be forced to accede to any reasonable requests. I was just about to get out of bed and go and see what my presents were, when a curious uproar broke out in the hall.

'Hold its head. Hold its *head*,' came Leslie's voice.

'Look out, you're spoiling the decorations,' wailed Margo.

'Damn the bloody decorations,' said Leslie. 'Hold its *head*.'

'Now, now, dears,' said Mother, 'don't quarrel.'

'Dear God,' said Larry in disgust, 'dung all over the floor.'

The whole of this mysterious conversation was accompanied by a strange pitter-pattering noise, as though someone were bouncing ping-pong balls on the tile floor of the hall. What on earth, I wondered, was the family up to now? Normally at this time they were still lying, semi-conscious, groping bleary-eyed for their early morning cups of tea. I sat up in bed, preparatory to going into the hall to join in whatever fun was afoot, when my bedroom door burst open and a donkey, clad in festoons of coloured crepe paper, Christmas decorations, and with three enormous feathers attached skilfully between its large ears, came galloping into the bedroom, Leslie hanging grimly on to its tail, shouting, 'Woa, you bastard!'

'Language, dear,' said Mother, looking flustered in the doorway.

'You're spoiling the decorations,' screamed Margo.

'The sooner that animal gets out of here,' said Larry, 'the better. There's dung all over the hall now.'

'You frightened it,' said Margo.

'I didn't do anything,' said Larry indignantly. 'I just gave it a little push.'

The donkey skidded to a halt by my bedside and gazed at me out of enormous brown eyes. It seemed rather surprised. It shook itself vigorously so that the feathers between its ears fell off and then very dexterously it hacked Leslie on the shin with its hind leg.

'Jesus!' roared Leslie, hopping around on one leg. 'It's broken my bloody leg.'

'Leslie, dear, there is no need to swear so much,' said Mother. 'Remember Gerry.'

'The sooner you get it out of that bedroom the better,' said Larry. 'Otherwise the whole place will smell like a midden.'

'You've simply *ruined* its decorations,' said Margo, 'and it took me hours to put them on.'

But I was taking no notice of the family. The donkey had approached the edge of my bed and stared at me inquisitively for a moment and then had given a little throaty chuckle and thrust in my outstretched hands a grey muzzle as soft as everything soft I could think of – silkworm cocoons, newly born puppies, sea pebbles, or the velvety feel of a tree frog. Leslie had now removed his trousers and was examining the bruise on his shin, cursing fluently.

'Do you like it dear?' asked Mother.

Like it! I was speechless.

The donkey was a rich dark brown, almost a plum colour, with enormous ears like arum lilies, white socks over tiny polished hooves as neat as a tap-dancer's shoes. Running along her back was the broad black cross that denotes so proudly that her race carried Christ into Jerusalem (and has since continued to be one of the most maligned domestic animals ever), and round each great shining eye she had a neat white circle which denoted that she came from the village of Gastouri.

'You remember Katerina's donkey that you liked so much?' said Margo. 'Well, this is her baby.'

This, of course, made the donkey even more special. The donkey stood there looking like a refugee from a circus, chewing a piece of tinsel meditatively, while I scrambled out of bed and flung on my clothes. Where, I inquired breathlessly of Mother, was I to keep her? Obviously I couldn't keep her in the villa in view of the fact that Larry had just pointed out to Mother that she could, if she so wished, grow a good crop of potatoes in the hall.

'That's what that house Costas built is for,' said Mother.

I was beside myself with delight. What a noble, kindly, benevolent family I had! How cunningly they had kept the secret from me! How hard they had worked to deck the donkey out in its finery! Slowly and gently, as though she were some fragile piece of china, I led my steed out through the garden and round into the olive grove, opened the door of the little bamboo hut, and took her inside. I thought I ought to just try her for size, because Costas was a notoriously bad workman. The little house was splendid. Just big enough for her. I took her out again and tethered her to an olive tree on a long length of rope, then I stayed for half an hour in a dreamlike trance admiring her from every angle while she grazed placidly. Eventually I heard Mother calling me in to breakfast and I sighed with satisfaction. I had decided that, without any doubt whatsoever, and without wishing in any way to be partisan, this donkey was the finest donkey in the whole of the island of Corfu. For no reason that I could think of, I decided to call her Sally. I gave her a quick kiss on her silken muzzle and then went in to breakfast.

After breakfast, to my astonishment, Larry, with a magnanimous air, said that if I liked he would teach me to ride. I said that I didn't know he could ride.

'Of course,' said Larry airily. 'When we were in India I was always galloping about on ponies and things. I used to groom them and feed them and so forth. Have to know what you're doing, of course.'

So, armed with a blanket and a large piece of webbing, we went out into the olive grove, placed the blanket on Sally's back, and tied it in position. She viewed these preparations with interest but a lack of enthusiasm. With a certain amount of difficulty, for Sally would persist in walking round and round in a tight circle, Larry succeeded in getting me onto her back. He then exchanged her tether for a rope halter and rope reins.

'Now,' he said, 'you just steer her as though she's a boat. When you want her to go faster, just simply kick her in the ribs with your heels.'

If that was all there was to riding, I felt, it was going to be simplicity itself. I jerked on the reins and dug my heels into Sally's ribs. It was unfortunate that my fall was broken by a large and exceptionally luxuriant bramble bush. Sally peered at me as I extricated myself, with a look of astonishment on her face.

'Perhaps,' said Larry, 'you ought to have a stick so then you can use your legs for gripping on to her and you won't fall off.'

He cut me a short stick and once again I mounted Sally. This time I wrapped my legs tightly round her barrel body and gave her a sharp tap with my switch. She bucked several times, indignantly, but I clung on like a limpet, and to my delight, within half an hour, I had her trotting to and fro between the olive trees, responding neatly to tugs on the rein. Larry had been lying under the olives smoking and watching my progress. Now, as I appeared to have mastered the equestrian art, he rose to his feet and took a penknife out of his pocket.

'Now,' he said, as I dismounted, 'I'll show you how to look after her. First of all, you must brush her down every morning. We'll get a brush for you in town. Then you must make sure her hooves are clean. You must do that every day.'

I inquired, puzzled, how did one clean donkeys' hooves?

'I'll show you,' said Larry nonchalantly.

He walked up to Sally, bent down, and picked up her hind leg.

'In here,' he said, pointing with the blade of the knife at Sally's hoof, 'an awful lot of muck gets trapped. This can lead to all sorts of things. Foot-rot and so forth, and it's very important to keep them clean.'

So saying, he dug his penknife blade into Sally's hoof. What Larry had not realized was that donkeys in Corfu were unshod and that a baby donkey's hoof is still, comparatively speaking, soft and very delicate. So, not unnaturally, Sally reacted as though Larry had jabbed her with a red-hot skewer. She wrenched her hoof out of his hands and as he straightened up and turned in astonishment, she did a pretty pirouette and kicked him neatly in the pit of the stomach with both hind legs. Larry sat down heavily, his face went white, and he doubled up, clasping his stomach and making strange rattling noises. The alarm I felt was not for Larry but for Sally, for I was quite sure that he would extract the most terrible retribution when he recovered. Hastily I undid Sally's rope and flicked her on the rump with the stick and watched her canter off into the olives. Then I ran into the house and informed Mother that Larry had had an accident. The entire family, including Spiro, who had just arrived, came running out into the olive grove where Larry was still writhing about uttering great sobbing, wheezing noises.

'Larry, dear,' said Mother distraught, 'what *have* you been doing?'

'Attacked,' gasped Larry between wheezes. 'Unprovoked . . . Creature mad . . . Probably rabies . . . Ruptured appendix.'

With Leslie on one side of him and Spiro on the other they carted Larry slowly back to the villa, with Mother and Margo fluttering commiseratingly and ineffectually around him. In a crisis of this magnitude, involving my family, one had to keep one's wits about one or all was lost. I ran swiftly round to the kitchen door where, panting but innocent, I informed our maid that I was going to spend the day out and could she give me some food to eat. She put half a loaf of bread, some onions, some olives, and a hunk of cold meat into a paper bag and gave it to me. Fruit I knew I could obtain from any of my peasant friends. Then I raced through the olive groves, carrying this provender, in search of Sally.

I eventually found her half a mile away, grazing on a succulent patch of grass. After several ineffectual attempts, I managed to scramble up onto her back and then, belabouring her behind with a stick, I urged her to a brisk trot as far away from the villa as possible.

I had to return to the villa for tea because Theodore was coming. When I got back I found Larry, swathed in blankets, lying on the sofa giving Theodore a graphic description of the incident.

'And then, absolutely unprovoked, it suddenly turned on me with slavering jaws, like the charge of the Light Brigade.' He broke off to glare at me as I entered the room. 'Oh, so you decided to come back. And what, may I inquire, have you done with that equine menace?'

I replied that Sally was safely bedded down in her stable and had, fortunately, suffered no ill effects from the incident. Larry glared at me.

'Well, I'm delighted to hear that,' he said caustically. 'The fact that I am lying here with my spleen ruptured in three places is of apparently little or no moment.'

'I have brought you . . . um . . . a little, you know . . . er . . . gift,' said Theodore, and he presented me with a replica of his own collecting box, complete with tubes and a fine muslin net. I could not have asked for anything nicer and I thanked him volubly.

'You had better go and thank Katerina too, dear,' said Mother. 'She didn't really want to part with Sally, you know.'

'I am surprised,' said Larry. 'I'd have thought she'd have been only too *glad* to get rid of her.'

'You'd better not go and see Katerina now,' said Margo. 'She's getting near her time.'

Intrigued by this unusual phrase, I asked what 'getting near her time' meant.

'She's going to have a baby, dear,' said Mother.

'The wonder of it is,' said Larry, 'as I thought when we went to the wedding, she didn't have it in the vestry.'

'Larry, dear,' said Mother. 'Not in front of Gerry.'

'Well, it's true,' said Larry. 'I've never seen such a pregnant bride in white.'

I said I thought it would be a good idea if I went to thank Katerina *before* she had the baby because after she had it she would probably be very busy. Reluctantly, Mother agreed to this, and so the following morning I mounted Sally and rode off through the olive trees in the direction of Gastouri, Roger trotting behind and indulging in a game which he and Sally had invented between them, which consisted of Roger darting in at intervals and nibbling her heels gently, growling furiously, whereupon Sally would give a skittish little buck and attempt to kick him in the ribs.

Presently we came to the little low white house, with the flattened area outside its front door neatly ringed with old rusty cans filled with flowers. To my astonishment I saw that we were not the only visitors that day. There were several elderly gentlemen sitting round a small table, hunched over glasses of wine, their enormous, swooping, nicotine-stained moustaches flapping up and down as they talked to each other. Clustered in the doorway of the house and peering eagerly through the one small window that illuminated its interior, there was a solid wedge of female relatives, all chattering and gesticulating at once.

From inside the house came a series of piercing shrieks, interspersed with cries for help from the Almighty, the Virgin Mary, and St Spiridion. I gathered from all this uproar and activity that I had arrived in the middle of a family row. This interfamily warfare was quite a common thing among the peasants and something I always found very enjoyable, for any quarrel, however trivial, was carried on with grim determination until it was sucked dry of the very last juices of drama, with people shouting abuse at one another through the olive trees and the men periodically chasing each other with bamboos.

I tethered Sally and made my way to the front door of the house, wondering, as I did so, what this particular row was about. The last one in this area that I remembered had lasted for a prodigious length of time (three weeks) and had all been started by a small boy who told his cousin that his grandfather cheated at cards. I wriggled and pushed my way determinedly through the knot of people who blocked the doorway and finally got inside, only to find the entire room seemed to be filled with Katerina's relatives, packed shoulder to shoulder like a football crowd. I had, quite early in life, discovered that the only way of dealing with a situation like this was to get down on one's hands and knees and crawl. This I did and by this means successfully achieved the front row in the circle of relatives that surrounded the great double bed.

Now I could see that something much more interesting than a family row was taking place. Katerina was lying on the bed with her cheap print frock rolled right up above her great, swollen breasts. Her hands were tightly clasping the head of the big brass bedstead, her white mound of a stomach quivered and strained with what appeared to be a life of its own, and she kept drawing her legs up and screaming, rolling her head from side to side, the sweat pouring down her face. Near her by the bedside, and obviously in charge of the proceedings, was a tiny, dirty, wizened little witch of a woman holding a bucket in one hand full of well water. Periodically she would dip a bundle of filthy rags into this and mop Katerina's face and her thighs with it. On the table by the bedstead a jug full of wine and a glass stood, and every time the old crone had finished the ablutions, she would put a drop of wine in the glass and force it into Katerina's mouth; then she would fill the glass and drain it herself, for presumably, in her capacity as midwife, she needed to keep up her strength as much as Katerina.

I congratulated myself warmly on the fact that I had not been deviated on my ride up to Katerina's house by several interesting things I had seen. If, for example, I had stopped to climb up to what I was pretty certain was a magpie's nest, I would probably have missed this whole exciting scene. Curiously enough, I was so used to the shrill indignation of the peasants over the most trivial circumstances that I did not really, consciously, associate Katerina's falsetto screams with pain. It was obvious that she was in some pain. Her face was white, crumpled, and old-looking, but I automatically subtracted ninety per cent of the screaming as exaggeration. Now and then, when she uttered a particularly loud scream and implored St Spiridion for his aid, all the relatives would scream in sympathy and also implore the Saint's intervention. The resulting cacophony in that tiny space had to be heard to be believed.

Suddenly Katerina clasped the bed-head still more tightly, the muscles in her brown arms showing taut. She writhed, drew up her legs and spread them wide apart.

'It is coming. It is coming. Praised be Saint Spiridion,' shouted all the relatives in chorus, and I noticed in the middle of the tangled, matted mass of Katerina's pubic hairs a round white object appear, rather like the top of an egg. There was a moment's pause and Katerina strained again and uttered a moaning gasp. Then, to my entranced delight, the baby's head suddenly popped out of her like a rabbit out of a hat, to be quickly followed by its pink, twitching body. Its face and its limbs were as crumpled and as delicate as a rose's petals. But it was its minuteness and the fact that it was so perfectly formed that intrigued me. The midwife shuffled forward shouting prayers and instructions to Katerina and seized the baby from between her blood-stained thighs. At that moment, to my intense annoyance, the ring of relatives all moved forward a pace in their eagerness to see the sex of the child, so that I missed the next piece of the drama, for all I could see were the large and extremely well-padded rumps of two of Katerina's larger aunts.

By the time I had burrowed between their legs and voluminous skirts and got to the front of the circle again, the midwife – at shouts of delight from everybody – declared the baby to be a boy and had severed the umbilical cord with a large and very ancient penknife she had extracted from a pocket in her skirt. One of the aunts surged forward and together she and the midwife tied the cord. Then, while the aunt held the squalling, twitching, pink blob of life, the midwife dipped her bundle of rags into the bucket and proceeded to swab the baby down. This done, she then filled a glass with wine and gave a couple of sips to Katerina and then filled her mouth with wine and proceeded to spit it from her toothless gums all over the baby's head, making the sign of the cross over its little body as she did so. Then she clasped the baby to her bosom and turned fiercely on the crowd of relatives.

'Come now, come now,' she shrilled. 'It is done. He has arrived. Go now, go now.'

Laughing and chattering excitedly, the relatives poured out of the little house and immediately started drinking wine and congratulating each other as though they had all personally been responsible for the successful birth of the baby. In the airless little room, smelling so strongly of sweat and garlic, Katerina lay exhausted on the bed, making feeble attempts to pull her dress down to cover her nakedness. I went to the edge of the bed and looked down at her.

'*Yasu*, Gerry mine,' she said and sketched a white travesty of her normal brilliant smile. She looked incredibly old, lying there.

I congratulated her politely on the birth of her first son and then thanked her for the donkey. She smiled again.

'Go outside,' she said. 'They will give you some wine.'

I left the little room and hurried after the midwife, for I was anxious to see what the next stage was in her treatment of the baby. Out at the back of the house she had spread a white linen cloth over a small table and placed the child on it. Then she picked up great rolls of previously prepared cloth, like very wide bandage, and with the aid of one of the more nimble and sober aunts, she proceeded to wind this round and round the baby's tiny body, pausing frequently to make sure its arms lay flat by its sides and its legs were together. Slowly and methodically she bound it up as straight as a guardsman. It lay there with only its head sticking out from this cocoon of webbing. Greatly intrigued by this, I asked the midwife why she was binding the baby up.

'Why? Why?' she said, her grizzled grey eyebrows flapping over her eyes, milky with cataracts, that peered at me fiercely. 'Because, if you don't bind up the baby, its limbs won't grow straight. Its bones are as soft as an egg. If you don't bind it up, its limbs will grow crooked or when it kicks and waves its arms about, it will break its bones, like little sticks of charcoal.'

I knew that babies in England were not bound up in this way, and I wondered whether this was because the British were in some way tougher-boned. Otherwise, it seemed to me, there would have been an awful lot of deformities inhabiting the British Isles. I made a mental note to discuss this medical problem with Theodore at the first opportunity.

After I had drunk several glasses of wine to honour the baby and eaten a large bunch of grapes, I got on Sally's back and rode slowly home. I would not have missed that morning for anything, I decided. But, thinking about it as we jogged through the dappled shade of the olives, the thing that amazed me was that anything so perfect and so beautiful should have matured and come forth from the interior of what, to me, was an old woman. It was like, I reflected, breaking open the old, brown, prickly husk of a chestnut and finding the lovely gleaming trophy inside.

PART TWO

Kontokali

Hospitality is, indeed, now no less than in classical times, a sacred duty in these islands, and it is a duty most conscientiously performed.

— PROFESSOR ANSTEAD

4

The Pygmy Jungle

It was a warm spring day, as blue as a jay's wing, and I waited impatiently for Theodore to arrive, for we were going to take a picnic lunch and walk two or three miles to a small lake that was one of our happiest hunting grounds. These days spent with Theodore, these 'excursions' as he called them, were of absorbing interest to me, but they must have been very exhausting for Theodore, for, from the moment of his arrival till his departure, I would ply him with a ceaseless string of questions.

Eventually, Theodore's cab clopped and tinkled its way up the drive and Theodore dismounted, clad, as always, in the most unsuitable attire for collecting: a neat tweed suit, respectable, highly polished boots, and a grey Homburg perched squarely on his head. The only ungracious note in this city gentleman's outfit was his collecting box, full of tubes and bottles, slung over one shoulder, and a small net with a bottle dangling from the end, attached to the end of his walking-stick.

'Ah, um,' he said, shaking me gravely by the hand. 'How are you? I see that we have got, um . . . a nice day for our excursion.'

As at that time of year one got weeks on end of nice days, this was scarcely surprising, but Theodore always insisted on mentioning it as though it was some special privilege that had been granted us by the gods of collecting. Quickly we gathered up the bag of food and the little stone bottles of ginger beer Mother had prepared for us, and slung these on our backs, together with my collecting equipment, which was slightly more extensive than Theodore's, since everything was grist to my mill and I had to be prepared for any eventuality.

Then, whistling for Roger, we went off through the sunlit olive groves, striped with shade, the whole island, spring-fresh and brilliant, lying before us. At this time of the year the olive groves would be full of flowers. Pale anemones with the tips of their petals dyed red as though they had been sipping wine, pyramid orchids that looked as though they had been made of pink icing, and yellow crocuses so fat, glossy, and waxy-looking you felt they would light like a candle if you set a match to their stamens. We would tramp through the rough stone paths among the olives, then for a mile or so follow the road lined with tall and ancient cypresses, each covered in a layer of white dust, like a hundred dark paint brushes loaded with chalk white. Presently we would strike off from the road and make our way over the crest of a small hill and there, lying below us, would be the lake, perhaps four acres in extent, its rim shaggy with reeds and its water green with plants.

On this particular day, as we made our way down the hillside towards the lake, I was walking a little ahead of Theodore and I suddenly came to an abrupt halt and stared with amazement at the path ahead of me. Alongside the edge of the path was the bed of a tiny stream which meandered its way down to join the lake. The stream was such a tiny one that even the early spring sun had succeeded in drying it up, so that there was only the smallest trickle of water. Through the bed of the stream and then up across the path and into the stream again lay what at first sight appeared to be a thick cable which seemed to be mysteriously possessed of a life of its own. When I looked closely I could see that the cable was made up of what looked like hundreds of small, dusty snakes. I shouted eagerly to Theodore and when he came I pointed this phenomenon out to him.

'Aha!' he said, his beard bristling and a keen light of interest in his eyes. 'Um, yes. Very interesting. Elvers.'

What kind of snake was an elver, I inquired, and why were they all travelling in a procession?

'No, no,' said Theodore. 'They are not snakes. They are baby eels and they appear to be, um . . . you know, making their way down to the lake.'

Fascinated, I crouched over the long column of baby eels, wriggling determinedly through the stone and grass and prickly thistles, their skins dry and dusty. There seemed to be millions of them. Who, in this dry, dusty place, would expect to find eels wriggling about?

'The whole, um . . . history of the eel,' said Theodore, putting his collecting box on the ground and seating himself on a convenient rock, 'is very curious. You see, at certain times the adult eels leave the ponds or rivers where they have been living and, er . . . make their way down to the sea. All the European eels do this and so do the North American eels. Where they went to was, for a long time, a mystery. The only thing, um . . . you know . . . scientists knew was that they never came *back*, but that eventually these baby eels would return and repopulate the same rivers and streams. It was not until after quite a number of years that people discovered what really happened.'

He paused and scratched his beard thoughtfully.

'All the eels made their way down to the sea and then swam through the Mediterranean, across the Atlantic, until they reached the Sargasso Sea, which is, as you know, off the north-eastern coast of South America. The . . . um . . . North American eels, of course, didn't have so far to travel, but they made their way to the same place. Here they mated, laid their eggs, and died. The eel larva, when it hatches out, is a very curious, um . . . you know . . . leaf-shaped creature and transparent, so unlike the adult eel that for a long time it was classified in a separate genus. Well, these larvae make their way slowly backwards to the place where their parents have come from and by the time they reach the Mediterranean or the North American shore, they look like these.'

Here Theodore paused and rasped his beard again and

delicately inserted the end of his cane into the moving column of elvers so that they writhed indignantly.

'They seem to have a very um . . . you know . . . strong homing instinct,' said Theodore. 'We must be some two miles from the sea, I suppose, and yet all these little elvers are making their way across this countryside in order to get back to the same lake that their parents left.'

He paused and glanced about him keenly and then pointed with his stick.

'It's quite a hazardous journey,' he observed, and I saw what he meant, for a kestrel was flying like a little black cross just above the line of baby eels, and as we watched he swooped and flew away with his claws firmly gripping a writhing mass of them.

As we walked on, following the line of eels, since they were going in the same direction, we saw other predators at work. Groups of magpies and jackdaws and a couple of jays flew up at our approach and we caught, out of the corner of our eye, the red glint of a fox disappearing into the myrtle bushes.

When we reached the lake-side, we had a set pattern of behaviour. First we would have a prolonged discussion as to which olive tree would be the best to put some of our equipment and our food under – which one would cast the deepest and the best shade at noon. Having decided on this, we would make a little pile of our possessions under it and then, armed with our nets and collecting boxes, we would approach the lake. Here we would potter happily for the rest of the morning, pacing with the slow concentration of a pair of fishing herons, dipping our nets into the weed-filigreed water. Here Theodore came into his own more than anywhere else. From the depths of the lake, as he stood there with the big scarlet dragon-flies zooming like arrows round him, he would extract magic that Merlin would have envied.

Here in the still, wine-gold waters, lay a pygmy jungle. On the lake bottom prowled the deadly dragon-fly larvae, as cunning predators as the tiger, inching their way through the debris of a million last year's leaves. Here the black tadpoles, sleek and shiny as licorice drops, disported in the shallows like plump herds of hippo in some African river. Through green forests of weed the multi-coloured swarms of microscopic creatures twitched and fluttered like flocks of exotic birds, while among the roots of the forests the newts, the leeches uncoiled like great snakes in the gloom, stretching out beseechingly, ever hungry. And here the caddis larvae, in their shaggy coats of twigs and debris, crawled dimly like bears fresh from hibernation across the sun-ringed hills and valleys of soft black mud.

'Aha, now, this is rather interesting. You see this, um . . . little maggot-like thing? Now this is the larva of the China-mark moth. I think, as a matter of fact, you have got one in your collection. What? Well, they're called China-mark moths because of the markings on the wing, which are said to resemble very closely marks that potters put on the base of, er . . . you know, very *good* china. Spode and so forth. Now the China-mark is interesting because it is one of the few moths that have aquatic larvae. The larvae live under water until they are . . . um . . . ready to pupate. The interesting thing about this particular species is that they have, er . . . um . . . you know, two forms of female. The male, of course, is fully winged and flies about when it hatches and er . . . so does one of the females. But the other female when it hatches out has, um . . . no wings and continues to live under the water, using its legs to swim with.'

Theodore paced a little farther along the bank on the mud that was already dried and jigsawed by the spring sun. A kingfisher exploded like a blue firework from the small willow, and out on the centre of the lake a tern swooped and glided on graceful, sickle-shaped wings. Theodore dipped his net into the weedy water, sweeping it to and fro gently, as though he were stroking a cat. Then the net was lifted and held aloft, while the tiny bottle that dangled from it would be subjected to a minute scrutiny through a magnifying glass.

'Um, yes. Some cyclopes. Two mosquito larvae. Aha, that's interesting. You see this caddis larva has made his case entirely out of baby ram's-horn snail shells. It is ... you know ... remarkably pretty. Ah now! Here we have, I think, yes, yes, here we have some rotifers.'

In a desperate attempt to keep pace with this flood of knowledge, I asked what rotifers were and peered into the little bottle through the magnifying glass at the twitching, wriggling creatures, as Theodore told me.

'The early naturalists used to call them wheel-animalcules, because of their curious limbs, you know. They wave them about in a very curious fashion, so that they almost look like, um ... you know, um ... er ... like the *wheels* of a watch. When you next come to see me I'll put some of these under the microscope for you. They are really extraordinarily beautiful creatures. These are, of course, all females.'

I asked why, of course, they should be females?

'This is one of the interesting things about the rotifer. The females produce virgin eggs. Um ... that is to say, they produce eggs without having come into contact with a male. Um ... er ... somewhat like a chicken, you know. But the difference is that the *rotifer* eggs hatch out into other females which in turn are capable of laying more eggs which ... um ... again hatch out into females. But at certain times, the females lay *smaller* eggs, which hatch out into males. Now, as you will see when I put these under the microscope, the female has a – how shall one say? – a quite *complex* body, an alimentary tract, and so on. The male has nothing at all. He is really just, er ... um ... a swimming bag of sperm.'

I was bereft of speech at the complexities of the private life of the rotifer.

'Another curious thing about them,' Theodore continued,

happily piling miracle upon miracle, 'is that at certain times, er . . . you know, if it is a hot summer or something like that and the pond is liable to dry up, they go down to the bottom and form a sort of hard shell round themselves. It's a sort of *suspended animation*, for the pond can dry up for, er . . . um . . . let us say seven or eight years, and they will just lie there in the dust. But as soon as the first rain falls and fills the pond, they come to life again.'

Again we moved forward, sweeping our nets through the balloon-like masses of frogs' spawn and the trailing necklace-like strings of the toad spawn.

'Here is, er . . . if you just take the glass a minute and look . . . an exceptionally fine hydra.'

Through the glass there sprang to life a tiny fragment of weed to which was attached a long slender coffee-coloured column, at the top of which was a writhing mass of elegant tentacles. As I watched, a rotund and earnest cyclops, carrying two large and apparently heavy sacks containing pink eggs, swam in a series of breathless jerks too close to the writhing arms of the hydra. In a moment it was engulfed. It gave a couple of violent twitches before it was stung to death. I knew, if you watched long enough, you could watch the cyclops being slowly and steadily engulfed and passing, in the shape of a bulge, down the column of the hydra.

Presently the height and the heat of the sun would tell us that it was lunch-time, and we would make our way back to our olive trees and sit there eating our food and drinking our ginger beer to the accompaniment of the sleepy zithering of the first-hatched cicadas of the year and the gentle, questioning coos of the collared doves.

'In Greek,' Theodore said, munching his sandwich methodically, 'the name for collared dove is *dekaoctur* – "eighteener," you know. The story goes that when Christ was . . . um . . . carrying the cross to Calvary, a Roman soldier, seeing that He was exhausted, took pity on Him. By the side of the road there was an old woman selling . . . um . . . you know . . . *milk*, and so the Roman soldier went to her and asked her how much a cupful would cost. She replied that it would cost eighteen coins. But the soldier had only seventeen. He . . . er . . . you know . . . pleaded with the woman to let him have a cupful of milk for Christ for seventeen coins, but the woman avariciously held out for eighteen. So, when Christ was crucified, the old woman was turned into a turtle dove and condemned to go about for the rest of her days repeating *dekaocto, dekaocto* – "eighteen, eighteen." If ever she agrees to say *deka-epta*, seventeen, she will regain her human form. If, out of obstinacy, she says *deka-ennaea*, nineteen, the world will come to an end.'

In the cool olive shade the tiny ants, black and shiny as caviare, would be foraging for our left-overs among last year's discarded olive leaves that the past summer's sun had dried and coloured a nut-brown and banana-yellow. They lay there as curled and as crisp as brandy-snaps. On the hillside behind us a herd of goats passed, the leader's bell clonking mournfully. We could hear the tearing sound of their jaws as they ate, indiscriminately, any foliage that came within their reach. The leader paced up to us and gazed for a minute with baleful, yellow eyes, snorting clouds of thyme-laden breath at us.

'They should not, er . . . you know, be left unattended,' said Theodore, prodding the goat gently with his stick. 'Goats do more damage to the countryside than practically anything else.'

The leader uttered a short sardonic 'bah' and then moved away, with his destructive troop following him.

We would lie for an hour or so, drowsing, and digesting our food, staring up through the tangled olive branches at a sky that was patterned with tiny white clouds like a child's finger-prints on a blue, frosty, winter window.

'Well,' Theodore would say at last, getting to his feet, 'I think perhaps we ought to . . . you know . . . just see what the *other* side of the lake has to offer.'

So once more we would commence our slow pacing of the rim of the shore. Steadily our test tubes, bottles, and jars would fill with a shimmer of microscopic life, and my boxes and tins and bags would be stuffed with frogs, baby terrapins, and a host of beetles.

'I suppose,' Theodore would say at last, reluctantly, glancing up at the sinking sun, 'I suppose . . . you know . . . we ought to be getting along home.'

And so we would laboriously hoist our now extremely heavy collecting boxes onto our shoulders and trudge homeward on weary feet, Roger, his tongue hanging out like a pink flag, trotting soberly ahead of us. Reaching the villa, our catches would be moved to more capacious quarters. Then Theodore and I would relax and discuss the day's work, drinking gallons of hot, stimulating tea and gorging ourselves on golden scones, bubbling with butter, fresh from Mother's oven.

It was when I paid a visit to this lake without Theodore that I caught, quite by chance, a creature that I had long wanted to meet. As I drew my net up out of the waters and examined the tangled weed mass it contained, I found crouching there, of all unlikely things, a spider. I was delighted, for I had read about this curious beast, which must be one of the most unusual species of spider in the world, for it lives a very strange aquatic existence. It was about half an inch long and marked in a rather vague sort of way with silver and brown. I put it triumphantly into one of my collecting tins and carried it home tenderly.

Here I set up an aquarium with a sandy floor and decorated it with some small dead branches and fronds of water-weed. Putting the spider on one of the twigs that stuck up above the water-level, I watched to see what it would do. It immediately ran down the twig and plunged into the water, where it turned a bright and beautiful silver, owing to the numerous minute air bubbles trapped in the hairs on its body. It spent five minutes or so running about below the surface of the water, investigating all the twigs and water-weed before it finally settled on a spot in which to construct its home.

Now the water-spider was the original inventor of the diving-bell, and sitting absorbed in front of the aquarium, I watched how it was done. First the spider attached several lengthy strands of silk from the weeds to the twigs. These were to act as guy ropes. Then, taking up a position roughly in the centre of these guy ropes, it proceeded to spin an irregular oval-shaped flat web of a more or less conventional type, but of a finer mesh, so that it looked more like a cobweb. This occupied the greater part of two hours. Having got the structure of its home built to its satisfaction, it now had to give it an air supply. This it did by making numerous trips to the surface of the water and into the air. When it returned to the water its body would be silvery with air bubbles. It would then run down and take up its position underneath the web and, by stroking itself with its legs, rid itself of the air bubbles, which rose and were immediately trapped underneath the web. After it had done this five or six times, all the tiny bubbles under the web had amalgamated into one big bubble. As the spider added more and more air to this bubble and the bubble grew bigger and bigger, its strength started to push the web up until eventually the spider had achieved success. Firmly anchored by the guy ropes between the weed and the twigs was suspended a bell-shaped structure full of air. This was now the spider's home in which it could live quite comfortably without even having to pay frequent visits to the surface, for the air in the bell would, I knew, be replenished by the oxygen given up by the weeds, and the carbon monoxide given out by the spider would soak through the silky walls of its house.

Sitting and watching this miraculous piece of craftsmanship, I wondered how on earth the very first water-spider (who wanted to *become* a water-spider) had managed to work out this ingenious method of living below the surface. But the habit of living in its own home-made submarine is not the only peculiar thing about this spider. Unlike the greater majority of species, the male is about twice the size of the female, and once they have mated, the male is not devoured by his wife, as happens so frequently in the married life of the spider. I could tell from her size that my spider was a female and I thought that her abdomen looked rather swollen. It seemed to me she might be expecting a happy event, so I took great pains to make sure that she got plenty of good food. She liked fat green daphnia, which she was extraordinarily adept at catching as they swam past; but probably her favourite food of all was the tiny, newly hatched newt efts which, although they were a bulky prey for her, she never hesitated to tackle. Having captured whatever titbit happened to be passing, she would then carry it up into her bell and eat it there in comfort.

Then came the great day when I saw that she was adding an extension to the bell. She did not hurry over this and it took her two days to complete. Then one morning, on peering into her tank, I saw to my delight that the nursery contained a round ball of eggs. In due course these hatched out into miniature replicas of the mother. I soon had more water-spiders than I knew what to do with and I found, to my annoyance, that the mother, with complete lack of parental feeling, was happily feeding off her own progeny. So I was forced to move the babies into another aquarium, but as they grew they took to feeding upon each other and so in the end I just kept the two most intelligent-looking ones and took all the rest down to the lake and let them go.

It was at this time, when I was deeply involved with the water-spiders, that Sven Olson at last turned up. Larry, to Mother's consternation, had developed the habit of inviting hordes of painters, poets, and authors to stay without any reference to her. Sven Olson was a sculptor, and we had had some warning of his impending arrival, for he had been bombarding us for several weeks with contradictory telegrams about his movements, which had driven Mother to distraction because she kept having to make and unmake his bed. Mother and I were having a quiet cup of tea on the veranda when a cab made its appearance, wound its way up the drive, and came to a stop in front of the house. In the back was seated an enormous man who bore a remarkable facial resemblance to the reconstructions of Neanderthal man. He was clad in a white singlet, a pair of voluminous brightly checked plus fours, and sandals. On his massive head was a broad-brimmed straw hat. The two holes situated one each side of the crown argued that this hat had been designed for the use of a horse. He got ponderously out of the cab, carrying a very large and battered Gladstone bag and an accordion. Mother and I went down to greet him. As he saw us approaching, he swept off his hat and bowed, revealing that his enormous cranium was completely devoid of hair except for a strange, grey, tattered duck's tail on the nape of his neck.

'Mrs Durrell?' he inquired, fixing Mother with large and child-like blue eyes. 'I am enchanted to meet you. My name is Sven.'

His English was impeccable, with scarcely any trace of an accent, but his voice was quite extraordinary, for it wavered between a deep rich baritone and a quavering falsetto, as though, in spite of his age, his voice was only just breaking. He extended a very large, white, spade-shaped hand to Mother and bowed once again.

'Well, I am glad you have managed to get here at last,' said Mother, brightly and untruthfully. 'Do come in and have some tea.'

I carried his accordion and his Gladstone bag and we all went and sat on the balcony and drank tea and stared at each other. There was a long, long silence while Sven munched on a piece of toast and occasionally smiled lovingly at Mother, while she smiled back and desperately searched her mind for suitable intellectual topics of conversation. Sven swallowed a piece of toast and coughed violently. His eyes filled with tears.

'I love toast,' he gasped. 'I simply love it. But it always does this to me.'

We plied him with more tea and presently his paroxysms of coughing died away. He sat forward, his huge hands folded in his lap, showing white as marble against the hideous pattern of his plus fours, and fixed Mother with an inquiring eye.

'Are you,' he inquired wistfully, 'are you, by any chance, musically inclined?'

'Well,' said Mother, startled, and obviously suffering from the hideous suspicion that if she said 'Yes' Sven might ask her to sing, 'I like music, of course, but I . . . can't play anything.'

'I suppose,' said Sven diffidently, 'you wouldn't like me to play something for you?'

'Oh, er, yes, by all means,' said Mother. 'That would be delightful.'

Sven beamed lovingly at her, picked up his accordion and unstrapped it. He extended it like a caterpillar and it produced noise like the tail-end of a donkey's bray.

'She,' said Sven, lovingly patting the accordion, 'has got some sea air in her.'

He settled his accordion more comfortably against his broad chest, arranged his sausage-like fingers carefully on the keys, closed his eyes, and began to play. It was a very complicated and extraordinary tune. Sven was wearing such an expression of rapture upon his ugly face that I was dying to laugh and was having to bite the insides of my cheeks to prevent it. Mother sat there with a face of frozen politeness like a world-famous conductor being forced to listen to somebody giving a recital on a penny whistle. Eventually the tune came to a harsh, discordant end. Sven heaved a sigh of pure delight, opened his eyes, and smiled at Mother.

'Bach is so beautiful,' he said.

'Oh, yes,' said Mother with well-simulated enthusiasm.

'I'm glad you like it,' said Sven. 'I'll play you some more.'

So for the next hour Mother and I sat there, trapped, while Sven played piece after piece. Every time Mother made some move to seek an escape, Sven would hold up one of his huge hands, as though arresting a line of imaginary traffic, and say, 'Just one more,' archly, and Mother, with a tremulous smile, would sit back in her chair.

It was with considerable relief that we greeted the rest of the family when they arrived back from town. Larry and Sven danced round each other, roaring like a couple of bulls and exchanging passionate embraces, and then Larry dragged Sven off to his room and they were closeted there for hours, the sound of gales of laughter occasionally drifting down to us.

'What's he like?' asked Margo.

'Well, I don't really know, dear,' said Mother. 'He's been playing to us ever since he arrived.'

'Playing?' said Leslie. 'Playing what?'

'His barrel organ, or whatever you call it,' said Mother.

'My God,' said Leslie. 'I can't stand those things. I hope he isn't going to play it all over the house.'

'No, no, dear. I'm sure he won't,' said Mother hastily, but her tone lacked conviction.

Just at that moment Larry appeared on the veranda again.

'Where's Sven's accordion?' he asked. 'He wants to play me something.'

'Oh, God,' said Leslie. 'There you are. I told you.'

'I hope he isn't going to play that accordion *all* the time, dear,' said Mother. 'We've already had an hour of it and it's given me a splitting headache.'

'Of course he won't play it all the time,' said Larry irritably, picking up the accordion. 'He just wants to play me one tune. What was he playing to you, anyway?'

'The most weird music,' said Mother. 'By some man – you know the one – something to do with trees.'

The rest of the day was, to say the least, harrying. Sven's

repertoire was apparently inexhaustible and when, during dinner, he insisted on giving us an impression of meal-time in a Scottish fortress by marching round and round the table playing one of the more untuneful Scottish reels, I could see the defences of the family crumbling. Even Larry was beginning to look a little pensive. Roger, who was uninhibited and straightforward in his dealings with human beings, summed up his opinion of Sven's performance by throwing back his head and howling dismally, a thing he only did normally when he heard the national anthem.

But by the time Sven had been with us three days, we had become more or less inured to his accordion, and Sven himself charmed us all. He exuded a sort of innocent goodness, so that whatever he did one could not be annoyed with him, any more than you can be annoyed with a baby for wetting its nappy. He quickly endeared himself to Mother, for, she discovered, he was an ardent cook himself and carried round an enormous leather-bound notebook in which he jotted down recipes. He and Mother spent hours in the kitchen, teaching each other how to cook their favourite dishes, and the results were meals of such bulk and splendour that all of us began to feel liverish and out of sorts.

It was about a week after his arrival that Sven wandered one morning into the room I proudly called my study. In that massive villa we had such a superfluity of rooms that I had succeeded in getting Mother to give me a special room of my own in which I could keep all my creatures.

My menagerie at this time was pretty extensive. There was Ulysses, the scops owl, who spent all day sitting on the pelmet above the window, imitating a decaying olive stump, and occasionally, with a look of great disdain, regurgitating a pellet onto the newspaper spread below him. The dog contingent had been increased to three by a couple of young mongrels who had been given to me for my birthday by a peasant family and who, because of their completely undisciplined behaviour, had been christened Widdle and Puke. There were rows and rows of jam jars, some containing specimens in methylated spirits, others containing microscopic life. And then there were six aquariums that housed a variety of newts, frogs, snakes, and toads. Piles of glass-topped boxes contained my collections of butterflies, beetles, and dragon-flies. Sven, to my astonishment, displayed a deep and almost reverent interest in my collection. Delighted to have somebody displaying enthusiasm for my cherished menagerie, I took him on a carefully conducted tour and showed him everything, even, after swearing him to secrecy, my family of tiny, chocolate-coloured scorpions that I had smuggled into the house unbeknownst to the family. One of the things that impressed Sven most was the underwater bell of the spider, and he stood quite silently in front of it, his great blue eyes fixed on it intensely, watching the spider as she caught her food and carried it up into the little dome. Seven displayed such enthusiasm that I suggested to him, rather tentatively, that he might like to spend a little time in the olive groves with me, so that I could show him some of these creatures in their natural haunts.

'But how kind of you,' he said, his great, ugly face lighting up delightedly. 'Are you sure I won't be interfering?'

No, I assured him he would not be interfering.

'Then I would be delighted,' said Sven. 'Absolutely delighted.'

So, for the rest of his stay, we would disappear from the villa after breakfast and spend a couple of hours in the olive groves.

On Sven's last day – he was leaving on the evening boat – we held a little farewell lunch party for him and invited Theodore. Delighted at having a new audience, Sven immediately gave Theodore a half-hour recital of Bach on his accordion.

'Um,' said Theodore, when Sven had finished, 'do you, you know, er . . . know any other tunes?'

'Just name it, Doctor,' said Sven, spreading out his hands expansively. 'I will play it for you.'

Theodore rocked thoughtfully for a moment on his toes.

'You don't by any chance, I suppose, er . . . happen to know a song called "There Is a Tavern in the Town"?' he inquired shyly.

'Of course!' said Sven and immediately crashed into the opening bars of the song.

Theodore sang vigorously, his beard bristling, his eyes bright, and when he had come to the end, Sven, without pause, switched into 'Clementine.' Emboldened by Theodore's Philistine attitude towards Bach, Mother asked Sven whether he could play 'If I Were a Blackbird' and 'The Spinning Wheel Song,' which he promptly executed in a masterly fashion.

Then the cab arrived to take him down to the docks, and he embraced each one of us fondly, his eyes full of tears. He climbed into the back of the cab with his Gladstone bag beside him and his precious accordion on his lap, and he waved to us extravagantly as the cab disappeared down the drive.

'Such a *manly* man,' said Mother with satisfaction, as we went inside. 'Quite one of the old school.'

'You should have told him that,' said Larry, stretching himself out on the sofa and picking up his book. 'There's nothing homo's like better than to be told they are virile and manly.'

'Whatever do you mean?' asked Mother, putting on her spectacles and glaring at Larry suspiciously.

Larry lowered his book and looked at her, puzzled.

'Homosexuals like to be told they are virile and manly,' he said at length, patiently, and with the air of one explaining a simple problem to a backward child.

Mother continued to glare at him, trying to assess whether or not it was one of Larry's elaborate leg-pulls.

'You are not trying to tell me,' she said at last, 'that that man is a – is a – is one of *those?*'

'Dear God, Mother, of course he is,' said Larry, irritably. 'He's a rampaging old queer – the only reason he's gone rushing back to Athens is because he's living with a ravishing seventeen-year-old Cypriot boy and he doesn't trust him.'

'Do you mean to say,' asked Margo, her eyes wide, 'that they get *jealous* of each other?'

'Of course they do,' said Larry, and dismissing the subject, he returned to his book.

'How extraordinary,' said Margo. 'Did you hear that, Mother? They actually get jealous –'

'Margo!' said Mother quellingly. 'We won't go into that. What *I* want to know, Larry, is why you invited him here if you knew he was, er, that way inclined?'

'Why not?' Larry inquired.

'Well, you might at least have thought of *Gerry*,' said Mother, bristling.

'Gerry?' asked Larry in surprise. 'Gerry? What's he got to do with it?'

'What's he got to *do* with it? Really, Larry, you do make me cross. That man could have been a bad influence on the boy if he had had much to do with him.'

Larry sat back on the sofa and looked at Mother. He gave a small exasperated sigh and put his book down.

'For the last three mornings,' he said, 'Gerry's been giving Sven natural history lessons in the olive groves. It doesn't appear to have done either of them irretrievable harm.'

'What?' squeaked Mother. 'What?'

I felt it was time to intervene. After all, I liked Sven. I explained how, early in his stay, he had wandered into my room and had become immediately absorbed and fascinated by my collection of creatures. Feeling that one convert was worth half a dozen saints, I had offered to take him into the olive groves and show him all my favourite haunts. So every morning we would set off into the olives and Sven would spend hours lying on his stomach peering at the busy lines of ants carrying their grass seeds or watching the bulbous-bodied female mantis laying her frothy egg case on a stone, or peering down the burrows of trap-door spiders, murmuring, 'Wonderful! Wonderful!' to himself, in such an ecstatic tone of voice that it warmed my heart.

'Well, dear,' said Mother, 'I think, in future, if you want to take one of Larry's friends for walks you should tell me first.'

5

Cuttlefish and Crabs

Each morning when I awoke the bedroom would be tiger-striped by the sun peering through the shutters. As usual, I would find that the dogs had managed to crawl onto the bed without my realizing it and would now be occupying more than their fair share, sleeping deeply and peacefully. Ulysses would be sitting by the window staring at the bars of golden sunlight, his eyes slit into malevolent disapproval. Outside, one could hear the hoarse, jeering crow of a cockerel and the soft murmuring of the hens (a sound soothing as bubbling porridge) as they fed under the orange and lemon trees, the distant clonk of goat bells, sharp chittering of sparrows in the eaves, and the sudden outburst of wheezing, imploring cries that denoted one of the parent swallows had brought a mouthful of food to their brood in the nest beneath my window. I would throw back the sheet and turf the dogs out onto the floor, where they would shake and stretch and yawn, their pink tongues curled like exotic leaves, and then I would go over to the window and throw back the shutters. Leaning out over the sill, the morning sun warm on my naked body, I would scratch thoughtfully at the little pink seals the dogs' fleas had left on my skin, while I got my eyes adjusted to the light. Then I would peer down over the silver olive tops to the beach and the blue sea which lay half a mile away. It was on this beach that, periodically, the fishermen would pull in their nets, and when they did so this was always a special occasion for me, since the net dragged to shore from the depths of the blue bay would contain a host of fascinating sea life which was otherwise beyond my reach.

If I saw the little fishing boats bobbing on the water I would get dressed hurriedly, and taking my collecting gear I would run through the olive trees down to the road and along it until I reached the beach. I knew most of the fishermen by name, but there was one who was my special friend, a tall, powerful young man with a mop of auburn hair. Inevitably, he was called Spiro after Spiridion, so in order to distinguish him from all the other Spiros I knew, I called him Kokino, or red. Kokino took a great delight in obtaining specimens for me, and although he was not a bit interested in the creatures himself, he got considerable pleasure from my obvious happiness.

One day I went down to the beach and the net was half-way in. The fishermen, brown as walnuts, were hauling on the dripping lines, their toes spreading wide in the sand as they pulled the massive bag of the net nearer and nearer to the shore.

'Your health, *kyrié* Gerry,' Kokino cried to me, waving a large freckled hand in greeting, his mop of hair glinting in the sun like a bonfire. 'Today we should get some fine animals for you, for we put the net down in a new place.'

I squatted on the sand and waited patiently while the fishermen, chattering and joking, hauled away steadily. Presently the top of the net was visible in the shallow waters, and as it broke surface you could see the glitter and wink of the trapped fish inside it. Hauled out onto the sand, it seemed as though the net were alive, pulsating with the fish inside it, and there was the steady, staccato purring noise of their tails, flapping futilely against each other. The baskets were fetched and the fish were picked out of the net and cast into them. Red fish, white fish, fish with wine-coloured stripes, scorpion fish like flamboyant tapestries. Sometimes there would be an octopus or a cuttlefish leering up from inside the net with a look of alarm in its human-looking eyes. Once all the edible contents of the net had been safely stowed away in the baskets, it was my turn.

In the bottom of the net would be a great heap of stones and seaweed and it was among these that I found my trophies: once a round flat stone from which grew a perfect coralline tree, pure white. It looked like a young beech tree in winter, its branches bare of leaves and covered with a layer of snow. Sometimes there would be cushion starfish, almost as thick as a sponge-cake and almost as large, the edges not forming pointed arms as with normal starfish, but rounded scallops. These starfish would be of a pale fawn colour, with a bright pattern of scarlet blotches. Once I got two incredible crabs, whose pincers and legs when pulled in tight fitted with immaculate precision the sides of their oval shells. These crabs were white with a rusty-red pattern on the back that looked not unlike an Oriental face. It was hardly what I would call protective colouration, and I imagine they must have had few enemies to be able to move about the sea-bed wearing such a conspicuous livery.

On this particular morning I was picking over a great pile of weed, and Kokino, having stowed away the last of the fish in the baskets, came over to help me. There was the usual assortment of tiny squids, the size of a match-box, pipe-fish, spider-crabs, and a variety of tiny fish which, in spite of their small size, had been unable to escape through the mesh of the net. Suddenly Kokino gave a little grunt, half surprise and half amusement, and picked something out of a tangled skein of seaweed and held it out to me on the calloused palm of his hand. I could hardly believe my eyes, for it was a sea-horse. Browny-green, carefully jointed, looking like some weird chess-man, it lay on Kokino's hand, its strange protruded mouth gasping and its tail coiling and uncoiling frantically. Hurriedly I snatched it from him and plunged it into a jar full of sea-water, uttering a mental prayer to St Spiridion that I was in time to save it. To my delight it righted itself, then hung suspended in the jar, the tiny fins on each side of its horse's head fluttering themselves into a blur. Pausing only to make sure that it really was all right, I scrabbled through the rest of the weed with the fervour of a gold prospector panning a river-bed where he had found a nugget. My diligence was rewarded, for in

a few minutes I had six sea-horses of various sizes hanging suspended in the jar. Enraptured by my good luck, I bid Kokino and
the other fishermen a hasty farewell and raced back to the villa.

Here I unceremoniously foreclosed on fourteen slowworms
and usurped their aquarium to house my new catches. I knew
that the oxygen in the jar in which the sea-horses were imprisoned
would not last for long and if I wanted to keep them alive I would
have to move quickly. Carrying the aquarium, I raced down to
the sea again, washed it out carefully, filled the bottom with sand
and dashed back to the villa with it; then I had to run down to
the sea again three times with buckets to fill it up with the
required amount of water. By the time I had poured the last
bucket into it, I was so hot and sweaty I began to wonder whether
the sea-horses were worth it. But as soon as I tipped them into
the aquarium I knew that they were. I had placed a small, twiggy,
dead olive branch in the aquarium, which I had anchored to the
sand, and as the sea-horses plopped out of the jar they righted
themselves and then, like ponies freshly released in a field, they
sped round and round the aquarium, their fins moving so fast
that you could not see them and each one gave the appearance
of being driven by some small internal motor. Having, as it were,
galloped round their new territory, they all made for the olive
branch, entwined their tails round it lovingly, and stood there
gravely at attention.

The sea-horses were an instant success. They were about the
only animal that I had introduced to the villa that earned the
family's unanimous approval. Even Larry used to pay furtive
visits to my study in order to watch them zooming and bobbing
to and fro in their tank. They took up a considerable amount of
my time, for I found that the sea-water soon grew rancid, and in
order to keep it clear and fresh I had to go down to the sea with
buckets four or five times a day. This was an exhausting process,
but I was glad that I kept it up, for otherwise I would not have
witnessed a very extraordinary sight.

One of the sea-horses, obviously an old specimen since he was nearly black, had a very well-developed paunch. This I merely attributed to age; then I noticed one morning there was a line along the paunch, almost as though it had been slit with a razor blade. I was watching this and wondering whether the sea-horses had been fighting and if so what they used as a weapon (for they seemed so defenceless), when to my complete and utter astonishment the slit opened a little wider and out swam a minute and fragile replica of the sea-horse. I could hardly believe my eyes, but as soon as the first baby was clear of the pouch and hanging in the clear water, another one joined it and then another and another until there were twenty microscopic sea-horses floating round their giant parent like a little cloud of smoke. Terrified lest the other adult sea-horses eat the babies, I hurriedly set up another aquarium and placed what I fondly imagined to be the mother and her offspring in it. Keeping two aquariums going with fresh water was an even more Herculean task and I began to feel like a pit-pony; but I was determined to continue until Thursday, when Theodore came to tea, so that I could show him my acquisitions.

'Aha,' he said, peering into the tanks with professional zeal, 'these are really most interesting. Sea-horses are, of course, according to the books, supposed to be found here, but I myself have er . . . you know . . . never seen them previously.'

I showed Theodore the mother with her swarm of tiny babies.

'No, no,' said Theodore. 'That's not the mother, that's the father.'

At first I thought that Theodore was pulling my leg, but he went on to explain that when the female laid the eggs and they had been fertilized by the male, they were taken into this special brood-pouch by the male and there they matured and hatched, so what I had thought was a proud mother was in reality a proud father.

Soon the strain of keeping my stable of sea-horses with a

supply of microscopic sea-food and fresh water became too great, and so with the utmost reluctance I had to take them down to the sea and release them.

It was Kokino who, as well as contributing specimens from his nets to my collection, showed me one of the most novel fishing methods I had ever come across.

I met him one day down by the shore putting a kerosene tin full of sea-water into his rickety little boat. Reposing in the bottom of the tin was a large and very soulful-looking cuttlefish. Kokino had tied a string round it where the head met the great egg-shaped body. I asked him where he was going and he said he was going to fish for cuttlefish. I was puzzled because his boat did not contain any lines or nets or even a trident. How then did he propose to catch cuttlefish?

'With love,' said Kokino mysteriously.

I felt it was my duty, as a naturalist, to investigate every method of capturing animals, so I asked Kokino whether it was possible for me to accompany him in order to see this mysterious process. We rowed the boat out into the blue bay until it hung over a couple of fathoms of crystal clear water. Here Kokino took the end of the long string that was attached to the cuttlefish and tied it carefully round his big toe. Then he picked up the cuttlefish and dropped it over the side of the boat. It floated in the water for a brief moment, looking up at us with what seemed to be an incredulous expression, and then, squirting out jets of water, it shot off in a series of jerks, trailing the string behind it, and soon disappeared in the blue depths. The string trailed gradually over the side of the boat, then tautened against Kokino's toe. He lit a cigarette and rumpled his flaming hair.

'Now,' he said, grinning at me, 'we will see what love can do.'

He bent to his oars and rowed the boat slowly and gently along the surface of the bay, with frequent pauses during which he stared with intense concentration at the string fastened to his toe. Suddenly he gave a little grunt, let the oars fold to the side of the boat like the wings of a moth, and grasping the line, he started to pull it in. I leaned over the side of the boat, staring down into the clear water, my eyes straining towards the end of the taut black line. Presently, in the depths, a dim blur appeared as Kokino hauled more quickly on the line and the cuttlefish came into sight. As it got closer, I saw, to my astonishment, it was not one cuttlefish but two, locked together in a passionate embrace. Swiftly Kokino hauled them alongside and with a quick flip of the line landed them in the bottom of the boat. So engrossed was the male cuttlefish with his lady-love that not even the sudden transition from his watery home to the open air seemed to worry him in the slightest. He was clasping the female so tightly that it took Kokino some time to prise him loose and then drop him into the tin of sea-water.

The novelty of this form of fishing greatly appealed to me, although I had the sneaking feeling that perhaps it was a little unsporting. It was rather like catching dogs by walking around with a bitch in season on the end of a long leash. Within an hour we had caught five male cuttlefish in a comparatively small area of the bay and it amazed me that there should be such a dense population of them in such a small area, for they were a creature that you very rarely saw unless you went fishing at night. The female cuttlefish, throughout this time, played her part with a sort of stoical indifference, but even so I felt that she should be rewarded, so I prevailed upon Kokino to let her go, which he did with obvious reluctance.

I asked him how he knew that the female was ready to attract the males, and he shrugged.

'It is the time,' he said.

Could you then at this time, I inquired, put any female on the end of a string and obtain results?

'Yes,' said Kokino. 'But of course, some females, like some women, are more attractive than others and so you get better results with those.'

My mind boggled at the thought of having to work out the comparative merits between two female cuttlefish. I felt it was a great pity that this method could not be employed with other creatures. The idea, for example, of dropping a female sea-horse over the side on a length of cotton and then pulling her up in a tangled entourage of passionate males was very appealing. Kokino was, as far as I knew, the only exponent of this peculiar brand of fishing, for I never saw any other fisherman employ it, and indeed, the ones I mentioned it to had never even heard of it and were inclined to treat my story with raucous disbelief.

This tattered coast-line near the villa was particularly rich in sea life, and as the water was comparatively shallow it made it easier for me to capture things. I had succeeded in inveigling Leslie into making me a boat, which greatly facilitated my investigations. This craft, almost circular, flat-bottomed, and with a heavy list to starboard, had been christened the *Bootle-Bumtrinket* and, next to my donkey, was my most cherished possession. Filling the bottom with jars, tins, and nets and taking a large parcel of food with me, I would set sail in the *Bootle-Bumtrinket* accompanied by my crew of Widdle, Puke, and Roger and, occasionally, Ulysses, my owl, should he feel so inclined. We would spend the hot, breathless days exploring remote little bays and rocky and weed-encrusted archipelagoes. We had many curious adventures on these expeditions. Once we found a whole acre of sea-bed covered with a great swarm of sea-hares, their royal-purple, egg-shaped bodies with a neat pleated frill along the edge and two strange protuberances on the head looking, in fact, extraordinarily like the long ears of a hare. There were hundreds of them gliding over the rocks and across the sand, all heading towards the south of the island. They did not touch each other or display any interest in each other, so I assumed it was not a mating gathering, but some form of migration.

On another occasion, a group of languid, portly, and good-natured dolphins discovered us riding at anchor in a small bay, and presumably attracted by the friendly colour scheme of orange and white in which the *Bootle-Bumtrinket* was painted, they disported themselves around us, leaping and splashing, coming up alongside the boat with their grinning faces, and breathing deep, passionate sighs at us from their blow-holes. A young one, more daring than the adults, even dived under the boat and we felt his back scrape along its flat bottom. My attention was equally divided between enjoying this delightful sight and trying to quell mutiny on the part of my crew, who had all reacted to the arrival of the dolphins in their individual ways. Widdle, never a staunch warrior, had lived up to his name copiously and crouched shivering in the bows, whining to himself. Puke had decided that the only way to save his life was to abandon ship and swim for the shore; he had to be restrained forcibly, as did Roger, who was convinced that if he was only allowed to jump into the sea with the dolphins, he would be able to kill them all, single-handedly, in a matter of moments.

It was during one of these expeditions that I came across a magnificent trophy that was, indirectly, responsible for leading Leslie into court, although I did not know it at the time. The family had all gone into town, with the exception of Leslie, who was recovering from a very severe attack of dysentery. It was his first day's convalescence and he lay on the sofa in the drawing-room as weak as a kitten, sipping iced tea and reading a large manual on ballistics. He had informed me, in no uncertain terms, that he did not want me hanging around making a nuisance of myself and so, as I did not want to go into the town, I had taken the dogs out in *Bootle-Bumtrinket*.

As I rowed along, I noticed on the smooth waters of the bay what I took to be a large patch of yellow seaweed. Seaweed was always worth investigating, as it invariably contained a host of small life and sometimes, if you were lucky, quite large creatures;

so I rowed towards it. But as I got closer, I saw that it was not seaweed, but what appeared to be a yellowish-coloured rock. But what sort of rock could it be that floated in some twenty feet of water? As I looked closer, I saw, to my incredulous delight, that it was a fairly large turtle. Shipping the oars and urging the dogs to silence, I poised myself in the bows and waited, tense with excitement as the *Bootle-Bumtrinket* drifted closer and closer. The turtle, outspread, appeared to be floating on the surface of the sea, sound asleep. My problem was to capture him before he woke up. The nets and various other equipment I had in the boat had not been designed for the capture of a turtle measuring some three feet in length, so the only way I felt I could achieve success was by diving in on him, grabbing him, and somehow getting him into the boat before he woke up. In my excitement it never occurred to me that the strength possessed by a turtle of this size was considerable and that it was unlikely he was going to give up without a struggle. When the boat was some six feet away I held my breath and dived. I decided to dive under him so as to cut off his retreat, as it were, and as I plunged into the lukewarm water I uttered a brief prayer that the splash I made would not awaken him and that, even if it did, he would still be too dozy to execute a rapid retreat. I had dived deep and now I turned on my back and there, suspended above me like an enormous golden guinea, was the turtle. I shot up under him and grabbed him firmly by his front flippers, which curved like horny sickles from out of his shell. To my surprise even this action did not wake him, and when I rose, gasping, to the surface, still retaining my grasp on his flippers, and shook the water from my eyes, I discovered the reason. The turtle had been dead for a fair length of time, as my nose and the host of tiny fish nibbling at his scaly limbs told me.

Disappointing though this was, a dead turtle was better than no turtle at all, and so I laboriously towed his body alongside the *Bootle-Bumtrinket* and made it fast by one flipper to the side of the boat. The dogs were greatly intrigued, under the impression that this was some exotic and edible delicacy I had procured for their special benefit. The *Bootle-Bumtrinket*, owing to her shape, had never been the easiest of craft to steer, and now, with the dead weight of the turtle lashed to one side of her, she showed a tendency to revolve in circles. However, after an hour's strenuous rowing, we arrived safely at the jetty, and having tied up the boat, I then hauled the turtle's carcass onto the shore where I could examine it. It was a hawks-bill turtle, the kind whose shell is used for the manufacture of spectacle frames and whose stuffed carcass you occasionally see in opticians' windows. His head was massive, with a great wrinkled jowl of yellow skin and a swooping beak of a nose that did give him an extraordinarily hawk-like look. The shell was battered in places, presumably by ocean storms or by the snap of a passing shark, and here and there it was decorated with little snow-white clusters of baby barnacles. His underside of pale daffodil-yellow was soft and pliable like thick, damp cardboard.

I had recently conducted a long and fascinating dissection of a dead terrapin that I had found and I felt this would be an ideal opportunity to compare the turtle's internal anatomy with that of his fresh-water brother, so I went up the hill, borrowed the gardener's wheelbarrow, and in it transported my prize up to the house and laid him out in state on the front veranda.

I knew there would be repercussions if I endeavoured to perform my dissection of the turtle inside the house, but I felt that nobody in his right mind would object to the dissection of the turtle on the front veranda. With my notebook at the ready and my row of saws, scalpels, and razor blades neatly laid out as though in an operating theatre, I set to work.

I found that the soft yellow plastron came away quite easily, compared with the underside of the terrapin, which had taken me three quarters of an hour to saw through. When the plastron was free, I lifted it off like a cover off a dish and there, underneath, were all the delicious mysteries of the turtle's internal organs displayed, multi-coloured and odoriferous to a degree. So consumed with curiosity was I that I did not even notice the smell. The dogs, however, who normally considered fresh cow dung to be the ideal scent to add piquancy to their love life, disappeared in a disapproving body, sneezing violently. I discovered, to my delight, that the turtle was a female and had a large quantity of half-formed eggs in her. They were about the size of ping-pong balls, soft, round, and as orange as a nasturtium. There were fourteen of them, and I removed them carefully and laid them in a gleaming, glutinous row on the flagstones. The turtle appeared to have a prodigious quantity of gut, and I decided that I should enter the exact length of this astonishing apparatus in my already blood-stained notebook. With the aid of a scalpel I detached the gut from the rear exit of the turtle and then proceeded to pull it out. It seemed never-ending, but before long I had it all laid out carefully across the veranda in a series of loops and twists, like a rather drunken railway line. One section of it was composed of the stomach, a rather hideous greyish bag like a water-filled balloon. This obviously was full of the turtle's last meal and I felt, in the interests of science, that I ought to check on what it had been eating just prior to its demise. I stuck a scalpel in the great wobbling mound and slashed experimentally. Immediately the whole stomach bag deflated with a ghastly sighing noise and a stench arose from its interior which made all the other smells pale into insignificance. Even I, fascinated as I was by my investigations, reeled back and had to retreat coughing to wait for the smell to subside.

I knew I could get the veranda cleaned up before the family got back from town, but in my excitement with my new acquisition, I had completely overlooked the fact that Leslie was convalescing in the drawing-room. The scent of the turtle's interior, so pungent that it seemed almost solid, floated in through the French windows and enveloped the couch on which he lay.

My first intimation of this catastrophe was a blood-curdling roar from inside the drawing-room. Before I could do anything sensible, Leslie, swathed in blankets, appeared in the French windows.

'What's that bloody awful stink?' he inquired throatily. Then, as his glance fell upon the dismembered turtle and its prettily arranged internal organs spread across the flagstones, his eyes bulged and his face took on a heliotrope tinge. 'What the hell's *that?*'

I explained, somewhat diffidently, that it was a turtle that I was dissecting. It was a female, I went on hurriedly, hoping to distract Leslie by detail. Here he could see the fascinating eggs that I had extracted from her interior.

'Damn her eggs,' shouted Leslie, making it sound like some strange medieval oath. 'Get the bloody thing away from here. It's stinking the place out.'

I said that I had almost reached the end of my dissection and that I had then planned to bury all the soft parts and merely keep the skeleton and shell to add to my collection.

'You're doing nothing of the sort,' shouted Leslie. 'You're to take the whole bloody thing and bury it. Then you can come back and scrub the veranda.'

Lugaretzia, our cook, attracted by the uproar, appeared in the French windows next to Leslie. She opened her mouth to inquire into the nature of this family quarrel when she was struck amidships by the smell of the turtle. Lugaretzia always had fifteen or sixteen ailments worrying her at any given moment, which she cherished with the same loving care that other people devote to window-boxes or Pekingese. At this particular time it was her stomach that was causing her the most trouble. In consequence she gasped two or three times, feebly, like a fish, uttered a strangled 'Saint Spiridion!' and fell into Leslie's arms in a well-simulated faint.

Just at that moment, to my horror, the car containing the rest of the family swept up the drive and came to a halt below the veranda.

'Hello, dear,' said Mother, getting out of the car and coming up to the steps. 'Did you have a nice morning?'

Before I could say anything, the turtle, as it were, got in before me. Mother uttered a couple of strange hiccuping cries, pulled out her handkerchief and clapped it to her nose.

'What,' she demanded indistinctly, 'is that terrible smell?'

'It's that bloody boy,' roared Leslie from the French windows, making ineffectual attempts to prop the moaning Lugaretzia against the door jamb.

Larry and Margo had now followed Mother up the steps and caught sight of the butchered turtle.

'What . . . ?' began Larry and then he too was seized with a convulsive fit of coughing.

'It's that damned boy,' he said, gasping.

'Yes, dear,' said Mother through her handkerchief. 'Leslie's just told me.'

'It's disgusting,' wailed Margo, fanning herself with her handkerchief. 'It looks like a railway accident.'

'What *is* it, dear?' Mother asked me.

I explained that it was an exceedingly interesting hawks-bill turtle, female, containing eggs.

'Surely you don't have to chop it up on the veranda?' said Mother.

'The boy's mad,' said Larry with conviction. 'The whole place smells like a bloody whaling ship.'

'I really think you'll have to take it somewhere else, dear,' said Mother. 'We can't have this smell on the front veranda.'

'Tell him to bury the damned thing,' said Leslie, clasping his blankets more firmly about him.

'Why don't you get him adopted by a family of Eskimos?' inquired Larry. 'They like eating blubber and maggots and things.'

'Larry, don't be disgusting,' said Margo. 'They can't eat anything like this. The very thought of it makes me feel sick.'

'I think we ought to go inside,' said Mother faintly. 'Perhaps it won't smell as much in there.'

'If anything, it smells worse in here,' shouted Leslie from the French windows.

'Gerry dear, you must clean this up,' said Mother as she picked her way delicately over the turtle's entrails, 'and disinfect the flagstones.'

The family went inside and I set about the task of clearing up the turtle from the front veranda. Their voices arguing ferociously drifted out to me.

'Bloody menace,' said Leslie. 'Lying here peacefully reading, and I was suddenly seized by the throat.'

'Disgusting,' said Margo. 'I don't wonder Lugaretzia fainted.'

'High time he had another tutor,' said Larry. 'You leave the house for five minutes and come back and find him disembowelling Moby Dick on the front porch.'

'I'm sure he didn't mean any harm,' said Mother, 'but it was rather silly of him to do it on the veranda.'

'Silly!' said Larry caustically. 'We'll be blundering round the house with gas-masks for the next six months.'

I piled the remains of the turtle into the wheelbarrow and took it up to the top of the hill behind the villa. Here I dug a hole and buried all the soft parts and then placed the shell and the bone structure near a nest of friendly ants, who had, on previous occasions, helped me considerably by picking skeletons clean. But the most they had ever tackled had been a very large green lizard, so I was interested to see whether they would tackle the turtle. They ran towards it, their antennae waving eagerly, and then stopped, thought about it for a bit, held a little consultation and then retreated in a body; apparently even the ants were against me, so I returned dispiritedly to the villa.

Here I found that a thin, whining little man, obviously made belligerent by wine, was arguing with Lugaretzia on the still-odoriferous veranda. I inquired what the man wanted.

'He says,' said Lugaretzia, with fine scorn, 'that Roger has been killing his chickens.'

'Turkeys,' corrected the man. 'Turkeys.'

'Well, turkeys then,' said Lugaretzia, conceding the point.

My heart sank. One calamity was being succeeded by another. Roger, we knew, had the most reprehensible habit of killing chickens. He derived a lot of innocent amusement in the spring and summer by chasing swallows. They would drive him into an apoplectic fury by zooming past his nose and then flying along the ground just ahead of him while he chased them, bristling with rage, uttering roars of fury. The peasants' chickens used to hide in the myrtle bushes and then, just as Roger was passing, they would leap out with a great flutter of wings and insane hysterical cackling right into his path. Roger, I was sure, was convinced that these chickens were a sort of ungainly swallow that he could get to grips with and so, in spite of yells of protest on our part, he would leap on them and kill them with one swift bite, all his hatred of the teasing summer swallows showing in his action. No punishment had any effect on him. He was normally an extremely obedient dog, except about this one thing, and so, in desperation, all we could do was to recompense the owners, but only on condition that the corpse of the chicken was produced as evidence.

Reluctantly I went in to tell the family that Roger had been at it again.

'Christ!' said Leslie, getting laboriously to his feet. 'You and your sodding animals.'

'Now, now, dear,' said Mother placatingly. 'Gerry can't help it if Roger kills chickens.'

'Turkeys,' said Leslie. 'I bet he'll want a hell of a lot for those.'

'Have you cleaned up the veranda, dear?' inquired Mother.

Larry removed a large handkerchief, drenched in eau-de-

Cologne, which he had spread over his face. 'Does it smell as though he's cleaned up the veranda?' he inquired.

I said hastily that I was just about to do it and followed Leslie to see the outcome of his conversation with the turkey owner.

'Well,' said Leslie belligerently, striding out onto the veranda, 'what do you want?'

The man cringed, humble, servile, and altogether repulsive.

'Be happy, *kyrié*, be happy,' he said, greeting Leslie.

'Be happy,' Leslie replied in a gruff tone of voice that implied he hoped the man would be anything but. 'What do you wish to see me about?'

'My turkeys, *kyrié*,' explained the man. 'I apologize for troubling you, but your dog, you see, he's been killing my turkeys.'

'Well,' said Leslie, 'how many has he killed?'

'Five, *kyrié*,' said the man, shaking his head sorrowfully. 'Five of my best turkeys. I am a poor man, *kyrié*, otherwise I wouldn't have dreamed . . .'

'Five!' said Leslie startled, and turned an inquiring eye on me.

I said I thought it was quite possible. If five hysterical turkeys had leaped out of a myrtle bush, I could well believe that Roger would kill them all. For such a benign and friendly dog, he was a very ruthless killer when he got started.

'Roger is a good dog,' said Lugaretzia belligerently.

She had joined us on the veranda and she obviously viewed the turkey owner with the same dislike as I did. Apart from this, in her eyes Roger could do no wrong.

'Well,' said Leslie, making the best of a bad job, 'if he's killed five turkeys, he's killed five turkeys. Such is life. Where are the bodies?'

There was a moment of silence.

'The bodies, *kyrié*?' queried the turkey owner tentatively.

'The bodies, the bodies,' said Leslie impatiently. 'You know, the bodies of the turkeys. You know we can't pay until you produce the bodies.'

'But that's not possible,' said the turkey owner nervously.

'What do you mean, not possible?' inquired Leslie.

'Well, it's not possible to bring the bodies, *kyrié*,' said the turkey owner with a flash of inspiration, 'because your dog has eaten them.'

The explosion that this statement provoked was considerable. We all knew that Roger was, if anything, slightly overfed, and that he was of a most fastidious nature. Though he would kill a chicken, nothing would induce him to feed upon the carcass.

'Lies! Lies!' shrilled Lugaretzia, her eyes swimming with tears of emotion. 'He's a good dog.'

'He's never eaten anything in his life that he's killed,' shouted Leslie. 'Never.'

'But five of my turkeys!' said the little man. 'Five of them he's eaten!'

'When did he kill them?' roared Leslie.

'This morning, *kyrié*, this morning,' said the man, crossing himself. 'I saw it myself, and he ate them all.'

I interrupted to say that Roger had been out that morning in the *Bootle-Bumtrinket* with me and, intelligent dog though he was, I did not see how he could be consuming the prodigious quantity of five turkeys on this man's farm and be out in the boat with me at the same time.

Leslie had had a trying morning. All he had wanted was to lie peacefully on the sofa with his manual of ballistics, but first he had been almost asphyxiated by my investigations into the internal anatomy of the turtle and now he was being faced by a drunken little man, trying to swindle us for the price of five turkeys. His temper, never under the best of control, bubbled over.

'You're a two-faced liar and a cheat,' he snarled. The little man backed away and his face went white.

'*You* are the liar and the cheat,' he said, with drunken belligerence. '*You* are the liar and the cheat. You let your dog kill everybody's chickens and turkeys and then when they come to you for payment, you refuse. *You* are the liar and the cheat.'

Even at that stage, I think that sanity could have prevailed, but the little man made a fatal mistake. He spat copiously and wetly at Leslie's feet. Lugaretzia uttered a shrill wail of horror and grabbed hold of Leslie's arm. Knowing his temper, I grabbed hold of the other one, too. The little man, appalled into a moment of sobriety, backed away. Leslie quivered like a volcano and Lugaretzia and I hung on like grim death.

'*Excreta* of a pig,' roared Leslie. 'Illegitimate son of a diseased whore . . .'

The fine Greek oaths rolled out, rich, vulgar, and biological, and the little man turned from white to pink and from pink to red. He had obviously been unaware of the fact that Leslie had such a command over the fruitier of the Greek insults.

'You'll be sorry,' he quavered. 'You'll be sorry.'

He spat once more with a pathetic sort of defiance and then turned and scuttled down the drive.

It took the combined efforts of the family and Lugaretzia three quarters of an hour to calm Leslie down, with the aid of several large brandies.

'Don't you worry about him, *kyrié* Leslie,' was Lugaretzia's final summing up. 'He's well known in the village as a bad character. Don't you worry about him.'

But we were forced to worry about him, for the next thing we knew, he had sued Leslie for not paying his debts and for defamation of character.

Spiro, when told the news, was furious.

'Gollys, Mrs Durrells,' he said, his face red with wrath. 'Why don'ts yous lets Masters Leslies shoot the son of a bitch?'

'I don't think that would really solve anything, Spiro,' said Mother. 'What we want to know now is whether this man has any chance of winning his case.'

'Winnings!' said Spiro with fine scorn. 'That bastard won't wins anythings. You just leaves it to me. I'll fixes it.'

'Now, don't go and do anything rash, Spiro,' said Mother. 'It'll only make matters worse.'

'I won'ts do anything rash, Mrs Durrells. But I'll fixes that bastard.'

For several days he went about with an air of conspiratorial gloom, his bushy eyebrows tangled in a frown of immense concentration, only answering our questions monosyllabically. Then, one day, a fortnight or so before the case was due to be heard, we were all in town on a shopping spree. Eventually, weighed down by our purchases, we made our way to the broad, tree-lined Esplanade and sat there having a drink and exchanging greetings with our numerous acquaintances who passed. Presently Spiro, who had been glaring furtively about him with the air of a man who had many enemies, suddenly stiffened. He hitched his great belly up and leaned across the table.

'Master Leslies, you sees that mans over there, that one with the white hair?'

He pointed a sausage-like finger at a small, neat little man who was placidly sipping a cup of coffee under the trees.

'Well, what about him?' inquired Leslie.

'He's the judges,' said Spiro.

'What judge?' said Leslie, bewildered.

'The judges who is going to tries your case,' said Spiro. 'I wants you go to over there and talks to him.'

'Do you think that's wise?' said Leslie. 'He might think I'm trying to muck about with the course of justice and give me ten years in prison or something.'

'Gollys, nos,' said Spiro, aghast at such a thought. 'He wouldn't puts Master Leslies in prison. He knows better than to do thats while I ams here.'

'But even so, Spiro, don't you think *he'll* think it a little funny if Leslie suddenly starts talking to him?' asked Mother.

'Gollys nos,' said Spiro. He glanced about him to make sure

that we weren't overheard, leaned forward, and whispered, 'He collects stamps.'

The family looked bewildered.

'You mean he's a philatelist?' said Larry at length.

'No, no, Master Larrys,' said Spiro. 'He's not one of them. He's a married man and he's gots two childrens.'

The whole conversation seemed to be getting even more involved than the normal ones that we had with Spiro.

'What,' said Leslie patiently, 'has his collecting stamps got to do with it?'

'I will takes you over there,' said Spiro, laying bare for the first time the Machiavellian intricacies of his plot, 'and yous tells hims that you will get him some stamps from England.'

'But that's bribery,' said Margo, shocked.

'It isn't bribery, Misses Margos,' said Spiro. 'He collects stamps. He *wants* stamps.'

'I should think if you tried to bribe him with stamps he'd give you about five hundred years' penal servitude,' said Larry to Leslie judiciously.

I asked eagerly whether, if Leslie was condemned, he would be sent to Vido, the convict settlement on a small island that lay in the sparkling sea half a mile or so from the town.

'No, no, dear,' said Mother, getting increasingly flustered. 'Leslie won't be sent to Vido.'

I felt this was rather a pity. I already had one convict friend, serving a sentence for the murder of his wife, who lived on Vido. He was a 'trusty' and so had been allowed to build his own boat and row home for the week-ends. He had given me a monstrous black-backed gull which tyrannized all my pets and the family. I felt that, exciting though it was to have a real murderer as a friend, it would have been better to have Leslie incarcerated on Vido so that he too could come home for the week-ends. To have a convict brother would, I felt, be rather exotic.

'I don't see that if I just go and *talk* to him it can do any harm,' said Leslie.

'I wouldn't,' said Margo. 'Remember, there's many a slip without a stitch.'

'I do think you ought to be careful, dear,' said Mother.

'I can see it all,' said Larry with relish. 'Leslie with a ball and chain; Spiro too, probably, as an accessory. Margo knitting them warm socks for the winter, Mother sending them food parcels and anti-lice ointment.'

'Oh, do stop it, Larry,' said Mother crossly. 'This is no laughing matter.'

'All you've gots to dos is to talks to him, Master Leslies,' said Spiro earnestly. 'Honest to Gods you've got to, otherwise I can't fixes it.'

Spiro had, prior to this, never let us down. His advice had always been sound, and even if it hadn't been legal, we had never so far come to grief.

'All right,' said Leslie. 'Let's give it a bash.'

'Do be careful, dear,' said Mother as Leslie and Spiro rose and walked over to where the judge was sitting.

The judge greeted them charmingly and for half an hour Leslie and Spiro sat at his table sipping coffee while Leslie talked to him in voluble, but inaccurate, Greek. Presently the judge rose and left them with much handshaking and bowing. They returned to our table where we waited agog for the news.

'Charming old boy,' said Leslie. 'Couldn't have been nicer. I promised to get him some stamps. Who do we know in England who collects them?'

'Well, your father used to,' said Mother. 'He was a very keen philatelist when he was alive.'

'Gollys, don't says that Mrs Durrells,' said Spiro, in genuine anguish.

A short pause ensued while the family explained to him the meaning of the word philatelist.

'I still don't see how this is going to help the case,' said Larry, 'even if you inundate him with penny blacks.'

'Never yous minds, Masters Larrys,' said Spiro darkly. 'I said I'd fixes it and I will. You just leaves it to me.'

For the next few days Leslie, convinced that Spiro could obstruct the course of justice, wrote to everybody he could think of in England and demanded stamps. The result was that our mail increased threefold and that practically every free space in the villa was taken up by piles of stamps which, whenever a wind blew, would drift like autumn leaves across the room, to the vociferous, snarling delight of the dogs. As a result of this, many of the stamps began to look slightly the worse for wear.

'You're not going to give him *those*, are you?' said Larry, disdainfully surveying a pile of mangled, semi-masticated stamps that Leslie had rescued from the jaws of Roger half an hour previously.

'Well, stamps are supposed to be old, aren't they?' said Leslie belligerently.

'Old, perhaps,' said Larry, 'but surely not covered with enough spittle to give him hydrophobia.'

'Well, if you can think of a better bloody plan, why don't you suggest it?' inquired Leslie.

'My dear fellow, *I* don't mind,' said Larry. 'When the judge is running around biting all his colleagues and you are languishing in a Greek prison, don't blame me.'

'All I ask is that you mind your own bloody business,' cried Leslie.

'Now, now, dear, Larry's only trying to be helpful,' said Mother.

'Helpful,' snarled Leslie, making a grab at a group of stamps that were being blown off the table. 'He's just interfering as usual.'

'Well, dear,' said Mother, adjusting her spectacles, 'I do think he may be right, you know. After all, some of those stamps do look a little, well, you know, second-hand.'

'He wants stamps and he's bloody well going to get stamps,' said Leslie.

And stamps the poor judge got, in a bewildering variety of sizes, shapes, colours, and stages of disintegration.

Then another thing happened that increased Leslie's confidence in winning the case a hundredfold. We discovered that the turkey man, whom Larry constantly referred to as Crippenopoulos, had been unwise enough to subpoena Lugaretzia as a witness for the prosecution. Lucretia, furious, wanted to refuse, until it was explained to her that she could not.

'Imagine that man calling me as a witness to help him,' she said. 'Well, don't you worry, *kyrié* Leslie, I'll tell the court how he forced you to swear at him and call him . . .'

The family rose in a body and vociferously informed Lugaretzia that she was not to do anything of the sort. It took us half an hour to impress upon her what she should and should not say. At the end of it, since Lugaretzia, like most Corfiotes, was not very strong on logic, we felt somewhat jaded.

'Well, with her as witness for the prosecution,' said Larry, 'I should think you'll probably get the death sentence.'

'Larry dear, don't say things like that,' said Mother. 'It's not funny even in a joke.'

'I'm not joking,' said Larry.

'Rubbish,' said Leslie uneasily. 'I'm sure she'll be all right.'

'I think it would be much safer to disguise Margo as Lugaretzia,' said Larry judicially. 'With her sweeping command over the Greek language she would probably do you considerably less harm.'

'Yes,' said Margo excitedly, struck for the first time by Larry's perspicacity, 'why can't I be a witness?'

'Don't be damned silly,' said Leslie. 'You weren't there. How can you be a witness?'

'I was almost there,' said Margo. 'I was in the kitchen.'

'That's all you need,' said Larry to Leslie. 'Margo and Lugaretzia in the witness-box and you won't even need a judge. You'll probably be lynched by the mob.'

When the day of the case dawned, Mother rallied the family.

'It's ridiculous for us all to go,' said Larry. 'If Leslie wants to get himself into prison, that's his affair. I don't see why we should be dragged into it. Besides, I wanted to do some writing this morning.'

'It's our duty to go,' said Mother firmly. 'We must put on a bold front. After all, I don't want people to think that I'm rearing a family of gaol-birds.'

So we all put on our best clothes and sat waiting patiently until Spiro came to collect us.

'Now, don'ts yous worrys, Master Leslies,' he scowled, with the air of a warder in the condemned cell. 'Everything's going to be OK's.'

But in spite of this prophecy, Larry insisted on reciting 'The Ballad of Reading Gaol' as we drove into town, much to Leslie's annoyance.

The court-room was a bustle of uncoordinated activity. People sipped little cups of coffee, other people shuffled through piles of papers in an aimless but dedicated way, and there was lots of chatter and laughter. Crippenopoulos was there in his best suit, but avoided our eye. Lugaretzia, for some reason best known to herself, was clad entirely in black. It was, as Larry pointed out, a premature move. Surely she should have reserved her mourning for after the trial.

'Now, Master Leslies,' said Spiro, 'you stands there, and I stands there and translates for you.'

'What for?' inquired Leslie, bewildered.

'Because you don'ts speaks Greeks,' said Spiro.

'Really, Spiro,' protested Larry, 'I admit his Greek is not Homeric, but it is surely perfectly adequate?'

'Masters Larrys,' said Spiro, scowling earnestly, 'Master Leslies mustn'ts speaks Greeks.'

Before we could inquire more deeply into this, there was a general scuffling and the judge came in. He took his seat and his eyes roved round the court and then, catching sight of Leslie, he beamed and bowed.

'Hanging judges always smile like that,' said Larry.

'Larry dear, do stop it,' said Mother. 'You're making me nervous.'

There was a long pause while what was presumably the Clerk of the Court read out the indictment. Then Crippenopoulos was called to give his evidence. He put on a lovely performance, at once servile and indignant, placating but belligerent. The judge was obviously impressed and I began to get quite excited. Perhaps I would have a convict for a brother after all. Then it was Leslie's turn.

'You are accused,' said the judge, 'of having used defamatory and insulting language to this man and endeavouring to deprive him of rightful payment for the loss of five turkeys, killed by your dog.'

Leslie stared blank-faced at the judge.

'What's he say?' he inquired of Spiro.

Spiro hitched his stomach up.

'He says, Masters Leslies,' and his voice was so pitched that it rumbled through the court-room like thunder, 'he says that you insults this mans and that you tries to swindle him out of moneys for his turkeys.'

'That's ridiculous,' said Leslie firmly.

He was about to go on when Spiro held up a hand like a ham and stopped him. He turned to the judge.

'The *kyrios* denies the charge,' he said. 'It would be impossible for him to be guilty anyway, because he doesn't speak Greek.'

'Christ!' groaned Larry sepulchrally. 'I hope Spiro knows what he's doing.'

'What's he saying? What's he doing?' said Mother nervously.

'As far as I can see, putting a noose round Leslie's neck,' said Larry.

The judge, who had had so many coffees with Leslie, who had received so many stamps from him, and who had had so many conversations in Greek with him, stared at Leslie impassively. Even if the judge had not known Leslie personally, it would have been impossible for him not to know that Leslie had some command over the Greek language. Nothing anyone did in Corfu was sacrosanct, and if you were a foreigner, of course, the interest in and the knowledge of your private affairs was that much greater. We waited with bated breath for the judge's reactions. Spiro had his massive head slightly lowered like a bull about to charge.

'I see,' said the judge dryly.

He shuffled some papers aimlessly for a moment and then glanced up.

'I understand,' he said, 'that the prosecution has a witness. I suppose we had better hear her.'

It was Lugaretzia's big moment. She rose to her feet, folded her arms, and stared majestically at the judge, her normally pale face pink with excitement, her soulful eyes glowing.

'You are Lugaretzia Condos and you are employed by these people as a cook?' inquired the judge.

'Yes,' said Lugaretzia, 'and a kinder, more generous family you could not wish to meet. Why, only the other day they gave me a frock for myself and for my daughter and it was only a month or two ago that I asked the *kyrios* . . .'

'Yes,' interrupted the judge, 'I see. Well, this has not got much relevance to the case. I understand that you were there when this man called to see about his turkeys. Now tell me in your own words what happened.'

Larry groaned.

'If she tells him in her own words, they'll get Leslie for sure,' he said.

432

'Well,' said Lugaretzia, glancing round the court to make sure she had everybody's attention. 'The *kyrios* had been very ill, very ill indeed. At times we despaired for his life. I kept suggesting cupping to his mother, but she wouldn't hear of it . . .'

'Would you mind getting to the point?' said the judge.

'Well,' said Lugaretzia, reluctantly abandoning the subject of illness, which was always a favourite topic with her, 'it was the *kyriós* first day up and he was very weak. Then this man,' she said, pointing a scornful finger at Crippenopoulos, 'arrived dead drunk and said that their dog had killed five of his turkeys. Now the dog wouldn't do that, *kyrié* judge. A sweeter, kinder, nobler dog was never seen in Corfu.'

'The dog is not on trial,' said the judge.

'Well,' said Lugaretzia, 'when the *kyrios* said, quite rightly, that he would have to see the corpses before he paid the man, the man said he couldn't show them because the dog had eaten them. This is ridiculous, as you can well imagine, *kyrié* judge, as no dog could eat five turkeys.'

'You are supposed to be a witness for the prosecution, aren't you?' said the judge. 'I ask only because your story doesn't tally with the complainant's.'

'Him,' said Lucretia, 'you don't want to trust him. He's a drunkard and a liar and it is well known in the village that he has got two wives.'

'So you are telling me,' said the judge, endeavouring to sort out this confusion, 'that the *kyrios* didn't swear at him in Greek and refuse payment for the turkeys.'

'Of course he didn't,' said Lucretia. 'A kinder, finer, more upstanding *kyrios* . . .'

'Yes, yes, all right,' said the judge.

He sat pondering for some time while we all waited in suspense, then he glanced up and looked at Crippenopoulos.

'I can see no evidence,' he said, 'that the Englishman behaved in the way you have suggested. Firstly he does not speak Greek.'

'He does speak Greek,' shouted Crippenopoulos wrathfully. 'He called me a . . .'

'Will you be quiet,' said the judge coldly. 'Firstly, as I was saying, he does not speak Greek. Secondly, your own witness denies all knowledge of the incident. It seems to me clear, however, that you endeavoured to extract payment for turkeys which had not, in fact, been killed and eaten by the defendant's dog. However, you are not on trial here for that, so I will merely find the defendant not guilty, and you will have to pay the costs.'

Immediately pandemonium reigned. Crippenopoulos was on his feet, purple with rage, shouting at the top of his voice and calling on St Spiridion's aid. Spiro, bellowing like a bull, embraced Leslie, kissed him on both cheeks, and was followed by the weeping Lugaretzia who did likewise. It was some time before we managed to extricate ourselves from the court, and jubilantly we went down to the Esplanade and sat at a table under the trees to celebrate.

Presently the judge came past and we rose in a body to thank him and invite him to sit and have a drink with us. He refused the drink shyly and then fixed Leslie with a penetrating eye.

'I wouldn't like you to think,' he said, 'that justice in Corfu is always dispensed like that, but I had a long conversation with Spiro about the case and after some deliberation I decided that your crime was not as bad as the man's. I hoped it might teach him not to swindle foreigners in future.'

'Well, I really am most grateful to you,' said Leslie.

The judge gave a little bow. He glanced at his watch.

'Well, I must be going,' he said. 'By the way, thank you so much for those stamps you sent me yesterday. Among them were two quite rare ones which were new to my collection.'

Raising his hat he trotted off across the Esplanade.

Interlude for Spirits

What seest thou else in the dark backward and abysm of time?

– SHAKESPEARE, *The Tempest*

Interlude for Spirits

Not very long after Leslie's court case, Margo was beset by another affliction to keep company with her acne. She suddenly started to put on weight and before long, to her horror, she was almost circular. Androuchelli, our doctor, was called in to view this mystery. He uttered a long series of distressed 'Po, po, po's' as he viewed Margo's obesity. He tried her on several pills and potions and a number of diets, to no effect.

'He says,' Margo confided to us tearfully at lunch one day, 'that he thinks it's glandular.'

'Glandular?' said Mother, alarmed. 'What does he mean, glandular?'

'I don't know,' wailed Margo.

'Must we always discuss your ailments at mealtimes?' inquired Larry.

'Larry dear, Androuchelli says it's glandular,' said Mother.

'Rubbish,' said Larry airily. 'It's puppy fat.'

'Puppy fat!' squeaked Margo. 'Do you know how much I weigh?'

'What you want is more exercise,' said Leslie. 'Why don't you take up sailing?'

'Don't think the boat's big enough,' said Larry.

'Beast,' said Margo, bursting into tears. 'You wouldn't say things like that if you knew how I felt.'

'Larry dear,' said Mother placatingly, 'that wasn't a very kind thing to say.'

'Well, I can't help it if she's wandering around looking like a water-melon covered with spots,' said Larry irritably. 'One would think it was *my* fault the way you all go on.'

437

'Something will have to be done,' said Mother. 'I shall see Androuchelli tomorrow.'

But Androuchelli repeated that he thought her condition might be glandular and that in his opinion Margo ought to go to London for treatment. So, after a flurry of telegrams and letters, Margo was dispatched to London and into the tender care of two of the only worth-while relatives with whom we were still on speaking terms, my mother's cousin Prudence and her mother, Great-Aunt Fan.

Apart from a brief letter saying she had arrived safely and that she, Cousin Prue, and Aunt Fan had taken up residence at a hotel near Notting Hill Gate and that she had been put in touch with a good doctor, we heard nothing further from Margo for a considerable length of time.

'I do wish she would write,' Mother said.

'Don't fuss, Mother,' said Larry. 'What's she got to write about, anyway, except to give you her new dimensions?'

'Well, I like to know what's going on,' said Mother. 'After all, she's in *London*.'

'What's London got to do with it?' asked Larry.

'In a big city like that anything can happen,' said Mother darkly. 'You hear all sorts of things about girls in big cities.'

'Really, Mother, you do worry unnecessarily,' said Larry in exasperation. 'What do you think's happened to her, for Heaven's sake? Do you think she's being lured into some den of vice? They'd never get her through the door.'

'It's no joking matter, Larry,' said Mother severely.

'But you get yourself into a panic about nothing,' said Larry. 'I ask you, what self-respecting white slaver is going to look at Margo twice? I shouldn't think there's one strong enough to carry her off, anyway.'

'Well, I'm worried,' said Mother, 'and I'm going to send a cable.'

So she sent a cable to Cousin Prudence, who replied at length saying that Margo was associating with people she didn't approve of, that she thought it would be a good thing if Mother came to talk some sense into her. Immediately pandemonium reigned. Mother, distraught, dispatched Spiro to buy tickets and started packing frantically, until she suddenly remembered me. Feeling it would do more harm than good to leave me in the tender care of my two elder brothers, she decided that I should accompany her. So Spiro was dispatched to get more tickets and yet more packing was done. I regarded the whole situation as heaven-sent, for I had just acquired a new tutor, Mr Richard Kralefsky, who was endeavouring – with grim determination in the face of my opposition – to instruct me in irregular French verbs, and this trip to England, I thought, would give me a much-needed respite from this torture.

The journey by train was uneventful, except that Mother was in constant fear of being arrested by the Fascist carabinieri. This fear increased a thousandfold when, at Milan, I drew a caricature of Mussolini on the steamy window of the carriage. Mother scrubbed at it for quite ten minutes with her handkerchief, with all the dedication of a washerwoman in a contest, before she was satisfied that it was obliterated.

Coming from the calm, slow, sunlit days of Corfu, our arrival in London, late in the evening, was a shattering experience. So many people were at the station that we did not *know*, all hurrying to and fro, grey-faced and worried. The almost incomprehensible language that the porters spoke, and London aglitter with lights and churning with people. The taxi nosing its way through Piccadilly like a beetle through a firework display. The cold air that made your breath float like a web of smoke in front of your mouth as you talked, so that you felt like a character in a cartoon strip.

Eventually the taxi drew up outside the fake, soot-encrusted Corinthian columns of Balaklava Mansions. We got our luggage into the hotel with the aid of an elderly, bowlegged, Irish porter, but there was no one to greet us, so apparently the telegram signalling our arrival had gone astray. The young lady, we were informed by the porter, had gone to her meeting, and Miss Hughes and the old lady had gone to feed the dogs.

'What did he say, dear?' asked Mother when he had left the room, for his accent was so thick that it sounded almost as though he were talking a foreign language. I said that Margo had gone to a meeting and that Cousin Prue and Aunt Fan were feeding the dogs.

'What *can* he mean?' said Mother, bewildered. 'What meeting has Margo gone to? What dogs is he talking about?'

I said I did not know but, from what I had seen of London, what it needed was a few more dogs around.

'Well,' said Mother, inexpertly putting a shilling in the meter and lighting the gas fire, 'I suppose we'll just have to make ourselves comfortable and wait until they come back.'

We had waited an hour when suddenly the door burst open and Cousin Prue rushed in, arms outstretched, crying 'Louise, Louise, Louise,' like some strange marsh bird. She embraced us both, her sloe dark eyes glowing with love and excitement. Her beautiful face, delicately scented, was soft as a pansy as I kissed her dutifully.

'I began to think that you were never coming,' she said. 'Mummy is on her way up. She finds the stairs trying, poor dear. Well, now, *don't* you both look well. You must tell me everything. Do you like this hotel, Louise? It's so cheap and convenient, but full of the most peculiar people.'

A gentle wheezing sound made itself heard through the open door.

'Ah, there's Mummy,' cried Prue. 'Mummy! Mummy! Louise's here.'

Through the door appeared my Great-Aunt Fan. At first glance she looked, I thought rather uncharitably, like a walking tent. She was enveloped in a rusty-red tweed suit of incredible style and dimensions. It made her look like a russet-red pyramid of tweed. On her head she wore a somewhat battered velveteen hat of the style that pixies are reputedly wont to use. Her spectacles, through which her eyes stared owlishly, glittered.

'Louise!' she cried throwing her arms wide and casting her eyes up as though Mother were some divine apparition. 'Louise and Gerald! You have come!'

Mother and I were kissed and embraced heartily. This was not the feathery, petal-soft embrace of Cousin Prue. This was a hearty, rib-cracking embrace and a firm kiss that left your lips feeling bruised.

'I am so sorry we weren't here to greet you, Louise dear,' said Prue, 'but we weren't sure when you were arriving and we had the dogs to feed.'

'What dogs?' asked Mother.

'Why, my Bedlington puppies, of course,' said Prue. 'Didn't you know? Mummy and I have become dog-breeders.' She gave a coy, tinkling laugh.

'But you had something else last time,' said Mother. 'Goats or something, wasn't it?'

'Oh, we've still got those,' said Aunt Fan. 'And my bees and the chickens. But Prudence here thought it would be a good thing to start dog-breeding. She's got such a head for business.'

'I really think it's a paying concern, Louise dear,' said Prue earnestly. 'I bought Tinkerbell and then Lucybell . . .'

'And then Tinybell,' interrupted Aunt Fan.

'And Tinybell,' said Prue.

'And Lucybell,' said Aunt Fan.

'Oh, Mummy, do be quiet. I've already said Lucybell.'

'And there's Tinkerbell too,' said Aunt Fan.

'Mummy is a little hard of hearing,' said Prue unnecessarily, 'and they have all had puppies. I brought them up to London to sell and at the same time we have been keeping an eye on Margo.'

'Yes, where is Margo?' asked Mother.

Prue tiptoed over to the door and closed it softly.

'She's at a *meeting*, dear,' she said.

'I know, but what sort of meeting?' asked Mother.

Prue glanced round nervously.

'A *spiritualist* meeting,' she hissed.

'And then there's Lucybell,' said Aunt Fan.

'Oh, Mummy, do be quiet.'

'Spiritualist meeting?' said Mother. 'What on earth's she gone to a spiritualist meeting for?'

'To cure her fatness and her acne,' said Prue. 'But mark my words, no good will come of it. It's an evil power.'

I could see Mother beginning to get alarmed.

'But I don't understand,' she said. 'I sent Margo home to see that doctor, what's his name?'

'I *know* you did, dear,' said Prue. 'Then, after she came to this hotel, she fell into the grasp of that evil woman.'

'What evil woman?' said Mother, now considerably alarmed.

'The goats are well too,' said Aunt Fan, 'but their milk yield is down a little this year.'

'Oh, Mummy, do shut up,' hissed Prue. 'I mean that evil woman, Mrs Haddock.'

'Haddock, haddock,' said Mother, bewildered. Her train of thought was always liable to be interrupted if anything culinary was mentioned.

'She's a medium, my dear,' said Prue, 'and she's got her hooks on Margo. She's told Margo that she's got a guide.'

'A guide?' said Mother feebly. 'What sort of guide?'

I could see, in her distraught condition, that she was now beginning to think Margo had taken up mountaineering or some similar occupation.

'A spirit guide,' said Prue. 'It's called Mawake. He's supposed to be a Red Indian.'

'I have ten hives now,' said Aunt Fan proudly. 'We get twice as much honey.'

'Mother, be quiet,' said Prue.

'I don't understand,' said Mother plaintively. 'Why isn't she still going to the doctor for her injections?'

'Because Mawake told her not to,' said Prue triumphantly. 'Three séances ago, he said – according to Margo, and of course the whole thing comes through Mrs Haddock so you can't trust it for a moment – according to Margo, Mawake said she was to have no more punctures.'

'Punctures?' said Mother.

'Well, I suppose it's Red Indian for injections,' said Prue.

'It is nice to see you again, Louise,' said Aunt Fan. 'I think we ought to have a cup of tea.'

'That's a very good idea,' said Mother faintly.

'I'm not going down there to order tea, Mummy,' said Prue, glancing at the door as if, behind it, were all the fiends of Hell. 'Not when they're having a meeting.'

'Why, what happens?' asked Mother.

'And some toast would be nice,' said Aunt Fan.

'Oh, Mummy, do be quiet,' said Prue. 'You have no idea what happens at these meetings, Louise. Mrs Haddock goes into a trance, then becomes covered with ectoplasm.'

'Ectoplasm?' said Mother. 'What's ectoplasm?'

'I've got a pot of my own honey in my room,' said Aunt Fan. 'I'm sure you will enjoy it, Louise. So much purer than these synthetic things you buy now.'

'It's a sort of stuff that mediums produce,' said Prue. 'It looks like . . . Well, it looks like, sort of like – I've never actually *seen* it, but I'm told that it looks like *brains*. Then they make trumpets fly about and things. I tell you, my dear, I never go into the lower regions of the hotel when they are holding a meeting.'

Fascinated though I was by the conversation, I felt the chance of seeing a woman called Mrs Haddock covered with brains, with a couple of trumpets floating about, was too good to miss, so I volunteered to go down and order tea.

However, to my disappointment, I saw nothing in the lower regions of the hotel to resemble remotely Cousin Prudence's description, but I did manage to get a tray of tea brought up by the Irish porter. We were sipping this, and I was endeavouring to explain to Aunt Fan what ectoplasm was, when Margo arrived, carrying a large cabbage under one arm, accompanied by a dumpy little woman with protruding blue eyes and wispy hair.

'Mother!' said Margo dramatically. 'You've come!'

'Yes, dear,' said Mother grimly. 'And not a moment too soon, apparently.'

'This is Mrs Haddock,' said Margo. 'She's *absolutely marvellous*.'

It became immediately apparent that Mrs Haddock suffered from a strange affliction. For some obscure reason she seemed to be incapable of breathing while talking. The result was that she would gabble, all her words latched together like a daisy chain and would then, when her breath ran out, pause and suck it in, making a noise that sounded like 'Whaaaha.'

Now she said to Mother, 'IamdelightedtomeetyouMrsDurrell. Ofcourse,myspiritguideinformedmeofyourcoming. Idohopeyou hadacomfortablejourney . . . Whaaaha.'

Mother, who had been intending to give Mrs Haddock a very frigid and dignified greeting, was somewhat put off by this strange delivery.

'Oh, yes. Did we?' she said nervously, straining her ears to understand what Mrs Haddock was saying.

'Mrs Haddock is a spiritualist, Mother,' said Margo proudly, as though she were introducing Leonardo da Vinci or the inventor of the first aeroplane.

'Really, dear?' said Mother, smiling frostily. 'How very interesting.'

'Itgivesonegreatcomforttoknowthathosewhohavegonebefore arestillintouchwithone . . . Whaaaha,' said Mrs Haddock earnestly. 'Somanypeoplereunaware . . . Whaa . . . aha . . . ofthe spiritworldthatliessoclose.'

'You should have seen the puppies tonight, Margo,' observed Aunt Fan. 'The little tinkers had torn up all their bedding.'

'Mummy, do be quiet,' said Prue, eyeing Mrs Haddock as though she expected her to grow horns and a tail at any moment.

'Yourdaughterisveryluckyinasmuchasshehas . . . Whaa . . . aha . . . managedtoobtainoneofthebetterguides,' said Mrs Haddock, rather as though Margaret had riffled through the *Debrett* before settling on her spirit counsellor.

'He's called Mawake,' said Margo. 'He's *absolutely marvellous!*'

'He doesn't appear to have done you much good so far,' said Mother tartly.

'But he has,' said Margo indignantly. 'I've lost three ounces.'

'Ittakestimeandpatienceandimplicitbeliefinthefuturelife . . . Whaaaha . . . mydearMrs Durrell,' said Mrs Haddock, smiling at Mother with sickly sweetness.

'Yes, I'm sure,' said Mother, 'but I really would prefer it if Margo were under a medical practitioner one could see.'

'I don't think they meant it,' said Aunt Fan. 'I think they're teething. Their gums get sore, you know.'

'Mummy, we are not *talking* about the puppies,' said Prue. 'We are talking about Margo's guide.'

'That will be nice for her,' said Aunt Fan, beaming fondly at Margo.

'Thespiritworldissomuchwiserthananyearthlybeing . . . Whaaaha,' said Mrs Haddock. 'Youcouldn'thaveyourdaughter inbetterhands. Mawakewasagreatmedicinemaninhisowntribe. OneofthemostknowledgeableinthewholeofNorthAmerica . . . Whaaah.'

'And he's given me such good advice, Mother,' said Margo. 'Hasn't he, Mrs Haddock?'

'Nomorepunctures. Thewhitegirlmusthavenomorepunctures . . . Whaaaha,' intoned Mrs Haddock.

'There you are,' hissed Prue triumphantly, 'I told you.'

'Have some honey,' said Aunt Fan companionably. 'It's not like that synthetic stuff you buy in the shops nowadays.'

'Mummy, be quiet.'

'I still feel, Mrs Haddock, that I would prefer my daughter to have sensible medical attention rather than this Mawake.'

'Oh, Mother, you're so narrow-minded and Victorian,' said Margo in exasperation.

'MydearMrsDurrellyoumustlearntotrustthegreatinfluencesof thespiritworldthatareafterallonlytryingtohelpandguideus . . . Whaaaha,' said Mrs Haddock. 'Ifeelthatifyoucametooneofour meetingsyouwouldbeconvincedofthegreatpowersofgoodthatour spiritguideshave . . . Whaaaha.'

'I prefer to be guided by my own spirit, thank you very much,' said Mother, with dignity.

'Honey isn't what it used to be,' said Aunt Fan, who had been giving the matter some thought.

'You are just prejudiced, Mother,' said Margo. 'You're condemning a thing without even *trying*.'

'IfeelsurethatifyoucouldpersuadeyourMothertoattendoneofour meetings . . . Whaaaha,' said Mrs Haddock, 'shewouldfinda wholenewworldopeningupbeforeher.'

'Yes, Mother,' said Margo, 'you must come to a meeting. I'm *sure* you'd be convinced. The things you see and hear! After all, there are no bricks without fire.'

I could see that Mother was suffering an inward struggle. For many years she had been deeply interested in superstitions, folk magic, witchcraft, and similar subjects, and now the temptation to accept Mrs Haddock's offer was very great. I waited breathlessly, hoping that she would accept. There was nothing I wanted more at that moment than to see Mrs Haddock covered with brains and with trumpets flying round her head.

'Well,' said Mother, undecided, 'we'll see. We'll talk about it tomorrow.'

'I'msurethatoncewebreakthroughthebarrierforyouwe'llbeable

togiveyoualotofhelpandguidance . . . Whaaaha,' said Mrs Haddock.

'Oh, yes,' said Margo. 'Mawake's simply *wonderful!*'

One would have thought she was talking about her favourite film star.

'Wearehavinganothermeetingtomorroweveninghereinthe hotel . . . Whaaaha,' said Mrs Haddock, 'andIdohopethatboth youandMargowillattend . . . Whaaaha.'

She gave us a pallid smile as though reluctantly forgiving us our sins, patted Margo on the cheek, and left.

'Really, Margo,' said Mother as the door closed behind Mrs Haddock, 'you do make me cross.'

'Oh, Mother, you are so *old-fashioned*,' said Margo. 'That doctor wasn't doing me any good with his injections, anyway, and Mawake is working miracles.'

'Miracles,' snorted Mother scornfully. 'You still look exactly the same size to me.'

'Clover,' said Aunt Fan, through a mouthful of toast, 'is supposed to be the best, although I prefer heather myself.'

'I tell you, dear,' said Prue, 'this woman's got a grip on you. She's malignant. Be warned before it's too late.'

'All I ask is that you just simply come to a meeting and *see*,' said Margo.

'Never,' said Prue, shuddering. 'My nerves wouldn't stand it.'

'It's interesting, too, that they have to have bumble-bees to fertilize the clover,' observed Aunt Fan.

'Well,' said Mother, 'I'm much too tired to discuss it now. We will discuss it in the morning.'

'Can you help me with my cabbage?' asked Margo.

'Do what?' inquired Mother.

'Help me with my cabbage,' said Margo.

'I have often wondered whether one could not cultivate bumble-bees,' said Aunt Fan, thoughtfully.

'What do you do with your cabbage?' inquired Mother.

'She puts it on her face,' hissed Prue. 'Ridiculous!'

'It isn't ridiculous,' said Margo, angrily. 'It's done my acne a world of good.'

'What? Do you mean you boil it or something?' asked Mother.

'No,' said Margo, 'I put the leaves on my face and you tie them on for me. Mawake advised it and it works wonders.'

'It's ridiculous, Louise dear. You should stop her,' said Prue, bristling like a plump kitten. 'It's nothing more than witchcraft.'

'Well, I'm too tired to argue about it,' said Mother. 'I don't suppose it can do you any harm.'

So Margo sat in a chair and held to her face large crinkly cabbage leaves which Mother solemnly fixed to her head with lengths of red twine. I thought she looked like some curious vegetable mummy.

'It's paganism. That's what it is,' said Prue.

'Nonsense, Prue, you do fuss,' said Margo, her voice muffled by cabbage leaves.

'I sometimes wonder,' said Mother, tying the last knot, 'whether my family's *all there*.'

'Is Margo going to a fancy-dress ball?' inquired Aunt Fan, who had watched the procedure with interest.

'No, Mummy,' roared Prue, 'it's for her spots.'

Margo got up and groped her way to the door. 'Well, I'm going to bed,' she said.

'If you meet anybody on the landing, you'll give them a terrible shock,' said Prue.

'Have a good time,' said Aunt Fan. 'Don't stay out till all hours. I know what you young things are like.'

After Margo had gone, Prue turned to Mother.

'You see, Louise dear? I didn't exaggerate,' she said. 'That woman is an evil influence. Margo's behaving like a mad thing.'

'Well,' said Mother, whose maxim in life was always defend your young regardless of how much in the wrong they are, 'I think she's being a little *unwise*.'

'Unwise!' said Prue. 'Cabbage leaves all over her face! Never doing anything that that Mawake doesn't tell her to! It's not healthy!'

'I shouldn't be a bit surprised if she didn't win first prize,' said Aunt Fan, chuckling. 'I shouldn't think there'd be other people there disguised as a cabbage.'

The argument waxed back and forth for a considerable time, interlaced with Aunt Fan's reminiscences of fancy-dress balls she had been to in India. At length Prue and Aunt Fan left us and Mother and I prepared for bed.

'I sometimes think,' said Mother, as she pulled the clothes up and switched off the light, 'I sometimes think that I'm the only *sane* member of the family.'

The following morning we decided to go shopping, since there were a great number of things unobtainable in Corfu that Mother wanted to purchase and take back with us. Prue said this would be an excellent plan, since she could drop her Bedlington puppies off with their new owner en route.

So at nine o'clock we assembled on the pavement outside Balaklava Mansions, and we must have presented a somewhat curious sight to passers-by. Aunt Fan, presumably to celebrate our arrival, had put on a pixie hat with a large feather in it. She stood on the pavement entwined like a maypole by the leashes of the eight Bedlington puppies that romped and fought and urinated round her.

'I think we'd better take a taxi,' said Mother, viewing the gambolling puppies with alarm.

'Oh, no, Louise,' said Prue. 'Think of the expense! We can go by tube.'

'With all the puppies?' asked Mother doubtfully.

'Yes, dear,' said Prue. 'Mummy's quite used to handling them.'

Aunt Fan, now bound almost immobile by the puppies' leashes, had to be disentangled before we could walk down the road to the tube station.

'Yeast and maple syrup,' said Margo. 'You mustn't let me forget yeast and maple syrup, Mother; Mawake says they're excellent for acne.'

'If you mention that man once again I shall get seriously angry,' said Mother.

Our progress to the tube station was slow, since the puppies circumnavigated any obstacle in their path in different ways, and we had to pause continually to unwind Aunt Fan from the lamp-posts, pillar-boxes, and occasional passers-by.

'Little tinkers!' she would exclaim breathlessly, after each encounter. 'They don't mean any harm.'

When we finally arrived at the ticket office, Prue had a pro-longed and acrimonious argument over the price charged for the Bedlingtons.

'But they're only eight weeks old,' she kept protesting. 'You don't charge for *children* under three.'

Eventually, however, the tickets were purchased and we made our way to the escalators to face a continuous warm blast of air from the bowels of the earth, which the puppies appeared to find invigorating. Yapping and snarling in a tangle of leads, they forged ahead, dragging Aunt Fan, like a massive galleon, behind them. It was only when they saw the escalators that they began to have misgivings about what, hitherto, had appeared to be an exciting adventure. They did not, it appeared, like to stand on things that move and they were unanimous in their decision. Before long we were all wedged in a tight knot at the top of the escalator, struggling with the screaming, hysterical puppies.

A queue formed behind us.

'It shouldn't be allowed,' said a frosty-looking man in a bowler hat. 'Dogs shouldn't be allowed on the tube.'

'I have paid for them,' panted Prue. 'They have as much right to travel by tube as you have.'

'Bloody 'ell,' observed another man. 'I'm in an 'urry. Can't you let me get by?'

'Little tinkers!' observed Aunt Fan, laughing. 'They're so high-spirited at this age.'

'Perhaps if we all picked up a puppy each?' suggested Mother, getting increasingly alarmed by the muttering of the mob.

At that moment Aunt Fan stepped backwards onto the first step of the escalator and slipped and fell in a waterfall of tweeds, dragging the shrieking puppies after her.

'Thank God for that,' said the man in the bowler hat. 'Perhaps now we can get on.'

Prue stood at the top of the escalator and peered down. Aunt Fan had now reached the half-way mark and was finding it impossible to rise, owing to the weight of puppies.

'Mummy, Mummy, are you all right?' screamed Prue.

'I'm sure she is, dear,' said Mother soothingly.

'Little tinkers!' said Aunt Fan faintly as she was carried down the escalator.

'Now that your dogs have gone, Madam,' said the man in the bowler hat, 'would it be possible for us, too, to use the amenities of this station?'

Prue turned, bristling to do battle, but Margo and Mother grabbed her and they slid downwards on the staircase towards the heaving heap of tweed and Bedlingtons that was Great-Aunt Fan.

We picked her up and dusted her down and disentangled the puppies. Then we made our way along to the platform. The puppies now would have made a suitable subject for an RSPCA poster. Never, at the best of times, a prepossessing breed, Bedlingtons can, in moments of crisis, look more ill-used than any other dog I know. They stood uttering quavering, high-pitched yelps like miniature sea-gulls, shivering violently, periodically squatting down bow-legged to decorate the platform with the results of their fear.

'Poor little things,' said a fat woman commiseratingly, as she passed. 'It's a shame the way some people treat animals.'

'Oh! Did you hear her?' said Prue belligerently. 'I've a good mind to follow her and give her a piece of my mind.'

Mercifully, at that moment the train arrived with a roar and a blast of hot air, and distracted everybody's attention. The effect on the puppies was immediate. One minute they had been standing there shivering and wailing like a group of half-starved grey lambs and the next minute they had taken off down the platform like a team of virile huskies, dragging Aunt Fan in their wake.

'Mummy, Mummy, come back,' screamed Prue as we started off in pursuit.

She had forgotten Aunt Fan's method of leading the dogs, which she had explained to me at great length. Never pull on the lead, because it might hurt their necks. Carrying out this novel method of dog-training, Aunt Fan galloped down the platform with the Bedlingtons streaming before her. We finally caught her and restrained the puppies just as the doors closed with a self-satisfied hiss and the train rumbled out of the station. So we had to wait in a pool of Bedlingtons for the next train to arrive. Once we finally got them in the train the puppies' spirits suddenly revived. They fought each other with enjoyment, snarling and screeching. They wound their leads round people's legs, and one of them, in a fit of exuberance, leaped up and tore a copy of *The Times* from the grasp of a man who looked as though he were the manager of the Bank of England.

We all had headaches by the time we arrived at our destination, with the exception of Aunt Fan, who was enchanted by the virility of the puppies. Acting on Mother's advice, we waited until there was a pause in the flow of human traffic before we attempted the escalator. To our surprise, we got the puppies to the top with little or no trouble. They were obviously becoming seasoned travellers.

'Thank goodness that's over,' said Mother as we reached the top.

'I'm afraid the puppies were a little bit trying,' said Prue, flustered. 'But then you see, they are used to the country. In town they think that everything's wrong.'

'Eh?' said Aunt Fan.

'Wrong,' shouted Prue. 'The puppies. They think that everything's wrong.'

'What a pity,' said Aunt Fan, and before we could stop her she had led the puppies onto the other escalator and they disappeared once again into the bowels of the earth.

Once we had got rid of the puppies, in spite of feeling somewhat jaded by our experiences, we had quite a satisfactory morning's shopping. Mother got all the things she needed, Margo got her yeast and maple syrup, and I, while they were purchasing these quite unnecessary items, managed to procure a beautiful red cardinal, a black-spotted salamander as fat and as shiny as an eiderdown, and a stuffed crocodile.

Each satisfied in our own way with our purchases, we returned to Balaklava Mansions.

At Margaret's insistence, Mother had decided that she would attend the séance that evening.

'Don't do it, Louise dear,' Cousin Prue said. 'It's dabbling with the unknown.'

Mother justified her action with a remarkable piece of logic.

'I feel I ought to meet this Mawake person,' she said to Prue. 'After all, he's giving Margo treatment.'

'Well, dear,' said Prue, seeing that Mother was adamant, 'I think it's madness, but I shall have to come with you. I can't let you attend one of those things on your own.'

I begged to be allowed to go too, for, as I pointed out to Mother, I had some little time previously borrowed a book from Theodore on the art of exposing fake mediums, so I felt that my knowledge thus acquired might come in exceedingly useful.

'I don't think we ought to take Mummy,' said Prue. 'I think it might have a bad effect on her.'

So at six o'clock that evening, with Prue palpitating in our midst like a newly caught bird, we made our way down to Mrs Haddock's basement room. Here we found quite a collection of people. There was Mrs Glut, the manageress of the hotel; a tall, saturnine Russian with an accent so thick that he sounded as though he were speaking through a mouthful of cheese; a young and very earnest blonde girl; and a vapid young man who, rumour had it, was studying to be an actor, but whom we had never seen do anything more strenuous than doze peacefully in the palm-fringed lounge. To my annoyance, Mother would not let me search the room before we started for hidden cords or fake ectoplasm. However, I did manage to tell Mrs Haddock about the book I had been reading, as I thought that if she was genuine it would be of interest to her. The look she bestowed upon me was anything but benevolent.

We sat in a circle holding hands and got off to a rather inauspicious start, since, as the lights were switched out, Prue uttered a piercing scream and leaped out of the chair she had been sitting in. It was discovered that the handbag she had leaned against the leg of the chair had slipped and touched her leg with a leathery clutch. When we had calmed Prue and assured her that she had not been assaulted by an evil spirit, we all returned to our chairs and held hands again. The illumination was from a night-light that guttered and blinked in a saucer and sent shadows rippling down the room and made our faces look as though they were newly arisen from a very old grave.

'NowIdon'twantanytalkingandImustaskyoualltokeepyourhands firmlyclaspedsothatwedon'tloseanyoftheessence . . . Whaaaha,' said Mrs Haddock. 'Iknowthereareunbelieversamongstus. NeverthelessIaskyoutomakeyourmindsquietandreceptive.'

'What does she mean?' whispered Prue to Mother. 'I'm not an unbeliever. My trouble is I believe *too much*.'

Having given us our instructions, Mrs Haddock then took up her position in an arm-chair, and with deceptive ease, went into a trance. I watched her narrowly. I was determined not to miss the ectoplasm. At first she just sat there with her eyes closed, and there was no sound except for the rustle and quiver of the agitated Prue. Then Mrs Haddock started to breathe deeply; presently she began to snore richly and vibrantly. It sounded like a sack of potatoes being emptied across a loft floor. I was not impressed. Snoring, after all, was one of the easiest things to fake. Prue's hand clutching mine was moist with perspiration and I could feel her shivers of apprehension running down her arm.

'Ahaaaaa,' said Mrs Haddock suddenly, and Prue leaped in her chair and uttered a small, despairing squeak as though she had been stabbed.

'Ahaaaaaaaa,' said Mrs Haddock, extracting the full dramatic possibilities from this simple utterance.

'I don't like it,' whispered Prue shakily. 'Louise, dear, I don't like it.'

'Be quiet or you'll spoil it all,' whispered Margo. 'Relax, and make your mind receptive.'

'I see strangers among us,' said Mrs Haddock suddenly, with such a strong Indian accent that it made me want to giggle. 'Strangers who have come to join our circle. To them I say "welcome".'

The only extraordinary thing about this, as far as I was concerned, was that Mrs Haddock was no longer stringing her words together and no longer uttering that strange inhalation of breath. She mumbled and muttered for a moment or so, incomprehensibly, and then said clearly, 'This is Mawake.'

'Ooo!' said Margaret, delighted. 'He's come! There you are, Mother! That's Mawake!'

'I think I'm going to faint,' said Prue.

I stared at Mrs Haddock in the dim, shaky light and I could not see any signs of ectoplasm or trumpets.

'Mawake says,' announced Mrs Haddock, 'that the white girl must have no more punctures.'

'There!' said Margaret triumphantly.

'White girl must obey Mawake. Must not be influenced by disbelievers.'

I heard Mother snort belligerently in the gloom.

'Mawake says that if white girl trusts him, before the coming of two moons she will be cured. Mawake says . . .'

But what Mawake was about to say was never vouchsafed to us, for, at that moment, a cat that had been drifting round the room, cloudlike and unobserved, jumped onto Prue's lap. Her scream was deafening. She leaped to her feet shouting, 'Louise, Louise, Louise!' and blundered like a bedazzled moth round the circle of people, screaming every time she touched anything.

Somebody had the good sense to switch on the lights before Prue, in her chicken-like panic, could do any damage.

'I say, it's a bit much, what?' said the vapid young man.

'You may have done her great harm,' said the girl, glaring at Prue and fanning Mrs Haddock with her handkerchief.

'I was touched by something. It touched me. Got into my lap,' said Prue tearfully. 'Ectoplasm.'

'You spoiled everything,' said Margo angrily. 'Just as Mawake was coming through.'

'I think we have heard quite enough from Mawake,' said Mother. 'I think it's high time you stopped fooling around with this nonsense.'

Mrs Haddock, who had remained snoring with dignity throughout this scene, suddenly woke up.

'Nonsense,' she said fixing her protuberant blue eyes on Mother. 'Youdaretocallitnonsense? . . . Whaaaha.'

It was one of the very few occasions when I had seen Mother really annoyed. She drew herself up to her full height of 4 feet 3½ inches and bristled.

'Charlatan,' she said uncharitably to Mrs Haddock. 'I said it was nonsense and it *is* nonsense. I am not having *my* family mixed up in any jiggery-pokery like this. Come Margo, come Gerry, come Prue. We will leave.'

So astonished were we by this display of determination on the part of our normally placid mother, that we followed her meekly out of the room, leaving the raging Mrs Haddock and her several disciples.

As soon as we reached the sanctuary of our room, Margo burst into floods of tears.

'You've spoiled it. You've spoiled it,' she said, wringing her hands. 'Mrs Haddock will never talk to us again.'

'And a good job, too,' said Mother grimly, pouring out a brandy for the twitching and still-distraught Prue.

'Did you have a nice time?' asked Aunt Fan, waking suddenly and beaming at us owlishly.

'No,' said Mother shortly, 'we didn't.'

'I can't get the thought of that ectoplasm out of my mind,' said Prue, gulping brandy. 'It was like a sort of . . . like . . . well, you know, squishy.'

'Just as Mawake was coming through,' howled Margo. 'Just as he was going to tell us something *important*.'

'I think you are wise to come back early,' said Aunt Fan, 'because even at this time of year it gets chilly in the evening.'

'I felt sure it was coming for my throat,' said Prue. 'I felt it going for my throat. It was like a sort of . . . a kind of . . . well a squishy sort of *hand* thing.'

'And Mawake's the only one that's done me any good.'

'My father used to say that at this time of the year the weather can be very treacherous,' said Aunt Fan.

'Margo, stop behaving so stupidly,' said Mother crossly.

'And Louise dear, I could feel this horrible sort of squishy fingers groping up towards my throat,' said Prue, ignoring Margo, busy with the embroidery of her experience.

'My father always used to carry an umbrella, winter and

summer,' said Aunt Fan. 'People used to laugh at him, but many's the time, even on quite hot days, when he found he needed it.'

'You always *spoil* everything,' said Margo. 'You always interfere.'

'The trouble is I don't interfere enough,' said Mother. 'I'm telling you, you're to stop all this nonsense, stop crying, and we are going back to Corfu immediately.'

'If I hadn't leaped up when I did,' said Prue, 'it would have fastened itself in my jugular.'

'There's nothing more useful than a pair of galoshes, my father used to say,' said Aunt Fan.

'I'm not going back to Corfu. I won't. I won't.'

'You will do as you're told.'

'It wound itself round my throat in such an evil way.'

'He never approved of gum-boots, because he said they sent the blood to the head.'

I had ceased listening. My whole being was flooded with excitement. We were going back to Corfu. We were leaving the gritty, soulless absurdity of London. We were going back to the enchanted olive groves and blue sea, to the warmth and laughter of our friends, to the long, golden, gentle days.

6

The Olive Merry-Go-Round

By May the olive-picking had been in progress for some time. The fruit had plumped and ripened throughout the hot summer days and now it fell and lay shining in the grass like a harvest of black pearls. The peasant women appeared in droves carrying tins and baskets on their heads. They would then crouch in circles round the base of the olive tree, chattering as shrilly as sparrows as they picked up the fruit and placed it in the containers. Some of the olive trees had been producing crops like this for five hundred years, and for five hundred years the peasants had been gathering the olives in precisely the same way.

It was a great time for gossip and for laughter. I used to move from tree to tree, joining the different groups, squatting on my haunches, helping them pick up the glossy olives, hearing gossip about all the relatives and friends of the olive-pickers and occasionally joining them as they ate under the trees, wolfing down the sour black bread and the little flat cakes wrapped in vine leaves that were made out of last season's dried figs. Songs would be sung, and it was curious that the peasants' voices, so sour and raucous in speech, could be plaintively sweet when raised in harmony together. At that time of year, with the yellow, waxy crocuses just starting to bubble up among the olive roots, and the banks purple with campanulas, the peasants gathered under the trees looked like a moving flower-bed and the songs would echo down the naves between the ancient olives, the sound as melancholy and as sweet as goat bells.

When the containers were piled high with the fruit, they would be hoisted up, and we would carry them down to the olive press in a long, chattering line. The olive press, a gaunt, gloomy building, was down in a valley through which ran a tiny, glittering stream. The press was presided over by Papa Demetrios, a tough old man, as twisted and bent as the olive trees themselves, with a completely bald head and an enormous moustache, snow-white except where it was stained yellow by nicotine, and reputed to be the biggest moustache in the whole of Corfu. Papa Demetrios was a gruff, bad-tempered old man, but for some reason he took a fancy to me and we got along splendidly. He even allowed me into the holy of holies itself, the olive press.

Here was a great circular trough like an ornamental fishpond and mounted in it a gigantic grindstone with a central strut of wood jutting from it. This strut was harnessed to Papa Demetrios' ancient horse, which, with a sack over its head so that it did not get giddy, would circle the trough, thus rolling the great grindstone round and round so that it could crush the olives as they were poured into it in a glinting cascade. As the olives were crushed, a sharp, sour smell rose in the air. The only sounds were the solid ploddings of the horse's hooves and the rumbling of the great grindstone and the steady drip, drip of the oil trickling out of the vents of the trough, golden as distilled sunlight.

In one corner of the press was a huge black crumbling mound that was the residue from the grinding: the crushed seeds, pulp, and skin of the olives forming black crusty cakes, like coarse peat. It had a rich, sweet-sour smell that almost convinced you it was good to eat. It was in fact fed to the cattle and horses with their winter food and it was also used as a remarkably efficient, if somewhat overpungent, fuel.

Papa Demetrios, because of his bad temper, was left severely alone by the peasants, who would deliver their olives and depart from the press with all speed. For you were never certain whether anybody like Papa Demetrios might not have the evil eye. In consequence, the old man was lonely and so he welcomed my intrusion into his domain. From me he would get all the local gossip: who had given birth and whether it was a boy or a girl; who was courting whom; and sometimes a more juicy item such as that Pepe Condos had been arrested for smuggling tobacco. In return for my acting as a sort of newspaper for him, Papa Demetrios would catch specimens for me. Sometimes it would be a pale-pink gulping gecko, or a praying mantis, or the caterpillar of an oleander hawk-moth, striped like a Persian carpet, pink and silver and green. It was Papa Demetrios who got me one of the most charming pets that I had at that time, a spade-footed toad, which I christened Augustus Tickletummy.

I had been down in the olive groves helping the peasants and I started to feel hungry. I knew that Papa Demetrios always kept a good supply of food at the olive press, so I went down to visit him. It was a sparkling day with a rumbustious, laughing wind that thrummed through the olive grove like a harp. There was a nip in the air, so I ran all the way with the dogs leaping and barking about me, and I arrived flushed and panting to find Papa Demetrios crouched over a fire that he had constructed out of slabs of olive 'cake'.

'Ah!' he said, glaring at me fiercely. 'So you've come, have you? Where have you been? I haven't seen you for two days. I suppose now spring is here you've got no time for an old man like me.'

I explained that I had been busy with a variety of things, such as making a new cage for my magpies, since they had just raided Larry's room and stood in peril of their lives if they were not incarcerated.

'Hum,' said Papa Demetrios. 'Ah, well. Do you want some corn?'

I said, as nonchalantly as I could, that there was nothing I would like better than corn.

He got up and strutted bow-legged to the olive press and reappeared carrying a large frying pan, a sheet of tin, a bottle of oil, and five golden-brown cobs of dried maize, like bars of bullion. He put the frying pan on the fire and scattered a small quantity of oil into it, then waited until the heat of the fire made the oil purr and twinkle and smoke gently in the bottom of the pan. Then he seized a cob of maize and twisted it rapidly between his arthritic hands so that the golden beads of corn pattered into the pan with a sound like rain on a roof. He put the flat sheet of tin over the top, gave a little grunt, and sat back, lighting a cigarette.

'Have you heard about Andreas Papoyakis?' he asked, running his fingers through his luxurious moustache.

No, I said I had not heard.

'Ah,' he said with relish. 'He's in hospital, that foolish one.'

I said I was sorry to hear it because I liked Andreas. He was a gay, kind-hearted, exuberant boy who inevitably managed to do the wrong things. They said of him in the village that he would ride a donkey backwards if he could. What, I inquired, was his affliction?

'Dynamite,' said Papa Demetrios, waiting to see my reaction.

I gave a slow whistle of horror and nodded my head slowly. Papa Demetrios, now assured of my undivided attention, settled himself more comfortably.

'This was how it happened,' he said. 'He's a foolish boy, Andreas is, you know. His head is as empty as a winter swallow's nest. But he's a good boy, though. He's never done anybody any harm. Well, he went dynamite fishing. You know that little bay down near Benitses? Ah, well, he took his boat there because he had been told that the country policeman had gone farther down the coast for the day. Of course, foolish boy, he never thought to check and make sure that the policeman *was* farther down the coast.'

I clicked my tongue sorrowfully. The penalty for dynamite fishing was five years in prison and a heavy fine.

'Now,' said Papa Demetrios, 'he got into his boat and was rowing slowly along when he saw ahead of him, in the shallow water, a big shoal of barbouni. He stopped rowing and lit the fuse on his stick of dynamite.'

Papa Demetrios paused dramatically, peered at the corn to see how it was doing, and lit another cigarette.

'That would have been all right,' he went on, 'but just as he was about to throw the dynamite, the fish swam away, and what do you think that idiot of a boy did? Still holding the dynamite he rowed after them. Bang!'

I said I thought that there could not be very much left of Andreas.

'Oh, yes,' said Papa Demetrios scornfully. 'He can't even dynamite properly. It was such a tiny stick all it did was blow off his right hand. But even so, he owes his life to the policeman, who *hadn't* gone farther down the coast. Andreas managed to row to the shore and there he fainted from loss of blood and he would undoubtedly have died if the policeman, having heard the bang, had not come down to the shore to see who was dynamiting. Luckily the bus was just passing and the policeman stopped it and they got Andreas into it and into the hospital.'

I said I thought it was a great pity that it should happen to anybody as nice as Andreas, but he was lucky to be alive. I presumed that when he was better he would be arrested and sent to Vido for five years.

'No, no,' said Papa Demetrios. 'The policeman said he thought Andreas had been punished quite enough, so he told the hospital that Andreas had caught his hand in some machinery.'

The corn had now started to explode, banging on to the tin like the explosions of miniature cannons. Papa Demetrios lifted the pan off the fire and took the lid off. There was each grain of corn exploded into a little yellow-and-white cumulus cloud, scrunchy and delicious. Papa Demetrios took a twist of paper from his pocket and unwrapped it. It was full of coarse grains of grey sea-salt, and into this we dipped the little clouds of corn and scrunched them up with relish.

'I've got something for you,' said the old man at last, wiping his moustache carefully with a large red-and-white handkerchief. 'Another one of those terrible animals that you are so eager to get.'

Stuffing my mouth with the remains of the popcorn and wiping my fingers on the grass, I asked him eagerly what it was.

'I'll fetch it,' he said, getting to his feet. 'It's a very curious thing. I've never seen one like it before.'

I waited impatiently while he went into the olive press and reappeared carrying a battered tin, the neck of which he had stuffed with leaves.

'There you are,' he said. 'Be careful, because it smells.'

I pulled out the plug of leaves and peered into the tin and discovered that Papa Demetrios was quite right; it smelt as strongly of garlic as a peasant bus on market day. In the bottom was crouched a medium-size, rather smooth-skinned, greenish-brown toad with enormous amber eyes and a mouth set in a perpetual, but rather insane, grin. As I put my hand into the tin to pick him up, he ducked his head between his forelegs, retracted his protuberant eyes into his skull in the odd way that toads have, and uttered a sharp bleating cry rather like that of a miniature sheep. I lifted him out of the tin and he struggled violently, exuding a terrible odour of garlic. I noticed that on each hind foot he had a horny black excrescence, blade-shaped, like a ploughshare. I was delighted with him, for I had spent a considerable amount of time and energy trying to track down spade-footed toads without success. Thanking Papa Demetrios profusely, I carried him home triumphantly and installed him in an aquarium in my bedroom.

I had placed earth and sand to a depth of two or three inches at the bottom of the aquarium and Augustus, having been christened and released, immediately set to work to build himself a home. With a curious movement of his hind legs, working backwards, using the blades of his feet as spades, he very rapidly dug himself a hole and disappeared from view with the exception of his protuberant eyes and grinning face.

Augustus, I soon discovered, was a remarkably intelligent beast and had many endearing traits of character which made themselves apparent as he got tamer. When I went into the room, he would scuttle out of his hole and make desperate endeavours to reach me through the glass walls of the aquarium. If I took him out and placed him on the floor, he would hop round the room after me and then, if I sat down, would climb laboriously up my leg until he reached my lap, where he would recline in a variety of undignified attitudes, basking in the heat of my body, blinking his eyes slowly, grinning up at me, and gulping. It was then that I discovered he liked to lie on his back and have his stomach gently massaged by my forefinger, and so from this unusual behaviour he derived the surname of Tickletummy. He would also, I learned, sing for his food. If I held a large, writhing earthworm over the top of the aquarium, Augustus would go into paroxysms of delight, his eyes seeming to protrude more and more with excitement, and he would utter a series of little pig-like grunts and the strange bleating cry he had given when I first picked him up. When the worm was finally dropped in front of him, he would nod his head vigorously, as if in thanks, grab one end of it and proceed to stuff it into his mouth with his thumbs. Whenever we had any guests, they were treated to an Augustus Tickletummy recital and they all agreed, gravely, that he had the best voice and repertoire of any toad they had met.

It was round about this time that Larry introduced Donald and Max into our life. Max was an immensely tall Austrian with curly blond hair, a blond moustache perched like an elegant butterfly on his lip, and intensely blue and kindly eyes. Donald, on the other hand, was short and pale-faced; one of those Englishmen who give you a first impression of being not only inarticulate, but completely devoid of personality.

Larry had run into this ill-assorted couple in the town and had lavishly invited them up to have drinks. The fact that they arrived, mellowed by a variety of alcoholic stimuli, at two o'clock in the morning did not strike any of us as being particularly curious, since, by that time, we were inured, or almost inured, to Larry's acquaintances.

Mother had gone to bed early with a severe cold, and the rest of the family had also retired to their rooms. I was the only member of the household awake. The reason for this was that I was waiting for Ulysses to return to the bedroom from his nightly wanderings and devour his supper of meat and minced liver. As I lay there reading, I heard a dim, blurred sound echoing through the olive groves. I thought at first it was a party of peasants returning late from a wedding, and took no notice. Then the cacophony grew closer and closer and from the clop and jingle accompanying it I realized it was some late night revellers passing on the road below in a cab. The song they were singing did not sound particularly Greek and I wondered who they could be. I got out of bed and leaned out the window, staring down through the olive trees. At that moment the cab turned off the road and started up the long drive towards the house. I could see it quite clearly because whoever was sitting in the back had apparently lighted a small bonfire. I watched this, puzzled and intrigued, as it flickered and shook through the trees on its way up to us.

At that moment Ulysses appeared out of the night sky, like a silently drifting dandelion clock, and endeavoured to perch on my naked shoulder. I shook him off and went and fetched his plate of food, which he proceeded to peck and gobble at, uttering tiny throaty noises to himself and blinking his brilliant eyes at me.

By this time the cab had made slow but steady progress and had entered the forecourt of the house. I leaned out the window enraptured by the sight.

It was not, as I had thought, a bonfire in the back of the

cab. There were two individuals sitting there, each clasping an enormous silver candelabra in which had been stuck some of the great white candles that one normally bought to put in the church of St Spiridion. They were singing loudly and untunefully, but with great panache, a song from *The Maid of the Mountains*, endeavouring, wherever possible, to harmonize.

The cab rolled to a halt at the steps that led up to the veranda.

'At seventeen . . .' sighed a very British baritone.

'At seventeen!' intoned the other singer in a rather heavy middle-European accent.

'He falls in love quite madly,' said the baritone, waving his candelabra about wildly, 'with eyes of tender blue.'

'Tender blue,' intoned the middle-European accent, giving a lechery to these simple words that had to be heard to be believed.

'At twenty-five,' continued the baritone, 'he thinks he's got it badly.'

'Badly,' said the middle-European accent dolefully.

'With eyes of different hue,' said the baritone, making such a wild gesture with his candelabra that the candles sped out of their sockets like rockets and fell sizzling onto the grass.

My bedroom door opened and Margo, clad in yards of lace and what appeared to be butter muslin, came in.

'What on earth's that *noise?*' she asked in a hoarse, accusing whisper. 'You *know* Mother's not well.'

I explained that the noise was nothing whatsoever to do with me, but apparently we had company. Margo leaned out the window and peered down at the cab where the singers had just reached the next verse of their song.

'I say,' she called, in muted tones, 'do you mind not making quite so much noise. My mother's sick.'

Immediate silence enveloped the cab and then a tall, gangling figure rose unsteadily to its feet. He held his candelabra aloft and gazed earnestly up at Margo.

'Must not dear lady,' he intoned sepulchrally, 'must not disturb Muzzer.'

'No, by Jove,' agreed the English voice from the interior of the cab.

'Who do you think they are?' Margo whispered to me in agitation.

I said that to me the thing was perfectly clear; they must be friends of Larry's.

'Are you friends of my brother's?' Margo fluted out the window.

'A noble being,' said the tall figure, waving the candelabra at her. 'He invited us for drinks.'

'Er . . . Just a minute, I'll come down,' said Margo.

'To look you closer would be to fulfil the ambition of a lifetime,' said the tall man, bowing somewhat uncertainly.

'See you closer,' corrected a quiet voice from the back of the cab.

'I'll go downstairs,' said Margo to me, 'and get them inside and keep them quiet. You go and wake Larry.'

I pulled on a pair of shorts, picked up Ulysses unceremoniously (who, with half-closed eyes, was digesting his food), and went to the window and threw him out.

'Extraordinary!' said the tall man, watching Ulysses fly away over the moon-silvered olive tops. 'Dis like the house of Dracula, no, Donald?'

'By Jove, yes,' said Donald.

I pattered down the corridor and burst into Larry's room. It took me some time to shake him awake, for, under the firm impression that Mother had been breathing her cold germs over him, he had taken the precaution of consuming half a bottle of whisky before he went to bed. Eventually he sat up blearily and looked at me.

'What the bloody hell do *you* want?' he inquired.

I explained about the two characters in the cab and that they had said they had been invited to drinks.

'Oh, Christ!' said Larry. 'Just tell them I've gone to Dubrovnik.'

I explained that I could not very well do this as by now Margo would have lured them into the house and that Mother, in her fragile condition, must not be disturbed. Groaning, Larry got out of bed and put on his dressing-gown and slippers and together we went down the creaking stairs to the drawing-room. Here we found Max, lanky, flamboyant, good-natured, sprawled in a chair waving his candelabra at Margo, all the candles of which had gone out. Donald sat hunched and gloomy in another chair, looking like an undertaker's assistant.

'Your eyes, they are tender blue,' said Max, waving a long finger at Margo. 'Ve vas singing about blue eyes, vere ve not, Donald?'

'We *were* singing about blue eyes,' said Donald.

'Dat's what I said,' said Max benevolently.

'You said "was,"' said Donald.

Max thought about this for a brief moment.

'Anyvay,' he said, 'de eyes vas blue.'

'Were blue,' said Donald.

'Oh, there you are,' said Margo, breathlessly, as Larry and I came in. 'I think these are friends of yours, Larry.'

'Larry!' bellowed Max, lurching up with the ungainly grace of a giraffe. 'Ve have come like you told us.'

'How very nice,' said Larry, forcing his sleep-crumpled features into something approaching an ingratiating smile. 'Do you mind keeping your voice down, because my mother's sick?'

'Muzzers,' said Max, with immense conviction, 'are de most important thing in de vorld.'

He turned to Donald, laid a long finger across his moustache, and said 'Shush' with such violence that Roger, who had sunk into a peaceful sleep, immediately leaped to his feet and started barking wildly. Widdle and Puke joined in vociferously.

'Damned bad form that,' observed Donald between the barks. 'Guest should not make his host's dogs bark.'

Max went down on his knees and engulfed the still barking Roger in his long arms, a manoeuvre that I viewed with
some alarm, since Roger, I felt, was quite capable of misinter-
preting it.

'Hush, Bow Wow,' said Max, beaming into Roger's bristling
and belligerent face.

To my astonishment, Roger immediately stopped barking and
started to lick Max's face extravagantly.

'Would you . . . er . . . like a drink?' said Larry. 'I can't ask you
to stop long, of course, because unfortunately my mother's ill.'

'Very civil of you,' said Donald. 'Very civil indeed. I must
apologize for him. Foreigner, you know.'

'Well, I think I'll just go back to bed,' said Margo, edging
tentatively towards the door.

'No, you won't,' Larry barked. 'Somebody's got to pour out
the drinks.'

'Do not,' said Max, reclining on the floor with Roger in his
arms and gazing at her piteously, 'do not remove doze eyes from
my orbit.'

'Well, I'll go and get the drinks, then,' said Margo breathlessly.

'And I vill help you,' said Max, casting Roger from him and
leaping to his feet.

Roger had been under the misguided impression that Max had
intended to spend the rest of the night cuddling him in front of
the dying fire, and so was not unnaturally put out when he was
thrown aside like this. He started barking again.

The door of the drawing-room burst open and Leslie, stark
naked except for a shot-gun under his arm, made his appearance.

'What the bloody hell's going on?' he asked.

'Leslie, *do* go and put some clothes on,' said Margo. 'These are
friends of Larry's.'

'Oh, God,' said Leslie dismally, 'not *more*.'

He turned and made his way back upstairs.

'Drinks!' said Max, rapturously seizing Margo in his arms and waltzing her round to the accompaniment of almost hysterical barks on the part of Roger.

'I do wish you would try to be more quiet,' said Larry. '*Max*, for Christ's sake.'

'Damned bad form,' said Donald.

'Remember my mother,' said Larry, since this reference had obviously struck a chord in Max's soul.

Immediately he ceased waltzing with the breathless Margo and came to a halt.

'Vere is your Muzzer?' he inquired. 'De lady is sick . . . take me to her dat I may secure her.'

'Succour,' said Donald.

'I'm here,' said Mother in a slightly nasal tone of voice from the doorway. 'What *is* going on?'

She was clad in her nightie and wearing, for reasons of her cold, a voluminous shawl over her shoulders. She carried under one arm the drooping, panting, apathetic figure of Dodo, her Dandie Dinmont terrier.

'Why, you're just in time, Mother,' said Larry. 'I want you to meet Donald and Max.'

With the first sign of animation that he had shown, Donald rose to his feet, marched swiftly across the room to Mother, seized her hand, and gave a slight bow over it.

'Enchanted,' he said. 'Terribly sorry about the disturbance. My friend, you know. Continental.'

'How nice to see you,' said Mother, summoning up all her resources.

At her entrance, Max had thrown his arms wide and was now gazing upon her with all the devoutness of a Crusader catching his first sight of Jerusalem.

'Muzzer!' he intoned dramatically. 'You are de Muzzer!'

'How do you do,' said Mother uncertainly.

'You are,' Max asked, getting his facts straight, 'de sick Muzzer?'

'Oh, it's just a bit of a cold,' said Mother deprecatingly.

'Ve have voked you,' said Max, clasping his breast, his eyes brimming with tears.

'Awoken or woken,' said Donald *sotto voce*.

'Come,' said Max and put his long arms round Mother and ushered her to a chair near the fire, pressing her into it with the utmost delicacy. He took off his coat and spread it gently about her knees. Then he squatted by her side, took her hand and peered earnestly into her face.

'Vhat,' he inquired, 'does Muzzer vant?'

'An uninterrupted night's sleep,' said Leslie, who had just returned, more conventionally garbed in a pair of pyjama trousers and sandals.

'Max,' said Donald sternly, 'stop monopolizing the conversation. Remember what we have come for.'

'Of course,' said Max delightedly. 'Ve have vunderful news, Larry. Donald has decided to become an author.'

'Had to,' murmured Donald modestly. 'Seeing all you chaps living in the lap of luxury. Royalties pouring in. Felt I must try my hand at it.'

'That's jolly good,' said Larry, with a certain lack of enthusiasm.

'I've just completed the first chapter,' said Donald, 'and so we came out hot-foot, as it were, so that I could read it to you.'

'Oh, God,' said Larry, horrified. 'No, Donald, really. My critical faculties are completely dehydrated at half past two in the morning. Can't you leave it here and I'll read it tomorrow?'

'It's short,' said Donald, taking no notice of Larry and producing a small sheet of paper from his pocket, 'but I think you will find the style interesting.'

Larry gave an exasperated sigh, and we all sat back and listened expectantly while Donald cleared his throat.

'Suddenly,' he began in a deep vibrant voice, 'suddenly, suddenly, suddenly, there he was and then suddenly, there she was, suddenly, suddenly, suddenly. And suddenly he looked at her, suddenly, suddenly, suddenly, and she suddenly looked at him, suddenly. She suddenly opened her arms, suddenly, suddenly, and he opened his arms, suddenly. Then suddenly they came together and, suddenly, suddenly, suddenly, he could feel the warmth of her body and suddenly, suddenly she could feel the warmth of his mouth on hers as they suddenly, suddenly, suddenly, suddenly fell on the couch together.'

There was a long pause while we waited for Donald to go on. He gulped once or twice as though overcome with emotion at his own writing, folded the piece of paper carefully and put it back in his pocket.

'What do you think?' he inquired of Larry.

'Well, it's a bit short,' said Larry cautiously.

'Ah, but what do you think of the style?' said Donald.

'Well, it's, um, interesting,' said Larry. 'I think you'll find it's been done before, though.'

'Couldn't have been,' explained Donald. 'You see, I only thought of it tonight.'

'I don't think he ought to have any more to drink,' said Leslie loudly.

'Hush, dear,' said Mother. 'What do you intend to call it, Donald?'

'I thought,' said Donald owlishly, 'I thought I would call it *The Suddenly Book*.'

'A very trenchant title,' said Larry. 'I feel, however, that your main characters could be padded out a little bit, in depth, as it were, before you get them all tangled up on the sofa.'

'Yes,' said Donald. 'You could well be right.'

'Well, that *is* interesting,' said Mother, sneezing violently. 'And now I think we really all ought to have a cup of tea.'

'I vill make de tea for you, Muzzer,' said Max, leaping to his feet and starting all the dogs barking again.

'I will help you,' said Donald.

'Margo, dear, you had better go with them and just make sure they find everything,' said Mother.

When the three of them had left the room, Mother looked at Larry.

'And these are the people,' she said coldly, 'you say are not eccentric.'

'Well, Donald's not eccentric,' said Larry. 'He's just a bit high.'

'And suddenly, suddenly, suddenly, suddenly he was drunk,' intoned Leslie, putting some more logs on the fire and kicking it into some semblance of a blaze.

'They are both of them very good chaps,' said Larry. 'Donald's already laid half of Corfu by its ears.'

'What do you mean?' said Mother.

'Well, you know how the Corfiotes love to worm every hidden secret out of you,' said Larry. 'They're all convinced that since he appears to have private means and is so incredibly British that he must have a terribly posh background. So he has been amusing himself by telling them all different stories. He has so far, I have been assured, been the elder son of a duke, the cousin of the Bishop of London, and the illegitimate son of Lord Chesterfield. He has been educated at Eton, Harrow, Oxford, Cambridge, and, to my delight, this morning Mrs Papanopoulos assured me that he had assured her that his formal education had been undertaken at Girton.'

Just at that moment Margo came back into the drawing-room, looking slightly distraught.

'I think you had better come and do something with them, Larry,' she said. 'Max has just lighted the kitchen fire with a five-pound note and Donald has disappeared and keeps shouting "Cooee" at us and we can't see where he's gone.'

All of us trooped down to the gigantic stone-flagged kitchen where a kettle was starting to sing on one of the charcoal fires and Max was contemplating, woefully, the charred remains of a five-pound note which he held in one hand.

'Really, Max,' said Mother, 'what a silly thing to do.'

Max beamed at her.

'No expense spared for Muzzer,' he said, and then, pressing the remains of the fiver into her hand, 'Keep it, Muzzer, as a souvenir.'

'Cooee,' came a doleful, echoing cry.

'That's Donald,' said Max proudly.

'Where is he?' said Mother.

'I don't know,' said Max. 'Ven he vants to hide, he vants to hide.'

Leslie strode to the back door and flung it open.

'Donald,' he called, 'are you there?'

'Cooee,' came a quavering cry from Donald with subtle, echoing overtones.

'Christ!' said Leslie. 'The silly bastard's fallen down the well.'

In the garden at the back of the kitchen there was a large well some fifty feet deep with a thick, round, iron pipe running right down the shaft. From the echoing qualities of Donald's voice, we were quite sure that Leslie's guess was right. Carrying a lamp, we made our way hurriedly up to the edge of the well and peered, in a circle, down into its dark depths. Half-way down the pipe was Donald, his arms and legs entwined firmly round it. He gazed up at us.

'Cooee,' he said coyly.

'Donald, don't be a bloody fool,' said Larry exasperatedly. 'Come up out of there. If you fall into that water you'll drown. Not that I worry about that, but you'll pollute our entire water supply.'

'Shan't,' said Donald.

'Donald,' said Max, 've vant you. Come. It is cold down dere. Come and have some tea with Muzzer and ve vill talk more about your book.'

'Do you insist?' asked Donald.

'Yes, yes, we insist,' said Larry impatiently.

Slowly and laboriously Donald climbed up the pipe, while we watched him breathlessly. When he was within easy reach, Max and the entire family leaned over the well, grabbed various portions of his anatomy, and hauled him to safety. Then we escorted our guests back into the house and plied them with vast quantities of hot tea until they seemed as sober as they were likely to be without having slept.

'I think you had better go home now,' said Larry firmly, 'and we'll meet you in town tomorrow.'

We escorted them out onto the veranda. The cab stood, with the horse drooping forlornly between the shafts. The cab driver was nowhere to be seen.

'Did they have a cab driver?' Larry asked of me.

I said that, quite honestly, I had been so captivated by the sight of their candelabras that I had not noticed.

'I vill drive,' said Max, 'and Donald shall sing to me.'

Donald arranged himself carefully in the back of the cab with the candelabras and Max took to the driving seat. He cracked the whip in a most professional manner and the horse aroused itself from its comatose condition, gave a sigh, and then shambled off down the drive.

'Good night,' shouted Max, waving his whip.

We waited until they had disappeared from sight behind the olive trees and then trooped back inside the house and with sighs of heartfelt relief, closed the front door.

'Really, Larry, you shouldn't invite people at this hour of night,' said Mother.

'I *didn't* invite them at this hour of the night,' said Larry, annoyed. 'They just *came*. I invited them for drinks.'

Just at that moment there was a thunderous knocking on the front door.

'Well, I'm off,' said Mother and scuttled upstairs with considerable alacrity.

476

Larry opened the front door and there stood the distraught figure of the cab driver.

'Where's my *carrochino*?' he shouted.

'Where were you?' retorted Larry. 'The *kyrios* have taken it.'

'They have stolen my *carrochino*?' shouted the man.

'Of course they haven't stolen it, foolish one,' said Larry, now tried beyond endurance. 'Because you weren't waiting here they took it to get back into town. If you run quickly you can catch them up.'

Imploring St Spiridion to help him, the man ran off through the olive trees and down towards the road.

Determined not to miss the last act in this drama, I ran to a vantage point where I got a clear view of the entrance to our drive and a stretch of moonlit roadway which led into town. The cab had just left the drive and arrived on the road at a brisk walk, Donald and Max singing happily together. At that moment the cab driver appeared through the olives, and screaming imprecations, he started to run after them.

Max, startled, looked over his shoulder.

'Volves, Donald,' he shouted. 'Hold tight!' He proceeded to belabour the behind of the unfortunate horse who, startled, broke into a gallop. But it was the sort of gallop that only a Corfu cab horse could achieve. It was just sufficiently fast to keep the cab owner running at full stretch some ten paces behind the cab. He was shouting and imploring and almost weeping with rage. Max, determined to save Donald, at all costs, was belabouring the horse unmercifully while Donald leaned over the back of the cab and shouted 'Bang!' at intervals, and thus they disappeared out of my sight along the Corfu road.

The following morning, at breakfast, all of us felt slightly jaded, and Mother was lecturing Larry severely for allowing people to turn up at two o'clock in the morning for drinks. Just at that moment, Spiro's car drove up to the front of the house and he waddled onto the veranda where we were sitting, clasping in his arms an enormous, flat brown-paper parcel.

'This is for yous, Mrs Durrells,' he said.

'For me?' said Mother, adjusting her spectacles. 'What on earth can it be?'

She unwrapped the brown paper cautiously and there inside, as bright as a rainbow, was the biggest box of chocolates I had ever seen in my life. Pinned to it was a little white card on which had been written in a rather shaky hand, 'With apologies for last night. Donald and Max.'

7

Owls and Aristocracy

Now winter was upon us. Everything was redolent with the smoke of olive-wood fires. The shutters creaked and slapped the sides of the house as the wind caught them, and the birds and leaves were tumbled across a dark lowering sky. The brown mountains of the mainland wore tattered caps of snow and the rain filled the eroded, rocky valleys, turning them into foaming torrents that fled eagerly to the sea carrying mud and debris with them. Once they reached the sea they spread like yellow veins through the blue water, and the surface was dotted with squill bulbs, logs and twisted branches, dead beetles and butterflies, clumps of brown grass and splintered canes. Storms would be brewed in among the whitened spikes of the Albanian mountains and then tumble across to us, great black piles of cumulus, spitting a stinging rain, with sheet lightning blooming and dying like yellow ferns across the sky.

It was at the beginning of the winter that I received a letter.

Dear Gerald Durrell,

I understand from our mutual friend, Dr Stephanides, that you are a keen naturalist and possess a number of pets. I was wondering, therefore, if you would care to have a white owl which my workmen found in an old shed they were demolishing? He has, unfortunately, a broken wing, but is otherwise in good health and feeding well.

If you would like him, I suggest you come to lunch on Friday and take him with you when you return home. Perhaps you

*would be kind enough to let me know. A quarter to one or one
o'clock would be suitable.*

*Yours sincerely,
Countess Mavrodaki*

This letter excited me for two reasons. Firstly, because I had
always wanted a barn owl, for that was what it obviously was,
and secondly, because the whole of Corfu society had been trying
unavailingly for years to get to know the Countess. She was the
recluse par excellence. Immensely wealthy, she lived in a gigantic,
rambling, Venetian villa deep in the country and never entertained
or saw anybody except the workmen on her vast estate. Her
acquaintance with Theodore was due only to the fact that he was
her medical adviser. The Countess was reputed to possess a large
and valuable library and for this reason Larry had been most anxious to try to get himself invited to her villa, but without success.

'Dear God,' he said bitterly when I showed him my invitation.
'Here I've been trying for months to get that old harpy to let me
see her books and she invites you to lunch – there's no justice in
the world.'

I said that after I had lunched with the Countess, maybe I
could ask her if he could see her books.

'After she's had lunch with *you* I shouldn't think she would be
willing to show me a copy of *The Times*, let alone her library,'
said Larry witheringly.

However, in spite of my brother's low opinion of my social
graces, I was determined to put in a good word for him if I saw
a suitable opportunity. It was, I felt, an important, even solemn
occasion, and so I dressed with care. My shirt and shorts were
carefully laundered and I had prevailed upon Mother to buy me
a new pair of sandals and a new straw hat. I rode on Sally – who
had a new blanket as a saddle to honour the occasion – for the
Countess's estate was some distance away.

The day was dark and the ground mushy under foot. It looked as though we would have a storm, but I hoped this would not be until after I had arrived, for the rain would spoil the crisp whiteness of my shirt. As we jogged along through the olives, the occasional woodcock zooming up from the myrtles in front of us, I became increasingly nervous. I discovered that I was ill-prepared for this occasion. To begin with, I had forgotten to bring my four-legged chicken in spirits. I had felt sure that the Countess would want to see this and in any case I felt it would provide a subject of conversation that would help us in the initial awkward stages of our meeting. Secondly, I had forgotten to consult anybody on the correct way to address a countess. 'Your Majesty' would surely be too formal, I thought, especially as she was giving me an owl? Perhaps 'Highness' would be better – or maybe just a simple 'Mam'?

Puzzling over the intricacies of protocol, I had left Sally to her own devices and so she had promptly fallen into a donkey-doze. Of all the beasts of burden, only the donkey seems capable of falling asleep while still moving. The result was that she ambled close to the ditch at the side of the road, suddenly stumbled and lurched and I, deep in thought, fell off her back into six inches of mud and water. Sally stared down at me with an expression of accusing astonishment that she always wore when she knew she was in the wrong. I was so furious, I could have strangled her. My new sandals oozed, my shorts and shirt – so crisp, so clean, so *well-behaved-looking* a moment before – were now bespattered with mud and bits of decaying water-weed. I could have wept with rage and frustration. We were too far from home to retrace our footsteps so that I could change; there was nothing for it but to go on, damp and miserable, convinced now that it did not matter how I addressed the Countess. She would, I felt sure, take one look at my gypsy-like condition and order me home. Not only would I lose my owl, but any chance I had of getting Larry in to see her library. I was a fool, I thought bitterly. I should have walked instead of trusting myself to this hopeless creature, who was now trotting along at a brisk pace, her ears pricked like furry arum lilies.

Presently we came to the Countess's villa, lying deep in the olive groves, approached by a drive lined with tall green-and-pink-trunked eucalyptus trees. The entrance to the drive was guarded by two columns on which were perched a pair of white-winged lions who stared scornfully at Sally and me as we trotted down the drive. The house was immense, built in a hollow square. It had at one time been a lovely, rich, Venetian red, but this had now faded to a rose-pink, the plaster bulged and cracked in places by the damp, and I noticed that a number of brown tiles were missing from the roof. The eaves had slung under them more swallows' nests – now empty, like small, forgotten, brown ovens – than I had ever seen congregated in one spot before.

I tied Sally up under a convenient tree and made my way to the archway that led into the central patio. Here a rusty chain hung down and when I pulled it I heard a bell jangle faintly somewhere in the depths of the house. I waited patiently for some time and was just about to ring the bell again when the massive wooden doors were opened. There stood a man who looked to me exactly like a bandit. He was tall and powerful, with a great jutting hawk-nose, sweeping flamboyant white moustaches, and a mane of curling white hair. He was wearing a scarlet tarboosh, a loose white blouse beautifully embroidered with scarlet-and-gold thread, baggy pleated black pants, and on his feet upturned *charukias* decorated with enormous red-and-white pom-poms. His brown face cracked into a grin and I saw that all his teeth were gold. It was like looking into a mint.

'*Kyrié* Durrell?' he inquired. 'Welcome.'

I followed him through the patio, full of magnolia trees and forlorn winter flower-beds, and into the house. He led me down a long corridor tiled in scarlet and blue, threw open a door, and ushered me into a great, gloomy room lined from ceiling to floor with bookshelves. At one end was a large fire-place in which a blaze flapped and hissed and crackled. Over the fire-place was an enormous gold-framed mirror, nearly black, with age. Sitting by the fire on a long couch, almost obliterated by coloured shawls and cushions, was the Countess.

She was not a bit what I had expected. I had visualized her as being tall, gaunt, and rather forbidding, but as she rose to her feet and danced across the room to me I saw she was tiny, very fat, and as pink and dimpled as a rosebud. Her honey-coloured hair was piled high on her head in a pompadour style and her eyes, under permanently arched and surprised eyebrows, were as green and shiny as unripe olives. She took my hand in both her warm little pudgy ones and clasped it to her ample breast.

'How kind, how *kind* of you to come,' she exclaimed in a musical, little girl's voice, exuding an overpowering odour of Parma violets and brandy in equal quantities. 'How very, *very* kind. May I call you Gerry? Of course I may. My friends call me Matilda . . . it isn't my *real* name, of course. That's Stephani Zinia . . . so uncouth – like a patent medicine. I *much* prefer Matilda, don't you?'

I said, cautiously, that I thought Matilda a very nice name.

'Yes, a comforting *old-fashioned* name. Names are *so* important, don't you think? Now he there,' she said, gesturing at the man who had shown me in, '*he* calls himself Demetrios. I call him Mustapha.'

She glanced at the man and then leaned forward, nearly asphyxiating me with brandy and Parma violets, and hissed suddenly, in Greek, 'He's a misbegotten Turk.'

The man's face grew red and his moustache bristled, making him look more like a bandit than ever. 'I am not a Turk,' he snarled. 'You lie.'

'You are a Turk and your name's Mustapha,' she retorted.

'It isn't . . . I'm not . . . It isn't . . . I'm not,' said the man, almost incoherent with rage. 'You are lying.'

483

'I'm not.'

'You are.'

'I'm not.'

'You are.'

'I'm *not*.'

'You're a damned elderly liar.'

'Elderly,' she squeaked, her face growing red. 'You dare to call me elderly . . . you . . . you *Turk* you.'

'You are elderly and you're fat,' said Demetrios-Mustapha coldly.

'That's too much,' she screamed. 'Elderly . . . fat . . . that's too much. You're sacked. Take a month's notice. No, leave this instant, you son of a misbegotten Turk.'

Demetrios-Mustapha drew himself up regally.

'Very well,' he said. 'Do you wish me to serve the drinks and lunch before I go?'

'Of course,' she said.

In silence he crossed the room and extracted a bottle of champagne from an ice bucket behind the sofa. He opened it and poured equal quantities of brandy and champagne into three large glasses. He handed us one each and lifted the third himself.

'I give you a toast,' he said to me solemnly. 'We will drink to the health of a fat, elderly liar.'

I was in a quandary. If I drank the toast it would seem that I was concurring in his opinion of the Countess, and that would scarcely seem polite; and yet, if I did *not* drink the toast, he looked quite capable of doing me an injury. As I hesitated, the Countess, to my astonishment, burst into delighted giggles, her smooth fat cheeks dimpling charmingly.

'You mustn't tease our guest, Mustapha. But I must admit the toast was a good touch,' she said, gulping at her drink.

Demetrios-Mustapha grinned at me, his teeth glittering and winking in the fire-light.

'Drink, *kyrié*,' he said. 'Take no notice of us. She lives for food, drink, and fighting, and it is my job to provide all three.'

'Nonsense,' said the Countess, seizing my hand and leading me to the sofa, so that I felt as though I were hitched to a small, fat, pink cloud. 'Nonsense, I live for a lot of things, a lot of things. Now, don't stand there drinking my drink, you drunkard. Go and see to the food.'

Demetrios-Mustapha drained his glass and left the room, while the Countess seated herself on the sofa, clasping my hand in hers, and beamed at me.

'This *is* cosy,' she said delightedly. 'Just you and I. Tell me, do you always wear mud all over your clothes?'

I hastily and embarrassedly explained about Sally.

'So you came by *donkey*,' she said, making it sound a very exotic form of transport. 'How *wise* of you. I distrust motorcars myself, noisy, uncontrollable things. Unreliable.

'I remember we had one when my husband was alive, a big yellow one. But my dear, it was a brute. It would obey my husband, but it would not do a thing I told it to do. One day it deliberately backed into a large stall containing fruit and vegetables – in spite of all I was trying to do to stop it – and then went over the edge of the harbour into the sea. When I came out of hospital, I said to my husband, "Henri," I said – that was his name – such a nice, *bourgeois* name, don't you think? Where was I? Oh, yes. Well, "Henri," I said, "that car's malevolent," I said. "It's possessed of an evil spirit. You must sell it." And so he did.'

Brandy and champagne on an empty stomach combined with the fire to make me feel extremely mellow. My head whirled pleasantly and I nodded and smiled as the Countess chattered on eagerly.

'My husband was a very cultured man, very cultured indeed. He collected books, you know. Books, paintings, stamps, beer-bottle tops, anything cultural appealed to him. Just before he died, he started collecting busts of Napoleon. You would be surprised how many busts they had made of that horrible little Corsican. My husband had five hundred and eighty-two. "Henri," I said to him. "Henri, this must stop. Either you give up collecting busts of Napoleon or I will leave you and go to St Helena." I said it as a joke, though, only as a joke, and you know what he said? He said he had been thinking about going to St Helena for a holiday – with all his busts. My God, what dedication! It was not to be borne! I believe in a little bit of culture in its place, but not to become *obsessed* with it.'

Demetrios-Mustapha came into the room, refilled our glasses and said, 'Lunch in five minutes,' and departed again.

'He was what you might call a *compulsive* collector, my dear. The times that I trembled when I saw that fanatical gleam in his eye. At a state fair once he saw a combine harvester, simply immense it was, and I could *see* the gleam in his eye, but I put my foot down. "Henri," I said to him. "Henri, we are not going to have combine harvesters all over the place. If you must collect, why not something sensible? Jewels or furs or something?" It may seem harsh, my dear, but what could I do? If I had relaxed for an *instant* he would have had the whole house full of farm machinery.'

Demetrios-Mustapha came into the room again. 'Lunch is ready,' he said.

Still chattering, the Countess led me by the hand out of the room, down the tiled corridor, then down some creaking wooden stairs into a huge kitchen in the cellars. The kitchen at our villa was enormous enough, but this kitchen simply dwarfed it. It was stone-flagged and at one end a positive battery of charcoal fires glowed and winked under the bubbling pots. The walls were covered with a great variety of copper pots, kettles, platters, coffee pots, huge serving dishes, and soup tureens. They all glowed with a pinky-red gleam in the fire-light, glinting and winking like tiger beetles. In the centre of the floor was a twelve-foot-long dining-table of beautiful polished walnut. This was carefully set for two with snowy-white serviettes and gleaming cutlery. In the centre of the table two giant silver candelabras each held a white forest of lighted candles. The whole effect of a kitchen and a state dining-room combined was very odd. It was very hot and so redolent with delicious smells they almost suffocated the Countess's scent.

'I hope you don't mind eating in the kitchen,' said the Countess, making it sound as though it were really the most degrading thing to eat food in such humble surroundings.

I said I thought eating in the kitchen was a most sensible idea, especially in winter, as it was warmer.

'Quite right,' said the Countess, seating herself as Demetrios-Mustapha held her chair for her. 'And, you see, if we eat upstairs I get complaints from this elderly Turk about how far he has to walk.'

'It isn't the distance I complain of, it's the weight of the food,' said Demetrios-Mustapha, pouring a pale green-gold wine into our glasses. 'If you didn't eat so much, it wouldn't be so bad.'

'Oh, stop complaining and get on with serving,' said the Countess plaintively, tucking her serviette carefully under her dimpled chin.

I, filled with champagne and brandy, was now more than a little drunk and ravenously hungry. I viewed with alarm the number of eating utensils that were flanking my plate, for I was not quite sure which to use first. I remembered Mother's maxim that you started on the outside and worked in, but there were so many utensils that I was uneasy. I decided to wait and see what the Countess used and then follow suit. It was an unwise decision for I soon discovered that she used any and every knife, fork, or spoon with a fine lack of discrimination and so, before long, I became so muddled I was doing the same.

The first course that Demetrios-Mustapha set before us was a fine, clear soup, sequinned with tiny golden bubbles of fat, with fingernail-sized croutons floating like crisp little rafts on an amber sea. It was delicious, and the Countess had two helpings, scrunching up the croutons, the noise like someone walking over crisp leaves. Demetrios-Mustapha filled our glasses with more of the pale, musky wine and placed before us a platter of minute baby fish, each one fried a golden brown. Slices of yellow-green lemons in a large dish and a brimming sauce-boat of some exotic sauce unknown to me accompanied it. The Countess piled her plate high with fish, added a lava flow of sauce, and then squeezed lemon juice lavishly over the fish, the table, and herself. She beamed at me, her face now a bright rose-pink, her forehead slightly beaded with sweat. Her prodigious appetite did not appear to impair her conversational powers one jot, for she talked incessantly.

'Don't you love these little fish? Heavenly! Of course, it's such a pity that they should die so *young*, but there we are. *So* nice to be able to eat *all* of them without worrying about the bones. *Such* a relief! Henri, my husband, you know, started to collect skeletons once. My dear, the house looked and smelt like a mortuary. "Henri," I said to him. "Henri, this must stop. This is an unhealthy death-wish you have developed. You must go and see a psychiatrist."'

Demetrios-Mustapha removed our empty plates, poured for us a red wine, dark as the heart of a dragon, and then placed before us a dish in which lay snipe, the heads twisted round so that their long beaks could skewer themselves and their empty eye-sockets look at us accusingly. They were plump and brown with cooking, each having its own little square of toast. They were surrounded by thin wafers of fried potatoes like drifts of autumn leaves, pale greeny-white candles of asparagus and small peas.

'I simply cannot understand people who are vegetarians,' said the Countess, banging vigorously at a snipe's skull with her fork so that she might crack it and get to the brain. 'Henri once tried to be a vegetarian. Would you believe it? But I couldn't endure it. "Henri," I said to him, "this must stop. We have enough food in the larder to feed an army, and I can't eat it single-handed." Imagine, my dear, I had just ordered two dozen hares. "Henri," I said, "you will have to give up this foolish fad."'

It struck me that Henri, although obviously a bit of a trial as a husband, had nevertheless led a very frustrated existence.

Demetrios-Mustapha cleared away the debris of the snipe and poured out more wine. I was beginning to feel bloated with food and I hoped that there was not too much more to come. But there was still an army of knives and forks and spoons, unused, beside my plate, so it was with alarm I saw Demetrios-Mustapha approaching through the gloomy kitchen bearing a huge dish.

'Ah!' said the Countess, holding up her plump hands in excitement. 'The main dish! What is it, Mustapha, what is it?'

'The wild boar that Makroyannis sent,' said Demetrios-Mustapha.

'Oh, the boar! The *boar!*' squeaked the Countess, clasping her fat cheeks in her hands. 'Oh, lovely! I had forgotten all about it. You do like wild boar, I hope?'

I said that it was one of my favourite meats, which was true, but could I have a very small helping, please?

'But of course you shall,' she said, leaning over the great, brown, gravy-glistening haunch and starting to cut thick pink slabs of it. She placed three of these on a plate – obviously under the impression that this was, by anyone's standards, a small portion – and then proceeded to surround them with the accoutrements. There were piles of the lovely little golden wild mushrooms, chanterelles, with their delicate, almost winy flavour; tiny marrows stuffed with sour cream and capers; potatoes baked in their skins, neatly split and anointed with butter; carrots red as a frosty winter sun, and great tree trunks of white leeks, poached in cream. I surveyed this dish of food and surreptitiously undid the top three buttons of my shorts.

'We used to get wild boar *such* a lot when Henri was alive. He used to go to Albania and shoot them, you know. But now we seldom have it. What a *treat!* Will you have some more mushrooms? No? *So* good for one. After this, I think we will have a pause. A pause is essential, I always think, for a good digestion,' said the Countess, adding naïvely, 'and it enables you to eat so much *more.*'

The wild boar was fragrant and succulent, having been marinaded well with herb-scented wine and stuffed with garlic cloves, but even so I only just managed to finish it. The Countess had two helpings, both identical in size, and then leaned back, her face congested to a pale puce colour, and mopped the sweat from her brow with an inadequate lace handkerchief.

'A pause, eh?' she said thickly, smiling at me. 'A pause to marshal our resources.'

I felt that I had not any resources to marshal, but I did not like to say so. I nodded and smiled and undid all the rest of the buttons on my shorts.

During the pause, the Countess smoked a long thin cheroot and ate salted peanuts, chatting on interminably about her husband. The pause did me good. I felt a little less solid and somnolent with food. When the Countess eventually decided that we had rested our internal organs sufficiently, she called for the next course, and Demetrios-Mustapha produced two mercifully small omelets, crispy brown on the outside and liquid and succulent on the inside, stuffed with tiny pink shrimps.

'What have you got for a sweet?' inquired the Countess, her mouth full of omelet.

'I didn't make one,' said Demetrios-Mustapha.

The Countess's eyes grew round and fixed.

'You didn't make a sweet?' she said, in tones of horror, as though he were confessing to some heinous crime.

'I didn't have time,' said Demetrios-Mustapha. 'You can't expect me to do all this cooking and all the housework.'

'But no *sweet*,' said the Countess despairingly. 'You can't have a lunch without a sweet.'

'Well, I bought you some meringues,' said Mustapha. 'You'll have to make do with those.'

'Oh, lovely!' said the Countess glowing and happy again. 'Just what's needed.'

It was the last thing I needed. The meringues were large and white and brittle as coral and stuffed to overflowing with cream. I wished fervently that I had brought Roger with me, as he could have sat under the table and accepted half my food, since the Countess was far too occupied with her own plate and her reminiscences really to concentrate on me.

'Now,' she said at last, swallowing the last mouthful of meringue and brushing the white crumbs from her chin. 'Now, do you feel replete? Or would you care for a little something more? Some fruit perhaps? Not that there's very much at this time of the year.'

I said no thank you very much, I had had quite sufficient.

The Countess sighed and looked at me soulfully. I think nothing would have pleased her more than to ply me with another two or three courses.

'You don't eat enough,' she said. 'A growing boy like you should eat more. You're far too thin for your age. Does your Mother feed you properly?'

I could imagine Mother's wrath if she had heard this innuendo. I said yes, Mother was an excellent cook and we all fed like lords.

'I'm glad to hear it,' said the Countess. 'But you still look a little peaky to me.'

I could not say so, but the reason I was beginning to look peaky was that the assault of food upon my stomach was beginning to make itself felt. I said, as politely as I could, that I thought I ought to be getting back.

'But of course, dear,' said the Countess. 'Dear me, a quarter past four already. How time flies!'

She sighed at the thought, then brightened perceptibly.

'However, it's nearly time for tea. Are you sure you wouldn't like to stay and have something?'

I said no, that Mother would be worried about me.

'Now, let me see,' said the Countess. 'What did you come for? Oh, yes, the owl. Mustapha, bring the boy his owl and bring me some coffee and some of those nice Turkish delights up in the lounge.'

Mustapha appeared with a cardboard box done up with string and handed it to me.

'I wouldn't open it until you get home,' he said. 'That's a wild one, that.'

I was overcome with the terrifying thought that if I did not hurry my departure, the Countess would ask me to partake of Turkish delight with her. So I thanked them both sincerely for my owl, and made my way to the front door.

'Well,' said the Countess, 'it has been enchanting having you, *absolutely enchanting*. You must come again. You must come in the spring or the summer when we have more choice of fruit and vegetables. Mustapha's got a way of cooking octopus which makes it simply melt in your mouth.'

I said I would love to come again, making a mental vow that if I did, I would starve for three days in advance.

'Here,' said the Countess, pressing an orange into my pocket, 'take this. You might feel peckish on the way home.'

As I mounted Sally and trotted off down the drive, she called, 'Drive carefully.'

Grim-faced, I sat there with the owl clasped to my bosom till we were outside the gates of the Countess's estate. Then the jogging I was subjected to on Sally's back was too much. I dismounted, went behind an olive tree, and was deliciously and flamboyantly sick.

When I got home I carried the owl up to my bedroom, untied the box and lifted him, struggling and beak-clicking, out onto the floor. The dogs, who had gathered round in a circle to view the new addition, backed away hurriedly. They knew what Ulysses could do when he was in a bad temper, and this owl was three times his size. He was, I thought, one of the most beautiful birds I had ever seen. The feathers on his back and wings were honeycomb golden, smudged with pale ash-grey; his breast was a spotless cream-white; and the mask of white feathers round his dark, strangely Oriental-looking eyes was as crisp and as starched-looking as any Elizabethan's ruff.

His wing was not as bad as I had feared. It was a clean break, and after half an hour's struggle, during which he managed to draw blood on several occasions, I had it splinted up to my satisfaction. The owl, which I had decided to call Lampadusa, simply because the name appealed to me, seemed to be belligerently scared of the dogs, totally unwilling to make friends with Ulysses, and viewed Augustus Tickletummy with undisguised loathing. I felt he might be happier, till he settled down, in a dark, secluded place, so I carried him up to the attic. One of the attic rooms was very tiny and lit by one small window which was so covered with cobwebs and dust that it allowed little light to penetrate the room. It was quiet and as dim as a cave, and I thought that here Lampadusa would enjoy his convalescence. I put him on the floor with a large saucer of chopped meat and locked the door carefully so that he would not be disturbed. That evening, when I went to visit him, taking him a dead mouse by way of a present, he seemed very much improved. He had eaten most of his meat and now hissed and beak-clicked at me with outspread wings and blazing eyes as he pitter-pattered about the floor. Encouraged by his obvious progress, I left him with his mouse and went to bed.

Some hours later I was awakened by the sound of voices emanating from Mother's room. Wondering, sleepily, what on earth the family could be doing at that hour, I got out of bed and stuck my head out of the bedroom door to listen.

'I tell you,' Larry was saying, 'it's a damned great polter-geist.'

'It can't be a poltergeist, dear,' said Mother. 'Poltergeists throw things.'

'Well, whatever it is, it's up there clanking its chains,' said Larry, 'and I want it exorcised. You and Margo are supposed to be the experts on the after-life. You go up and do it.'

'I'm not going up there,' said Margo tremulously. 'It might be anything. It might be a malignant spirit.'

'It's bloody malignant all right,' said Larry. 'It's been keeping me awake for the last hour.'

'Are you sure it isn't the wind or something, dear?' asked Mother.

'I know the difference between wind and a damned ghost playing around with balls and chains,' said Larry.

'Perhaps it's burglars,' said Margo, more to give herself confidence than anything else. 'Perhaps it's burglars and we ought to wake Leslie.'

Half-asleep and still bee-drowsy from the liquor I had consumed that day, I could not think what the family were talking about. It seemed as intriguing as any of the other crises that they seemed capable of evoking at the most unexpected hours of the day or night, so I went to Mother's door and peered into the room. Larry was marching up and down, his dressing-gown swishing imperially.

'Something's got to be done,' he said. 'I can't sleep with rattling chains over my head, and if I can't sleep I can't write.'

'I don't see what you expect *us* to do about it, dear,' said Mother. 'I'm sure it must be the wind.'

'Yes, you can't expect us to go up there,' said Margo. 'You're a man, *you* go.'

'Look,' said Larry, 'you are the one who came back from London covered with ectoplasm and talking about the infinite. It's probably some hellish thing you've conjured up from one of your séances that's followed you here. That makes it *your* pet. You go and deal with it.'

The word 'pet' penetrated. Surely it could not be Lampadusa? Like all owls, barn owls have wings as soft and as silent as dandelion clocks. Surely he could not be responsible for making a noise like a ball and chain?

I went into the room and inquired what they were all talking about.

'It's only a ghost, dear,' said Mother. 'Larry's found a ghost.'

'It's in the attic,' said Margo, excitedly. 'Larry thinks it followed me from England. I wonder if it's Mawake?'

'We're not going to start *that* all over again,' said Mother firmly.

'I don't care *who* it is,' said Larry, 'which one of your dis-embodied friends. I want it removed.'

I said I thought there was just the faintest possibility that it might be Lampadusa.

'What's that?' inquired Mother.

I explained that it was the owl the Countess had given me.

'I might have known it,' said Larry. 'I might have known it. Why it didn't occur to me instantly, I don't know.'

'Now, now, dear,' said Mother. 'It's only an owl.'

'Only an owl!' said Larry. 'It sounds like a battalion of tanks crashing about up there. Tell him to get it out of the loft.'

I said I could not understand why Lampadusa was making a noise since owls were the quietest of things . . . I said they drifted through the night on silent wings like flakes of ash . . .

'This one hasn't got silent wings,' said Larry. 'It sounds like a one-owl jazz band. Go and get it *out*.'

Hurriedly I took a lamp and made my way up to the attic. When I opened the door I saw at once what the trouble was. Lampadusa had devoured his mouse and then discovered that there was a long shred of meat still lying in his saucer. This, during the course of the long, hot day, had solidified and become welded to the surface of the saucer. Lampadusa, feeling that this shred of meat would do well as a light snack to keep body and soul together until dawn, had endeavoured to pick it off the plate. The curve of his sharp amber beak had gone through the meat, but the meat had refused to part company with the saucer, so that there he was, effectively trapped, flapping ineffectually round the floor, banging and clattering the saucer against the wooden boards in an effort to disentangle it from his beak. So I extricated him from this predicament and carried him down to my bedroom where I shut him in his cardboard box for safe-keeping.

PART THREE

Criseda

This place is wonderfully lovely. I wish you could see it; if you came I could put you up beautifully, and feed you on ginger-beer and claret and prawns and figs.

– Edward Lear

8

Hedgehogs and Sea-dogs

When spring came, we moved to a new villa, an elegant, snow-white one shaded by a huge magnolia tree, that lay in the olive groves not far from where our very first villa had been. It was on a hillside overlooking a great flat area marked out like a gigantic chess-board by irrigation ditches, which I knew as the fields. They were in fact the old Venetian salt-pans used long ago for collecting the brine that floated into the channels from the big salt-water lake on whose shores they lay. The lake had long since silted up and the channels, now flooded by fresh water from the hills, provided a grid-work of lush fields. This was an area overflowing with wildlife, and so it was one of my happiest hunting grounds.

Spring in Corfu never seemed to be half-hearted. Almost overnight, it seemed, the winter winds had blown the skies clean of clouds, so that they shone a clear delphinium blue, and overnight the winter rains had flooded the valleys with wildflowers; the pink of pyramid orchids, yellow of crocus, tall pale spikes of the asphodels, the blue eyes of the grape hyacinths peering at you from the grass, and the wine-dipped anemones that bowed in the slightest breeze. The olive groves were alive and rustling with the newly arrived birds: the hoopoes, salmon-pink and black with surprised crests, probed their long, curved beaks at the soft earth between the clumps of emerald grass; goldfinches, chiming and wheezing, danced merrily from twig to twig, their plumage glowing gold and scarlet and black. In the irrigation ditches in the fields, the waters became green with weed, interlaced with the strings of toad spawn, like black-pearl necklaces; emerald-green frogs croaked at each other, and the water tortoises, their shells as black as ebony, crawled up the banks to dig their holes and lay their eggs. Steel-blue dragon-flies, slender as threads, hatched and drifted like smoke through the undergrowth, moving in a curious stiff flight. Now was the time when the banks at night were lit by the throbbing, green-white light of a thousand glow-worms and in the day-time by the glint of wild strawberries hanging like scarlet lanterns in the shade. It was an exciting time, a time for explorations and new discoveries, a time when an overturned log might reveal almost anything from a field-vole's nest to a wriggling glitter of baby slow-worms, looking as though they were cast in burnished bronze.

I was down in the fields one day, endeavouring to catch some of the brown water-snakes that inhabited the irrigation ditches, when an old woman, whom I knew slightly, called me from some six fields away. She had been digging up the ground with her short-handled, broad-bladed hoe, standing up to her ankles in the rich loam, wearing the thick, ungainly sheep's-wool stockings the peasants put on for this operation.

'I've found you something,' she called. 'Come quickly.'

It was impossible for me to get there quickly, for each field was surrounded by an irrigation ditch on all four sides and finding the bridges across these was like finding your way through a maze.

'Quickly! Quickly!' screamed the old woman. 'They are running away. Quickly!'

I ran and leaped and scuttled, almost falling into the ditches, racing across the rickety plank bridges, until, panting, I reached her side.

'There,' she said, pointing. 'There. Mind they don't bite you.'

I saw that she had dug up a bundle of leaves from under the earth in which something white was moving. Gingerly I parted the leaves with the handle of my butterfly net and saw to my delight four fat, newly born, baby hedgehogs, pink as cyclamen, with soft, snow-white spines. They were still blind and they wriggled and nosed at each other like a litter of tiny pigs. I picked them up and put them carefully inside my shirt, thanked the old woman, and made my way homewards. I was excited about my new pets, principally because they were so young. I already had two adult hedgehogs, called Itch and Scratch because of the vast quantities of fleas they harboured, but they were not really tame. These babies I thought would grow up differently. I would be, as far as they were concerned, their mother. I visualized myself walking proudly through the olive groves, preceded by the dogs, Ulysses, and my two magpies, and trotting at my heels, four tame hedgehogs, all of which I would have taught to do tricks.

The family were arranged on the veranda under the grapevine, each occupied with his or her own affairs. Mother was knitting, counting the stitches audibly at intervals to herself and saying 'damn' periodically when she went wrong. Leslie was squatting on the flag-stones, carefully weighing gunpowder and little piles of silver shot as he filled shiny red cartridge cases. Larry was reading a massive tome and occasionally glancing irritably at Margo, who was clattering away at her machine, making some diaphanous garment, and singing, off key, the only line she knew of her favourite song of the moment.

'She wore her little jacket of blue,' she warbled. 'She wore her little jacket of blue, She wore her little jacket of blue, She wore her little jacket of blue.'

'The only remarkable thing about your singing is your tenacity,' said Larry. 'Anybody else, faced with the fact that they could not carry a tune and couldn't remember the simplest lyric, would have given up, defeated, a long time ago.'

He threw his cigarette butt down on the flag-stones and this produced a roar of rage from Leslie.

'Watch the gunpowder,' he shouted.

'Leslie dear,' said Mother, 'I do wish you wouldn't shout like that, you've made me lose count.'

I produced my hedgehogs proudly and showed them to Mother.

'Aren't they sweet,' she said, peering at them benignly through her spectacles.

'Oh, God! He hasn't got something new has he?' asked Larry. He peered at my pink progeny in their white fur coats with distaste.

'What are they?' he inquired.

I explained that they were baby hedgehogs.

'They can't be,' he said. 'Hedgehogs are all brown.'

My family's ignorance of the world they lived in was always a source of worry to me, and I never lost an opportunity of imparting information. I explained that female hedgehogs could not, without suffering the most refined torture, give birth to babies covered with hard spines, and so they were born with these little rubbery white spikes which could be bent between the fingers as easily as a feather. Later, as they grew, the spines would darken and harden.

'How are you going to feed them, dear? They've got such tiny mouths,' said Mother, 'and they must still be drinking milk, surely?'

I said that I had seen, in a shop in the town, a complete do-it-yourself baby outfit for children, which consisted of several worthless items such as a celluloid doll, nappies, a potty, and so forth, but one article had caught my attention: a miniature feeding bottle with a supply of tiny red teats. This, I said, would be ideal for feeding the baby hedgehogs with, but the potty, doll, and other accoutrements could be given to some deserving peasant child. There was only one slight snag, and that was that I had had some rather heavy expenses to meet recently (such as the wire for the magpie cage) and so I had overspent on my pocket-money.

'Well, dear,' said Mother doubtfully, 'if it isn't too expensive I suppose I could buy it for you.'

I said it was not expensive at all, when you considered that it was more like an investment, for not only would you be getting an invaluable feeding bottle which would come in useful for other animals, but you would be rearing four tame hedgehogs and getting a grateful peasant child into the bargain. What finer way, I asked, of spending money? So the outfit was purchased. A young peasant girl, whom I rather fancied, received with the most satisfactory joy the doll, potty, and other rubbish, and I went about the stern task of rearing my babies.

They lived in a large cardboard box, full of cotton wool, under my bed, and at night, in order to keep them warm, I placed their box on top of a hot-water bottle. I had wanted to have them sleeping in the bed with me, but Mother pointed out that this was not only unhygienic, but that I risked rolling on them in the night and killing them. I found they thrived best on watered cow's milk and I fed them assiduously three times a day and once in the middle of the night. The night feed proved to be a little difficult, for in order to make sure that I woke up I had borrowed a large tin alarm clock from Spiro. This used to go off like a rattle of musketry, and unfortunately woke not only me but the entire family as well. Eventually, so vociferous were the family in their complaints, Mother suggested I give them an extra feed late at night when I went to bed, in lieu of the feed at two o'clock in the morning that woke everybody up. This I did and the hedgehogs thrived and grew. Their eyes opened and their spines turned from snow-white to grey and became firmer. They had now, as I anticipated, convinced themselves that I was their mother, and would come scrambling onto the edge of the box when I opened it, jostling and pushing for first suck at the bottle, uttering tiny wheezy squeaks and grunts. I was immensely proud of them and looked forward happily to the day when they would trot at my heels through the olive groves.

Then Mother and I were invited to spend a week-end with some friends in the extreme south of the island, and I found myself in a quandary. I longed to go, for the sandy, shallow coasts of the south were a fine place for finding heart-urchins which, in fact, looked not unlike baby hedgehogs. Heart-shaped, they were covered with soft spines which formed a tufted tail at one end and a spiky Red-Indian-like head-dress along the back. I had found only one of these, and that had been crushed by the sea and was scarcely recognizable, but I knew from Theodore that they were found in abundance two or three inches under the sand in the south of the island. However, I had my brood of hedgehogs to consider, for I could not very well take them with me, and as Mother was coming too, there was nobody I really trusted to look after them.

'I'll look after them,' offered Margo. 'Dear little things.'

I was doubtful. Did she realize, I asked, the intricacies of looking after the hedgehogs? The fact that, for example, the cotton wool in their box had to be changed three times a day? That they must have only diluted cow's milk? That the milk had to be warmed to blood heat and no more? And most important of all, that they were allowed only half a bottle of milk each at every feed? For I had very soon found out that, if you let them, they would drink themselves comatose at every meal, with the most dire results that entailed the changing of the cotton wool even more frequently.

'Don't be silly,' said Margo. 'Of course I can look after them. I know about babies and things. You just write down on a piece of paper what I am supposed to do, and they'll be quite all right.'

I was torn. I desperately wanted to search for heart-urchins in the golden sands covered by the warm, shallow sea, and yet I doubted Margo's proclivities as a nursemaid. However, Margo grew so indignant at my doubting her that eventually, reluctantly, I gave in. I had prevailed upon Larry, who happened to be in a good mood, to type out a detailed list of do's and don't's for hedgehog-rearers and I gave Margo a practical course in bottle warming and cotton wool changing.

'They seem awfully hungry,' she said as she lifted each writhing, squeaking baby out of the box and pushed the end of the teat into its groping, eager mouth.

I said that they were always like that. One should take no notice of it. They were just naturally greedy.

'Poor little things,' said Margo.

I should have been warned.

I spent an exhilarating week-end. I got myself badly sunburnt, for the fragile spring sun was deceptive, but I came back, triumphant, with eight heart-urchins, four shells new to my collection, and a baby sparrow that had fallen out of its nest. At the villa, after I had suffered the barks and licks and nibbles of greeting that the dogs always bestowed upon you if you had been away for more than two hours, I asked Margo eagerly how my baby hedgehogs were.

'They're doing all right now,' she said. 'But really, Gerry, I do think you ill-treat your pets. You were starving those poor little things to death. They were so hungry. You've no idea.'

With a sinking feeling in the pit of my stomach, I listened to my sister.

'Ravenous, poor little dears. Do you know, they've been taking two bottles each at every feed?'

Horrified, I rushed up to my bedroom and pulled the cardboard box out from under my bed. In it lay my four hedgehogs, bloated beyond belief. Their stomachs were so large that they could only paw feebly with their legs without making any progress. They had degenerated into pink sacks full of milk, frosted with spines. They all died that night and Margo wept copiously over their balloon-like corpses. But her grief did not give me any pleasure, for never would my hedgehogs trot obediently at my heels through the olive groves. As a punishment to my overindulgent sister, I dug four little graves and erected four little crosses in the garden as a permanent reminder, and for four days I did not speak to her.

My grief over the death of my hedgehogs was, however,

short-lived, for at that time Donald and Max reappeared on the island, triumphantly, with a thirty-foot yacht, and Larry introduced into our midst Captain Creech.

Mother and I had spent a very pleasant afternoon in the olive groves, she collecting wildflowers and herbs and I collecting newly emerged butterflies. Tired but happy, we made our way back to the villa for tea. When we came in sight of the villa, she came to a sudden halt.

'Who's that man sitting on the veranda?' she asked.

I had been busy throwing sticks for the dogs, so I was not really concentrating. Now I saw, stretched out on the veranda, a strange figure in crumpled white ducks.

'Who is he? Can you see?' asked Mother, agitated.

At that time she was suffering under the delusion that the manager of our bank in England was liable, at any moment, to pay a flying visit to Corfu for the express purpose of discussing our overdraft, so this unknown figure on the veranda fermented her fears.

I examined the stranger carefully. He was old, almost completely bald, and what little hair he had adhering to the back of his skull was long and as white and wispy as late summer thistle-down. He had an equally unkempt white beard and moustache. I assured Mother that, as far as I could see, he bore no resemblance to the bank manager.

'Oh, dear,' said Mother, annoyed. 'He would arrive now. I've got absolutely nothing for tea. I wonder who he is?'

As we got nearer, the stranger, who had been dozing peacefully, suddenly woke up and spotted us.

'Ahoy!' he shouted, so loudly and suddenly that Mother tripped and almost fell down. 'Ahoy! You must be Mother Durrell, and the boy, of course. Larry told me all about you. Welcome aboard.'

'Oh, dear,' whispered Mother to me, 'it's another one of Larry's.'

As we got closer, I could see that our guest had a most

extraordinary face, pink and as carunculated as a walnut. The cartilage of his nose had obviously received, at one time or another, so many severe blows that it twisted down his face like a snake. His jaw too had suffered the same fate and was now twisted to one side, as though hitched up to his right ear-lobe by an invisible thread.

'Delighted to meet you,' he said, as though he owned the villa, his rheumy eyes beaming. 'My, you're a better-looking wench than your son described.'

Mother stiffened and dropped an anemone from the bunch of flowers she carried.

'I,' she said with frigid dignity, 'am Mrs Durrell, and this is my son Gerald.'

'My name's Creech,' said the old man. 'Captain Patrick Creech.' He paused and spat accurately and copiously over the veranda rail into Mother's favourite bed of zinnias. 'Welcome aboard,' he said again, exuding bonhomie. 'Glad to know you.'

Mother cleared her throat nervously. 'Is my son Lawrence here?' she inquired, adopting her fruity, aristocratic voice, which she did only in moments of extreme stress.

'No, no,' said Captain Creech. 'I left him in town. He told me to come out here for tea. He said he would be aboard shortly.'

'Well,' said Mother, making the best of a bad job, 'do sit down. If you will excuse me a moment I'll just go and make some scones.'

'Scones, eh?' said Captain Creech, eyeing Mother with such lasciviousness that she dropped two more wildflowers. 'I like scones, and I like a woman that's handy in the galley.'

'Gerry,' said Mother frostily, 'you entertain Captain Creech while I get the tea.'

She made a hurried and slightly undignified exit and I was left to cope with Captain Creech.

He had reslumped himself in his chair and was staring at me with watery eyes from under his tattered white eyebrows. His stare was so fixed that I became slightly unnerved. Conscious of my duties as host, however, I offered him a box full of cigarettes. He peered into it, as though it were a well, his jaw moving to and fro like a ventriloquist's dummy.

'Death!' he shouted so suddenly and so vigorously that I almost dropped the cigarettes. He lay back in his chair and fixed me with his blue eyes.

'Cigarettes are death, boyo,' he said. He felt in the pocket of his white ducks and produced a stubby pipe as blackened and as gnarled as a piece of charcoal. He stuck it between his teeth, which made his jaw look even more lop-sided than ever.

'Never forget,' he said, 'a man's best friend is his pipe.'

He laughed uproariously at his own joke and dutifully I laughed too. He got up and spat copiously over the veranda rail and then flopped back into his chair. I searched my mind for a topic of conversation. Nothing seemed to present itself. He would surely not be interested in the fact that today I had heard the first cicada, nor that Agathi's chicken laid six eggs the size of hazel-nuts. Since he was nautically inclined, I wondered whether the news would excite him that Taki, who could not afford a boat, had been night-fishing (holding a light above his head with one hand and a trident in the other) and had successfully driven the trident through his own foot, imagining it was an exotic form of fish? But Captain Creech, peering at me from behind the oily fumes of his pipe, started the conversation himself.

'You're wondering about my face, aren't you boyo?' he said accusingly, and I noticed that the skin on his cheeks became pinker and more shiny, like satin, as he said it. Before I could voice a denial, he went on.

'Wind-jammers. That's what did it. Wind-jammers. Going round the Horn. Tearing wind, straight out of the arsehole of the earth. I fell, see? The canvas flapping and roaring like God's thunder. The rope slipped through my fingers like an oiled snake. Straight onto the deck. They did what they could with it . . . of course, we hadn't a doctor on board.' He paused and felt his jaw meditatively. I sat riveted in my chair, fascinated. 'By the time we got round to Chile the whole thing had set as hard as Portland,' he said, still fondling his jaw. 'I was sixteen years old.'

I wondered whether to commiserate with him or not, but he had fallen into a reverie, his blue eyes blank. Mother came onto the veranda and paused, struck by our immobility.

'Chile,' said the Captain with relish. 'Chile. That was the first time I got gonorrhoea.'

Mother started and then cleared her throat loudly.

'Gerry, come and help me bring out the tea,' she said.

Together we brought out the teapot, milk jug and cups, and the plates with golden-yellow scones and toast Mother had prepared.

'Tucker,' said Captain Creech, filling his mouth with scone. 'Stops your belly rumbling.'

'Are you, um, staying here long?' asked Mother, obviously hoping that he was not.

'Might retire here,' said Captain Creech indistinctly, wiping scone crumbs off his moustache. 'Looks a pretty little place. Might go to anchor here.'

He was forced, because of his jaw, to slurp his tea noisily. I could see Mother getting increasingly alarmed.

'Don't you, um, have a ship?' she asked.

'No bloody fear,' said Captain Creech, seizing another scone. 'Retired, that's me. Got time now to look a little more closely at the wenches.'

He eyed Mother meditatively as he spoke, masticating his scone with great vigour.

'A bed without a woman is like a ship without a hold,' he observed.

Mercifully Mother was saved from having to reply to this remark by the arrival of the car containing the rest of the family and Donald and Max.

'Muzzer, we have come,' announced Max, beaming at her and embracing her tenderly. 'And I see we are in time for tea. Strumpets! How lovely! Donald, we have strumpets for tea!'

'Crumpets,' corrected Donald.

'They're scones,' said Mother.

'I remember a strumpet in Montevideo,' said Captain Creech. 'Marvellous bitch. Kept the whole ship entertained for two days. They don't breed them with stamina like that nowadays.'

'Who is this disgusting old man?' asked Mother as soon as she had an opportunity of backing Larry into a corner away from the tea-party, which was now in full swing.

'He's called Creech,' said Larry.

'I know *that*,' said Mother, 'but what did you bring him here for?'

'He's an interesting old boy,' said Larry, 'and I don't think he's got a lot of money. He's come here to retire on a minute pension, I think.'

'Well, he's not going to retire on *us*,' said Mother firmly. 'Don't invite him again.'

'I thought you'd like him,' said Larry. 'He's travelled all over the world. He's even been to India. He's full of the most fascinating stories.'

'As far as I am concerned he can go on travelling,' said Mother. 'The stories he's been telling up to now aren't what *I* call fascinating.'

Captain Creech, once having discovered our 'anchorage,' as he put it, became a frequent visitor. He would arrive generally, we noticed, just in time for a meal, shouting, 'Ahoy there! Can I come aboard and have a chin-wag?' As he had obviously walked two and a half miles through the olive groves to reach us, it was difficult to deny him this privilege, and so Mother, muttering evilly, would rush into the kitchen and water the soup and bisect the sausages so that Captain Creech could join us. He would regale us with tales of his life at sea and the names of the places that he had visited. Names that I knew only from maps would slide enticingly out of his disjointed mouth. Trincomalee, Darwin and Durban, Buenos Aires, Wellington and Calcutta, the Galapagos, the Seychelles and the Friendly Islands. It seemed that there was no corner of the globe that he had not penetrated. He would intersperse these stories with prolonged and exceptionally vulgar sea-shanties and limericks of such biological complexity that, fortunately, Mother could not understand them.

Then came the never-to-be-forgotten day when Captain Creech arrived, uninvited, for tea as we were entertaining the local English minister and his wife, more out of a sense of duty than of religion. To our amazement, Captain Creech behaved remarkably well. He exchanged views on sea-serpents and the height of tidal waves with the padre and explained the difference between longitude and latitude to the padre's wife. His manners were exemplary and we were quite proud of him, but towards the end of tea the padre's wife had, with extreme cunning, managed to steer the conversation onto her children. This subject was all-absorbing to her. You would have thought that not only was she the only woman in the world to have given birth, but that they had been immaculately conceived as well. Having treated us to a ten-minute monologue on the incredible perspicacity of her offspring, she paused momentarily to drink her tea.

'I'm a bit too old to have babies,' said Captain Creech.

The padre's wife choked.

'But,' he went on with satisfaction, 'I have a lot of fun trying.'

The tea-party was not a success.

Shortly after this, Donald and Max turned up one day at the villa.

'Muzzer,' said Max, 'we are going to carry you away.'

'Yacht party,' said Donald. 'Fabulous idea. Max's idea, of course.'

'Yacht party where?' inquired Mother.

'Round ze island,' said Max, throwing out his long arms in an all-embracing gesture.

'But I thought you didn't know how to sail her,' said Leslie.

'No, no. We don't sail her. Larry sails her,' said Max.

'Larry?' said Leslie incredulously. 'But Larry doesn't know the first thing about boats.'

'Oh, no,' said Donald earnestly. 'Oh, no. He's quite an expert. He's been taking lessons from Captain Creech. The Captain's coming along too, as crew.'

'Well, that settles it then,' said Mother. 'I'm not coming on a yacht with that disgusting old man, apart from the danger involved if Larry's going to sail it.'

They tried their best to persuade her, but Mother was adamant. The most she would concede was that the rest of the family, with Theodore, would drive across the island and rendezvous with them at a certain bay where we could picnic and, if it was warm enough, bathe.

It was a bright, clean morning when we set off and it looked as though it were going to be ideal for both sailing and picnicking; but by the time we reached the other side of the island and had unpacked the picnic things, it began to look as though we were in for a sirocco. Theodore and I made our way down through the trees to the edge of the bay. The sea had turned a cold steel-grey and the wind had stretched and starched a number of white clouds across the blue sky. Suddenly, along the rim of the sea, three water-spouts appeared, loping along the horizon like the huge undulating necks of some prehistoric monsters. Bowing and swaying, graceful as swans they danced along the horizon and disappeared.

'Aha,' said Theodore, who had been watching this phenomenon interestedly, 'I have never seen *three* of them together. Very curious. Did you notice how they moved together, almost as if they were . . . er . . . you know, animals in a herd?'

I said that I wished they had been closer.

'Um,' said Theodore rasping his beard with his thumb. 'I don't think water-spouts are things one wants to get on . . . er . . . um . . . intimate terms with. I remember once I visited a place in Macedonia where one had . . . er . . . you know, come ashore. It had left a trail of damage about two hundred yards wide and a quarter of a mile long, that is to say *inland*. Even quite big olive trees had been, er, you know, damaged and the smaller ones were broken up like matchwood. And of course, at the point where the water-spout finally broke up, the ground was saturated by tons of salt water and so it was . . . you know . . . completely unsuitable for agriculture.'

'I say, did you see those bloody great water-spouts?' asked Leslie, joining us.

'Yes, very curious,' said Theodore.

'Mother's in a panic,' said Leslie. 'She's convinced they're heading straight for Larry.'

'I don't think there's any danger of that,' said Theodore, 'they look too far out to me.'

By the time we had installed ourselves in the olive groves at the edge of the bay, it was obvious that we were in for one of those sudden and exceedingly sharp siroccos which blew up at that time of the year. The wind lashed the olive trees and churned up the bay to white-capped rollers.

'We might as well go home,' said Leslie. 'It isn't going to be much fun picnicking in this.'

'We can't, dear,' said Mother. 'We promised to meet Larry here.'

'If they've got any sense, they'll have put in somewhere else,' said Leslie.

'I can't say I envy them being out in this,' said Theodore, gazing at the waves pounding the rocks.

'Oh, dear, I do hope they will be all right,' said Mother. 'Larry really is foolish.'

We waited an hour, with Mother getting increasingly panicky

with each passing moment. Then Leslie, who had climbed to a neighbouring headland, came back with the news that he could see them.

'I must say I think it's surprising they got this far,' said Leslie. 'The boom's swinging about all over the place and they're tacking practically in circles.'

Presently the yacht headed into the narrow mouth of the bay and we could see Donald and Max dodging about, pulling at ropes and canvas while Larry and Captain Creech clung to the tiller and were obviously shouting instructions. We watched their progress interestedly.

'I hope they remember that reef,' said Leslie.

'What reef?' said Mother in alarm.

'There's a damn great reef just there where that white water is,' said Leslie.

Spiro had been standing gazing out to sea like a brown gargoyle, his face scowling.

'I don't likes it, Master Leslies,' he said in a hoarse whisper. 'They don't looks as though they knows how to sails.'

'Oh, dear,' said Mother. 'Why ever did I agree to this?'

At that moment (owing to the fact, we discovered later, that Donald and Max misinterpreted their instructions and had hauled up a length of canvas instead of taking it down) several things happened simultaneously. The yacht's sails were suddenly caught by an errant gust of wind. They puffed out. The boom came over with a splintering crash that one could hear quite clearly on shore and knocked Max overboard. The yacht turned almost on her side and, propelled by the gust of wind, ran with a remarkably loud scrunching noise straight onto the reef, where she remained upright for a brief moment and then, as if despairing of the yachtsmen on board, she lay down languidly on her side. Immediately all was confusion.

Mother shouting 'Oh, my God! Oh, my God!' had to sit down hurriedly on an olive root. Margo burst into tears, waving her hands and screaming, 'They'll drown! They'll down!' Spiro, Leslie, and I made our way to the edge of the bay. There was not much we could do as there was no boat available to launch as a rescue vessel. But presently we saw the four expert sailors swimming away from the wreck of the yacht, Larry and Donald apparently propelling Captain Creech through the water. Leslie and I and Spiro stripped off our clothes hurriedly and plunged into the sea. The water was icy cold and the waves had considerably more force in them than I gave them credit for.

'Are you all right?' shouted Leslie as the flotilla of shipwrecked mariners came towards us.

'Yes,' said Max. 'Right as rain.'

He had a four-inch gash on his forehead and the blood was running down his face and into his moustache. Larry had one eye bruised and scraped and rapidly swelling. Captain Creech's face, bobbing between Larry's and Donald's, had achieved an extraordinary mauve colour, rather like the bloom of a plum.

'Give us a hand with the Captain,' said Larry. 'Silly old bastard only told me as we went over that he couldn't swim.'

Spiro, Leslie, and I laid hands upon Captain Creech and relieved the panting Donald and Larry of their rescue work. We must have made an arresting tableau as we staggered, gasping, through the shallows and out onto the shore. Leslie and Spiro were supporting Captain Creech, one on each side of him, as his legs seemed in imminent danger of buckling.

'Ahoy there!' he called to Mother. 'Ahoy there, my wench.'

'Look at Max's head!' screamed Margo. 'He'll bleed to death!'

We staggered up into the shelter of the olive groves, and while Mother, Margo, and Theodore did hasty first-aid on Max's head and Larry's eye, we laid Captain Creech under an olive tree, since he seemed incapable of standing up.

'Port at last,' he said with satisfaction. 'Port at last. I'll make sailors of you lads yet.'

It became obvious, now that we had time to concentrate, that Captain Creech was extremely drunk.

'Really, Larry, you do make me cross,' said Mother. 'You might all have been drowned.'

'It wasn't my fault,' said Larry aggrievedly. 'We were doing what the Captain told us to do. Donald and Max went and pulled the wrong ropes.'

'How can you take instructions from him?' said Mother. 'He's drunk.'

'He wasn't drunk when he started,' said Larry. 'He must have had a secret supply somewhere on board. He did seem to pop down to the cabin rather a lot, now I come to think about it.'

'Do not trust him, gentle maiden,' sang Captain Creech in a wavering baritone. 'Though his heart be pure as gold, He'll leave you one fine morning, With a cargo in your hold.'

'Disgusting old brute,' said Mother. 'Really, Larry, I'm extremely cross with you.'

'A drink, me boyos,' called Captain Creech hoarsely, gesturing at the dishevelled Max and Donald. 'You can't sail without a drink.'

At length we had dried ourselves as best we could and wrung the water out of everybody's clothes; then we made our way, shivering, up the hill to the car.

'What are we going to do about the yacht?' said Leslie, since Donald and Max, as the owners, appeared to be unperturbed by her fate.

'We'll stops at the next village,' said Spiro. 'I knows a fishermans there. He'll fix it.'

'I think, you know,' said Theodore, 'if we've got any stimulant with us, it would be an idea to give some to Max. He may possibly suffer from concussion after a blow like that.'

'Yes, we've got some brandy,' said Mother, delving into the car.

She produced a bottle and a cup.

'Darling girl,' said Captain Creech, fixing his wavering eye upon the bottle. 'Just what the doctor ordered.'

'You're not having any of this,' said Mother firmly. 'This is for Max.'

We had to dispose ourselves in the car as best we could, sitting on each other's laps, trying to give as much space as possible to Max, who had now gone a very nasty leaden colour and was shivering violently in spite of the brandy. To Mother's annoyance, she found herself, willy-nilly, having to be wedged in alongside Captain Creech.

'Sit on my lap,' said the Captain hospitably. 'Sit on my lap and we can have a little cuddle to keep warm.'

'Certainly not,' said Mother primly. 'I'd rather sit on Donald's lap.'

As we drove back across the island to town, the Captain regaled us with his version of some sea-shanties. The family argued acrimoniously.

'I do wish you'd stop him singing these songs, Larry,' said Mother.

'How can I stop him? *You're* in the back. *You* stop him.'

'He's *your* friend,' said Mother.

'Ain't it a pity, she's only one titty to feed the baby on. The poor little bugger will never play rugger and grow up big and strong.'

'Might have killed you all, filthy old brute,' said Mother.

'Actually, most of it was Larry's fault,' said Leslie.

'It was not,' said Larry indignantly. 'You weren't there, so you don't know. It's extremely difficult when someone shouts at you to luff your helm, or whatever it is, when there's a howling gale blowing.'

'There was a young lady from Chichester,' observed Captain Creech with relish, 'who made all the saints in their niches stir.'

'The one I'm sorry for is poor Max,' said Margo, looking at him commiseratingly.

'I don't know why he should get the sympathy,' said Larry, whose eye had now almost completely disappeared and was a rich shiny black. 'He's the fool who caused it all. I had the boat under perfect control till he hauled up that sail.'

'Well, I don't call you a sailor,' said Margo. 'If you'd been a sailor you wouldn't have told him to haul it up.'

'That's just the point,' snarled Larry. 'I didn't tell him to haul it up. He hauled it up on his own.'

'It was the good ship Venus,' began the Captain, whose repertoire appeared to be inexhaustible.

'Don't argue about it, dear,' said Mother. 'I've got a severe headache. The sooner we get into town, the better.'

We got to town eventually and dropped Donald and Max at their hotel and the still carolling Captain Creech at his and drove home, wet and cold and acrimonious.

The following morning we were sitting, all feeling slightly wilted, finishing our breakfast on the veranda. Larry's eye had now achieved sunset hues which could only have been captured by the brush of Turner. Spiro drove up honking his horn, the dogs racing in front of the car, snarling and trying to bite the wheels.

'I do wish Spiro wouldn't make quite so much noise when he arrives,' said Larry.

Spiro stumped up onto the veranda and went through his normal morning routine.

'Morning, Mrs Durrells, morning Missy Margo, morning Master Larrys, morning Master Leslies, morning Master Gerrys. How's your eyes, Master Larrys?' he said, screwing up his face into a commiserating scowl.

'At the moment I feel as if I shall probably be going round with a white stick for the rest of my days,' said Larry.

'I've got a letters for yous,' said Spiro to Mother.

Mother put on her glasses and opened it. We waited expectantly. Her face went red.

'The impertinence! The insolence! Disgusting old *brute!* Really, I have never heard anything like it.'

'What on earth's the matter?' asked Larry.

'That revolting old Creech creature,' said Mother, waving the letter at him.

'It's *your* fault, *you* introduced him to the house.'

'What have I done now?' asked Larry, bewildered.

'That filthy old brute has written and proposed to me,' said Mother.

There was a moment's stunned silence while we took in this remarkable information.

'Proposal?' said Larry cautiously. 'An indecent proposal, I presume?'

'No, no,' said Mother. 'He says he wants to marry me. What a fine little woman I am and a lot of sentimental twaddle like that.'

The family, united for once, sat back and laughed until tears came.

'It's no laughing matter,' said Mother, stamping about the veranda. 'You've got to *do* something about it.'

'Oh,' said Larry, mopping his eyes. 'Oh, this is the best thing that's happened for ages. I suppose he thinks since he took his trousers off in front of you yesterday to wring them out, he must make an honest woman of you.'

'Do stop laughing,' said Mother angrily. 'It isn't *funny.*'

'I can see it all,' said Larry unctuously. 'You in white muslin, Leslie and me in toppers to give you away, Margo as your bridesmaid, and Gerry as your page. It will be a very affecting scene. I expect the church will be full of jaded ladies of pleasure, all waiting to forbid the banns.'

Mother glared at him. 'When there's a *real* crisis,' she said angrily, 'you children are of absolutely no use whatsoever.'

'But I think you would look lovely in white,' said Margo, giggling.

'Where have you decided on for your honeymoon?' asked Larry. 'They say Capri is awfully nice at this time of year.'

But Mother was not listening. She turned to Spiro, registering determination from top to toe.

'Spiro, you are to tell the Captain the answer is *no*, and that I never want him to set foot in this house again.'

'Oh, come now, Mother,' protested Larry. 'What we children *want* is a father.'

'And you all,' said Mother, rounding on us in a fury, 'are not to tell anybody about this. I will not have my name linked with that disgusting . . . disgusting *reprobate*.'

And so that was the last we saw of Captain Creech. But what we all referred to as Mother's great romance made an auspicious start to the year.

9

The Talking Head

Summer gaped upon the island like the mouth of a great oven. Even in the shade of the olive groves it was not cool and the incessant, penetrating cries of the cicadas seemed to swell and become more insistent with each hot, blue noon. The water in the ponds and ditches shrank and the mud at the edges became jigsawed, cracked and curled by the sun. The sea lay as breathless and still as a bale of silk, the shallow waters too warm to be refreshing. You had to row the boat out into deep water, you and your reflection the only moving things, and dive over the side to get cool. It was like diving into the sky.

Now was the time for butterflies and moths. In the day, on the hillsides, which seemed sucked free of every drop of moisture by the beating sun, you would get the great languid swallow-tails, flapping elegantly and erratically from bush to bush; fritillaries, glowing almost as hot and angry an orange as a live coal, skittered quickly and efficiently from flower to flower; cabbage whites; clouded yellows; and the lemon-yellow-and-orange brimstones bumbled to and fro on untidy wings. Among the grasses the skippers, like little brown furry aeroplanes, would skim and purr, and on glittering slabs of gypsum the red admirals, as flamboyant as a cluster of Woolworth jewellery, would sit opening and closing their wings as though expiring from the heat. At night the lamps would become a teeming metropolis of moths, and the pink geckos on the ceiling, big-eyed and splay-footed, would gorge until they could hardly move. Oleander hawk-moths, green and silver, would zoom into the room suddenly, from nowhere, and in a frenzy of love, dive at the lamp, hitting it with such force that the glass shattered. Death's-head hawk-moths, mottled ginger and black, with the macabre skull and cross-bones embroidered on the plush fur of their thoraxes, would come tumbling down the chimney to lie fluttering and twitching in the grate, squeaking like mice.

Up on the hillsides where the great beds of heather were burnt crisp and warm by the sun, the tortoises, lizards, and snakes would prowl, and praying mantises would hang among the green leaves of the myrtle, swaying slowly and evilly from side to side. The afternoon was the best time to investigate life on the hills, but it was also the hottest. The sun played a tattoo on your skull, and the baked ground was as hot as a griddle under your sandalled feet. Widdle and Puke were cowards about the sun and would never accompany me in the afternoons, but Roger, that indefatigable student of natural history, would always be with me, panting vigorously, swallowing his drooling saliva in great gulps.

Together we shared many adventures. There was the time when we watched, entranced, two hedgehogs, drunk as lords on the fallen and semi-fermented grapes they had eaten from under the vines, staggering in circles, snapping at each other belligerently, uttering high-pitched screams and hiccups. There was a time we watched a fox cub, red as an autumn leaf, discover his first tortoise among the heather. The tortoise, in the phlegmatic way they have, folded himself up in his shell, tightly closed as a portmanteau. But the fox had seen a movement and, prick-eared, it moved round him cautiously. Then, for it was still only a puppy, it dabbed quickly at the tortoise's shell with its paw and then jumped away, expecting retaliation. Then it lay down and examined the tortoise for several minutes, its head between its paws. Finally it went forward rather gingerly and after several unsuccessful attempts managed to pick the tortoise up with its jaws, and with head held high, trotted off proudly through the heather. It was on these hills that we watched the baby tortoises hatching out of their papery-shelled eggs, each one looking as wizened and as crinkled as though it were a thousand years old at the moment of birth, and it was here that I witnessed for the first time the mating dance of the snakes.

Roger and I were sitting under a large clump of myrtles that offered a small patch of shade and some concealment. We had disturbed a hawk in a cypress tree near by and were waiting patiently for him to return so that we could identify him. Suddenly, some ten feet from where we had crouched, I saw two snakes weaving their way out of a brown web of heather stalks. Roger, who for some obscure reason was frightened of snakes, uttered an uneasy little whine and put his ears back. I shushed him violently and watched to see what the snakes would do. One appeared to be following close on the heels of the other. Was he, I wondered, perhaps in pursuit of it in order to eat it? They slid out of the heather and into some clumps of sun-whitened grass and I lost sight of them. Cursing my luck, I was just about to shift my position in the hopes of seeing them again when they reappeared on a comparatively open piece of ground.

Here the one that was leading paused and the one that had been following it slid up alongside. They lay like this for a moment or so and then the pursuer started to nose tentatively at the other one's head. I decided that the first snake was a female and that her follower was her mate. He continued butting his head at her throat until eventually he had raised her head and neck slightly off the ground. She froze in that position and the male, backing away a few inches, raised his head also and they stayed like that, immobile, staring at each other for some considerable time. Then slowly the male slid forward and twined himself round the female's body and they both rose as high as they could without overbalancing, as entwined together as two convolvulus. Again they remained motionless for a time and then started to sway like two wrestlers pushing against each other in the ring, their tails curling and grasping at the grass roots around them to give themselves better purchase. Suddenly they flopped sideways, the hinder ends of their bodies met and they mated lying there in the sun, as entangled as streamers at a carnival.

At this moment Roger, who had viewed with increasing distress my interest in the snakes, got to his feet and shook himself before I could stop him, indicating that, as far as he was concerned, it would be far better if we moved on. The snakes unfortunately saw his movement. They convulsed in a tangled heap for a moment, their skins gleaming in the sun, and then the female disentangled herself and sped rapidly towards the sanctuary of the heather, dragging the male, still fastened to her, helplessly behind her. Roger looked at me, gave a small sneeze of pleasure, and wagged his stumpy tail. But I was annoyed with him and told him so in no uncertain terms. After all, as I pointed out to him, on the numerous occasions when he was latched to a bitch how would *he* like to be overtaken by some danger and dragged so ignominiously from the field of love?

With the summer came the bands of gypsies to the island to help harvest the crops and to steal what they could while they were there. Sloe-eyed, their dusky skins burnt almost black by the sun, their hair unkempt and their clothing in rags, you would see them moving in family groups along the white, dusty roads, riding on donkeys or on lithe little ponies, shiny as chestnuts. Their encampments were always a squalid enchantment, with a dozen pots bubbling with different ingredients over the fires, the old women squatting in the shadow of their grubby lean-tos with the heads of the younger children in their laps, carefully searching them for lice, while the older children, tattered as dandelion leaves, rolled and screamed and played in the dust. Those of the men who had a side-line would be busy with it, one twisting and tying multi-coloured balloons together, so that they screeched in protest, making strange animal shapes. Another, perhaps, who was the proud possessor of a Karaghiozi shadow show, would be refurbishing the highly coloured cut-out figures and practising some of Karaghiozi's vulgarities and innuendoes to the giggling delight of the handsome young women who stirred the cooking pots or knitted in the shade.

I had always wanted to get on intimate terms with the gypsies, but they were a shy and hostile people, barely tolerating the Greeks. So that my mop of hair, bleached almost white by the sun, and my blue eyes made me automatically suspect, and although they would allow me to visit their camps, they were never forthcoming, in the way that the peasants were in telling me about their private lives and their aspirations. But it was, nevertheless, the gypsies who were indirectly responsible for an uproar in the family. For once I was entirely innocent.

It was the tail-end of an exceptionally hot summer's afternoon. Roger and I had been having an exhausting time pursuing a large and indignant king snake along a length of dry stone wall. No sooner had we dismantled one section of it than the snake would ease himself fluidly along into the next section, and by the time we had rebuilt the section we had pulled down, it would take half an hour or so to locate him again in the jigsaw of rocks. Finally we had to concede defeat and we were now making our way home to tea, thirsty, sweating, and covered with dust. As we rounded an elbow of the road, I glanced into the olive grove that sloped down the hillside into a small valley, and saw what, at first glance, I took to be a man with an exceptionally large dog. A closer look, however, and I realized, incredulously, that it was a man with a bear. I was so astonished that I cried out involuntarily. The bear stood up on its hind legs and turned to look up at me, as did the man. They stared at me for a moment and then the man waved his hand in casual greeting and turned back to the task of spreading his belongings under the olive tree while the bear got down again on its haunches and squatted, watching him with interest. I made my way hurriedly down the hillside, filled with excitement. I had heard that there were dancing bears in Greece, but I had never actually seen one. This was an opportunity too good to be missed. As I drew near, I called a greeting to the man and he turned from his jumble of possessions and replied courteously enough. I saw that he was indeed a gypsy, with the dark, wild eyes and the blue-black hair, but he was infinitely more prosperous-looking than most of them, for his suit was in good repair and he wore shoes, a mark of distinction in those days, even among the landed peasantry of the island.

I asked whether it was safe to approach, for the bear, although wearing a leather muzzle, was untethered.

'Yes, come,' called the man. 'Pavlo won't hurt you, but leave your dog.'

I turned to Roger and I could see that, brave though he was, he did not like the look of the bear and was staying by me only out of a sense of duty. When I told him to go home, he gave me a grateful look and trotted off up the hillside, trying to pretend that he was ignorant of the whole scene. In spite of the man's assurances that Pavlo was harmless, I approached with caution, for although it was only a youngster, the bear, when it reared on its hind legs, was a good foot or so taller than I was and possessed on each broad, furry paw a formidable and very serviceable array of glittering claws. It squatted on its haunches and peered at me out of tiny, twinkling brown eyes, panting gently. It looked like a large pile of animated, unkempt seaweed. To me it was the most desirable animal I had ever set eyes on and I walked round it, viewing its excellence from every possible vantage point.

I plied the man with eager questions. How old was it? Where did he get it? What was he doing with it?

'He dances for his living and for my living,' said the man, obviously amused by my enthusiasm over the bear. 'Here, I'll show you.'

He picked up a stick with a small hook at the end and slid it into a ring set into the leather muzzle the bear wore.

'Come, dance with your papa.'

In one swift movement the bear rose on its hind legs. The

man clicked his fingers and whistled a plaintive tune, starting to shuffle his feet in time to the music and the bear followed suit. Together they shuffled in a slow, stately minuet among the electric blue thistles and the dried asphodel stalks. I could have watched them forever. When the man reached the end of his tune, the bear, as of habit, got down on all fours again and sneezed.

'Bravo!' said the man softly. 'Bravo!'

I clapped enthusiastically. Never, I said earnestly, had I seen such a fine dance, nor such an accomplished performer as Pavlo. Could I, perhaps, pat him?

'You can do what you like with him,' said the man, chuckling, as he unhooked his stick from the bear's muzzle. 'He's a fool, this one. He wouldn't even hurt a bandit who was robbing him of his food.'

To prove it he started scratching the bear's back and the bear, pointing its head up into the sky, uttered throaty, wheezy murmurings of pleasure and sank gradually down onto the ground in ecstasy, until he was spread out looking almost, I thought, like a bearskin rug.

'He likes to be tickled,' said the man. 'Come and tickle him.'

The next half hour was pure delight for me. I tickled the bear while he crooned with delight. I examined his great claws and his ears and his tiny bright eyes and he lay there and suffered me as though he were asleep. Then I leaned against his warm bulk and talked to his owner. A plan was forming in my mind. The bear, I decided, had got to become mine. The dogs and my other animals would soon get used to it and together we could go waltzing over the hillsides. I convinced myself that the family would be overjoyed at my acquisition of such an intelligent pet. But first I had to get the man into a suitable frame of mind for bargaining. With the peasants, bargaining was a loud, protracted, and difficult business. But this man was a gypsy and what they did not know about bargaining would fit conveniently into an acorn cup. The man seemed much less taciturn and reticent than the other gypsies I had come into contact with, and I took this as a good sign. I asked him where he had come from.

'Way beyond, way beyond,' he said, covering his possessions with a shabby tarpaulin and shaking out some threadbare blankets which were obviously going to serve as his bed. 'Landed at Lefkimi last night and we've been walking ever since, Pavlo, the Head, and I. You see, they wouldn't take Pavlo on the buses; they were frightened of him. So we got no sleep last night, but tonight we'll sleep here and then tomorrow we'll reach the town.'

Intrigued, I asked him what he meant by 'he, Pavlo, and the Head' walking up from Lefkimi?

'My Head, of course,' he said. 'My little talking Head.' And he picked up the bear stick and slapped it on a pile of goods under the tarpaulin, grinning at me.

I had unearthed the battered remains of a bar of chocolate from the pocket of my shorts and I was busy feeding this to the bear, who received each fragment with great moans and slobberings of satisfaction. I said to the man that I did not understand what he was talking about. He squatted on his haunches in front of me and lit a cigarette, peering at me out of dark eyes, as enigmatic as a lizard's.

'I have a Head,' he said, jerking his thumb towards his pile of belongings, 'a living Head. It talks and answers questions. It is without doubt the most remarkable thing in the world.'

I was puzzled. Did he mean, I asked, a head without a body?

'Of course without a body. Just a head,' and he cupped his hands in front of him, as though holding a coconut.

'It sits on a little stick and talks to you. Nothing like it has ever been seen in the world.'

But how, I inquired, if the head were a disembodied head, could it live?

'Magic,' said the man solemnly. 'Magic that my great-great-grandfather passed down to me.'

I felt sure that he was pulling my leg, but intriguing though the discussion on talking heads was, I felt we were wandering away from my main objective, which was to acquire the immediate freehold of Pavlo, now sucking in through his muzzle, with wheezy sighs of satisfaction, my very last bit of chocolate. I studied the man carefully as he squatted, dreamy-eyed, his head enveloped in a cloud of smoke. I decided that with him the bold approach was the best. I asked him bluntly whether he would consider selling the bear and for how much.

'Sell Pavlo?' he said. 'Never! He's like my own son.'

Surely, I said, if he went to a good home? Somewhere where he was loved and allowed to dance, surely then he might be tempted to sell? The man looked at me, meditatively puffing on his cigarette.

'Twenty million drachmas?' he inquired, and then laughed at my look of consternation. 'Men who have fields must have donkeys to work them,' he said. 'They don't part with them easily. Pavlo is my donkey. He dances for his living and he dances for mine, and until he is too old to dance, I will not part with him.'

I was bitterly disappointed, but I could see that he was adamant. I rose from my recumbent position on the broad, warm, faintly snoring back of Pavlo and dusted myself down. Well, I said, there was nothing more I could do. I understood his wanting to keep the bear, but if he changed his mind, would he get in touch with me? He nodded gravely. And if he was performing in town, could he possibly let me know where, so that I could attend?

'Of course,' he said, 'but I think people will tell you where I am, for my Head is extraordinary.'

I nodded and shook his hand. Pavlo got to his feet and I patted his head.

When I reached the top of the valley I looked back. They were both standing side by side. The man waved briefly and Pavlo, swaying on his hind legs, had his muzzle in the air, questing after me with his nose. I liked to feel it was a gesture of farewell.

I walked slowly home thinking about the man and his talking head and the wonderful Pavlo. Would it be possible, I wondered, for me to get a bear cub from somewhere and rear it? Perhaps if I advertised in a newspaper in Athens it might bring results.

The family were in the drawing-room having tea and I decided to put my problem to them. As I entered the room, however, a startling change came over what had been a placid scene. Margo uttered a piercing scream, Larry dropped a cup full of tea into his lap and then leaped up and took refuge behind the table, while Leslie picked up a chair and Mother gaped at me with a look of horror on her face. I had never known my presence to provoke quite such a positive reaction on the part of the family.

'Get it out of here,' roared Larry.

'Yes, get the bloody thing out,' said Leslie.

'It'll kill us all!' screamed Margo.

'Get a gun,' said Mother faintly. 'Get a gun and save Gerry.'

I couldn't, for the life of me, think what was the matter with them. They were all staring at something behind me. I turned and looked and there, standing in the doorway, sniffing hopefully towards the tea-table, was Pavlo. I went up to him and caught hold of his muzzle. He nuzzled at me affectionately. I explained to the family that it was only Pavlo.

'I am not *having* it,' said Larry throatily. 'I am not *having* it. Birds and dogs and hedgehogs all over the house and now a bear. What does he think this is, for Christ's sake? A bloody Roman arena?'

'Gerry, dear, do be careful,' said Mother quaveringly. 'It looks rather fierce.'

'It will kill us all,' quavered Margo with conviction.

'I can't get past it to get to my guns,' said Leslie.

'You are *not* going to have it. I forbid it,' said Larry. 'I will *not* have the place turned into a bear pit.'

'Where did you get it, dear?' asked Mother.

'I don't care *where* he got it,' said Larry. 'He's to take it back this instant, quickly, before it rips us to pieces. The boy's got no sense of responsibility. I am not going to be turned into an early Christian martyr at my time of life.'

Pavlo got up on his hind legs and uttered a long wheezing moan which I took to mean that he desired to join us in partaking of whatever delicacies there were on the tea-table. The family interpreted it differently.

'Ow!' screeched Margo, as though she had been bitten. 'It's attacking.'

'Gerry, *do* be careful,' said Mother.

'I'll not be responsible for what I do to that boy,' said Larry.

'If you survive,' said Leslie. 'Do shut up, Margo, you're only making matters worse. You'll provoke the bloody thing.'

'I can scream if I want to,' said Margo indignantly.

So raucous in their fear were the family that they had not given me a chance to explain. Now I attempted to. I said that, first of all, Pavlo was not mine, and secondly, he was as tame as a dog and would not hurt a fly.

'Two statements I refuse to believe,' said Larry. 'You pinched it from some flaming circus. Not only are we to be disembowelled, but arrested for harbouring stolen goods as well.'

'Now, now, dear,' said Mother, 'let Gerry explain.'

'Explain?' said Larry. 'Explain? How do you explain a bloody great bear in the drawing-room?'

I said that the bear belonged to a gypsy who had a talking head.

'What do you mean, a talking head?' asked Margo.

I said that it was a disembodied head that talked.

'The boy's mad,' said Larry with conviction. 'The sooner we have him certified the better.'

The family had now all backed away to the farthest corner of the room in a trembling group. I said, indignantly, that my story was perfectly true and that, to prove it, I'd make Pavlo dance. I seized a piece of cake from the table, hooked my finger into the ring on his muzzle, and uttered the same commands as his master had done. His eyes fixed greedily on the cake, Pavlo reared up and danced with me.

'Oo, look!' said Margo. 'Look! It's dancing!'

'I don't care if it's behaving like a whole *corps de ballet*,' said Larry. 'I want the damn thing out of here.'

I shovelled the cake in through Pavlo's muzzle and he sucked it down greedily.

'He really is rather sweet,' said Mother, adjusting her spectacles and staring at him with interest. 'I remember my brother had a bear in India once. She was a very nice pet.'

'No!' said Larry and Leslie simultaneously. 'He's not having it.'

I said I could not have it anyway, because the man did not want to sell it.

'A jolly good thing, too,' said Larry.

'Why don't you now return it to him, if you have quite finished doing a cabaret act all over the tea-table?'

Getting another slice of cake as a bribe, I hooked my finger once more in the ring on Pavlo's muzzle and led him out of the house. Half-way back to the olive grove, I met the distraught owner.

'There he is! There he is! The wicked one. I couldn't think where he had got to. He never leaves my side normally, that's why I don't keep him tied up. He must have taken a great fancy to you.'

Honesty made me admit that I thought the only reason Pavlo had followed me was because he viewed me in the light of a purveyor of chocolates.

'Phew!' said the man. 'It is a relief to me. I thought he might have gone down to the village and that would have got me into trouble with the police.'

Reluctantly, I handed Pavlo over to his owner and watched them make their way back to their camp under the trees. And then, in some trepidation, I went back to face the family. Although it had not been my fault that Pavlo had followed me, I'm afraid that my activities in the past stood against me, and the family took a lot of convincing that, on this occasion, the guilt was not mine.

The following morning, my head still filled with thoughts of Pavlo, I dutifully went into town – as I did every morning – to the house of my tutor, Richard Kralefsky. Kralefsky was a little gnome of a man with a slightly humped back and great, earnest, amber eyes, who suffered from real tortures in his unsuccessful attempts to educate me. He had two most endearing qualities: one was a deep love for natural history (the whole attic of his house was devoted to an enormous variety of canaries and other birds); the other was the fact that, for at least a part of the time, he lived in a dream-world where he was always the hero. These adventures he would relate to me. He was inevitably accompanied in them by a heroine who was never named, but known simply as 'a lady'.

The first half of the morning was devoted to mathematics, and with my head full of thoughts of Pavlo, I proved to be even duller than usual, to the consternation of Kralefsky, who had hitherto been under the impression that he had plumbed the depths of my ignorance.

'My dear boy, you simply aren't concentrating this morning,' he said earnestly. 'You don't seem able to grasp the simplest fact. Perhaps you are a trifle overtired? We'll have a short rest from it, shall we?'

Kralefsky enjoyed these short rests as much as I did. He would potter about in the kitchen and bring back two cups of coffee and some biscuits, and we would sit companionably while he told me highly coloured stories of his imaginary adventures. But this particular morning he did not get a chance. As soon as we were sitting comfortably, sipping our coffee, I told him all about Pavlo and the man with the talking head and the bear.

'Quite extraordinary!' he said. 'Not the sort of thing one expects to find in an olive grove. It must have surprised you, I'll be bound.'

Then his eyes glazed and he fell into a reverie, staring at the ceiling, tipping his cup of coffee so that it slopped into the saucer. It was obvious that my interest in the bear had set off a train of thought in his mind. It had been several days since I had had an instalment of his memoirs, and so I waited eagerly to see what the result would be.

'When I was a *young* man,' began Kralefsky, glancing at me earnestly to see whether I was listening, 'when I was a young man, I'm afraid I was a bit of a harum-scarum. Always getting into trouble, you know.'

He chuckled reminiscently and brushed a few biscuit crumbs from his waistcoat. With his delicately manicured hands and his large, gentle eyes it was difficult to imagine him as a harum-scarum, but I tried dutifully.

'I thought at one time I would even join a *circus*,' he said, with the air of one confessing to infanticide. 'I remember a large circus came to the village where we were living and I attended every performance. Every single performance. I got to know the circus folk quite well, and they even taught me some of their tricks. They said I was *excellent* on the trapeze.' He glanced at me, shyly, to see how I would take this. I nodded seriously, as though there were nothing ludicrous in the thought of Kralefsky, in a pair of spangled tights, on a trapeze.

'Have another biscuit?' he inquired. 'Yes? That's the ticket! I think I'll have one, too.'

Munching my biscuit I waited patiently for him to resume.

'Well,' he continued, 'the week simply flew past and the evening came for the final performance. I wouldn't have missed it for the world. I was accompanied by a lady, a young friend of mine, who was desirous of seeing the performance. How she laughed at the clowns! *And* admired the horses. She little knew of the horror that was soon to strike.'

He took out his delicately scented handkerchief and patted his moist brow with it. He always tended to get a trifle overexcited as he reached the climax of a story.

'The final act,' he said, 'was the lion-tamer.' He paused so that the full portent of this statement could sink in. 'Five beasts he had. Huge Nubian lions with black manes, fresh from the jungle, so he told me. The lady and I were sitting in the front row where we could obtain the best possible view of the ring. You know the sort of cage affair that they put up in the ring for the lion act? Well, in the middle of the act, one of the sections, which had not been securely bolted, fell inwards. To our horror, we saw it fall on the lion-tamer, knocking him unconscious instantly.' He paused, took a nervous sip of coffee and then wiped his brow once more.

'What was to be done?' he inquired rhetorically. 'There were five huge, snarling lions and I had a lady by my side. My thoughts worked fast. If the lady was to be saved, there was only one thing I could think of. Seizing my walking-stick, I leaped into the ring and marched into the cage.'

I made just audible sounds, indicative of admiration.

'During the week when I had been visiting the circus, I had studied the lion-tamer's method with great care, and now I thanked my lucky stars for it. The snarling beasts on their pedestals towered over me, but I looked them straight in the eye. The human eye, you know, has great power over the animal world. Slowly, fixing them with a piercing gaze and pointing my walking-stick at them, I got them under control and drove them inch by inch out of the ring and back into their cage. A dreadful tragedy had been averted.'

I said that the lady must have been grateful to him.

'She was indeed. She was indeed,' said Kralefsky, pleased. 'She even went so far as to say that I gave a better performance than the lion-tamer himself.'

Had he, I wondered, during his circus days, ever had anything to do with dancing bears?

'All sorts of animals,' said Kralefsky lavishly. 'Elephants, seals, performing dogs, bears. They were all there.'

In that case, I said tentatively, would he not like to come and see the dancing bear. It was only just down the road, and although it was not exactly a circus, I felt it might interest him.

'By Jove, that's an idea,' said Kralefsky. He pulled his watch out of his waistcoat pocket and consulted it. 'Ten minutes, eh? It'll help blow the cobwebs away.'

He got his hat and stick and together we made our way eagerly through the narrow, crowded streets of the town, redolent with the smell of fruits and vegetables, drains, and freshly baked bread. By dint of questioning several small boys, we discovered where Pavlo's owner was holding his show. It was a large, dim barn at the back of a shop in the centre of town. On the way there I had borrowed some money from Kralefsky and purchased a bar of sticky nougat, for I felt I could not go to see Pavlo without taking him a present.

'Ah, Pavlo's friend! Welcome,' said the gypsy as we appeared in the doorway of the barn.

To my delight, Pavlo recognized me and came shuffling forward, uttering little grunts, and then reared up on his hind legs in front of me. Kralefsky backed away, rather hurriedly, I thought, for one of his circus training, and took a firmer grip on his stick.

'Do be careful, my boy,' he said.

I fed the nougat to Pavlo and when finally he had squelched the last sticky lump off his back teeth and swallowed it, he gave a contented sigh and lay down with his head between his paws.

'Do you want to see the Head?' asked the gypsy. He gestured towards the back of the barn where there was a plain deal table on which was a square box, apparently made out of cloth.

'Wait,' he said, 'and I'll light the candles.'

He had a dozen or so large candles soldered to the top of a box in their own wax, and these he now lit so they flickered and quivered and made the shadows dance. Then he went forward to the table and rapped on it with his bear stick.

'Head, are you ready?' he asked.

I waited with a delicate prickle of apprehension in my spine. Then from the interior of the cloth box a clear treble voice said, 'Yes, I'm ready.'

The man lifted the cloth at one side of the box and I saw that the box was formed of slender lathes on which thin cloth had been loosely tacked. The box was about three feet square. In the centre of it was a small pedestal with a flattened top and on it, looking macabre in the flickering light of the candles, was the head of a seven-year-old boy.

'By Jove!' said Kralefsky in admiration. 'That is clever!'

What astonished me was that the head was *alive*. It was obviously the head of a young gypsy lad, made up rather crudely with black grease paint to look like a Negro. It stared at us and blinked its eyes.

'Are you ready to answer questions now?' asked the gypsy, looking, with obvious satisfaction, at the entranced Kralefsky. The Head licked its lips and then said, 'Yes, I am ready.'

'How old are you?' asked the gypsy.

'Over a thousand years old,' said the Head.

'Where do you come from?'

'I come from Africa and my name is Ngo.'

The gypsy droned on with his questions and the Head answered them, but I was not interested in that. What I wanted to know was *how* the trick was done. When he first told me about the Head, I had expected something carved out of wood or plaster which, by ventriloquism, could be made to speak, but this was a living head perched on a little wooden pedestal, the circumference of a candle. I had no doubt that the Head was alive for its eyes wandered to and fro as it answered the questions automatically, and once, when Pavlo got up and shook himself, a look of apprehension came over its face.

'There,' said the gypsy proudly when he had finished his questioning. 'I told you, didn't I? It's the most remarkable thing in the world.'

I asked him whether I could examine the whole thing more closely. I had suddenly remembered that Theodore had told me of a similar illusion which was created with the aid of mirrors. I did not see where it was possible to conceal the body that obviously belonged to the Head, but I felt that the table and the box needed investigation.

'Certainly,' said the gypsy, somewhat to my surprise. 'Here, take my stick. But all I ask is that you don't touch the Head itself.'

Carefully, with the aid of the stick, I poked all round the pedestal to see if there were any concealed mirrors or wires, and the Head watched me with a slightly amused expression in its black eyes. The sides of the box were definitely only of cloth and the floor of the box was, in fact, the top of the table on which it stood. I walked round the back of it and I could see nothing. I even crawled under the table, but there was nothing there and certainly no room to conceal a body. I was completely mystified.

'Ah,' said the gypsy in triumph. 'You didn't expect that, did you? You thought I had a boy concealed in there, didn't you?'

I admitted the charge humbly and begged him to tell me how it was done.

'Oh, no. I can't tell you,' he said. 'It's magic. If I told you, the head would disappear in a puff of smoke.'

I examined both the box and the table for a second time, but, even bringing a candle closer to aid my investigations, I still could not see how it was possible.

'Come,' said the gypsy. 'Enough of the Head. Come and dance with Pavlo.'

He hooked the stick into the bear's muzzle and Pavlo rose on his hind legs. The gypsy handed the stick to me and then picked up a small wooden flute and started to play, and Pavlo and I did a solemn dance together.

'Excellent, by Jove! Excellent!' said Kralefsky, clapping his hands with enthusiasm. I suggested that he might like to dance with Pavlo too, since he had such vast circus experience.

'Well, now,' said Kralefsky. 'I wonder whether it would be altogether wise? The animal, you see, is not familiar with me.'

'Oh, he'll be all right,' said the gypsy. 'He's tame with anyone.'

'Well,' said Kralefsky reluctantly, 'if you're sure. If you insist.'

He took the bear stick gingerly from me and stood facing Pavlo, looking extremely apprehensive.

'And now,' said the gypsy, 'you will dance.'

And he started to play a lilting little tune on his pipe.

I stood enchanted by the sight. The yellow, flickering light of the candles showed the shadows of Kralefsky's little humpbacked figure and the shaggy form of the bear on the wall as they pirouetted round and round, and squatting on its pedestal in the box, the Head watched them, grinning and chuckling to itself.

10

The Angry Barrels

At the tail-end of the summer came the grape harvest. Throughout the year you had been aware of the vineyards as part of the
scenery, but it was only when the grape harvest came that you
remembered the sequence of events that led up to it: the vineyards in winter, when the vines looked dead, like so many pieces
of driftwood stuck in lines in the soil; and then the day in spring
when you first noticed a green sheen on each vine as the delicate,
frilly little leaves uncurled. And then the leaves grew larger and
hung on the vines, like green hands warming themselves in the
heat of the sun. After that the grapes started to appear, tiny
nodules on a branched stem, which gradually grew and plumped
themselves in the sunlight until they looked like the jade eggs of
some strange sea-monster. Then was the time for the washing of
the vines. The lime and copper sulphate in big barrels would be
dragged to the vineyards in little wooden carts pulled by the
ever-patient donkeys. The sprayers would appear in their uniforms that made them look like visitors from another planet:
goggles and masks, a great canister strapped on their backs from
which led a rubber pipe, as mobile as an elephant's trunk, through
which the liquid would run. This mixture was of a blue that put
the sky and the sea to shame. It was the distilled blueness of
everything blue in the world. Tanks would be filled and the
sprayers would move through the frilly groves of vine, covering
each leaf, wrapping each bunch of green grapes in a delicate web
of Madonna blue. Under this protective blue mantle, the grapes
swelled and ripened until at last, in the hot dog-days of summer,
they were ready to be plucked and eased of their juice.

The grape harvest was so important that it naturally became

a time of visiting, a time of picnics and of celebrations, a time when you brought out last year's wine and mused over it.

We had been invited to attend a wine harvest by a Mr Stavrodakis, a tiny, kindly, wizened little man with a face like that of a half-starved tortoise, who owned a villa and some big vineyards towards the north of the island. He was a man who lived for his wine, who thought that was the most important thing in the world; and so his invitation was delivered with all the solemnity befitting such an occasion and was received with equal solemnity by the family. In his note of invitation, written in bold copper plate, embellished with little frills and flourishes so that it looked like a wrought-iron tracery, he had said, 'Do please feel free to bring those of your friends that you think might enjoy this.'

'Wonderful,' said Larry. 'He's supposed to have the best cellar in Corfu.'

'Well, I suppose we can go if you want to,' said Mother doubtfully.

'Of course I want to,' said Larry. 'Think of all that wine. I tell you what, we'll hire a *benzina* and make up a party.'

'Oh, yes,' said Margo eagerly. 'He's got that marvellous beach on his estate. We must get in some more swimming before the summer ends.'

'We can invite Sven,' said Larry. 'He should be back by then. And we'll ask Donald and Max to come along.'

'And Theodore,' said Leslie.

'Larry dear,' said Mother, 'the man's only invited us to watch his grapes being pressed or whatever it is they do; you can't take a whole assortment of people along with you.'

'He says in his letter to bring any of our friends we want to,' said Larry.

'Yes, but you can't take a whole circus,' said Mother. 'How's the poor man going to feed us all?'

'Well, that's easily solved,' said Larry. 'Write and tell him that we'll bring our own food.'

'I suppose that means I'll have to cook it,' said Mother.

'Nonsense,' said Larry vaguely. 'We'll just take a few chops or something and grill them over an open fire.'

'I know what *that* means,' said Mother.

'Well, surely you can organize it somehow,' said Larry. 'After all, it seems to me a perfectly simple thing to do.'

'Well,' said Mother reluctantly, 'I'll have a word with Spiro in the morning and see what can be done.'

The result was that Mother penned a careful note to Mr Stavrodakis saying that we would be delighted to accept his invitation and bring a few friends. We would bring our own food and picnic on the beach, if we might. Mr Stavrodakis sent back another piece of copper-plate topiary expressing himself overwhelmed at our kindness in accepting his invitation and saying that he looked forward to seeing us. He added, 'Do please come undressed as we are in the family way.' The phrase puzzled us all considerably – since he was a bachelor of long standing – until we realized he had translated it literally from the French.

The party finally consisted of Donald and Max, Theodore, Kralefsky, Sven, who had turned up in the nick of time from Athens, Spiro, and the family. We assembled at six thirty in the morning at the sunken steps behind the king's palace in the town, where a dumpy, freshly painted *benzina* waited, bobbing a greeting to us on the tiny ripples. Getting on board took us quite some time. There were the numerous hampers of food and wine, the cooking utensils, and Mother's enormous umbrella which she refused to travel without during the summer months. Then Kralefsky, bowing and beaming, had to go through the performance of handing Mother and Margo on board.

'Gently now. Don't stumble. That's the ticket!' he said as he escorted them both onto the boat with all the courtesy of a doge handing his latest mistress into a gondola.

'Fortunately,' said Theodore, peering up at the blue sky penetratingly from under the brim of his Homburg, 'fortunately it looks as though it's going to be er . . . um . . . you know, a fine day. I'm glad of that, for, as you know, the slightest motion upsets me.'

Sven missed his footing as he was getting on board and almost dropped his precious accordion into the sea, but it was retrieved from a watery death by Max's long arm. Eventually we were all on board. The *benzina* was pushed out, the engine was started, and we were off. In the pale, pearly, early morning haze, the town looked like a child's town, built of toppling bricks. The façades of tall, elderly Venetian houses of the town, crumbling gently, coloured in pale shades of cream and brown and white and cyclamen pink, were blurred by the haze so they looked like a smudged pastel drawing.

'A life on the ocean wave!' said Kralefsky, inhaling the warm, still air dramatically. 'That's the ticket!'

'Although the sea *looks* so calm,' observed Theodore, 'there is, I think, a slight – almost imperceptible – motion.'

'What rubbish, Theodore,' said Larry. 'You could lay a spirit level on this sea and you wouldn't get a wink out of the bubble.'

'Is Muzzer comfortable?' inquired Max lovingly of Mother.

'Oh, yes, dear, thank you, quite comfortable,' she said, 'but I'm a little bit worried. I'm not sure whether Spiro remembered the garlic.'

'Don't you worries Mrs Durrells,' said Spiro, who had overheard the remark. 'I gots all the things that you tells me to get.'

Sven, having examined his accordion with the utmost care to make sure that it had come to no harm, now lashed it round himself and ran an experimental series of fingers up its keyboard.

'A rousing sea-shanty,' said Donald. 'That's what we need. Yo, ho, ho, and a bottle of rum.'

I left them and made my way up into the bow of the *benzina* where I lay, staring down over the prow as it sheared its way through the glassy blue sea. Occasionally little flocks of flying fish would break the surface ahead of us, glittering blue and moon silver in the sun, as they burst from the water and skimmed along the surface, like insect-gleaning summer swallows across a blue meadow.

At eight o'clock we reached our destination, a half-mile-long beach that lay under the flanks of Pandokrator. Here the olive grove came almost to the sea, separated from it only by a wide strip of shingle. As we approached the shore, the engine was switched off and we drifted in gently under our own momentum. Now that there was no engine noise we could hear the cries of the cicadas welcoming us to land. The *benzina*, with an enormous sigh, pressed its bow into the pebbles of the shallows. The lithe, brown boy, whose boat it was, came forward from the engine and leaped from the bow with the anchor, which he lodged firmly in the shingle. Then he piled a collection of boxes alongside the bow of the *benzina* in a sort of tottering staircase down which Mother and Margo were escorted by Kralefsky, who bowed elegantly as each reached the shingle, but somewhat marred the effect by inadvertently stepping backwards into six inches of sea-water and irretrievably ruining the crease of his elegant trousering. Eventually we and all our goods and chattels were ashore, and leaving our possessions under the olive trees, strewn haphazardly like something from a wrecked ship that had been disgorged by the sea, we made our way up the hill to Stavrodakis' villa.

The villa was large and square, faded red with green shutters and built up high so that the lower floor formed a spacious cellar. Streams of peasant girls were walking up the drive carrying baskets of grapes on their heads, moving with the lithe graceful-ness of cats. Stavrodakis came scuttling among them to greet us.

'So kind, so kind! Really so kind!' he kept repeating as each introduction was made.

He seated us all on his veranda under a great carnival-red wig of bougainvillæa and opened several bottles of his best wine. It was heavy and sharp and glowed a sullen red as though he were pouring garnets into our glasses. When we were fortified and slightly light-headed with this brew, he led us, skittering ahead like an amiable black beetle, down to his cellars.

The cellars were so big that their dimmest recesses had to be lit by oil lamps, little flickering wicks floating in pots of amber oil. The cellar was divided into two parts, and he led us first to where the treading was taking place. Looming over everything else in the dim light were three gigantic barrels. One of them was being filled with grapes by a constant procession of peasant women. The other two were occupied by the treaders. In the corner, seated on an upturned keg, was a grey, fragile-looking old man who, with great solemnity, was playing on a fiddle.

'That's Taki and that's Yani,' said Stavrodakis, pointing to the two wine-treaders.

Taki's head could only just be seen above the rim of the barrel, whereas Yani's head and shoulders were still visible.

'Taki's been treading since last night,' said Stavrodakis, glancing nervously at Mother and Margo, 'so I'm afraid he's a little bit inebriated.'

Indeed, from where we stood we could smell the heady fumes of the grape pulp and they were intoxicating enough, so their force must have been trebled when concentrated in the warm depths of the barrel. From the base of the barrel the crude young wine dribbled out into a trough, where it lay smouldering with patches of froth on top as pink as almond blossom. From here it was syphoned off into barrels.

'This is, of course, the end of the harvest,' Stavrodakis was explaining. 'These are the last of the red grapes. They come from a little vineyard high up and produce, I venture to think, one of the better wines of Corfu.'

Taki momentarily stopped his jig on the grapes, hooked arms over the side of the barrel and hung there like a drunken swallow on its nest, his arms and hands stained with wine and covered with a crust of grape skins and seeds.

'It's time I came out,' he said thickly, 'or I shall be as drunk as a lord.'

'Yes, yes, in a minute, my Taki,' said Stavrodakis, looking round him nervously. 'In a minute Costos will be here to relieve you.'

'One must pee,' Taki explained aggrievedly. 'A man can't work unless he pees.'

The old man put down his fiddle, and presumably by way of compensation, handed Taki a lump of coarse bread, which he ate wolfishly.

Theodore was giving Sven an erudite lecture on wines, pointing at both treaders and the barrels with his walking-stick as though they had been objects in a museum.

'Who was it?' said Max to Larry, 'that drownded in a butt of malmsey?'

'One of Shakespeare's more sensible heroes,' said Larry.

'I remember once,' Kralefsky said to Donald, 'taking a lady round one of the biggest cellars in France. Half-way round the cellar I began to feel uneasy. I had a premonition of danger and so I escorted the lady out and at that moment fourteen of the barrels burst with a roar like cannons . . .'

'Here, as you have seen, we do the treading,' said Stavrodakis. 'Now if you will just follow me this way, I'll show you where the wine is stored.'

He led us through an archway into the other gloomy section of the cellar. Here rank after rank of barrels lay on their sides and the noise was incredible. At first I thought it must have some outside source, until I realized that it emanated from the barrels. As the wine fermented in their brown bellies, the barrels gurgled and squeaked and growled at each other like an angry mob. The sound was fascinating, but slightly horrific. It was as though in each barrel there were incarcerated some frightful demon mouthing incomprehensible abuse.

'The peasants say,' said Theodore with macabre relish, tapping one of the barrels lightly with his stick, 'the peasants say that it sounds like a drowning man.'

'Malmsey!' said Max excitedly. 'Barrels and barrels of malmsey! Larry, we'll get drownded together!'

'Drowned,' said Donald.

'Most interesting,' Mother was saying insincerely to Stavrodakis, 'but if you will excuse us, I think Margo and I had better go back to the beach and see about lunch.'

'I wonder what force it generates in there,' said Leslie, glancing round moodily. 'I mean, if it generated sufficient force to push one of those bungs out, I wonder what power it would have?'

'Quite considerable,' said Theodore. 'I remember once seeing a man who was quite badly injured by the bung from a barrel.' As if to demonstrate this, he tapped a barrel sharply with his stick and we all jumped.

'Yes, well, if you will excuse us,' said Mother nervously, 'I think Margo and I had better be going.'

'But the rest of you, the rest of you will come up to the house and have some wine?' pleaded Stavrodakis.

'Of course we will,' said Larry, as though he were doing him a favour.

'Malmsey!' said Max, rolling his eyes in ecstasy. 'We will have malmsey!'

So while Margo and Mother went back to the beach to help Spiro in the preparations for lunch, Stavrodakis fussily hurried us back onto the veranda and plied us with wine, so that when it was time for us to go back to the beach, we were mellow, warm, and flushed.

' "I dreamt," ' carolled Max as we walked through the olives, taking a delighted Stavrodakis with us to share our lunch, ' "I dreamt that I dwelt in marble halls" with vessels and turfs by my side.'

'He just does it to annoy me,' Donald confided to Theodore. 'He knows that song perfectly well.'

Under the trees at the edge of the sea, three charcoal fires had been lighted and they glowed, shuddered, and smoked gently, and over them popped and sizzled a variety of foods. Margo had laid a great cloth in the shade and was putting cutlery and glasses on it, singing untunefully to herself while Mother and Spiro crouched like witches over the fires, larding the brown sizzling carcass of a kid with oil and squeezed garlic and anointing the great body of a fish – its skin bubbled and crisped enticingly by the heat – with lemon juice.

Lunch we ate in a leisurely fashion, sprawled round the bright cloth, the glasses glowing with wine. The mouthfuls of kid were rich and succulent, woven with herbs, and the sections of fish melted like snow-flakes in your mouth. The conversation drifted and sprang up and then coiled languidly again, like the smoke from the fires.

'You have to be in love with a piece of stone,' said Sven solemnly. 'You see a dozen pieces of stone. You say, "Pah! That's not for me," and then you see a piece, delicate and elegant, and you fall in love with it. It's like women. But then comes the marriage and that can be terrible. You fight with it and you find that the stone is hard. You are in despair, then suddenly, like wax, it melts under your hands and you create a shape.'

'I remember,' said Theodore, 'being asked by Berlincourt – you know, that French painter who lives over at Paleocastritsa – being asked by him to go and look at his work. He said, er, you know, quite distinctly, "come and see my *paintings*." So I went one afternoon and he was most hospitable. He gave me, um, you know, little cakes and tea and then I said I would like to see his paintings, and he pointed to one large canvas which was on the, um, what is it, that thing that painters use? Ah, yes, *easel*. It was quite a pretty painting, really. It showed the bay at Paleocastritsa with the monastery quite clearly and when I had admired it, I looked round to see where the rest of his work was, but there didn't appear to be any. So I, um, asked him where the *rest* of his paintings were and he pointed to the easel and said, um, "under there". It appeared that he couldn't afford canvases and so he painted one picture on top of another.'

'Great artists have to suffer,' said Sven lugubriously.

'When winter comes, I'll take you over to the Butrinto marshes,' said Leslie with enthusiasm. 'Masses of duck there and damned great wild boars up in the hills.'

'Ducks I like, but vild boars I think are a bit big for me,' said Max, with the conviction of one who knows his limitations.

'I don't think Max is up to it,' said Donald. 'He'd probably cut and run at a crucial moment. A foreigner, you know.'

'And then,' said Mother to Kralefsky, 'you put your bay leaf and sorrel in just *before* it starts to simmer.'

'So I says to him, Misses Margos, I says, I don't care if he is the French Ambassador, he's a bastard.'

'Then, at the edge of the marsh – it's a bit difficult walking, of course, because the ground's so mushy – you can get woodcock and snipe.'

'I remember once I visited a village in Macedonia where they did very curious, um, you know, wood sculptures.'

'I knew a lady once who used to make it without the bay leaf, but with a pinch of mint.'

It was the hottest hour of the day when even the cicadas seem to slow down and falter occasionally in their song. The black ants moved busily across the cloth, gathering the crumbs of our food. A horse-fly, its eyes gleaming like malevolent emeralds, settled for a brief moment on Theodore's beard and then zoomed away.

Slowly, full of food and wine, I got up and made my way down to the sea. 'And sometimes,' I could hear Stavrodakis say to Margo, 'sometimes the barrels really *shout*. They make a noise as if they were fighting. It keeps me awake.'

'Oh, don't,' said Margo, shuddering. 'It makes me creepy just to think of it.'

The sea was still and warm, looking as though it had been varnished, with just a tiny ripple patting languidly at the shore. The shingle scrunched and shifted, hot under my bare feet. The rocks and pebbles that made up this beach were incredible in shape and colour, moulded by the waves and the gentle rubbing and polishing one against the other. They had been sculptured into a million shapes. Arrow-heads, sickles, cockerels, horses, dragons, and starfish. Their colouring was as bizarre as their shapes, for they had been patterned by the earth's juices millions of years before and now their decorations had been buffed and polished by the sea. White with gold or red filigree, blood-red with white spots, green, blue, and pale fawn, hen's-egg brown with a deep rusty-red pattern like a fern sprawled across them, pink as a peony with white Egyptian hieroglyphics forming a mysterious, undecipherable message across them. It was like a vast treasure trove of jewels spread along the rim of the sea.

I waded into the warm shallows and then dived and swam out to cooler water. Here, if you held your breath and let yourself sink to the bottom, the soft velvety blanket of the sea momentarily stunned and crippled your ears. Then, after a moment, they became attuned to the underwater symphony. The distant throb of a boat engine, soft as a heart-beat, the gentle whisper of the sand as the sea's movement shuffled and rearranged it and, above all, the musical clink of the pebbles on the shore's edge. To hear the sea at work on its great store of pebbles, rubbing and polishing them lovingly, I swam from the deep waters into the shallows. I anchored myself with a handful of multi-coloured stones, then, ducking my head below the surface, listened to the beach singing under the gentle touch of the small waves. If walnuts could sing, I reflected, they would sound like this. Scrunch, tinkle, squeak, mumble, cough (silence while the wave retreats) and then the whole thing in different keys repeated with the next wave. The sea played on the beach as though it were an instrument. I lay and dozed for a time in the warm shallows and then, feeling heavy with sleep, I made my way back into the olive groves.

Everyone lay about disjointedly, sleeping round the ruins of our meal. It looked like the aftermath of some terrible battle. I curled up like a dormouse in the protective roots of a great olive and drifted off to sleep myself.

I woke to the gentle clinking of tea-cups as Margo and Mother laid the cloth for tea. Spiro brooded with immense concentration over a fire on which he had set a kettle. As I watched drowsily, the kettle lifted its lid and waved pertly at him, hissing steam. He seized it in one massive hand and poured the contents into a teapot, then, turning, he scowled at our recumbent bodies.

'Teas,' he roared thunderously. 'Teas is readys.'

Everybody started and woke.

'Dear God! Must you yell like that, Spiro?' asked Larry plaintively, his voice thickened by sleep.

'Tea,' said Kralefsky, waking up and glancing round him, looking like a dishevelled moth. 'Tea, by Jove. Excellent.'

'God, my head aches,' said Leslie. 'It must be that wine. It's got a kick like a mule.'

'Yes, I'm feeling a bit fragile myself,' said Larry, yawning and stretching.

'I feel as though I've been drowned,' said Max with conviction. 'Drowned in malmsey and then brought back by artificial inspiration.'

'Must you always massacre the English tongue?' said Donald irritably. 'God knows it's bad enough having thousands of Englishmen doing it, without you foreigners starting.'

'I remember reading somewhere' – began Theodore, who had awakened instantly, like a cat, and who, having slept like one, looked as immaculate as though he had not been to sleep at all – 'I remember reading once that there's a tribe up in the mountains of Ceylon that speaks a language that nobody can understand.

I mean to say, not even expert linguists have been able to understand it.'

'It sounds just like Max's English,' said Donald.

Under the influence of tea, buttered toast, salt biscuits, water-cress sandwiches, and an enormous fruit-cake as damp and as fragile and as rich-smelling as loam, we started to wake up. Presently we went down to the sea and swam in the warm waters until the sun sank and pushed the mountain's shadow over the beach suddenly, making it look cold and drained of colour. Then we went up to Stavrodakis' villa and sat under the bougainvillæa watching the sunset colours blur and mingle over the sea. We left Stavrodakis, who insisted on giving us a dozen great jars of his best wine to commemorate our visit, and made our way back to the *benzina*.

As we headed out to sea we left the shadow of the mountain and came into the warm glow of the sun again, which was sinking, smudged blood-red behind the bulk of Pandokrator, casting a shimmering reflection across the water like a flaming cypress tree. A few tiny clouds turned pink and vine-yellow, then the sun dipped behind the mountain and the sky turned from blue to pale green and the smooth surface of the sea became for a brief moment all the magical colours of a fire-opal. The engine throbbed as we edged our way back towards the town, unroll-ing a white bale of lace wake behind us. Sven played the open-ing of 'The Almond Tree' very softly and everyone started to sing.

> 'She shook the flowering almond tree one sunny day
> With her soft little hands,
> The snowy blossoms on her breast and shoulders lay
> And in her hair's dark strands
> The snowy blossoms on her breast and shoulders lay
> And in her hair's dark strands . . .'

Spiro's voice, deep, rich, and smooth as black velvet, harmonizing with Theodore's pleasant baritone and Larry's tenor. Two flying fish skimmed up from the blue depths beneath our bow, skittered along the water, and were lost in the twilight sea.

Now it was getting dark enough to see the tiny green coruscations of phosphorus as our bow slid through the water. The dark wine glugged pleasantly from the earthenware pitchers into the glasses, the red wine that, last year, had lain snarling to itself in the brown barrels. A tiny wind, warm and soft as a kitten's paw, stroked the boat. Kralefsky, his head thrown back, his large eyes full of tears, sang at the velvet blue sky, shuddering with stars. The sea crisped itself along the sides of the boat with the sound of winter leaves, wind-lifted, rubbing themselves affectionately against the trunks of the trees that gave them birth.

'But when I saw my darling thus in snow arrayed,
To her sweet side I sped.
I brushed the gleaming petals from each lock and braid,
I kissed her and I said:
I brushed the gleaming petals from each lock and braid,
I kissed her and I said . . .'

Far out in the channel between Corfu and the mainland, the darkness was freckled and picked out with the lights of the fishing boats. It was as though a small section of the Milky Way had fallen into the sea. Slowly the moon edged up over the carapace of the Albanian mountains, at first red like the sun, then fading to copper, to yellow, and at last to white. The tiny wind-shimmers on the sea glittered like a thousand fish scales.

The warm air, the wine, and the melancholy beauty of the night filled me with a delicious sadness. It would always be like this, I thought. The brilliant, friendly island, full of secrets, my family and my animals round me and, for good measure, our friends. Theodore's bearded head outlined against the moon wanting only horns to make him Pan; Kralefsky crying unashamedly now like a black gnome weeping over his banishment from fairyland; Spiro with his scowling brown face, his voice becoming as richly vibrant as a million summer bees; Donald and Max, frowning as they endeavoured to remember the words of the song and harmonize at the same time. Sven, like a great ugly white baby, gently squeezing the soulful music from his ungainly instrument.

> 'Oh, foolish one, to deck your hair so soon with snow,
> Long may you have to wait;
> The dreary winter days when chilling north winds blow
> Do not anticipate!
> The dreary winter days when chilling north winds blow
> Do not anticipate!'

Now, I thought, we were edging into winter, but soon it would be spring again, burnished, glittering, bright as a goldfinch; and then it would be summer, the long, hot, daffodil-yellow days.

> 'Oh, foolish one, to deck your hair so soon with snow,
> Long may you have to wait;
> The dreary winter days when chilling north winds blow
> Do not anticipate!
> The dreary winter days when chilling north winds blow
> Do not anticipate!'

Lulled by the wine and the throbbing heart of the boat's engine, lulled by the warm night and the singing, I fell asleep while the boat carried us back across the warm, smooth waters to our island and the brilliant days that were not to be.

Epilogue

Corfu is of such importance to me that its loss would deal a fatal blow to my projects. Remember this: in the present state of Europe, the greatest misfortune which could befall me is the loss of Corfu.

— NAPOLEON

Mail

Letter

Dear Mrs Durrell,

It seems at last war can no longer be avoided and I think perhaps you were wise to leave Corfu. One can only hope that we can all meet in happier times when mankind has regained its senses. I will look forward to that.

Should you wish to reach me, my address is c/o The Ionian Bank, Athens.

I wish you and your family the very best of luck in the future.

Love to you all,
Yours,
Theodore

Postcard

Mother,

Have moved to Athens, so keep in touch. Place marvellous. Acropolis like pink flesh in the sun. Have sent my things to you. In a trunk marked '3' you will find book called An Evaluation of Marlowe. *Can you send it to me? Everyone here wearing tin hats and looking like war. Am buying myself large spear.*

Love,
Larry

Letter

Dear Mother,

    I have had all my travellers' cheques pinched by some bloody Italian. They nearly arrested me because I punched him in the snoot. Give me the Greeks any day.

    Can you send some more money to me at the Magnifica Hotel, Plaza de Contina, Milan? Will be home soon. Don't worry.

Love,

Les

P.S. It looks like war, doesn't it?

Letter

Darling Mother,

    Just a hurried note to tell you I'm leaving on the boat on Monday so I should be in England in about three weeks.

    Things here are rather hectic, but what can you expect? It never rains but it snows. I think it's simply disgusting the way the Germans are carrying on. If I had my way I'd tell them.

Will see you soon.

Love to you,

Margo

P.S. I enclose a letter from Spiro. Most odd.

Letter

Dear Missy Margo,

    This is to tell you that war has been declared. Don't tell a soul.

Spiro

The Garden of the Gods

This book is for Ann Peters,
at one time my secretary and
always my friend,
because she loves Corfu and
probably knows it better than I do

Contents

I

Dogs, Dormice, and Disorder

The unspeakable Turk should immediately be struck out
of the question.

– CARLYLE

That summer was a particularly rich one; it seemed as if the
sun had drawn up a special bounty from the island for never
had we had such an abundance of fruit and flowers, never had
the sea been so warm and filled with fish, never had so many
birds reared their young, or butterflies and other insects hatched
and shimmered across the countryside. Watermelons, their
flesh as crisp and cool as pink snow, were formidable botanical
cannonballs, each one big enough and heavy enough to obliterate
a city; peaches, as orange or pink as a harvest moon, loomed
huge in the trees, their thick, velvety pelts swollen with sweet
juice; the green and black figs burst with the pressure of their
sap, and in the pink splits the gold-green rose beetles sat dazed
by the rich, never-ending largesse. Trees had been groaning with
the weight of cherries, so that the orchards looked as though
some great dragon had been slain among the trees, bespattering
the leaves with scarlet and wine-red drops of blood. The maize
cobs were as long as your arm and as you bit into the canary-
yellow mosaic of seeds, the white milky juice burst into your
mouth; and in the trees, swelling and fattening themselves for
autumn, were the jade-green almonds and walnuts, and olives,
smoothly shaped, bright and shining as birds' eggs strung among
the leaves.

Naturally, with the island thus a-burst with life, my collecting activities redoubled. As well as my regular weekly afternoon spent with Theodore, I now undertook much more daring and comprehensive expeditions than I had been able to before, for now I had acquired a donkey. This beast, Sally by name, had been a birthday present; and as a means of covering long distances and carrying a lot of equipment I found her an invaluable, if stubborn, companion. To offset her stubbornness she had one great virtue; she was, like all donkeys, endlessly patient. She would gaze happily into space while I watched some creature or other or else would simply fall into a donkey doze, that happy, trance-like state that donkeys can attain when, with half-closed eyes, they appear to be dreaming of some nirvana and become impervious to shouts, threats, or even whacks with sticks. The dogs, after a short period of patience, would start to yawn and sigh and scratch and show by many small signs that they felt we had devoted enough time to a spider or whatever it was and should move on. Sally, however, once she was in her doze, gave the impression that she would happily stay there for several days if the necessity arose.

One day a peasant friend of mine, a man who had obtained a number of specimens for me and who was a careful observer, informed me that there were two huge birds hanging about in a rocky valley some five miles north of the villa. He thought that they must be nesting there. From his description they could only be eagles or vultures and I was most anxious to try to get some young of either of these birds. My birds of prey collection now numbered three species of owl, a sparrowhawk, a merlin, and a kestrel, so I felt the addition of an eagle or vulture would round it off. Needless to say I did not vouchsafe my ambition to the family, as already the meat bill for my animals was astronomical. Apart from this I could imagine Larry's reaction to the suggestion of a vulture being inserted into the house. When acquiring new pets I always found it wiser to face him with a *fait accompli*, for once the animals were introduced to the villa I could generally count on getting Mother and Margo on my side.

I prepared for my expedition with great care, making up loads of food for myself and the dogs, a good supply of *gasoza* as well as the normal complement of collecting tins and boxes, my butterfly net and a large bag to put my eagle or vulture in. I also took Leslie's binoculars; they were of a higher magnification than my own. He, luckily, was not around for me to ask, but I felt sure he would happily have lent them to me had he been at home. Having checked my equipment for the last time to make sure nothing was missing I proceeded to festoon Sally with the various items. She was in a singularly sullen and recalcitrant mood, even by donkey standards, and annoyed me by deliberately treading on my foot and then giving me a sharp nip on the buttock when I bent down to pick up my fallen butterfly net. She took grave offence at the clout I gave her for this misbehaviour, so we started this expedition barely on speaking terms. Coldly, I fixed her straw hat over her furry lily-shaped ears, whistled to the dogs and set off.

Although it was still early the sun was hot and the sky clear, burning blue, like the blue you get by scattering salt on a fire, blurred at the edges with heat haze. To begin with we made our way along the road thick with white dust, as clinging as pollen, and we passed many of my peasant friends on their donkeys, going to market or down to their fields to work. This inevitably held up the progress of the expedition, for good manners required that I passed the time of day with each one. In Corfu one must always gossip for the right length of time and perhaps accept a crust of bread, some dry watermelon seeds, or a bunch of grapes as a sign of love and affection. So when it was time to turn off the hot, dusty road and start climbing through the cool olive groves I was laden with a variety of edible commodities, the largest of which was a watermelon, a generous present pressed upon me by Mama Agathi, a friend of mine whom I had not seen for a week, an unconscionable length of time, during which she presumed I had been without food.

The olive groves were dark with shadows and as cool as a well after the glare of the road. The dogs went ahead as usual, foraging around the great pitted olive boles and occasionally, maddened by their audacity, chasing skimming swallows, barking vociferously. Failing, as always, to catch one, they would then attempt to vent their wrath on some innocent sheep or vacant-faced chicken, and would have to be sternly reprimanded. Sally, her previous sulkiness forgotten, stepped out at a good pace, one ear pricked forward and the other one backward, so that she could listen to my singing and comments on the passing scene.

Presently we left the shade of the olives and climbed upwards through the heat-shimmered hills, making our way through thickets of myrtle bushes, small copses of holm oak, and great wigs of broom. Here Sally's hooves crushed the herbs underfoot and the warm air became redolent with the scent of sage and thyme. By midday, the dogs panting, Sally and I sweating profusely, we were high up among the gold and rust-red rocks of the central range, while far below us lay the sea, blue as flax. By half past two, pausing to rest in the shade of a massive outcrop of stone, I was feeling thoroughly frustrated. We had followed the instructions of my friend and had indeed found a nest, which to my excitement proved to be that of a griffon vulture, moreover, the nest perched on a rocky ledge contained two fat and almost fully fledged youngsters at just the right age for adoption. The snag was that I could not reach the nest, either from above or below. After having spent a fruitless hour trying to kidnap the babies I was forced, albeit reluctantly, to give up the idea of adding vultures to my birds of prey collection. We moved down the mountainside and stopped to rest and eat in the shade. While I ate my sandwiches and hard-boiled eggs, Sally had a light lunch of dry maize cobs and watermelon, and the dogs assuaged their thirst with a mixture of watermelon and grapes, gobbling the juicy fruit eagerly and occasionally choking and coughing as a melon seed got stuck. Because of their voraciousness and total lack of table manners, they had finished their lunch long before Sally or I, and having reluctantly come to the conclusion that I did not intend to give them any more to eat they left us and slouched down the mountainside to indulge in a little private hunting.

I lay on my tummy eating crisp, cool watermelon, pink as coral, and examined the hillside. Fifty feet or so below where I lay were the ruins of a small peasant house. Here and there on the hillside I could just discern the crescent shaped, flattened areas which had once been the tiny fields of the farm. Eventually, it must have become obvious that the impoverished soil would no longer support maize or vegetables on the pocket handkerchief fields, and so the owner had moved away. The house had tumbled down and the fields become overrun with weeds and myrtle. I was staring at the remains of the cottage, wondering who had lived there, when I saw something reddish moving through the thyme at the base of one of the walls.

Slowly I reached out for the field glasses and put them to my eyes. The tumbled mass of rocks at the base of the wall sprang into clear view, but for a moment I could not see what it was that had attracted my attention. Then, to my astonishment, from behind a clump of thyme appeared a lithe, tiny animal, as red as an autumn leaf. It was a weasel, and to judge by its behaviour, a young and rather innocent one. It was the first weasel I had seen on Corfu and I was enchanted by it. It peered about with a slightly bemused air and then stood up on its hind legs and sniffed the air vigorously. Apparently not smelling anything edible, it sat down and had an intensive and, from the look of it, very satisfying scratch. Then it suddenly broke off from its toilet and carefully stalked and attempted to capture a vivid canary-yellow brimstone butterfly. The insect, however, slipped out from under its jaws and flipped away, leaving the weasel snapping at thin air and looking slightly foolish. It sat up on its hind legs once more, to see where its quarry had gone and, overbalancing, almost fell off the stone on which it was sitting.

I watched it, entranced by its diminutive size, its rich colouring, and its air of innocence. I wanted above all things to catch it and take it home with me to add to my menagerie but I knew this would be difficult. While I was musing on the best method of achieving this result a drama unfolded in the ruined cottage below. I saw a shadow, like a Maltese cross, slide over the low scrub, and a sparrowhawk appeared, flying low and fast towards the weasel who was sitting up on his stone sniffing the air and apparently unaware of his danger. I was just wondering whether to shout or clap my hands to warn him when he saw the hawk. With an incredible turn of speed he turned, leaped gracefully on to the ruined wall and disappeared into a crack between two stones that I would have thought would not have allowed the passage of a slow-worm, let alone a mammal the size of the weasel. It was like a conjuring trick; one minute he had been sitting on his rock, the next he vanished into the wall like a drop of rain water. The sparrowhawk checked with fanned tail and hovered briefly, obviously hoping the weasel would reappear. After a moment or so it got bored and slid off down the mountainside in search of less wary game. After a short time the weasel poked his little face out of the crack. Seeing the coast was clear he emerged cautiously. Then he made his way along the wall and, as though his recent escape into the crack had given him the idea, he proceeded to investigate and disappear into every nook and cranny that existed between the stones. As I watched him I was wondering how to make my way down the hill so as to throw my shirt over him before he was aware of my presence. In view of his expert vanishing trick when faced with the hawk, it was obviously not going to be easy.

At that moment he slid, sinuous as a snake, into a hole in the base of the wall. From another hole a little higher up there emerged a second animal in a great state of alarm, which made its way along the top of the wall and disappeared into a crevice. I was greatly excited, for even with the brief glimpse I had got of it, I recognized it as a creature that I had tried for many months to track down and capture, a garden dormouse, probably one of the most attractive of the European rodents. It was about half the size of a full-grown rat, with cinnamon-coloured fur, brilliant white underparts, a long furry tail ending in a brush of black and white hair, and a black mask of fur beneath the ears, running across the eyes and making it look ridiculously as though it was wearing an old-fashioned mask of the sort that burglars were reputed to indulge in.

I was now in something of a quandary, for there below me were two animals I dearly wanted to possess, one hotly pursuing the other, and both of them exceedingly wary. If my attack was not well planned I stood a good chance of losing both animals. I decided to tackle the weasel first, as he was the more mobile of the two, and I felt that the dormouse would not move from its new hole if undisturbed. On reflection I decided that my butterfly net was a more suitable instrument than my shirt, so armed with it I made my way down the hillside with the utmost caution, freezing immobile every time the weasel appeared out of the hole and looked around. Eventually I got to within a few feet of the wall without being detected. I tightened my grip on the long handle of my net and waited for the weasel to come out from the depths of the hole he was now investigating. When he did emerge he did so with such suddenness that I was unprepared. He sat up on his hind legs and stared at me with interest untinged by alarm. I was just about to take a swipe at him with my net when, crashing through the bushes, tongues lolling, tails wagging, came the three dogs, as vociferously pleased to see me as if we had been separated for months. The weasel vanished. One minute he was sitting there, frozen with horror at this avalanche of dogs, the next he was gone. Bitterly I cursed the dogs and banished them to the higher reaches of the mountain, where they went to lie in the shade, hurt and puzzled at my bad temper. Then I set about trying to capture the dormouse.

Over the years the mortar between the stones had grown frail and heavy winter rains had washed it away so that now, to all intents and purposes, the remains of the house was a series of dry-stone walls. With its maze of intercommunicating tunnels and caves, it formed the ideal hideout for any small animal. There was only one way to hunt for an animal in this sort of terrain and that was to take the wall to pieces, so rather laboriously this was what I started to do. After having dismantled a good section of it I had unearthed nothing more exciting than a couple of indignant scorpions, a few woodlice, and a young gecko who fled, leaving his writhing tail behind him. It was hot and thirsty work and after an hour or so I sat down in the shade of the, as yet, undismantled wall to have a rest.

I was just wondering how long it would take me to demolish the rest of the wall when from a hole some three feet from me, the dormouse appeared. It scrambled up like a somewhat overweight mountain climber and then, having reached the top, sat down on its fat bottom and began to wash its face with great thoroughness, totally ignoring my presence. I could hardly believe my luck. Slowly and with great caution I manoeuvred my butterfly net towards him, got it into position, and then clapped it down suddenly. This would have worked perfectly if the top of the wall had been flat, but it was not. I could not press the rim of the net down hard enough to avoid leaving a gap. To my intense annoyance and frustration, the dormouse, recovering from its momentary panic, squeezed out from under the net, galloped along the wall and disappeared into another crevice. However this proved to be its undoing, for it had chosen a 'cul de sac' and before it had discovered its mistake I had clamped the net over the entrance.

The next thing was to get it out and into the bag without

getting bitten. This was not easy and before I had finished it had sunk its exceedingly sharp teeth into the ball of my thumb, so that I, the handkerchief, and the dormouse were liberally bespattered with gore. Finally, however, I got it into the bag. Delighted with my success, I mounted Sally and rode home in triumph with my new acquisition.

On arrival at the villa I carried the dormouse up to my room and housed it in a cage which had, until recently, been the home of a baby black rat. This rat had met an unfortunate end in the claws of my scops owl, Ulysses, who was of the opinion that all rodents had been created by a beneficent providence in order to fill his stomach. I therefore made quite sure that my precious dormouse could not escape and meet a similar fate. Once it was in the cage I was able to examine it more closely. I discovered it was a female with a suspiciously large tummy, which led me to believe that she might be pregnant. After some consideration I called her Esmerelda (I had just been reading *The Hunchback of Notre Dame* and had fallen deeply in love with the heroine), and provided her with a cardboard box full of cotton waste and dried grass in which to have her family.

For the first few days Esmerelda would leap at my hand like a bulldog when I went to clean her cage or feed her, but within a week she had grown tame and tolerated me, though still viewing me with a certain reserve. Every evening Ulysses, on his special perch above the window, would wake up and I would open the shutters so that he could fly off into the moonlit olive groves and hunt, only returning for his plate of mincemeat at about two in the morning. Once he was safely out of the way I could let Esmerelda out of her cage for a couple of hours' exercise. She proved to be an enchanting creature with enormous grace in spite of her rotundity, and would take prodigious and breath-taking leaps from the cupboard on to the bed (where she bounced as if it was a trampoline), and from the bed to the bookcase or table, using her long tail with its bushy end as a balancing rod.

She was vastly inquisitive and nightly would subject the room and its contents to a minute scrutiny, scowling through her black mask with whiskers quivering. I discovered that she had a consuming passion for large brown grasshoppers and she would often come and sit on my bare chest, as I lay in bed, and scrunch these delicacies. The result was that my bed always seemed to contain a prickly layer of wing cases, bits of leg, and chunks of horny thorax, for she was a greedy and not particularly well-mannered feeder.

The came the exciting evening when, after Ulysses had floated on silent wings into the olive groves and commenced to call 'toink, toink' after the manner of his kind, I opened the cage door to find that she would not come out but lurked inside the cardboard box and made angry chittering noises at me. When I tried to investigate her bedroom she fastened onto my forefinger like a tiger and I had great difficulty in getting her to let go. Eventually I managed to get her off and, holding her firmly by the scruff of the neck, investigated the box. I found there, to my infinite delight, eight babies, each the size of a hazelnut and as pink as a cyclamen bud. Delighted with Esmerelda's happy event I showered her with grasshoppers, melon seeds, grapes, and other delicacies of which I knew she was particularly fond, and followed the progress of the babies with breathless interest.

Gradually the babies developed. Their eyes opened and their fur grew. Within a short time the more powerful and adventurous of them would climb laboriously out of their cardboard nursery and wobble about on the floor of the cage when Esmerelda was not looking. This filled her with alarm, and she would pick the errant baby up in her mouth, and uttering peevish growling noises, transfer it to the safety of the bedroom. This was all very well with one or two, but as soon as all eight babies reached the inquisitive stage, it was impossible for her to control them and so she had to let them wander at will. They started to follow her out of the cage and it was then that I discovered that dormice, like shrews, have a habit of caravanning. That is to say Esmerelda would go first; hanging on to her tail would be baby number one, hanging on to his or hers would be baby number two, on to his baby number three, and so on. It was a magical sight to see these nine diminutive creatures, each wearing his little black mask, wending their way around the room like an animated furry scarf, flying over the bed or shillying up the table leg. A scattering of grasshoppers on the bed or floor, and the babies, squeaking excitedly, would gather round to feed, looking ridiculously like a convention of bandits.

Eventually, when the babies were fully adult, I was forced to take them into the olive grove and let them go. The task of providing sufficient food for nine rapacious dormice was proving too time-consuming. I released them at the edge of the olive grove, near a thicket of holm oak, and these they colonized successfully. In the evenings, when the sun was setting and the sky was getting as green as a leaf, striped with sunset clouds, I used to go down to watch the little masked dormice flitting through the branches with a ballerina-like grace, chittering and squeaking to each other as they pursued moths, or fireflies or other delicacies through the shadowy branches.

It was a result of one of my many forays on donkey-back that we became infested by dogs. We had been up in the hills where I had been endeavouring to catch some agamas on the glittering gypsum cliffs. We returned towards evening, when the shadows lay everywhere, charcoal black, and everything was bathed in the slanting, soft golden light of the sinking sun. We were hot and tired, hungry and thirsty, for we had long since eaten and drunk everything that we had brought with us. The last vineyard we had passed had only yielded some bunches of very black wine-grapes whose sharp vinegariness had made the dogs curl back their lips and screw up their eyes and had left me feeling hungrier and thirstier than ever.

I decided that as leader of the expedition it was up to me to provide sustenance for the rest of the crew. I reined in and thought about the problem. We were equidistant between three sources of food. There was the shepherd, old Yani, who would, I knew, give us cheese and bread, but his wife would probably be still in the fields and Yani himself might not have returned from grazing his goat flock. There was Agathi, who lived alone in a tiny, tumbledown cottage, but she was so poor that I felt guilty at accepting anything from her, and, in fact, always made a point of sharing my food with her when I was around that way. Finally, there was sweet and gentle Mama Kondos, a widow of some eighty summers, who lived with her three unmarried and, as far as I could see, unmarriageable daughters on an untidy but prosperous farm in a valley to the south. They were quite well off by peasant standards, owning, apart from five or six acres of olives and agricultural land, two donkeys, four sheep, and a cow. They were what one might call the landed gentry of the area, and so I decided that the honour of revictualling my expedition would fall to them.

The three inordinately fat, ill-favoured but good-natured girls had just returned from working in the fields and were gathered round the small well, bright and shrill as parrots, washing their fat, hairy brown legs. Mama Kondos herself, like a diminutive clockwork toy, was trotting to and fro scattering maize for the squawking tousled flock of chickens. There was nothing straight about Mama Kondos; her diminutive body was bent like a sickle blade, her legs were bowed with years of carrying heavy loads on her head, her arms and hands permanently bent from picking things up; even her upper and lower lips curved inwards over her toothless gums, and her snow-white, dandelion-seed eyebrows curved over her black eyes, blue-rimmed, which in their turn were guarded on each side by a fence of curved wrinkles in a skin as delicate as a baby mushroom's.

The daughters, on seeing me, gave shrill cries of joy and

gathered round me like benign shire horses, clasping me to their mammoth bosoms and kissing me, exuding affection, sweat, and garlic in equal quantities. Mama Kondos, a small, bent David among these aromatic Goliaths, beat them aside, shouting shrilly: 'Give him to me, give him to me! My golden one, my heart, my love! Give him to me.' She clasped me to her and covered my face with bruising kisses, for her gums were as hard as a tortoise's mouth.

At length, after I had been thoroughly kissed and patted and pinched all over to make sure I was real, I was allowed to sit down and to offer some explanations as to why I had deserted them for so long. Did I not realize that it was a whole week since I had visited them? How could my love be so cruel, so tardy, so ephemeral? Still, since I was here at last, would I like some food? I said yes, I would love some, and some for Sally as well. The dogs, more ill-mannered, had helped themselves; Widdle and Puke had torn sweet white grapes off the vine that trailed over part of the house and were gulping them down greedily, while Roger, who appeared to be more thirsty than hungry, had gone beneath the fig and almond trees and had disembowelled a watermelon. He was laying with his nose stuck into its cool pink interior, his eyes closed in ecstasy, sucking the sweet icy juice through his teeth. Immediately, Sally was given three cobs of ripe corn to chew on and a bucket of water to slake her thirst, while I was presented with a mammoth sweet potato, its skin black and deliciously charcoaly from the fire, its sweet flesh beautifully soggy, a bowl of almonds, some figs, two enormous peaches, a hunk of yellow bread, olive oil and garlic.

Once I had engulfed this provender and thus taken the edge off my hunger, I could concentrate on exchanging gossip. Pepi had fallen out of an olive tree and broken his arm, silly boy; Leonora was going to have another baby to replace the one that died; Yani – no, not that Yani, the Yani over on the other side of the hill – had quarrelled with Taki over the price of a donkey and

Taki had got so angry he had fired his shotgun at the side of Yani's house, only it had been a very dark night and Taki was drunk and it had turned out to be Spiro's house, so now none of them were speaking. For some time we discussed the foibles and dissected the characters of our fellow men with great relish and then I noticed that Lulu was missing from the scene. Lulu was Mama Kondos' dog, a lean and long-legged bitch with huge soulful eyes and long floppy ears like a spaniel. Like all peasant dogs, she was gaunt and scabby, her ribs sticking out like the strings of a harp, but she was an endearing creature and I was fond of her. Normally, she was one of the first to greet me but now she was nowhere to be seen. Had anything happened to her, I asked.

'Puppies!' said Mama Kondos. '*Po, po, po, po*. Eleven! Would you believe it?'

They had tied Lulu up to an olive tree near the house when the birth had become imminent and she had crawled into the depths of the tree trunk to have her young. After she had greeted me with enthusiasm she watched with interest as I crawled into the olive tree on hands and knees and extracted the puppies to look at. As always, I was amazed that such scrawny, half-starved mothers could produce such plump, powerful puppies, with squashed, belligerent faces and loud seagull voices. They were, as usual, in a wide variety of colours – black and white, white and tan, silver and bluish-grey, all black and all white. Any litter of Corfu puppies displays such a wide variety of colour schemes that to settle the question of paternity is virtually impossible. I sat with the mewling patchwork of puppies in my lap and told Lulu how clever she was. She wagged her tail furiously.

'Clever, huh?' said Mama Kondos sourly. 'Eleven puppies isn't clever, it's wanton. We shall have to get rid of all but one.'

I was well aware that Lulu could not possibly be allowed to keep her full complement of puppies and, in fact, she was lucky that they were going to leave her one. I felt I might be of use. I said that I felt sure that my mother would not only be delighted at the thought of having a puppy but would be overwhelmed with gratitude to the Kondos family and Lulu for providing her with one. I therefore, after much thought, chose the one I liked best, a slug-fat, screaming little male who was black, white, and grey with bright, corn-coloured eyebrows and feet. I asked them to save this one for me until he was old enough to leave Lulu; in the meantime, I would apprise Mother of the exciting fact that we had acquired another dog, which would bring our complement up to five; a nice round figure, I considered.

To my astonishment, Mother was not a bit pleased with the suggested increase in our dog tribe.

'No, dear,' she said firmly, 'we are not having another dog. Four is quite enough. And what with all your owls and everything it's costing a fortune in meat anyway. No, I'm afraid another dog is out of the question.'

In vain I argued that the puppy would be killed if we did not intervene. Mother remained firm. There was only one thing to be done. I had noticed in the past that Mother, faced with a hypothetical question like, 'Would you like a nestful of baby redstarts?' would say 'no' firmly and automatically. Faced, however, with the nestful of baby birds, she would inevitably waver and then say yes. Obviously, there was only one thing to be done and that was to show her the puppy. I was confident that she would never be able to resist his golden eyebrows and socks. I sent a message down to the Kondoses asking if I could borrow the puppy to show Mother, and one of the fat daughters obligingly brought it up the next day. But when I unwrapped it from the cloth in which she had brought it I found to my annoyance that Mama Kondos had sent the wrong puppy. I explained this to the daughter, who said that she could do nothing about it as she was on her way to the village. I had better go and see her mother. She added that I had better make haste as Mama Kondos had mentioned that she was intending to destroy the puppies that morning. Hastily, I mounted Sally and galloped through the olive groves.

When I reached the farm I found Mama Kondos sitting in the sun stringing garlic heads together into white, knobbly plaits, while around her the chickens scratched and purred contentedly. After she had embraced me, asked after the health of myself and the family and given me a plate of green figs, I produced the puppy and explained my errand.

'The wrong one?' she exclaimed, peering at the yelling puppy and prodding it with her forefinger. 'The wrong one? How stupid of me. *Po po po po*, I quite thought it was the one with white eyebrows you wanted.' Had she, I inquired anxiously, destroyed the rest of the puppies?

'Oh yes,' she said absently, still staring at the puppy. 'Yes, this morning, early.'

Well then, I said resignedly, since I could not have the one I had set my heart on, I had better have the one she had saved.

'No, I think I can get you the one you want,' she said, getting to her feet and fetching a broad-bladed hoe.

How, I wondered, could she get me my puppy if she had destroyed them? Perhaps she was going to retrieve the corpse for me. I had no desire for that. I was just going to say so when Mama Kondos, mumbling to herself, trotted off to a field nearby the house, where the stalks of the first crop of maize stood yellow and brittle in the hot sun-cracked ground. Here she cast about for a moment and then started to dig. With the second sweep of the hoe she dug up three screaming puppies, their legs paddling frantically, ears, eyes, and pink mouths choked with earth.

I was paralysed with horror. She checked the puppies she had dug up, found they were not the one that I wanted, threw them to one side, and recommenced digging. It was only then that the full realization of what Mama Kondos had done swept over me. I felt as though a great scarlet bubble of hate burst in my chest and tears of rage poured down my cheeks. From my not uncomprehensive knowledge of Greek insults, I dragged up the worst in my vocabulary. Yelling these at Mama Kondos, I pushed her out of the way so hard that she sat down suddenly, bewildered among the corn stalks. Still calling down the curses of every saint and deity I could think of, I seized the hoe and rapidly but carefully dug up the rest of the gasping puppies. Mama Kondos was too astonished by my sudden change from calm to rage to say anything; she just sat there, open-mouthed. I stuffed the puppies unceremoniously into my shirt, collected Lulu and the pup that had been left to her, and rode off on Sally, shouting curses over my shoulder at Mama Kondos, who had now got to her feet and was running after me shouting: 'But, golden one, what's the matter? Why are you crying? You can have all the puppies. What's the matter?'

I burst into the house, hot, tear-stained, covered with mud, my shirt bulging with puppies, Lulu trotting at my heels, delighted with this sudden and unexpected outing for herself and her offspring. Mother was, as usual, embedded in the kitchen making various delicacies for Margo who had been away touring the mainland of Greece to recover from yet another unfortunate affair of the heart. Mother listened to my incoherent and indignant account of the puppies' premature burial and was duly shocked.

'Really!' she exclaimed indignantly. 'These peasants! I can't understand how they can be so cruel. Burying them alive! I never heard of such a barbarous thing. You did quite right to save them, dear. Where are they?'

I ripped open my shirt, as though committing hara-kiri, and a cascade of wriggling puppies fell out on to the kitchen table where they started to grope their way blindly about, squeaking.

'Gerry, dear, not on the table where I'm rolling pastry,' said Mother. 'Really, you children! Yes, well, even if it's clean mud we don't want it in the pies. Get a basket.'

I got a basket and we put the puppies into it. Mother peered at them.

'Poor little things,' she said. 'There do seem to be an awful lot of them. *How* many? Eleven! Well, I don't know what we'll do with them. We can't have eleven dogs with the ones we've got.'

I said hastily that I had got it all worked out; as soon as the puppies were old enough we would find homes for them. I added that Margo, who would be home by then, could help me; it would be an occupation for her and keep her mind off sex.

'Gerry, dear!' said Mother, aghast. 'Don't say things like that. Whoever told you that?'

I explained that Larry had said that she needed her mind taken off sex and so I thought that the puppies' arrival would achieve this happy result.

'Well, you mustn't talk like that,' said Mother. 'Larry's got no business to say things like that. Margo's just . . . just . . . a bit . . . emotional, that's all. Sex has nothing to do with it; that's something *quite* different. Whatever would people think if they heard you? Now go and put the puppies somewhere safe.'

So I took the puppies to a convenient olive tree near the veranda, tied Lulu to it and cleaned the puppies with a damp cloth. Lulu, deciding that baskets were very effete places in which to bring up puppies, immediately excavated a burrow between the friendly roots of the tree and carefully transferred her puppies to it one by one. To his annoyance, I spent more time cleaning up my special puppy than the others and tried to think of a name for him. Finally, I decided to call him Lazarus, Laz for short. I placed him carefully with his brothers and sisters and went to change my mud- and urine-stained shirt.

I arrived at the lunch table in time to hear Mother telling Leslie and Larry about the puppies.

'It's extraordinary,' said Leslie, 'I don't think they mean to be cruel; they just don't think. Look at the way they shove wounded birds into their game bags. So what happened? Did Gerry drown the puppies?'

'No he did *not*,' said Mother indignantly. 'He brought them here, of course.'

'Dear God!' said Larry. 'Not more dogs! We've got four already.'

'They're only puppies,' said Mother, 'poor little things.'

'How many are there?' asked Leslie.

'Eleven,' said Mother reluctantly.

Larry put down his knife and fork and stared at her. 'Eleven?' he repeated. 'Eleven? Eleven puppies! You must be mad.'

'I keep telling you, they're only puppies – tiny little things,' said Mother, flustered. 'And Lulu's very good with them.'

'Who the hell's Lulu?' asked Larry.

'Their mother – she's a dear,' said Mother.

'So that's twelve bloody dogs.'

'Well, yes, I suppose it is,' said Mother. 'I hadn't really counted.'

'That's the trouble round here,' snapped Larry. 'Nobody counts! And before you know where you are you're knee deep in animals. It's like the bloody creation all over again, only worse. One owl turns into a battalion before you know where you are; sex-mad pigeons defying Marie Stopes in every room of the house; the place is so full of birds it's like a bloody poulterer's shop, to say nothing of snakes and toads and enough small fry to keep Macbeth's witches in provender for years. And on top of all that you go and get twelve more dogs. It's a perfect example of the streak of lunacy that runs in this family.'

'Nonsense, Larry, you do exaggerate,' said Mother. 'Such a lot of fuss over a few puppies.'

'You call eleven puppies a *few*? The place will look like the Greek branch of Crufts' Dog Show and they'll probably all turn out to be bitches and come into season simultaneously. Life will deteriorate into one long canine sexual orgy.'

'Oh yes,' said Mother, changing the subject. 'You're not to

go around saying Margo's sex mad. People will get the wrong idea.'

'Well, she is,' said Larry. 'I see no reason to cover up the truth.'

'You know perfectly well what I mean,' said Mother firmly; 'I won't have you saying things like that. Margo's just romantic. There's a lot of difference.'

'Well, all I can say is,' said Larry, 'when all those bitches you've brought into the house come into season together Margo's going to have a lot of competition.'

'Now, Larry, that's quite enough,' said Mother. 'Anyway I don't think we ought to discuss sex at lunch.'

A few days after this, Margo returned from her travels, bronzed and well and with her heart apparently healed. She talked incessantly about her trip and gave us graphic thumbnail pictures of the people she had met, inevitably ending with, 'and so I told them if they came to Corfu to come and see us'.

'I do hope you didn't invite everyone you met, Margo dear,' said Mother, slightly alarmed.

'Oh, of course not, Mother,' said Margo impatiently, having just told us about a handsome Greek sailor and his eight brothers to whom she had issued this lavish invitation. 'I only asked the *interesting* ones. I would have thought you'd be glad to have some *interesting* people around.'

'I get enough interesting people that Larry invites, thank you,' said Mother acidly, 'without *you* starting.'

'This trip has opened my eyes,' concluded Margo dramatically. 'I've realized that you're all simply stagnating here. You're becoming narrow-minded and . . . and . . . insulated.'

'I don't see that objecting to unexpected guests is being narrow-minded, dear,' said Mother. 'After all, I'm the one that has to do the cooking.'

'But they're not unexpected,' explained Margo haughtily, 'I invited them.'

'Well, yes,' said Mother, obviously feeling that she was not making much headway with this argument. 'I suppose if they write and let us know they're coming we can manage.'

'Of course they'll let us know,' said Margo coldly. 'They're my friends; they wouldn't be so ill-mannered as not to let us know.'

As it happened, she was wrong.

I returned to the villa after a very pleasant afternoon spent drifting up the coast in my boat looking for seals and, bursting, sun-glowing and hungry, into the drawing-room in search of tea and the mammoth chocolate cake I knew Mother had made, I came upon a sight so curious that I stopped in the doorway, my mouth open in amazement while the dogs, clustered round my legs, started to bristle and growl with astonishment. Mother was seated on the floor, perched uncomfortably on a cushion, gingerly holding in one hand a piece of rope to which was attached a small, black, and excessively high-spirited ram. Sitting around Mother, cross-legged on cushions, were a fierce-looking old man in a tarboosh and three heavily veiled women. Also ranged on the floor were lemonade, tea, and plates of biscuits, sandwiches, and the chocolate cake. As I entered the room, the old man had leaned forward, drawn a huge, heavily ornate dagger from his sash, and cut himself a large hunk of cake which he stuffed into his mouth with every evidence of satisfaction. It looked rather like a scene out of the *Arabian Nights*. Mother cast me an anguished look.

'Thank goodness you've come, dear,' she said, struggling with the ram, who had gambolled into her lap by mistake. 'These people don't speak English.'

I inquired who they were.

'I don't know,' said Mother desperately. 'They just appeared when I was making tea; they've been here for hours. I can't understand a word they say. They insisted on sitting on the floor. I think they're friends of Margo's; of course, they may be friends of Larry's but they don't look highbrow enough.'

I tried tentatively talking in Greek to the old man and he leaped to his feet, delighted that someone understood him. He had a swooping, eagle nose, an immense white moustache like a frosty sheaf of corn, and black eyes that seemed to snap and crackle with his mood. He was wearing a white tunic with a red sash in which his dagger reposed, enormous baggy pants, long white cotton socks, and red, upturned *charukias* with immense pom-poms on the toes. So I was the adorable signorina's brother, was I, he roared excitedly, bits of chocolate cake trembling on his moustache as he talked. What an honour to meet me. He clasped me to him and kissed me so fervently that the dogs, fearing for my life, all started barking. The ram, faced with four vociferous dogs, panicked; it ran round and round Mother, twisting the rope around her. Then, at a particularly snarling bark from Roger, it uttered a frantic bleat and fled towards the French windows and safety, pulling Mother onto her back in a welter of spilled lemonade and chocolate cake. Things became confused.

Roger, under the impression that the old Turk was attacking both myself and Mother, launched an assault on the Turk's *charukias* and got a firm grip on one of the pom-poms. The old boy aimed a kick at Roger with his free foot and promptly fell down. The three women were sitting absolutely still, cross-legged on their cushions, screaming loudly behind their *yashmaks*. Mother's dog, Dodo, who had long ago decided that anything in the nature of a rough house was acutely distressing to a Dandie Dinmont of her lineage, sat soulfully in a corner and howled. The old Turk, who was surprisingly lithe for his age, had drawn his dagger and was making wild but ineffectual swipes at Roger, who was darting from pom-pom to pom-pom growling savagely, evading the blade with ease. Widdle and Puke were trying to round up the ram, and Mother, desperately unravelling herself, was shouting incoherent instructions to me.

'Get the lamb! Gerry, get the lamb! They'll kill it,' she squeaked, covered with lemonade and bits of chocolate cake.

'Black son of the devil! Illegitimate offspring of a witch! My shoes! Leave my shoes! I will kill you . . . destroy you!' panted the old Turk, slashing away at Roger.

'Ayii! Ayii! Ayii! His shoes! His shoes!' screamed the women in a chorus, immobile on their cushions.

With difficulty avoiding a stab wound myself, I managed to tear the ravening Roger off the old Turk's pom-poms and get him and Widdle and Puke out onto the veranda. Then I opened the sliding doors and shut the lamb in the dining-room as a temporary measure while I soothed the old Turk's wounded feelings. Mother, smiling nervously and nodding vigorously at everything I said although she did not understand it, was making an attempt to clean herself up, but this was rather ineffectual as the chocolate cake had been one of her larger and more glutinous creations, oozing cream, and she had put her elbow into the exact centre of it as she fell backwards. At length I managed to soothe the old man, and while Mother went up to change her dress I dished out brandy to the Turk and his three wives. My helpings were liberal, so by the time Mother came back faint hiccups were coming from behind at least one of the veils and the Turk's nose had turned fiery red.

'Your sister is . . . how shall I tell you? . . . magical . . . God-given. Never have I seen a girl like her,' he said, holding out his glass eagerly. 'I, who, as you see, have three wives, I have never seen a girl like your sister.'

'What's he saying?' asked Mother, eyeing his dagger nervously. I repeated what the Turk had said.

'Disgusting old man,' said Mother. 'Really, Margo should be more careful.'

The Turk drained his glass and held it out again, beaming convivially at us.

'Your maid here,' he said, jerking a thumb at Mother, 'she is a little bit soft, huh? She doesn't speak Greek.'

'What does he say?' asked Mother.

Dutifully, I translated.

'Impertinent man!' said Mother indignantly. 'Really, I could smack Margo. Tell him who I am, Gerry.'

I told the Turk, and the effect on him was more than Mother could have wished. With a roar, he leaped to his feet, rushed across to her, seized her hands and covered them with kisses. Then, still holding her hands in a vice-like grip, he peered into her face, his moustache trembling.

'The mother,' he intoned, 'the mother of my Almond-blossom.'

'What's he say?' asked Mother tremulously.

But before I could translate, the Turk had barked out an order to his wives, who showed their first sign of animation. They leaped from their cushions, rushed to Mother, lifted their *yash-maks*, and kissed her hands with every symptom of veneration.

'I do wish they wouldn't keep kissing me,' gasped Mother. 'Gerry, tell them it's quite unnecessary.'

But the Turk, having got his wives re-established on their cushions, turned once again to Mother. He threw a powerful arm round her shoulders, making her squeak and threw out his other arm oratorically.

'Never did I think,' he boomed, peering into Mother's face, 'never did I think that I should have the honour of meeting the mother of my Almond-blossom.'

'What's he saying?' asked Mother agitatedly, trapped in the Turk's bear-like hug.

Again I translated.

'Almond-blossom? What's he talking about? The man's mad,' she said.

I explained that the Turk was apparently greatly enamoured of Margo and that this was his name for her. This confirmed Mother's worst fears about the Turk's intentions.

'Almond-blossom, indeed!' she said indignantly. 'Just wait until she gets back – I'll give her Almond-blossom!'

Just at that moment, cool and fresh from a swim, Margo herself appeared in a very revealing bathing costume.

'Ooooh!' she screamed delightedly. 'Mustapha! And Lena, and Maria, and Telina! How lovely!'

The Turk rushed across to her and kissed her hands reverently while his wives clustered round making muffled noises of pleasure.

'Mother, this is Mustapha,' said Margo, glowing.

'We have already met,' said Mother grimly, 'and he's ruined my new dress, or, rather his lamb has. Go and put some clothes on.'

'His lamb?' asked Margo, bewildered. 'What lamb?'

'The lamb he brought for his Almond-blossom, as he calls you,' said Mother accusingly.

'Oh, it's just a nickname,' said Margo colouring, 'he doesn't mean any harm.'

'I know what these dirty old men are,' said Mother ominously. 'Really, Margo, you should know better.'

The old Turk was listening to this exchange with quick glances from his bright eyes and a beatific smile on his face; however, I could see that my powers of translation would be stretched to their limit if Mother and Margo started arguing so I opened the sliding doors and let the lamb in. He came in pertly, prance-footed, black and curly as a storm cloud.

'How dare you!' said Margo. 'How dare you insult my friends. He's not a dirty old man; he's one of the cleanest old men I know.'

'I don't care whether he's clean or not,' said Mother, coming to the end of her patience. 'He can't stay here with all his . . . his . . . women. I'm not cooking for a harem.'

'It is wonderful to hear the mother and daughter talk together,' the Turk confided to me. 'It's like the sound of sheep bells.'

'You're beastly,' said Margo, 'you're beastly! You don't want me to have any friends. You're narrow-minded and suburban!'

'You can't call it suburban to object to three wives,' said Mother indignantly.

'It reminds me,' said the Turk, his eyes moist, 'of the singing of the nightingales in my valley.'

'He can't help it if he's a Turk,' shrilled Margo. 'He can't help it if he's got to have three wives.'

'Any man can avoid having three wives if he puts his mind to it,' said Mother firmly.

'I expect,' said the Turk confidingly, 'Almond-blossom is telling her mother what a happy time we had in my valley, huh?'

'You always try to repress me,' said Margo. 'Everything I do is wrong.'

'The trouble is I give you too much licence. I let you go away for a few days and you come back with this . . . this . . . old roué and his dancing girls,' said Mother.

'There you are, that's what I mean – you repress me,' said Margo triumphantly. 'Now you expect me to have a licence for a Turk.'

'How I would like to take them back to my village,' said the Turk, gazing at them fondly. 'Such wonderful time we would have . . . dancing, singing, wine . . .'

The lamb seemed disappointed that no one was taking any notice of him; he had gambolled a little, decorated the floor, and done two nicely executed pirouettes, but he felt that no one was paying him the attention he deserved, so he put down his head and charged Mother. It was a beautifully executed charge. I could speak with some authority, for during my expeditions through the surrounding olive groves I had frequently met with eager and audacious young rams and fought them matador fashion, using my shirt as a cloak, to our mutual satisfaction. While deploring the result, I had to confess that the charge was excellent, well thought out, as it was, and with the full power of the ram's wiry body and bony head landing with precision on the back of Mother's knees. Mother was projected on to our extremely uncomfortable horsehair sofa as if propelled by a cannon, and she lay there gasping. The Turk, horrified at what his gift had done, leaped in front of her, arms outstretched, to protect her from further attack, which seemed imminent, for the ram, pleased with itself, had retreated to a corner of the room and was prancing and bucking rather in the manner of a boxer limbering up in his corner of the ring.

'Mother, Mother, are you all right?' screamed Margo.

Mother was too breathless to answer her.

'Ah-ha! You see, he has spirit like me, Almond-blossom,' cried the Turk. 'Come on then, my brave one, come on!'

The ram accepted the invitation with a speed and suddenness that took the Turk by surprise. It moved across the room in a black blur, its feet machine-gunning on the scrubbed boards, hit the Turk on his shins with a crack, and precipitated him onto the sofa with Mother, where he lay uttering loud cries of rage and pain. I had been charged in the shins like that and so I could sympathize.

The Turk's three wives, aghast at their master's downfall, were standing immobile, uttering noises like three minarets at sundown. It was into this interesting situation that Larry and Leslie intruded. They stood riveted in the doorway, drinking in the scene with unbelieving eyes. There was I pursuing a recalcitrant lamb round the room, Margo comforting three ululating ladies in veils, and Mother apparently rolling around on the sofa with an elderly Turk.

'Mother, don't you think you're getting a little old for this sort of thing?' Larry asked with interest.

'By Jove, look at that marvellous dagger,' said Leslie, eyeing the still-writhing Turk with interest.

'Don't be stupid, Larry,' said Mother angrily, massaging the backs of her legs. 'It's all Margo's Turk's fault.'

'You can't trust Turks,' said Leslie, still eyeing the dagger. 'Spiro says so.'

'But what are you doing rolling about with a Turk at this hour?' Larry inquired. 'Practising to be Lady Hester Stanhope?'

'Now, Larry, I've had quite enough this afternoon. Stop making me angry. The sooner this man is out of here, the better I'll be pleased,' said Mother. 'Kindly ask him to go.'

'You can't, you can't. He's my Turk,' squeaked Margo tearfully. 'You can't treat my Turk like that.'

'I'm going upstairs to put some witch hazel on my bruises,' said Mother, hobbling towards the door, 'and I want that man out of here by the time I come down.'

By the time she had returned, both Larry and Leslie had struck up a firm friendship with the Turk and to Mother's annoyance he and his wives stayed on for several hours, imbibing gallons of sweet tea and biscuits before we could finally manage to get them into a *caraccino* and back to town.

'Well, thank heaven *that's* over,' said Mother, limping towards the dining-room for our evening meal. 'At least they're not staying here, and that's one mercy. But really, Margo, you should be careful who you invite.'

'I'm sick of the way you criticize my friends,' said Margo. 'He's a perfectly ordinary, harmless Turk.'

'He would have made a charming son-in-law, don't you think?' asked Larry. 'Margo could have called the first son Ali Baba and the daughter Sesame.'

'Don't joke like that, Larry dear,' said Mother.

'I'm not joking,' said Larry. 'The old boy told me his wives were getting a bit long in the tooth and that he rather fancied Margo as number four.'

'Larry! he didn't! Disgusting old brute,' said Mother. 'It's a good thing he didn't say that to me. I'd have given him a piece of my mind. What did *you* say?'

'He was rather put off when I told him what Margo's dowry was,' said Larry.

'Dowry? What dowry?' asked Mother, mystified.

'Eleven unweaned puppies,' explained Larry.

2

Ghosts and Spiders

Take heed o' the foul fiend.

– SHAKESPEARE, *King Lear*

Throughout the year Thursday was, as far as I was concerned, the most important day of the week, for that was the day that Theodore visited us. Sometimes it would be a long family day – a drive down south and a picnic on a remote beach, or something similar; but, normally, Theo and I would set off alone on one of our excursions, as Theodore insisted on calling them. Bedecked with our collecting equipment and bags, nets, bottles, and test tubes and accompanied by the dogs, we would set out to explore the island in much the same spirit of adventure as filled the bosoms of Victorian explorers who ventured into Darkest Africa.

But not many of the Victorian explorers had the benefit of Theodore as a companion; as a handy encyclopaedia to take along on a trip, he could not be bettered. To me, he was omniscient as a god, but much nicer since he was tangible. It was not only his incredible erudition that astonished everyone who met him but his modesty. I remember how we would sit on the veranda, surrounded by the remnants of one of Mother's sumptuous teas, listening to the tired cicadas singing the evening in, plying Theodore with questions. Meticulously dressed in his tweed suit, his blonde hair and beard immaculate, his eyes would sparkle with interest as each new subject was introduced.

'Theodore,' Larry would ask, 'there's a painting up in the

monastery at Paleocastritsa that the monks say was done by Panioti Dokseras. D'you think it is?'

'Well,' Theodore would say cautiously, 'I'm afraid it's a subject about which I know very little. But I believe I'm right in saying that it's more likely to be the work of Tsadzanis . . . er . . . he did that most interesting little picture . . . in the Patera Monastery . . . you know, the one on the upper road leading north of Corfu. Now, he of course . . .'

During the next half-hour he would give an all-embracing and succinct lecture on the history of painting in the Ionian Islands since about 1242 and then end by saying: 'But if you want an *expert* opinion, there's Doctor Paramythiotis who'd give you much more information than I can.'

It was small wonder that we treated him like an oracle. The phrase 'Theo says' set the seal of authenticity on whatever item of information the person was going to vouchsafe; it was the touchstone for getting Mother's agreement to anything from the advisability of living entirely on fruit to the innocuousness of keeping scorpions in one's bedroom. Theodore was everything to everyone. With Mother he could discuss plants, particularly herbs and recipes, while keeping her supplied with reading matter from his capacious library of detective novels. With Margo he could talk of diets, exercises, and the various unguents supposed to have a miraculous effect on spots, pimples, and acne. He could keep pace effortlessly with any idea that entered the mercurial mind of my brother Larry, from Freud to peasant belief in vampires; while Leslie he could enlighten on the history of firearms in Greece or the winter habits of the hare. As far as I was concerned, with a hungry, questing, and ignorant mind, Theodore represented a fountain of knowledge on every subject from which I drank greedily.

On Thursday, Theodore would generally arrive at about ten, sitting sedately in the back of the horse-drawn cab, silver Homburg on his head, his collecting box on his knees, his walking-stick with its little gauze net on the end by his side. I, who had been up since six and peering down through the olive groves to see if he were coming, would by now have decided in despair that he had forgotten what day it was or that he had fallen down and broken his leg or that some other catastrophe had overtaken him. My relief at seeing him, grave, sedate, and intact in the back of the cab, would be considerable. The sun, up until then suffering from an eclipse, would start to shine again. Having shaken me by the hand courteously, Theodore would pay the cab-man and remind him to return at the appropriate hour in the evening. Then, hoisting his collecting bag onto his shoulders, he would contemplate the ground, rising and falling on his well-polished boots.

'I think . . . er . . . you know . . .' he would say, 'we might investigate those little ponds near . . . er . . . Kontokali. That is to say, unless there is somewhere else . . . er . . . you know . . . that you would prefer to go.'

I would say happily that the little ponds near Kontokali would suit me fine.

'Good,' Theodore would say. 'One of the reasons I particularly want to go . . . er . . . that way . . . is because the path takes us past a very good ditch . . . er . . . you know . . . that is to say, a ditch in which I have found a number of rewarding specimens.'

Talking cheerfully, we would set out, and the dogs, tongues lolling, tails wagging, would leave the shade of the tangerine trees and follow us. Presently, a panting Lugaretzia would catch up with us, carrying the bag containing our lunch which we had both forgotten.

We would make our way through the olive groves, chattering together, stopping periodically to examine a flower or a tree, bird or caterpillar; everything was grist to our mill, and Theodore knew something about everything.

'No I don't know of any way you could preserve mushrooms for your collection; whatever you use, they would . . . um . . . er

. . . you know . . . shrivel up. The best way would be to draw or paint them, or, perhaps, you know, *photograph* them. You could collect the spore patterns, though, and they are remarkably pretty. What . . . ? Well, you remove the cup of the . . . er . . . you know . . . the mushroom or toadstool and place it on a white card. The fungus must be ripe, of course, or it won't drop its spores. After a time, you remove the cap carefully from the card . . . that is to say, you take care not to smudge the spores, and you will find an attractive . . . er . . . sort of pattern is left.'

The dogs would fan out ahead of us, cocking their legs, snuffling in the dark holes that honeycombed the great, ancient olive trees, and dashing off in noisy and futile pursuit of the swallows that skimmed millimetres high over the ground down the long meandering avenues of trees. Presently, we would reach more open country where the olive groves would give way to small fields of fruit trees and maize or vineyards.

'Aha!' Theodore would say, stopping by a weedy, water-filled ditch and peering into it, his eyes gleaming, his beard bristling with enthusiasm. 'Now here's something interesting. There, do you see? Just by the end of my stick.'

I would strain my eyes but see nothing. Theodore, attaching his net to the end of his walking-stick, would make a neat dipping motion, like a man taking a fly out of his soup, and would then haul in the net.

'There, you see? It's the egg sac of the *Hydrophilus piceus* . . . er . . . that is to say, the great silver water beetle. It's the female, as you know, that spins . . . er . . . makes this sac. It may have up to fifty eggs in it; the curious thing is . . . Just a minute, while I get my forceps . . . Um . . . there . . . you see? Now, this . . . um . . . you might say, chimney, though perhaps "mast" would be better, is filled with air so the whole thing is rather like a little boat which can't capsize. The . . . er . . . air-filled mast prevents it . . . Yes, if you put it in your aquarium it should hatch out, though I must warn you that the larvae are very . . . er . . . you know . . . very *fierce* and will probably eat your other specimens. Let's see if we can catch an adult.'

Patiently as any wading bird, Theodore would pace the edge of the ditch, dipping his net in at intervals and sweeping it to and fro.

'Aha! Success!' he would exclaim at last, and carefully place a large black beetle, legs thrashing indignantly, into my eager hands.

I would admire the strong, ribbed wing cases, the bristly legs, the whole body with a faint olive green sheen.

'It's a rather slow swimmer compared with the other . . . er . . . you know . . . aquatic beetles, and it has a very curious method of swimming. Um . . . um . . . instead of using the legs together, like any other aquatic species, it uses them alternately. It gives it a . . . you know . . . very jerky appearance.'

The dogs, on these occasions, were somewhat of a mixed blessing. Sometimes they would distract us by rushing into a peasant's farmyard and attacking all his chickens, the ensuing altercation with the chicken owner wasting at least half an hour; at other times they would be quite useful, surrounding a snake so that it could not escape and barking prodigiously until we came to investigate. For me, at any rate, they were comforting to have around; Roger, like a stocky, unclipped black lamb; Widdle, elegant in his silky coat of fox-red and black; and Puke, looking like a miniature liver and white-spotted bull terrier. Occasionally they would get bored if we stopped for too long, but generally they lay patiently in the shade, pink tongues flicking, lolling, tails wagging amicably whenever they caught our eye.

It was Roger that first introduced me to one of the most beautiful spiders in the world, with the elegant sounding name of *Eresus niger*. We had walked a considerable distance and at noon, when the sun was at its hottest, decided to stop and eat our picnic in the shade. We sat down at the edge of an olive grove and started feasting on sandwiches and ginger beer.

Normally, when Theodore and I had our meal the dogs would sit around, panting and gazing at us imploringly, since they were always of the opinion that our food was in some way superior to theirs, and so having finished their rations would try to obtain largesse from us, using all the wiles of an Asiatic beggar. On this particular occasion, Widdle and Puke rolled their eyes, panted and gasped, and tried by every means possible to show us that they were at death's door from starvation. Unusually, Roger did not join in. Instead he was sitting out in the sunshine in front of a patch of brambles watching something with great intentness. I went over to see what was intriguing him to such an extent that he was ignoring my sandwich crusts. At first I could not see what it was; then suddenly I saw something so startlingly beautiful that I could hardly believe my eyes. It was a tiny spider, the size of a pea, and at first glance it looked like an animated ruby or a moving drop of blood. Uttering a whoop of joyous enthusiasm, I rushed to my collecting bag and got a glass-topped pill box in which to catch this brilliant creature. He was not easily caught however, for he could take prodigious jumps for his size, and I had to pursue him round and round the bramble bush for some time before I had him safely locked in my pill box. Triumphantly I carried this gorgeous spider over to Theodore.

'Aha!' said Theodore, taking a swig of ginger beer, before producing his magnifying glass the better to examine my capture. 'Yes an *Eresus niger* . . . um . . . yes . . . this is of course the male, such a pretty creature, the female is . . . er . . . you know . . . all black, but the male is very brightly coloured.'

On close examination through a magnifying glass, the spider turned out to be even more beautiful than I had thought. Its forequarters, or cephalo-thorax, were velvety black with little specks of scarlet at the edges. Its rather stocky legs were ringed with white bands, so that it looked ridiculously as though it was wearing striped pants. But it was its abdomen that was really eye-catching; this was vivid huntsman's red, marked with three round black spots rimmed with white hairs. It was the most spectacular spider that I had ever seen and I was determined to try to get it a mate and see if I could breed them. I subjected the bramble bush and the terrain around it to a minute scrutiny, but with no success. Theodore explained to me that the female spider digs a burrow about three inches long, lined with tough silk. 'You can distinguish it from other spiders' burrows,' he said, 'because the silk at one point is protruded like an apron and this forms a sort of roof over the mouth of the tunnel. Moreover, the outside is covered with bits and pieces of the female spider's past meals, in the shape of grasshopper legs and wing cases and the remains of beetles.'

Armed with this knowledge I went the following day and combed the entire area round the bramble bush once again. After spending the whole afternoon on it, I still did not meet with success. Irritably I started on my way home to tea. I took a short cut that led me over some small hills covered with the giant Mediterranean heath which seemed particularly to flourish in this sandy and rather desiccated terrain. It was the sort of wild, dry country, favoured by ant lions, fritillaries and other sun-loving butterflies, lizards and snakes. As I walked along I suddenly came upon the ancient skull of a sheep. In one of its empty eye sockets a praying mantis had laid its curious egg cases, which to me always looked like an oval pudding of some sort, made out of ribbed sponge cake. I was squatting down examining this and wondering whether to take it to the villa to add it to my collection, when I suddenly saw a burrow of a female spider, just as Theodore had described it.

I pulled out my knife and with great care excavated a large wedge of soil, which when levered out, contained not only the spider, but her burrow as well. Delighted with my success, I placed it carefully in my collecting bag and hurried back to the villa. I had already got the male installed in a small aquarium, but I felt that the female was worthy of better things.

I unceremoniously evicted two frogs and a baby tortoise from my largest aquarium, and made it ready for her. When it was finished, decorated with bits of heather and interesting branches of moss, I carefully placed the wedge of earth containing her and her nest on the bottom and left her to recover from this sudden and unexpected house move.

Three days later I introduced the male. At first it was very dull, because he did nothing more romantic than rush about like an animated hot ember, trying to catch the various insects I had put in the aquarium as provender. But then, early one morning when I went to look, I discovered that he had found the lair of the female. He was walking to and fro around it, in a curious jerky fashion, his striped legs stiff, his body trembling with what one could only conclude was passion. He strutted about in great excitement for a minute or so, then approached the burrow and disappeared under the roof. Here to my annoyance I could no longer observe him, but I presumed that he must be mating with the female. He was in the burrow for about an hour, and then he emerged jauntily and continued his carefree pursuit of the bluebottles and grasshoppers that I had provided for him. However, I removed him to another aquarium as a precautionary measure since I knew that in some species, the female had cannibalistic habits and was not averse to making a light snack of her husband.

The rest of the drama I could not witness in detail, but I saw bits of it. The female eventually laid a bunch of eggs which she carefully encapsulated in a web. This balloon of eggs she stored down her tunnel, but brought up each day to hang under the roof. Whether she did this so that the eggs could get more heat from the sun, or to allow them access to more fresh air I was not certain. The egg case was disguised by having small morsels of beetle and grasshopper remains attached to the outside.

As the days passed she proceeded to add to the roof over the tunnel and finally constructed a silken roof above ground. I watched this architectural achievement for some considerable time and then, as I could see nothing, I grew impatient. With the aid of a scalpel and a long darning needle I carefully opened up the silken room. To my astonishment I found that it was surrounded by cells in which all the young spiders sat, while in the central hall lay the corpse of their mother. It was a macabre, yet touching sight; the babies all sitting round the mortal remains of their mother, in a sort of spiders' wake. When the babies hatched, however, I was forced to let them all go. Providing food for some eighty minute spiders was a problem in catering which even I, enthusiastic though I was, could not solve.

Among the numerous friends that Larry saw fit to inflict us with was a strange pair of painters called Lumis Bean and Harry Bunny. They were both American and deeply devoted to each other, so much so that within twenty-four hours they were known privately to the family as Lumy Lover and Harry Honey. They were young, very good looking, with the fluid boneless grace of movement that you expect from coloured people but rarely get in Europeans. They wore perhaps a shade too many gold bangles and a *soupçon* too much scent and hair cream, but they were nice and, what was unusual in the painters who came to stay, hard-working. Like so many Americans, they were possessed of a charming *naïveté* and earnestness and these qualities, as far as Leslie was concerned at any rate, made them ideal subjects for practical jokes. I used to participate in these and then relate the results to Theodore, who used to get as much innocent pleasure as Leslie and I did out of the result. Every Thursday I had to report progress and I sometimes got the feeling that Theodore looked forward to the jokes with more interest than he did the news of my menagerie.

Leslie had a genius for practical jokes and the child-like innocence of our two guests inspired him to new heights. It was shortly after their arrival that he got them to congratulate

Spiro most prettily on his final success in taking out Turkish naturalization papers. Spiro, who, like most Greeks, considered the Turks to be slightly more malevolent than Satan himself and who had spent several years fighting them, exploded like a volcano. Fortunately, Mother was near at hand and moved swiftly between the white-faced protesting, bewildered Lumy and Harry and Spiro's barrel-shaped, muscular bulk. She looked not unlike a diminutive Victorian missionary facing a charging rhino.

'Gollys, Mrs Durrells,' Spiro roared, his gargoyle features purple with rage, his ham-like hands clenched. 'Lets me pokes them one.'

'Now, now, Spiro,' said Mother, 'I'm sure it's all a mistake. I'm sure there's an explanation.'

'They calls me a bastard Turks!' roared Spiro. 'I'm Greeks. I'm no bastard Turks.'

'Of course you're not,' said Mother soothingly, 'I'm sure it was just a mistake.'

'Mistakes!' bellowed Spiro, his plurals coming thick and fast with rage. 'Mistakes! I'm nots goings to be called a bastards Turks by these bloody fairies, if you'll excuse my language, Mrs Durrells.'

It was some considerable time before Mother could calm Spiro and get a coherent story out of the terrified Lumy Lover and Harry Honey. The episode gave her a severe headache and she was very cross with Leslie.

Some time later Mother had to move them out of the bedroom we had given them because it was going to be decorated. She put them temporarily into one of our large, gloomy attics. This gave Leslie the opportunity of telling them the story of the headless bell-ringer of Kontokali who died in the attic. He was the fiend who in 1604, or thereabouts, was official executioner and torturer to Corfu. First he would torture his victims and then he would ring his bell before they were finally beheaded. Getting slightly fed up with him, the villagers of Kontokali broke into the villa one night and beheaded him. Now, as a prelude to seeing his ghost, headless and with a gory stump, you would hear him frantically ringing his bell.

Having convinced our earnest couple of the authenticity of this fable by getting it vouched for by Theodore, Leslie borrowed fifty-two alarm clocks from a friendly clock-maker in town, prised up two floor boards in the attic, and placed the clocks, all set to go off at three in the morning, carefully between the joists.

The effect of fifty-two alarm clocks all going off simultaneously was most gratifying. Not only did Lumy and Harry vacate the attic with all speed, uttering cries of terror, but in their haste they tripped each other up and, clasped in each other's arms, fell heavily down the attic stairs. The resulting turmoil woke the whole house and it was some time before we could convince them that it was a joke and soothe them with brandy. Mother, together with our guests, once again had a severe headache next day and would hardly talk to Leslie at all.

The affair of the invisible flamingoes came about one day quite casually as we were sitting having tea on the veranda. Theodore had asked our pair of Americans how their work was progressing.

'Darling Theo,' said Harry Honey, 'we're getting on divinely, simple divinely, aren't we, lover?'

'We sure are,' said Lumy Lover, 'we sure are. The light here is fantastic, simply fantastic. It's as though the sun were closer to the earth somehow, you know.'

'It sure does seem that way,' Harry Honey agreed. 'It seems just like, as Lumy says, the sun is right down low, beaming straight at little old us.'

'I said that to you this morning, Harry Honey, didn't I?' said Lumy Lover.

'You did, Lumy, you did. Right up there by that little barn, do you remember, you said to me . . .'

'Have another cup of tea,' Mother interrupted, for she knew

from experience that these post-mortems to prove the together-
ness of these two could go on indefinitely.

The conversation drifted on into the realms of art and I scarcely
listened until suddenly my attention was riveted by Lumy Lover
saying:

'Flamingoes! Ooh, Harry Honey, flamingoes! My favourite
birds. Where, Les, where?'

'Oh, over there,' said Leslie, giving a wave that embraced
Corfu, Albania, and the better half of Greece. 'Great flocks of
them.'

Theodore, I could see, was holding his breath, as was I, in
case Mother, Margo, or Larry should say anything to upset this
outrageous lie.

'Flamingoes?' said Mother interestedly. 'I didn't know there
were any flamingoes here.'

'Yes,' said Leslie solemnly, 'hundreds of them.'

'Did you know there were flamingoes, Theodore?' asked
Mother.

'I . . . er . . . you know . . . caught a glimpse of them down on
Lake Hakiopoulos,' said Theodore, not deviating from the truth
but omitting to mention that this had been three years previously
and the only time flamingoes had ever visited Corfu. I had a
handful of pink feathers to commemorate it.

'Jee-hovah!' said Lumy Lover. 'Could we catch a glimpse of
them, Les, dear? D'you suppose we could sneak up on them?'

'Sure,' said Leslie airily, 'easiest thing in the world. They
migrate over the same route every day.'

The following morning Leslie came into my room carrying
what looked like a strange form of trumpet made out of a cow's
horn. I asked him what it was and he grinned.

'It's a flamingo decoy,' he said with satisfaction.

I was deeply interested and said I had never heard of a flamingo
decoy.

'Neither have I,' Leslie admitted. 'It's an old cow's horn powder container, for muzzle-loaders, you know. But the end's broken off so you can blow on it.'

By way of illustration, he raised the pointed end of the cow's horn to his lips and blew. The horn produced a long, sonorous sound somewhere between a foghorn and a raspberry, with very vibrant overtones. I listened critically and said that it did not sound a bit like a flamingo.

'Yes, but I bet Lumy Lover and Harry Honey don't know that,' said Leslie. 'Now all I need is to borrow your flamingo feathers.'

I was somewhat reluctant to part with such rare specimens from my collection until Leslie explained why he wanted them and promised that they would come to no harm.

At ten o'clock Lumy and Harry appeared, having been dressed by Leslie for flamingo hunting. Each wore a large straw hat and gumboots, for, as Leslie explained, we might have to follow the flamingoes into the swamps. Lumy and Harry were flushed and excited at the prospect of this adventure and their enthusiasm when Leslie demonstrated the flamingo decoy knew no bounds. They blew such resounding blasts on it that the dogs went mad and howled and barked and Larry, furious, leaned out of his bedroom window and said that if we were all going to carry on like a meet of the bloody Quorn hunt he was going to move.

'And you're old enough to know better!' was his parting shot as he slammed the window, addressed to Mother who had just joined us to see what the noise was all about.

We eventually got our bold hunters into the field and walked them about two miles, by which time their enthusiasm for flamingo hunting was on the wane. Then we scrambled them up to the top of an almost inaccessible hillock, stationed them inside a bramble bush and told them to keep calling to attract the flamingoes. For half an hour they blew on the horn in turns with great dedication, but their wind started to give out. Towards the end the noise they were making was beginning to sound more like the despairing cry of a mortally wounded bull elephant than anything in the bird line.

Then it was my turn. Panting and excited, I rushed up the hillock and told our hunters that their efforts had not been in vain. The flamingoes had indeed responded but, unfortunately, they had settled in a valley below a hill half a mile to the east. If they hurried there, they would find Leslie waiting. I was lost in admiration at their American tenacity. Thumping along in their ill-fitting gumboots, they galloped off to the farther hill, pausing periodically as per my instructions to blow gaspingly on the flamingo decoy. When, in an ocean of sweat, they reached the top of the hill, they found Leslie. He said that if they remained there and continued to blow on the decoy he would make his way around the valley and drive the flamingoes up to them. He gave them his gun and game bag so that, as he explained, he could stalk more easily. Then he faded away.

It was at this point that our favourite policeman, Filimona Kontakosa entered the act. Filimona was without doubt the fattest and most somnambulistic of all the Corfu policemen; he had been in the force for thirty-odd years and owed his lack of promotion to the fact that he had never made an arrest. He had explained to us at great length that he was, in fact, physically incapable of doing so; the mere thought of being harsh to a criminal would fill his pansy-dark eyes with tears, and on feast days the slightest sign of altercation among the wine-happy villagers and you could see him waddling resolutely in the opposite direction. He preferred to lead a gentle life and every fortnight or so he would pay us a visit to admire Leslie's gun collection (for which we had no permits) and bring gifts of smuggled tobacco to Larry, flowers to Mother and Margo, and sugared almonds to me. He had, in his youth, been a deck hand on a cargo boat and had acquired a tenuous command of the English language, and this, combined with the fact that all Corfiotes adore practical jokes, made him perfect for our purposes. He rose to the occasion magnificently.

He waddled to the top of the hill, resplendent in his uniform, every kilo of him looking the personification of law and order and a credit to the force. He found our hunters blowing in a desultory fashion on their decoy. Benignly, he asked them what they were doing. Responding to kindness like two puppies, Lumy Lover and Harry Honey were only too delighted to compliment Filimona on his truncated English and explain matters to him. To the Americans' consternation, he suddenly changed from a kindly, twinkling, fat policeman to the cold, brutal personification of officialdom.

'You no know flamongoes you no shoot?' he snapped at them. 'Is forbidden to shoot flamongoes!'

'But, darling, we're not shooting them,' said Lumy Lover falteringly. 'We only want to *see* them.'

'Yes. Gee, you got it all wrong,' said Harry Honey ingratiatingly. 'We don' wanna shoot the little fellas; we just wanna see 'em. No shoot, see?'

'If you no shoot, why you have gun?' asked Filimona.

'Oh, that,' said Lumy Lover, reddening. 'That belongs to a friend of ours . . . er . . . amigo . . . savvy?'

'Yeah, yeah,' said Harry Honey, 'friend of ours. Les Durrell. Maybe you know him? He's well known around these parts.'

Filimona stared at them coldly and implacably.

'I no know this friend,' he said at last. 'Please to open bag.'

'Well, now, steady on, see here,' protested Lumy Lover. 'This isn't *our* bag, officer.'

'No, no,' said Harry Honey. 'It belongs to this friend of ours, Durrell.'

'You have gun. You have bag,' Filimona pointed out. 'Please to open bag.'

'Well, I must say I think you're exceeding your duty just a tiny bit, officer, I really do,' said Lumy Lover, while Harry Honey nodded eager assent. 'But if it'll make you feel any easier, well then, I don't suppose there's much harm in letting you have a little peek.'

He wrestled briefly with the straps of the bag, opened it, and handed it to Filimona. The policeman peered into it, gave a triumphant grunt, and pulled from the interior the plucked and headless body of a chicken to which were adhering numerous bright pink feathers. Both the stalwart flamingo hunters went white with emotion.

'But see here now . . . er . . . wait a moment . . .' Lumy Lover began, and his voice trailed away before Filimona's accusing look.

'Is forbidden shoot flamongo, I tell you,' said Filimona. 'I arrest you both.'

He herded them, alarmed and protesting, down to the village police station and kept them there for several hours, during which they nearly went mad writing out statements and getting so muddled through nerves and frustration that they kept contradicting each other's stories. To add to their alarm Leslie and I had assembled a crowd of our village friends who shouted and roared in the terrifying way Greeks have, periodically bellowing 'Flamongo!' and throwing the odd stone at the police station.

Eventually Filimona allowed his captives to send a note to Larry, who stormed down into the village, told Filimona it would be more to the point if he caught some evil-doers rather than indulged in practical jokes, and brought our two flamingo hunters back to the bosom of the family.

'This has got to stop!' said Larry angrily. 'I will not have my guests subjected to ill-bred japes perpetrated by a pair of half-witted brothers.'

I must say Lumy Lover and Harry Honey were wonderful.

'Don't be angry, Larry darling,' said Lumy Lover. 'It's just high spirits. It's just as much our fault as Les'.'

'Yes,' said Harry Honey. 'Lumy's right. It's our fault for being so gullible, silly old us.'

To show that there was no ill-feeling, they even went down to the town and brought back a crate of champagne to have a party and they went down to the village themselves to fetch Filimona up to the house for it. They sat on the terrace, one on each side of the policeman, toasting him coyly in champagne while Filimona, in a surprisingly good tenor, sang love songs that brightened his great dark eyes with tears.

'You know,' Lumy Lover confided to Larry at the height of the party, 'he'd be really very good looking if he went on a diet. But don't tell Harry I said so, darling, will you?'

3

The Garden of the Gods

Behold, the Heavens do open, the Gods look down and the
unnatural scene they laugh at.

– SHAKESPEARE, *Coriolanus*

The island lay bent like a misshapen bow, its two tips nearly
touching the Greek and Albanian coastlines, and the blue waters
of the Ionian Sea were caught in its curve like a blue lake. Outside
our villa was a wide flagstoned veranda roofed with an ancient
vine from which the great green clusters of grapes hung like
chandeliers; from here one looked out over the sunken garden
full of tangerine trees and the silver-green olive groves to the sea,
blue and smooth as a flower petal.

In fine weather we always had our meals on the veranda at
the rickety marble-topped table and it was here that all the major
family decisions were taken. It was at breakfast that there was
liable to be most acrimony and dissension, for it was then that
letters, if any, were read and plans for the day made, remade,
and discarded; it was during these early morning sessions that
the family fortunes were organized, albeit haphazardly, so that a
simple request for an omelet might end in a three-month camping
expedition to a remote beach, as had happened on one occasion.
So when we assembled in the brittle morning light we were
never quite sure how the day was going to get on its feet. To
begin with, one had to step warily for tempers were fragile but,
gradually, under the influence of tea, coffee, toast, home-made
marmalade, eggs and bowls of fruit, a lessening of the early

morning tension would be felt and a more benign atmosphere begin to permeate the veranda.

The morning that heralded the arrival of the Count among us was no different from any other. We had all reached the final cup of coffee stage and each was busy with his own thoughts; Margo, my sister, her blonde hair done up in a bandana, was musing over two pattern books, humming gaily but tunelessly to herself; Leslie had finished his coffee and produced a small automatic pistol from his pocket, dismantled it, and was absent-mindedly cleaning it with his handkerchief; my mother was perusing the pages of a cookery book in pursuit of a recipe for lunch, her lips moving soundlessly, occasionally breaking off to stare into space while she tried to remember if she had the necessary ingredients; Larry, clad in a multi-coloured dressing gown, was eating cherries with one hand and reading his mail with the other.

I was busy feeding my latest acquisition, a young jackdaw, who was such a singularly slow eater that I had christened him Gladstone, having been told that that statesman always chewed everything several hundred times. While waiting for him to digest each mouthful I stared down the hill at the beckoning sea and planned my day. Should I take my donkey, Sally, and make a trip to the high olive groves in the centre of the island to try to catch the agamas that lived on the glittering gypsum cliffs, where they basked in the sun, tantalizing me by wagging their yellow heads and puffing out their orange throats? Or should I go down to the small lake in the valley behind the villa, where the dragon-fly larvae should be hatching? Or, should I perhaps – happiest thought of all – take my latest acquisition, my boat, on a major sea trip?

In spring the almost enclosed sheet of water that separated Corfu from the mainland would be a pale and delicate blue; then, as spring settled into hot, crackling summer, it seemed to stain the still sea a deeper and more unreal colour that in some lights was like the violet blue of a rainbow, a blue that faded to a rich jade-green in the shallows. In the evening when the sun sank it was as if it were drawing a brush across the sea's surface, streaking and blurring it to purples smudged with gold, silver, tangerine, and pale pink.

To look at this placid, land-locked sea in summer it seemed mild-mannered, a blue meadow that breathed gently and evenly along the shoreline; it was difficult to believe that it could be fierce; but even on a still, summer's day, somewhere in the eroded hills of the mainland, a hot fierce wind would suddenly be born and leap, screaming, at the island, turning the sea so dark it was almost black, combing each wave crest into a sheaf of white froth and urging and harrying them like a herd of panic-stricken blue horses until they crashed exhausted on the shore and died in a hissing shroud of foam. And in winter, under an iron-grey sky, the sea would lift sullen muscles of almost colourless waves, ice-cold and unfriendly, veined here and there with mud and debris that the winter rains swept out of the valleys and into the bay.

To me, this blue kingdom was a treasure-house of strange beasts which I longed to collect and observe. At first it was frustrating for I could only peck along the shoreline like some forlorn sea-bird, capturing the small fry in the shallows and occasionally being tantalized by something mysterious and wonderful cast upon the shore. But then I got my boat, the good ship *Bootle-Bumtrinket*, and the whole of this kingdom was opened up for me, from the golden red castles of rock and their deep pools and underwater caves in the north to the long, glittering white sand dunes lying like snow drifts in the south.

I decided on the sea trip, and so intent was I on planning it that I had quite forgotten Gladstone, who was wheezing at me with the breathless indignation of an asthmatic in a fog.

'If you *must* keep that harmonium covered with feathers,' said Larry, glancing up irritably, 'you might at least teach it to sing properly.'

He was obviously not in the mood to receive a lecture on the jackdaw's singing abilities so I kept quiet and shut Gladstone up with a mammoth mouthful of food.

'Marco's sending Count Rossignol for a couple of days,' Larry said casually to Mother.

'Who's he?' asked Mother.

'I don't know,' said Larry.

Mother straightened her glasses and looked at him.

'What do you mean, you don't know?' she asked.

'What I say,' said Larry. 'I don't know; I've never met him.'

'Well, who's Marco?'

'I don't know; I've never met him either. He's a good artist though.'

'Larry, dear, you can't start inviting people you don't know to stay,' said Mother. 'It's bad enough entertaining the ones you *do* know without starting on the ones you don't.'

'What's knowing them got to do with it?' asked Larry, puzzled.

'Well, if you know them, at least they know what to expect,' Mother pointed out.

'Expect?' said Larry coldly. 'You'd think I was inviting them to stay in a ghetto or something, the way you go on.'

'No, no, dear, I don't mean *that*,' said Mother, 'but it's just that this house so seldom seems normal. I do try but we don't seem able to live like other people somehow.'

'Well if they come to stay here they must put up with us,' said Larry. 'Anyway, you can't blame *me*; I didn't invite him. Marco's sending him.'

'But that's what I mean,' said Mother. 'Complete strangers sending complete strangers to us, as if we were an hotel or something.'

'Trouble with you is you're anti-social,' said Larry.

'And so would you be if you had to do the cooking,' said Mother indignantly. 'It's enough to make one want to be a hermit.'

'Well, as soon as the Count's been, you can *be* a hermit if you want to. No one's stopping you.'

'A lot of chance *I* get to be a hermit, with you inviting streams of people to stay.'

'Of course you can, if you organize yourself,' said Larry. 'Leslie will build you a cave down in the olive groves; you can get Margo to stitch a few of Gerry's less-smelly animal skins together, collect a pot of blackberries, and there you are. I can bring people down to see you. "This is my mother," I shall say, "she has deserted us to become a hermit."'

Mother glared at him.

'Really, Larry, you do make me cross sometimes,' she said.

'I'm going down to see Leonora's baby,' said Margo. 'Is there anything you want from the village?'

'Oh yes,' said Larry, 'that reminds me. Leonora's asked me to be a god-parent to the brat.'

Leonora was our maid Lugaretzia's daughter, who used to come up to the house and help us when we had a party and who, because of her sparkling good looks, was a great favourite of Larry's.

'You? A godfather!' said Margo in astonishment. 'I thought godfathers were supposed to be pure and religious and things.'

'How nice of her,' said Mother doubtfully. 'But it's a bit odd, isn't it?'

'Not half so odd as it would be if she asked him to be father,' said Leslie.

'Leslie, dear, don't say things like that in front of Gerry, even in fun,' said Mother. 'Are you going to accept, Larry?'

'Yes. Why shouldn't the poor little thing have the benefit of my guidance?'

'Ha!' said Margo derisively. 'Well, I shall tell Leonora that if she thinks you're going to be pure and religious she's trying to make a pig's poke out of a sow's ear.'

'If you can translate that into Greek, you're welcome to tell her,' said Larry.

'My Greek's just as good as yours,' replied Margo belligerently.

'Now, now, dears, don't quarrel,' said Mother. 'I do wish you wouldn't clean your guns with your handkerchief, Leslie; the oil is impossible to get out.'

'Well, I've got to clean them with *something*,' said Leslie aggrievedly.

At this point I told Mother I was going to spend the day exploring the coast and could I have a picnic?

'Yes, dear,' she said absently. 'Tell Lugaretzia to organize something for you. But do be careful, dear, and don't go into very deep water. Don't catch a chill and . . . watch out for sharks.'

To Mother, every sea, no matter how shallow or benign, was an evil and tumultuous body of water, full of tidal waves, water spouts, typhoons, and whirlpools, inhabited entirely by giant octopus and squids and savage, sabre-toothed sharks, all of whom had the killing and eating of one or other of her progeny as their main objective in life. Assuring her that I would take great care, I hurried off to the kitchen, collected the food for myself and my animals, assembled my collecting equipment, whistled the dogs, and set off down the hill to the jetty where my boat was moored.

The *Bootle-Bumtrinket*, being Leslie's first effort in boatbuilding was almost circular and flat-bottomed, so that, with her attractive colour scheme of orange and white stripes, she looked not unlike an ornate celluloid duck. She was a friendly, stalwart craft but owing to her shape and her lack of keel she became very flustered in anything like a heavy sea and would threaten to turn upside down and proceed that way, a thing she was prone to do in moments of stress. When I went on any long expeditions in her I always took plenty of food and water in case we were blown off course and shipwrecked, and I hugged the coastline as much as possible so that I could make a dash for safety should the

Bootle-Bumtrinket be assaulted by a sudden sirocco. Owing to my boat's shape, she could not wear a tall mast without turning over and her pocket-handkerchief-sized sail could only garner and harvest the tiniest cupfuls of wind; thus, for the most part, she was propelled from point to point with oars. When we had a full crew on board – three dogs, an owl, and sometimes a pigeon – and were carrying a full cargo – some two dozen containers full of seawater and specimens – she was a back-aching load to push through the water.

Roger was a fine dog to take to sea and he thoroughly enjoyed it; he also took a deep and intelligent interest in marine life and would lie for hours, ears pricked, watching the strange convolutions of the brittle starfish in a collecting bottle. Widdle and Puke, on the other hand, were not sea dogs and were really most at home tracking down some not-too-fierce quarry in the myrtle groves; when they came to sea they tried to be helpful but rarely succeeded and in a crisis would start howling or jumping overboard, or, if thirsty, drinking seawater and then vomiting over your feet just as you were doing a tricky bit of navigation. I could never really tell if Ulysses, my scops owl, liked sea trips; he would sit dutifully wherever I placed him, his eyes half-closed, wings pulled in, looking like one of the more malevolent carvings of oriental deities. My pigeon, Quilp – he was the son of my original pigeon, Quasimodo – adored boating: he would take over the *Bootle-Bumtrinket*'s minute foredeck and carry on as though it were the promenade deck of the *Queen Mary*. He would pace up and down, pausing to do a quick waltz occasionally and, with pouting chest, would give a contralto concert, looking strangely like a large opera singer on a sea voyage. Only if the weather became inclement would he get nervous and would then fly down and nestle in the captain's lap for solace.

On this particular day I had decided to pay a visit to a small bay, one side of which was formed by a tiny island surrounded by reefs in which there dwelled a host of fascinating creatures.

My particular quarry was a peacock blenny which I knew lived in profusion in that shallow water. Blennies are curious looking fish with elongated bodies, some four inches long, shaped rather like an eel; with their pop eyes and thick lips they are vaguely reminiscent of a hippopotamus. In the breeding season the males became most colourful, with a dark spot behind the eyes edged with sky blue, a dull orange hump-like crest on the head, and a darkish body covered with ultramarine or violet spots. The throat was pale sea-green with darkish stripes on it. In contrast, the females were light olive with pale blue spots and leaf-green fins. I was anxious to capture some of these colourful little fish, since it was their breeding season, and I was hoping to establish a colony of them in one of my aquariums so that I could watch their courtship.

After half an hour's stiff rowing we reached the bay which was rimmed with silvery olive groves and great golden tangles of broom that sent its heavy musky scent out over the still clear waters. I anchored the *Bootle-Bumtrinket* in two feet of water near the reef, and then, taking off my clothes, and armed with my butterfly net and a wide-mouthed jar, I stepped into the gin-clear sea which was as warm as a bath.

Everywhere there was such a profusion of life that it required stern concentration not to be diverted from one's task. Here the sea-slugs, like huge warty brown sausages, lay in battalions among the multi-coloured weeds. On the rocks were the dark purple, black pin-cushions of the sea urchins, their spines turning to and fro like compass needles. Here and there, stuck to the rocks like enlarged woodlice, were the chitons and the brightly freckled top shells, moving about, each containing either its rightful owner or else a usurper in the shape of a red-faced, scarlet-clawed hermit crab. A small weed-covered rock would suddenly walk away from under your foot, revealing itself as a spider crab, with his back a neatly planted garden of weeds, to camouflage him from his enemies.

Soon I came to the area of the bay that I knew the blennies favoured. It was not long before I spotted a fine male, brilliant and almost iridescent in his courting outfit of many colours. Cautiously I edged my net towards him and he retreated suspiciously, gulping at me with his pouting lips. I made a sudden sweep with the net but he was too wary and avoided it with ease. Several times I tried and failed and after each attempt he retreated a little further. Finally, tiring of my attentions, he flipped off and took refuge in his home, which was the broken half of a terracotta pot of the sort that fishermen put down to trap unwary octopuses in. Although he was under the impression he had reached safety, it was in fact his undoing, for I simply scooped him up, pot and all, in my net and then transferred him and his home to one of the bigger containers in the boat.

Flushed with success I continued my hunting, and by lunch-time had caught two green wives for my blenny, as well as a baby cuttlefish and an interesting species of starfish, which I had not seen previously. The sun was now blistering hot and most of the sea life had disappeared under rocks to lurk in the shade. I went on shore, to sit under the olive trees and eat my lunch. The air was heavy with the scent of broom and full of the zinging cries of cicadas. As I ate, I watched a huge dragon-green lizard with bright blue eye markings along his body, carefully stalk and catch a black and white striped swallowtail butterfly. No mean feat, since swallowtails rarely sit still for long and their flight is erratic and unpredictable. Moreover the lizard caught the butterfly on the wing – leaping some sixteen inches off the ground to do so.

Presently, having finished my lunch, I loaded up the boat and getting my canine crew on board, began to row home so that I could settle my blennies in their aquariums. Reaching the villa, I placed the male blenny, together with his pot, in the centre of the larger of my aquariums and then carefully introduced the two females. Although I watched them for the rest of the afternoon they did nothing spectacular. The male merely lay, gulping and pouting, in the entrance of his pot while the females gulped and pouted with equal zest at either end of the aquarium.

The following morning when I got up I found, to my intense annoyance, that the blennies must have been active at dawn for a number of eggs had been laid inside, on the roof of the pot. Which female was responsible for this I did not know, but the male was a very protective and resolute father, attacking my finger ferociously when I picked up the pot to look at the eggs.

Determined not to miss any of the drama I rushed to get my breakfast and ate it squatting in front of the aquarium, my gaze fixed on the blennies. The family, who had hitherto regarded fish as the least of potential trouble-makers among my pets, began to have doubts about the blennies, for as the morning wore on I would importune each passing member of the household to bring me an orange, or a drink of water, or to sharpen my pencil for me, for I was whiling away the time drawing the blennies in my diary. My lunch was served at the aquarium and as the long, hot afternoon wore on I began to feel sleepy. The dogs, long since bored with a vigil they could not understand, had gone off into the olive groves and left me and the blennies to our own devices.

The male blenny was deep in his pot, scarcely visible. One of the females had wedged herself behind some small rocks, while the other sat gulping on the sand. Occupying the aquarium with the fish were two small spider crabs, each encrusted with weeds, and one wearing a small, pink sea anemone like a rakish bonnet on his head. It was this crab who really precipitated the romance of the blennies. He was wandering about the floor of the aquarium, delicately popping bits of debris into his mouth with his claws, like a finicky spinster eating cucumber sandwiches, when he happened to wander up to the entrance of the pot. Immediately the male blenny emerged, glowing with iridescent colours, ready for battle. He swooped down onto the spider crab and bit at it viciously time after time. The crab, after a few ineffectual attempts to ward off the fish with its claws, meekly turned tail and scuttled off. This left the blenny, glowing virtuously, as the victor and he sat just outside his pot looking smug.

Now a very unexpected thing happened. The female on the sand had had her attention attracted by the fight with the crab and now she swam over and stopped some four or five inches away from the male. At the sight of her he became very excited and his colouring seemed to glow all the more. Then suddenly he attacked the female. He dashed at her and bit at her head, at the same time curving his body like a bow and giving her blows with his tail. I watched this behaviour in amazement until I realized that throughout this beating and buffeting the female was completely passive and made no attempt at retaliation. What I was witnessing was not an unprovoked attack, but a belligerent courtship display. As I watched I saw that, with slaps from his tail and bites at the female's head, the male blenny was in fact herding her towards his pot as a sheepdog herds sheep.

Realizing that once they entered the pot I should lose sight of them, I dashed into the house and came back with an instrument I normally used for examining birds' nests. It was a bamboo pole with a small mirror set at an angle on the end. If there was a birds' nest out of reach you could use the mirror as a periscope to enable you to examine the eggs or fledglings. Now I used it in the same way, but upside down. By the time I got back the blennies were disappearing into the pot. With great caution, so as not to disturb them, I lowered the mirror on the bamboo into the water and manoeuvred it until it was at the entrance of the pot. When I had jiggled it into position, I found I not only got a good view of the interior of the pot, but that the sunlight reflected off the mirror and lit up the inside beautifully.

To begin with the two fish stayed close together, there was a lot of fin waving but nothing much else. The male's attacks on the female ceased, now she was safely in the pot, and he seemed more conciliatory towards her. After about ten minutes the female moved from the position alongside him and proceeded to lay a small cluster of transparent eggs which were stuck to the smooth side of the pot like frog spawn. This done she moved and the male took up his position over the eggs. Unfortunately, the female got between me and him, so I could not see him actually fertilize the eggs, but it was obvious that that was what he was doing. Then the female, feeling that her part of the procedure was over, swam out of the pot and across the aquarium, displaying no further interest in the eggs. The male, however, spent some time fussing around them and came to lay in the mouth of the pot on guard.

I waited eagerly for the baby blennies to appear, but there must have been something wrong with the aeration of the water for only two of the eggs hatched. One of the diminutive babies was, to my horror, eaten by his own mother, before my eyes. Not wishing to have a double case of infanticide on my conscience, and lacking aquarium space, I put the second baby in a jar and rowed down the coast to the bay where I had caught his parents. Here I released him with my blessing, in the clear tepid water ringed with golden broom, where I hoped that he would rear many multi-coloured offspring of his own.

Three days later the Count appeared. He was tall and slender, with tightly curled hair as golden as a silkworm cocoon, shining with oil, a delicately curled moustache of a similar hue, and slightly protuberant eyes of a pale and unpleasant green. He alarmed Mother by arriving with a huge wardrobe trunk and she was convinced that he had come to stay for the summer. But we soon found that the Count found himself so attractive he felt it necessary to change his clothes about eight times a day to do justice to himself. His clothes were such elegant confections, beautifully hand-stitched and of such exquisite materials, that Margo was torn between envy at his wardrobe and disgust at his effeminacy. Combined with this narcissistic preoccupation with himself, the Count had other equally objectionable character-istics. He drenched himself in a scent so thick that it was almost visible and he had only to spend a second in a room to permeate the whole atmosphere, while the cushions he leaned against and the chairs he sat in reeked for days afterwards. His English was limited, but this did not prevent him from expounding on any subject with a sort of sneering dogmatism that made everyone's hackles rise. His philosophy, if any, could be summed up in the phrase, 'We do it better in France', which he used repeatedly about everything. He had such a thoroughly Gallic interest in the edibi-lity of everything with which he came in contact that one could have been pardoned for thinking him the reincarnation of a goat.

He arrived, unfortunately, in time for lunch, and by the end of the meal, without really trying, he had succeeded in alienating everybody including the dogs. It was, in its way, quite a *tour de force* to be able to irritate five people of such different character apparently without even being aware of doing so, inside two hours of arrival. During the course of lunch, he said, having just eaten a soufflé as delicate as a cloud in which were embedded the pale pink bodies of freshly caught shrimps, that it was obvious that Mother's chef was not French. Having discovered that Mother was the chef, he showed no embarrassment but merely said that she would then be glad of his presence for it would enable him to give her some guidance in the culinary arts. Leaving her speechless with rage at his audacity, he turned his attention to Larry, to whom he vouchsafed the information that the only good writers were French. At the mention of Shakespeare, he merely shrugged; '*le petit poseur*,' he said. To Leslie, he offered the information that anyone who was interested in hunting must assuredly have the instincts of a criminal; in any case, it was well known that the French produced the best guns, swords, and other offensive weapons. To Margo he gave the advice that it was a woman's job to keep beautiful for men and, in particular, not to be greedy and eat too many things that would ruin the figure.

As Margo was suffering from a certain amount of puppy fat at that time and was on a rigid diet in consequence, this information was not at all well received. He condemned himself in my eyes by calling the dogs 'village curs' and compared them unfavourably to his selection of labradors, setters, retrievers, and spaniels, all French-bred, of course. Furthermore, he was puzzled why I kept so many pets, all of which were uneatable. 'In France we only shoot zis kind of thing,' he said.

Small wonder then that after lunch, when he went upstairs to change, the family were quivering like a suppressed volcano. Only Mother's golden rule that a guest must not be insulted on the first day kept us in check. But such was the state of our nerves that if anyone had started to whistle the 'Marseillaise' we would have torn him limb from limb.

'You see,' said Mother accusingly to Larry, 'this is what comes of letting people you don't know send people you don't know to stay. The man's insufferable!'

'Well . . . he's not so bad,' said Larry feebly trying to argue against an attitude that he agreed with. 'I thought some of his comments were valid.'

'Which?' asked Mother ominously.

'Yes, which?' asked Margo, quivering.

'Well,' said Larry vaguely, 'I thought that soufflé *was* a bit on the rich side, and Margo is beginning to look a bit circular.'

'Beast!' said Margo, and burst into tears.

'Now, that's quite enough, Larry,' said Mother. 'How we're going to endure this . . . this . . . scented *lounge-lizard* of yours for another week I don't know.'

'Well, I've got to put up with him too, don't forget,' said Larry, irritated.

'Well, he's *your* friend . . . I mean, your friend's friend . . . I mean, well, whatever he is, he's *yours*,' said Mother, 'and it's up to you to keep him out of the way as much as possible.'

'Or I'll pepper his arse for him,' said Leslie, 'the smelly little . . .'

'Leslie,' said Mother, 'that's quite enough.'

'Well, he is,' said Leslie doggedly.

'I know he is, dear, but you shouldn't say so,' Mother explained.

'Well, I'll try,' said Larry, 'but don't blame me if he comes down to the kitchen to give you a cookery lesson.'

'I'm warning you,' said Mother mutinously, 'if that man sets foot in my kitchen, I shall walk out . . . I shall go . . . I shall go and . . .'

'Be a hermit?' suggested Larry.

'No, I shall go and stay in an hotel until he's gone,' said Mother, uttering her favourite threat. 'And this time I really *mean* it.'

To give Larry his due, he did strive manfully with Count Rossignol for the next few days. He took him to the library and museum in town, he showed him the Kaiser's summer palace with all its repulsive statuary, he even took him to the top of the highest point in Corfu, Mount Pantocrator, and showed him the view. The Count compared the library unfavourably with the Bibliothèque Nationale, said that the museum was not a patch on the Louvre, noted the Kaiser's palace was inferior in size, design, and furnishings to the cottage he had for his head gardener, and finally observed that the view from Pantocrator was not to be mentioned in the same breath as *any* view to be seen from *any* high spot in France.

'The man's intolerable,' said Larry, refreshing himself with brandy in Mother's bedroom, where we had all repaired to escape the Count's company. 'He's got an obsession with France; I can't think why he ever left the place. He even thinks their telephone service is the best in the world! And he's so *humourless* about everything, one would think he were a Swede.'

'Never mind, dear,' said Mother. 'It's not for long now.'

'I'm not sure I shall last the course,' said Larry. 'So far about the only thing he hasn't claimed for France is God.'

'Ah, but they probably believe in him better in France,' Leslie pointed out.

'Wouldn't it be wonderful if we could do something really nasty to him?' said Margo wistfully. 'Something really horrible.'

'No, Margo,' said Mother firmly, 'we've never done anything nasty to anyone that's stayed with us – I mean, except as a joke or by accident – and we're not going to start. We'll just have to put up with him; after all, it's only for a few more days. It'll soon pass.'

'Dear God!' said Larry suddenly. 'I've just remembered. It's the bloody christening on Monday!'

'I do wish you wouldn't swear so much,' said Mother. 'What's that got to do with it?'

'Can you imagine taking him to a *christening*?' asked Larry. 'No, he'll just have to go off somewhere on his own.'

'I don't think we ought to let him go wandering off on his own,' said Mother, as if she were talking about a dangerous animal. 'I mean he might meet one of our friends.'

We all sat and thought about the problem.

'Why doesn't Gerry take him somewhere?' said Leslie suddenly. 'After all, he doesn't want to come to a boring christening.'

'That's a brainwave,' said Mother delightedly. 'The very thing!'

Immediately all my instincts for self-preservation came to the fore. I said that I *did* want to go to the christening, I *had* been looking forward to it, it was the only chance I would ever have of seeing Larry being a godfather, and he might drop the baby or something and I would miss it; and anyway, the Count didn't like snakes and tortoises and birds and things, so what could *I* do with him? There was silence while the family, like a jury, examined the strength of my case.

'I know, take him out in your boat,' suggested Margo brightly.

'Excellent!' said Larry, 'I'm sure he's got a straw hat and a striped blazer among his sartorial effects. Perhaps we can borrow a banjo.'

'It's a very good idea,' said Mother. 'After all, it's only for a couple of hours, dear. You surely wouldn't mind that.'

I stated in no uncertain terms that I would mind it very much indeed.

'I tell you what,' said Leslie. 'They're having a fish drive down at the lake on Monday. If I get the chap who's in charge to let you go, will you take the Count?'

I wavered, for I had long wanted to see a fish drive. I knew I was going to have the Count for the afternoon so it was simply a matter of what I could get out of it.

'And then we can see about that new butterfly cabinet you want,' said Mother.

'And Margo and I will give you some money for books,' said Larry, generously anticipating Margo's participation in the bribery.

'And I'll give you that clasp-knife you wanted,' said Leslie.

I agreed. If I had to put up with the Count for an afternoon I was at least being fairly compensated. That evening at dinner, Mother explained the situation and went into such detailed eulogies about the fish drives that you would have thought she had personally invented them.

'Ees eating?' asked the Count.

'Yes, yes,' said Mother. 'The fish are called *kefalias* and they're delicious.'

'No, ees eating on ze lack?' asked the Count. 'Ees eating wiz sun?'

'Oh . . . oh, I see,' said Mother. 'Yes, it's very hot. Be sure to wear a hat.'

'We go in ze *enfant*'s yacht?' asked the Count, who liked to get things clear.

'Yes,' said Mother.

The Count outfitted himself for the expedition in pale blue linen trousers, elegant chestnut-bright shoes, a white silk shirt with a blue and gold cravat knotted carelessly at the throat, and an elegant yachting cap. While the *Bootle-Bumtrinket* was ideal for my purposes, I would have been the first to admit that she had none of the refinements of an ocean-going yacht, and this the Count was quick to perceive when I led him down to the canal in the maze of old Venetian salt pans below the house, where I had the boat moored.

'Zis . . . is yacht?' he asked in surprise and some alarm.

I said that indeed this was our craft, stalwart and stable, and, he would note, a flat bottom to make it easier to walk about in. Whether he understood me, I do not know; perhaps he thought the *Bootle-Bumtrinket* was merely the dinghy in which he was to be rowed out to the yacht, but he climbed in delicately, spread his handkerchief fastidiously over the seat, and sat down gingerly. I leaped aboard and with the aid of a pole started punting the craft down the canal which, at this point, was some twenty feet wide and two feet deep. I congratulated myself on the fact that only the day before I had decided that the *Bootle-Bumtrinket* was starting to smell almost as pungently as the Count, for over a period a lot of dead shrimps, seaweed, and other debris had collected under her boards. I had sunk her in some two feet of sea water and given her bilges a thorough cleaning so that she was sparkling clean and smelt beautifully of sun-hot tar and paint and salt water.

The old salt pans lay along the edge of the brackish lake, forming a giant chessboard with the cross-hatching of these placid canals, some as narrow as a chair, some thirty feet wide. Most of these waterways were only a couple of feet deep but below the water lay an almost unplumbable depth of fine black silt. The *Bootle-Bumtrinket*, by virtue of her shape and flat bottom, could be propelled up and down these inland waterways with comparative ease, for one did not have to worry about gusts of wind or a sudden, bouncing cluster of wavelets, two things that always made her a bit alarmed. But the disadvantage of the canals was that they were fringed on each side with tall, rustling bamboo breaks which, while providing shade, shut out the wind, so that the atmosphere was still, dark, hot, and as richly odiferous as a manure heap. For a time the artificial smell of the Count vied with the scents of nature and eventually nature won.

'Ees smell,' the Count pointed out. 'In France ze water ees hygiene.'

I said it would not be long before we left the canal and were out on the lake, where there would be no smell.

'Ees eating,' was the Count's next discovery, mopping his face and moustache with a scent-drenched handkerchief. 'Ees eating much.'

His pale face had, as a matter of fact, turned a light shade of heliotrope. I was just about to say that that problem, too, would be overcome once we reached the open lake when, to my alarm, I noticed something wrong with the *Bootle-Bumtrinket*. She had settled sluggishly in the brown water and hardly moved to my punting. For a moment I could not imagine what was wrong with her; we had not run aground and I knew that there were no sand banks in this canal. Then suddenly I noticed the swirl of water coiling up over the boards in the bottom of the boat. Surely, I thought, she could not have sprung a leak.

Fascinated, I watched the water rise, to engulf the bottom of the oblivious Count's shoes. I suddenly realized what must have happened. When I had cleaned out the bilges I had, of course, removed the bung in the *Bumtrinket*'s bottom to let the fresh sea water in; apparently, I had not replaced it with enough care and now the canal water was pouring into the bilges. My first thought was to pull up the boards, find the bung and replace it, but the Count was now sitting with his feet in about two inches of water and it seemed imperative to turn the *Bootle-Bumtrinket* towards the bank while I could still manoeuvre a trifle and get my exquisite passenger on shore. I did not mind being deposited in the canal by the *Bootle-Bumtrinket* – after all I was always in and out of the canals like a water rat in pursuit of water snakes, terrapins, frogs, and other small fry – but I knew that the Count would look askance at gambolling in two feet of water and an undetermined amount of mud. My efforts to turn the leaden waterlogged boat towards the bank were superhuman. Gradually, I felt the dead weight of the boat responding and her bows turning sluggishly towards the shore. Inch by inch, I eased her towards the bamboos and we were within ten feet of the bank when the Count noticed what was happening.

'*Mon Dieu!*' he cried shrilly, ''ve are submerge. My shoe is submerge. Ze boat, she ave sonk.'

I briefly stopped poling to soothe the Count. I told him that there was no danger; all he had to do was to sit still until I got him to the bank.

'My shoe! *Regardez* my shoe!' he cried, pointing at his now dripping and discoloured footwear with such an expression of outrage that it was all I could do not to giggle.

A moment, I said to him, and I should have him on dry land. Indeed if he had done what I had said, this would have been the case, for I had managed to get the *Bootle-Bumtrinket* to within six feet of the bamboos. But the Count was too worried about the state of his shoes and this prompted him to do something very silly. In spite of my warning shout, he looked over his shoulder, saw land looming close, got to his feet and leaped onto the *Bootle-Bumtrinket*'s minute foredeck. His intention was to leap from there to safety when I had manoeuvred the boat a little closer, but he had not reckoned with the *Bootle-Bumtrinket*'s temperament. A placid boat, she had nevertheless a few quirks, and one thing she did not like was anyone standing on her foredeck; she simply gave an odd sort of bucking twist, rather like a trained horse in a cowboy film, and slid you over her shoulder. She did this to the Count now.

He fell into the water with a yell, spread-eagled like an ungainly frog, and his proud yachting cap floated towards the bamboo roots while he thrashed about in a porridge of water and mud. I was filled with a mixture of alarm and delight; I was delighted that the Count had fallen in – though I knew my family would never believe that I had not engineered it – but I was alarmed at the way he was thrashing about. To try to stand up is an instinctive reaction when finding one is in shallow water, but in this case the effort only made one sink deeper into the glutinous mud. Once Larry had fallen into one of these canals while out shooting and had got himself so deeply embedded that it had required the united efforts of Margo, Leslie, and myself to extricate him. If the Count got himself wedged in the canal bottom I would not have the strength to extricate him single-handed and by the time I got help the Count might well have disappeared altogether beneath the gleaming mud. I abandoned ship and leaped into the canal to help him. I knew how to walk in mud and, anyway, only weighed a quarter of what the Count weighed so I did not sink in so far. I shouted to him to keep still until I got to him.

'*Merde!*' said the Count, proving that he was at least keeping his mouth above water.

He tried to get up once but, at the terrible, gobbling clutch of the mud, uttered a despairing cry like a bereaved seagull and lay still. Indeed, he was so frightened of the mud that when I reached him and tried to pull him shorewards he screamed and shouted and accused me of trying to push him in deeper. He was so absurdly childlike that I had a fit of the giggles and this of course only made him worse. He had relapsed into French, which he was speaking with the rapidity of a machine gun so, with my tenuous command of the language, I was unable to understand him. Eventually, I got my unmannerly laughter under control, once more seized him under the armpits and started to drag him shorewards. Then it suddenly occurred to me how ludicrous our predicament would seem to an onlooker, a twelve-year-old boy trying to rescue a six-foot man, and I was overcome again and sat down in the mud and laughed till I cried.

'Vy you laughing? Vy you laughing?' screamed the Count, trying to look over his shoulder at me. 'You no laughing, you pulling, *vite, vite!*'

Eventually, swallowing great hiccups of laughter, I started to pull at the Count again and eventually got him fairly close to the shore. Then I left him and climbed out onto the bank. This provoked another bout of hysteria.

'No going avay, no going avay!' he yelled, panic-stricken. 'I am sonk. No going avay!'

I ignored him. Choosing seven of the tallest bamboos in the vicinity, I bent them over one by one until their stems splintered but did not snap; then I twisted them round until they reached the Count and formed a sort of green bridge between him and the shore. Acting on my instructions, he turned on his stomach and pulled himself along until at last he reached dry land. When he eventually got shakily to his feet he looked as though the lower half of his body had been encased in melting chocolate. Knowing that this glutinous mud could dry hard in record time, I offered to scrape some of it off him with a piece of bamboo. He gave me a murderous look.

'*Espèce de con!*' he said vehemently.

My shaky knowledge of the Count's language did not allow me to translate this but the enthusiasm with which it was uttered led me to suppose that it was worth retaining in my memory. We started to walk home, the Count simmering vitriolically. As I had anticipated, the mud on his legs dried at almost magical speed and within a short time he looked as though he were wearing a pair of trousers made out of a pale brown jigsaw puzzle. From the back, he reminded me so much of the armour-clad rear of an Indian rhinoceros that I almost got the giggles again.

It was unfortunate, perhaps, that the Count and I should have arrived at the front door of the villa just as the huge Dodge driven by our scowling, barrel-shaped self-appointed guardian angel, Spiro Hakiopoulos, drew up with the family, flushed with wine, in the back of it. The car came to a halt and the family stared at the Count with disbelieving eyes. It was Spiro who recovered first.

'Gollys, Mrs Durrells,' he said, twisting his massive head round and beaming at Mother, 'Master Gerrys fixes the bastards.'

This was obviously the sentiment of the whole family but Mother threw herself into the breach.

'My goodness, Count,' she said in well-simulated tones of horror, 'what *have* you been doing with my son?'

The Count was so overcome with the audacity of this remark that he could only look at Mother open-mouthed.

'Gerry dear,' Mother went on, 'go and change out of those wet things before you catch cold, there's a good boy.'

'Good boy!' repeated the Count, shrilly and unbelievingly. '*C'est un assassin! C'est une espèce de . . .*'

'Now, now, my dear fellow,' said Larry, throwing his arm round the Count's muddy shoulders, 'I'm sure it's been a mistake. Come and have a brandy and change your things. Yes, yes, rest assured that my brother will smart for this. Of course he will be punished.'

Larry led the vociferous Count into the house and the rest of the family converged on me.

'What did you do to him?' asked Mother.

I said I had not done anything; the Count and the Count alone was responsible for his condition.

'I don't believe you,' said Margo. 'You always say that.'

I protested that had I been responsible I would be proud to confess. The family were impressed by the logic of this.

'It doesn't matter a damn if Gerry did it or not,' said Leslie. 'It's the end result that counts.'

'Well, go and get changed, dear,' said Mother, 'and then come to my room and tell us all about how you did it.'

But the affair of the *Bootle-Bumtrinket* did not have the effect that everyone hoped for; the Count stayed on grimly, as if to punish us all, and was twice as offensive as before. However, I had ceased feeling vindictive towards the Count; whenever I thought of him thrashing about in the canal I was overcome with helpless laughter; which was worth any amount of insults. Furthermore, the Count had unwittingly added a fine new phrase to my French vocabulary. I tried it out one day when I made a mistake in my French composition and I found it tripped well off the tongue. The effect on my tutor, Mr Kralefsky, was, however, very different. He had been pacing up and down the room, hands behind him, looking like a humpbacked gnome in a trance. At my expression, he came to a sudden stop, wide-eyed, looking like a gnome who had just had an electric shock from a toadstool.

'*What* did you say?' he asked in a hushed voice.

I repeated the offending phrase. Mr Kralefsky closed his eyes, his nostrils quivered, and he shuddered.

'*Where* did you hear that?' he asked.

I said I had learned it from a Count who was staying with us.

'Oh. Well, you must never say it again, do you understand,' Mr Kralefsky said, 'never again! You . . . you must learn that in this life sometimes even *aristocrats* let slip an unfortunate phrase in moments of stress. It does not behove us to imitate them.'

I did see what Kralefsky meant. Falling into a canal, for a Count, could be called a moment of stress, I supposed.

But the saga of the Count was not yet over. A week or so after he had departed, Larry, one morning at breakfast, confessed to feeling unwell. Mother put on her glasses and stared at him critically.

'How do you mean, unwell?' she asked.

'Not my normal, manly, vigorous self.'

'Have you got any pains?'

'No,' Larry admitted, 'no actual pains. Just a sort of lassitude, a feeling of ennui, a debilitated, drained feeling, as if I had spent the night with Count Dracula, and I feel that, for all his faults, our late guest was not a vampire.'

'Well, you look all right,' said Mother, 'though we'd better get you looked at. Dr Androuchelli is on holiday, so I'll have to get Spiro to bring Theodore.'

'All right,' said Larry listlessly, 'and you'd better tell Spiro to nip in and alert the British cemetery.'

'Larry, don't say things like that,' said Mother, getting alarmed. 'Now, you go up to bed and, for heaven's sake, stop there.'

If Spiro could be classified as our guardian angel to whom no request was impossible of fulfilment, Dr Theodore Stephanides was our oracle and guide to all things. He arrived, sitting sedately in the back of Spiro's Dodge, immaculately dressed in a tweed suit, his Homburg at just the correct angle, his beard twinkling in the sun.

'Yes, it was really . . . um . . . very curious,' said Theodore, having greeted us all, 'I was just thinking to myself how nice a trip . . . er . . . was an especially beautiful day . . . um . . . not too hot, and that sort of thing, you know . . . er . . . and suddenly Spiro turned up at the laboratory. Most fortuitous.'

'I'm so glad that my agony is of benefit to *someone*,' said Larry.

'Aha! What . . . er . . . you know . . . seems to be the trouble?' asked Theodore, eyeing Larry with interest.

'Nothing concrete,' Larry admitted. 'Just a general feeling of death being imminent. All my strength seems to have drained away. I've probably, as usual, been giving too much of myself to my family.'

'I don't think *that's* what's wrong with you,' said Mother decisively.

'I think you've been eating too much,' said Margo; 'what you want is a good diet.'

'What he wants is a little fresh air and exercise,' contributed Leslie. 'If he took the boat out a bit . . .'

'Yes, well, Theodore will tell us what's wrong,' said Mother.

'I can't find anything . . . er . . . you know . . . organically wrong,' said Theodore judiciously, rising and falling on his tiptoes, 'except that he is perhaps a trifle overweight.'

'There you are! I told you he needed a diet,' said Margo triumphantly.

'Hush, dear,' said Mother. 'So what do you advise, Theodore?'

'I should keep him in bed for a day or so,' said Theodore. 'Give him a light diet, you know, nothing very oily, and I'll send out some medicine . . . er . . . that is to say . . . a *tonic* for him. I'll come out the day after tomorrow and see how he is.'

Spiro drove Theodore back to town and in due course reappeared with the medicine.

'I won't drink it,' said Larry eyeing the bottle askance. 'It looks like essence of bat's ovaries.'

'Don't be silly, dear,' said Mother, pouring some into a spoon, 'it will do you good.'

'It won't. It's the same stuff as my friend Dr Jekyll took, and look what happened to him.'

'What happened to him?' asked Mother, unthinkingly.

'They found him hanging from the chandelier, scratching himself and saying he was Mr Hyde.'

'Come on now, Larry, stop fooling about,' said Mother firmly.

With much fussing, Larry was prevailed upon to take the medicine and retire to bed.

The following morning we were all woken at an inordinately early hour by roars of rage coming from Larry's room.

'Mother! Mother!' he was roaring. 'Come and look what you've done!'

We found him prancing round his room, naked, a large mirror in one hand. He turned on Mother belligerently and she gasped at the sight of him. His face was swollen up to about twice normal size and was the approximate colour of a tomato.

'*What* have you been doing dear?' asked Mother faintly.

'Doing? It's what *you've* done,' he shouted, articulating with difficulty. 'You and bloody Theodore and your damned medicine – it's affected my pituitary. Look at me! It's worse than Jekyll and Hyde.'

Mother put on her spectacles and gazed at Larry.

'It looks to me as though you've got mumps,' she said puzzled.

'Nonsense! That's a child's disease,' said Larry impatiently.

'No, it's that damned medicine of Theodore's, I tell you, it's affected my pituitary. If you don't get the antidote straight away I shall grow into a giant.'

'Nonsense, dear, I'm sure it's mumps,' said Mother. 'But it's very funny because I'm sure you've had mumps. Let's see, Margo had measles in Darjeeling in 1920 . . . Leslie had sprue in Rangoon – no, I'm wrong, that was 1900 in Rangoon and *you* had sprue, then Leslie had chickenpox in Bombay in 1911 . . . or was it 12? I can't quite remember, and then *you* had your tonsils out in Rajputana in 1922, or it may have been 1923, I can't remember exactly, and then after that, Margo got . . .'

'I hate to interrupt this Old Moore's Almanac of Family Ailments,' said Larry coldly, 'but would somebody like to send for the antidote before I get so big that I can't leave the room?'

Theodore, when he appeared, agreed with Mother's diagnosis.

'Yes . . . er . . . clearly a case of mumps,' he said.

'What do you mean, *clearly*, you charlatan?' said Larry, glaring at him from watering and swollen eyes. 'Why didn't you know what it was yesterday? And anyhow, I can't get mumps, it's a child's disease.'

'No, no,' said Theodore. 'Children generally get it but quite often adults get it too.'

'Why didn't you recognize a common disease like that when you saw it?' demanded Larry. 'Can't you even recognize a mump? You ought to be drummed out of the medical council or whatever it is that they do for malpractice.'

'Mumps are very difficult to diagnose in the . . . er . . . early stages,' said Theodore, 'until the swellings appear.'

'Typical of the medical profession,' said Larry bitterly. 'They can't even spot a disease until the patient is twice life size. It's a scandal.'

'As long as it doesn't affect your . . . um . . . you know . . . um . . . your . . . er . . . lower quarters,' said Theodore thoughtfully, 'you should be all right in a few days.'

'Lower quarters?' Larry asked, mystified, 'what lower quarters?'

'Well, er . . . you know . . . mumps causes swelling of the glands,' explained Theodore, 'and so if it travels down the body and affects the glands in your . . . um . . . lower quarters it can be very painful indeed.'

'You mean I'll swell up and start looking like a bull elephant?' asked Larry in horror.

'Mmm, er . . . yes,' said Theodore, finding he could not better this description.

'It's a plot to make me sterile!' shouted Larry. 'You and your bloody tincture of bat's blood! You're jealous of my virility.'

To say that Larry was a bad patient was putting it mildly. He had an enormous hand-bell by the bed which he rang incessantly for attention and Mother had to examine his nether regions about twenty times a day to assure him that he was not in any way affected. When it was discovered that it was Leonora's baby that had given him mumps he threatened to excommunicate it!

'I'm its godfather,' he said. 'Why can't I excommunicate the ungrateful little bastard?'

By the fourth day, we were all beginning to feel the strain. Captain Creech then appeared to see Larry. Captain Creech, a retired mariner of lecherous habits, was mother's *bête noire*. His determined pursuit of anything female, and Mother in particular, in spite of his seventy-odd years, was a constant source of annoyance to her, as was the captain's completely uninhibited behaviour and one-track mind.

'Ahoy!' he shouted, staggering into the bedroom, his lopsided jaw waggling, his wispy beard and hair standing on end, his rheumy eyes watering. 'Ahoy, there! Bring out your dead!'

Mother, who was examining Larry for the fourth time that day, straightened up and glared at him.

'Do you mind, captain?' she said coldly. 'This is supposed to be a sick-room, not a bar parlour.'

'Got you in the bedroom at last!' said Creech, beaming, taking no notice of Mother's expression. 'Now, if the boy moves over we can have a little cuddle.'

'I'm far too busy to cuddle, thank you,' said Mother frostily.

'Well, well,' said the captain, seating himself on the bed, 'what's this namby-pamby mumps thing you've got, huh, boy? Child stuff! If you want to be ill, be ill properly, like a man. Why, when I was your age nothing but a dose of clap would have done for me.'

'Captain, I would be glad if you would not reminisce in front of Gerry,' said Mother firmly.

'It hasn't affected the old manhood, has it?' asked the captain with concern. 'Terrible when it gets you in the crutch. Can ruin a man's sex life, mumps in the crutch.'

'Larry is perfectly all right, thank you,' said Mother with dignity.

'Talking of crutches,' said the captain, 'have you heard about the young Hindu virgin from Kutch, who kept two tame snakes in her crutch, she said when they wriggle, it's a bit of a giggle, but my boyfriends don't like my crutch much. Ha ha ha!'

'Really, captain!' said Mother, outraged, 'I do wish you wouldn't recite poetry in front of Gerry.'

'Got your mail when I was passing the post office,' the captain went on, oblivious of Mother's strictures, pulling some letters and cards out of his pocket and tossing them on to the bed. 'My, they've got a nice little bit serving in there now. She'd win a prize for the best marrows in any horticultural show.'

But Larry was not listening; he had extracted a postcard from the mail Captain Creech had brought. Having read it, he started to laugh uproariously.

'What is it, dear?' asked Mother.

'A postcard from the Count,' said Larry, wiping his eyes.

'Oh, him,' sniffed Mother, 'well, I don't want to know about *him*.'

'Oh yes you will,' said Larry. 'It's worth being ill just to be able to get this. I'm starting to feel better already.'

He picked up the postcard and read it out to us. The Count had obviously got someone to write the card for him whose command of English was fragile but inventive.

'I have reeching Rome,' it began. 'I am in clinic inflicted by disease called moops. Have inflicted all over. I finding I cannot arrange myself. I have no hunger and impossible I am sitting. Beware yourself the moops. Count Rossignol.'

'Poor man,' said Mother without conviction when we had all stopped laughing. 'We shouldn't laugh really.'

'No,' said Larry. 'I'm going to write and ask him if Greek moops are inferior in virulence to French moops.'

4

The Elements of Spring

A habitation of dragons, and a court for owls.

ISAIAH 34:13

Spring, in its season, came like a fever; it was as though the island shifted and turned uneasily in the warm, wet bed of winter and then, suddenly and vibrantly, was fully awake, stirring with life under a sky as blue as a hyacinth bud into which a sun would rise, wrapped in mist as fragile and as delicately yellow as a newly completed silkworm cocoon. For me, spring was one of the best times, for all the animal life of the island was astir and the air full of hope. Maybe today I would catch the biggest terrapin I had ever seen or fathom the mystery of how a baby tortoise, emerging from its egg as crushed and wrinkled as a walnut, would, within an hour, have swelled to twice its size and have smoothed out most of its wrinkles in consequence. The whole island was a-bustle and ringing with sound. I would awake early, breakfast hurriedly under the tangerine trees already fragrant with the warmth of the early sun, gather my nets and collecting boxes, whistle for Roger, Widdle, and Puke, and set off to explore my kingdom.

Up in the hills, in the miniature forests of heather and broom, where the sun-warmed rocks were embossed with strange lichens like ancient seals, the tortoises would be emerging from their winter sleep, pushing aside the earth under which they had slept and jerking slowly out into the sun, blinking and gulping. They would rest until the sun had warmed them, and then would move slowly off towards the first meal of clover or dandelion, or maybe a fat, white puff-ball. Like other parts of my territory, I had the tortoise hills well organized; each tortoise possessed a number of distinguishing marks so that I could follow its progress. Each nest of stonechats or black-caps was carefully marked so that I could watch progress, as was each papery mound of mantis eggs, each spider's web, and each rock under which lurked some beast dear to me.

But it was the heavy emergence of the tortoises that would really tell me that spring had started, for it was not until winter was truly over that they lumbered forth in search of mates, cumbersome and heavily armoured as any medieval knight in search of a damsel to succour. Having once satisfied their hunger, they became more alert – if such a word can be used to describe a tortoise. The males walked on their toes, their necks stretched out to the fullest extent, and at intervals they would pause and utter an astonishing, loud, and imperative yap. I never heard a female answer this ringing, Pekinese-like cry, but by some means the male would track her down and then, still yapping, do battle with her, crashing his shell against hers, trying to bludgeon her into submission, while she, undeterred, would try to go on feeding in between the bouts of buffeting. So the hills would resound to the yaps and slithering crashes of the mating tortoises and the stonechats' steady 'tak tak' like a miniature quarry at work, the cries of pink-breasted chaffinches like tiny, rhythmic drops of water falling into a pool, and the gay, wheezing song of the goldfinches as they tumbled through the yellow broom like multi-coloured clowns.

Down below the tortoise hills, below the old olive groves filled with wine-red anemones, asphodels, and pink cyclamen, where the magpies made their nests and the jays would startle you with their sudden harsh, despairing scream, lay the old Venetian salt pans, spread out like a chessboard. Each field, some only the size of a small room, was bounded by wide, shallow, muddy canals of brackish water. It consisted of a little jungle of vines, maize, fig trees, tomatoes as acrid-smelling as stinkbugs, watermelons like the huge green eggs of some mythical bird, trees of cherry, plum, apricot, and loquat, strawberry plants, and sweet potatoes, all forming the larder of the island. On the seaward side, each brackish canal was fringed with cane breaks and reed beds sharply pointed as an army of pikes; but inland, where the streams fell from the olive groves into the canals and the water was sweet, you got lush plant growth and the placid canals were emblazoned with water lilies and fringed with golden king-cups.

It was here that in the spring the two species of terrapin – one black with gold spots and one pin-striped delicately with grey – would whistle shrilly, almost like birds, as they pursued their mates. The frogs, green and brown, with leopard-patched thighs, looked as though they were freshly varnished. They would clasp each other with passionate, pop-eyed fervour or gurk an endless chorus and lay great cumulus clouds of grey spawn in the water. In places where the canals were bordered by shade-giving cane breaks, fig and other fruit trees, the diminutive tree frogs, vivid green, with skin as soft as a damp chamois leather, would puff up their little yellow throat pouches to the size of walnuts and croak in a monotonous tenor voice. In the water, where the pigtails of weed moved and undulated gently in the baby currents, the tree frogs' spawn would be laid in yellowish lumps the size of a small plum.

Along one side of the fields lay a flat grassland area which, with the spring rains, would be inundated and turn into a large shallow lake some four inches deep, lined with grass. Here, in this warm water, the newts would assemble, hazelnut-brown with yellow bellies. A male would take up his station facing the female, tail curved round, and then, with a look of almost laughable concentration on his face, he would wag his tail ferociously, ejaculating sperm and wafting it towards the female. She, in her turn, would place the fertilized egg, white and almost as transparent as the water, yolk black and shining as an ant, onto a leaf and then, with her hind legs, bend the leaf and stick it so that the egg was encased.

In spring the herds of strange cattle would appear to graze on this drowned lake. Huge, chocolate-coloured animals with massive, backward-slanting horns as white as mushrooms, they looked like the Ankole cattle from the centre of Africa but they must have been brought from somewhere nearer, Persia or Egypt perhaps. They were tended by strange, wild, gypsy-like bands who in long, low, horse-drawn wagons would camp by the grazing area: the savage-looking men, dusky as crows, and the handsome women and girls with velvet black eyes and hair like mole-skin would sit gossiping or basket-making round the fire, speaking a language I could not understand, while the raggedly dressed boys, thin and brown, jay-shrill and jackal suspicious, would act as herdsmen. The great beasts' horns would clack and rattle together like musketry as they barged each other out of the way in their eagerness to feed. The sweet cattle-smell of their brown coats lingered in the warm air after them like the scent of flowers. One day the grazing area would be empty; the next day, as if they had always been there, there would be the jumbled encampment caught in a perpetual spider's web of smoke from its pink, glittering fires and the herds of cattle moving slowly through the shallow water, their probing, tearing mouths and splashing hooves frightening the newts and sending the frogs and baby terrapins off in panic-stricken flight at this mammoth invasion.

I greatly coveted one of these huge, brown cattle, but I knew that my family would not under any circumstances allow me to have anything so large and fierce looking, no matter how much I pleaded that they were so tame that they were herded by mere toddlers of six or seven. The nearest I got to possessing one of these animals was quite close enough so far as the family was concerned. I had been down in the fields just after the gypsies had killed a bull; the still-bloody hide was stretched out and a group of girls were scraping it with knives and rubbing wood ash into it. Nearby was piled its gory, dismembered carcass already shining and humming with flies and next to it was the massive head, the fringed ears lying back, the eyes half-closed as if musing, a trickle of blood from one nostril. The sweeping white horns were some four feet long and as thick as my thigh and I gazed at them longingly, as covetous as any early big game hunter.

It would be impractical, I decided, to buy the whole head; even though I was convinced of my mastery of the art of taxidermy the family did not share this belief. Besides, there had recently been a bit of unpleasantness over a dead turtle I had unthinkingly dissected on the veranda and so everyone was inclined to view my interest in anatomy with a jaundiced eye. It was a pity, really, for the bull's head, carefully mounted, would have looked magnificent over the door of my bedroom and have been the *pièce de résistance* of my collection, surpassing even my stuffed flying fish and my almost complete goat skeleton. However, knowing how implacable my family could be, I decided reluctantly I would have to settle for the horns. After a spirited piece of bargaining – the gypsies knew enough Greek for that – I purchased the horns for ten drachmas and my shirt. The absence of the shirt I explained to Mother by saying I had ripped it so badly falling out of a tree that the remnants were not worth bringing back. Then, triumphantly, I carried the massive horns up to my room and spent the morning polishing them, nailing them to a plaque of wood, and then hanging the whole thing with great care on a hook over my door.

I stood back to admire the effect and at that moment heard Leslie's voice raised in anger.

'Gerry!' he shouted. 'Gerry! Where are you?'

I remembered that I had borrowed a tin of gun oil from his room to polish the horns with, meaning to restore it before he noticed. But before I could do anything the door burst open and he appeared belligerently.

'Gerry! Have you got my bloody gun oil?' he inquired.

The door, returning on the impetus of his entrance, swung back and slammed. My magnificent pair of horns leaped off the wall as if propelled by the ghost of the bull that had possessed them and landed on top of Leslie's head, felling him as though he had been pole-axed.

My first fear was that my beautiful horns might be broken; my second, that my brother might be dead. Both proved to be erroneous. My horns were intact and my brother, his eyes still glazed, hoisted himself into a sitting position and stared at me.

'Christ! My head!' he moaned, clasping his temples and rocking to and fro. 'Bloody hell!'

As much as to dilute his wrath as anything, I went in search of Mother. I found her in her bedroom brooding over the bed, which was covered with what appeared to be a library of knitting patterns. I explained that Leslie had been, as it were, accidentally gored by my horns. As usual, Mother looked upon the gloomy side and was convinced that I had secreted a bull in my room which had disembowelled Leslie. Her relief at finding him sitting on the floor apparently intact was considerable but tinged with annoyance.

'Leslie; dear, what have you been doing?' she asked.

Leslie gazed up at her, his face slowly taking on the colour of a sun-mellowed plum. He had some difficulty in finding his voice.

'That bloody boy,' he said at last, in a sort of muted roar. 'He tried to brain me . . . hit me with a pair of sodding great deer horns!'

'Language, dear,' said Mother automatically. 'I'm sure he didn't mean to.'

I said, no, I had intended no harm, but in the interests of accuracy I would point out that they were not deer horns, which were a different shape, but the horns of a species of bull which I had not as yet identified.

'I don't care what bleeding species it is,' snarled Leslie, 'I don't care whether it's a bloody bastard brontosaurus horn!'

'Leslie, *dear*,' said Mother, 'it's quite unnecessary to swear so much.'

'It *is* necessary,' shouted Leslie. 'And if you'd been hit on the head by something like a whale's ribcage you'd swear too.'

I started to explain that a whale's ribcage did not, in fact, resemble my horns in the least but I was quelled by a terrible look from Leslie and my anatomical lecture dried in my throat.

'Well, dear, you can't keep them over the door,' said Mother, 'it's a most dangerous place. You might have hit Larry.'

My blood ran cold at the thought of Larry felled by the horns of my bull.

'You'll have to hang them somewhere else,' Mother continued.

'No,' said Leslie. 'If he must keep the bloody things, he's not to hang them up. Put them in a cupboard or somewhere.'

Reluctantly, I accepted this restriction, and so my horns reposed on the window-sill, doing no further damage than to fall regularly on to our maid Lugaretzia's foot every evening when she closed the shutters, but as she was a professional hypochondriac of no mean abilities she enjoyed the bruises she sustained. But this incident put a blight on my relationship with Leslie for some time, which was the direct cause of my unwittingly arousing Larry's ire.

Early in the spring I had heard echoing and booming from the reed beds around the salt pans the strange roaring of a bittern. I was wildly excited about this for I had never seen one of these birds and I was hopeful that they would nest, but pinpointing the exact area in which the birds were operating was difficult for the reed beds were extensive. However, by spending some considerable time perched in the higher branches of an olive tree on a hill commanding the reeds, I succeeded in narrowing down the field of search to an acre or two. Soon the bitterns stopped calling and I felt sure they were nesting. I set off early one morning leaving the dogs behind. I soon reached the fields and plunged into the reed beds, moving to and fro like a questing hound, refusing to be tempted away from my objective by the sudden ripple of a water snake, the clop of a jumping frog, or the tantalizing dance of a newly hatched butterfly. Soon I was in the heart of the cool, rustling reeds, and I then found, to my consternation, that the area was so extensive and the reeds so high that I was completely lost. On every side I was surrounded by a fence of reeds and their leaves made a flickering green canopy above me through which I could see the vivid blue sky. Being lost did not worry me, for I knew, if I walked long enough in any direction, I would hit the sea or the road; but what did worry me was that I could not be sure if I were searching the right area. I found some almonds in my pocket and sat down to eat them while I considered the problem.

I had just eaten the last one and decided that my best course was to go back to the olive trees and re-establish my bearings when I discovered that without knowing it I had been sitting within eight feet of a bittern for the last five minutes. He was standing there, stiff as a guardsman, his neck stretched up straight, his long, greenish-brown beak pointing skywards, while from each side of his narrow skull his dark, protuberant eyes gazed at me with a fierce watchfulness. His body, pale fawn, mottled with dark brown, merged into the shimmering shadow-flecked reeds perfectly, and to add to the illusion that he was part of the moving background, the bird swayed from side to side. I was enchanted and sat watching him, hardly daring to breathe. Then there was a sudden commotion among the reeds and the bittern abruptly stopped looking like a reed and launched himself heavily into the air as Roger, with lolling tongue and eyes beaming with *bonhomie*, came crashing into view.

I was torn between remonstrating with Roger for having

frightened the bittern and praising him for his undoubted feat of having tracked me down by scent over a difficult route of about a mile and a half. However, Roger was obviously so delighted with his own achievement that I had not the heart to scold him. I found two almonds I had overlooked in my pocket and gave them to him as a reward. Then we set to work to search for the bitterns' nest. We soon found it, a neat pad of reeds with the first greenish egg lying in the cup. I was delighted and determined to keep a close watch on the nest to note the progress of the young; then, carefully bending the reeds to mark the trail, I followed Roger's stumpy tail. He obviously had a much better sense of direction than I had, for within a hundred yards we had reached the road and Roger was shaking the water off his woolly coat and rolling in the fine, dry, white dust.

As we left the road and made our way up the hillside through the olive groves sparkling with light and shade, coloured with a hundred wild flowers, I stopped to pick some anemones for Mother. While I gathered the wine-coloured flowers I brooded on the problem of the bitterns. When the hen bird had reared her brood to the stage where they were fully feathered, I would dearly have liked to kidnap two and add them to my not inconsiderable menagerie. The trouble was, the fish bill for my present creatures – a black-backed gull, twenty-four terrapins, and eight water snakes – was considerable and I felt that Mother would view the addition of two hungry young bitterns with mixed feelings, to say the least. Pondering this problem, it was some time before I became aware that someone was piping an urgent, beckoning call on a flute.

I glanced down at the road below and there was the Rose-Beetle Man. He was a strange, itinerant pedlar I frequently met on my expeditions through the olive groves. Slender, foxy-faced, and dumb, he wore the most astonishing garb – a huge, floppy hat to which were pinned many strings tied to glittering gold-green rose beetles, his clothes mended with many multi-coloured bits of cloth so that it looked almost as though he were wearing a patch-work quilt. A great, bright blue cravat completed his ensemble. On his back were bags and boxes, cages full of pigeons, and from his pockets he could produce anything from wooden flutes, carved animals or combs, to bits of the sacred robe of St Spiridion.

One of his chief charms as far as I was concerned was that, being dumb, he had to rely on a remarkable ability for mimicry. He used his flute as his tongue. When he saw that he had caught my attention he took the flute from his mouth and beckoned. I hurried down the hill, for I knew that the Rose-Beetle Man sometimes had things of great interest. It was he, for example, who had got me the biggest clam shell in my collection and, moreover, with the two tiny parasitic pea-crabs still inside.

I stopped by him and said 'good morning'. He smiled, showing discoloured teeth, and doffing his floppy hat with an exaggerated bow, setting all the beetles that were tied to it buzzing sleepily on the end of their strings like a flock of captive emeralds. Presently, after inquiring after my health by leaning forward and peering questioningly and anxiously, wide-eyed, into my face, he told me that he was well by playing a rapid, gay, rippling tune on his flute and then drawing in great lungfuls of warm spring air and exhaling them, his eyes closed in ecstasy. Thus having disposed of the courtesies, we got down to business.

What, I inquired, did he want of me? He raised his flute to his lips, gave a plaintive, quavering hoot, prolonged and mournful, and then, taking the flute from his lips, opened his eyes wide and hissed, swaying from side to side and occasionally snapping his teeth together. As an imitation of an angry owl it was so perfect that I almost expected the Rose-Beetle Man to fly away. My heart beat with excitement, for I had long wanted a mate for my scops owl, Ulysses, who spent his days sitting like a carved totem of olive wood above my bedroom window and his nights decimating the mouse population around the villa. But when I asked him the Rose-Beetle Man laughed to scorn my idea of anything so common as a scops owl. He removed a large cloth bag from the many bundles with which he was encumbered, opened it, and carefully tipped the contents at my feet.

To say that I was struck speechless was putting it mildly, for there in the white dust tumbled three huge owlets, hissing and swaying and beak-cracking in what seemed to be a parody of the Rose-Beetle Man, their tangerine-golden eyes enormous with a mixture of rage and fear. They were baby eagle owls and, as such, so rare as to be a prize almost beyond the dreams of avarice. I knew that I must have them. The fact that the acquisition of the three fat and voracious owls would send the meat bill up in the same way as the addition of the bitterns to my collection would have affected the fish bill was neither here nor there. Bitterns were things of the future, which might or might not materialize, but the owls, like large, greyish-white snowballs, beak-clicking and rumba-ing in the dust, were solid fact.

I squatted down by the owlets and as I stroked them into a state of semi-somnolence I bargained with the Rose-Beetle Man. He was a good bargainer, which made the whole thing much more interesting, but it was also very peaceful bargaining with him for it was done in complete silence. We sat opposite one another like two great art connoisseurs at Agnew's haggling, say, over a trio of Rembrandts. The lift of a chin, the minutest inclination or half-shake of the head was sufficient, and there were long pauses during which the Rose-Beetle Man tried to undermine my determination with the aid of music and some indigestible nougat which he had in his pocket. But it was a buyer's market and he knew it; who else in the length and breadth of the island would be mad enough to buy not one but three baby eagle owls? Eventually the bargain was struck.

As I was temporarily embarrassed financially, I explained to the Rose-Beetle Man that he would have to wait for payment until the beginning of the next month when my pocket money was due. The Rose-Beetle Man had frequently been in this predicament himself so he understood the situation perfectly. I would, I explained, leave the money with our mutual friend Yani at the café on the crossroads where the Rose-Beetle Man could pick it up during one of his peregrinations across the countryside. Thus having dealt with the sordid, commercial side of the transaction, we shared a stone bottle of ginger beer from the Rose-Beetle Man's capacious pack. Then I placed my precious owls carefully in their bag and continued on my way home, leaving the Rose-Beetle Man lying in the ditch among his wares and the spring flowers, playing on his flute.

It was the lusty cries the owlets gave on the way back to the villa that suddenly brought home to me the culinary implications of my new acquisitions. It was obvious that the Rose-Beetle Man had not fed his charges. I did not know how long he had had them, but judging from the noise they were making they were extremely hungry. It was a pity, I reflected, that my relations with Leslie were still slightly strained, for otherwise I could have persuaded him to shoot some sparrows or perhaps a rat or two for my new babies. As it was, I could see I would have to rely on my mother's unfailing kindness of heart.

I found her ensconced in the kitchen, stirring frantically at a huge, aromatically bubbling cauldron, frowning at a cookbook in one hand, her spectacles misty, her lips moving silently as she read. I produced my owls with the air of one who is conferring a gift of inestimable value. My mother straightened her spectacles and glanced at the three hissing, swaying balls of down.

'Very nice, dear,' she said in an absent-minded tone of voice, 'very nice. Put them somewhere safe, won't you?'

I said they would be incarcerated in my room and that nobody would know that I had got them.

'That's right,' said Mother, glancing nervously at the owls. 'You know how Larry feels about more pets.'

I did indeed, and I intended to keep their arrival a secret from him at all costs. There was just one minor problem, I explained, and that was that the owls were hungry – were, in fact, starving to death.

'Poor little things,' said Mother, her sympathies immediately aroused. 'Give them some bread and milk.'

I explained that owls ate meat and that I had used up the last of my meat supply. Had Mother perhaps a fragment of meat that she could lend me so that the owls did not die?

'Well, I'm a bit short of meat,' said Mother. 'We're having chops for lunch. Go and see what's in the icebox.'

I went to the massive icebox in the larder that contained our perishable foodstuffs and peered into its icy, misty interior. All I could unearth were the ten chops for lunch and even these were hardly meal enough for three voracious eagle owls. I went back with this news to the kitchen.

'Oh dear,' said Mother. 'Are you sure they won't eat bread and milk?'

I was adamant. Owls would only eat meat.

At that moment, one of the babies swayed so violently he fell over and I was quick to point this out to Mother as an example of how weak they were getting.

'Well, I suppose you'd better take the chops then,' said Mother, harassed. 'We'll just have to have vegetable curry for lunch.'

Triumphantly, I carried the owls and the chops to my bedroom and stuffed the hungry babies full of meat.

As a consequence of the owls' arrival we sat down to lunch rather late.

'I'm sorry we're not earlier,' said Mother, uncovering a tureen and letting loose a cloud of curry-scented steam, 'but the potatoes wouldn't cook for some reason.'

'I thought we were going to have chops,' complained Larry aggrievedly. 'I spent all morning getting my taste buds on tiptoe with the thought of chops. What happened to them?'

'I'm afraid it's the owls, dear,' said Mother apologetically. 'They have such huge appetites.'

Larry paused, a spoonful of curry halfway to his mouth.

'Owls?' he said, staring at Mother. 'Owls? What do you mean, owls? What owls?'

'Oh!' said Mother, flustered, having realized that she had made a tactical error. 'Just owls . . . birds, you know . . . nothing to worry about.'

'Are we having a plague of owls?' Larry inquired. 'Are they attacking the larder and zooming out with bunches of chops in their talons?'

'No, no, dear, they're only babies. They wouldn't do that. They have the most beautiful eyes, and they were simply starving, poor little things.'

'Bet they're some new creatures of Gerry's,' said Leslie sourly. 'I heard him crooning to something before lunch.'

'Then he's got to release them,' barked Larry.

I said I could not do this as they were babies.

'Only babies, dear,' said Mother placatingly. 'They can't help it.'

'What do you mean, can't help it?' said Larry. 'The damned things, stuffed to the gills with my chops . . .'

'*Our* chops,' Margo interrupted. 'I don't know why you have to be so selfish.'

'It's got to stop,' Larry went on, ignoring Margo. 'You indulge the boy too much.'

'They're just as much our chops as yours,' said Margo.

'Nonsense, dear,' said Mother to Larry, 'you do exaggerate. After all, it's only some baby owls.'

'Only!' said Larry bitingly. 'He's already got one owl and we know *that* to our cost.'

'Ulysses is a very sweet bird and no trouble,' put in Mother defensively.

'Well, he might be sweet to you,' said Larry, 'but he hasn't come and vomited up all the bits of food he has no further use for all over *your* bed.'

'That was a long time ago, dear, and he hasn't done it again.'

'And what's it got to do with *our* chops, anyway?' asked Margo.

'It's not only owls,' said Larry, 'though, God knows, if this goes on, we'll start to look like Athene. You don't seem to have any control over him. Look at that business with the turtle last week.'

'That was a mistake, dear. He didn't mean any harm.'

'A mistake!' said Larry witheringly. 'He disembowelled the bloody thing all over the veranda. My room smelled like the interior of Captain Ahab's boat. It's taken me a week and the expenditure of about five hundred gallons of eau de cologne to freshen it up to the extent where I can enter it without fainting.'

'We smelled it just as much as you did,' said Margo indignantly. 'Anyone would think that *you* were the only one to smell it.'

'Yes!' exclaimed Leslie. 'It smelled worse in my room. I had to sleep out on the back veranda. I don't know why you think you're the only one who ever suffers.'

'I don't,' said Larry witheringly. 'I'm just not interested in the suffering of lesser beings.'

'The trouble with you is you're selfish,' said Margo, clinging to her original diagnosis.

'All right,' snapped Larry. 'Don't listen to me. You'll all complain soon enough when your beds are waist-deep in owl vomit. I shall go and stay in a hotel.'

'I think we've talked quite enough about the owls,' said Mother firmly. 'Who's going to be in for tea?'

It transpired that we were all going to be in for tea.

'I'm making some scones,' said Mother, and sighs of satisfaction ran round the table, for Mother's scones, wearing cloaks of home-made strawberry jam, butter, and cream, were a delicacy all of us adored. 'Mrs Vadrudakis is coming to tea so I want you to behave,' Mother went on.

Larry groaned.

'Who the hell is Mrs Vadrudakis?' he asked. 'Some old bore, I suppose?'

'Now, don't start,' said Mother severely. 'She sounds a very nice woman. She wrote me such a nice letter; she wants my advice.'

'What on?' asked Larry.

'Well, she's very distressed by the way the peasants keep their animals. You know how thin the dogs and cats are, and those poor donkeys with sores that we see. Well, she wants to start a society for the elimination of cruelty to animals here in Corfu, rather like the RSPCA, you know. And she wants us to help her.'

'She doesn't get *my* help,' said Larry firmly. 'I'm not helping any society to prevent cruelty to animals. I'd help them to promote cruelty.'

'Now, Larry, don't say things like that,' said Mother severely. 'You know you don't mean it.'

'Of course I do,' said Larry, 'and if this Vadrudakis woman spent a week in this house she'd feel the same. She'd go round strangling owls with her bare hands, if only to survive.'

'Well, I want you all to be polite,' said Mother firmly, adding, 'and you're not to mention owls, Larry. She might think we're peculiar.'

'We are,' concluded Larry with feeling.

After lunch I discovered that Larry, as he so often did, had alienated the two people who might have been his allies in his anti-owl campaign, Margo and Leslie. Margo, on seeing the owlets, went into raptures. She had just acquired the art of knitting and, with lavish generosity, offered to knit anything I wanted for the owls. I toyed with the idea of having them all dressed in identical, striped pullovers but discarded this as impractical and reluctantly refused the kind suggestion.

Leslie's offer of help was more practical. He said he would shoot a supply of sparrows for me. I asked whether he could do this every day.

'Well, not every day,' said Leslie. 'I might not be here; I might be in town or something. But I will when I can.'

I suggested that he might do some bulk shooting for me, procuring enough sparrows to last me a week, perhaps.

'That's a good idea,' said Leslie, struck by this. 'You work out how many you need for the week and I'll get 'em for you.'

Laboriously, for mathematics was not my strong point, I worked out how many sparrows (supplemented with meat) I would need a week and took the result to Leslie in his room, where he was cleaning the latest addition to his collection, a magnificent old Turkish muzzle-loader.

'Yes . . . OK,' he said, looking at my figures. 'I'll get 'em for you. I'd better use the air rifle; if I use the shotgun we'll have bloody Larry complaining about the noise.'

So, armed with the air rifle and a large paper bag, we went round the back of the villa. Leslie loaded the gun, leaned back against the trunk of an olive tree, and started shooting. It was as simple as target shooting, for that year we had a plague of sparrows and the roof of the villa was thick with them. As they were picked off by Leslie's excellent marksmanship they rolled down the roof and fell to the ground, where I would collect them and put them in my paper bag.

After the first few shots, the sparrows grew a little uneasy and retreated higher up until they were sitting on the apex of the roof. Here Leslie could still shoot them but they were precipitated over the edge of the roof and rolled down to fall on the veranda on the other side of the house.

'Wait until I shoot a few more before you collect 'em,' said Leslie, and so I dutifully waited.

He continued shooting for some time, rarely missing, and

the faint 'thunk' of the rifle coincided with the collapse and disappearance of a sparrow from the rooftop.

'Damn,' he said suddenly. 'I've lost count. How many's that?'

I said that I hadn't been counting either.

'Well, go and pick up the ones on the veranda and wait there. I'll pick off another six. That should do you.'

Clasping my paper bag, I went around to the front of the house, and saw, to my consternation, that Mrs Vadrudakis, whom we had forgotten, had arrived for tea. She and Mother were sitting somewhat stiffly on the veranda clasping cups of tea, surrounded by the bloodstained corpses of numerous sparrows.

'Yes,' Mother was saying, obviously hoping that Mrs Vadrudakis had not noticed the rain of dead birds, 'yes, we're all great animal lovers.'

'I hear this,' said Mrs Vadrudakis, smiling benevolently. 'I hear you lof the animals like me.'

'Oh yes,' said Mother. 'We keep so many pets. Animals are a sort of passion with us, you know.'

She smiled nervously at Mrs Vadrudakis, and at that moment a dead sparrow fell into the strawberry jam.

It was impossible to cover it up and equally impossible to pretend it was not there. Mother stared at it as though hypnotized; at last, she moistened her lips and smiled at Mrs Vadrudakis, who was sitting with her cup poised, a look of horror on her face.

'A sparrow,' Mother pointed out weakly. 'They ... er ... seem to be dying a lot this year.'

At that moment, Leslie, carrying the air rifle, strode out of the house.

'Have I killed enough?' he inquired.

The next ten minutes were fraught with emotion. Mrs Vadrudakis said she had never been so upset in her life and that we were all fiends in human shape. Mother kept saying that she was sure Leslie had not meant to cause offence and that, anyway, she was sure the sparrows had not suffered. Leslie, loudly and belligerently, went on repeating that it was a lot of bloody fuss about nothing and, anyway, owls ate sparrows and did Mrs Vadrudakis want the owls to starve, eh? But Mrs Vadrudakis refused to be comforted. She wrapped herself, a tragic and out-raged figure, in her cloak, shudderingly picked her way through the sparrows' corpses, got into her cab, and was driven away through the olive groves at a brisk trot.

'I do wish you children wouldn't do things like that,' said Mother, shakily pouring herself a cup of tea while I picked up the sparrows. 'It really was most . . . careless of you, Leslie.'

'Well, how was I to know the old fool was out here?' said Leslie indignantly. 'I can't be expected to see through the house, can I?'

'You should be more careful, dear,' said Mother. 'Heaven knows what she must think of us.'

'She thinks we're savages,' said Leslie, chuckling. 'She said so. She's no loss, silly old fool.'

'Well, the whole thing's given me a headache. Go and ask Lugaretzia to make some more tea, Gerry, will you?'

Two pots of tea and several aspirins later, Mother was begin-ning to feel better. I was sitting on the veranda giving her a lecture on owls, to which she was only half-listening, saying, 'Yes, dear, how interesting,' at intervals, when she was suddenly galvanized by a roar of rage from inside the villa.

'Oh dear, I can't stand it,' she moaned. 'Now what's the matter?'

Larry strode out onto the veranda.

'Mother!' he shouted 'This has got to stop. I won't put up with it.'

'Now, now, dear don't shout. What's the matter?' Mother inquired.

'It's like living in a bloody natural history museum!'

'What is, dear?'

'This is! Life here. It's intolerable. I won't put up with it!' shouted Larry.

'But what's the matter, dear?' Mother asked, bewildered.

'I go to get myself a drink from the icebox and what do I find?'

'What do you find, dear?' asked Mother with interest.

'Sparrows!' bellowed Larry. 'Bloody great bags of suppurating unhygienic sparrows!'

It was not my day.

5

Fakirs and Fiestas

The Prince of Darkness is a Gentleman.

– SHAKESPEARE, *King Lear*

It was always during the late spring that my collection of animals swelled to a point where even Mother occasionally grew alarmed, for it was then that everything was arriving and hatching, and baby animals are, after all, easier to acquire than adults. It was also the time when the birds, newly arrived to nest and rear their young, were harried by the local gentry with guns in spite of the fact that it was out of season. Everything was grist to their mill, these townee sportsmen, for whereas the peasants would stick to the so-called game birds – thrushes, blackbirds, and the like – the hunters from the town would blast everything that flew. You would see them returning triumphantly, weighed down with guns and bandoliers of cartridges, their game bags full of a sticky, bloody, feathery conglomeration of anything from robins to redstarts, from nuthatches to nightingales. So in the spring my room and that portion of the veranda set aside for the purpose always had at least half a dozen cages and boxes containing gape-mouthed baby birds or birds that I had managed to rescue from the sportsmen and which were recuperating with makeshift splints on wings or legs.

The only good thing about this spring slaughter was that it gave me a pretty good idea of what birds were to be found in the island. Realizing I could not stop the killing, I at least turned it to good account. I would track down the brave and noble

Nimrods and ask to see the contents of their game bags. I would then make a list of all the dead birds and, by pleading, save the lives of those that had only been wounded. It was by this means that Hiawatha came into my possession.

I had spent an interesting and energetic morning with the dogs. We had been up early and out in the olive groves while everything was still dawn-chilly and misted with dew; I had found this an excellent time for collecting insects, for the coldness made them lethargic and unwilling to fly, and thus more easily acquired. I had obtained two butterflies and a moth new to my collection, two unknown beetles, and seventeen locusts which I collected to feed my baby birds with. By the time the sun was well up in the sky and had gathered some heat we had unsuccessfully chased a snake and a green lizard, milked Agathi's goat (unbeknownst to her) into a collecting jar as we were all thirsty, and dropped in on my old shepherd friend Yani who provided us with some bread and fig cake and a straw hat full of wild strawberries to sustain us.

We made our way down to a small bay where the dogs lay panting or crab-hunted in the shallows while I, spread-eagled like a bird in the warm, transparent water, lay face downwards holding my breath and drifting over the landscape of the sea. When it grew close to midday and my stomach told me lunch would be ready I dried off in the sun, the salt forming in patches on my skin like a silky pattern of delicate lace, and started off home. As we meandered through the olive groves, shady and cool as a well between the great trunks, I heard a series of explosions in the myrtle groves away to the right. I moved over to investigate, keeping the dogs close to me, for Greek hunters were jumpy and would in most cases shoot before stopping to identify what they were shooting at. The danger applied to me too so I talked loudly to the dogs as a precaution. 'Here, Roger . . . heel! Good boy. Puke, Widdle! Widdle, come here! Heel . . . that's a good boy. Puke, come back . . .' I spotted the hunter sitting on a giant olive root and mopping his brow and, as soon as I knew he had seen us, I approached him.

He was a plump, white little man, with a moustache like an elongated black toothbrush over his prim little mouth, and dark glasses covered eyes as round and as liquid as a bird's. He was dressed in the height of fashion for hunting – polished riding boots, new breeches in white cord, an atrociously cut hacking jacket in mustard and green tweed, beset with so many pockets that it looked like the eaves of a house hung with swallows' nests. His green Tyrolean hat, with its bunch of scarlet and orange feathers, was tilted to the back of his curly head, and he was mopping his ivory brow with a large handkerchief that smelled strongly of cheap cologne.

'*Kalimera, kalimera*,' he greeted me, beaming and puffing. 'Welcome. Houf! It's a hot day, isn't it?'

I agreed, and offered him some of the strawberries that remained in my hat. He looked at them rather apprehensively, as if fearing they were poisoned, took one delicately in his plump fingers and smiled his thanks as he popped it into his mouth. I got the impression that he had never before eaten strawberries out of a hat with his fingers and was not quite sure about the rules.

'I've had a good morning's hunt,' he said proudly, pointing to where his game bag lay, bulging ominously, blood-bespattered and feathery. From the mouth of it protruded the wing and head of a lark, so blasted and mangled it was difficult to identify.

Would he, I inquired, mind if I examined the contents of his bag?

'No, no, of course not,' he said. 'You will see I'm quite a marksman.'

I did see. His bag consisted of four blackbirds, a golden oriole, two thrushes, eight larks, fourteen sparrows, two robins, a stone-chat, and a wren. The last, he admitted, was a bit small but very sweet to eat if cooked with paprika and garlic.

'But this,' he said proudly, 'is the best. Be careful, because it's not quite dead.'

He handed me a bloodstained handkerchief and I unwrapped it carefully. Inside, gasping and exhausted, a great, hard seal of blood on its wing, was a hoopoe.

'That is not, of course, good to eat,' he explained to me, 'but the feathers will look good in my hat.'

I had long wanted to possess one of these splendid, heraldic-looking birds, with their fine crests and their salmon-pink and black bodies, and I had searched everywhere for their nests so that I could hand-rear some young ones. Now here was a live hoopoe in my hands or, to be more exact, a half-dead one. I examined it carefully and found that it in fact looked worse than it was, for all it had was a broken wing, and this was a clean break as far as I could judge. The problem was how to get my proud, fat hunter to part with it.

Suddenly I had an inspiration. I started by saying that it made me feel bitter and annoyed that my mother was not there at that moment for she was, I explained, a world-famous authority on birds. (Mother could, with difficulty, distinguish between a sparrow and an ostrich). She had, in fact, written the definitive work on birds for the hunters of England. To prove it, I produced from my collecting bag a battered and much-consulted copy of *A Bird Book for the Pocket* by Edmund Sanders, a book I was never without.

My fat friend was most impressed. He turned over the pages muttering appreciative '*po po po po*'s' to himself. My Mother, he said, must be a remarkable woman to have written such a book. The reason I wished she was there at this moment, I went on, was because she had never seen a hoopoe. She had seen every other bird on the island, including the rare kingfisher; to prove it I took the scalp of a dead kingfisher I had found and used as a talisman in my collecting bag and laid it in front of him. He was struck with this little skull-cap of bright blue feathers. They were much prettier than hoopoe feathers when one considered it, I said. It took a little time for the thought to penetrate but I soon had him begging that I would take the hoopoe to my mother, in exchange for the scrap of velvety blue feathers. I put on a nice display of astonished reluctance fading into grovelling gratitude, put the wounded hoopoe inside my shirt and hurried home with it, leaving my hunter friend sitting on his olive root looking like Tweedledum and trying happily to fix the kingfisher scalp to his hat with a pin.

When I got home I took my new acquisition to my room and examined it carefully. To my relief, its long, curved rubbery beak, like a slender scimitar, was intact, for without the use of this delicate organ I knew that the bird could not survive. Apart from exhaustion and fright the only thing wrong with it appeared to be a broken wing. The break was high in the upper wing and, on investigating it gently, I found that it was a clean break, the bone having been snapped like a dry twig and not smashed and splintered like a green one. I carefully cut away the feathers with my dissecting scissors, washed the scab of blood and feathers away with warm water and disinfectant, splinted the bone with two curved slivers of bamboo, and bound the whole thing up tight. It was quite a professional job and I was proud of it. The only trouble was that it was too heavy and when I released the bird it fell over on its side, dragged down by the weight of the splint. After some experiment, I managed to make a much lighter splint out of bamboo and sticking plaster, and with a thin strip of bandage bound the whole thing firmly to the bird's side. Then, with a pipette, I gave it a drink of water and placed it in a cardboard box covered with a cloth to recover.

I called the hoopoe Hiawatha and the family greeted its arrival in our midst with unqualified approval, for they liked hoopoes and, moreover, it was the only exotic bird species they could all recognize at twenty paces. Finding things to eat for Hiawatha kept me very busy during the first few days of her convalescence, for she was a finicky patient, would only eat live food and was choosy about that. I had to release her on the floor of my room and throw the tit-bits at her – the succulent grasshoppers, as green as jade, locusts with plump thighs, their wings as crisp as biscuits, small lizards and tiny frogs. These she would grab and bang vigorously on any suitable hard surface – a chair or bed leg, the edge of the door or table – until she was sure that they were dead. Then, a couple of quick gulps and she would be ready for the next course. One day, when the family had all assembled in my room to watch Hiawatha feed, I gave her an eight-inch slow-worm. With her delicate beak, her finely banded crest, and her beautiful pink and black colour scheme, she looked a very demure bird, even more so because she generally kept her crest folded back against her skull. But now she took one look at the slow-worm and changed into a predatory monster. Her crest rose and spread itself, quivering like a peacock's tail, her throat puffed out, she uttered a strange little purring grunt deep in her throat and hopped rapidly and purposefully towards where the slow-worm was dragging along its burnished copper body, oblivious of its fate. Hiawatha paused and, with her splinted and her good wings spread out, she leaned forward and pecked at the slow-worm – a rapid, rapier-thrust of her beak, so quick it was difficult to see. The slow-worm, at the blow, writhed into a lashing figure of eight and I saw to my amazement that Hiawatha's first blow had completely crushed the reptile's egg-shell fragile skull.

'Good Lord!' said Larry, equally amazed. 'Now, that's what I call a *useful* bird to have around the house. A few dozen of those around and we wouldn't have to worry about snakes.'

'I don't think they could tackle a big one,' said Leslie judiciously.

'Well, I wouldn't mind if they just cleaned up the small ones,' said Larry. 'That'd be a start.'

'You talk as if the house were full of snakes, dear,' put in Mother.

'It is,' answered Larry austerely. 'What about the Medusa-wig of snakes Leslie found in the bath?'

'They were only water snakes,' said Mother.

'I don't care what they were. If Gerry's going to be allowed to fill the bath with snakes then I shall carry a brace of hoopoes around with me.'

'Ooh, look at it now!' squeaked Margo.

Hiawatha had delivered a number of rapid blows down the length of the slow-worm's body and she was now picking up the still-writhing length and dashing it onto the floor rhythmically, as the fishermen would beat an octopus against the rocks to make it tender. After a time there was no discernible life left in the body; Hiawatha stared down at it, crest up, head on one side. Satisfied, she seized the head in her beak. Slowly, gulping and throwing her head back, she swallowed it inch by inch. In a couple of minutes there was only half an inch of tail protruding from the corner of her beak.

Hiawatha never grew really tame and she was always nervous, but she learned to tolerate human beings in fairly close proximity to her. When she had settled down I used to take her out onto the veranda where I kept various other birds and let her walk about in the shade of the grape vine. It was not unlike a hospital ward, for at that time I had six sparrows recovering from concussion brought about by being caught in break-back mousetraps set by peasant boys, four blackbirds and a thrush who had been caught by baited fish-hooks set in the olive groves, and half a dozen assorted birds ranging from a tern to a magpie recovering from the effects of gunshot wounds. In addition, there was a nest of young goldfinches and an almost-fledged greenfinch which I was hand-rearing. Hiawatha did not seem to mind the proximity of these other birds but she kept herself to herself, pacing slowly up and down the flagstones, brooding with half-closed eyes, aloofly aristocratic like a beautiful queen imprisoned in some castle. At the sight of a worm, frog, or grasshopper, of course, her behaviour would become anything but queenly.

About a week after Hiawatha had entered my avian clinic I set off one morning to meet Spiro. This was a sort of daily ritual; he would blow loud blasts on his horn when he reached the edge of the property, which was some fifty acres in extent, and I and the dogs would tear through the olive groves to intercept him somewhere along the drive. Panting for breath, I would burst out of the olive groves, the dogs barking hysterically in front of me, and we would hold up the great, gleaming Dodge, its hood back, Spiro in his peaked cap crouching, massive, brown, and scowling behind the wheel. I would take my place on the running board, holding tight to the windscreen, and Spiro would drive on, the dogs in an ecstasy of mock fierceness trying to bite the front tyres. The conversation every morning was also a ritual that never varied.

'Good mornings, Master Gerrys,' Spiro would say. 'Hows are yous?'

Having ascertained that I had not developed any dangerous disease during the night, he would inquire after the rest of us.

'And hows the familys?' he would ask. 'Hows your mothers? And Master Larrys? And Master Leslies? And Missy Margos?'

By the time I had reassured him as to their health we would have reached the villa, where he would lumber from one member of the family to the other checking as to whether my information was correct. I was rather bored by the daily, almost journalistic interest Spiro took in the family's health, as if they were royalty, but he persisted as if some awful fate might have overtaken them during the night. One day, in a fit of devilry, I told him, in response to his earnest inquiry, that they were all dead; the car swerved off the drive and crashed straight into a large oleander bush, showering Spiro and myself with pink blossoms and nearly knocking me off the running board.

'Gollys, Master Gerrys! You mustn't say things like thats!' he roared, pounding the wheel with his fist. 'You makes me scarce when you say things likes that. You makes me sweats! Don't you ever say that agains.'

This particular morning, having reassured himself as to the health of each member of the family, he lifted a small strawberry basket covered with a fig leaf from the seat by his side.

'Here,' he said, scowling at me. 'I gots a presents for you.'

I took the leaf off the basket. Inside crouched two naked and repulsive-looking birds. I was enchanted and thanked Spiro profusely, for they were baby jays, as I could see by their sprouting wing-feathers. I had never had jays before. I was so pleased with them that I took them with me when I went to my studies with Mr Kralefsky. This was the advantage of having a tutor who was as mad about birds as I was. Together we spent an exciting and interesting morning trying to teach them to open their mouths and feed, when we should have been committing the glittering pageantry of English history to memory. But the babies were singularly stupid and refused to accept either Kralefsky or myself as a substitute mother.

I took them back home at lunch-time and during the afternoon tried to get them to behave sensibly, but without success. They would only take food if I forced their beaks open and pushed it down their throats with my finger, a process that they strongly objected to, as well they might. Eventually, having shoved enough down them to keep them more or less alive, I left them in their strawberry basket on the veranda and went to fetch Hiawatha, who had shown a marked preference for having her food served on the veranda rather than in the privacy of my room. I placed her on the flagstones and started to throw her the grasshoppers I had caught for her. She hopped eagerly, snapped up the first, killed it, and swallowed it with almost indecent haste.

As she sat there gulping, looking rather like an elderly, angular dowager duchess who had swallowed a sorbet the wrong way at a ball, the two baby jays, lolling their heads, bleary-eyed, over the edge of their basket, caught sight of her. Immediately, they started to call wheezily, open-mouthed, their heads wobbling from side to side like two very old men looking over a fence. Hiawatha put up her crest and stared at them. I did not expect her to take much notice, for she always ignored the other baby birds when they called out to be fed, but she hopped nearer the basket and surveyed the baby jays interestedly. I threw her a grasshopper and she grabbed it, killed it, and then, to my complete astonishment, hopped up to the basket and crammed the insect down the gaping maw of one of the jays. Both babies wheezed and screamed and flapped their wings in delight and Hiawatha looked as startled as I was at what she had done. I threw her another grasshopper and she killed it and fed the other baby. After this, I would feed Hiawatha in my room and then bring her down onto the veranda periodically where she would act the part of mother to the baby jays.

She never showed any other maternal feelings for the babies; she would not, for example, seize the little encapsulated blobs of excreta from the babies' behinds when they cocked them over the edge of the nest. This task of cleaning up was left to me. Once she had fed the babies so that they stopped screaming, she lost all interest in them. I concluded it must be something in the timbre of their call that aroused her maternal instincts, for although I experimented with the other babies I possessed and they screamed their lungs out, she took no notice at all. Gradually, the baby jays decided to let me feed them and as soon as they stopped calling at her appearance Hiawatha took no further notice of them. It was not simply that she ignored them; she seemed unaware of their existence.

When her wing had healed, I removed the splint and found that although the bone had set well the wing muscles had become weak with lack of use, and Hiawatha tended to favour the wing, always walking rather than flying. To make her exercise it I used to take her down into the olive groves and throw her up into the air so that she was forced to use her wings to make a safe landing. Gradually, she started to take short flights as the wing strengthened and I began to think that I would be able to release her, when she met her death. I had taken her out onto the veranda one day and while I was feeding my assortment of babies Hiawatha flew or, rather, glided down to a nearby olive grove to practise her flying and make a light snack on some daddy long-legs that were just hatching.

I was absorbed in feeding the babies and was not taking much notice when suddenly I heard hoarse, despairing cries from Hiawatha. I vaulted over the veranda rail and raced through the trees, but I was too late. A large, mangy, battle-scarred feral cat was standing with the limp form of the hoopoe in his mouth, his great green eyes staring at me over her pink body. I gave a shout and ran forward; the cat turned with oil-like fluidity and leaped into the myrtle bushes carrying Hiawatha's body with him. I gave chase but once the cat had reached the tangled sanctuary of the myrtles it was impossible to track him down. I returned, furious and upset, to the olive grove, where all that was left to remind me of Hiawatha were some pink feathers and a few drops of blood scattered like rubies on the grass. I swore that if I ever came across the cat again I would kill it if I could. Apart from anything else, it presented a threat to the rest of my bird collection.

But my mourning for Hiawatha was cut short by the arrival in our midst of something slightly more exotic than a hoopoe and much more trouble. Larry had suddenly announced that he was going to stay with some friends of his in Athens and do some research work. After the flurry of his departure, tranquillity descended on the villa. Leslie spent most of his time pottering about with a gun and Margo, who at that moment was not engaged in any hectic affair of the heart, had taken up soap sculpture. Ensconced in the attic, she was producing somewhat lopsided and slippery pieces of sculpture out of an acrid-smelling yellow soap and appearing in a flowered smock and an artistic trance at mealtimes.

Mother, seizing on this unexpected period of calm, decided to do a job that had long wanted doing. The previous year had been an exceptionally good one for fruit and Mother had spent hours preparing various jams and chutneys, some from her grandmother's recipes from India dating back to the early eighteen hundreds. Everything went fine and the big cool larder was a-glint with battalions of bottles. Unfortunately, during a particularly savage storm in the winter, the larder roof had leaked and in consequence Mother had come down one morning and found all the labels had come off. She was faced with several hundred jars, the contents of which were difficult to identify unless you opened the jar. Now, given a moment's respite by her family, she determined to do this necessary job. Since it involved tasting, I offered to help. Between us we had got some hundred and fifty jars of preserves on the kitchen table, armed ourselves with spoons and new labels, and were just about to start on the mammoth tasting when Spiro arrived.

'Good afternoons, Mrs Durrells. Goods afternoons, Master Gerrys,' he rumbled, lumbering into the kitchen like a chestnut-brown dinosaur. 'I's gots a telegrams for you, Mrs Durrells.'

'A telegram, Spiro?' Mother quavered. 'Who from, I wonder? I hope it's not bad news.'

'No, don't you worry, it's not bad news, Mrs Durrells,' he said, handing her the telegram. 'I gots the man in the post office to reads it to me. It's from Master Larrys.'

'Oh dear,' said Mother, with foreboding.

The telegram said simply: 'Forgot to tell you Prince Jeejeebuoy arriving eleventh short stay. Athens wonderful. Love. Larry.'

'Really, Larry is the most annoying creature!' Mother exclaimed angrily. 'What does he go and invite a prince for? He knows we haven't got the right rooms for royalty. And he won't be here to entertain him. What am I supposed to do with a prince?'

She gazed at us in a distraught fashion but neither Spiro nor I could give her any intelligent advice. We could not even telegraph Larry and demand his return, for, characteristically, he had gone off and omitted to give us his friends' address.

'The eleventh is tomorrow, isn't it? He'll be coming on the boat from Brindisi, I expect. Spiro, would you meet him and bring him out? And will you bring some lamb for lunch? Gerry, go and tell Margo to put some flowers in the spare room and to make sure the dogs haven't put any fleas in there, and tell Leslie he must go down to the village and tell Red Spiro we want some fish. Really, it's too bad of Larry . . . I shall give him a piece of my mind when he gets back. I can't be bothered with entertaining princes at my age.' Mother bustled angrily and aimlessly around the kitchen, banging saucepans and frying pans about.

'I'll brings you some of my dahlias for the tables. Do you wants any champagne?' asked Spiro, who obviously felt that the prince should be treated properly.

'No, if he thinks I'm paying a pound a bottle for champagne, he's mistaken. He can just drink ouzo and wine like the rest of us, prince or no prince,' said Mother firmly, and then added, 'Well, I suppose you'd better bring a crate. We needn't give him any and it always comes in useful.'

'Don'ts you worrys, Mrs Durrells,' said Spiro comfortingly, 'I fixes anythings you wants. You wants I gets the King's butler again?'

The King's butler, an ancient and aristocratic old boy, was dragged out of retirement by Spiro every time we had a big party.

'No, no, Spiro, we're not going to go to a lot of trouble. After all, he's coming unexpectedly so he'll just have to take us as he finds us. He'll just have to take pot-luck . . . and . . . and . . . muck in. And if he doesn't like it . . . well, it's just too bad,' said Mother, shelling peas with trembling hands and dropping more on the floor than into the colander. 'And, Gerry, go and ask Margo if she could run up those new curtains for the dining-room. The material's in my bedroom. The old ones don't look the same since Les set fire to them.'

So the villa was transformed into a hive of activity. The wooden floor of the spare room was scrubbed until it was a pale cream colour, just in case the dogs had put any fleas in there; Margo ran up the new curtains in record time and did flower arrangements everywhere; and Leslie cleaned his guns and boat in case the prince should want to go shooting or yachting. Mother, scarlet with heat, trotted frantically around the kitchen making scones, cakes, apple turnovers, and brandysnaps, stews, pies, jellies, and trifles. I was merely told to remove all my animals from the veranda and to keep them under control, to go and have my hair cut and to make sure I put on a clean shirt. So the following day, all dressed up by Mother's orders, we sat on the veranda and waited patiently for the prince to be brought out to us by Spiro.

'What's he a prince *of* ?' asked Leslie.

'Well, I don't really know,' said Mother. 'One of those small states the maharajas have, I expect.'

'It's a very odd name, Jeejeebuoy,' said Margo, 'are you sure it's real?'

'Of course it's real, dear,' said Mother. 'There are lots of Jeejeebuoys in India. It's a very old family, like . . . um . . . like . . .'

'Smith?' suggested Leslie.

'No, no, not nearly as common as that. No, the Jeejeebuoys go right back in history. There must have been Jeejeebuoys long before my grandparents went to India.'

'His ancestors probably organized the Mutiny,' suggested Leslie with relish. 'Let's ask him if his grandfather invented the Black Hole of Calcutta.'

'Oh, yes, let's,' said Margo. 'D'you think he did? What was it?'

'Leslie, dear, you shouldn't say things like that,' said Mother. 'After all, we must forgive and forget.'

'Forgive and forget what?' asked Leslie, bewildered, not having followed Mother's train of thought.

'Everything,' said Mother firmly, adding, rather obscurely, 'I'm sure they *meant* well.'

Before Leslie could investigate this further, the car roared up the drive and drew up below the veranda with an impressive squeal of brakes. Sitting in the back, dressed in black, and with a beautifully arranged turban as white as a snowdrop bud, sat a slender, diminutive Indian with enormous, glittering almond-shaped eyes that were like pools of liquid agate fringed with eyelashes as thick as a carpet. He opened the door deftly and leaped out of the car. His smile of welcome was like a lightning flash of white in his brown face.

'Vell, vell, here ve are at last,' he cried excitedly, spreading his slender brown hands like butterfly wings and dancing up onto the veranda. 'You must be Mrs Durrell, of course. Such charm. And you are the hunter of the family . . . Leslie. And Margo, the beauty of the island, vitout doubt . . . And Gerry the savant, the naturalist *par excellence*. I can't tell you how hot it makes me to meet you all.'

'Oh . . . well . . . er . . . er . . . yes, we're delighted to meet you, Your Highness,' Mother began.

Jeejeebuoy uttered a yelp and slapped his forehead.

'Desh and demnation!' he said. 'My foolish name again! My dear Mrs Durrell, how can I apologize? Prince is my Christian name. A vhim on my mother's part to make our humble family royal, you understand? A mother's love, hm? Dream son vill aspire to golden heights, huh? No, no, poor voman, ve must forgive her, uh? I am plain Prince Jeejeebuoy, at your service.'

'Oh,' said Mother, who having geared herself to cope with royalty, felt somewhat let-down. 'Well, what do we call you?'

'My friends, of which I have an inordinate number,' said the new arrival earnestly, 'call me Jeejee. I do hope that you vill call me the same.'

So Jeejee took up residence and during the short time he was there created greater havoc and endeared himself more to us than any other guest we had had. With his pedantic English, his earnest, gentle air, he took such a deep and genuine interest in everything and everyone that he was irresistible. For Lugaretzia he had various pots of evil-smelling sticky substances with which to anoint her numerous imaginary aches and pains; with Leslie he would discuss in grave detail the state of hunting in the world and give graphic and probably untrue stories of tiger and wild boar hunts he had been on. For Margo he procured some lengths of cloth and made them into saris and taught her how to wear them; Spiro he would enthral with tales of the riches and mysteriousness of the East, of bejewelled elephants wrestling with each other and maharajas worth their weight in precious stones. He was proficient with his pencil and as well as taking a deep and genuine interest in all my pets completely won me over by doing delicate little sketches of them for me to stick in my natural history diary, a document which was, to my mind, considerably more important than a combination of the *Magna Carta*, *The Book of Kells* and the *Gutenberg Bible*, and was treated as such by our discerning guest. But it was Mother that Jeejee really charmed into submission, for not only did he have endless mouth-watering recipes for her to write down and a fund of folklore and ghost stories, but his visit enabled Mother to talk endlessly about India, where she had been born and bred and which she considered her real home.

In the evening we would sit long over our meal at the big, creaking dining table, the clusters of oil lamps in the corners of the great room blooming in pools of primrose yellow light, the drifts of small moths fluttering against them like snow; the dogs lying in the doorway – now their numbers had risen to four they were never allowed into the dining-room – would yawn and sigh at our tardiness, but we would be oblivious to them. Outside the ringing cries of the crickets and the crackle of tree frogs would make the velvety night alive. In the lamplight Jeejee's eyes would seem to grow bigger and blacker like an owl's, with a strange liquid fire in them.

'Of course, in your day, Mrs Durrell, things vere different. You could not intermingle. No, no, strict segregation, vasn't it? But now things are better. First the maharajas got their toes in the doors and nowadays even some of us humbler Indians are allowed to intermingle and thus accrue some of the advantages of civilization,' said Jeejee one evening.

'In my day,' said Mother, 'it was the Eurasians that they felt most strongly about. We wouldn't be allowed even to play with them by my grandmother. Of course we always did.'

'Children are singularly insensitive to the correct civilized behaviour,' said Jeejee smiling. 'Still there vere some difficulties at first, you know. Rome, however, vas not built in a day. Did you hear about the Babu in my town who vas invited to the ball?'

'No, what happened?'

'Vell, he saw that after the gentlemen had finished dancing with the ladies they escorted them back to their chairs and fanned them with the ladies' fan. So, having conducted a sprightly valtz with a European lady of some eminence he conducted her safely back to her seat, took her fan, and said, "Madam, may I make vind in your face?"'

'That sounds the sort of thing Spiro would say,' said Leslie.

'I remember once,' said Mother throwing herself into reminiscence with pleasure, 'when my husband was Chief Engineer in Rourki. We had the most terrible cyclone. Larry was only a baby. The house was a long, low one and I remember we ran from room to room trying to hold the doors shut against the wind. As we ran from room to room, the house simply collapsed behind us. We eventually ended up in the butler's pantry. But when we had the house repaired the Babu contractor sent in a bill which was headed "For repairs to Chief Engineer's backside".'

'India must have been fascinating then,' said Jeejee, 'because, unlike most Europeans, you vere part of the country.'

'Oh yes,' said Mother, 'even my grandmother was born there. When most people talked of home and meant England, when *we* said home we meant India.'

'You must have travelled extensively,' said Jeejee enviously. 'I suppose you've seen more of my country than I have.'

'Practically every nook and cranny,' said Mother. 'My husband being a civil engineer, of course, he had to travel. I always used to go with him. If he had to build a bridge or a railway right out in the jungle, I'd go with him and we'd camp.'

'That must have been fun,' said Leslie enthusiastically, 'a primitive life under canvas.'

'Oh it was. I loved the simple life in camp. I remember the elephants used to go ahead with the marquees, the carpets and the furniture, and then the servants would follow in the ox-carts with the linen and silver . . .'

'You call that camping?' interrupted Leslie incredulously. 'With marquees?'

'We only had three,' said Mother defensively. 'A bedroom, dining-room and a drawing-room. And they were built with fitted carpets anyway.'

'Well, I don't call that camping,' said Leslie.

'It was,' said Mother. 'It was right out in the jungle. We could hear tigers and all the servants were terrified. Once they killed a cobra under the dining table.'

'And that was before Gerry was born,' said Margo.

'You should write your memoirs, Mrs Durrell,' said Jeejee gravely.

'Oh no,' laughed Mother, 'I couldn't possibly write. Besides, what would I call it?'

'How about "It Took Fourteen Elephants"?' suggested Leslie.

'Or, "Through the Forest on a Fitted Carpet",' suggested Jeejee.

'The trouble with you boys is you never take anything seriously,' said Mother severely.

'Yes,' said Margo, '*I* think it was jolly brave of Mother to camp with only three marquees and cobras and things.'

'Camping!' snorted Leslie derisively.

'Well, it *was* camping dear. I remember once one of the elephants went astray and we had no clean sheets for three days. Your father was most annoyed.'

'I never knew anything as big as an elephant *could* go astray,' said Jeejee, surprised.

'Oh, yes,' said Leslie, 'easily mislaid, elephants.'

'Well, anyway, you wouldn't like it if *you* were without clean sheets,' said Mother with dignity.

'Of course they wouldn't,' put in Margo, 'and I think it's fun hearing about ancient India, even if they don't.'

'But I do find it most educational,' Jeejee protested.

'You're always making fun of Mother,' said Margo. 'I don't see why you should be so superior just because your father invented the Black Hole or whatever it was.'

It says much for Jeejee that he almost fell under the table laughing, and all the dogs started barking vociferously at his mirth.

But probably the most endearing thing about Jeejee was his intense enthusiasm for anything he happened to take up, even when it was demonstrated beyond a shadow of a doubt that he could not achieve success in that sphere of activity. When Larry had first met him he had decided to be one of India's greatest poets and with the aid of a compatriot who spoke little English ('he vas my compositor,' Jeejee explained) he started a magazine called *Poetry for the People*, or *Potry for the Peeple* or *Potery for the Peopeople*, depending on whether Jeejee was supervising his compositor or not. This little magazine was published once a month, with contributions from everyone that Jeejee knew, and some of them made strange reading, as we discovered, for Jeejee's

luggage was full of blurred copies of his magazine which he
would hand out to anyone who displayed interest.

Perusing them we discovered such interesting items as 'The
Potry of Stiffen Splendour – a creetical evaluation'. Jeejee's compositor friend apparently believed in printing words as they
sounded, or, rather, as they sounded to him at that moment.
Thus there was a long and eulogistic article by Jeejee on 'Tees
Ellyot, Pot Supreme'. The compositor's novel spelling combined
with the misprints naturally to be found in such a work, made
reading it a pleasurable though puzzling occupation. 'Whye
Notte a Black Pot Lorat?', for example, posed an almost un-
answerable question, written apparently in Chaucerian English;
while the article entitled 'Roy Cambill, Ball Fighter and Pot',
made one wonder what poetry was coming to. However, Jeejee
was undaunted by the difficulties, including the fact that his
compositor never pronounced the letter 'h' and so never used it.
His latest enthusiasm was to start a second magazine (printed on
the same hand-press with the same carefree compositor), devoted
to his newly evolved study of what he called 'Fakyo', which was
described in the first copy of *Fakyo for All* as 'an amalgam of the
misterious East, bringing together the best of Yoga and Fakirism,
giving details and tiching people ow'.

Mother was greatly intrigued by Fakyo, until Jeejee started to
practise it. Clad in a loincloth and covered in ashes, he meditated
for hours on the veranda or else walked in a well-simulated
trance through the house, leaving a trail of ashes behind him. He
fasted religiously for four days, and on the fifth day worried
Mother to death by fainting and falling down the stairs.

'Really, Jeejee,' said Mother crossly, 'this has got to stop.
There's not enough *of* you to fast.'

Putting him to bed, Mother concocted huge strength-giving
curries, only to have Jeejee complain that there was no Bombay
duck, the dried fish which was such a pungent and attractive
addition to any curry.

'But you can't get it here, Jeejee; I've tried,' Mother protested.

Jeejee waved his hands like pale bronze moths against the white of the sheet.

'Fakyo tells that in life there is a substitute for everything,' he said firmly.

When he recovered sufficiently, he paid a visit to the fish market in the town and purchased a vast quantity of fresh sardines. We came back from a pleasant morning's shopping in the town to find the kitchen and its environs untenable. Jeejee, brandishing a knife with which he was gutting the fish before laying them out in the sun to dry outside the back door, was doing battle with what appeared to be every fly, bluebottle and wasp in the Ionian Islands. He had been stung about five times and one eye was swollen and partially closed. The smell of rapidly decomposing sardines was overwhelming and the kitchen floor and table were covered in snowdrifts of silver fish skin and bits of entrails. It was only when Mother showed him the article on Bombay duck in the *Encyclopaedia Britannica* that he reluctantly gave up the idea of sardines as a substitute. It took Mother two days, with buckets of hot water and disinfectant, to rid the kitchen of the smell, and even then there was still the odd wasp blundering in hopefully through the windows.

'Perhaps I'd better find you a substitute in Athens or Istanbul,' said Jeejee hopefully. 'I vas thinking that lobster baked and crushed to a powder . . .'

'I wouldn't worry about it, Jeejee dear,' said Mother hurriedly. 'We've done without it for some time now and it hasn't hurt us.'

Jeejee was *en route* for Persia via Turkey in order to visit an Indian fakir practising there.

'From him I shall learn many things to add to Fakyo,' said Jeejee. 'He is a great man. In particular, he is a great exponent of holding his breath and going into a trance. He vas vunce buried for a hundred and twenty days.'

'Extraordinary,' said Mother, deeply interested.

'You mean buried alive?' asked Margo. 'Buried alive for a hundred and twenty days? How horrible! It doesn't seem natural somehow.'

'But he's in a trance, dear Margo; he feels nothing,' explained Jeejee.

'I'm not so sure,' said Mother musingly. 'That's why I want to be cremated, you know. Just in case I happen to slip into a trance and no one notices.'

'Don't be ridiculous, Mother,' said Leslie.

'It's not ridiculous,' replied Mother firmly. 'People are so careless nowadays.'

'And what else does a fakir do?' asked Margo. 'Can he make mango trees grow from seeds? You know, straight away? I saw them do that in Simla once.'

'That is simple conjuring,' said Jeejee. 'Vhat Andrawathi does is much more complex. He is an expert in levitation, for example, and it is vun of the things I vant to see him about.'

'But I thought levitation was card tricks,' said Margo.

'No,' said Leslie, 'it's floating about, sort of flying, isn't it, Jeejee?'

'Yes,' said Jeejee. 'A vonderful ability. A lot of the early Christian saints could do it. I myself have not yet reached that stage of proficiency; that is vhy I vant to study under Andrawathi.'

'How lovely to be able to float like a bird,' said Margo delightedly. 'What fun you could have.'

'I believe it to be a truly tremendous experience,' said Jeejee, his eyes shining. 'You feel as if you are being lifted tovards heaven.'

The following day, just before lunch, Margo came rushing into the drawing-room in a state of panic.

'Come quickly! Come quickly!' she screamed. 'Jeejee's committing suicide!'

We hurried outside and there, perched on the window-sill of his room, was Jeejee, clad in nothing but a loincloth.

'He's got one of those trances again,' said Margo, as if it were an infectious disease.

Mother straightened her glasses and stared upwards. Jeejee started to sway gently.

'Go upstairs and grab him, Les,' said Mother. 'Quickly. I'll keep him talking.'

The fact that Jeejee was raptly silent did not occur to her. Leslie rushed into the house. Mother cleared her throat.

'Jeejee, dear,' she fluted, 'I don't think it's very *wise* of you to be up there. Why don't you come down and have lunch?'

Jeejee did come down, but not quite as Mother intended. He stepped gaily out into space and, accompanied by horrified cries from Mother and Margo, fell earthwards. He crashed into the grapevine some ten feet beneath his window, sending a shower of grapes on to the flagstones. Fortunately, the vine was an old and sinewy one and it held Jeejee's slight weight.

'My God!' he shouted. 'Vere am I?'

'In the grapevine,' screamed Margo excitedly. 'You agitated yourself there.'

'Don't move till we get a ladder,' said Mother faintly.

We got a ladder and extricated the tousled Jeejee from the depths of the vine. He was bruised and scratched but otherwise unhurt. Everyone's nerves were soothed with brandy and we sat down to a late lunch. By the time evening came, Jeejee had convinced himself that he had in fact succeeded in levitating himself.

'If my toes had not become entangled in the pernicious vine, I vould have gone sailing around the house,' he said, lying bandaged but happy on the sofa. '*Vhat* an achievement!'

'Yes, well, I'll be happier if you don't practise while you are staying here,' said Mother. 'My nerves won't stand it.'

'I vill come back from Persia and spend my birthday with you, my dear Mrs Durrell,' said Jeejee, 'and I vill then report progress.'

'Well, I don't want a repetition of today,' said Mother severely. 'You might have killed yourself.'

Two days later Jeejeebuoy, still covered with sticking plaster but undaunted, left for Persia.

'I wonder if he will come back for his birthday,' said Margo. 'If he does, let's have a special party for him.'

'Yes, that's a good idea,' said Mother. 'He's such a sweet boy, but so . . . erratic, so . . . *unsafe.*'

'Well, he's the only guest we've had who could really be described as having paid a flying visit,' said Leslie.

6

The Royal Occasion

Kings and Bears oft worry their keepers.

Scottish Proverb

In those halcyon days we spent in Corfu it could be said that every day was a special day, specially coloured, specially arranged, so that it differed completely from the other three hundred and sixty-four and was memorable because of this. But there is one day in particular which stands out in my mind, for it involved not only the family and their circle of acquaintances but the entire population of Corfu.

It was the day that King George returned to Greece and nothing like it for colour, excitement and intrigue had ever been experienced in the island. Even the difficulties of organizing St Spiridion's procession paled into insignificance beside this event.

I first heard about the honour that was to fall on Corfu from my tutor, Mr Kralefsky. He was so overwhelmed with excitement that he took scant interest in the cock linnet I had been at considerable pains to procure for him.

'Great news, dear boy, great news! Good morning, good morning,' he greeted me, his large soulful eyes brimming with tears of emotion, his shapely hands flapping to and fro and his head bobbing with excitement below his hump-back. 'A proud day for this island, by Jove! Yes indeed, a proud day for Greece, but an especially proud one for this, our island. Er . . . what? Oh, the linnet . . . Yes. Nice birdie . . . tweet, tweet. But, as I was saying, what a triumph for us here in this little realm set in a sea of blue, as Shakespeare has it, to have the King visit us.'

This, I thought, was more like it. I could raise a faint enthusiasm for a real king, if only for the fringe benefits that might accrue. Which king was it, I inquired, and would I have a holiday when he came?

'Why, the King of Greece, King George,' said Mr Kralefsky, shocked by my ignorance. 'Didn't you know?'

I pointed out that we did not have the dubious benefits of a wireless and so, for the most part, lived in a state of blissful ignorance.

'Well,' said Mr Kralefsky, gazing at me rather worriedly, as if blaming himself for my lack of knowledge, 'well, we had Metaxas, as you know, and he was a dictator. Now, mercifully, they've got rid of him, odious man, so now His Majesty can come back.'

When, I inquired, had they got rid of Metaxas? Nobody had told me.

'Why, you remember, surely!' cried Kralefsky. 'You *must* remember – when we had the revolution and that cake shop was so badly damaged by the machine-gun bullets. Such unsafe things, I always think, machine-guns.'

I did remember the revolution because it had given me three days' blissful holiday from my lessons and the cake shop had been one of my favourite shops. But I had not connected this with Metaxas. Would there, I inquired hopefully, be another shop disembowelled by machine-gun fire when the King came?

'No, no,' said Kralefsky shocked. 'No, it'll be a most gay occasion. Everyone *en fête*, as they say. Well, it's such exciting news that I think we might be forgiven if we take the morning off to celebrate. Come upstairs and help me feed the birds.'

So we made our way up to the huge attic in which Kralefsky kept his collection of wild birds and canaries and spent a satisfying morning feeding them, Kralefsky dancing about the room waving the watering-can, his feet scrunching on the fallen seed as if it were a shingle beach, singing snatches of the 'Marseillaise' to himself.

Over lunch I imparted the news of the King's visit to the family. They each received it in their characteristic ways.

'That'll be nice,' said Mother, 'I'd better start working out menus.'

'He's not coming to stay *here*, thank God,' Larry pointed out.

'I know that, dear,' said Mother, 'but . . . er . . . there'll be all sorts of parties and things I suppose.'

'I don't see why,' said Larry.

'Because they always do,' said Mother. 'When we were in India we always had parties during the durbar.'

'This is not India,' said Larry, 'so I don't intend to waste my time working out the stabling for elephants. The whole thing will have a disruptive enough effect on the even tenor of our ways as it is, mark my words.'

'If we're having parties, can I have some new clothes, Mother?' asked Margo eagerly. 'I really haven't got a thing to wear.'

'I wonder if they'll fire a salute,' mused Leslie. 'They've only got those old Venetian cannons, but I should think they'd be damned dangerous. I wonder if I ought to pop in and see the Commandant of the Fort.'

'You keep out of it,' Larry advised. 'They want to welcome the man, not assassinate him.'

'I saw some lovely red silk the other day,' said Margo, 'in that little shop . . . you know, the one where you turn right by Theodore's laboratory?'

'Yes, dear, how nice,' said Mother, not listening. 'I wonder if Spiro can get me some turkeys?'

But the effect of the Royal Visit on the family paled into insignificance in comparison with the traumatic effect it had on Corfu as a whole. It was pointed out, by somebody who should have known better, that not only was the island going to be

graced by a visit from the monarch but the whole episode would
be particularly symbolic as when the King arrived in Corfu he
would be setting foot on Greek soil for the first time since his
exile. At this thought the Corfiotes lashed themselves into a fever
of activity and before long so complicated and so acrimonious
had the preparations become that we were forced to go into
town each day to sit on the Platia with the rest of Corfu to learn
the news of the latest scandal.

The Platia, laid out with its great arches to resemble the Rue
de Rivoli by French architects in the early days of the French
occupation of Corfu, was the hub of the island. Here you would
sit at little tables under the arches or beneath the shimmering
trees and, sooner or later, you would see everyone on the island
and hear every facet of every scandal. One sat there drinking
quietly and, sooner or later, all the protagonists in the drama
were washed up at one's table.

'I *am* Corfu,' said Countess Malinopoulos. 'Therefore it is
incumbent upon me to form the committee that works out how
we are to welcome our gracious King.'

'Yes, indeed, I do see that,' Mother agreed nervously.

The Countess, who resembled a raddled black crow wearing an orange wig, was a formidable force, there was no doubt,
but the matter was too important to allow her to ride rough-
shod over everyone. Within a very short time there were no less
than six welcoming committees, all struggling to persuade the
Nomarch that their plans ought to take preference over all others.
It was rumoured that he had an armed guard and slept in a locked
room after an attempt by one of the female committee members
to sacrifice her virginity in order to get his approval to her
committee's schemes.

'Disgusting!' trumpeted Lena Mavrokondas, rolling her black
eyes and smacking her red lips as she wished that she had thought
of the idea herself. 'Imagine, my dears, a woman of her age trying
to break into the Nomarch's room, naked!'

'It does seem a curious way to try to get his ear,' Larry agreed innocently.

'No, no, it is too absurd,' Lena went on, deftly popping olives into her scarlet mouth as though she were loading a gun. 'I've seen the Nomarch and I am sure he will agree to my committee being the official one. It is such shame the British flit is not in port; we could then have arrange a guard of honour. Oh, those lovely sailors in their uniform, they always look so clean and so virulent.'

'The incidence of infectious diseases in the Royal Navy . . .' Larry began, when Mother hastily interrupted.

'Do tell us what your plans are, Lena,' she said, glaring at Larry, who was on his eighth ouzo and inclined to be somewhat unreliable.

'Soch plans, my dears, soch plans ve 'ave! This whole Platia vill be decorate in blue and vite, but alvays ve 'ave troubles with that fool Marko Paniotissa.' Lena's eyes rolled in despair.

Marko, we knew, was a sort of inspired madman and we wondered how he had got on to the committee at all.

'What does Marko want to do?' asked Larry.

'Donkeys!' hissed Lena, as if it were an obscene word.

'Donkeys?' repeated Larry. 'He wants to have donkeys? What does he think it is? An agricultural show?'

'This I explain 'im,' said Lena, 'but alvays 'e wants to 'ave donkeys. 'E says it is symbolic, like Christ's ride into Jerusalem, so 'e vants blue and vite donkeys.'

'Blue and white ones? You mean dyed?' asked Mother. 'Whatever for?'

'To match the Greek flags,' said Lena, rising to her feet and facing us grimly, shoulders back, hands clenched; 'but I tell 'im, "Marko," I say, "you 'ave donkeys over my dead corpse."'

She strode off down the Platia, every inch a daughter of Greece.

The next one to stop at our table was Colonel Velvit, a tall, rather beautiful old man with a Byronic profile and an angular body that twitched and moved like a windblown marionette. With his curling white hair and flashing dark eyes, he looked incongruous in his Scout's uniform, but he carried it off with dignity. Since his retirement his one interest in life was the local Scout troop and, while there were those unkind enough to say that his interest in Scouts was not entirely altruistic, he worked hard and had certainly never yet been caught.

He accepted an ouzo and sat mopping his face with a lavender-scented handkerchief.

'Those boys,' he said plaintively, 'those boys of mine will be the death of me. They are so high spirited.'

'What they probably need is a bevy of nubile Girl Guides,' said Larry. 'Have you thought of that?'

'It is no joke, my dear,' said the Colonel, eyeing Larry morosely. 'They are so full of high spirits I fear they will get up to some prank or other. I was simply horrified at what they did today and the Nomarch was most annoyed.'

'The poor Nomarch appears to be getting it in the neck from every direction,' said Leslie.

'What did your Scouts do?' asked Mother.

'Well, as you know, my dear Mrs Durrell, I am training them to put on a special demonstration for His Majesty on the evening of his arrival.' The Colonel sipped his drink delicately like a cat. 'First, they march out, some dressed in blue and some in white, in front of the . . . how do you call it? . . . dais! Exactly so, the dais. And they form a square and salute the King. Then, at the word of command they change positions and form the Greek flag. It's a very striking sight, though I say it myself.'

He paused, drained his glass and sat back.

'Well, the Nomarch wanted to see how we were progressing so he came along and stood on the dais, representing the King, as it were. Then I gave the command and the troop marched out.'

He closed his eyes and a small shudder shook him.

'Do you know what they did?' he asked, in a small voice. 'I have never felt so ashamed. They marched out, stopped in front of the Nomarch and gave the Fascist salute. Boy Scouts! The Fascist salute!'

'Did they shout "*Heil* Nomarch"?' asked Larry.

'Mercifully, no,' said Colonel Velvit. 'For a moment I was paralysed with shock and then, hoping that the Nomarch had not noticed, I gave the command to form the flag. They moved about and then, to my horror, the Nomarch was confronted by a blue and white swastika. He was furious. He almost cancelled our part in the proceedings. What a blow to the Scout movement that would have been!'

'Yes, indeed,' said Mother, 'but they're only children, after all.'

'That's true, my dear Mrs Durrell, but I cannot have people saying that I am training a group of Fascists,' said Colonel Velvit earnestly. 'They'll be saying next that I plan to take over Corfu.'

During the ensuing days, as the time of the great event grew nearer, the island's inhabitants became more and more frenzied and tempers grew shorter and shorter. Countess Malinopoulos was now no longer speaking to Lena Mavrokondas and she in her turn was not speaking to Colonel Velvit because his Boy Scouts had given her a gesture of unmistakably biological nature as they passed by her house. All the leaders of the village bands, who always took part in the St Spiridion's procession, had quarrelled bitterly with each other over procedure in the march past, and one evening on the Platia we were treated to the sight of three incensed tuba players chasing a bass drummer, all in full uniform and carrying their instruments. The tuba players, obviously driven beyond endurance, cornered the drummer, tore his instrument from him and jumped on it. Immediately, the Platia was a seething mass of infuriated bandsmen locked in combat. Mr Kralefsky, who was an innocent bystander, received a nasty cut on the back of the head from a flying cymbal and old Mrs Kukudopoulos, who was exercising her two spaniels between the trees, had to pick up her skirts and run for it. This incident (everybody said, when she died the next year), took years off her life, but as she was ninety-five when she died this was scarcely credible. Soon nobody was on speaking terms with anybody, though they all talked to us for we kept strictly neutral. Captain Creech, whom no one suspected of possessing a patriotic streak of any sort, was wildly excited by the whole thing, and, to everyone's annoyance, went from committee to committee spreading gossip, singing bawdy songs, pinching unsuspecting and unprotected bosoms and buttocks, and generally making a nuisance of himself.

'Disgusting old creature!' said Mother, her eyes flashing; 'I do wish he'd behave himself. After all, he is meant to be British.'

'He's keeping the committees on their toes, if I may use the phrase,' said Larry. 'Lena tells me that her bottom was black and blue after the last meeting he attended.'

'Filthy old brute,' said Mother.

'Don't be so harsh, Mother,' said Larry. 'You know you're only jealous.'

'Jealous!' squeaked Mother, bristling like a diminutive terrier. 'Jealous! . . . of that . . . old . . . old . . . *libertine*! Don't be so disgusting. I won't have you say things like that, Larry, even in joke.'

'But it's unrequited love for you that makes him drown his sorrows in wine and women,' Larry pointed out. 'If you'd make an honest man of him, he'd reform.'

'He was drowning his sorrows in wine and women long before he met me,' said Mother, 'and as far as I'm concerned, he can go on doing so. He's one person I'm not interested in reforming.'

The captain, however, was oblivious to all criticism.

'Darling girl!' he said to Mother the next time he met her, 'you haven't by any chance a Union Jack in your bottom drawer?'

'No, captain, I'm afraid I haven't,' said Mother with dignity. 'Neither have I a bottom drawer.'

'What? A fine wench like you? No bottom drawer? No nice collection of frilly black knickers to drive your next husband mad?' asked Captain Creech, eyeing Mother with a lecherous and rheumy eye.

Mother blushed and stiffened.

'I have no intention of driving *anyone* mad, with or without knickers!' she said with great dignity.

'That's my wench,' said the captain. 'Game, that's what you are, game. I like a little nudity myself, to tell the truth.'

'What d'you want a Union Jack for?' asked Mother, frigidly changing the subject.

'To wave, of course,' said the captain. 'All these wogs will be waving their flag, so we must show 'em the good old Empire's not to be overlooked.'

'Have you tried the Consul?' asked Mother.

'Him?' replied the captain scornfully. 'He said there was only one on the island and *that* was only to be used for special occasions. If this is not a special occasion, what in the name of the testicles of St Vitus *is*? So I told him to use his flagpole as an enema.'

'I do wish you wouldn't encourage that dirty old man to come and sit with us, Larry,' said Mother plaintively when the captain had staggered off in pursuit of the Union Jack. 'His conversation is obscene and I don't like him saying things like that in front of Gerry.'

'It's your fault, you encourage him,' said Larry. 'All this talk about removing your knickers.'

'Larry! You know perfectly well what I meant. It was a slip of the tongue.'

'But it gave him hope,' went on Larry. 'You'd better watch out or he'll be into your bottom drawer like a truffle hound choosing nighties for the wedding night.'

'Oh, do be quiet!' said Mother crossly. 'Really, Larry, you make me angry sometimes.'

The island became more and more tense. From the remote mountain villages where the older women were polishing up their cow's-horn head-dresses and ironing their handkerchiefs, to the town where every tree was being pruned and every table and chair on the Platia repainted, all was a-seethe with acrimonious activity. In the old part of the town, where the streets were two-donkeys narrow and the air always redolent of freshly baked bread, fruit, sunshine and drains in equal quantities, was the tiny café belonging to a friend of mine, Costi Avgadrama.

The café was justly famous for producing the best ice-cream in Corfu, for Costi had been to Italy and had learned all the dark arts of ice-cream making. His confections were much in demand and there was scarcely a party worth calling a party given on the island that did not include one of Costi's enormous, tottering, multi-coloured creations. Costi and I had a good working agreement; I would go to his café three times a week to collect all the cockroaches in his kitchen to feed my birds and animals, and in return for this service I was allowed to eat as many ice-creams as I could during my work. Determined that his shops should be clean for the Royal Visit, I went along to Costi's café about three days before the King was due and found him in a mood of suicidal despair such as only a Greek, with the aid of ouzo, can acquire and sustain. I asked him what was the matter.

'I am ruined,' he said sepulchrally, setting before me a stone bottle of ginger beer and a gleaming white ice-cream big enough to sink the *Titanic*. 'I am a ruined man, *kyria* Gerry. I am a laughing stock. No longer will people say "Ah, Corfu, that is where Costi's ice-cream comes from." No, they will say instead, "Corfu? That's where that fool Costi's ice-cream comes from." I shall have to leave the island, there is no other course. I shall go to Zante or maybe Athens, or perhaps I shall join a monastery.

My wife and children will starve, my poor old parents will feel burning shame as they beg for their bread . . .'

Interrupting these gloomy prophecies, I asked what had happened to bring about this state of despair.

'I am a genius,' said Costi simply and without boastfulness, seating himself at my table and absent-mindedly pouring himself out another ouzo. 'No one in Corfu could produce ice-creams like mine, so succulent, so beautiful, so . . . so *cold*.'

I said this was true. I went further, for he obviously needed encouragement, and said that his ice-creams were famous throughout Greece, maybe even throughout Europe.

'True,' groaned Costi. 'So it was natural that when the King was to visit Corfu the Nomarch wanted him to taste my ice-cream.'

I was greatly impressed and said so.

'Yes,' said Costi, 'twelve kilos of ice-cream I was to deliver to the Palace at *Mon Repos* and one special ice-cream for the great banquet on the night His Majesty arrives. Aghh! it was this special ice that was my undoing. This is why my wife and children must starve. Ah, cruel and relentless fate!'

'Why?' I asked bluntly, through a mouthful of ice-cream. I was in no mood for the frills; I wanted to get to the core of the story.

'I decided that this ice-cream must be something new, something unique, something never dreamed of before,' said Costi, draining his ouzo. 'All night I lay awake waiting for a sign.'

He closed his eyes and turned his head from side to side on a hot, unyielding, imaginary pillow.

'I did not sleep, I was in a fever. Then, just as the first cocks crowed, "Ku-ka-ra-ka, koo," I was blinded by a flash of inspiration.'

He smote himself so hard on the forehead he almost fell out of his chair. Shakily, he poured out another ouzo.

'I saw before my hot and tired eyes the vision of a flag, a flag of Greece, the flag for which we have all suffered and died, but the flag made in my *best superior, quality, full cream ice-cream,*' he said triumphantly, and sat back to see its effect on me.

I said I thought the idea was the most brilliant I had ever heard of. Costi beamed, and then, remembering, his expression became one of despair again.

'I leaped out of bed,' he continued dolefully, 'and ran into my kitchen. There I discovered that I had not the ingredients to carry out my plan. I had chocolate to colour the cream brown, I had dyes to make it red or green or even yellow, but I had nothing, nothing at all, to make the blue stripes in the flag.' He paused, drank deeply, and then drew himself up proudly.

'A lesser man . . . a Turk or an Albanian . . . would have abandoned the plan. But not Costi Avgadrama. You know what I did?'

I shook my head and took a swig of ginger beer.

'I went to see my cousin Michaeli. You know, he works for the chemist's down by the docks. Well, Michaeli – may St Spiridion's curse fall upon him and his offspring – gave me some stuff to make the stripes blue. Look!'

Costi went to his cold room and disappeared inside; then he came staggering out bearing a mammoth dish and laid it in front of me. It was full of ice-cream with blue and white stripes and did look remarkably like the Greek flag, even if the blue was a little on the purple side. I said I thought it was magnificent.

'Deadly!' hissed Costi. 'Deadly as a bomb.'

He sat down and stared malevolently at the huge dish. I could see nothing wrong with it except that the blue was more the colour of methylated spirits than true blue.

'Disgraced! By my own cousin, by that son of an unmarried father!' said Costi. 'He gave me the powder, he said it would be fine; he promised me, the viper tongue, that it would work.'

But it had worked, I pointed out, so what was the trouble?

'By God and St Spiridion's mercy,' said Costi piously, 'I had the idea of making a small flag for my family, just so they could celebrate their father's triumph. I cannot bear to think what would have happened if I had not done this.'

He rose to his feet and opened the door leading from the café to his private quarters.

'I will show you what that monster, my cousin, has done,' he said, and called up the stairs, 'Katarina! Petra! Spiro! Come!'

Costi's wife and his two sons came slowly and reluctantly down the stairs and stood in front of me. To my astonishment I saw that they all had bright purple mouths, the rich, royal purple of a summer beetle's wing case.

'Put out your tongue,' Costi commanded.

The family opened their mouths and poked out tongues the colour of a Roman's robe. They looked like macabre orchids, or a species of mandrake, perhaps. I could see Costi's problem. In the helpful, unthinking way that Corfiotes have, his cousin had given him a packet of gentian violet. I had once had to paint a sore on my leg with this substance and I knew that, among its many properties, it was an extremely tenacious dye. Costi would have a purple wife and children for some weeks to come.

'Just imagine,' he said to me in a hushed whisper, having sent his discoloured wife and brood back upstairs, 'just imagine if I'd sent this to the Palace. Imagine all those church dignitaries, their beards purple! A purple Nomarch and a purple King! I would have been shot.'

I said I thought it would have been rather funny. Costi was greatly shocked. When I grew up, he said severely, I would realize that some things in life were very serious, not comical.

'Imagine the reputation of the *island* . . . imagine *my* reputation if I had turned the King purple,' he said, as he gave me another ice-cream to show that there was no ill-feeling. 'Imagine how the foreigners would have laughed if the Greek King had turned purple. *Po! po! po! po!* St Spiridion save us!'

And how about the cousin, I inquired; how had he taken the news?

'He doesn't know yet,' said Costi, grinning evilly, 'but he will soon. I've just sent him an ice-cream shaped like the Greek flag.'

So the island was wound up to a pitch of unbearable excitement when the great day dawned. Spiro had organized his huge and ancient Dodge with the hood down as a sort of combination grandstand and battering ram, determined that the family at any rate were going to get a good view of the proceedings. In a festive mood, we drove into town and had a drink on the Platia to pick up news of the final preparations. Lena, resplendent in green and purple, told us that Marko had finally, if reluctantly, given up his idea of blue and white donkeys but now had another plan only slightly less bizarre.

'You know 'e 'as 'is father's printing works, huh?' said Lena. 'Vell, 'e say 'e is to print thousands and thousands of Greek flags and take them out in 'is yacht and then scatter them over the vater so that the King's ship 'as a carpet of Greek flags to sail on, no?'

Marko's yacht was the joke of Corfu; a once rather lush cabin cruiser, Marko had added so much superstructure to it that, as Leslie rightly said, it looked like a sort of sea-going Crystal Palace with a heavy list to starboard. Every time Marko set sail in it bets were laid as to when and if he would return.

'So,' continued Lena, 'first 'e 'ave the flags print, then 'e finds they don't float – they sink. So 'e makes little crosses of vood and sticks the flags on them so that they vill float.'

'It sounds rather a nice idea,' said Mother.

'If it works,' said Larry. 'You know Marko's genius for organization. Remember Constantine's birthday.'

In the summer Marko had organized a sumptuous picnic for his nephew Constantine's birthday. It would have been a splendid event, with everything from roast suckling pig to watermelons filled with champagne. The élite of Corfu were invited. The only snag was that Marko had got his beaches muddled and while he sat in solitary splendour surrounded by enough food to feed an army on a beach far down south, the élite of Corfu, hot and hungry, waited on a beach in the far north of the island.

'Vell,' said Lena, with an expressive shrug, 've cannot stop him. All the flags are loaded on his boat. He has sent a man with a rocket to Coloura.'

'A man with a rocket?' asked Leslie. 'What for?'

Lena rolled her eyes expressively.

'When the man sees the King's ship he fires the rocket,' she said. 'Marko sees the rocket and this gives him time to rush out and cover the sea with flags.'

'Well, I hope he succeeds,' said Margo. 'I like Marko.'

'My dear, so do ve all,' said Lena. 'In my village where I 'ave my villa ve have a village idiot. He is charming, *très sympathique*, but ve do not want to make him the mayor.'

With this waspish parting shot, she left us. The next one to arrive was Colonel Velvit in an agitated state.

'You haven't by any chance seen three small, fat Boy Scouts?' he asked. 'No, I didn't think you would have. Little brutes! They went off into the country *in their uniforms*, the little savages, and came back looking like pigs! I sent them off to the cleaners to get their uniforms cleaned and they've disappeared.'

'If I see them, I'll send them to you,' said Mother soothingly. 'Don't worry.'

'Thank you, my dear Mrs Durrell. I would not worry, but the little devils are an important part of the proceedings,' said Colonel Velvit, preparing to go in search of the missing Scouts. 'You see, not only do they form part of the stripe in the flag but they have to demolish the bridge as well.'

With this mysterious remark, he departed, loping off like a hound.

'Bridge? What bridge?' asked Mother, bewildered.

'Oh, it's part of the show,' said Leslie. 'Among other things, they build a pontoon bridge over an imaginary river, cross it, and then blow it up to prevent the enemy following.'

'I always thought Boy Scouts were peaceful,' said Mother.

'Not the Corfiote ones,' said Leslie. 'They're probably the most war-like inhabitants of Corfu.'

At that moment Theodore and Kralefsky, who were to share the car with us, arrived.

'There has been . . . er . . . you know . . . a slight hiatus over the salute,' Theodore reported to Leslie.

'I knew it!' said Leslie angrily. 'That fool of a Commandant! He was too airy-fairy when I spoke to him. I told him those Venetian cannons would burst.'

'No, no . . . er . . . the cannons haven't burst. Er . . . um . . . at least, not *yet*,' said Theodore. 'No, it is a problem of timing. The Commandant was very insistent that the salute should be fired the moment the King's foot touches Greek soil. The . . . er . . . um . . . difficulty was apparently to arrange a signal from the docks that could be seen by the . . . gunners in the . . . er . . . you know . . . the fort.'

'So what have they arranged?' asked Leslie.

'They have sent a corporal down to the docks with a forty-five,' said Theodore. 'He is to fire it the moment *before* the King sets foot on the shore.'

'Does he know how to fire it?' asked Leslie sceptically.

'Well . . . er . . .' said Theodore, 'I had to spend quite some time trying to make him see that it was dangerous to put it . . . um . . . you know . . . loaded *and* cocked into his holster.'

'Silly fool, he'll shoot himself through the foot like that,' said Leslie.

'Never mind,' said Larry, 'there's bound to be some blood-letting before the day is out. I hope you brought your first aid kit, Theodore.'

'Don't say things like that, Larry,' begged Mother. 'You make me feel quite nervous.'

'Ifs you're readys, Mrs Durrells, we oughts to gets going,' said Spiro, who had appeared, brown, scowling, looking like a gargoyle on holiday from Notre Dame. 'The crowd's getting very tense.'

'Dense, Spiro, *dense*,' said Margo.

'That's what I says, Misses Margo,' said Spiro. 'But don'ts you worry. I'll fix 'em. I'll scarce them out of the way with my horn.'

'Spiro really ought to write a dictionary,' said Larry as we climbed into the Dodge and wedged ourselves on to the capacious leather seats.

Since early morning the white dusty roads had been jammed with carts and donkeys bringing peasants into the capital for the great event, and a great pall of dust covered the countryside, turning the plants and trees by the roadside white, hanging in the air like microscopic flakes of snow. The town was now as full or fuller than it was on St Spiridion's day and great bevies of people were eddying across the Platia in their best clothes like clouds of wind-swept blossoms. Every back street was jammed with humanity mixed with donkeys, the whole moving at a glacier pace, and the air was full of excited chatter and laughter, the pungent smell of garlic, and the all-pervading smell of mothballs, the sign of special clothes carefully extracted from their places of safe-keeping. On every side you could hear brass bands tuning up, donkeys braying, the cries of the street vendors, and the excited screams of children. The town quivered and throbbed like a great, multi-coloured, redolent beehive.

Driving at a snail's pace, honking his great, rubber-bulbed horn to 'scarce' the uncaring populace out of the way, Spiro drove us down to the docks. Here all was bustle and what passed for efficiency; a band was lined up, its instruments sparkling, its uniforms immaculate, its air of respectability only slightly marred by the fact that two of its members had black eyes. Next to it was a battalion of local soldiery, looking remarkably clean and neat. Church dignitaries, with their carefully combed, white, silver, and iron-grey beards, bright and gay as a flock of parrots in their robes, chatted animatedly to each other, stomachs bulging, beards wagging, plump, well-manicured hands moving in the most delicate of gestures. Near the dockside where the King would come ashore stood a forlorn-looking corporal; obviously his responsibilities were weighing heavily on him for he kept fingering his revolver holster nervously and biting his nails.

Presently, there was a surge of excitement and everyone was saying, 'The King! The King! The King is coming!' The corporal adjusted his hat and stood a little straighter. What had given rise to this rumour was the sight of Marko Paniotissa's yacht putting out into the bay and lumbering to and fro while Marko, in the stern, could be seen unloading bundle after bundle of Greek flags.

'I didn't see the rocket, did you?' asked Margo.

'No, but you can't see the headland from here,' said Leslie.

'Well, I think Marko's doing splendidly,' said Margo.

'It's certainly a very pretty effect,' said Mother.

And indeed it was, for several acres of the smooth sea were covered with a carpet of tiny flags which looked most impressive. Unfortunately, as we were to learn within the next hour and a half, Marko's timing had been at fault. The man he had stationed up in the north of the island to fire the signal rocket was most reliable but his identification of ships left a lot to be desired and so what eventually appeared was not the ship conveying the King but a rather grubby little tanker on its way to Athens. This in itself would not have been such a grave error but Marko, carried away as so many Corfiotes were that day, had failed to check on the glue with which the flags were stuck to the little wooden pieces that allowed them to float. As we waited for the King we were treated to the sight of the glue disintegrating under the influence of sea water and several thousand Greek flags sinking ignominiously to the bottom of the bay.

'Oh, poor Marko, I feel so sorry for him,' said Margo, almost in tears.

'Never mind,' said Larry consolingly, 'perhaps the King likes little bits of wood.'

'Um . . . I don't . . . you know . . . think so,' said Theodore. 'You see how they're all shaped like a little cross. That in Greece is considered a very bad omen.'

'Oh dear,' said Mother. 'I do hope the King won't realize that Marko did it.'

'If Marko is wise, he'll go into voluntary exile,' contributed Larry.

'Ah, here he comes at last,' said Leslie as the King's ship sailed majestically across several acres of little wooden crosses, as though ploughing its way through a marine war cemetery.

The gang-plank was lowered, the band struck up blaringly, the Army came to attention, and the crowd of church dignitaries moved forward like a suddenly uprooted flower bed. They reached the bottom of the gang-plank, the band stopped playing, and to a chorus of delighted 'Ah's' the King made his appearance, paused briefly to salute, and then made his way slowly down the gangway. It was the little corporal's great moment. Sweating profusely, he had moved as close to the gang-plank as he could and he had his gaze riveted on the King's feet. His instructions had been explicit; three paces before the King stepped off the gangway and on to Greek soil he was to give the signal. This would give the fort enough time to fire the cannon as the King stepped ashore.

The King descended slowly. The atmosphere was tense with emotion. The corporal fumbled with his holster and then, at the crucial moment, drew his forty-five and fired five rounds approximately two yards away from the King's right ear. It immediately became obvious that the fort had not thought to tell the Welcoming Committee about its signal and so the Committee, to say the least, was taken aback, as was the King and, indeed, as were we all.

'My God, they've amputated him,' screamed Margo, who always lost both her head and her command over English in moments of crisis.

'Don't be a fool, it's the signal,' snapped Leslie, training his field glasses on the fort.

But it was obvious that the Welcoming Committee thought much the same as my sister. As one man, they fell on the unfortunate corporal. He, white-faced and protesting, was pummelled and thumped and kicked, his revolver was torn from his grasp and he was hit smartly on the head with it. It is probable that he would have come to some serious harm if at that moment the cannons had not blared out in an impressive cumulus cloud of smoke from the ramparts of the fort and vindicated his action.

After this all was smiles and laughter, for the Corfiotes had a keen sense of humour. Only the King looked a trifle pensive. He climbed into the official open car and a snag made its appearance; for some reason the door would not lock. The chauffeur slammed it, the sergeant in charge of the troops slammed it, the band leader slammed it, and a passing priest slammed it but it refused to stay shut. The chauffeur, not to be defeated, backed up, and took a run and kicked it violently. The car shuddered but the door remained obdurate. They tried string, but there was nothing to tie it to. Eventually, since there could be no further delay, they were forced to drive off with the Nomarch's secretary hanging over the back of the seat and holding the door shut with one hand.

Their first stop was at St Spiridion's Church so that the King could make his obeisances to the mummified remains of the saint. Surrounded by a forest of ecclesiastical beards, he disappeared into the dark depths of the church, where a thousand candles bloomed like a riot of primroses. It was a hot day and the chauffeur of the King's car was feeling a bit exhausted after his fight with the door so, without telling anyone, he left the car parked in front of the church and nipped round the corner for a drink. And who is to blame him? Who, on occasions such as this, has not felt the same? However, his estimation of the time the

King would take to visit the saint was inaccurate so when the King, surrounded by the cream of the Greek church, suddenly emerged from the church and took his place in the car, the chauffeur was conspicuous by his absence. As was usual in Corfu when a crisis was reached, everyone blamed everyone else for the chauffeur's disappearance. A quarter of an hour passed while accusations were hurled, fists were shaken, and runners were sent in all directions in search of the chauffeur. There was some delay because no one knew which café he was honouring with his presence, but eventually he was tracked down and a stream of vituperation was poured on his head as he was dragged ignominiously away in the middle of his second ouzo.

The next stop was the Platia, where the King was to see the march past of troops and bands and the exhibition by the Scouts. By driving cacophonously through the narrow back streets, Spiro got us to the Platia long before the King's car.

'Surely they can't do anything else wrong,' said Mother worriedly.

'The island has surpassed itself,' said Larry. 'I had hoped they might get a puncture between the docks and the church, but that was asking too much, I suppose.'

'Well, I'm not so sure,' said Theodore, his eyes twinkling. 'Remember, this is Corfu. They might well have something more in store for us.'

'I do hope not,' said Kralefsky. 'Really! Such organization! It makes one blush.'

'They can't think up anything more, Theo, surely,' Larry protested.

'I wouldn't like to be ... er ... um ... bank on it ... you know ...' said Theodore.

As it turned out, he was perfectly right.

The King arrived and took his place on the dais. The troops marched past with great vigour and all of them managed to be more or less in step. Corfu was rather a remote garrison in those days and the recruits did not get much practice but, nevertheless, they acquitted themselves creditably. Next came the mass bands – bands from every village in the island, their variously coloured uniforms glowing, their instruments so polished that the gleam of them hurt the eyes. If their delivery quavered a little and was slightly off-key, it was more than made up for by the volume and force of their playing.

Then it was the turn of the Scouts and we all clapped and cheered as Colonel Velvit, looking like an extremely nervous and attenuated Old Testament prophet in Scout's uniform, led his diminutive troops onto the dusty Platia. They saluted the King and then, obeying a rather strangled falsetto order from the colonel, shuffled to and fro and formed the Greek flag. Such a wave of clapping and cheering broke out that it must surely have been heard in the remotest vastnesses of the Albanian mountains. After a short display of gymnastics the troop then went over to where two white lines represented the two banks of a river. Here half the troop hurried away and reappeared with planks necessary for making a pontoon bridge while the other half were busy getting a line across the treacherous waters. So fascinated were the crowd by the mechanics of this that they drifted closer and closer to the 'river', accompanied by the policemen who were supposed to be keeping them back.

In record time, the Scouts, none of whom were more than eight-years-old, created their pontoon across the imaginary river and then led by one small boy blowing vociferously and inaccurately on a trumpet, jog-trotted across the bridge and stood to attention on the opposite side. The crowd were enchanted; they clapped, cheered, whistled and stamped. Colonel Velvit allowed himself a small, tight, military smile and cast a proud look in our direction. Then he barked out a word of command. Three small fat Scouts detached themselves from the troop and made their way to the bridge, carrying fuses, a plunger and other demolition equipment. They fixed everything up and then rejoined the troop, unwinding the fuse wire as they came. They stood at attention and waited. Colonel Velvit savoured his big moment; he glanced round to make sure he had everyone's undivided attention. The silence was complete.

'Demolish bridge!' roared Colonel Velvit, and one of the Scouts crouched and pressed the plunger home.

The next few minutes were confused, to say the least. There was a colossal explosion; a cloud of dust, gravel and bits of bridge was thrown into the air, to descend like hail upon the population. The first three rows of the crowd, all the policemen and Colonel Velvit, were thrown flat on their backs. The blast, carrying with it gravel and splinters of wood, reached the car where we were sitting, battered against the coachwork like machine-gun fire and blew Mother's hat off.

'Christ Almighty!' said Larry. 'What the hell's that fool Velvit playing at?'

'My hat,' panted Mother. 'Somebody get my hat!'

'I'll gets it, Mrs Durrells, don'ts you worrys,' roared Spiro.

'Most unnerving, most unnerving,' said Kralefsky, his eyes closed, mopping his brow with his handkerchief. 'Far too militant for small boys.'

'Small boys! Bloody little fiends,' cried Larry angrily, shaking gravel out of his hair.

'I felt sure something else would happen,' added Theodore with satisfaction, happy now that Corfu's reputation for calamities was secure.

'They must have had some sort of explosive,' said Leslie. 'I can't think what Colonel Velvit was playing at. Damned dangerous.'

It became obvious a little later that it was not the colonel's fault. Having rather shakily lined up his troop and marched them away, he returned to the scene of the carnage to apologize to Mother.

'I cannot tell you how mortified I am, Mrs Durrell,' he said, tears in his eyes. 'Those little brutes got some dynamite from some fishermen. I assure you, I knew absolutely nothing about it, nothing.'

In his dust-stained uniform and battered hat, he looked very pathetic.

'Oh, don't worry, Colonel,' said Mother, shakily lifting a brandy and soda to her lips. 'It's the sort of thing that could happen to anyone.'

'Happens all the time in England,' said Larry. 'Never a day passes . . .'

'Do come and have dinner with us,' interrupted Mother, giving Larry a quelling look.

'Thank you, dear lady, you are too kind,' said the colonel. 'I must go and change.'

'I was very interested in the reaction of the spectators,' said Theodore, with scientific relish. 'You know . . . er . . . the ones who were blown down.'

'I should think they were damned annoyed,' said Leslie.

'No,' went on Theodore proudly, 'this is Corfu. They all . . . you know . . . helped each other up, brushed each other down, and remarked on how good the whole thing was . . . er . . . how realistic. It didn't seem to occur to them that there was anything strange in Boy Scouts having dynamite.'

'Well, if you live long enough in Corfu, you cease to be surprised at anything,' said Mother with conviction.

Eventually, after a prolonged and delicious meal in town, during which we tried to convince Colonel Velvit that his bridge demolition had been the high spot of the day, Spiro drove us home through the cool, velvety night. The scops owls called 'toink toink' to each other, chiming like strange bells among the trees; the white dust billowed behind the car and remained suspended like a summer's cloud in the still air; the dark cathedral groves of the olives were pricked out with the pulsing green lights of fireflies. It had been a good, if exhausting, day, and we were glad to be home.

'Well,' said Mother, stifling a yawn as she picked up her lamp and made her way to the stairs, 'King or no King, I'm staying in bed until twelve tomorrow.'

'Oh . . .' said Larry contritely, 'didn't I tell you?'

Mother paused halfway up the stairs and looked at Larry, the wavering lamplight making her shadow quiver and leap on the white wall.

'Tell me what?' she asked suspiciously.

'About the King,' said Larry. 'I'm sorry I should have told you before.'

'Told me what?' said Mother, now seriously alarmed.

'I've asked him to lunch,' said Larry.

'Larry! You haven't! Really, you are thoughtless . . .' Mother began, and then realized that she was having her leg pulled.

She drew herself up to her full five foot.

'I don't think that's funny,' she said frigidly. 'Anyway, the laugh would have been on him for I've only got eggs in the house.'

With great dignity, ignoring our laughter, she made her way to bed.

7

The Paths of Love

Stay me with flagons, comfort me with apples for I am
sick of love.

SONG OF SOLOMON 5

It had been one of those prodigious, desiccating, earth-cracking summers that was so hot it even bleached the sky to a pale end-of-summer, forget-me-not colour and flattened the sea so that it lay like a great blue pool, unmoving, warm as fresh milk. At night you could hear the floors and shutters and beams of the villa shifting and groaning and cracking in the warm air as the last juices were sucked out of them. The full moon would rise like a red coal, glowering down at us from the hot, velvety sky, and in the morning the sun was already too warm to be comfortable ten minutes after it appeared. There was no wind and the heat pressed down on the island like a lid. On the hillside in the breathless air, the plants and grasses withered and died until they stood there, bleached and blonde as honey, crisp as wood shavings. The days were so hot that even the cicadas started singing earlier and siestaed during the heat of the day, and the ground was baked so that there was nowhere you could walk without shoes.

The villa represented to the local animal life a series of large wooden caves which were perhaps half a degree cooler than the surrounding olive, orange and lemon groves, and so they flocked to join us. At first I was naturally blamed for this sudden influx of creatures but eventually the invasion became so

707

comprehensive that even my family realized I could not be responsible for quite such a large quantity and variety of life forms. Battalions of black ticks marched into the house and beset the dogs, massing in such numbers on their ears and heads that they looked like chain-mail and were just as difficult to remove. In desperation we had to douse them with kerosene, which made the ticks drop off. The dogs, deeply insulted by this treatment, slouched, panting, round the house, reeking of kerosene, shedding ticks in vast quantities. Larry suggested that we put up a notice saying 'Danger – inflammable dogs' for, as he rightly pointed out, if anyone lit a match near one of them the whole villa was liable to go up in flames like a tinder box.

The kerosene only gave us a temporary respite. More and more ticks marched into the house until at night one could lie in bed and watch rows of them performing strange route marches around the room. The ticks, fortunately, did not attack us but confined themselves to driving the dogs mad. However, the hordes of fleas that decided to take up residence with us were another matter. They arrived suddenly, out of nowhere, it seemed, like the Tartar hordes, and over-ran us before we realized what was happening. They were everywhere and you could feel them hopping on to you and running up your legs as you walked around the house. The bedrooms became untenable and for a time we took our beds out on to the broad verandas and slept there.

But the fleas were not the most objectionable of the lesser inhabitants of the house. The tiny scorpions, black as ebony, infested the bathroom where it was cool. Leslie going in late one night to clean his teeth was ill-advised enough to go barefoot and was stung on the toe. The scorpion was only half an inch long but the agony of the bite was out of all proportion to the size of the beast and it was some days before Leslie could walk. The larger scorpions preferred the kitchen area, where they would quite blatantly sit on the ceiling looking like misshapen aerial lobsters.

At night when the lamps were lit, thousands of insects appeared; moths of all shapes, from tiny fawn-coloured ones with wings shaped like tattered feathers, to the great big, striped, pink and silver hawk moths, whose death dives at the light were capable of breaking the lantern chimney. Then there were the beetles, some as black as mourners, some gaily striped and patterned, some with short, club-shaped antennae, others with antennae as long and thin as a Mandarin's moustache. With these came a multitude of lesser forms of life, most of them so small that you needed a magnifying glass to make out their incredible shapes and colours.

Naturally, this conglomeration of insects was marvellous as far as I was concerned. Each evening I hung about the lights, my collecting boxes and bottles at the ready, vying with the other predators for choice specimens. I had to look sharp, for the competition was brisk. On the ceiling were the geckoes, pale, pink-skinned, spread-fingered, bulbous-eyed, stalking the moths and beetles with minuscule care. Alongside them were the green, swaying, hypocritical mantis with their mad eyes and chinless faces, moving on slender, prickly legs like green vampires.

On ground level I had to contend with enormous chocolate-coloured spiders like lanky, furry wolves, who would lurk in the shadows and scuttle out and snatch a specimen almost from my very fingers. They were aided and abetted by the fat map toads in their handsome patchwork skins of green and silvery grey who hopped and gulped their way, wide-eyed with astonishment, through this largesse of food, and the swift, furtive, and some-how sinister scutigera. This form of centipede had a body some three inches long and as thick as a pencil and flattened; around the perimeter was a hedge, a fringe of long, slender legs. When it moved, as each pair of legs came into action, these fringes appeared to undulate in waves, and the animal progressed as smoothly as a stone on ice, silent and unnerving, for scutigera were among the most ferocious and skilful of hunters.

One evening, the lights had been lit and I was waiting patiently to see what they were going to add to my collection; it was still fairly early so that most of the predators, apart from myself and a few bats, had not put in an appearance. The bats whipped up and down the veranda as fast as whiplashes, taking the moths and other succulent dainties from within inches of the lamp, the wind from their wings making the flames shudder and leap. Gradually, the pale dragon-green afterglow of the sunset faded, the crickets started their prolonged musical trills, the gloom of the olive trees was lit by the cold lights of the fireflies, and the great house, creaking and groaning with sunburn, settled down for the night.

The wall behind the lamp was already covered by a host of various insects which, after an unsuccessful suicide attempt, were clinging there to recover themselves before trying again. At the base of the wall, from a minute crack in the plaster, emerged one of the smallest and fattest geckoes I had ever seen. He must have been newly hatched for he measured only about an inch and a half in length, but obviously the short time he had been in the world had not prevented him from eating prodigiously for his body and tail were so fat as to make him appear almost circular. His mouth was set in a wide, shy smile and his large dark eyes were wide and wondering, like the eyes of a child that sees a table set for a banquet. Before I could stop him he had waddled slowly up the wall and started his supper with a lacewing fly; these creatures, with their transparent wings like green lace and their large green-gold eyes, were favourites of mine and so I was annoyed with him.

Gulping down the last bit of gauzy wing, the baby gecko paused, clinging to the wall, and mused for a bit, occasionally blinking his eyes. I could not think why he had chosen the lacewing, which was a bulky thing to handle, when he was surrounded on all sides by a variety of small insects which would have been easier for him to catch and eat. But it soon became apparent that he was a glutton whose eyes were bigger than his stomach. Having hatched from an egg – and, therefore, lacking a mother's guidance – he was under the strong but erroneous impression that all insects were edible and that the bigger they were the quicker they would assuage his hunger. He did not even seem to be aware of the fact that for a creature of his size some insects could be dangerous. Like an early missionary, he was so concerned with himself that it never occurred to him that somebody might look upon him simply as a meal.

Ignoring a convention of small and eminently edible moths sitting near him, he stalked a great, fat, hairy oak eggar whose body was almost bigger than his own; he misjudged his run-in, however, and merely caught her by the tip of one wing. She flew off and such was the power of her brown wings that she almost tore the gecko's grip from the wall and carried him with her. Nothing daunted, after a brief rest, the gecko launched an assault on a longicorn beetle his own size. He would never have been able to swallow such a hard, prickly monster, but this apparently did not occur to him. However, he could not get a grip on the beetle's hard and polished body, and all he succeeded in doing was knocking it to the floor.

He was just having another brief rest and surveying the battle-field when, with a crisp rustle of wings, an enormous mantis flew on to the veranda and alighted on the wall some six inches away. She folded her wings with a noise like the crumpling of tissue paper and, with viciously pronged arms raised in mock prayer, stared about her with lunatic eyes, twisting her head from side to side as she surveyed the array of insects assembled for her benefit.

The gecko, it was fairly obvious, had never seen a mantis before and did not realize how lethal they could be; as far as he was concerned, it was an enormous green dinner of the sort that he had dreamed about but never hoped to obtain. Without more ado, and ignoring the fact that the mantis was some five times his size, he began to stalk her. The mantis, meanwhile, had singled out a silver-Y moth and was moving towards it on its attenuated, elderly spinster legs, pausing occasionally to sway to and fro, the personification of evil. Hard in her wake came the gecko, head down, grimly determined, pausing whenever the mantis did, and lashing his ridiculous little fat tail to and fro like an excited puppy.

The mantis reached the oblivious moth, paused, swaying, then lashed out with her foreclaws and seized it. The moth, which was a large one, started fluttering frantically and it required all the strength of the mantis' cruelly barbed forelegs to hold it. As she was struggling with it, looking like a rather inept juggler, the gecko, who had lashed himself into a fury with his fat tail, launched his attack. He darted forward and laid hold of the mantis' wing case like a bulldog. The mantis was busy trying to juggle the moth round in her claws and so this sudden attack from the rear knocked her off balance. She fell to the ground, carrying with her the moth and the gecko. When she landed she still had the gecko hanging grimly to her wing case. She relinquished the moth, which was by now almost dead, so as to leave her sabre-sharp front claws free to do battle with the gecko.

I had just decided that this was the point where I should step in to add a mantis and a gecko to my menagerie when another protagonist entered the arena. From the shadows of the grapevine a scutigera slid into view, a moving carpet of legs, skimming purposefully towards the still-twitching moth. It reached it, poured itself over the body, and sank its jaws into the moth's soft thorax. It was a fascinating scene; the mantis bent almost double, slashing downwards with her needle-sharp claws at the gecko who, with eyes protruding with excitement, was hanging on grimly though he was being whipped to and fro by his large antagonist. The scutigera meanwhile, deciding it could not move the moth, lay draped over it like a pelmet, sucking out its vital juices.

It was at that point that Theresa Olive Agnes Dierdre, known as Dierdre for short, made her appearance. Dierdre was one of a pair of enormous common toads that I had found, tamed with comparative ease, and established in the tiny walled garden below the veranda. Here they lived a blameless life among the geraniums and tangerine trees, venturing up onto the veranda when the lights were lit to take their share of the insect life.

So taken up was I by the strange foursome in front of me that I had forgotten all about Dierdre and when she appeared on the scene I was unprepared, lying as I was on my stomach with my nose some six inches from the battlefield. Unbeknownst to me, Dierdre had been watching the skirmishing from beneath a chair. She now hopped forward fatly, paused for a brief second, then, before I could do anything, leaped forward in the purposeful way that toads have, opened her huge mouth and with the aid of her tongue flipped both scutigera and moth into her capacious maw. She paused again, gulping so that her protuberant eyes disappeared briefly, and then turned smartly to the left and flapped both mantis and gecko into her mouth. Only for a moment did the gecko's tail protrude, wriggling like a worm between Dierdre's thick lips, before she stuffed it firmly into her mouth, toad-fashion, with her thumbs.

I had read about food chains and the survival of the fittest but this I felt was carrying things too far.

Apart from anything else, I was annoyed with Dierdre for spoiling what was proving to be an absorbing drama. So that she would not interfere with anything else I carried her back to the walled garden she shared with her husband, Terence Oliver Albert Dick, under a stone trough full of marigolds. I reckoned she had eaten quite enough for one evening anyway.

So it was to a house baked crisp as a biscuit, hot as a baker's oven, and teeming with animal life that Adrian Fortescue Smythe made his appearance. Adrian, a school friend of Leslie's, had spent one holiday with us in England and as a result had fallen deeply and irrevocably in love with Margo, much to her annoyance. We were all spread out on the veranda reading our fortnightly mail when the news of Adrian's imminent arrival was broken to us by Mother.

'Oh, how nice,' she said. 'That will be nice.'

We all stopped reading and looked at her suspiciously.

'*What* will be nice?' asked Larry.

'I've had a letter from Mrs Fortescue Smythe,' said Mother.

'I don't see anything nice about *that*,' said Larry.

'What does the old hag want?' Leslie inquired.

'Leslie, dear, you mustn't call her an old hag. She was very kind to you, remember.'

Leslie grunted derisively

'What's she want anyway?'

'Well, she says Adrian's doing a tour of the Continent and could he come to Corfu and stay with us for a bit.'

'Oh good,' said Leslie, 'it'll be nice to have Adrian to stay.'

'Yes, he's a nice boy,' admitted Larry magnanimously.

'Isn't he!' said Mother enthusiastically. 'Such nice manners.'

'Well, *I'm* not pleased he's coming,' contributed Margo. 'He's one of the most boring people I know. He makes me yawn just to look at him. Can't you say we're full up, Mother?'

'But I thought you liked Adrian,' said Mother, surprised. 'He certainly liked you, if I remember.'

'That's just the point. I don't want him drooling all over the place like a sex-starved spaniel.'

Mother straightened her spectacles and looked at Margo.

'Margo, dear, I don't think you ought to talk about Adrian like that, I don't know where you get these expressions. I'm sure you're exaggerating. I never saw him look like a . . . like a . . . well . . . like what you said. He seemed perfectly well behaved to me.'

'Of course he was,' said Leslie belligerently. 'It's just Margo; she thinks every man is after her.'

'I don't,' said Margo indignantly. 'I just don't like him. He's squishy. Every time you looked around, there he was, dribbling.'

'Adrian never dribbled in his life.'

'He did. Nothing but dribble, dribble, drool.'

'*I* never saw him dribbling,' said Mother, 'and anyway I can't say he mustn't stay just because he dribbles, Margo. Do be reasonable.'

'He's Les' friend. Let him dribble over Les.'

'He doesn't dribble. He's never dribbled.'

'Well,' said Mother, with the air of one solving a problem. 'There'll be plenty for him to do so I dare say he won't have time to dribble.'

A fortnight later a starving, exhausted Adrian arrived, having cycled with practically no money all the way from Calais on a bicycle, which had given up the unequal struggle and fallen to bits at Brindisi. For the first few days we saw little of him since Mother insisted he went to bed early, got up late, and had another helping of everything. When he did put in an appearance I watched him narrowly for signs of dribbling, for of all the curious friends we had had staying with us, we had never had one that dribbled before and I was anxious to witness this phenomenon. But apart from a tendency to go scarlet every time Margo entered the room and to sit looking at her with his mouth slightly open (when honesty compelled me to admit he did look rather like a spaniel), he betrayed no other signs of eccentricity. He had extravagantly curly hair, large, very gentle hazel eyes, and his hormones had just allowed him to achieve a hairline moustache of which he was extremely proud. He had bought, as a gift for Margo, a record of a song which he obviously considered to be the equivalent of Shakespearian sonnets set to music. It was called 'At Smokey Joe's' and we all grew to hate it intensely, for Adrian's day was not complete unless he had played this cacophonous ditty at least twenty times.

'Dear God,' Larry groaned at breakfast one morning as he heard the hiss of the record, 'not *again*, not at this hour.'

'At Smokey Joe's in Havana,' the gramophone proclaimed loudly in a nasal tenor voice, 'I lingered quenching my thirst . . .'

'I can't bear it. Why can't he play something else?' Margo wailed.

'Now, now, dear. He likes it,' said Mother placatingly.

'Yes, and he bought it for *you*,' said Leslie. 'It's your bloody present. Why don't you tell him to stop?'

'No, you can't do that, dear,' said Mother. 'After all, he is a guest.'

'What's that got to do with it?' snapped Larry. 'Just because he's tone deaf, why should we all have to suffer? It's Margo's record. It's her responsibility.'

'But it seems so impolite,' said Mother worriedly. 'After all, he brought it as a present; he thinks we like it.'

'I know he does. I find it hard to credit such depths of ignorance,' said Larry. 'D'you know he took off Beethoven's Fifth yesterday *halfway through* to put on that emasculated yowling! I tell you he's about as cultured as Attila the Hun.'

'Sshh, he'll hear you, Larry dear,' said Mother.

'What, with that row going on? He'd need an ear trumpet.'

Adrian, oblivious to the family's restiveness, now joined the recorded voice to make a duet. As he had a nasal tenor voice remarkably similar to the vocalist's the result was pretty horrible.

'I saw a damsel there . . . That was really where . . . I saw her first . . . Oh, Mama Inez . . . Oh, Mama Inez . . . Oh, Mama Inez . . . Mama Inez . . .' warbled Adrian and the gramophone more or less in unison.

'God in heaven!' Larry exploded. 'That's really too much! Margo, you've got to speak to him.'

'Well, do it politely, dear,' said Mother. 'We don't want to hurt his feelings.'

'I feel just like hurting his feelings,' said Larry.

'I know,' said Margo, 'I'll tell him Mother's got a headache.'

'That will only give us a temporary respite,' pointed out Larry.

'*You* tell him Mother's got a headache and *I'll* hide the needle,' suggested Leslie triumphantly. 'How about that?'

'Oh, that's a brainwave,' Mother exclaimed, delighted that the problem had been solved without hurting Adrian's feelings.

Adrian was somewhat mystified by the disappearance of the needles and the fact that everyone assured him they could not be obtained in Corfu. However, he had a retentive memory, if no ability to carry a tune, so he hummed 'At Smokey Joe's' all day long, sounding like a hive of distraught tenor bees.

As the days passed, his adoration for Margo showed no signs of abating; if anything, it grew worse, and Margo's irritation waxed with it. I began to feel very sorry for Adrian, for it seemed that nothing he could do was right. Because Margo said she thought his moustache made him look like an inferior gentlemen's hairdresser, he shaved it off, only to have her proclaim that moustaches were a sign of virility. Furthermore, she was heard to say in no uncertain terms that she much preferred the local peasant boys to any English import.

'They're so handsome and so sweet,' she said to Adrian's obvious chagrin. 'They all sing so well. They have such nice manners. They play the guitar. Give me one of them instead of an Englishman any day. They have a sort of ordure about them.'

'Don't you mean aura?' asked Larry.

'Anyway,' Margo continued, ignoring this, 'they're what I call *men*, not namby-pamby dribbling wash-outs.'

'Margo, dear,' said Mother, glancing nervously at the wounded Adrian. 'I don't think that's very kind.'

'I'm not trying to be kind,' said Margo, 'and most of cruelty is kindness if it's done in the right way.'

Leaving us with this baffling piece of philosophy, she went off to see her latest conquest, a richly tanned fisherman with a luxuriant moustache. Adrian was so obviously mortified that the family felt it must try and alleviate his mood of despair.

'Don't take any notice of Margo, Adrian dear,' said Mother soothingly. 'She doesn't mean what she says. She's very head-strong, you know. Have another peach.'

'Pig-headed,' said Leslie. 'And *I* ought to know.'

'I don't see *how* I can be more like the peasant boys,' mused Adrian, puzzled. 'I suppose I could take up the guitar.'

'No, no, don't do that,' said Larry hastily, 'that's quite unnecess-ary. Why not try something simple? Try chewing garlic.'

'Garlic?' asked Adrian, surprised. 'Does Margo like garlic?'

'Sure to,' said Larry, 'you heard what she said about those peasant lads' auras. Well, what's the first bit of their aura that hits you when you go near them? Garlic!'

Adrian was much struck by the logic of this and chewed a vast quantity of garlic, only to be told by Margo, with a handkerchief over her nose, that he smelled like the local bus on market day.

Adrian seemed to me to be a very nice person; he was gentle and kind and always willing to do anything that anyone asked of him. I felt it my duty to do something for him, but short of locking Margo in his bedroom – a thought which I dismissed as impractical and liable to be frowned on by Mother – I could think of nothing very sensible. I decided to discuss the matter with Mr Kralefsky in case he could suggest anything. When we were having our coffee break I told him about Adrian's unsuccessful pursuit of Margo, a welcome respite for us both from the insol-uble mysteries of the square on the hypotenuse.

'Aha!' he said. 'The paths of love never run smooth. One is tempted to wonder, indeed, if life would not be a trifle dull if the road to one's goal were always smooth.'

I was not particularly interested in my tutor's philosophical flights but I waited politely. Mr Kralefsky picked up a biscuit delicately in his beautifully manicured hands, held it briefly over his coffee cup and then christened it in the brown liquid before popping it into his mouth. He chewed methodically, his eyes closed.

'It seems to me,' he said at last, 'that this young Lochinvar is trying too hard.'

I said that Adrian was English but, in any case, how could one try too hard; if one didn't try hard one didn't achieve success.

'Ah,' said Mr Kralefsky archly, 'but in matters of the heart things are different. A little bit of indifference sometimes works wonders.'

He put his fingertips together and gazed raptly at the ceiling. I could tell that we were about to embark on one of his flights of fancy with his favourite mythological character, 'a lady'.

'I remember once I became greatly enamoured of a certain lady,' said Kralefsky. 'I tell you this in confidence, of course.'

I nodded and helped myself to another biscuit. Kralefsky's stories were apt to be a bit lengthy.

'She was a lady of such beauty and accomplishments that every eligible man flocked round her, like . . . like . . . bees round a honey pot,' said Mr Kralefsky, pleased with this image. 'From the moment I saw her I fell deeply, irrevocably, inconsolably in love and felt that she in some measure returned my regard.'

He took a sip of coffee to moisten his throat, then he trellised his fingers together and leaned across the desk, his nostrils flaring, his great, soulful eyes intense.

'I pursued her relentlessly as a . . . as a . . . hound on the scent, but she was cold and indifferent to my advances. She even mocked the love that I offered her.'

He paused, his eyes full of tears, and blew his nose vigorously.

'I cannot describe to you the torture I went through, the burning agony of jealousy, the sleepless nights of pain. I lost twenty-four kilos; my friends began to worry about me, and, of course, they all tried to persuade me that the lady in question was not worthy of my suffering. All except one friend . . . a . . . an experienced man of the world, who had, I believe, had several affairs of the heart himself, one as far away as Baluchistan. He told me that I was trying too hard, that as long as I was casting my heart at the lady's feet she would be, like all females, bored by her conquest. But if I showed a little indifference, aha! my friend assured me, it would be a very different tale.'

Kralefsky beamed at me and nodded his head knowingly. He poured himself out more coffee.

And had he shown indifference, I asked.

'Indeed I did,' said Kralefsky. 'I didn't lose a minute. I embarked on a boat for China.'

I thought this was splendid; no woman, I felt, could claim to have you enslaved if you suddenly leaped on a boat for China. It was sufficiently remote to give the vainest woman pause for thought. And what happened, I inquired eagerly, when Mr Kralefsky returned from his travels?

'I found she had married,' said Mr Kralefsky, rather shamefacedly, for he realized that this was somewhat of an anticlimax.

'Some women are capricious and impatient, you know. But I managed to have a few moments of private conversation with her and she explained it all.'

I waited expectantly.

'She said,' Mr Kralefsky continued, 'that she had thought I had gone for good to become a Lama so she married. Yes, the little dear would have waited for me had she known, but, torn with grief, she married the first man who came along. If I had not misjudged the length of the voyage she would have been mine today.'

He blew his nose violently, a stricken look on his face. I digested this story, but it did not seem to give any very clear clues as to how to help Adrian. Should I perhaps lend him my boat, the *Bootle-Bumtrinket*, and suggest that he rowed over to Albania? Apart from the risk of losing my precious boat, I did not think that Adrian was strong enough to row that far. No, I agreed with Kralefsky that Adrian was being too eager but, knowing how capricious my sister was, I felt she would greet her admirer's disappearance from the island with delight rather than with despair. Adrian's real difficulty lay in the fact that he could never get Margo alone. I decided that I would have to take Adrian in hand if he was going to achieve anything like success.

The first thing was for him to stop following Margo around like a lamb following a sheep and to feign indifference, so I inveigled him into accompanying me when I went out to explore the surrounding countryside. This was easy enough to do. Margo, in self-defence, had taken to rising at dawn and disappearing from the villa before Adrian put in an appearance so he was left pretty much to himself. Mother had tried to interest him in cooking but after he had left the icebox open and melted half our perishable foodstuffs, set fire to a frying pan full of fat, turned a perfectly good joint of lamb into something closely resembling biltong, and dropped half a dozen eggs on to the kitchen floor, she was only too glad to back up my suggestion that Adrian should accompany me.

I found Adrian an admirable companion, considering that he had been brought up in a city. He never complained, he would patiently obey my terse instructions to 'Hold that!' or 'Don't move – it'll bite you!' to the letter, and seemed genuinely interested in the creatures we pursued.

As Mr Kralefsky had predicted, Margo became intrigued by Adrian's sudden absence. Although she did not care for his attentions she felt perversely piqued when she was not receiving them. She wanted to know what Adrian and I did all day long. I replied rather austerely that Adrian was helping me in my zoological investigations. I said that moreover he was shaping up very well and if this went on I would have no hesitation in proclaiming him a very competent naturalist by the end of the summer.

The Garden of the Gods

'I don't know how you can go around with anyone so wet,' she said. 'I find him an incredible bore.'

I said that was probably just as well as Adrian had confessed to me that he was finding Margo a bit boring too.

'What?' said Margo, outraged. 'How dare he say that, how dare he!'

Well, I pointed out philosophically, she had only herself to blame. After all, who would not find someone boring if they carried on like she did, never going swimming with him, never going walking with him, always being rude.

'I'm not rude,' said Margo angrily. 'I just speak the truth. And if he wants a walk I'll give him one. Boring indeed!'

I was so pleased with the success of my scheme that I over-looked the fact that Margo, like the rest of my family, could be a powerful antagonist when aroused. That evening she was so unexpectedly polite and charming to Adrian that everyone, with the victim's exception, was amazed and alarmed. Skilfully, Margo steered the conversation round to walks and then said that, as Adrian's time in the island was growing short, it was essential that he saw more of it. What better method than walking? Yes, stammered Adrian, that was really the best way of seeing a country.

'I intend to go for a walk the day after tomorrow,' said Margo airily, 'a lovely walk. It's a pity you're so busy with Gerry, otherwise you could have come with me.'

'Oh, don't let that worry you. Gerry can fend for himself,' said Adrian, with what I privately considered to be callous and impolite indifference. 'I'd love to come!'

'Oh good,' fluted Margo. 'I'm sure you'll enjoy it; it's one of the nicest strolls around here.'

'Where?' inquired Leslie.

'Liapades,' said Margo airily, 'I haven't been there for ages.'

'Liapades?' echoed Leslie. 'A stroll? It's right the other side of the island. It'll take you hours.'

722

'Well, I thought we'd take a picnic and make a day of it,' said Margo, adding archly, 'that is, if Adrian doesn't mind.'

It was obvious that Adrian would not mind if Margo had suggested swimming underwater to Italy and back in full armour. I said I thought I would accompany them, as it was an interesting walk from a zoological point of view. Margo shot me a baleful look.

'Well, if you come you must behave yourself,' she said enigmatically.

Adrian was, needless to say, full of the walk and Margo's kindness in asking him. I was not so sure. I pointed out that Liapades was a long way and that it was very hot, but Adrian said he did not mind a bit. Privately, I wondered, since he was rather frail, whether he would last the pace but I could not say this without insulting him. At five o'clock on the appointed day we assembled on the veranda. Adrian was wearing an enormous pair of hob-nailed boots he had acquired from somewhere, long trousers and a thick flannel shirt. To my astonishment, when I ventured to suggest that this ensemble was not suitable for a walk across the island in a temperature of over a hundred in the shade, Margo disagreed. Adrian was wearing perfect walking kit, chosen by herself, she said. The fact that she was clad in a diaphanous bathing suit and sandals and I was in shorts and an open-necked shirt did not deter her. She was armed with a massive pack on her back, which I imagined contained our food and drink, and a stout stick. I was carrying my collecting bag and butterfly net.

Thus equipped, we set out, Margo setting an unreasonably fast pace, I thought. Within a short space of time Adrian was sweating profusely and his face turned pink. Margo, in spite of my protests, stuck to open country and shunned the shade-giving olive groves. In the end I kept pace with them but walked in the shade of the trees a few hundred yards away. Adrian, afraid of being accused of being soft, followed doggedly and moistly at

Margo's heels. After four hours, he was limping badly and dragging his feet; his grey shirt was black with sweat and his face was an alarming shade of magenta.

'Would you like a rest?' Margo inquired at this point.

'Just a drink, perhaps,' said Adrian in a parched voice like a corncrake.

I said I thought this was a splendid idea so Margo stopped and sat down on a red hot rock in the open sun-soaked ground on which you could have roasted a team of oxen. She fumbled surreptitiously in her pack and produced three small bottles of *Gazoza*, a fizzy and extremely sweet local lemonade.

'Here,' she said, handing us a bottle each. 'This'll buck you up.'

In addition to being fizzy and over-sweet, the *Gazoza* was very warm so, if anything, it increased rather than assuaged our thirst. By the time it was nearing midday we were in sight of the opposite coast of the island. The news brought a spark of hope into the lacklustre eyes of Adrian. Once we reached the sea we could rest and swim, Margo explained. We reached the wild coastline and made our way down through the jumble of gigantic red and brown rocks strewn along the sea shore like an uprooted giants' cemetery. Adrian threw himself down in the shade of an enormous block of rock topped with a wig of myrtle and a baby umbrella pine and tore off his shirt and boots. His feet, we discovered, were almost the same startling red as his face, and badly blistered. Margo suggested that he soak them in a rock pool to harden them and this he did while Margo and I swam. Then, much refreshed, we squatted in the shade of the rocks and I said I thought some food and drink would be welcome.

'There is none,' said Margo.

There was a stunned silence for a moment. 'What d'you mean, there is none?' asked Adrian. 'What's in that pack?'

'Oh, those are just my bathing things,' said Margo. 'I decided I wouldn't bring any food because it was so heavy to carry in this heat, and anyway, we'll be back for supper if we start soon.'

'And what about something to drink?' inquired Adrian hoarsely. 'Haven't you got any more *Gazoza*?'

'No, of course not,' said Margo irritably. 'I brought *three*. That's one each, isn't it? And they're terribly heavy to carry. I don't know what you're fussing about anyway; you eat far too much. A little rest'll do you good. It'll give you a chance to un-bloat.'

Adrian came as close to losing his temper as I had ever seen him.

'I don't *want* to un-bloat, whatever that means,' he said icily, 'and if I did I wouldn't walk half across the island to do it.'

'That's just the trouble with you. You're namby-pamby,' snorted Margo. 'Take you for a little walk and you're screaming for food and wine. You just want to live in the hub of luxury all the time.'

'I don't think a drink on a day like this is a luxury,' said Adrian. 'It's a necessity.'

Finding this argument profitless, I took the three empty *Gazoza* bottles half a mile down the coast to where I knew there was a tiny spring. When I reached it I found a man squatting by it, having his midday meal. He had a brown, seamed, wind-patterned face, and a sweeping black moustache. He was wearing the thick, sheepswool socks that the peasants wore when working in the fields and beside him lay his short, wide-bladed hoe.

'*Kalimera*,' he greeted me without surprise, and waved his hand in a courteous gesture towards the spring, as if he owned it.

I greeted him and then lay face downwards on the small carpet of green moss that the moisture had created, and lowered my face to where the bright spring throbbed like a heart under some maidenhair ferns. I drank long and deeply and I could never remember water having tasted so good. I soaked my head and neck with it and sat up with a satisfied sigh.

'Good water,' said the man. 'Sweet, huh? Like a fruit.'

I said the water was delicious and started to wash the *Gazoza* bottles and fill them.

'There's a spring up there,' said the man, pointing up the precipitous mountainside, 'but the water is different, bitter as a widow's tongue. But this is sweet, kind water. You are a foreigner?'

While I filled the bottles I answered his questions but my mind was busy with something else. Nearby lay the remains of his food – half a loaf of maize bread, yellow as a primrose, some great fat white cloves of garlic and a handful of large, wrinkled olives as black as beetles. At the sight of them my mouth started to water and I became acutely aware of the fact that I had been up since dawn with nothing to eat. Eventually the man noticed the glances I kept giving his food supply and, with the typical generosity of the peasants, pulled out his knife.

'Bread?' he asked. 'You want bread?'

I said that I would love some bread but that the problem was that there were three of me, as it were. My sister and her husband, I lied, were also starving somewhere among the rocks. He snapped his knife shut, gathered together the remains of his lunch and held it out to me.

'Take it for them,' he said grinning. 'I've finished and it's not right for the good name of Corfu that foreigners should starve.'

I thanked him profusely, put the olives and garlic into my handkerchief, tucked the bread and the *Gazoza* bottles under my arm and set off.

'Go to the good,' the man called after me. 'Keep away from the trees, we'll be having a storm later.'

Looking up at the blue and burnished sky, I thought the man was wrong but did not say so. When I got back I found Adrian sitting glumly with his feet in a rock pool and Margo sunbathing on a rock and singing tunelessly to herself. They greeted the food and water with delight and fell on it, tearing at the golden bread and gulping the olives and garlic like famished wolves.

'There,' said Margo brightly when we had finished, as if she had been responsible for providing the viands, 'that was nice. Now I suppose we'd better be getting back.'

Immediately, a snag became apparent; Adrian's feet, cool and happy from the rock pool, had swollen and it took the united efforts of Margo and myself to get his boots on again. Even when we had succeeded in forcing his feet into the boots he could only progress at a painfully slow pace, limping along like an elderly tortoise.

'I do wish you'd hurry up,' shouted Margo irritably after we had progressed a mile or so and Adrian was lagging behind.

'I can't go any faster. My feet are killing me,' Adrian said miserably.

In spite of our protests, that he would get sunburned, he had taken off his flannel shirt and exposed his milk-white skin to the elements. It was when we were a couple of miles from the villa that the peasant's prophecy about the storm became fact. These summer storms would be hatched in a nest of cumulus clouds in the Albanian mountains and ferried rapidly across to Corfu by a warm, scouring wind like the blast from a baker's oven. The wind hit us now, stinging our skins and blinding us with dust and bits of leaf. The olives changed from green to silver like the sudden gleam of a turning school of fish, and the wind roared its way through a million leaves with a noise like a giant breaker on the shore. The blue sky was suddenly, miraculously, blotted out by bruise-coloured clouds that were splintered by jagged spears of lavender-coloured lightning. The hot, fierce wind increased and the olive groves shook and hissed as though shaken by some huge, invisible predator. Then came the rain, plummeting out of the sky in great gouts, hitting us with the force of sling-shot. A background to all this was the thunder, stalking imperiously across the sky, rumbling and snarling above the scudding clouds like a million stars colliding, crumbling and avalanching through space.

This was one of the best storms we had ever experienced and Margo and I were thoroughly enjoying it, for after the heat and stillness we found the stinging rain and the noise exhilarating. Adrian did not share our view; he was one of those unfortunate people who were terrified of lightning, so to him the whole thing was monstrous and alarming. We tried to take his mind off the storm by singing but the thunder was so loud that he could not hear us. We struggled on grimly and at last, through the gloomy, rain-striped, olive groves we saw the welcoming lights of the villa. As we reached it and Adrian staggered in through the front door, seeming more dead than alive, Mother appeared in the hall.

'Where *have* you children been? I was getting quite worried,' she said, and then, catching sight of Adrian; 'Good heavens, Adrian dear, what *have* you been doing?'

She might well have asked, for those parts of Adrian's anatomy that were not scarlet with sunburn were interesting shades of blue and green; he could hardly walk and his teeth were chattering so violently that he could not talk. Being scolded and commiserated in turns, he was whisked away to bed by Mother, where he lay, with mild sun-stroke, a severe cold and septic feet, for the next few days.

'Really, Margo, you do make me angry sometimes,' said Mother. 'You know he's not strong. You might have killed him.'

'Serves him jolly well right,' said Margo callously. 'He shouldn't have said I was boring. It's an eye for an ear.'

Adrian, however, unwittingly got his own back; when he recovered he found a shop in the town that stocked gramophone needles.

8

The Merriment of Friendship

The sound of cornet, flute, harp, sackbut, psaltery, dulcimer,
and all kinds of musick.

EZEKIEL 5

It was towards the end of summer that we held what came to
be known as our Indian party. Our parties, whether carefully
planned or burgeoning on the spur of the moment out of nothing,
were always interesting affairs since things seldom went exactly
as we planned them. In those days, living as we did in the country,
without the dubious benefits of radio or television, we had to
rely on such primitive forms of amusement as books, quarrelling, parties, and the laughter of our friends, so naturally parties
– particularly the more flamboyant ones – became red-letter
days, preceded by endless preparations. Even when they were
successfully over, they provided days of delightfully acrimonious
argument as to how they could have been better managed.

We had had a fairly tranquil patch for a month or so; we had
not had a party, and no one had turned up to stay, so Mother
had relaxed and become very benign. We were sitting on the
veranda one morning reading our mail when the party was
hatched. In her mail Mother had just received a mammoth
cookery book entitled *A Million Mouthwatering Oriental Recipes*,
lavishly illustrated with colour reproductions so lurid and glossy
that you felt you could eat them. Mother was enchanted with it
and kept reading bits aloud to us.

'Madras Marvels!' she exclaimed delightedly. 'Oh, they're lovely. I remember them, they were a favourite of your father's when we lived in Darjeeling. And, look! Konsarmer's Delights! I've been looking for a recipe for them for *years*. They're simply delicious, but so rich.'

'If they're anything like the illustrations,' said Larry, 'you'd have to live on a diet of bicarbonate of soda for the next twenty years after you ate one.'

'Don't be silly, dear. The ingredients are absolutely pure – four pounds of butter, sixteen eggs, eight pints of cream, the flesh of ten young coconuts . . .'

'God!' said Larry, 'it sounds like a breakfast for a Strasbourg goose.'

'I'm sure you'll like them, dear. Your father was very fond of them.'

'Well, I'm supposed to be on a diet,' said Margo. 'You can't go forcing *me* to have stuff like that.'

'Nobody's forcing you, dear,' said Mother. 'You can always say no.'

'Well, you know I can't say no, so that's forcing.'

'Go and eat in another room,' suggested Leslie, flipping through the pages of a gun catalogue, 'if you haven't got the will power to say no.'

'But I *have* got the will power to say no,' said Margo indignantly. 'I just can't say no when Mother offers it to me.'

'Jeejee sends his salaams,' said Larry, looking up from the letter he was perusing. 'He says he's coming back here for his birthday.'

'His birthday!' exclaimed Margo. 'Ooh, good! I'm glad he remembered.'

'Such a *nice* boy,' said Mother. 'When's he coming?'

'As soon as he gets out of hospital,' said Larry.

'Hospital? Is he ill?'

'No, he's just having trouble with his levitation; he's got a busted leg. He says his birthday's on the sixteenth so he'll try and make it by the fifteenth.'

'I *am* glad,' said Mother. 'I grew very fond of Jeejee and I'm sure he'll love this book.'

'I know, let's give him a huge birthday party,' said Margo excitedly. 'You know, a really *huge* party.'

'That's a good idea,' said Leslie. 'We haven't had a decent party for ages.'

'And I could make some of the recipes out of this book,' contributed Mother, obviously intrigued by the thought.

'An oriental feast,' exclaimed Larry. 'Tell everyone to come in turbans, with jewels in their navels.'

'No, I think that's going too far,' said Mother. 'No, let's just have a nice, quiet little . . .'

'You can't have a nice, quiet little party for Jeejee,' said Leslie. 'Not after you told him you always travelled with four hundred elephants. He expects something a bit spectacular.'

'It wasn't four hundred elephants, dear. I only said we went *camping* with elephants. You children do exaggerate. And, anyway, we can't produce elephants here; he wouldn't expect *that*.'

'No, but you've got to put on some sort of show,' said Leslie.

'I'll do all the decorations,' offered Margo. 'Everything will be oriental – I'll borrow Mrs Papadrouya's Burmese screens and there are the ostrich feathers that Lena's got . . .'

'We've still got a wild boar and some duck and stuff left in the cold room in town,' said Leslie. 'Better use it up.'

'I'll borrow Countess Lefraki's piano,' said Larry.

'Now, look all of you . . . stop it,' cried Mother, alarmed. 'It's not a durbar we're having, just a birthday party.'

'Nonsense, Mother, it'll do us good to let off a little steam,' said Larry indulgently.

'Yes, in for a penny, in for a pound,' said Leslie.

'And you might as well be hung for an ox as an ass,' contributed Margo.

'Or your neighbour's wife, if it comes to that,' added Larry.

'Now it's a question of who to invite,' said Leslie.

'Theodore, of course,' said the family in unison.

'Then there's poor old Creech,' said Larry.

'Oh no, Larry,' Mother protested. 'You know what a disgusting old brute he is.'

'Nonsense, Mother, the old boy loves a party.'

'And then there's Colonel Ribbindane,' said Leslie.

'No!' Larry exclaimed vehemently. 'We're not having that quintessence of boredom, even if he is the best shot on the island.'

'He's not a bore,' said Leslie belligerently. 'He's no more boring than your bloody friends.'

'None of my friends is capable of spending an entire evening telling you in words of one syllable and a few Neanderthal grunts how he shot a hippo on the Nile in 1904.'

'It's jolly interesting,' retorted Leslie hotly. 'A damned sight more interesting than listening to all your friends going on about bloody art.'

'Now, now, dears,' said Mother peaceably, 'there'll be plenty of room for everyone.'

I left them to the normal uproar that went on while the guest list for any party was being compiled; as far as I was concerned, so long as Theodore was coming the party was assured of success. I could leave the choice of other guests to my family.

The preparations for the party gathered momentum. Larry succeeded in borrowing Countess Lefraki's enormous grand piano and a tiger-skin rug to place alongside it. The piano was conveyed to us with the utmost tenderness, for it had been the favourite instrument of the late Count, on the back of a long, flat cart drawn by four horses. Larry, who had been to supervise the removal, removed the tarpaulins that had been covering the instrument against the sun, mounted the cart and ran off a quick rendering of 'Walking My Baby Back Home', to make sure that it had not suffered from its journey. It seemed in good shape, if a trifle jangly, and after a prodigious effort we managed to get it into the drawing-room. Planted, black and gleaming as an agate, in the corner, the magnificent tiger skin lying in front of it, the mounted head snarling in defiance, it gave the whole room a rich, oriental air.

This was added to by Margo's decorations – tapestries that she had painted on huge sheets of paper and hung on the walls, pictures of minarets, peacocks, cupola-palaces, and bejewelled elephants. Everywhere there were vases of ostrich feathers dyed all the colours of the rainbow, and bunches of multi-coloured balloons like crops of strange tropical fruit. The kitchen, of course, was like the interior of Vesuvius; in the flickering ruby light of half a dozen charcoal fires, Mother and her minions scurried to and fro. The sound of beating and chopping and stirring was so loud that it precluded speech, while the aromatic smells that drifted upstairs were so rich and heavy it was like being wrapped in an embroidered cloak of scent.

Over all this, Spiro presided, like a scowling, brown genie; he seemed to be everywhere, bull-voiced, barrel-bodied, carrying enormous boxes of food and fruit to the kitchen in his ham-like hands, sweating and roaring and cursing as three dining-tables were insinuated into the dining-room and joined together, appearing with everlasting flowers for Margo, strange spices and other delicacies for Mother. It was during moments like this that you realized Spiro's true worth, for you could ask the impossible of him and he would achieve it. 'I'll fixes that,' he would say, and fix it he would, whether it was out-of-season fruit or procuring such a thing as a piano tuner, a species of human being that had been extinct in the island since 1890 so far as anyone knew. It was extremely unlikely, in fact, that any of our parties would have got beyond the planning stage if it had not been for Spiro.

At last everything was ready. The sliding doors between the dining-room and drawing-room had been pulled back and the vast room thus formed was a riot of flowers, balloons and paintings, the long tables with their frost-white cloths sparkling with silver, the side tables groaning under the weight of the cold dishes. A suckling pig, brown and polished as a mummy, with an orange in his mouth, lay beside a haunch of wild boar, sticky with wine and honey marinade, thick with pearls of garlic and the round seeds of coriander; a bank of biscuit-brown chickens and young turkeys was interspersed with wild duck stuffed with wild rice, almonds and sultanas, and woodcock skewered on lengths of bamboo; mounds of saffron rice, yellow as a summer moon, were treasure-troves that made one feel like an archaeologist, so thickly were they encrusted with fragile pink strips of octopus, toasted almonds and walnuts, tiny green grapes, carunculated hunks of ginger and pine seeds. The *kefalia* I had brought from the lake were now browned and charcoal blistered, gleaming in a coating of oil and lemon juice, spattered with jade-green flecks of fennel; they lay in ranks on the huge plates, looking like a flotilla of strange boats tied up in harbour.

Interspersed with all this were the plates of small things – crystallized orange and lemon rind, sweet corn, flat thin oat cakes gleaming with diamonds of sea salt, chutney and pickles in a dozen colours and smells and tastes to tantalize and soothe the taste buds. Here was the peak of the culinary art – here a hundred strange roots and seeds had given up their sweet essence; vegetables and fruits had sacrificed their rinds and flesh to wash the fowl and the fish in layers of delicately scented gravies and marinades. The stomach twitched at this bank of edible colour and smell; you felt you would be eating a magnificent garden, a multi-coloured tapestry, and that the cells of your lungs would be so filled with layer upon layer of fragrance that you would be drugged and immobile like a beetle in the heart of a rose. The dogs and I tiptoed several times into the room to look at this succulent display; we would stand until the saliva filled our mouths and then reluctantly go away. We could hardly wait for the party.

Jeejee, whose boat had been delayed, arrived on the morning of his birthday, dressed in a ravishing peacock-blue outfit, his turban immaculate. He was leaning heavily on a stick but otherwise showed no signs of his accident, and was as ebullient as ever. To our embarrassment, when showed the preparation we had made for his birthday, he burst into tears.

'To think that I, the son of a humble sweeper, an untouchable, should be treated like this,' he sobbed.

'Oh, it's nothing really,' said Mother, rather alarmed by his reaction. 'We often have little parties.'

As our living-room looked like a cross between a Roman banquet and the Chelsea Flower Show, this gave the impression that we always entertained on the scale that would have been envied by the Tudor court.

'Nonsense, Jeejee,' said Larry. 'You an untouchable! Your father was a lawyer.'

'Vell,' said Jeejee, drying his eyes, 'I vould have been untouchable if my father had been a different caste. The trouble with you, Lawrence, is that you have no sense of the dramatic. Think vhat a poem I could have vritten, "The Untouchable Banquet".'

'What's an untouchable?' Margo asked Leslie in a penetrating whisper.

'It's a disease, like leprosy,' he explained solemnly.

'My God!' said Margo dramatically. 'I hope he's sure he hasn't got it. How does he know his father isn't infected?'

'Margo, dear,' said Mother quellingly. 'Go and stir the lentils, will you?'

We had a riotous picnic lunch on the veranda, with Jeejee regaling us with stories of his trip to Persia, singing Persian love songs to Margo with such verve that all the dogs howled in unison.

'Oh, you *must* sing one of those tonight,' said Margo delighted. 'You *must*, Jeejee. Everyone's going to do something.'

'Vat you mean, Margo dear?' asked Jeejee, mystified.

'We've never done it before – it's a sort of cabaret. Everyone's going to do something,' Margo explained. 'Lena's going to do a bit of opera – something out of the *Rosy Cavalier* . . . Theodore and Kralefsky are going to do a trick by Houdini . . . you know, everyone's going to do something . . . so you must sing in Persian.'

'Vy couldn't I do something more in keeping with Mother India?' said Jeejee, struck by the thought. 'I could levitate.'

'No,' said Mother, interrupting firmly, 'I want this party to be a success. No levitation.'

'Why don't you be something typically Indian?' suggested Margo. 'I know, be a snake charmer!'

'Yes,' said Larry, 'the humble, typical, untouchable, Indian snake charmer.'

'My God! Vat a vonderful idea!' cried Jeejee, his eyes shining. 'I vill do so.'

Anxious to be of service, I said I could lend him a basket of small and harmless slow-worms for his act, and he was delighted with the idea that he would have some real snakes to charm. Then we all went to siesta and to prepare ourselves for the great evening.

The sky was striped green, pink and smoke-grey, and the first owls had started to chime in the dark olives when the guests began to arrive. Among the first was Lena, clasping a huge book of operatic music under her arm and wearing a flamboyant evening dress of orange silk in spite of the fact that she knew the party was informal.

'My dears,' she said thrillingly, her black eyes flashing, 'I'm in great voice tonight. I feel I shall do justice to the master. No, no, not ouzo, it might afflict my vocal chord. I will have a tiny champagne and brandy. Yes, I can feel my throat vibrate, you know – like a harp.'

'How nice,' said Mother insincerely. 'I'm sure we shall all enjoy it.'

'She's got a lovely voice, Mother,' said Margo. 'It's a mezzotint.'

'Soprano,' said Lena coldly.

Theodore and Kralefsky arrived together, carrying a coil of ropes and chains and several padlocks.

'I hope,' said Theodore, rocking up and down on his toes, 'I hope our . . . er . . . little . . . you know . . . our little illusion will be successful. We have, of course, never done it before.'

'*I* have done it before,' said Kralefsky with dignity. 'It was Houdini himself who showed me. He even went so far as to compliment me on my dexterity. "Richard," he said – for we were on intimate terms, you understand, "Richard, I've never seen anyone except myself so nimble-fingered."'

'Really?' said Mother. 'Well, I'm sure it will be a great success.'

Captain Creech arrived wearing a battered top hat, his face strawberry-red, his thistledown hair looking as though the slightest breeze would blow it from his head and chin. He staggered even more than usual and his broken jaw looked particularly lop-sided; it was obvious that he had been priming himself well prior to his arrival. Mother stiffened and gave a forced smile as he lurched through the front door.

'My! You look really sumptuous tonight,' said the Captain, leering at Mother and rubbing his hands, swaying gently. 'You've put on some weight lately, haven't you?'

'I don't think so,' said Mother primly.

The captain eyed her up and down critically.

'Well, you seem to have a better handful in your bustle than you used to have,' he said.

'I would be glad if you would refrain from making personal remarks, Captain,' said Mother coldly.

The captain was unabashed.

'It doesn't worry *me*,' he confided. 'I like a woman with a bit of something you can get your hands on. A thin woman's no good in bed – like riding a horse with no saddle.'

'I have no interest in your preference, either in or out of bed,' said Mother with asperity. 'Now if you'll excuse me, I have to go and attend to the food.'

More and more carriages clopped up to the front door, more and more cars disgorged guests. The room filled up with the strange selection of people the family had invited. In one corner, Kralefsky, like an earnest hump-backed gnome, was telling Lena about his experiences with Houdini.

' "Harry," I said to him – for we were intimate friends, you understand, "Harry show me what secrets you like, they are safe with me. My lips are sealed." '

Kralefsky took a sip of his wine and pursed his lips to show how they were sealed.

'Really?' said Lena, with total lack of interest. 'Vell, of course it's different in the singing vorld. Ve singers pass on our secrets. I remember Krasia Toupti saying to me, "Lena your voice is so beautiful I cry vhen I hear it; I have taught you all I know. Go, carry the torches of our genius to the vorld." '

'I didn't mean to imply that Harry Houdini was secretive,' said Kralefsky stiffly; 'he was the most generous of men. Why, he even showed me how to saw a woman in half.'

'My dear, how curious it must feel to be cut in half,' mused Lena. 'Think of it, your bottom half could be having an affair in one room while your other half was entertaining an archbishop. How droll.'

'It's only an illusion,' said Kralefsky, going pink.

'So is life,' replied Lena soulfully. 'So is life, my friend.'

The noise of drinking was exhilarating. Champagne corks popped and the pale, chrysanthemum-coloured liquid, whispering gleefully with bubbles, hissed into the glasses; heavy red wine glupped into the goblets, thick and crimson as the blood of some mythical monster, and a swirling wreath of pink bubbles formed on the surface; the frosty white wine tiptoed into the glasses, shrilling, gleaming, now like diamonds, now like topaz; the ouzo lay transparent and innocent as the edge of a mountain pool until the water splashed in and the whole glass curdled like a conjuring trick, coiling and blurring into a summer cloud of moonstone white.

Presently we moved down the room to where the vast array of food awaited us. The King's butler, fragile as a mantis, superintended the peasant girls in the serving. Spiro, scowling more than normal with concentration, meticulously carved the joints and the birds. Kralefsky had been trapped by the great, grey, walrus-like bulk of Colonel Ribbindane, who loomed over him, his giant moustache hanging like a curtain over his mouth, his bulbous blue eyes fixed on Kralefsky in a paralysing stare.

'The hippopotamus, or river horse, is one of the largest of the quadrupeds to be found in the continent of Africa . . .' he droned, as though lecturing a class.

'Yes, yes . . . fantastic beast. Truly one of nature's wonders,' said Kralefsky, looking round desperately for escape.

'When you shoot a hippopotamus or river horse,' droned Colonel Ribbindane, oblivious to interruption, 'as I have had the good fortune to do, you aim between the eyes and the ears, thus ensuring that the bullet penetrates the brain.'

'Yes, yes,' Kralefsky agreed, hypnotized by the Colonel's protuberant blue eyes.

'Bang!' said the Colonel, so suddenly and loudly that Kralefsky nearly dropped his plate. 'You hit him between the eyes . . . Splash! Crunch! . . . straight into the brain, d'you see?'

'Yes, yes,' said Kralefsky, swallowing and going white.

'Splosh!' said the Colonel, driving the point home. 'Blow his brains out in a fountain.'

Kralefsky closed his eyes in horror and put down his half-eaten plate of suckling pig.

'He sinks then,' the colonel went on, 'sinks right down to the bottom of the river . . . glug, glug, glug. Then you wait twenty-four hours – d'you know why?'

'No . . . I . . . uh . . .' said Kralefsky, swallowing frantically.

'Flatulence,' explained the colonel with satisfaction. 'All the semi-digested food in its belly, d'you see? It rots and produces gas. Up puffs the old belly like a balloon and up she pops.'

'H-How interesting,' said Kralefsky faintly. 'I think, if you will just excuse me . . .'

'Funny things, stomach contents . . .' mused the colonel, ignoring Kralefsky's attempts at escape. 'Belly is swollen up to twice its natural size; when you cut it open, whoosh! like slicing up a zeppelin full of sewage, d'you see?'

Kralefsky put his handkerchief over his mouth and gazed round in an anguished manner.

'Different with the elephant, the *largest* land quadruped in Africa,' the colonel droned on, filling his mouth with crisp suckling pig. 'D'you know the pygmies cut it open, crawl into the belly and eat the liver all raw and bloody . . . still quivering sometimes. Funny little chaps, pygmies . . . negroes, of course . . .'

Kralefsky, now a delicate shade of yellow-green, escaped to the veranda, where he stood in the moonlight taking deep breaths.

The suckling pig had vanished, the bones gleamed white in the joints of lamb and boar, and the rib cages and breast bones of the chickens and turkeys and ducks lay like the wreckage of upturned boats. Jeejee, having sampled a little of everything, at Mother's insistence, and having declared it infinitely superior to anything he had ever eaten before, was vying with Theodore to see how many Taj Mahal Titbits they could consume.

'Delicious,' muttered Jeejee indistinctly, his mouth full. 'Simply delicious, my dear Mrs Durrell. You are the apotheosis of culinary genius.'

'Yes indeed,' said Theodore, popping another Taj Mahal Titbit into his mouth and scrunching it up. 'They're really excellent. They make something similar in Macedonia . . . er . . . um . . . but with goat's milk.'

'Jeejee, did you really break your leg levitating, or whatever it's called?' asked Margo.

'No,' said Jeejee sorrowfully. 'I vouldn't mind if I had, it vould have been in a good cause. No, the damned stupid hotel vere I stayed had French vindows in the bedrooms but they couldn't afford a balcony.'

'Sounds like a Corfu hotel,' said Leslie.

'So one evening I was overcome with forgetfulness and I stepped out onto the balcony to do some deep breathing; and of course there vas no balcony.'

'You might have been killed,' said Mother. 'Have another titbit.'

'Vat is death?' asked Jeejee oratorically. 'A mere sloughing of the skin, a metamorphosis. I vent into a deep trance in Persia and my friend got incontrovertible proof that in a previous life I vas Ghengis Khan.'

'You mean the film star?' asked Margo, wide-eyed.

'No, dear Margo, the great varrior,' said Jeejee.

'You mean you could remember being him?' asked Leslie, interested.

'Alas, no. I vas in a trance,' said Jeejee sadly. 'One is not allowed to remember one's previous lives.'

'You . . . khan have your cake and eat it,' explained Theodore, delighted at having found an opportunity for a pun.

'I wish everybody would hurry up and finish eating,' said Margo, 'then we could get on with the acts.'

'To hurry such a meal vould be an insult,' said Jeejee. 'There is time, the whole night stretches before us. Besides, Gerry and I have to go and organize my supporting cast of reptiles.'

It took quite some time before the cabaret was ready, for everyone was full of wine and good food and refused to be hurried. Eventually, however, Margo got the cast assembled. She had tried to get Larry to be master of ceremonies but he had refused; he said that if she wanted him to be part of the cabaret he was not going to be master of ceremonies as well. In desperation, she had had to step into the breach herself. Blushing slightly, she took up her place on the tiger skin by the piano and called for silence.

'Ladies and gentlemen,' she said. 'Tonight, for your entertainment, we have a cabaret of the best talent on the island and I'm sure that you will all enjoy the talents of these talented talents.'

She paused, blushing, while Kralefsky gallantly led the applause.

'I would like to introduce Constantino Megalotopolopopoulos,' she continued, 'who is going to act as accompanist.'

A tiny, fat little Greek, looking like a swarthy ladybird, trotted into the room, bowed, and sat down at the piano. This had been one of Spiro's achievements, for Mr Megalotopolopopoulos, a draper's assistant, could not only play the piano but read music as well.

'And now,' said Margo, 'it is with great pleasure that I present to you that very talented artiste Lena Mavrokondas accompanied by Constantino Megalotopolopopoulos on the piano. Lena will sing that great area from *Rosy Cavalier*, "The Presentation of the Rose".'

Lena, glowing like a tiger-lily, swept to the piano, bowed to Constantino, placed her hands carefully over her midriff as though warding off a blow, and began to sing.

'Beautiful, beautiful,' said Kralefsky as she finished and bowed to our applause. 'What virtuosity.'

'Yes,' said Larry, 'it used to be known as the three-vee method at Covent Garden.'

'Three-vee?' asked Kralefsky, much interested. 'What's that?'

'Vim, vibrato, and volume,' said Larry.

'Tell them I will sing encore,' whispered Lena to Margo after a whispered consultation with Constantino Megalotopolopopoulos.

'Oh yes. How nice,' said Margo flustered and unprepared for

this largesse. 'Ladies and gentlemen, Lena will now sing another song, called "The Encore".'

Lena gave Margo a withering look and swept into her next song with such vigour and so many gestures that even Creech was impressed.

'By George, she's a good-looking wench, that!' he exclaimed, his eyes watering with enthusiasm.

'Yes, a true artiste,' agreed Kralefsky.

'What chest expansion,' said Creech admiringly. 'Bows like a battleship.'

Lena finished on a zither-like note and bowed to the applause which was loud but nicely judged in warmth and length to discourage another encore.

'Thank you Lena, that was wonderful. Just like the real thing,' said Margo, beaming. 'And now, ladies and gentlemen, I present the famous escape artists, Krafty Kralefsky and his partner, Slithery Stephanides.'

'Dear God,' said Larry, 'who thought of those names?'

'Need you ask?' said Leslie; 'Theodore. Kralefsky wanted to call the act "The Mysterious Escapologist Illusionists" but Margo couldn't guarantee to say it properly.'

'One must be thankful for small mercies,' said Larry.

Theodore and Kralefsky clanked on to the floor near the piano carrying their load of ropes, chains and padlocks.

'Ladies and gentlemen,' said Kralefsky. 'Tonight we will show you tricks that will baffle you, tricks so mysterious that you will be agog to know how they are done.'

He paused to frown at Theodore, who had dropped a chain on the floor by mistake.

'For my first trick I will ask my assistant not only to bind me securely with rope but chain as well.'

We clapped dutifully and watched, delighted, while Theodore wound yards and yards of rope and chain around Kralefsky. Occasional whispered altercations drifted to the audience.

'I've . . . er . . . you know . . . um . . . forgotten precisely the knot . . . Um . . . yes . . . you mean the padlock *first*? Ah yes, I have it . . . hm . . . er . . . just a second.'

At length, Theodore turned apologetically to the audience.

'I must apologize for . . . er . . . you know . . . er . . . taking so long,' he said, 'but, unfortunately, we didn't have time to . . . er . . . practise, that is to say . . .'

'Get on with it!' hissed Krafty Kralefsky.

At length, Theodore had wound so many lengths of rope and chain around Kralefsky that he looked as though he had stepped straight out of Tutankhamen's tomb.

'And now,' said Theodore, with a gesture at the immobile Kralefksy, 'would anyone like to . . . er . . . you know . . . examine the knots?'

Colonel Ribbindane lumbered forward.

'Er . . . um . . .' said Theodore, startled, not having expected his offer to be taken up. 'I'm afraid I must ask you to . . . um . . . that is to say . . . if you don't actually *pull* on the knots . . . er . . . um . . .'

Colonel Ribbindane made an inspection of the knots that was so minute one would have thought he were chief warder in a prison. At length, and with obvious reluctance, he pronounced the knots good. Theodore looked relieved as he stepped forward and gestured at Kralefsky again.

'And now, my assistant, that is to say, my *partner*, will show you how . . . easy it is to . . . er . . . you know . . . um . . . rid yourself of . . . er . . . um . . . several yards . . . feet, I should say . . . though, of course, being in Greece, perhaps one should say metres . . . er . . . um . . . several metres of . . . er . . . rope and chains.'

He stepped back and we all focused our attention on Kralefsky.

'Screen!' he hissed at Theodore.

'Ah! Hm . . . yes,' said Theodore, and laboriously moved a screen in front of Kralefsky.

There was a long and ominous pause, during which we could hear panting and the clanking of chains from behind the screen.

'Oh dear,' said Margo, 'I do hope he can do it.'

'Shouldn't think so,' said Leslie, 'all those padlocks look rusty.'

But at that moment, to our astonishment, Theodore whipped away the screen and revealed Kralefsky, slightly purple of face and dishevelled, standing free in a pool of ropes and chains.

The applause was genuine and surprised, and Kralefsky basked in the adulation of his audience.

'My next trick, a difficult and dangerous one, will take some time,' he said portentously. 'I shall be roped and chained by my assistant and the knots can be examined by – ha ha – the sceptics among you, and then I shall be cast into an airtight box. In due course you will see me emerge miraculously, but it takes some time for me to achieve this . . . er . . . miracle. The next act will kindly entertain you.'

Spiro and Megalotopolopopoulos appeared dragging a large and extremely heavy olive-wood chest of the sort that used to be used for storing linen. It was ideal for the purpose, for when Kralefsky had been roped and chained and the knots examined minutely by a suspicious Colonel Ribbindane, he was lifted into it by Theodore and Spiro and slid into the interior as neatly as a snail into its shell. Theodore, with a flourish, slammed the lid shut and locked it.

'Now, when my assis . . . er . . . my . . . er . . . um . . . partner, this is to say . . . signals, I will release him,' he said. 'On with the show!'

'I don't like it,' said Mother. 'I hope Mr Kralefsky knows what he's doing.'

'I shouldn't think so,' said Leslie gloomily.

'It's too much like . . . well . . . premature burial.'

'Perhaps when we open it he'll have changed into Edgar Allan Poe,' suggested Larry hopefully.

'It's perfectly all right, Mrs Durrell,' said Theodore. 'I can communicate with him by a series of knocks . . . um . . . a sort of Morse code.'

'And now,' said Margo, 'while we are waiting for Krafty

Kralefsky to escape, we have that incredible snake charmer from the East, Prince Jeejeebuoy.'

Megalotopolopopoulos played a series of thrilling chords and Jeejee trotted into the room. He had removed his finery and was clad simply in a turban and loincloth. As he could not find a suitable snake-charming pipe, he was carrying a violin which he had got Spiro to borrow from a man in the village; in his other hand he held his basket containing his act. He had rejected with scorn my slow-worms when he had seen them as being far too small to aid in the cultivation of the image of Mother India. He had insisted instead on borrowing one of my water snakes, an elderly specimen some two and a half feet long and of an extremely misanthropic disposition. As he bowed to the audience the top fell off the basket and the snake, looking very disgruntled, fell out on to the floor. Everyone panicked except Jeejee, who squatted down cross-legged near the coiled snake, tucked the violin under his chin and started to play. Gradually, the panic subsided and we all watched entranced as Jeejee swayed to and fro, extracting the most agonizing noises from the fiddle, watched by the alert and irritated snake. Just at that moment came a loud knock from the box in which Kralefsky was incarcerated.

'Aha!' said Theodore. 'The signal.'

He went to the box and bent over, his beard bristling as he tapped on it like a woodpecker. Everyone's attention was on him, including Jeejee's, and at that moment the water snake struck. Fortunately, Jeejee moved so that the water snake only got a firm hold on his loincloth; however, it hung on grimly and pugnaciously.

'Ow! My God!' screamed the incredible snake charmer from the East. 'Hey, Gerry, quick, quick, it's biting me in the crutch.'

It was some minutes before I could persuade him to stand still so that I could disentangle the snake from his loincloth. During this time, Theodore was having a prolonged Morse code conversation with Kralefsky in the box.

'I do not think I can do any more,' said Jeejee, shakily accepting a large brandy from Mother. 'It tried to bite me below the belt!'

'He will apparently be a minute or two yet,' announced Theodore. 'He's had a little trouble . . . er . . . difficulty, that is, with the padlocks. At least, that's what I understand him to say.'

'I'll put the next act on,' said Margo.

'Think,' said Jeejee faintly, 'it might well have been a cobra.'

'No, no,' said Theodore. 'Cobras are not found here in Corfu.'

'And now,' said Margo, 'we have Captain Creech, who will give us some old-time songs and I'm sure you'll want to join in with him. Captain Creech.'

The captain, his top hat tilted at a rakish angle, strutted across to the piano and did a little bow-legged to and fro shuffle, twirling the cane he had procured.

'Old sea shanty,' he bellowed, putting his top hat on the end of his cane and twirling it round dextrously. 'Old sea shanty. You all join in the chorus.'

He did a short dance, still twirling his hat, and came in on the beat of the song which Megalotopolopopoulos was thumping out,

> 'O Paddy was an Irishman,
> He came from Donegal,
> And all the girls they loved him well,
> Though he only had one ball,
> For the Irish girls are girls of sense,
> And they didn't mind at all,
> For, as Paddy pointed out to them,
> 'Twas better than none at all.
> O folderol and folderay,
> A sailor's life is grim,
> So you're only too delighted,
> If you get a bit excited,
> Whether it's with her or him.'

'Really, Larry!' said Mother, outraged, 'is this your idea of entertainment?'

'Why pick on me?' asked Larry, astounded. 'It's nothing to do with me.'

'You invited him, disgusting old man. He's your friend.'

'I can't be responsible for what he *sings*, can I?' asked Larry irritably.

'You must put a stop to it,' declared Mother. 'Horrible old man.'

'He certainly twirls his hat round very well,' said Theodore enviously. 'I wonder how . . . he . . . er . . . does it?'

'I'm not interested in his hat – it's his songs.'

'It's a perfectly good music hall ditty,' said Larry. 'I don't know what you're going on about.'

'It's not the sort of music hall ditty *I'm* used to,' said Mother.

> 'O, Blodwyn was a Welsh girl,
> She came from Cardiff city,
> And all the boys they loved her well,
> Though she only had one titty,'

carolled the captain, getting into his stride.

'Repulsive old fool!' spat out Mother.

> 'For the Welsh boys there,
> Are boys of sense,
> And didn't they all agree,
> One titty is better than two sometimes,
> For it leaves you one hand free.
> O folderol and folderay,
> A sailor's life is grim . . .'

'Even if you don't consider me, you might consider Gerry,' said Mother.

'What d'you want me to do? Write the verses down for him?' asked Larry.

'D'you ... you know ... hear a sort of *tapping*?' asked Theodore.

'Don't be ridiculous, Larry, you know perfectly well what I mean.'

'I wondered if he might be ready ... um ... the trouble is, I can't quite remember the signal,' Theodore confessed.

'I don't know why you always have to pick on me,' said Larry. 'Just because *you're* narrow-minded.'

'I'm as broad-minded as anybody,' protested Mother indignantly. 'In fact, sometimes I think I'm too broad.'

'I *think* it was two slow and three quick,' mused Theodore, 'but I may be mistaken.'

> 'O, Gertrude was an English lass,
> She came from Stoke-on-Trent,
> But when she loved a nice young lad,
> She always left him bent.'

'Listen to that!' said Mother. 'It's beyond a joke. Larry, you must stop him.'

'*You're* objecting, *you* stop him,' said Larry.

> 'But the boys of Stoke
> They loved a poke,
> And suffered in the bed,
> For they said that Gert
> Was a real prime skirt,
> But she had a left-hand thread.'

'Really, Larry, you carry things too far. It's not funny.'

'Well, he's been through Ireland, Wales and England,' Larry pointed out. 'He's only got Scotland to go, unless he branches out into Europe.'

'You must stop him doing that!' said Mother, aghast at the thought.

'I think, you know, perhaps I ought just to open the box and have a look,' said Theodore thoughtfully. 'You know, just as a *precaution*.'

'I wish you'd stop carrying on like a female Bowdler,' said Larry. 'It's all good clean fun.'

'Well, it's not *my* idea of good clean fun,' exclaimed Mother, 'and I want it stopped.'

> 'O, Angus was a Scottish lad,
> He came from Aberdeen . . .'

'There you are, he's got to Scotland now,' said Larry.

'Er . . . I'll try not to disturb the captain,' said Theodore, 'but I thought perhaps just to take a quick glance . . .'

'I don't care whether he's got to John o'Groats,' said Mother. 'It's got to stop.'

Theodore had tiptoed over to the box and was now feeling in his pockets worriedly; Leslie joined him and they discussed the problem of the entombed Kralefsky. I saw Leslie trying ineffectually to raise the lid when it became obvious that Theodore had lost the key. The captain sang on unabated.

> 'O, Fritz, he was a German lad,
> He came from old Berlin . . .'

'There!' said Mother. 'He's started on the Continent! Larry, you must stop him!'

'I wish you'd stop carrying on like the Lord Chamberlain,' said Larry, annoyed. 'It's Margo's cabaret, tell *her* to stop him.'

'It's a mercy that most of the guests don't speak good enough English to understand,' said Mother. 'Though what the others must think . . .'

'Folderol and folderay,
A sailor's life is grim . . .'

'I'd make life grim for him if I could,' said Mother. 'Depraved old fool!'

Leslie and Theodore had now been joined by Spiro, carrying a large crowbar; together they set about the task of trying to open the lid.

'O, Françoise was a French girl,
She came from the town of Brest,
And, oh, she lived up to its name,
And gave the boys no rest.'

'I do try to be broad-minded,' said Mother, 'but there *are* limits.'

'Tell me, my dears,' asked Lena, who had been listening to the captain with care. 'What is left-hand thread?'

'It's a . . . it's a . . . it's a sort of English joke,' said Mother desperately. 'Like a pun, you know?'

'Yes,' explained Larry. 'Like you say a girl's got a pun in the oven.'

'Larry, that's quite enough,' said Mother quellingly. 'The captain's bad enough without *you* starting.'

'Mother,' said Margo, having just noticed. 'I think Kralefsky's suffocating.'

'I do not understand this pun in oven,' said Lena. 'Explain me.'

'Take no notice, Lena, it's only Larry's joke.'

'If he's suffocating, ought I to go and stop the captain's song?' asked Margo.

'An excellent idea! Go and stop him at once,' said Mother.

There were loud groaning noises as Leslie and Spiro struggled with the heavy lid of the chest. Margo rushed up to the captain.

'Captain, Captain, please stop,' she said. 'Mr Kralefsky's . . . Well, we're rather worried about him.'

'Stop?' said the captain startled. 'Stop? But I've only just begun.'

'Yes, well, there are more urgent things than your songs,' said Mother frigidly. 'Mr Kralefsky's stuck in his box.'

'But it's one of the best songs I know,' said the captain aggrievedly. 'It's the longest, too – one hundred and forty countries it deals with – Chile, Australia, the Far East, the lot. A hundred and forty verses!'

I saw Mother flinch at the thought of the captain singing the other hundred and thirty-four verses.

'Yes, well, some other time perhaps,' she promised untruthfully. 'But this is an emergency.'

With a splintering noise like a giant tree being felled, the lid of the chest was finally wrenched open. Inside lay Kralefsky still swathed in ropes and chains, his face an interesting shade of blue, his hazel eyes wide and terrified.

'Aha, I see we're a bit ... er ... you know ... premature,' said Theodore. 'He hasn't succeeded in untying himself.'

'Air! Air!' croaked Kralefsky. 'Give me air!'

'Interesting,' said Colonel Ribbindane. 'Saw a pygmy like that once in the Congo ... been trapped in an elephant's stomach. The elephant is the largest African quadruped ...'

'Do get him out,' said Mother agitatedly. 'Get some brandy.'

'Fan him! Blow on him!' shrilled Margo, and burst into tears. 'He's dying, he's dying, and he never finished his trick.'

'Air ... air,' moaned Kralefsky as they lifted him out of the box.

In his shroud of ropes and chains, his face leaden, his eyes closed, he certainly looked a macabre sight.

'I think perhaps, you know, the ropes and chains are a little constricting,' said Theodore judiciously, becoming the medical man.

'Well, *you* put them on him, you get them off him,' said Larry. 'Come on, Theodore, you've got the key for the padlocks.'

'I seem, rather unfortunately, to have mislaid it,' Theodore confessed.

'Dear God!' exclaimed Leslie. 'I knew they shouldn't be allowed to do this. Damned silly. Spiro, can you get a hacksaw?'

They laid Kralefsky on the sofa and supported his head on the cushions; he opened his eyes and gasped at us helplessly. Colonel Ribbindance bent and stared into Kralefsky's face.

'This pygmy I was telling you about,' he said. 'His eyeballs filled up with blood.'

'Really?' said Theodore, much interested. 'I believe you get the same when someone is . . . er . . . you know . . . garrotted. A rupturing of the blood vessels in the eyeballs sometimes bursts them.'

Kralefsky gave a small, despairing squeak like a field mouse.

'Now, if he had taken a course in Fakyo,' said Jeejee, 'he vould have been able to hold his breath for hours, perhaps even days, possibly even months or *years*, vith practice.'

'Would that prevent his eyeballs filling with blood?' asked Ribbindane.

'I don't know,' said Jeejee honestly. 'It vould probably prevent them *filling* with blood; they might just go pink.'

'Are my eyes full of blood?' asked Kralefsky agitatedly.

'No, no, of course they're not,' said Mother soothingly. 'I do wish you all would stop talking about blood and worrying poor Mr Kralefsky.'

'Yes, take his mind off it,' said Captain Creech. 'Shall I finish my song?'

'No,' said Mother firmly, 'no more songs. Why don't you get Mr Maga . . . whatever his name is to play something soothing and all have a nice dance while we unwrap Mr Kralefsky?'

'That's an idea, my lovely wench,' said Captain Creech to Mother. 'Waltz with me! One of the quickest ways of getting intimate, waltzing.'

'No,' said Mother coldly. 'I'm much too busy to get intimate with anyone, thank you very much.'

'You, then,' said the captain to Lena, 'you'll give me a cuddle round the floor, huh?'

'Vell, I must confess it, I like the valtz,' said Lena, puffing out her chest, to the captain's obvious delight.

Megalotopolopopoulos swung himself into a spirited rendering of 'The Blue Danube' and the captain whisked Lena off across the room.

'The trick *would* have worked perfectly, only Dr Stephanides should have only *pretended* to lock the padlocks,' Mr Kralefsky was explaining, while a scowling Spiro hacksawed away at the locks and chains.

'Of course,' said Mother, 'we quite understand.'

'I was never . . . er . . . you know . . . very good at conjuring,' admitted Theodore contritely.

'I could feel the air running out and hear my heartbeats getting louder and louder. It was horrible, quite horrible,' said Kralefsky, closing his eyes with a shudder that made all his chains jangle. 'I began to think I'd never get out.'

'And you missed the rest of the cabaret too,' put in Margo sympathetically.

'Yes, by God!' exclaimed Jeejee. 'You didn't see my snake-charming. Damned great snake bit me in the loincloth, and me an unmarried man!'

'And then the blood started pounding in my ears,' said Kralefsky, hoping to remain the focus of attention. 'Everything went black.'

'But . . . er . . . you know . . . it *was* dark in there,' Theodore observed.

'Don't be so literal, Theo,' said Larry. 'One can't embroider a story properly with you damned scientists around.'

'I'm not embroidering,' said Kralefsky with dignity, as the last padlock fell away and he could sit up. 'Thank you, Spiro. No, I assure you, everything went as black as . . . as black as . . .'

'A nigger's bottom?' offered Jeejee helpfully.

'Jeejee, dear, don't use that word,' said Mother, shocked. 'It's not polite.'

'Vhat? Bottom?' asked Jeejee, mystified.

'No, no,' said Mother, 'that other word.'

'Vhat? Nigger?' he asked. 'But vhat's vrong with it? I'm the only nigger here and *I* don't object.'

'Spoken like a white man,' declared Colonel Ribbindane admiringly.

'Well *I* object,' said Mother firmly. 'I won't have you calling yourself a nigger. To me, you're just as, just as . . .'

'White as driven snow?' suggested Larry.

'You know perfectly well what I mean, Larry,' said Mother crossly.

'Well,' went on Kralefsky, 'there was I with the blood pounding in my ears . . .'

'Oooh,' squeaked Margo suddenly, 'just look what Captain Creech has done to Lena's lovely dress.'

We turned to look at that section of the room where several couples were gyrating merrily to the waltz, none with greater enthusiasm than the captain and Lena. Unfortunately, unbeknownst to either of them, the captain at some point must have trodden on the deep layer of frills that decorated the edge of Lena's gown and wrenched them away; now they were waltzing away oblivious to the fact that the captain had both feet inside Lena's dress.

'Good heavens! Disgusting old man!' said Mother.

'He was right about the waltz being intimate,' said Larry. 'Another couple of whirls and they'll be wearing the same dress.'

'D'you think I ought to tell Lena?' asked Margo.

'I shouldn't,' said Larry. 'It's probably the nearest she's been to a man in years.'

'Larry, that's quite unnecessary,' said Mother.

Just at that moment, with a flourish, Megalotopolopopoulos brought the waltz to an end, Lena and the captain spun round and round like a top and then stopped. Before Margo could say anything, the captain stepped backwards to bow and fell flat on his back, ripping a large section of Lena's skirt away. There was a moment's terrible silence while every eye in the room was riveted, fascinated, on Lena, who stood there frozen. The captain broke the spell, speaking from his recumbent position on the floor.

'My, that's a fine pair of knickers you're wearing,' he observed jovially.

Lena uttered what can only be described as a Greek screech, a sound that has all the blood-curdling qualities of a scythe blade scraped across a hidden rock; part lamentation, part indignation, with a rich, murderous overtone, a noise wrenched up, as it were, from the very bowels of the vocal chords. Galli-Curci would have been proud of her. It was, strangely enough, Margo who leaped into the breach and avoided what could have been a diplomatic crisis, though her method of doing so was perhaps a trifle flamboyant. She simply snatched a cloth from a side table, rushed to Lena and swathed her in it. This gesture in itself would have been all right except that she chose a cloth on which there were reposing numerous dishes of food and a large twenty-four-branch candelabra. The crash of breaking china and the hissing of candles falling into chutneys and sauces successfully distracted the guests from Lena, and under cover of the pandemonium she was rushed upstairs by Margo.

'I hope you're satisfied now!' said Mother accusingly to Larry.

'Me? What have I done?' he inquired.

'That man,' said Mother. 'You invited him; now look what he's done.'

'Given Lena the thrill of her life,' said Larry. 'No man ever tried to tear her skirt off before.'

'It's not funny, Larry,' said Mother severely, 'and if we have any more parties I will not have that . . . that . . . licentious old libertine.'

'Never mind, Mrs Durrell, it's a lovely party,' said Jeejee.

'Well, as long as you're enjoying it, I don't mind,' said Mother, mollified.

'If I have another hundred reincarnations, I'm sure I shall never have another birthday party like this.'

'That's very sweet of you, Jeejee.'

'There's only one thing,' said Jeejee soulfully, 'I hesitate to mention it . . . but . . .'

'What?' asked Mother. 'What was wrong?'

'Not wrong,' said Jeejee sighing, 'just *lacking*.'

'*Lacking?*' asked Mother, alarmed. 'What was lacking?'

'Elephants,' said Jeejee earnestly, 'the largest quadrupeds in India.'

GERALD DURRELL

A MESSAGE FROM DURRELL WILDLIFE CONSERVATION TRUST

Gerald Durrell's childhood efforts at zoo-keeping, which so bemused his long-suffering family, were the beginning of a lifelong dedication to saving endangered species. What he learned on Corfu from mentors such as Theo inspired his crusade to preserve the rich diversity of animal life on our planet.

This crusade to preserve endangered species did not end with Gerald Durrell's death in 1995. His work goes on through the untiring efforts of the Durrell Wildlife Conservation Trust.

Over the years many readers of Gerald Durrell's books have been so motivated by his experiences and vision that they have wanted to continue the story for themselves by supporting the work of his Trust. We hope that you will feel the same way today because through his books and life, Gerald Durrell set us all a challenge. 'Animals are the great voteless and voiceless majority,' he wrote, 'who can only survive with our help'.

Please don't let your interest in conservation end when you turn this page. Visit our website to find out how you can be part of our crusade to save animals from extinction.

For further information, or to send a donation, write to:

Durrell Wildlife

Les Augrès Manor

Jersey,

Channel Islands, JE3 5BPUK

Website: www.durrell.org

Email: info@durrell.org

He just wanted a decent book to read ...

Not too much to ask, is it? It was in 1935 when Allen Lane, Managing Director of Bodley Head Publishers, stood on a platform at Exeter railway station looking for something good to read on his journey back to London. His choice was limited to popular magazines and poor-quality paperbacks – the same choice faced every day by the vast majority of readers, few of whom could afford hardbacks. Lane's disappointment and subsequent anger at the range of books generally available led him to found a company – and change the world.

'We believed in the existence in this country of a vast reading public for intelligent books at a low price, and staked everything on it'
Sir Allen Lane, 1902–1970, founder of Penguin Books

The quality paperback had arrived – and not just in bookshops. Lane was adamant that his Penguins should appear in chain stores and tobacconists, and should cost no more than a packet of cigarettes.

Reading habits (and cigarette prices) have changed since 1935, but Penguin still believes in publishing the best books for everybody to enjoy. We still believe that good design costs no more than bad design, and we still believe that quality books published passionately and responsibly make the world a better place.

So wherever you see the little bird – whether it's on a piece of prize-winning literary fiction or a celebrity autobiography, political tour de force or historical masterpiece, a serial-killer thriller, reference book, world classic or a piece of pure escapism – you can bet that it represents the very best that the genre has to offer.

Whatever you like to read – trust Penguin.